Microsoft®
Office XP
Developer's Guide

Version 2002

PUBLISHED BY
Microsoft Press
A Division of Microsoft Corporation
One Microsoft Way
Redmond, Washington 98052-6399

Library of Congress Cataloging-in-Publication Data
Microsoft Office XP Developer's Guide / Microsoft Corporation
      p. cm.
   Includes index.
   ISBN 0-7356-1242-0
   1. Microsoft Office.   2. Business--Computer programs.   I. Microsoft Corporation.

   HF5548.4.M525 M538   2001
   005.369--dc21   2001022224

Printed and bound in the United States of America.

1 2 3 4 5 6 7 8 9   QWT   6 5 4 3 2 1

Distributed in Canada by Penguin Books Canada Limited.

A CIP catalogue record for this book is available from the British Library.

Microsoft Press books are available through booksellers and distributors worldwide. For further information about international editions, contact your local Microsoft Corporation office or contact Microsoft Press International directly at fax (425) 936-7329. Visit our Web site at mspress.microsoft.com. Send comments to *mspinput@microsoft.com.*

Active Directory, ActiveX, BackOffice, BizTalk, FrontPage, IntelliMouse, IntelliSense, JScript, MapPoint, Microsoft, Microsoft Press, MS-DOS, MSDN, MSN, Outlook, PivotChart, PivotTable, PowerPoint, SharePoint, Visio, Visual Basic, Visual C++, Visual InterDev, Visual SourceSafe, Visual Studio, Win32, Win32s, Win64, Windows, and Windows NT are either registered trademarks or trademarks of Microsoft Corporation in the United States and/or other countries. Other product and company names mentioned herein may be the trademarks of their respective owners.

Unless otherwise noted, the example companies, organizations, products, people, and events depicted herein are fictitious. No association with any real company, organization, product, person, or event is intended or should be inferred.

Acquisitions Editor: Juliana Aldous
Project Editor: Denise Bankaitis

Part No. X08-04902

CONTENTS

Foreword

Congratulations! If you are reading this foreword, you are part of the strong community of professional developers who either are using Microsoft® Office as a part of a custom business solution or are very interested in learning how to utilize Office as a great platform for solutions. This book is the best available resource for learning how to take advantage of the new programmability features of Office XP.

More than 2.6 million developers currently are using Office as a part of their custom business solutions. Why are so many developers building solutions with Office? For starters, Office can now be found on more than 125 million users' desktops. In addition, developers have recognized that leveraging the Office platform found on users' desktops is the best way to build business solutions that integrate into the environment already familiar to users—thus reducing expenses, such as training efforts and support calls.

With the release of Office XP, Microsoft has worked hard to augment the award winning work in previous versions of Office with new features that make it possible for broader solution types to be built with Office. With this release, Microsoft has continued to improve the Office Component Object Model (COM) and to integrate Microsoft® Visual Basic® for Applications (VBA) throughout Office. Having a consistent development language and environment greatly simplifies developers' efforts in building solutions and working with the objects and the services Office provides. In addition, in this release, Microsoft has provided a broad new set of tools and services that work hand-in-hand with VBA:

- **Extensible Markup Language (XML) Support** Microsoft® Excel and Microsoft® Access can natively read and write XML documents.

- **Smart Tag Technology** Smart Tags are COM objects that dynamically associate relevant words or terms with relevant user actions. This technology is extensible and makes it possible for e-mail, spreadsheets, and documents to "come alive."

- **Office Web Components** In an effort to bring the richness of Office to the Web, Microsoft has updated the Office Web Components and made it possible for broader customization and distribution of data solutions.

- **Workflow Designers** Found in Office XP Developer, the new workflow designers for Microsoft® Exchange Server and Microsoft® SQL Server™ provide a quick and easy design surface to build workflow applications.

- **Data Access Page Designer** Updated since last version based on customer feedback, the Data Access Page Designer makes it possible for Access developers to build web-based applications leveraging the Access skills they already have.

- **Digital Dashboards**   Digital Dashboards provide a simply way to quickly see all the information that is relevant to a user. By using Office XP Developer, you can build Web Parts and Digital Dashboards quickly and easily.

There are plenty more updates and improvements that make Office XP the best release of Office yet. However, the question is this: With all these new updates, tools, and platform services, how do you get started? That is where this book comes in.

The *Microsoft Office XP Developer's Guide* is intended specifically to help professional developers take advantage of the platform services and tools in the Office suite. This book was designed from the ground up to be a comprehensive guide to building custom solutions that profit from the powerful technologies available in Office. The authors assume you know the basics of VBA and understand something about what it means to work with Office objects, object models, and components, as well as Internet related technologies, such as XML, HTML, and HTTP. There is no fluff or filler here. This is not a user's guide. This is a roll-up-your-sleeves-and-get-productive-quickly resource designed to help you build your custom Office solutions. The *Microsoft Office XP Developer's Guide* was written by a team of experienced and talented writers and developers who have worked closely with the Office XP team throughout the entire development cycle. That experience and knowledge has been included here in the form of insights, tips, tricks, and sample code that will make you productive immediately.

So, whether you have been developing solutions with Office for years or are starting now, whether you are an Office developer looking to incorporate Internet technologies into your solutions or a Web developer looking to leverage Office, by opening this book you have taken the most important first step in capitalizing on everything Office XP has to offer. The *Microsoft Office XP Developer's Guide* is truly the "developer's owner's manual" to Office XP.

Anders Brown

Lead Product Manager
Microsoft Office Developer and Solutions Group
Microsoft Corporation
http://www.microsoft.com/office/developer/
May 2001

Getting Started with Office XP Developer

Microsoft® Office XP Developer provides everything for developers building solutions with Office XP. Office Developer includes professional productivity tools, documentation, and sample code for quickly building, managing, and deploying solutions with Office and Office components.

Office XP makes it possible for developers to take advantage of application programmability to access a rich platform of pre-built functionality on which they can build custom solutions. Application programmability refers to the extent to which an application can be customized and integrated with other applications to deliver a seamless, tailored solution with which users are familiar. Building solutions on top of productivity applications results in faster development cycles and satisfied users, because organizational data can be delivered directly into productivity applications that users work with every day.

Introduction

Developers have been able to build custom solutions based on the applications in Microsoft Office for a long time. Each new version of Office brings new tools and technologies that make it easier to develop and deliver custom Office-based solutions. As companies have standardized on the Office suite of applications, users have become more familiar with these applications, and developers have learned to take advantage of the Office tools and technologies to create customized and integrated solutions on top of the Office suite of applications. These are solutions designed to improve users' abilities to gather, analyze, customize, publish, and share information.

More than 2.6 million developers currently use Office as a part of the custom solutions they build. After all, Office can now be found on more than 40 million users' desktops. Developers have long recognized that Office exposes hundreds of reusable objects that can be automated and integrated programmatically to create custom solutions. Furthermore, developers know they can save time and effort by taking advantage of the pre-built objects, functionality, and services provided by the Office applications.

With the Office XP Developer release, Microsoft has continued to simplify the process of customizing and automating Office and creating collaborative knowledge management solutions. Having a consistent development language and environment greatly simplifies developers' efforts in building solutions and working with the objects and services Office provides. However, the major challenge of developing solutions generally revolves around knowing which objects to create instances of, which properties to set, and the appropriate and available methods to call.

With more than 600 programmable objects exposed to the developer, Office provides incredible flexibility; however, there must be some way of identifying the appropriate objects, knowing the most efficient way to access them, and understanding the syntax required for developing solutions with them.

Typographic Conventions

The following typographic conventions are used in Help:

Example of convention	Description
On the **File** menu, click **Open**.	Elements that appear in the user interface are bold when the steps for performing a procedure are detailed.
expr, path	In syntax, italics indicate placeholders for information you supply. In text, italic letters are used for defined terms, usually the first time they occur in a topic. In addition, italics are used occasionally for emphasis.
ReadOnly, FileName	In text and syntax, the use of bold and italic together indicates named arguments.
[expressionlist]	In syntax, items in square brackets are optional.
**{While	Until}**	In syntax, braces and a vertical bar indicate a choice between two or more items. You must choose one of the items unless all of the items are enclosed in square brackets.
`Dim rstCust As ADODB.Recordset`	A monospace font indicates code.
`Set olNewItem = _` `    ol.CreateItem(olMailItem)`	The line-continuation character (_) is used to break long lines of code.

`Sub StockSale()`
`    .`
`    .`
`    .`
`End Sub`
	A column of three periods indicates that part of an example has been omitted intentionally.

Code Samples and Programming Style

Microsoft® Office XP Developer Help contains numerous code samples that you can use to experiment with the concepts covered. Unless otherwise noted, the code is compatible with Microsoft® Visual Basic® for Applications (VBA) 6.0 as it is implemented in Visual Basic 6.0, Microsoft® Access, Microsoft® Excel, Microsoft® FrontPage®, Microsoft® Outlook®, Microsoft® PowerPoint®, Microsoft® Word, and other applications that host VBA 6.0. Additional code samples are written in Visual Basic Scripting Edition (VBScript), Microsoft® JScript®, HTML, and DHTML.

The documentation uses the following conventions in VBA sample code:

- Keywords appear with an initial letter capitalized; concatenated words might contain other capital letters. Variables appear in mixed case, constants in uppercase.

```
Dim objDatabase As Object
    Const PROP_NOT_FOUND_ERROR = 3270


    Set objDatabase = CurrentDb
```

- In full procedures, all variables are declared locally or are listed with an initialization procedure that declares public variables. All code has been tested with the VBA Option Explicit statement to make sure there are no undeclared variables.

- An apostrophe (') introduces a comment:

```
' This is a comment.
Dim intNew As Integer   ' This is also a comment.
```

- Control-flow blocks and statements in Sub, Function, and Property procedures are indented:

```
Sub MyCode ()
    Dim intX As Integer
    Dim intP As Integer
    Dim intQ As Integer

    If intX > 0 Then
        intP = intQ
    End If
End Sub
```

- Naming conventions are used to make it easier to identify objects and variables in the code samples. For more information about naming conventions, see "Writing Solid Code."

The Documentation also uses the following convention in HTML script samples:

- The HTML and DHTML naming conventions use a lowercase or lowercase and uppercase concatenated style for object, variable, method, event, function, and property names. For example, the name of the document object is lowercase, whereas the name of the srcElement property is a concatenated lowercase and uppercase combination.

Using the Code Samples

Microsoft® Office XP Developer comes with numerous code samples that you can use for experimenting and becoming acquainted with features. Many of these samples, along with a sample application, have been collected in the Samples folder on the Office XP Developer CD-ROM. Wherever possible, these code samples were written not only for you to learn from studying how they work but also so you can use them directly in your custom applications.

The CD-ROM contains code samples illustrating Office programmability features, including samples that highlight each of the Office applications and demonstrate how to create useful forms, reports, and interfaces for them, samples that illustrate how add-ins can be loaded and used, information on how to work with shared components, and details about how to automate one application from another. In addition, several sample Office applications are included that you can use in your solutions. These sample applications include a progress bar that you can use in any Office application, an audit trail example that acts as a means of tracking all activities affecting a piece of information, and an Installer sample that makes it possible for developers to get the component IDs for Office features they want to be available on users' machines.

Some of the examples use data in Northwind.mdb, a sample database that ships with Microsoft® Access. If you have not installed the Northwind sample database, you must do so to take full advantage of these examples.

A sample workflow application for Microsoft® SQL Server™ is included on the CD-ROM that shows how to create a simple Issue Tracking application that consists of a Web-based user interface and a SQL Server database. The sample demonstrates how to track an issue through a basic series of states or steps in a business process.

Also included with Office XP Developer is the Code Librarian. The Code Librarian contains a large starter database of prewritten code for standard routines for Office, Microsoft® Visual Basic® for Applications (VBA), Office XP Developer projects, and the development environment. Each code snippet is associated with a category and multiple keywords, making it easy to find the code you are looking for. When you have located a desired piece of code in the Code Librarian, you can add that code to your code module.

In Microsoft® Word, security is set by default to High, which means that the code will not run when you open the Word sample files. To use these files, you must change the security setting.

To change the security setting in Word

1. Point to **Macro** on the **Tools** menu.

2. Click **Security**, and then click either **Medium** or **Low** on the **Security Level** tab.

To run the scripting examples that use scriptlets, your browser's security settings must be set to Medium or Low.

For more information and samples, see the Office Developer Web site at http://msdn.microsoft.com/office.

What's New in Office XP Developer

With the release of Office XP Developer, Microsoft has worked hard to augment the award winning work in previous versions of Office with new features that make it possible for broader solution types to be built with Office. With this release, Microsoft has continued to improve the Office Component Object Model (COM) and to integrate Microsoft® Visual Basic® for Applications (VBA) throughout Office. Having a consistent development language and environment greatly simplifies developers' efforts in building applications and working with the objects and the services Office provides. In addition, in this release, Microsoft has provided a broad new set of tools and services that work hand-in-hand with VBA.

Office Developer provides the productivity tools professional developers must have to build solutions faster, the integration tools to make their solutions work seamlessly with data and the Web, and the management tools to simplify deploying and managing the solutions they build with Office. Here are some of the features that have been added or enhanced in this version.

- **Extensible Markup Language (XML) Support** Microsoft® Excel and Microsoft® Access can natively read and write XML documents.

- **Smart Tag Technology** Smart Tags are COM objects that dynamically associate relevant words or terms with relevant user actions. This technology is extensible and makes it possible for e-mail, spreadsheets, and documents to "come alive".

- **Office Web Components** In an effort to bring the richness of Office to the Web, Microsoft has updated the Office Web Components and made it possible for broader customization and distribution of data solutions.

- **Workflow Designers** Found only in Office XP Developer, the new workflow designers for Microsoft® Exchange Server and Microsoft® SQL Server™ provide a quick and easy design surface to build workflow applications.

- **Data Access Page Designer** Updated since last version based on customer feedback, the Data Access Page Designer makes it possible for Access developers to build web-based applications leveraging the Access skills they already have.

- **Digital Dashboards**   Digital Dashboards provide a simply way to quickly see all the information that is relevant to a user. By using Office XP Developer, you can build Web Parts and Digital Dashboards quickly and easily.

There are plenty more updates and improvements that make Office XP the best release of Office yet.

- **Integrated development environment**   The development components of Office XP Developer have been integrated into a shell environment that is designed to be convenient to use and familiar to anyone who works with other Microsoft professional development tools. The new integrated development environment includes features such as the Solution Explorer, a properties window, an object browser, and a task list. In addition, a Web browser package is included that makes it possible for you to work on HTML pages and preview them in the development environment.

- **Integrated Code Librarian**   You can use the Code Librarian to store and manage reusable code in a centralized database. You can add your own code to the existing Code Librarian database, or you can create new code databases. The Code Librarian has been redesigned for Office Developer, providing more efficient code management and functionality as part of the integrated development environment.

- **Improved Packaging wizard**   The Packaging wizard makes it easy for you to build and deploy setup programs for your Office Developer applications. The wizard guides you through the steps of creating a setup program that contains all of the information required to install your applications on users' computers.

Setting up the Developer Design Environment

To install the Office Productivity tools, the Workflow Designer for SQL Server, the Workflow Designer for Exchange Server, and Dashboard Developer tools, your computer must meet the following system requirements.

System Requirements

The developer workstation must meet the following system requirements:

- Microsoft® Windows® 2000, Microsoft® Windows NT4® Service Pack 6, Windows 98, or Windows Millennium edition

  Note   You must be a member of the Administrators group or Power Users group in Windows to have access to all of the features of Microsoft® Office XP Developer.

- Office XP

- For Workflow for SQL Server Developer tools: a version of Microsoft® SQL Server™ is required on the developer computer to use the workflow tools. If the server contains SQL Server 7.0, then the developer workstation must contain SQL Server 7.0 or Microsoft® SQL Server™ Desktop Engine 7.0. If the server contains SQL Server 2000, then the developer workstation can contain either SQL Server version 7.0 or version 2000.

  Note   If you install SQL Server 2000, you must install to the default SQL Named Instance.

Installing the Developer Tools

After meeting system prerequisites, launch Office XP Developer Setup to install the developer tools.

To Install the Developer Tools

1. Verify that all system requirements have been satisfied. Install any missing prerequisites before launching Office XP Developer Setup.

2. Install Office XP from the Office XP CD-ROM. The default installation installs Microsoft® Visual Basic® for Applications 6.3; if you customize your installation, be sure to include this as well.

3. Install Microsoft SQL Server or SQL Server Desktop Engine to use the Workflow Tools for SQL Server.

4. Launch the Office XP Developer Setup program from the Office XP Developer CD-ROM.

5. Click **Windows Component Update**. This installs operating system components required by Office XP Developer.

    Note   The Windows Component Update does not install other system prerequisite components, such as Office XP.

6. Click **Install Office Developer**.

7. From the feature list, accept the default options, or select the check box next to the desired component.

    - To install all available productivity tools, open the **Office Developer Tools** node, and select the **Office Developer Tools** check box. To install only individual tools, clear the check box next to the tools you do not want to install.

    - To install workflow components for SQL Server, open the **Workflow Developer Tools** node, and select the **Workflow Designer for SQL Server** check box to install the development tools. Select the **Workflow Manager for SQL Server** check box to install the administrative tools.

    - To install workflow components for Exchange Server, open the **Workflow Developer Tools** node, and select the **Workflow Designer for Exchange Server** check box.

    - To install Dashboard Developer tools, select the **Dashboard Developer Tools** check box.

    - To install Software Developer Kits, open the **Office Developer Tools**, and select the **Software Developer Kits** check box.

8. Click **Install Now!** to continue with Setup.

9. When Office Developer setup is complete, you are returned to the Office Developer Setup window. Click **Exit** to close the window.

Setting up the Server Environment

To take advantage of all Microsoft® Office XP Developer features, you must have access to servers that have the appropriate configuration. For the latest details about setting up the servers, see Readme.htm on the root of the Office Developer CD-ROM.

To create workflow applications using Microsoft® Exchange and Digital Dashboards, you must have access to a server running Exchange 2000 Server. To create workflow applications using Microsoft® SQL Server™, you must have access to a server running SQL Server 7.0 or SQL Server 2000 and the Workflow Services for SQL Server, which is installed using the Office Developer CD-ROM.

Setting up the Exchange Server

It is recommended you develop workflow applications on a computer set aside for development before moving them to a production Exchange 2000 Server. For specific instructions about setting up an Exchange Server, refer to the Exchange 2000 Server documentation. Here are some tips specific to setting up and configuring an Exchange Server for workflow applications. If you have a test version of Exchange 2000 set up, you can adjust your own configuration. On a production Exchange 2000 Server, the server administrator makes the adjustments.

System Requirements

The Exchange Server must meet the following system requirements:

- Microsoft® Windows® 2000 Server

- Windows 2000 Service Pack 1

- Exchange 2000 Server

Configuring Server Components

By default, Microsoft Exchange 2000 Server includes a workflow engine that controls the state changes to documents in a workflow folder. The workflow event sink (CDOWFEVT.DLL) calls the engine when an event fires in your workflow enabled folder. Before creating Exchange workflow applications, the workflow event sink has to be configured to run under the identity of a user with appropriate permissions. To do this, you must create a user with the appropriate permissions, add them as the identity of the workflow event sink, and then add this user to the appropriate groups and roles on the Exchange 2000 Server.

To create users

1. On the domain controller for your Exchange 2000 Server, from the **Start** button point to **Programs**, point to **Microsoft Exchange**, and then click **Active Directory Users and Computers**.

2. Expand the server node.

3. Right-click **Users**, point to **New,** and click **User**.

4. Enter **First name**, **Last name**, and **User logon name**. Do not include spaces in the logon name. Click **Next**.

5. Enter and confirm a password. For test accounts, it is reasonable to enable the **Password Never Expires** option. Click **Next**.

6. All the options for creating a new mailbox are set for you. Click **Next**.

7. Click **Finish**.

To assign an identity for the workflow event sink

1. In the **Active Directory Users and Computers** window, right-click the **Exchange Domain Servers** group, and select **Properties**.

2. Click on the **Members** tab.

3. Click **Add**.

4. Type *<user alias>*.

5. Press **Enter**, click **Apply**, and click **OK**.

6. From the **Start** button, point to **Programs**, point to **Administrative Tools**, and then click **Component Services**.

7. Under the **Console Root**, expand **Component Services**.

8. Expand **Computers**, **My Computer**, **COM+ Applications**, **Workflow Event Sink**.

9. Right-click **Workflow Event Sink**, and select **Properties**.

10. Select the **Identity** tab.

11. Under **Account**, next to the **This User** text box, click **Browse**.

12. In the **Name** text box, enter <user alias>, and press **Enter**.

13. The **User** option is set to <domain>\<user alias>.

14. Enter and confirm the password for the account.

15. Click **OK** to confirm settings.

> **Note** If you return to the **Identity** tab, the **Password** field will be blank, but your password will still be valid.

The user account that is used for the Workflow Event Sink user account has to be part of the following two COM+ roles:

- Can Register Workflow

- Privileged Workflow Authors

> **Note** To make administration easier, it is recommended you create a single group and add that group to the roles and Exchange Domain Servers group. Then, you can make it possible for users to run workflow applications simply by adding them to the group.

To add the user to the two COM+ roles

1. From the **Start** menu, point to **Programs**, point to **Administrative Tools**, and then click **Component Services**.

2. In the **Component Services** dialog box, open the **Component Services** node, then **Computers**, then **My Computer**, then **COM+ Applications**, then **Workflow Event Sink**, and then **Roles**.

    There are two workflow roles there—**Can Register Workflow** and **Privileged Workflow Authors**.

3. Add the user to both of these roles by right-clicking the role name and adding the user.

The user account that is used in the Workflow Event Sink must be a member of the Exchange Domain Servers group.

To make user a member of the Exchange Domain Servers group

1. From the **Start** menu, point to **Programs**, point to **Administrative Tools**, and then click **Active Directory Users and Computers**.

2. In the **Domain Users** folder, right-click the user name, and select **Properties**.

3. Select the **Member Of** tab, and click **Add**.

4. Find the Exchange Domain Servers group, and add the user.

You might have to shut down and restart the application for these changes to be applied. To do that right-click the Workflow Event Sink node, and select Shut Down, then right-click the node, and select Start.

To set script execution permissions

When the server users have been configured, you must permit script execution on the Exchange Server. This is not the default.

1. Log onto Exchange 2000 Server as **Administrator**.

2. From the **Start** button, point to **Programs**, point to **Microsoft Exchange**, and then click **System Manager**.

3. Expand your server.

4. Expand **Protocols**.

5. Expand **HTTP**.

6. Expand **Exchange Virtual Server**.

7. Right-click **Public**, and select **Properties**.

8. Click the **Access** tab.

9. Under **Execute Permissions**, enable **Scripts** and **Executables**.

10. Click **Authentication**.

11. Under **Select the authentication method to use for this resource**, make sure **Anonymous** is not enabled.

12. Under **Basic authentication**, set the default domain to the domain name for your Exchange Server.

13. Click **OK**.

> **Note** Do not set script execution permissions by right-clicking **My Computer** and selecting **Manage**. When the Active Directory synchronizes, the settings in Manage are overruled by the settings in the System Manager.

Setting up the SQL Server

To create and run workflow applications using SQL Server, you must have a server containing SQL Server 7.0 or SQL Server 2000 and the Workflow Services for SQL Server to host and manage the workflow applications.

System Requirements

The SQL Server must meet the following system requirements:

Windows 2000 Server

- System Administrator privileges on the Windows 2000 Server. To obtain System Administer privileges, add yourself to the Administrators group on the server.

- Internet Information Services (IIS) with Front Page server extensions. Windows 2000 Server installs IIS by default.

- Windows 2000 Service Pack 1

SQL Server 7.0 or SQL Server 2000

You can use either SQL Server 7.0 or SQL Server 2000. The developer workstation must be using the same version of SQL Server as the server.

Requirements for SQL Server 2000

- The service account setting must be set to use a Domain User account. This is the default in SQL Server Setup.

- Security mode can be set to Windows authentication or Mixed mode.

Requirements for SQL Server 7.0

- The service account setting must be set to use a Domain User account. This is the default in SQL Server setup.

- SQL Server 7.0 must use Integrated Security.

  If your SQL Server currently uses SQL Security, reinstall SQL Server, and select the Integrated Security option.

- SQL Server 7.0 Service Pack 2, available on the Office Developer CD-ROM.

After meeting system prerequisites, launch Office XP Developer Setup to install the Workflow Services for SQL Server.

Note If you are upgrading from a previous version of SQL Server workflow server components, uninstall all previous SQL Server workflow components before running Setup. You must run an uninstall procedure that you will find in the Readme file before you uninstall, or any applications and templates that you created previously will be lost.

Installing Server Components

To install the Workflow Services for SQL Server

1. Verify that the server is configured correctly and that all system requirements are met.

2. Install SQL Server. See prerequisite information earlier.

3. Insert the Office XP Developer CD-ROM, and launch the Office XP Developer Setup program.

4. Click **Windows Component Update**. This installs operating system components required by Office Developer. Insert the Windows Component Update CD-ROM, and enter the path to the CD-ROM.

   Note The Windows Component Update does not install other system prerequisite components, such as Office XP.

5. Click **Install Office Developer**.

6. From the feature list, select **Workflow Services for SQL Server**.

7. Click **Install Now!** to continue with Setup.

PART 2

Developing Office Developer Applications

Microsoft® Office XP Developer provides the productivity tools professional developers must have to build applications faster, integration tools to make their applications work seamlessly with data and the Web, and management tools to simplify deploying and managing the applications they build with Microsoft Office.

To develop applications using Office Developer

1. Design your application before starting. Numerous considerations make application development much easier if they are addressed from the start—for example, choosing a data store, security, and schema. For more information, see "Designing Applications."

2. Create an Office Developer project and develop your application. Workflow applications and dashboard projects are created using the Microsoft development environment. Applications using Microsoft® Visual Basic® for Applications (VBA) are created using the Visual Basic Editor in the Office application you are using. For more information, see "Developing Applications with Microsoft Office Developer."

3. Debug your code and create errors handlers. Successfully debugging code is more of an art than a science. The best results come from writing understandable and maintainable code and using the available debugging tools. Writing good error handlers is a matter of anticipating problems or conditions that are beyond your immediate control and that will prevent your code from executing correctly at run time. For more information, see "Debugging and Error Handling."

4. Add online Help to your application to reduce the amount of time required to train and support users.

5. Localize your application, adapting it for countries or parts of the world in which it will be used. You must translate the strings in the user interface, and it might involve changing the application itself where necessary. For more information, see "Localizing Your Application."

6. Deploy your application with one of the many alternatives, ranging from copying a file to a common share on a network server to building a full-fledged setup program. How you choose to deploy the application depends largely on what type of application you have created. For more information, see "Deploying Your Application."

CHAPTER 1

Designing Applications

It is important for developers to go through the process of planning and design to be able to begin coding with a clear goal in mind. Spending a few hours up front on design can mean the difference between delivering the application that customers must have a few months down the road or backtracking to try to convert many hours of coding work into the application that should have been designed in the first place.

In This Section

The Design Process
Identify your customers and their requirements before you begin designing an application.

Which Technologies Should You Use?
Determine the type of application you want to create and which application or technologies to use as the basis for your application.

Thinking About User Interface Design
Understand how an effective user interface is an important aspect to application design.

Designing Code for Reusability
Maximize the reusability of your code by spending some time thinking about how to structure your code within the application.

Security Considerations
Protect your intellectual property by securing your code and protect your application from viruses and unwelcome users.

Testing Your Application
Test your code to make sure that each part of the application works as expected.

Application Deployment
After you develop an application, you can distribute it to users.

The Design Process

The first thing that you must do when you begin designing an application is to identify your customers. Who will be using the application? It might be just one person, a small workgroup within your company, or an entire department. Perhaps you are a consultant building custom applications for other companies. Maybe you are building Office-based applications to package and sell through a retail outfit or over the Internet. Whoever your customers are, you should have a thorough understanding of their business processes and their requirements before you begin building your application.

What Do Your Customers Want?

The first step in the design process is to get a clear idea of what your customers want. This can take some time and patience, especially if your customers are not technical people by nature.

Have your customers tell you in their own words what they want, and ask lots of questions to clarify your customers' goals for yourself. It is a good idea to rephrase your customers' requests and repeat them back to make sure that you are communicating on the same plane. For example, if your customers say they want to be able to create reports from a set of data, you must know: Who will be using the reports? Can they be read-only, or must users be able to manipulate the data in the report to present it in new ways? Should the reports be available over a corporate intranet, will they be printed, or will they be e-mailed? The answers to these kinds of questions will begin to eliminate certain design possibilities and shift your focus to others.

You might have to ask the same question several times in several different ways. It might be helpful to diagram or demonstrate multiple possibilities to your customers and ask them to choose the one that best fits what they have in mind. Keep in mind your customers probably find the planning and design process difficult, and they would rather you just went away and came back with what they want. Simplifying choices for your customers, while keeping their goals in mind, might make the process easier for everyone.

What Do Your Customers Need?

What your customers want and what your customers require is not always the same thing. Customers might say they want a particular type of application, because that is what they are familiar with, or because they have seen the technology and think it is cool. As the developer, you must figure out what application will best fit your customers' requirements and offer persuasive evidence to your customers. That said, keep in mind that in the end, the application your customers want takes priority over the application that you want to build. If you cannot understand why your customers want a particular application, it is possible you do not understand their requirements well enough.

To figure out what your customers require, look at your customers' existing applications, if there are any, and their business process. For example, if your customers want to create a database to track accounting information that to date has been managed on paper, review the paper system carefully, so you can model the application on the existing system. Of course, in the process of modeling the existing system, you might find ways to enhance the system within the application and make your customers' business process more efficient.

Next, find out who will be using the application and how they will use it. Interview as many people as you can who have used the existing system or who will use your application when it has been created. If you are dealing with only one person to create an application that will be used by several people, it is possible you are getting a narrow perspective on what the application must do.

Who will use the application and how they will use it can make a big difference in your design. For example, a database in which multiple users might be entering data simultaneously across a network requires a different design than a database that is managed by one or two people who enter data and then generate reports for other users. The first application might require record-locking management, full-fledged security, and a means of distributing the front end across a corporate network. The second application probably can get by with no locking management, minimal security, and a common network share for those using it.

At the Drawing Table

When you have gathered as much information as you can from your customers, sit down with a pencil and paper, and sketch out the initial design for the application—the technologies to be used, the user interface, the organization of the code. Doing this gives you a basis to begin working, and it is likely to bring up all kinds of new questions you must ask your customers. Nailing down as many issues as you can before you start coding will save you time in the long run.

If your application is complex, you might want to write a specification for it. A specification is a document that outlines your goals in creating the application, discusses the details of the application's implementation, and notes unresolved technical and design issues. It is a valuable document and helps both you and your customers agree on how the application will work before you begin creating it. It also provides you and any other programmers working on the project with a road map for the development process.

Of course, you might not be able to foresee every aspect of your application's design ahead of time. As you develop the application, you most likely will learn new ways to do things, encounter unplanned obstacles, and refine your understanding of your customers' requirements. The key is to create a flexible design, so making a change does not send you all the way back to the beginning. For example, creating custom objects is a good way to build in flexibility. If you must modify an object, you only have to do so once within that object's class module. Using constants in your code is another way to make your code more organized and easier to modify.

If you suspect there might be a more efficient way to do something, indulge your intuition before you dive into the code. There is no point in re-creating the wheel if someone has already built the component you must have.

Building a Prototype

For most Microsoft® Office XP applications, you are not required to build a full-fledged prototype—the application you are building can act as the prototype you show to your customers. When you begin building the application, however, it is useful to approach it as though it were a prototype, so you can demonstrate quickly to your customers how the application is going to work.

Map out a general user interface, but do not spend hours laying out controls and adding graphics if the user interface might have to be altered. Also, forego work on the fine details of navigation through the application, unless that is a critical part for your customers to see.

Build the core part of the application first. For example, if you are building a wizard, focus on the code that generates the basic result, rather than adding in the various options that users will be able to select to fine-tune the outcome. This way, you can determine whether you are on the right track for creating the application your customers must have. Also, when you have tackled the hard problems, you will have more insight into the way that the final application will work and a better understanding of your customers' business process.

Use sample data to test your initial design. Do not use live data or your customer's only copy of the data if your application might modify it. Create a local copy of the data that you can isolate until you have tested the application thoroughly.

Which Technologies Should You Use?

The first critical design decisions you must make are what type of application you want to create and which application or technologies to use as the basis for your application. Applications you create with Microsoft® Office XP are likely to fall into one of the following broad categories: data-management applications, document templates, add-ins, and Web applications—either with or without a data-management component.

Each of the Office applications is better suited to some applications than to others. Deciding which to use requires some familiarity with the strengths and weaknesses of each of them.

In This Section

Workflow: Technology Backgrounder
> You generally use the term workflow to describe applications that are modeled as business processes.

Where Should You Store Data?
> Access existing data directly through OLE DB or through Open Database Connectivity (ODBC).

Building Add-ins, Wizards, and Templates
> Learn how add-ins, wizards, and templates help users do their jobs more efficiently.

Workflow: Technology Backgrounder

You generally use the term workflow to describe applications that are modeled as business processes. Typical workflow applications include forms routing/approval, document review/publishing, and issue tracking. While you can implement such applications in nearly any programming language or development environment, you can simplify the task with the use of a workflow engine and specialized workflow modeling tools.

- Modeling tools make it possible for the overall design, or flow, of a business process to be specified in a simple, high-level representation called a process definition. You can modify or extend the process definition without rewriting all of the low-level application code.

- The workflow engine executes and manages individual instances of a process definition, also known as process instances.

The conceptual model for a workflow process includes states and events. A state is a discrete value of the state property of an item. For example, the state of an issue defines where that issue is in the workflow process, such as Resolved or Closed. An event defines the operations that can be performed on an item. One special type of event is a transition, which moves the item from one state to another.

The core services provided by the Workflow Designer tools that you can use to create applications are Workflow and Security.

Workflow

Workflow processes are used to enforce business rules, such as who sees an item, the sequence of events an item goes through, the routing of an item, or even when an item can be created or deleted. Microsoft® Office XP Developer creates workflow processes specifically for Microsoft® Exchange folders or for Microsoft® SQL Server™ databases. When workflow is applied, all items in that folder must conform to the information flow created by the workflow process.

A workflow process is made up of a series of tasks and events, the order in which they must occur, and (optionally) the script that is executed for each event. In its simplest form, a workflow process automates and enforces the order of tasks. For example, a user can create a new item in a folder and assign it to another user. This user can resolve the item and assign it to the original user who then can close the issue.

Office Developer uses a graphical user interface (GUI) to represent the workflow process as a diagram that can be automated, extended, and edited. The conceptual model for a workflow process includes states, events, and transitions.

Workflow component	Description
State	A state defines the current status of an item in the workflow process, such as Resolved.
Event	An event defines the operations that can be performed on an item, such as Create. In addition, workflow events can be used to trigger scripts.
Transition	A transition, which is a special type of event, moves an item from one state to another, such as Change. When creating a transition, in addition to selecting the event, you must specify the next state.

Workflow Data Stores

A key part of designing your workflow process is determining how your application should get data from users, validate it, and move it through the workflow process. The extent to which your application must control user input is a factor in choosing which data store to use as the basis for your application.

You must make a decision about the level of security your workflow must have. You might want to restrict the ability to view or change information at different steps in your workflow. Your workflow process can be secured in several different ways. The following is list of some of the security methods and the required data store.

Security method	Data store
Role-based permissions	SQL Server
Server security	Exchange 2000 Server
Back-end business process logic component	Exchange 2000 Server
Front-end security for the application user interface	Exchange 2000 Server SQL Server

Security

The ability to view or change certain pieces of information often must be restricted based on a user's role. For example, in a payroll application, an employee and manager both might be permitted to view the employee's salary, but only the payroll clerk has the permissions to change the salary in the application.

Permissions specify what kind of access a user has to objects in the folder. For example, if a user has read permissions for an item, data can be viewed or retrieved but not edited.

The security model you follow for the user interface of your application will depend on the type of application you are creating and the security requirements of your team or company.

SQL Server

Workflow Designer for Microsoft® SQL Server™ provides role-based security based on security information from SQL Server and Microsoft® Windows NT®. Roles are defined by the developer using Microsoft® Access database security tools and are based on the SQL Server database roles.

Permissions specify what kind of access a user has to data or objects in the team application database. For example, if a user has read permissions for a table, the user can view or retrieve but not edit data in the table. Permissions can be modified using Access.

Security can be managed at the team application level by adding or removing users from the application. Setting security at the application level controls access to both the team database and the team Web site. In addition, permissions can be applied at a table level or row level.

These security features leverage the database-, table-, and column-level security that SQL Server provides. Workflow Designer for SQL Server also extends the SQL Server security model by enabling row-level security and workflow action security.

Row-level permissions make it possible for users to set permissions on individual rows on a table. Only main user tables can have row-level permissions set. When you define permissions for a main table, those permissions are enforced on related rows in any detail user tables.

Row-level permissions are enforced for write operations using triggers on the associated table. Read permissions are enforced by requiring all access to the table to be performed through a base view that Workflow Designer for SQL Server creates and by locking the base table.

The workflow application also can implement NTFS permissions on the team Web site. This provides an additional layer of security. See the Windows NT documentation for more details.

The permissions and roles you define for your application are preserved when you create a template based on it. The Workflow Template Creation wizard provides the option of removing existing database users before storing the database in the template. If you plan to make a template based on the workflow application, make sure all permissions are applied to roles rather than to users, because the specific users of an application might change from instance to instance.

Exchange 2000

There are three tiers to the security model for a workflow application. The first is the server security, the second is the security for the back-end business process logic component, and the third is the front-end security for the application user interface.

Server Security

Setting up and maintaining a secure server is the job of the server administrator. This job includes creating objects and users on the server and managing the permissions for these objects and users. Typically, this includes creating roles, adding users to roles, and assigning role permission to objects on the server. For an overview of security topics for Microsoft® Exchange 2000 Server, refer to *Implementing your Administrative Model* in the Exchange 2000 Server online Help.

Back-End Permissions

Using Workflow Designer for Exchange Server, developers can assign role-based security on workflow actions. The server administrator or folder owner, using the Exchange 2000 security tools, defines these roles and permissions.

Permissions specify what kind of access a user has to objects in the folder. For example, if a user has read permissions for an item, the user can view or retrieve but not edit data. These permissions can be modified using Exchange 2000 Server.

Roles are groups of Exchange users. Assigning permissions to roles rather than directly to users is the preferred method for setting up security. It is easier to maintain and scale applications using role-based security.

By default, all roles are granted permissions to perform all workflow actions. Limiting actions based on a user's role can ensure that only appropriate persons are making changes to items in a folder. For example, in an order-entry scenario, order clerks might be the only employees with permissions to create a new order, while the shipping clerks might be the only employees with permissions to close an order or to mark it as filled.

For an overview of security topics for Exchange 2000 Server, refer to *Implementing your Administrative Model* in the Exchange 2000 Server online Help.

Where Should You Store Data?

Many applications involve storing and managing data at some level. Microsoft's OLE DB technology makes it easier to access data in any format. If you must work with existing data, you can access it directly through OLE DB or through Open Database Connectivity (ODBC). If you are creating an application to store new data or if your customer wants to move existing data into the new application, you can choose the data-storage strategy that makes the most sense for your application.

Where should you store your data if you have the freedom to design your data storage from scratch? Although there are many options if you are building an Office-based application, you are most likely going to store data in a Microsoft® Excel workbook, in a Microsoft® Access database (.mdb), or on a database server, such as Microsoft® SQL Server™.

Should You Store Data in Excel or in a Relational Database?

Many people are comfortable with Microsoft® Visual Basic® for Applications (VBA) programming in Excel but are intimidated by relational databases, such as Access and SQL Server, which require an understanding of relational database design concepts. Some developers end up using Excel to build data-management applications that would be better off as relational databases.

Excel is best for storing small amounts of data on which you must perform calculations, or that you want to present in a grid format. In addition, Excel is good for storing disparate types of information—numeric, text, and graphical data, such as charts, that does not conform easily to a particular structure.

For larger data sets, Excel might not be the ideal application for storing the data, but it is a superior tool for analyzing and presenting data that is stored in another format. You can import data into Excel from any OLE DB or ODBC data source and use the Excel calculation and analysis tools to analyze the data however you choose.

Here are a few questions to ask when trying to decide whether to use a relational database or Excel to store data:

- Does your data duplicate items that could be stored in one place? For example, are you typing a customer's address repeatedly each time you take an order for that customer? If so, you would be better off storing your data in a relational database, where you can enter customer information in a single table and create relationships with other tables that use that data.

- Must you be able to expand the system with more data or more users in the future? If so, it is likely your application will become extremely complicated as you add data. Again, you would be better off storing your data in a relational database and using queries to get to the data that you require. A relational database is a better choice for scalability.

- Must you store or archive old data? Access is better suited to this task than Excel. On the other hand, if you regularly replace data without archiving it, Excel might be sufficient. For example, if your application pulls daily stock quotes from a Web page but does not have to track stock histories, Excel is ideal.

- Must your application be multiuser? If more than one person might have to access the data at the same time, you can take advantage of the built-in multiuser features in Access.

- Do you have to be able to control and validate data entry? Generally, Access is better suited for this than Excel. Access provides controls with built-in data binding with which you can impose validation rules easily. You can create bound controls and perform data validation on a UserForm in Excel, but it is more work.

If you decide to store your data in a relational database, you have several options. If you are building either a single-user application or a multiuser application for a small workgroup, you can store the data in an Access database (.mdb) or in a Microsoft® SQL Server™ 2000 Desktop Engine database.

A Microsoft SQL Server 2000 Desktop Engine database uses a database engine that is similar to the one found in SQL Server, however, a desktop engine database cannot support as many users; best performance is achieved with five or fewer users. The advantage to using the desktop engine is you can use it to create a SQL Server database from Access without actually having SQL Server on your computer. It is a good tool for prototyping and designing an enterprise solution. You eventually will migrate to SQL Server, because you can run a desktop engine database under SQL Server without modification. A database server such as SQL Server can support hundreds to thousands of simultaneous users. A properly optimized Access database (.mdb) can support up to 255 simultaneous users, although best performance is achieved with 25 to 50 users. An Access database is best for small workgroup-based applications.

Designing a Relational Database

If you decide to store the data for your application in a Microsoft® Access database (.mdb), Microsoft® SQL Server™ database, or other relational database, designing the database structure likely will be the most challenging part of building the application. To understand how the tables in the database should be structured and how they should relate to one another, you must understand the data—perfectly. Although it is easy to modify the data model while you are developing the application, it is much more difficult when your customers are using the application. It is important to put as much effort as necessary into the process of designing the data model before you begin writing code. Developing an application based on a well-designed data model is much more rewarding than working with one that is designed poorly.

Thinking About Data Entry and User Input

If your application requires users to enter data, a key part of your design process is determining how your application should get data from users and validate it. The extent to which your application must control user input is another factor in choosing which application to use as the basis for your application.

If you decide to store the data in a relational database, such as a Microsoft® Access or Microsoft® SQL Server™ database, it is a good idea to separate the application into two parts: a back-end database and a front-end data-entry component. The back-end database contains the tables, where all of the data is stored, while the front end displays the data and manages data entry. By designing the application this way, you can store the data in a central location on a network server and distribute a copy of the front-end file or files to each user. You can build the front-end data-entry component in any Microsoft® Office XP application or in Microsoft® Visual Basic®.

Using Access to Create a Data-Entry Component

An Access database makes a good front-end data-entry component for data stored in a relational database. If your back-end database is an Access .mdb file, you can create another .mdb file to function as the front-end and link it to the tables in the back-end database. In the front-end component, create the queries, forms, reports, data access pages, macros, and modules that you must have to build the application and to manipulate and display the data.

If your back-end database is a SQL Server database, you can create an Access Data Project (.adp) to function as the front-end data-entry component. In an Access project, you can create forms, reports, data access pages, macros, and modules, just as you can in an .mdb file. In addition, you can create SQL-specific objects, such as views, stored procedures, and database diagrams. By using an Access project, you can display the data in a SQL Server database, and you can create a database or modify the database structure.

Creating either an Access database or an Access project file is the best approach if your application requires users to enter data and if you must control the way data is stored. The design of your database itself enforces certain rules on the way users can enter data. For example, a user cannot violate a table's primary key by adding a duplicate record. In addition, you can establish custom validation rules in Access that prevent users from entering invalid data.

Validating User Input from Excel, Word, and PowerPoint-Based Applications

Microsoft® Excel, Microsoft® Word, and Microsoft® PowerPoint® are good tools for displaying data stored in a relational database, but they do not provide much flexibility for entering data into the database. However, if your data is stored in Excel, Word, or PowerPoint and your application requires that you control and validate the data that users enter, you still might have to perform data validation. Here are some ways to control and validate user input from these applications:

- Use the InputBox function to prompt users to input small amounts of information. Verify within code that users entered data, and make sure it is the type of data you are expecting. For example, you can use the IsNumeric and IsDate functions to determine whether users entered a number or a date.

- Create a custom dialog box that prompts users to enter data or select options. Using this approach provides more flexibility than using the InputBox function. By using a combo box, for example, you can force users to choose an existing value from a list, thus preventing errors that might occur if users typed the value in.

- Disable controls on the form until users have entered the data you are expecting. For example, within the Change event procedure for a text box control, you can check whether the value of the text box is a zero-length string (""). If it is, you can disable the command buttons on the form, so users cannot proceed without entering text or canceling, as shown in the following procedure:

```
' The Len function returns zero if there is no data in the text box,
' and a nonzero value if there is, so using the CBool function
' converts the numeric value to True (nonzero) or False (zero).
Private Sub txtGetData_Change()
    cmdOK.Enabled = CBool(Len(txtGetData.Value))
End If
```

- Create a wizard that walks users through an operation, prompting them at each step to supply the necessary data. Again, you can prevent users from proceeding by disabling the command buttons that the wizard uses for navigation.

You also can use these strategies for controlling and validating data input through script in a Web page.

Retrieving, Analyzing, and Presenting Data

When you have designed the data-storage and data-entry components of your application, you should begin thinking about how to present and summarize the data in a format that makes sense to users. Although generally not as difficult as database design, determining which data users want to see and building reports to display the data in a usable format can be a more challenging task than it initially seems.

Here are some questions to ask as you design the reporting component of an application:

- Must the report be linked dynamically to the data source, or can it be a static report? If the report must display the most up-to-date data, it should be linked dynamically to the data source. On the other hand, if the data is not updated frequently, or if the report must be re-created regularly because the structure of the underlying data source changes, you can create a static report.

- Do users have to interact with the data in the report, or can the report be read-only? If users must perform calculations on the data or manipulate the data to display it in novel ways, you probably want to create the report in Microsoft® Excel or use the Office Web Components to create it in a Web page.

- Do users have to be able to view the report from a Web page or from within one of the Microsoft® Office XP applications?

- Must the report be formatted nicely?

The following table describes some common types of reports that you can create with Office XP applications and their advantages. There are other ways to create reports in addition to those described here.

Type of report	Application or technology	Advantages
Static (not dynamically linked to data)	Access report snapshot	You can create a report snapshot by exporting an Access report to a snapshot file (.snp). A report snapshot retains the formatting of the report from which it is created. You can view it in the Snapshot Viewer application or embedded in a Web page by using the Snapshot Viewer control (Snapview.ocx). In addition, it can be e-mailed as a stand-alone file to someone who does not have Access. To view a snapshot file, a user must have the Snapshot Viewer, which is included with Access. Users who do not have Access can download it free of charge from the Office Developer Forum Web site at http://www.microsoft.com/officedev/index/snapshot.htm.
	Access object saved as HTML	Saving a Microsoft® Access table, query, form, or report as HTML creates a static, unformatted HTML table in a Web page.
Dynamic (linked to data)	Access report	The data in the report is refreshed each time you close and reopen it. An Access report can be formatted nicely, so it might be a good choice for printed reports.
	Excel query table	A query table is a table in Microsoft® Excel that is linked dynamically to an Excel range or to an external data source. You can filter a query table and use it as the data source for a chart, PivotTable report, or Microsoft® PivotChart™ report.

Type of report	Application or technology	Advantages
	Excel PivotTable report or PivotChart report	A PivotTable report can be linked dynamically to an Excel range or to an external data source. You can use a PivotTable report to view a single set of data in a variety of configurations. To display the data graphically, you can create a PivotChart report that is linked dynamically to a PivotTable report. In addition, you can save a PivotTable report or PivotChart report to a Web page to create a dynamic report on a Web page.
	XML in Access	Through XML, Access can move information between a variety of sources without losing the meta data required to update the original source and/or any intermediate sources. Further, XML not only provides the mechanism for moving information among various products on the client, XML also enables the movement of information between the client and the server, and even across servers themselves.

Building Add-ins, Wizards, and Templates

Many design considerations are for applications that store and display data, which companies often require. Other common applications are those that might not involve data storage but help users do their jobs more efficiently. Add-ins, wizards, and templates fall into that category.

There are two types of add-ins you can create for Microsoft® Office XP applications: Component Object Model (COM) add-ins and application-specific add-ins. COM add-ins take advantage of COM technology and can be designed to work in multiple Office XP applications and in the Microsoft® Visual Basic® Editor. For example, you could create a COM add-in that displays a set of images to be inserted into a Microsoft® Word document, a Microsoft® Excel worksheet, or a Microsoft® PowerPoint® presentation. You can build COM add-ins in Visual Basic 5.0 or 6.0, or with Office XP Developer.

Application-specific add-ins, on the other hand, function only in the application in which they were created. For example, you could create an Excel add-in to perform calculations you must have to run repeatedly on different sets of data. Both types of add-ins can be integrated into the users' environment, so they become part of the application.

A wizard is a special type of add-in, and you can create a wizard as either a COM add-in or an application-specific add-in. A wizard walks a user through a process, one step at a time. The Mail Merge Helper in Word is a good example of a wizard that walks a user through a complicated process. Creating a wizard is a good way both to control how users enter information into a document and to speed up the process of formatting the document correctly.

A template forms the basis for a new document and can contain text, graphics, predefined styles, macros, and code. Templates make it easier for users to create common documents in a standardized format. For example, you could create a Word template displaying your company's logo and address, so all correspondence from your company has the same look.

Digital Dashboards and Web Parts

Microsoft® Office XP Developer provides a Digital Dashboard project based on Web Parts rendered in Microsoft® Outlook® and stored in Microsoft® Exchange 2000 Server. The architecture is extensible, so other storage providers can be integrated through standard interfaces.

Web Parts are reusable portal components that wrap web-based content fragments (XML, HTML, and scripting) with a standard property schema. The property schema controls how Web Parts are rendered in a Digital Dashboard.

The combination of Web Parts and the Digital Dashboard provides an easy-to-use way to present line-of-business, collaboration, and business intelligence data stored in Exchange Server and other stores.

The Digital Dashboard uses an Active Server Pages (ASP) to generate the visual (DHTML) representation of a dashboard. This ASP uses an Exchange (Web) store, which supports the personality types and is achieved by standardizing the API between the Dashboard Factory and the Store Access Services components

Thinking About User Interface Design

An important aspect of application design is the design of an effective user interface. A good user interface should be attractive, neatly laid out, and well organized. In addition, it should be easy to use and understand. The best applications are those that users can work with fairly intuitively, without extensive training or documentation.

Any way in which users interact with your application is part of the user interface. Here are some suggestions for designing an effective user interface:

- Strive for consistency in the way the application looks and in the way that users work with it. Be consistent with colors, fonts, and formatting. The application should be appealing visually and not overwhelming.

- Make it easy for users to navigate through the application. For example, when the application starts, you might want to display a switchboard form that provides users with a set of choices.

- Make the application equally accessible through the mouse or the keyboard. Set the tab order for controls on a form or Web page, so users can move from one control to the next predictably. Take into account users who might have difficulty seeing the screen or using the mouse or keyboard.

- Whenever possible, provide clear visual clues, so users can figure out what is happening. For example, it is a good idea to change the mouse pointer to an hourglass during lengthy operations, so users do not think the application has stopped working.

- Validate data that users enter, so you can prompt users immediately to correct wrong data.

- When you create custom toolbars and menus, make sure they are displayed when the application is available and hidden when it is not.

- Implement thorough error handling, and anticipate as many different types of errors as you can. Provide error messages that are clear and succinct.

Designing Code for Reusability

When you have mapped out the overall design for your application, spend some time thinking about how to structure your code within the application. There is always more than one way to write the code, and with a little additional effort, you can maximize the reusability of your code. The work you do now to make your code reusable, when possible, can save you and other developers time in the future. If you write code with the intention of reusing it in other scenarios, your code might be easier to maintain, because you will tend to write smaller, more compact procedures that are easier to modify.

- Whenever practical, write procedures that are atomic—that is, each procedure performs one task. Procedures written in this manner are easier to reuse.

- Adopt a set of coding standards, and stick to them.

- Document your procedures and modules well by adding comments, so you and other developers can figure out later what your code is doing.

- Group similar procedures or procedures that are called together in a module. Not only does this help you to organize your code functionally, it can enhance your application's performance. By default, Microsoft® Visual Basic® for Applications (VBA) compiles code on demand, meaning that when you run a procedure, VBA compiles that module and the modules containing any procedures that are called by that procedure. Compiling fewer modules results in improved performance. (To further improve performance, be sure to save your code in a compiled state.)

- Develop a library of procedures that you can reuse. Use a code library tool to store procedures and code snippets, so they are available immediately when you must have them. Microsoft® Office XP Developer includes such a tool, the Code Librarian, which is an add-in for the Visual Basic Editor and the common development environment.

- Create custom objects by encapsulating related code in class modules. You can add properties, methods, and events to custom objects, as well as organize them into custom hierarchical object models. When you have built and tested a custom object, you can treat it as a "black box"—you and other developers can use the object without thinking about the code that it contains. When you must maintain the code, you only have to modify it once within the class module.

- Develop interfaces to extend custom objects. An interface provides a basic set of properties, methods, and events to any custom object that implements the interface. By using an interface, you can create sets of closely related, yet distinct, objects that share common code.

- If you have Visual Basic, you can create Automation servers, which are .dll or .exe files that contain custom objects. The advantage to packaging custom objects in separate .dll or .exe files is that you can call them from any VBA project, just as you would call any Automation server, without having to include the code for the object in your project.

Security Considerations

While security might not be the most exciting topic, the fact is security is taking on an ever-greater importance for programmers as computers become increasingly connected through corporate networks and the Internet. Be sure to discuss the security requirements for your application with your customers.

As a Microsoft® Office XP application developer, you should concern yourself with two aspects of security. The first is protecting your intellectual property by securing your code. The second is protecting your application from viruses and unwelcome users.

To secure your intellectual property, you have the following options:

- You can password-protect the VBA project.

- If your application involves creating an add-in, you can build a COM add-in, which is compiled into a .dll file. The code contained in the .dll file cannot be viewed, so you can distribute the file without worrying about others stealing your code.

- If you are building an application in Microsoft® Access, you can create an .mde file from the database and distribute that file. Saving your database as an .mde file removes all editable source code and prevents users from viewing or modifying the design of forms, reports, data access pages, or modules. Your VBA code will continue to run, but it cannot be viewed or edited. If your application is an Access project (.adp) rather than an Access database, you can create an .ade file, which is similar to an .mde file.

    Note Although saving a database as an .mde or .ade file prevents users from modifying a data access page from within Access, if they have access to the HTML file, they can still modify the HTML file in another HTML editor. To prevent users from modifying a data access page, you should save the HTML file to a network share and specify read-only permissions for users who must view the data access page but who should not be able to modify it.

To protect your application from viruses and from undesired users, you have the following options:

- You can install a VBA virus scanner.

- You can define trusted sources for code. A trusted source is an individual or company that has been certified by a certification authority. Then, you can set the security level for each Office XP application to High to run code only from trusted sources, to Medium to permit users to choose whether to run potentially unsafe code, or to Low to run all code, whether trusted or not.

- You can use Microsoft® Jet security to secure a Microsoft Jet database (.mdb). Microsoft Jet makes it possible for you to implement user-level security for each object in a database.

Testing Your Application

Testing your code is a fundamental part of building a Microsoft® Office XP application. Thorough testing will save you time and effort later on.

In general, you probably find you test code as you go to make sure that each part of the application works as expected before you move onto the next part. In addition, it is a good idea to test the application thoroughly when you are done building it to find things that you missed and to try new or unexpected scenarios. If you have access to other computers, test your application there to make sure it behaves as expected on different system configurations.

When you have tested the application yourself, get someone else to test it as well. Ideally, you would recruit another developer or a professional tester, but if that is not an option, have your customers begin testing the application.

Before you deploy your application to all users, choose a subset of users to act as beta testers. Have them keep track of all the bugs they encounter—how they caused the bug, what they expected the application to do, and what it actually did. You can log run-time errors from within the application, either in a text file on the users' computers or to a centrally located database.

Finally, consider how you will deal with a serious bug should one be discovered after you have deployed your application fully. If your application includes a file that might have to be modified for a bug fix—for example, an .mdb file that is the front end for a database application—you have little choice but to distribute a new version of that file to all users to fix the bug. If your application is Web-based, however, you might be able to fix the bug in the Web page on the Web server; the next time a user accesses that Web page, the user will see the new version containing the bug fix.

Application Deployment

After you develop an application, you can distribute it to users. The type of application that you develop might determine the way in which you will deploy it. For example, you might distribute a Microsoft® Excel-based application for individual user to client desktops, while a corporate information tool might be best viewed on the corporate intranet by using a web browser.

Determine your method of deployment during your initial planning process to help make distribution as efficient as possible.

When you distribute your application to client desktops, you should provide users with a Setup program to perform some or all of the following tasks:

- Copy the required files to the user's computer.
- Place the files in the appropriate folders.
- Register components.
- Create a Start menu item or group.
- Create an icon on the user's desktop.

When you deploy your application to users, you can distribute the setup program from:

- A Network server using automatic installation or client request.
- A Web site in an intranet or on the Internet.
- Removable media such as a CD-ROM.

The option, or set of options, that you choose depends on the location of the users (whether they are in the same physical location or geographically dispersed), the users' network access, and the users' skill levels (whether they are comfortable locating and installing software on their systems).

The Packaging Wizard is a great tool that can help you create a setup package you can then deploy to users. For information, see Creating a Setup Package Using the Packaging Wizard.

Developing Office Applications Using VBA

Microsoft® Office application development is typically the process of customizing an Office application to perform some function or service. Developing an Office application can range from writing a simple Microsoft® Visual Basic® for Applications (VBA) procedure to creating a sophisticated financial analysis and reporting application. An Office developer is anyone who uses the programmability features of Office to make an application do something better, faster, or more efficiently than it could be done before. An Office application is an application that uses an Office application or component as part of its overall architecture.

Every custom application is, in some sense, an answer to a particular problem or requirement. When you understand the problem, the success of your application will depend on your ability to deliver a response that uses appropriate tools tailored to the experience level of the people who will be using your application.

In This Section

Office Objects and Object Models
    Integrate the features from two or more Office applications into a single application to amplify and focus users' productivity.

Working with Office Applications
    Take advantage of different objects, collections of objects, properties, methods, and events to build your application.

Working with Shared Office Components
    Search for files, use the Office Assistant, manipulate command bars, read and write document properties, read and write script, and hook add-ins to your Office application using a set of shared objects available in all Office applications.

Getting the Most Out of Visual Basic for Applications
    Write code that is fast, efficient, easy to read and maintain, and, if possible, reusable with a solid working knowledge of Visual Basic for Applications (VBA)—what features the language includes and what you can do with it.

Add-ins, Templates, Wizards, and Libraries
    Create and use COMAddIn objects (a shared Office component in the Microsoft Office XP object library).

The Benefits of Office Programmability

There are currently more than 2.5 million Office developers creating custom applications that use the applications or components in Microsoft® Office. The term "Office developer" includes developers who work exclusively in one or more of the Office applications. It also includes developers working in any language that can access the objects exposed by Office applications. For more than ten years, Microsoft has been making improvements to the Office suite that make it possible for developers to quickly and easily build and deploy custom desktop applications. These improvements are the reason why Office applications continue to play such an important role in custom application development:

- **Users and businesses already use the Microsoft Office suite of applications.** Most users already have Office on their desktop. The most recent surveys indicate that more than 40 million people regularly use Office to get their work done. Building applications based on the Office platform makes it possible for developers to target this large base of users. Also, even if you are not developing within the Office development environment, it is still a good idea to take advantage of the objects exposed by Office applications so that your custom applications can leverage existing, proven, and tested Office functionality.

- **Office supports programmable objects and an integrated development environment.** Each Office application exposes its functionality through programmable objects, and each also supports the ability to integrate with other applications by using Automation (formerly OLE Automation). Most applications share the same programming language (Visual Basic for Applications) and integrated development environment (the Visual Basic Editor). Applications created with VBA run in the same memory space as the host application and therefore execute faster. The programmable objects and powerful development tools in Office let developers build applications that tightly integrate applications and seamlessly share data and information. In addition, distribution of Office-based applications is simplified because VBA code and Microsoft® ActiveX® controls are part of the application document or project.

- **Faster development cycles mean more affordable applications.** The use of a single language and development environment also makes application development faster. What you learn while programming one application applies when working with another application. VBA code written for one application can often be reused in an application that works with a different application. Developers' skills become more valuable because they can work across many applications. Reducing the number of development environments or languages that developers must learn means that the time and cost of creating custom applications is reduced. Reliance on existing components eliminates the need to develop or test large portions of the application. This lets developers quickly build robust applications that previously might have been cost-prohibitive.

- **Users become part of the application.** Because applications are created and run in an environment familiar to the user, support costs are kept to an absolute minimum. Building an application based on Office technologies makes it possible for you define the application in a context with which your users are already familiar. This makes it possible for greater user participation in the application-design process and can dramatically reduce training and support costs. It takes less time and effort to customize applications your users already own than to build new applications from scratch. The more familiar users are with the application, the easier it is going to be for them to understand and use your application.

Office Objects and Object Models

Each Microsoft® Office XP application contains a powerful set of tools designed to help you accomplish a related set of tasks. For example, Microsoft® Access provides powerful data-management and query capabilities, Microsoft® Excel provides mathematical, analytical, and reporting tools, Microsoft® Outlook® provides tools for sending and receiving e-mail, for scheduling, and for contact and task management, and Microsoft® Word makes it possible for you create and manage documents, track versions of documents among different users, and create forms and templates. As powerful as these and the other Office applications are on their own, you also can integrate the features from two or more Office applications into a single solution to amplify and focus users' productivity.

The key technology that makes individual Office applications programmable and makes creating an integrated Office solution possible is the Component Object Model (COM) technology known as automation.

Automation makes it possible for a developer to use Microsoft® Visual Basic® for Applications (VBA) code to create and control software objects exposed by any application, dynamic-link library (DLL), or Microsoft® ActiveX® control that supports the appropriate programmatic interfaces. VBA and automation make it possible for you to program individual Office applications, as well as to run other applications from within a host application. For example, you can run a hidden instance of Excel from within Access to perform mathematical and analytical operations on your Access data. The key to understanding automation is to understand objects and object models: what they are, how they work, and how they work together.

> **Note** To master the use of automation in your Office solutions, you must have a detailed working knowledge of the applications you are integrating. That is the kind of knowledge and experience that can be gained only with further application-specific training and hands-on experience.

In This Section

Integrated Office Solution Development
    Use the COM software architecture or VBA to develop an integrated Office solution.

Objects, Collections, and Object Models: Technology Backgrounder
    Understand how to reference objects in an application's object model and how to use the objects and features available to build your solution.

Office Application Automation
    Learn how to automate one Office application from another.

Integrated Office Solution Development

The ability to develop an integrated Office solution heavily depends on two technologies:

- The Component Object Model (COM) software architecture

- Microsoft® Visual Basic® for Applications (VBA)

The COM software architecture makes it possible for software developers to build their applications and services from individual software components collectively referred to as COM components or simply components. COM components consist of the physical, compiled files that contain classes, which are code modules that define programmable objects. There are two types of COM components: in-process components and out-of-process components. In-process components are either DLLs or Microsoft® ActiveX® controls (.ocx files) and can run only within the process of another application. Out-of-process components are .exe files and run as freestanding applications. A COM component can serve either or both of the following roles in application development:

- Sharing its objects with other applications. This role is called being an Automation server.

- Using other components' objects. This role is called being an Automation client. In earlier documentation, this role was called being an Automation controller.

The Microsoft® Windows® operating system and Microsoft® Office XP suite of applications are examples of products that have been developed by using the COM software architecture. Just because software is developed by using COM does not mean that it can be programmed by using VBA. However, if an application or service supports automation, it can expose interfaces to the features of its components as objects that can be programmed from VBA, as well as many other programming languages. To support automation, an application or service must provide either or both of two methods of exposing its custom interfaces:

- By providing the IDispatch interface. In this way, the application or service can be queried for further information about its custom interfaces. Applications and services that support the IDispatch interface provide information about their custom interfaces at run time by using a method called late binding.

- By making it possible for direct access at design time to the member functions in its virtual function table, or vtable, that implement its interfaces. Applications and services that support direct access to custom interfaces support what is called vtable binding or early binding.

An application can be said to support automation if it supports either one, but not necessarily both, of these methods. Most contemporary applications and services provide support for both methods and are referred to as supporting dual interfaces.

To support early or late binding, an application or service also must supply a type library (also known as an object library). A type library is a file or part of a file that describes the type of one or more objects. Type libraries do not store objects; they store type information. By accessing a type library, a programming environment can determine the characteristics of an object, such as the interfaces supported by the object and the names and addresses of the members of each interface. With this information, the programming language can be used to work with the exposed interfaces.

In the VBA programming environment, you can establish a connection to a type library, which is called establishing a reference to a type library. After you establish a reference to a type library, you can view information about the objects made available through the type library by using the Object Browser. Establishing a reference to a type library also makes it possible for VBA to perform error-checking at compile time to ensure code written against the type library is free from errors because of improper declarations or from passing values of the wrong type. Additionally, referencing a type library makes it possible for you to take advantage of VBA features that simplify writing code, such as automatic listing of the properties and methods of objects exposed by the type library. Furthermore, referencing a type library makes your code run faster, because information about the objects you are programming is available to VBA at design time; this information can be used to optimize your code when it is compiled.

The VBA programming environment can be incorporated into applications that support automation to make them programmable. The suite of Microsoft® Office XP applications, incorporate the VBA programming environment and are written to support both kinds of automation interfaces. Additionally, many other software components, such as Microsoft® ActiveX® controls and DLLs, expose their functionality to VBA programmers through automation interfaces.

Using the objects, properties, and methods exposed through automation interfaces, you can use VBA code running in modules associated with the currently open document, template, database, Microsoft® FrontPage®-based web, or add-in to automate that application. VBA and automation make it possible to record simple macros to automate keystrokes and mouse actions (in applications that support macro recording), and to create sophisticated integrated solutions, such as document management, accounting, and database applications.

To produce even more powerful integrated applications, you can use VBA code running in one application to create and work with objects from another installed application or component. For example, if you are developing a solution in Microsoft® Access and you want to use mathematical or other functions available only in Microsoft® Excel, you can use VBA to create an instance of Excel and use its features from code running in Access.

You can think of automation as a nervous system that makes programmatic communication and feedback between applications and components possible, and as "glue" that makes it possible for you integrate features from Office applications and other software components into a custom solution.

The VBA support for automation provides Office developers with incredible flexibility and power. By taking advantage of automation, you can use the features exposed through the object models of the entire Office suite of applications (as well as any third-party applications and components that support automation interfaces) as a set of business-application building blocks. By taking advantage of the pre-built components exposed through automation, you do not have to develop your own custom components and procedures every time you want to get something done. In addition to shortening the development time for your solution, using pre-built components means you can take advantage of the thousands of hours of design, development, and testing that went into producing them.

By using VBA and objects exposed through automation, you can select the best set of features to use to perform the tasks you want to accomplish, you can provide the data users must have to accomplish their jobs, and you can manage workflow to provide an effective and productive solution.

Objects, Collections, and Object Models: Technology Backgrounder

Microsoft® Office XP applications expose their functionality to the Microsoft® Visual Basic® for Applications (VBA) language through a hierarchical system of objects and collections of objects called an object model. When you understand how to reference objects in an application's object model, you can use the objects and features available to build your solution.

An application fundamentally consists of two things: content and functionality. Content refers to the information within an application, that is, the documents, worksheets, tables, or slides and the information they contain. Content also refers to information about the attributes of individual elements in that application, such as the size of a window, the color of a graphic, or the font size of a word. Functionality refers to all the ways you can work with the content in the application, for example, opening, closing, adding, deleting, sending, copying, pasting, editing, or formatting the content in the application.

The content and functionality that make up an application are represented to the Visual Basic language as discrete units called objects. For the most part, the set of objects exposed by an application to VBA corresponds to all the objects that you can work with by using the application's user interface. You probably are familiar with many of these objects, such as Microsoft® Access databases, tables, queries, forms, and reports; Microsoft® Excel workbooks, worksheets, and cell ranges; Word documents, sections, paragraphs, sentences, and words; Microsoft® Outlook® messages, appointments, and contacts; Microsoft® PowerPoint® presentations and slides; and Microsoft® FrontPage®-based webs and web pages.

The objects exposed by an application are arranged relative to each other in hierarchical relationships. The top-level object in a Microsoft® Office XP application is the Application object, which represents the application itself. The Application object contains other objects that you have access to only when the Application object exists (that is, when an instance of the application itself is running). For example, the Excel Application object contains Workbook objects, and the Word Application object contains Document objects. Because the Document object depends on the existence of the Word Application object for its own existence, the Document object is said to be the child of the Application object; conversely, the Application object is said to be the parent of the Document object.

Many child objects have children of their own. For example, the Excel Workbook object contains, or is parent to, the Worksheets object. The Worksheets object is a special kind of object called a collection that represents a set of objects - in this case, all the worksheets in the workbook, which in turn are represented as individual Worksheet objects within that collection. A parent object can have multiple children; for instance, the Word Window object has as children the Document, Panes, Selection, and View objects. Additionally, identically named child objects might belong to more than one parent object; for instance, in Word, both the Application object and the Document object have a Windows collection as a child object. However, even though the child objects have the same name, typically, their functionality is determined by the parent object; for example, the Microsoft® Windows® collection for the Application object contains all the current document windows in the application, whereas the Windows collection for the Document object contains only the windows that display the specified document.

In addition to containing child objects, each object in the hierarchy contains content and functionality that apply both to the object itself and to all its child objects. The higher an object is in a hierarchy of nested objects (that is, the more child objects an object has), the wider the scope of its content and functionality. For example, in Excel, the Application object contains the size of the application window and the ability to quit the application; the Workbook object contains the file name and format of the workbook and the ability to save the workbook; the Worksheets collection contains Worksheet object names and the ability to add and delete worksheets.

You often do not get to the actual contents of a file, such as the values on an Excel worksheet or the text in a Word document, until you have navigated through several levels in the object hierarchy. This is because the scope of this specific content belongs to a particular functionality of the application. For example, the value in a cell on a worksheet applies only to that cell, not to all cells on the worksheet, so you cannot store the value directly in a Worksheet object.

To work with the content and functionality exposed by an object, you use properties and methods of that object. You use properties to determine or change some characteristic of an object, such as its color, dimensions, or state. For example, you can set the Visible property of an Excel Worksheet object to specify whether a worksheet is visible to the user. You use methods to perform a particular action on an object. For example, you use the PrintOut method of the Word Document object to print the document.

Some objects also respond to events. An event is an action that typically is performed by a user such as clicking a mouse, pressing a key, changing data, or opening a document or form but also can be performed by program code or by the system itself. You can write code, called an event procedure, which will run whenever an event occurs. For example, you can write code in a form's Open event to size or position the form whenever it is opened.

In summary, the representation of content and functionality in an application is divided among the objects in the application's object model. Together, the objects in the object model's hierarchy represent all the content and functionality in the application that is exposed to Visual Basic. Separately, the objects provide access to very specific areas of content and functionality. To determine or set a characteristic of an object, you read or set one of the object's properties. To perform an action on or with an object, you use one of the object's methods. Additionally, some objects provide events that are typically triggered by a user's action, so you can write code that will run in response to that action.

Objects Exposed by an Object Model

To work with the objects exposed by an object model, you first must declare an object variable and set a reference to the object you want to work with. When you have established a reference to an object, you can work with its properties, methods, or events.

To set a reference, you must build an expression that gains access to one object in the object model and then use properties or methods to move up or down the object hierarchy until you get to the object you want to work with. The properties and methods you use to return the object you start from and to move from one object to another are called "object accessors" or just "accessors."

Accessors typically have the same name as the object they are used to access; for example, the Word Documents property is used to access the Documents collection. Accessors are typically properties, but in some object models, accessors are methods.

This topic includes the following sections:

- The Application Object

- Navigating the Object Hierarchy

- Shortcut Accessors

- Referencing the Document or Workbook in Which Code Is Running

- The Parent Property

- Accessing an Embedded OLE Object's Application

- Creating Your Own Objects and Object Models

The Application Object

A common place to gain access to the object model is the top-level object. In all Microsoft® Office XP applications and in most applications that support Microsoft® Visual Basic® for Applications (VBA), the top-level object is the Application object. However, some applications and components might have a different top-level object. For example, when you are programming the Visual Basic Editor (by using a reference to the Visual Basic for Applications Extensibility 5.3 library), the top-level object is the VBE object.

Note The following code assumes you are running Microsoft® Word.

You use the Application property to return a reference to the Application object. The following code fragment returns a reference to the Application object and then sets properties to display scroll bars, ScreenTips, and the status bar:

```
Dim wdApp As Application
Set wdApp = Application
With wdApp
    .DisplayScrollBars = True
    .DisplayScreenTips = True
    .DisplayStatusBar = True
End With
```

If you have established references to more than one type library that contains an Application object, the Application property will always return the Application object for the host application. In addition, for any other object that has the same name in two or more referenced type libraries, the accessor property or method will return the object from the first type library referenced in the Available References list of the References dialog box (Tools menu).

For example, the Microsoft® ActiveX® Data Objects (ADO) and Data Access Objects (DAO) type libraries both have Recordset objects. If you have a reference to the ADO type library followed by the DAO type library, a declaration such as the following will always return the ADO Recordset object:

```
Dim rstNew As Recordset
```

While you might be able to adjust the priority of references in the References dialog box to correct this, a better solution, which eliminates any ambiguity and prevents errors, is to declare an object variable by using the fully qualified class name, also called the programmatic identifier or ProgID, of the object. To do this, combine the name of the application or component that contains the object (as it appears in the Object Browser's Project/Library box) with the name of the object separated by a period.

For example, to declare an object variable that will be used to work with the Word Application object from another application, you must declare the object variable this way:

```
Dim wdApp As Word.Application
```

Similarly, if you have both the ADO and the DAO type libraries referenced in your project, you should declare object variables to work with Recordset objects this way:

```
Dim rstADO As ADODB.Recordset
Dim rstDAO As DAO.Recordset
```

> **Note** You can view the ProgIDs of all installed applications and components on a computer by running the Registry Editor and looking under the \HKEY_CLASSES_ROOT\CLSID subkey.

Navigating the Object Hierarchy

To get to an object from the top-level object, you must step through all the objects above it in the hierarchy by using accessors to return one object from another. Many objects, such as workbooks, worksheets, documents, presentations, and slides, are members of collections. A collection is an object that contains a set of related objects. You can work with the objects in a collection as a single group rather than as separate entities. Because collections are always one level higher than individual objects in the hierarchy, you usually have to access a collection before you can access an object in that collection. The accessor that returns a collection object usually has the same name as the collection object itself. For example, the Documents property of the Word Application object returns the Documents collection object, which represents all open documents. The following expression returns a reference to the Word Documents collection object:

```
Application.Documents
```

You reference an item in a collection either by using a number that refers to its position in the collection or by using its name. For example, if a document named Report.doc is the first open document in the Documents collection, you can reference it in either of the following ways:

```
Application.Documents(1)
```

-or-

```
Application.Documents("Report.doc")
```

To get to an object further down the object hierarchy, simply add additional accessors and objects to your expression until you get to the desired object. For example, the following expression returns a reference to the second paragraph in the Paragraphs collection of the first open document:

```
Application.Documents(1).Paragraphs(2)
```

Shortcut Accessors

There are shortcut accessors you can use to gain direct access to objects in the model without having to navigate from the Application object. These shortcuts include accessors, such as the Documents, Workbooks, Items, and Presentations properties, that you can use to return a reference to the document collection for the corresponding application. For example, in Word, you can use either of the following statements to open MyDoc.doc:

```
Application.Documents.Open Filename:="c:\docs\mydoc.doc"
```

-or-

```
Documents.Open Filename:="c:\docs\mydoc.doc"
```

There are other shortcut accessors, such as the ActiveWindow, ActiveDocument, ActiveWorksheet, or ActiveCell properties that return a direct reference to an active part of an application. The following statement closes the active Word document. Note that the Application object and the Documents collection object are not explicitly specified.

```
ActiveDocument.Close
```

> **Tip**   When <globals> is selected in the Classes list in the Object Browser, you can use any accessor that appears in the Members of list as a shortcut. That is, you do not have to return the object that the property or method applies to before you use the property or method, because VBA can determine that information from the context in which your code is running.

Referencing the Document or Workbook in Which Code Is Running

When you are using the ActiveDocument and ActiveWorkbook accessor properties, it is important to remember that the reference returned is to the document or workbook that is currently in use (the topmost window of all open documents or workbooks). In many circumstances, you can reference an active object implicitly, that is, without including the entire hierarchy above the object to which you are referring. For example, you can create a reference to the active workbook's Worksheets collection without preceding the collection with ActiveWorkbook. or an explicit reference to the workbook's name or number in the Workbooks collection:

```
Worksheets("MySheet")
```

However, using implicit references or references to the ActiveDocument or ActiveWorkbook accessor properties can create problems if you are developing a global template or add-in and need to make sure your code refers to the add-in or global template itself. Word and Excel provide two special accessor properties that return a reference to the document or workbook in which the VBA code is running: ThisDocument and ThisWorkbook. Use the ThisDocument or ThisWorkbook property whenever you need to make sure that your code refers to the document or workbook that contains the code that is running.

For example, both of the following Set statements reference the worksheet named Addin Definition. The first makes an explicit reference to the active workbook by using the ActiveWorkbook property. The second makes an implicit reference; because it doesn't explicitly refer to a specific workbook, the reference is assumed to be to the active workbook. In either case, the reference made in the Set statement will be to the worksheet in whatever workbook happens to be active when the code runs.

```
Set rngMenuDef = ActiveWorkbook.Worksheets("Addin Definition"). _
    Range("MenuDefinition")
Set rngMenuDef = Worksheets("Addin Definition").Range("MenuDefinition")
```

References such as these will work correctly while you are developing an add-in or template if you have no other documents or workbooks open while you are testing your code, or if the add-in or template is in the active window when the code is running. However, when your add-in or template is in use, these types of references can cause errors. To make sure that you are referencing the workbook in which code is running, use the ThisWorkbook property as shown in the following Set statement:

```
Set rngMenuDef = ThisWorkbook.Worksheets("Addin Definition"). _
    Range("MenuDefinition")
```

The Parent Property

To access an object higher up in the object hierarchy from the current object, you can often use the Parent property of the object. Using an object's Parent property makes it possible for you to reference the higher object that contains the current object. For example, if you write a function to work with a control on a form (the function takes an argument of type Control), you can use the control's Parent property to reference the form that contains the control.

Note that the Parent property doesn't always return the object immediately above the current object in the hierarchy, it might return a higher object, especially if the object immediately above the current object is a collection. For example, the Parent property of a Word Document object returns the Application object, not the Documents collection. You can use the TypeName function to find out what kind of object to which the Parent property of an object refers. For example, in Word, the following statement displays the type of object that the Parent property of the Document object refers to:

```
MsgBox TypeName(Documents("Document1").Parent)
```

Tip You can use the TypeName function to determine the type of object returned by any expression, not just expressions that use the Parent property. The TypeName function can also be used to determine the kind of data type returned by an expression, such as Byte, Integer, or Long.

Creating Your Own Objects and Object Models

You can create your own objects and object models by creating and using class modules. For example, you might need to work with complex sets of data that need to be managed in a consistent and reliable way. By creating your own objects, properties, and methods to work with this data in a class module, you can create an object model to make working with your data simpler and less error-prone. Similarly, you can create class modules to create wrapper functions around Windows application programming interface (API) calls or even complex parts of existing object models to make them easier to use.

Collections

Although collections and the objects they contain, such as the Workbooks collection and the Workbook object are distinct objects each with their own properties and methods, they're grouped as one unit in most object model graphics to reduce complexity.

To return a single member of a collection, you usually use the Item property or method and pass the name or index number of the member as the index argument. For example, in Excel, the following expression returns a reference to an open workbook by passing its name "Sales.xls" to the Item property and then invokes the Close method to close it:

```
Workbooks.Item("Sales.xls").Close
```

The Item property or method is the default for most collections, so you can usually omit it from your expression. For example, in Excel, the following two expressions are equivalent:

```
Workbooks.Item("Sales.xls")
```

-or-

```
Workbooks("Sales.xls")
```

To reference items in a collection by using an index number, simply pass the number of the item to the Item property or method of the collection. For example, if Sales.xls is the second workbook in the Workbooks collection, the following expression will return a reference to it:

```
Workbooks(2)
```

> **Note** Most collections used in Office applications (except Access) are *one-based*, that is, the index number of the first item in the collection is 1. However, the collections in Access and some components, such as ADO and DAO, are *zero-based*, which is, the index number of the first item is 0. For more information, refer to the Visual Basic Reference Help topic for the collection you want to work with.

Adding Objects to a Collection

You can also create new objects and add them to a collection, usually by using the Add method of that collection. The following code fragment creates a new document by using the Professional Memo.dot template and assigns it to the object variable docNew:

```
Const TEMPLATE_PATH   As String = "c:\program files\microsoft
office\templates\1033\"
Dim docNew            As Word.Document


Set docNew = Documents.Add(Template:=TEMPLATE_PATH & "memos\professional
memo.dot")
```

Working with Objects in a Collection

You can find out how many objects there are in a collection by using the Count property. The following Excel example displays a message box with the number of workbooks that are open:

```
MsgBox Workbooks.Count & " workbooks are open."
```

You can perform an operation on all the objects in a collection, or you can set or test a value for all the objects in a collection. To do this, you use a For Each…Next structure, or a For…Next structure in conjunction with the Count property to loop through all the objects in the collection.

Whenever possible, you should use a For Each…Next loop when you need to work with all the items in a collection. A For Each…Next loop generally performs faster and doesn't require you to use or test a loop counter, which can introduce errors. The following Excel example contains a For Each…Next structure that loops through the Worksheets collection of a workbook and appends " - By Automation" to the name of each worksheet:

```
Sub CreateExcelObjects()
    Dim xlApp           As Excel.Application
    Dim wkbNewBook      As Excel.Workbook
    Dim wksSheet        As Excel.Worksheet
    Dim strBookName     As String


    ' Create new hidden instance of Excel.
    Set xlApp = New Excel.Application
    ' Add new workbook to Workbooks collection.
    Set wkbNewBook = xlApp.Workbooks.Add
    ' Specify path to save workbook.
    strBookName = "c:\my documents\xlautomation.xls"
    ' Loop through each worksheet and append " - By Automation" to the
    ' name of each sheet. Close and save workbook to specified path.
```

```
With wkbNewBook
    For Each wksSheet In .Worksheets
        wksSheet.Name = wksSheet.Name & " - By Automation"
    Next wksSheet
    .Close SaveChanges:=True, FileName:=strBookName
End With


Set wkbNewBook = Nothing
Set xlApp = Nothing
End Sub
```

Under some circumstances, you must use a For...Next loop to work with items in a collection. For example, if you try to use a For Each...Next loop to delete all the objects in a collection, only every other object in the collection will be deleted. This is because after deleting the first item, all items in the collection are re-indexed so that what was the second item is now the first. When the Next statement runs at the end of the first execution of the loop, the pointer is advanced one, skipping that item for the next iteration of the loop. For this reason, to delete all items in a collection, you must use a For...Next loop that starts from the end of the collection and works backwards.

Another situation that requires you to use a For...Next loop to work with items in a collection is if you need to work with only a specific number of items, say the first ten, or every tenth item.

Properties and Methods

To work with the content and functionality exposed by an object, you use properties and methods of that object. The following Excel example uses the Value property of the Range object to set the contents of cell B3 on the Sales worksheet in the Current.xls workbook to 3:

```
Workbooks("Current.xls").Worksheets("Sales").Range("B3").Value = 3
```

The following example uses the Bold property of the Font object to apply bold formatting to cell B3 on the Sales worksheet:

```
Workbooks("Current.xls").Worksheets("Sales").Range("B3").Font.Bold = True
```

The following Word example uses the Close method of the Document object to close the file named Draft3.doc:

```
Documents("Draft3.doc").Close
```

In general, you use properties to set or read the content, which can include the text or value contained in an object, or other attributes of the object, and you use methods to work with an application's (or the Microsoft® Visual Basic® for Applications) built-in functionality to perform operations on the content. Be aware, however, that this distinction doesn't always hold true; there are a number of properties and methods in every object model that are exceptions to this rule.

Events

An event is an action that is typically performed by a user, such as clicking a mouse button, pressing a key, changing data, or opening a document or form, but the action can also be performed by program code, or by the system itself. You can write event procedure code to respond to such actions at either of two levels:

- **Document-level or subdocument-level events**   These events occur for open documents and in some cases, for objects within them. For example, the Word Document object can respond to the Open, New, and Close events; the Excel Workbook object can respond to events such as the Open, BeforeClose, and BeforeSave events; and the Excel Worksheet object can respond to events, such as the Activate and Calculate events. Microsoft® PowerPoint® supports only application-level events.

- **Application-level events**   These events occur at the level of the application itself, for example, when a new Microsoft® Word document, Microsoft® Excel workbook, or PowerPoint presentation is created, for which the corresponding events are the NewDocument, NewWorkbook, and NewPresentation events.

Microsoft® Access provides a different model that responds to events on Form and Report objects, and most of the controls on them, such as ListBox and TextBox objects. UserForms, which can be used from Excel, Word, and PowerPoint, provide a similar event model to Access forms.

The Microsoft® Outlook® Application object provides events that can be used from the ThisOutlookSession module or a COM add-in running from an installation of the Outlook application, such as ItemSend, NewMail, OptionsPagesAdd, Quit, Reminder, and Startup. To create code that responds to a user's actions in the Outlook user interface, you can use the WithEvents keyword to declare object variables that can respond to Outlook Explorer, Inspector, and MAPIFolder object events. All Outlook item objects, except the NoteItem object, can respond to events, such as the Open, Read, and Reply events.

The Microsoft® FrontPage® Application object provides events that make it possible for your solution to respond to the creation and editing of pages and FrontPage-based webs, such as OnPageNew, OnPageOpen, OnBeforePageSave, OnAfterPageSave, and OnPageClose, and OnWebNew, OnWebOpen, OnBeforeWebPublish, OnAfterWebPublish, and OnWebClose.

In addition to the events supported by each Office application, the CommandBarButton object, CommandBarComboBox object, and CommandBars collection support events.

Responding to Document-Level Events

To create event procedures for events in Excel workbooks and Word documents, you need to work with the ThisWorkbook or ThisDocument modules. For example, to write an event procedure that will run when a Word document is opened, open the document and then open the Visual Basic Editor. In the Project Explorer, double-click ThisDocument to open the ThisDocument module. In the Object box in the Code window, click Document, and then click Open in the Procedure box. The Microsoft® Visual Basic® Editor will create an event procedure template for the document's Open event. You can then enter any code you want to run whenever the document is opened. For example, the following event procedure sets certain features of the active window and view of a Word document when it is opened:

```
Private Sub Document_Open()
' Set Window and View properties to display document with document map
' in page layout view.
    With ActiveWindow
        .DisplayVerticalScrollBar = True
        .DisplayRulers = False
        .DisplayScreenTips = True
        .DocumentMap = True
        .DocumentMapPercentWidth = 25
        With .View
            .Type = wdPageView
            .WrapToWindow = True
            .EnlargeFontsLessThan = 11
            .ShowAll = False
            .ShowPicturePlaceHolders = False
            .ShowFieldCodes = False
            .ShowBookmarks = False
        End With
    End With
End Sub
```

If you want to prevent code written in a document's Open event from running when the document is opened programmatically from another application, you can check the Application object's UserControl property to determine if a user opened the application.

Responding to Application-Level Events

Microsoft® Office XP includes a comparable set of events for Word and PowerPoint with similar names across each application. For example, where Excel provides NewWorkbook and WorkbookOpen events, Word provides NewDocument and DocumentOpen events, and PowerPoint provides NewPresentation and PresentationOpen events. Providing consistent event handling and similar names across Word, Excel, and PowerPoint makes it easier to create a COM add-in that works across these applications. FrontPage doesn't supply as extensive a set of application-level events as the other Office applications, but FrontPage events also have similar names; for example, OnPageNew, OnWebNew, OnPageOpen, and OnWebOpen.

The NewDocument, NewWorkbook, NewPresentation, and OnPageNew events are useful for tasks such as automatically formatting new documents and inserting content such as the date, time, author, or latest company logo off the intranet. Similarly, the OnWebNew event can be used to automatically apply themes or to add pages and content to new FrontPage-based webs. The

DocumentOpen, WorkbookOpen, PresentationOpen, and OnPageOpen events can be used to retrieve information from the document and update command bar customizations. The DocumentClose, DocumentSave, and DocumentPrint events in Word (and comparable events in Excel and PowerPoint) can be used to ensure that document properties, such as the author or subject, are entered in the document before the document can be closed, saved, or printed. Similarly, the FrontPage OnBeforePageSave, OnBeforeWebPublish, OnPageClose, and OnWebClose events can be used to check page properties or to check the sizes of image files on the page, and to verify hyperlinks before publishing a FrontPage-based web.

To write event procedures for the Application object, you must create a new class module and declare an object variable as type Application by using the WithEvents keyword. For example, you can create a class module named XLEvents and add the following declaration to create a private Excel Application object variable to respond to events:

```
Private WithEvents xlApp As Excel.Application
```

When you have done this, you can click xlApp in the Object box of the class module's Code window, and then click any of the events in the Procedure box to write event procedures to respond to Excel Application object events. However, because you can't use the New keyword to create an instance of the Application object variable when you are declaring it by using the WithEvents keyword, you'll need to write a Set statement to do so in the class module's Initialize event this way:

```
Private Sub Class_Initialize
    Set xlApp = Excel.Application
End Sub
```

This process is called creating an event sink. To activate the event sink, you declare in another module a public (or private) object variable for your event sink class, and then run a procedure that will create an instance of your class before the events you want to handle occur. For example:

```
Public evtEvents As XLEvents


Public Sub InitXLEvents()
    Set evtEvents = New XLEvents
End Sub
```

Creating an event sink in a class module provides a way for you to create an independent object that will respond to application-level events. The VBA project that contains the class module and procedure used to initialize your event sink must be running before any of the events you want to trap occur. Because application-level events are triggered by events that occur while the application itself is being used to open and work with documents, you will most typically implement an event sink in an add-in to trap an application's application-level events, or in automation code running from another application.

Using the Object Browser

The Object Browser is available in all Microsoft products that contain the Microsoft® Visual Basic® for Applications (VBA) programming environment. The Object Browser makes it possible for you to view all objects, methods, properties, events, and constants of all COM components whose type libraries are referenced by the application you are working with. By default, each Microsoft® Office XP application references a set of type libraries. For example, Word references by default Visual Basic for Applications, Microsoft® Word, OLE automation, and Microsoft® Office XP type libraries.

To manually reference any additional type libraries available on your system

- From the **Tools** menu in the **Visual Basic Editor**, click **References**.

To display the Object Browser

- Open the **Visual Basic Editor**, and then click **Object Browser** on the **View** menu.

The Object Browser

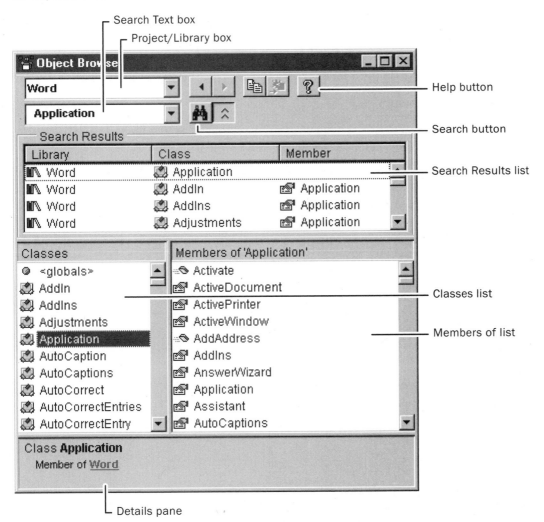

The Project/Library box shows all the available referenced type libraries. These libraries make it possible for you to use early binding with the corresponding applications.

The Search Text box shows any keywords you have searched for by using the drop-down list. You can also type a word in this box, and then click the Search button to search the available libraries for that word. The Search Results list displays any classes, properties, methods, events, or constants that contain the word you searched for.

The Classes list displays all objects and collections in the library, and the Members of list displays all methods, properties, events, and constants associated with the selected object in the Classes list. The bottom pane of the dialog box (the Details pane) displays other information about the currently selected item, such as what kind of object it is, its data type, what arguments it might take, and what library or collection of which the item is a member.

If a Help file has been associated with the objects in the type library, you can display a Help topic by clicking the item in either the Classes or Members of list, and then pressing F1 or clicking the Help button in the upper-right corner of the dialog box.

Working with the Outlook Object Model

The programming model of Microsoft® Outlook® differs somewhat from the other Microsoft® Office applications. You can work with Outlook's object model in three ways:

- You can write Microsoft® Visual Basic® for Applications (VBA) code that runs from a local project file or a COM add-in that is associated with the local installation of Outlook.

- You can use the native scripting environment available within the Outlook forms that are used to display items such as messages and appointments.

- You can use automation to work with Outlook from other Office applications and applications that support VBA.

To write VBA code that runs from a local project file (VBAProject.OTM), open Outlook, point to Macro on the Tools menu, and then click Visual Basic Editor. In Outlook, the Visual Basic Editor makes it possible for you to write code that can be run from this installation of Outlook only. For example, by adding code to the ThisOutlookSession module, you can write code against the following Application object events: ItemSend, NewMail, OptionsPagesAdd, Quit, Reminder, and Startup. Just as with other Office applications, you can insert code modules, class modules, and UserForms to further customize your solution, and you can run procedures from menu items or toolbar buttons.

To distribute a solution created by using a local Outlook VBA project, you can export your modules and objects to files and then import them on other machines where Outlook is installed. However, a much better way to distribute your solution is to compile and install your solution as a COM add-in by using the COM add-in designer available in Microsoft® Office XP Developer or in Microsoft® Visual Basic® 6.0.

To write script that runs within Outlook items, you use the Outlook Script Editor. Outlook forms (that is, all items you can open in Outlook, such as messages, appointments, and contacts) support scripting in Microsoft® Visual Basic® Scripting Edition (VBScript) by using the Outlook Script Editor. Because VBScript is a subset of VBA, there are limitations to what you can do; for example, VBScript supports only one data type, the Variant data type, and a number of VBA keywords and features aren't supported. To access the Outlook Script Editor, you must be in form design mode.

To open the Outlook Script Editor

1.   Open the Outlook item you want to base your form on.

2.   On the **Tools** menu, point to **Forms**, and then click **Design This Form**. To start from an existing custom form, point to **Forms** on the **Tools** menu, click **Design a Form**, and then select a form.

3.   Make any changes you want to the design of the form.

4.   On the **Form** menu, click **View Code**.

When working with scripting in Outlook forms, you will most typically be writing event procedures. For example, you might want to write an event procedure for your form's Open event to initialize the form to display a particular tab page and enter default values in certain fields.

To add an event handler stub to the Outlook Script Editor

1.   From the **Script** menu, click **Event Handler.**

2.   Select the event you want to work with, and then click **Add**.

For more information about the Outlook object model, click Microsoft® Outlook® Object Library Help on the Help menu in the Outlook Script Editor.

To work with Outlook from another application, you can use automation code with either early binding or late binding. To use early binding, establish a reference to the Microsoft® Outlook® object library and then declare and initialize an object variable that references the Outlook Application object. For example:

```
Dim olApp As Outlook.Application
Set olApp = New Outlook.Application
```

Similarly, you can use the CreateObject function with an object variable declared as type Object to initialize a late-bound object variable. For example:

```
Dim olApp As Object
Set olApp = CreateObject("Outlook.Application")
```

Either way, you can then use this object variable to work with the other objects, properties, methods, and events of the Outlook object model.

Office Application Automation

Automating one application from another is often referred to as running code from a host application to automate another application. Although automating one Office application from another is generally accomplished in the same way, there are some important differences regarding how you work with each application.

When Microsoft® Visual Basic® for Applications (VBA) code references an object that is not installed, the Windows installer technology will attempt to install the required feature. In all Microsoft® Office applications except Microsoft® Outlook® and Microsoft® FrontPage®, you can use the FeatureInstall property to control what happens when an uninstalled object is referenced. When this property is set to the default (msoFeatureInstallOnDemand), any attempt to use an uninstalled object causes the Microsoft® Windows® installer to try to install the requested feature.

In some circumstances, this might take some time, and the user might believe that the machine has stopped responding to additional commands. To address this, you can set the FeatureInstall property to msoFeatureInstallOnDemandWithUI to display a progress meter so that users can see that something is happening as the feature is being installed.

If you want to trap the error that is returned and display your own dialog box to the user or take some other custom action, you can set the FeatureInstall property to msoFeatureInstallNone. For more information and details about application-specific behavior, search the Office application's Help index for "FeatureInstall property."

Setting References

The first step in automating one Microsoft® Office application from another is referencing the application you want to automate. This reference lets your application "see" the objects exposed by the other application. In most cases, this means setting a reference to the application's type library by using the References dialog box.

Before you work with objects exposed by an Office application, you should set a reference to that application by using the References dialog box.

To open the References dialog box

- Click **References** on the **Tools** menu in the **Visual Basic Editor**.

In your custom solutions, you must reference only the application that contains the objects you want to manipulate by using automation. Including unnecessary references will increase the time it takes for your solution to load and will consume some additional memory resources.

You can use the objects of another Office application (or the objects exposed by any other application or component that supports automation) without setting a reference in the References dialog box by using the CreateObject or GetObject function and declaring object variables as the generic Object type.

If you use this technique, the objects in your code will be late-bound, and as a result you will not be able to use design-time tools such as automatic statement completion or the Object Browser, and your code will not run as fast.

Tip Because the Application object of every Office XP application includes accessor properties to work with some of the shared Office components such as the Assistant and FileSearch objects, you can work with these objects without having a reference to the Microsoft Office XP object library. You might want to do this if your application must load quickly. However, when you are using a shared Office component without a reference to the Microsoft® Office XP object library, your code can't use enumerated constants; if it does, an error will be displayed. For example, when you are using the Assistant object with a reference to the Microsoft® Office XP object library, you can use a line of code such as the following to animate the Office Assistant:

```
Application.Assistant.Animation = msoAnimationGreeting
```

Tip To use the same line of code without a reference to the Microsoft® Office XP office library, you must use the actual value of the msoAnimationGreeting constant, which is 2, as in the following line of code:

```
Application.Assistant.Animation = 2
```

Tip However, this is not a recommended coding procedure, because these numbers could change during the next revision. Using the constant makes sure your code will not break because of a change in the number. To determine the values for constants such as msoAnimationGreeting, you must temporarily establish a reference to the Microsoft® Office XP office library and use the Object Browser to look up the numeric values of the constants you want work with. Using the numeric values will make your code less readable, and Microsoft doesn't guarantee that the same value will be used in future versions of Microsoft® Office, so code written in this manner might not work correctly in future versions of Office. The VBA projects for all Office applications except Access include a reference to the Microsoft® Office XP office library by default. Therefore, if you want to prevent a reference to the Microsoft® Office XP office library from being loaded when your solution is opened, you must remove the reference in your solution's VBA project.

When you refer to an object in code, VBA determines what type of object it is by searching the type libraries selected in the References dialog box in the order in which they are displayed. If an object has the same name in two or more referenced type libraries, VBA uses the definition provided by the type library listed higher in the Available References list.

To change the order in which the libraries are searched, you can use the Priority buttons to move the type libraries (except for the Visual Basic for Applications and the host application's type library) up or down the list. However, a better way to eliminate ambiguous object references is to fully qualify type declarations by including the programmatic identifier in front of the object name; for example, `Dim docNew As Word.Document`. Qualifying type declarations by using the programmatic identifier eliminates a potential source of errors and also makes your code more self-documenting.

If you have established a reference to an application or component's type library, you can learn about the exposed objects by using the Object Browser and the Help system.

Object Variable Declaration

Before one application can work with the objects exposed by another application's type library, it must first determine what information is contained in that type library. The process of querying the objects, methods, and properties exposed by another application is called binding. Microsoft® Visual Basic® for Applications (VBA) programming in Microsoft® Office applications supports two kinds of binding: early binding and late binding. How and when binding occurs can have a great impact on how your solution performs.

If you establish a reference to the application's or component's type library, you can use early binding. When early binding is used, VBA retrieves information at design time about the application's objects directly from the type library, thus making it possible for you to declare object variables as specific types. For example, if you establish a reference to the Microsoft® Word object library when you are working with Word documents, you can declare object variables by using data types that are specific to Word, such as the Documents or Document types. Early binding reduces the amount of communication that needs to occur when your solution is running, thereby enhancing your solution's performance.

Late binding queries the application you are automating at run time, which makes it possible for you to declare object variables by using the generic Object or Variant data type. In general, late binding is useful if you are writing generic code to run against any of several applications and won't know the type of object you are working with until run time. Note that the additional overhead of querying an application at run time can slow down the performance of your solution.

Note Some applications and components that support automation support only late binding. All Office XP applications and most contemporary applications that support automation support both early and late binding. However, scripting languages such as VBScript and Microsoft® JScript® don't support early binding because they don't support references or specific object data types (for example, in VBScript only the Variant data type is supported).

Early-Bound Declarations

Early binding makes it possible for you to declare an object variable as a programmatic identifier, or class name, rather than as an Object or a Variant data type. The programmatic identifier of an application is stored in the Microsoft® Windows® registry as a subkey below the \HKEY_CLASSES_ROOT subtree. For example, the programmatic identifier for Microsoft® Access is "Access.Application"; for Microsoft® Excel it is "Excel.Application."

When you are using early binding, you can initialize the object variable by using the CreateObject or GetObject function or by using the New keyword if the application supports it. All Office XP applications can be initialized by using the New keyword. Because the Microsoft® Outlook® programming environment for Outlook items supports only scripting, you can't use early binding declarations of any sort in its VBScript programming environment; however, you can use early binding in VBA code in a local Outlook VBA project or COM add-in, or in automation code that works with Outlook from another host application.

Early binding is the friendly name for what C programmers call virtual function table binding, or vtable binding. To use early binding, the host application must establish a reference to a type library (.tlb) or an object library (.olb), or an .exe, .dll, or .ocx file that contains type information about the objects, methods, properties, and events of the application or service you want to automate.

In the following code fragment, an Application variable is declared by using the programmatic identifier for Word (Word.Application) and a new instance of Word is created by using the Set statement with the New keyword:

```
Dim wdApp As Word.Application

Set wdApp = New Word.Application
```

If the code following these lines doesn't set the Application object's Visible property to True, the new instance of Word will be hidden. All Office applications are hidden by default when they are automated from another application.

Use early binding whenever possible. Early binding has the following advantages:

Syntax checking When you use early binding, VBA checks the syntax of your statements against the syntax stored in the object library during compilation rather than checking it at run time, so that you can catch and address errors at design time. For example, VBA can determine if you are using valid properties or methods of an object, and if you are passing valid arguments to those properties and methods.

Support for statement-building tools   When you use early binding, the Visual Basic Editor supports features that make writing code much easier and less prone to errors, such as automatic listing of an object's properties and methods, and pop-up tips for named arguments.

Support for built-in constants   When you use early binding, your code can refer to the built-in constants for method arguments and property settings because this information is available from the type library at design time. If you use late binding, you must define these constants in your code by looking up the values in the application's documentation.

Better performance   Performance is significantly faster with early binding than with late binding.

Late-Bound Declarations

Late binding makes it possible for you to declare a variable as an Object or a Variant data type. The variable is initialized by calling the GetObject or CreateObject function and specifying the application's programmatic identifier. For example, in the following code fragment, an Object variable is declared and then set to an instance of Microsoft® Access by using the CreateObject function:

```
Dim objApp As Object
Set objApp = CreateObject("Access.Application")
```

Late binding is the friendly name for what C programmers used to call IDispatch binding, and was the first method of binding implemented in applications that can control other applications through automation. For this reason, you can use late binding to maintain backward compatibility with older applications. However, late binding uses a lot of overhead; it is faster than dynamic data exchange (DDE), but slower than early binding.

> **Tip**   DDE is a protocol that was established before OLE for exchanging data between Windows applications. There is no need to use DDE to exchange data between Office applications because of their support for automation. However, you might have to use DDE from some other application that doesn't support automation code to work with data from an Office application. For more information about using DDE, search the Visual Basic Reference Help for the Office application you want to work with.

The CreateObject function must also be used to work with objects from any automation component from script. This is because scripting has no method of establishing references to type libraries to support early binding.

Creation of Object Variables to Automate Another Office Application

Working with the objects from one Microsoft® Office application to another Office application through Microsoft® Visual Basic® for Applications (VBA) code is very similar to using code to work with the objects within the code's host application. In most cases, you begin by creating an object variable that points to the Application object representing the Office application that contains the objects you want to work with. In general, you create an early-bound object variable by using the New keyword. However, there are limited circumstances where you might choose to use the CreateObject or GetObject function to create an object variable.

When you write VBA code in an application that manipulates objects within that same application, the reference to the Application object is implicit. When you are automating another application, the reference to the Application object generally must be explicit. The following two examples illustrate this difference. The first example contains VBA code intended to be run in Microsoft® Word. The second example contains VBA code intended to be run from another Office application (or any application that supports automation through VBA). For the second example to work, a reference must be set to the Microsoft® Word object library in the application the code is run from.

```
Sub CodeRunningInsideWord()
    Dim docNew As Word.Document


    ' Add new document to Documents collection.
    Set docNew = Documents.Add
    ' Type text into document.
    Selection.TypeText "Four score and seven years ago"
    ' Display document name and count of words, and then close document
without
    ' saving changes.
    With docNew
        MsgBox "'" & .Name & "' contains " & .Words.Count & " words."
        .Close wdDoNotSaveChanges
    End With
    Set docNew = Nothing
End Sub


Sub CodeRunningOutsideWord()
    Dim wdApp      As Word.Application
    Dim docNew     As Word.Document


    ' Create new hidden instance of Word.
    Set wdApp = New Word.Application
    ' Create a new document.
    Set docNew = wdApp.Documents.Add
```

```
' Add text to document.
wdApp.Selection.TypeText "Four score and seven years ago"
' Display document name and count of words, and then close
' document without saving changes.
With docNew
    MsgBox "'" & .Name & "' contains " & .Words.Count & " words."
    .Close wdDoNotSaveChanges
End With
wdApp.Quit
Set wdApp = Nothing
End Sub
```

In most cases, you will create an object variable that refers to the top-level object representing the application you want to access through automation, the Application object. When you have the reference to the Application object, you use additional references to that object's child objects to navigate to the object or method you want to manipulate. You assign object variables to child objects by using a method of a higher-level object with the Set statement.

However, Microsoft® Excel and Word also make it possible for you to create a top-level reference to certain child objects of the Application object. For this reason, it is possible to rewrite the previous CodeRunningOutsideWord procedure to start from a reference to a Word Document object, this way:

```
Sub CodeRunningOutsideWord2()
    Dim docNew As Word.Document

    Set docNew = New Word.Document
    Set docNew = Documents.Add
    ' The following line uses the Application property to access the
    ' implicit instance of the Word Application object.
    docNew.Application.Selection.TypeText "Four score and seven years ago"
    With docNew
        MsgBox "'" & .Name & "' contains " & .Words.Count & " words."
        .Close wdDoNotSaveChanges
    End With
    docNew.Application.Quit
    Set docNew = Nothing
End Sub
```

Similarly, Excel makes it possible for you to create a top-level reference starting from the Workbook object. You can do this in either of two ways:

- By using the Excel.Sheet class name to create a workbook that contains a single worksheet.

  -or-

- By using the Excel.Chart class name to create a workbook that contains a worksheet with an embedded Chart object and another worksheet that contains a default data set for the chart.

To create a Workbook object either way, you must use the CreateObject function, because the Excel.Sheet and Excel.Chart class names don't support the New keyword. For example, to automate Excel starting with a top-level reference to a Workbook object that contains a single worksheet, use code such as this:

```
Dim wbkSheet As Excel.Workbook
Set wbkSheet = CreateObject("Excel.Sheet")
```

To automate Excel starting with a top-level reference to a Workbook object that contains a worksheet with a chart and another worksheet containing a default data set for the chart, use code such as this:

```
Dim wbkChart As Excel.Workbook
Set wbkChart = CreateObject("Excel.Chart")
```

When you are automating Word starting from a Document object or automating Excel starting from a Workbook object, an implicit reference is created to the Application object. If you must access properties and methods of the Application object, you can use the Application accessor property of the Document or Workbook objects. While using the Document or Workbook objects as top-level objects might reduce the amount of code you have to write somewhat, in most cases your code will be easier to understand and more consistent if you start from a reference to the Application object.

The following table shows all the top-level Office objects you can reference and their class names.

Object type	Class name
Access application	Access.Application
Excel application	Excel.Application
Excel workbook	Excel.Sheet
	Excel.Chart
FrontPage application	FrontPage.Application
Outlook application	Outlook.Application
PowerPoint application	PowerPoint.Application
Word application	Word.Application
Word document	Word.Document

Automating the Visual Basic Editor

In addition to using code to work with other Microsoft® Office applications, you can also use automation code to work with the objects exposed by the Microsoft® Visual Basic® Editor object model. You can use the Visual Basic Editor's object model to work with the objects in its user interface, such as its windows and command bars, which makes it possible for you to develop add-ins to customize and extend the Visual Basic Editor's user interface. Additionally, you can use the Visual Basic Editor's object model to work with your Microsoft® Visual Basic® for Applications (VBA) project itself to add and delete references, to set and read project properties, and to work with the components that make up your project, such as standard modules, class modules, and UserForms. This feature makes it possible for you to write code to maintain references, to document and set properties for projects, and to work with existing components and add new ones.

To work with the Visual Basic Editor's objects, first you must establish a reference to its type library, which is named Microsoft® Visual Basic® for Applications Extensibility 5.3. To write code to work with the Visual Basic Editor, you must initialize a variable to work with the Visual Basic Editor's top-level object, the VBE object. However, you can't reference the VBE object directly. This is because the Visual Basic Editor isn't an independent application or service; it's running as part of the host application's process. To initialize an object variable to work with the Visual Basic Editor, you must use the VBE accessor property of the host application's Application object. The VBE property is available in all Office applications except Outlook. The following example shows how to initialize an object variable to work with the Visual Basic Editor:

```
Dim objVBE As VBIDE.VBE
Set objVBE = Application.VBE
```

For an overview of working with the Visual Basic Editor's object model, see the *Visual Basic Language Developer's Handbook* by Ken Getz and Mike Gilbert (Sybex, 1999).

> **Note** The Microsoft® Access Application object provides a References collection and Reference object that make it possible for you to work with references in an Access VBA project without requiring you to establish a reference to the Microsoft Visual Basic for Applications Extensibility 5.3 type library. For more information about the Access References collection, search the Microsoft Access Visual Basic Reference Help index for "References collection."

The Set Statement and the New Keyword in Automation

You start automation code by declaring object variables with a specific object type that represents the top-level object and then declaring any child objects you want to reference. You then create an instance of the top-level object by using the Set statement and the New keyword. However, the New keyword can't be used to create a new instance of a child object. To create an instance of a child object, use the appropriate method of the parent object along with the Set statement.

In the following example, the top-level Microsoft® Excel Application object variable is assigned by using the Set statement and the New keyword. The object variable representing the Workbook child object is assigned by using the parent object's Add method and the Set statement.

```
Sub CreateExcelObjects()
    Dim xlApp          As Excel.Application
    Dim wkbNewBook     As Excel.Workbook
    Dim wksSheet       As Excel.Worksheet
    Dim strBookName    As String

    ' Create new hidden instance of Excel.
    Set xlApp = New Excel.Application
    ' Add new workbook to Workbooks collection.
    Set wkbNewBook = xlApp.Workbooks.Add
    ' Specify path to save workbook.
    strBookName = "c:\my documents\xlautomation.xls"
    ' Loop through each worksheet and append " - By Automation" to the
    ' name of each sheet. Close and save workbook to specified path.
    With wkbNewBook
        For Each wksSheet In .Worksheets
            wksSheet.Name = wksSheet.Name & " - By Automation"
        Next wksSheet
        .Close SaveChanges:=True, FileName:=strBookName
    End With

    Set wkbNewBook = Nothing
    XlApp.Quit
    Set xlApp = Nothing
End Sub
```

Note The CreateExcelObjects procedure uses three Excel object variables, but only the first two are instantiated by using the Set statement. You do not need to use the Set statement to create an object variable that will be used only inside a For…Each loop.

In the next example, the top-level Microsoft® Outlook® Application object is created by using the Set statement and the New keyword. The MailItem child object variable is created by using the Application object's CreateItem method. The Recipient child object is created by using the Add method of the MailItem object's Recipients collection.

```
Sub CreateOutlookMail()
    Dim olApp              As Outlook.Application
    Dim olMailMessage      As Outlook.MailItem
    Dim olRecipient        As Outlook.Recipient
    Dim blnKnownRecipient  As Boolean
    ' Create new instance of Outlook or open current instance.
    Set olApp = New Outlook.Application
    ' Create new message.
    Set olMailMessage = olApp.CreateItem(olMailItem)
    ' Prompt for message recipient, attempt to resolve address, and
    ' then send or display.
    With olMailMessage
        Set olRecipient = .Recipients.Add(InputBox("Enter name of message recipient", _
            "Recipient Name"))
        blnKnownRecipient = olRecipient.Resolve
        .Subject = "Testing mail by Automation"
        .Body = "This message was created by VBA code running " _
            & "Outlook through Automation."
        If blnKnownRecipient = True Then
            .Send
        Else
            .Display
        End If
    End With
    Set olMailMessage = Nothing
    olApp.Quit
    Set olApp = Nothing
End Sub
```

Note At the end of this procedure, each object variable is destroyed by explicitly setting it equal to the Nothing keyword.

You can also use the New keyword to create a new instance of the object at the same time you declare its object variable. For example:

```
Dim olApp As New Outlook.Application
```

If you do this, there is no need to use a Set statement to instantiate the object. However, this technique is not recommended because you have no control over when the object variable is created. For example, if your code must test to see if an object exists by using a statement such as

`If olApp Is Nothing Then`, this test will return True if you have created an instance of the object in the Dim statement. Additionally, you might not need to use an object except at the user's request. If you create an instance of the object by using New in the Dim statement, the object will be created even if it isn't used. To maintain control over when an object is created, don't use the New keyword in the Dim statement, and instantiate the object by using a Set statement at the point in your code where you must use the object.

Single-Use vs. Multi-Use Applications

Whether you return a reference to a new instance of the Application object or an existing instance depends on whether the application's default behavior is as a single-use or a multi-use application. A single-use application causes a new instance of that application to be created whenever an object variable is instantiated in any host application. For example, Microsoft® Word is a single-use application, so the following code creates a new instance of Microsoft® Word regardless of how many instances of Word might be running already:

```
Dim wdApp aAs Word.Application
Set wdApp = New Word.Application
```

A multi-use application makes it possible for host applications to share the same instance of the application. The next example creates a new instance of Microsoft® Outlook® only if Outlook is not running when the code is executed. Because Outlook is a multi-use application, if Outlook is running already when this code is run, the object variable points to the currently running instance.

```
Dim olApp As Outlook.Application
Set olApp = New Outlook.Application
```

The following table shows the default behavior for each Office application.

Application	Application type
Access	Single-use
Excel	Single-use
FrontPage	Single-use
Outlook	Multi-use
PowerPoint	Multi-use
Word	Single-use

You can use the GetObject function to create an object variable that references a currently running instance of a single-use application.

If you create an object variable that points to a multi-use application (Outlook or Microsoft® PowerPoint®) and an instance of the application is running already, any method you use to create the object variable will return a reference to the running instance. For example, if Outlook is running already, the following lines of code all return a reference to the same instance of Outlook:

```
Dim olApp1 As Outlook.Application
Dim olApp2 As Outlook.Application
Dim olApp3 As Outlook.Application
Set olApp1 = New Outlook.Application
Set olApp2 = CreateObject("Outlook.Application")
Set olApp3 = GetObject(, "Outlook.Application")
```

Using the CreateObject and GetObject Functions

You can use the Set statement with the CreateObject and GetObject functions to create a top-level object variable that represents a Microsoft® Office application. These functions should be used only in those situations where the New keyword does not provide the functionality you require.

You use the CreateObject function to create a top-level object variable that represents an Office application in the following two situations:

- The Office application for which you want to create an Application object is not available on the local computer but is available on some other computer on your network. For example, you can run Microsoft® Visual Basic® for Applications (VBA) code that prints reports from a Microsoft® Access database that is located on a network server even though Access is not installed on the computer from which the code is run. If Access is installed on the network server, you can create an Access Application object that runs on the server by specifying the name of the server in the CreateObject function's optional servername argument. For example:

```
Dim objAcApp As Object
Set objAcApp = CreateObject("Access.Application", "MyServer1")
```

The servername argument of the CreateObject function is the same as the machine name portion of a share name. Therefore, for a share named \\MyServer1\Public, the servername argument is "MyServer1".

To successfully run an Office application as a remote server, you must configure Distributed Component Object Model (DCOM) settings on the computer that is acting as a server, and also possibly on the client computers. To configure DCOM, run the Distributed COM Configuration utility (Dcomcnfg.exe) from the Run box on the Startup menu. For more information about configuring DCOM, search the Microsoft Technical Support Web site (http://support.microsoft.com) for "Configure DCOM."

- The CreateObject function is also useful when you are not sure if the Office application you want to automate will be installed on the computer that runs your code. The following example illustrates how to use the CreateObject function to make sure an application is available for automation:

```
Sub CreateObjectExample()
    Dim objApp As Object

    Const ERR_APP_NOTFOUND As Long = 429

    On Error Resume Next
    ' Attempt to create late-bound instance of Access application.
    Set objApp = CreateObject("Access.Application")
    If Err = ERR_APP_NOTFOUND Then
        MsgBox "Access isn't installed on this computer. " _
            & "Could not automate Access."
        Exit Sub
    End If
    With objApp
        ' Code to automate Access here.
        .Quit
    End With
    Set objApp = Nothing
End Sub
```

Note The Application object variable in this procedure is declared by using the Object data type and is late-bound to the application by using the CreateObject function. The code must be written this way, because, if an object variable is declared as a specific Application object type and that application is not present, the code will break.

Note The CreateObject function also must be used to work with objects from any automation component from script. This is because scripting has no method of establishing references to type libraries to support early binding. However, for security reasons, you wouldn't typically use the CreateObject function from script to create an instance of an Office application.

You can use the GetObject function in these situations:

• You must create a reference to a running instance of an application. For example, the following code creates a reference to the running instance of Access. If Access is not running when the code executes, a Set statement is used to create an object variable for the Access Application object.

```
Sub GetObjectExample()
    Dim acApp As Access.Application

    Const ERR_APP_NOTRUNNING As Long = 429
```

```
On Error Resume Next


' Attempt to reference running instance of Access.
Set acApp = GetObject(, "Access.Application")
' If Access isn't running, create a new instance.
If Err = ERR_APP_NOTRUNNING Then
    Set acApp = New Access.Application
End If
With acApp
    ' Code to automate Access here.
End With
' If instance of Access was started by this code,
' shut down application.
If Not acApp.UserControl Then
    acApp.Quit
    Set acApp = Nothing
End If
End Sub
```

If multiple instances of the application you want to automate are running, there is no way to guarantee which instance the GetObject function will return. For example, if two sessions of Access are running and you use the GetObject function to retrieve an instance of Access from code running in Excel, there's no way to guarantee which instance of Access will be used.

There are few circumstances where it makes sense to use the GetObject function to return a reference to a running instance of an Office application. If a user opened the running instance, you would rarely want your code to be manipulating the objects in that instance of the application. However, when you use the Shell function to start an Access application (so that you can supply a password and workgroup information file to open a secured database), it does make sense to work with the running instance of Access by using the GetObject function to return a reference to the instance of Access that you started.

- You also use the GetObject function when you must open an Office file and return a reference to the host application object at the same time. The following example shows how to use the GetObject function to open an Access database from disk and return a reference to the Access application. When HTML is passed as the value for the lngRptType argument, the procedure creates a Web page from a report and displays that page in a Web browser.

```
Function GetReport(Optional lngRptType As opgRptType) As Boolean
    ' This function outputs a report in the format specified by
    ' the optional lngRptType argument. If lngRptType is specified,
    ' the report is automatically opened in the corresponding
    ' application.
```

```
' lngRptType can be any of the following constants defined
' by Enum opgRptType in the Declarations section of this
' module:
' XLS = output to Excel
' RTF = output to Rich Text Format
' SNAPSHOT = output to Access snapshot report format
' HTML = output to HTML
' If lngRptType is not specified, the report is opened in
' Access and displayed in Print Preview.

Dim acApp            As Access.Application
Dim strReportName    As String
Dim strReportPath    As String

   Const SAMPLE_DB_PATH As String = "c:\program files\" _
   & "microsoft office\office\samples\northwind.mdb"

strReportName = "Alphabetical List of Products"
strReportPath = "c:\my documents\"
' Start Access and open Northwind Traders database.
   Set acApp = GetObject(SAMPLE_DB_PATH, "Access.Application")
With acApp
   ' Output or display in specified format.
   With .DoCmd
      Select Case lngRptType
         Case XLS
         .OutputTo acOutputReport, strReportName, _
            acFormatXLS, strReportPath & "autoxls.xls", True
         Case RTF
         .OutputTo acOutputReport, strReportName, _
            acFormatRTF, strReportPath & "autortf.rtf", True
         ' Snapshot Viewer must be installed to view snapshot
         ' output.
         Case SNAPSHOT
         .OutputTo acOutputReport, strReportName, _
            acFormatSNP, strReportPath & "autosnap.snp", True
```

```
            Case HTML
            .OutputTo acOutputReport, strReportName, _
                acFormatHTML, strReportPath & "autohtml.htm", _
                True, "NWINDTEM.HTM"
            Case Else
            acApp.Visible = True
            .OpenReport strReportName, acViewPreview
        End Select
    End With
    ' Close Access if this code created current instance.
    If Not .UserControl Then
        acApp.Quit
        Set acApp = Nothing
    End If
    End With
End Function
```

Working with Documents That Contain Startup Code

Using automation to open a document does not prevent a document's startup code from running.
Startup code can be defined in various ways in Microsoft® Office applications, as explained in the
following table.

Application	Startup code location
Word	Startup code is contained in the event procedures for the Open or New events in the ThisDocument module of a document or template.
Excel	Startup code is contained in the event procedure for the Open event in the ThisWorkbook module of a workbook or template.
Outlook	Startup code is contained in the event procedure for the Startup event in the ThisOutlookSession of the local Outlook VBA project.
Access	If you create an Access macro named AutoExec, this macro's actions will run on startup. You can also place startup code in the event procedure for the startup form's Open event. To specify a form to be opened on startup, use the Startup command on the Tools menu.

Note Microsoft® PowerPoint® and Microsoft® FrontPage® documents don't have a way to
define startup code.

Because startup code might display message boxes or modal forms that act as dialog boxes, these message or dialog boxes might prevent your code from proceeding until a user closes or responds to them. If you have startup code in a Microsoft® Excel workbook or a Microsoft® Access database that you don't want to run if the document is opened programmatically from another application, you can use the UserControl property of the Application object to determine how a document is being opened and then act accordingly. If you can't use the UserControl property, you might need to use a SendKeys statement to send keystrokes to close the message or dialog box.

In Excel, the UserControl property will return False only when the document or workbook is opened from automation by using a hidden instance of the Excel Application object (Application.Visible = False). For example, the following code defined in an Excel workbook's Open event procedure will run only if the workbook is opened by a user or a visible instance of the Excel Application object. If you open the workbook by using a hidden instance of the Excel Application object from code running in another application, the message box won't be displayed.

```
Private Sub Workbook_Open()
    Dim strMsg As String

    strMsg = "This message was triggered by this workbook's " & _
            "Open event." & vbCrLf & _
            "It won't be displayed if this workbook " & _
            "is opened by using a hidden" & vbCrLf & _
            "instance of the Excel Application object " & _
            "from Automation code."

    ' If opened through Automation by using a hidden instance,
    ' the UserControl property will be False.
    If Application.UserControl = True Then
        MsgBox strMsg
    End If
End Sub
```

Note In Microsoft® Word 97 and later, there is no way to prevent Open event code from running with the UserControl property. If Word is visible to the user, or if you call the UserControl property of a Word Application or Document object from within a Word code module, this property will always return True. However, you can still use the Word UserControl property from automation code (that creates a hidden instance of Word) running from another application to determine if a document was opened programmatically or by the user.

In Access, you don't have to check or keep track of whether the instance of the Application object is hidden or visible because the UserControl property is False whenever the application is started from code. To control whether code in the startup form's Open event is executed, Access provides a Cancel argument for the Open event. As shown in the following example, you can set the Cancel argument to True to keep a startup form from opening if you open the database by using automation code:

```
Private Sub Form_Open (Cancel As Integer)
   ' If database is opened from Automation,
   ' cancel the Open event of the form.
   If Application.UserControl = False Then
      Cancel = True
   Else
   ' Any startup code that needs to run when the
   ' database is opened by a user goes here.
   End If
End Sub
```

You can also use the UserControl property of the Access Application object to control whether actions in a database's AutoExec macro will run when the database is opened from another program by using automation. To do this, you must enter `Application.UserControl = True` in the Condition column for each action you want to cancel. (To display the Condition column, click Conditions on the View menu.)

> **Tip**   You can also use COM add-ins to implement a startup form or code. COM add-ins support events that you can use to determine how an application was loaded before connecting the add-in.

Shutting Down Objects Created by Using Automation

A local variable is normally destroyed when the procedure in which it is declared is finished executing. However, it is good programming practice to explicitly destroy an application-level object variable used to automate another application by setting it equal to the Nothing keyword. Doing this frees any remaining memory used by the variable. For some Application objects, you might also have to use the object's Quit method to completely destroy an object variable and free up the memory it is using. As a general rule, it's safest to do both: Use the Quit method and then set the object variable equal to the Nothing keyword.

There might be situations where you must determine if the instance of an application you are working with was created by your code before shutting it down. Generally, you can inspect the UserControl property of the Application object to determine if your code opened the current instance. However, there are cases where the value of the UserControl property can change from False to True as your code executes. For example, if you start Microsoft® Excel through automation, make it visible, and make it possible for the user to interact with this instance, such as by typing something in a cell, the UserControl property will return True even though your code started the instance. To handle this situation, assign the value of the UserControl property to a variable right after you create the instance of the Application object, and use this variable to test the value of the UserControl property before closing the application, as shown in the following example:

```
Sub GetObjectXL()
    Dim xlApp            As Excel.Application
    Dim blnUserControl   As Boolean

    Const ERR_APP_NOTRUNNING As Long = 429

    ' Set blnUserControl to True as default.
    blnUserControl = True
    On Error Resume Next
    ' Attempt to open current instance of Excel.
    Set xlApp = GetObject(, "Excel.Application")
    ' If no instance, create new instance.
    If Err = ERR_APP_NOTRUNNING Then
        Set xlApp = New Excel.Application
        ' Store current state of UserControl property.
        blnUserControl = xlApp.UserControl
    End If
    With xlApp
        ' Code to automate Excel here.
        ' Check original value of UserControl property.
        If blnUserControl = False Then
            xlApp.Quit
            Set xlApp = Nothing
        End If
    End With
End Sub
```

Note Microsoft® PowerPoint®, Microsoft® Outlook®, and Microsoft® FrontPage® have no method of determining if an instance of the Application object has been started by a user or program.

Working with Office Applications

Each Microsoft® Office XP application exposes an object model with hundreds of different objects, collections of objects, properties, methods, and events that you can take advantage of to build your application.

This section introduces the objects that you will use most often in each of the Office applications. This introduction helps you become immediately productive when you are working with Microsoft® Visual Basic® for Applications (VBA) in any Office application or when you are driving another application through Automation (formerly called OLE Automation).

In This Section

Working with Microsoft Access Objects
> Use Form, Report, and DataAccessPage objects and the controls they contain to format and display data and make it possible to add or edit data in a database.

Working with Microsoft Excel Objects
> Use Microsoft® Visual Basic® for Applications (VBA) to work with Microsoft® Excel objects, from within either Excel itself or another Microsoft® Office XP application to gain access to every part of Excel.

Working with Microsoft FrontPage Objects
> Create, deploy, modify, and manage Web sites using Microsoft® FrontPage®.

Working with Microsoft Outlook Objects
> Create custom Microsoft® Outlook® objects and manipulate those objects from within Outlook or from another application using VBA code from within Outlook or another Microsoft® Office XP application by using Automation.

Working with Microsoft PowerPoint Objects
> Automate Microsoft® PowerPoint® by using the Application object, from which you can open an existing Presentation object or create a new presentation.

Working with Microsoft Project Objects
> Build powerful custom applications easily with the Microsoft® Project object model.

Working with Microsoft Publisher Objects
> Use Microsoft® Visual Basic® for Applications (VBA) to work with t he Microsoft® Publisher object model.

Working with Microsoft Word Objects
> Use Microsoft® Visual Basic® for Applications (VBA) to work with the Microsoft® Word Document object, Application object, and Documents collection.

Working with Microsoft Visio Objects
> Design, model, and manage complex enterprise-level systems with the sophisticated tool set provided by Microsoft® Visio® products.

Working with Microsoft Access Objects

Working with Microsoft® Access objects primarily means working with Form, Report, and DataAccessPage objects and the controls they contain. You can use these powerful Access objects to format and display data and make it possible for the user to add or edit data in a database. In addition, Access exposes many other objects you can use to work with your Access application; among the most important are the CurrentProject, CurrentData, CodeProject, CodeData, Screen, and DoCmd objects and the Modules and References collections. This section presents an overview of how to work with Access objects by using Microsoft® Visual Basic® for Applications (VBA).

> **Note**   You can use the Object Browser and Access Visual Basic Reference Help to learn more about individual objects, properties, methods, and events.

Tables and relationships, the data in tables, and queries are managed and maintained by a database engine. For .mdb-type databases, Access uses the Microsoft® Jet database engine. For .adp-type databases, Access uses the Microsoft® SQL Server database engine or any other ActiveX Data Objects (ADO) data source. You programmatically work with tables, data in tables, or queries by using ADO or Data Access Objects (DAO).

In This Section

Understanding the Access Application Object
Use the properties and methods provided by the Application objects to create and work with other Access objects.

Built-in Access Functions and Methods
Learn about functions and methods that appear in the Object Browser as methods of the Application object.

Working with Reports, Forms, and Data Access Pages
Use reports, forms, and data access pages provided by Access to display data to the user.

Understanding the Access Application Object

The Application object is the top-level object in the Microsoft® Access® object model. It provides properties and methods you can use to create and work with other Access objects. It also provides several built-in functions you can use to work with the objects in your database. In essence, the Application object serves as the gateway to all other Access objects.

Application-wide options are available through the Options dialog box and the Startup dialog box. The commands to open these dialog boxes are located on the Tools menu. You can use the Options dialog box to specify or determine application-wide settings, such as whether the status bar is displayed, the new database sort order, and the default record-locking settings. You use the Startup dialog box to specify or determine settings such as which form opens automatically when your database opens and your database application's title and icon. The following sections discuss how you can use Microsoft® Visual Basic® for Applications (VBA) to access all of these settings.

Working with the Options Dialog Box Settings

Use the Application object's SetOption and GetOption methods to specify or determine the settings in the Options dialog box. Both methods use a string argument that identifies the option you want to access. The SetOption method takes an additional argument representing the value you want to set. For example, the following code displays a message box that indicates whether datasheet gridlines are turned on:

```
MsgBox "Horizontal Gridlines On = " & _
    CBool(GetOption("Default Gridlines Horizontal")) & vbCrLf _
    & "Vertical Gridlines On = " & CBool(GetOption("Default Gridlines
Vertical"))
```

The next example illustrates how you can use the SetOption method to specify a new default database folder:

```
SetOption "Default Database Directory", "C:\NewMDBs"
```

To see a list of all the string arguments used to access settings in the Options dialog box, search the Microsoft® Access Visual Basic Reference Help index for "options, setting," open the topic "Set Startup Properties and Options in Code," and then jump to the topic "Set Options from Visual Basic."

The value returned by the GetOption method and the value you pass to the SetOption method as the setting argument depend on the type of option you are using. The following table establishes some guidelines for Options dialog box settings.

If the option is	Then the value of the option is
A text box	A string or numeric value
A check box	An integer that will be True (-1) (selected) or False (0) (not selected)
An option button in an option group, or an item in a combo box or a list box	An integer corresponding to the item's position in the option group or list (starting with 0 for the first item, 1 for the second item, and so on)

Note If you use the SetOption method to change a user's Options dialog box settings, be sure to restore those settings when your code is finished executing or when your application ends. Otherwise, the settings you specify will be applied to any database the user opens. Note that the settings in the Options dialog box are stored in the Microsoft® Windows® registry in the \HKEY_CURRENT_USER\Software\Microsoft\Office\10.0\Access\Settings subkey. As a result, changes to these settings will not persist if the database is run on a different machine.

Understanding Startup Properties

You use startup properties to customize how a database application appears when it is opened. You work with startup properties differently than you do the settings in the Options dialog box. Each option in the Startup dialog box has a corresponding Access property, but you won't find these properties in the Object Browser. In a new database, the startup properties do not exist until a user makes a change to the default settings in the Startup dialog box.

To set these properties programmatically for an .mdb-type database, you must first add each property to the Properties collection of the Database object. This is true whether you are using DAO or ADO. In other words, even without a reference to DAO, you still use the Properties collection of the Database object to work with these properties. In an .adp-type database, startup properties are stored in the Properties collection of the CurrentProject object.

In the following sample, the AddCustomProperty sample procedure is used to set the AppTitle property in an .mdb-type database. Note that if the property does not exist when the AddCustomProperty procedure is called, the property is created and appended to the Properties collection of the Database object.

```
Const TEXT_VALUE As Integer = 10
If AddCustomProperty("AppTitle", TEXT_VALUE, "MyDatabase") Then
    ' Property added to collection.
End If


Function AddCustomProperty(strName As String, _
                           varType As Variant, _
                           varValue As Variant) As Boolean
    ' The following generic object variables are required
    ' when there is no reference to the DAO 3.6 object library.
    Dim objDatabase As Object
    Dim objProperty As Object

    Const PROP_NOT_FOUND_ERROR = 3270

    Set objDatabase = CurrentDb
    On Error GoTo AddProp_Err
    objDatabase.Properties(strName) = varValue

    AddCustomProperty = True

AddProp_End:
    Exit Function
```

```
AddProp_Err:
   If Err = PROP_NOT_FOUND_ERROR Then
      Set prpProperty = objDatabase.CreateProperty(strName, varType,
varValue)
      objDatabase.Properties.Append objProperty
      Resume
   Else
      AddCustomProperty = False
      Resume AddProp_End
   End If
End Function
```

Note Changes you make to any of the startup properties by using VBA will be available programmatically but will not take effect until the next time the database is opened.

For more information about setting startup properties, search the Microsoft® Access Visual Basic® Reference Help index for "startup options, setting," open the Help topic "Set Startup Properties and Options in Code," and then jump to "Set Startup Properties from Visual Basic."

Built-in Access Functions and Methods

The Microsoft® Access Application object contains several functions and methods you can use to work with data, Access objects, or the application itself. These functions and methods appear in the Object Browser as methods of the Application object, although they might be referred to as "functions." These functions and methods can be used within Access or from another application by using Automation.

Calling Built-in Access Functions and Methods Without Using an Application Object Variable

To use Automation, you usually have to create an instance of the Application object, but you can call built-in Access functions and methods of the Application object from other Microsoft® Office applications without first creating an Access Application object variable. The only requirements are that you set a reference to the Microsoft® Access object library in the calling application's Microsoft® Visual Basic® for Applications (VBA) project, and that you call the function or method by using the Access qualifier, as illustrated in the following example. For example, you could use the following VBA code to call the built-in Access Eval function to evaluate a string expression contained in a Microsoft® Word bookmark:

```
Dim rngResults As Word.Range
Set rngResults = ActiveDocument.Bookmarks("MathMark").Range
rngResults.Text = Access.Eval(rngResults.Text)
```

Note Direct calls to built-in Access functions and methods, such as the one illustrated in the preceding example, automatically create a new instance of Access that remains in memory until the document containing the code that called the function or method is closed. If you want more control over when the instance of Access is created and destroyed, create it by using the New keyword or the CreateObject or GetObject function, and close it by setting the Application object variable equal to Nothing.

The following table summarizes some of the Access functions and methods available to you from the Application object and descriptions of how they might be used.

Function or method	Description
Domain aggregate functions	A domain is simply a set of records defined by a table or query. You use domain aggregate functions to get statistical information about a set of records, for example, to count the number of records or to determine the sum of values in a particular field. These functions use a naming convention that begins with a capital "D", for example, DAvg, DCount, DLookup, DSum, and so on. You can use these functions in VBA code, in a query expression, or in a calculated control on a form or report.
Eval function	You use this function to evaluate a string expression that results in a text string or numeric value. The Eval function uses a single argument that either is a string expression that returns a value or is the name of a built-in or user-defined function that returns a string. You can use the Eval function in a calculated control, a query expression, a macro, or VBA code.
GUIDFromString and StringFromGUID functions	You use these functions to convert a globally unique identifier (GUID) to a String value or a String value to a GUID. A GUID is a 16-byte value used to uniquely identify an object.
hWndAccessApp method	You can use this method to determine the handle (a unique Long Integer value) assigned by Microsoft® Windows® to the main Access window. You can use the hWnd property to determine the handle assigned by Microsoft Windows to an Access Form or Report window.
HyperlinkPart function	The HyperlinkPart function returns information about data stored in a field that has the Hyperlink data type. This information is similar to the information contained in the properties of a Hyperlink object. You can use this function in VBA code, a query expression, or a calculated control.
LoadPicture method	This method loads a graphic file stored on disk into the Picture property of a control. You use this method to set or change the Picture property of a control at run time.

Function or method	Description
Nz function	You use the Nz function to evaluate a value and return a specified value if the evaluated value is Null. This function is useful when you are assigning values from a field in a recordset to a control that cannot use Null values.
SysCmd method	This is the Swiss army knife of Access methods. It can perform a variety of tasks depending on the value of the acSysCmdAction constant supplied in its action argument. For example, you can use this method to display a progress meter or text in the status bar, return information about Access (such as the directory where Msaccess.exe is located), or to get information about an Access object (such as whether a form is open).

For more information about these functions and methods, search for them by name in the Microsoft® Access Visual Basic Reference Help index.

Note In addition to working with built-in Access methods and functions, you can use the Application object's Run method to call custom procedures stored in an Access database.

Creating, Opening, and Closing an Access Application

You can create a new database, or open and close an existing database, from within Microsoft® Access® or by using Automation from another application. The methods discussed in this section are typically used in Automation from another application. If your code is running inside Access, the code typically works with the currently open database, and using these methods is not necessary.

Note If you are working in another application and you must access only the data in a database (tables or queries), and not objects such as forms or reports, you use ADO to access the data you require.

You use the NewCurrentDatabase method to create a new .mdb-type database. You use the OpenCurrentDatabase and CloseCurrentDatabase methods to open and close an existing .mdb-type database. The following sample is designed to be run from any Microsoft® Office application. It opens the Northwind Traders sample database and prints the portion of the Product Catalog report specified in the OpenReport method:

```
Sub PrintReport(strCategoryName As String)
    Dim acApp        As Access.Application
    Dim strDBPath    As String

    Const DB_PATH As String = _
        "c:\program files\microsoft office\office\samples\northwind.mdb"

    Set acApp = New Access.Application
```

```
With acApp
    .OpenCurrentDatabase DB_PATH
    ' Print the Product Catalog report.
    .DoCmd.OpenReport "Catalog", acViewNormal, , _
        "CategoryName = '" & strCategoryName & "'"
End With
acApp.Quit
Set acApp = Nothing
End Sub
```

You use the NewAccessProject, OpenAccessProject, or CreateAccessProject method to open or create an .adp-type database. The NewAccessProject method creates a new .adp-type database and causes it to become active, whereas the CreateAccessProject method only creates an .adp file on disk. You use the OpenAccessProject method to open an existing .adp-type database and the CloseCurrentDatabase method to close an .adp-type database.

When you create a new database or have a database open, you can use other methods of the Application object to create new Access objects. For example, you use the CreateForm and CreateControl methods to create forms and controls on forms. You use the CreateReport and CreateReportControl methods to create reports and controls on reports. You use the CreateDataAccessPage method to create data access pages. To programmatically add controls to a data access page, you must use script or the Dynamic HTML (DHTML) object model to work with HTML directly.

> **Note**   Although the methods discussed above let you programmatically create a database and the objects it contains, these methods typically are used only in wizards or add-ins. Generally, you create the database and its objects through the Access user interface and then work with these objects programmatically by using Microsoft® Visual Basic® for Applications (VBA) code run from Access or another Office application.

The CurrentData and CurrentProject Objects

In previous versions of Microsoft® Access, you can use Data Access Objects (DAO's) and their methods and properties to get information about forms, reports, macros, tables, fields, relationships, and queries. For example, you can use Document objects to get information about the tables and queries in a database. There are separate Container objects representing forms, reports, scripts (Access macros), tables (tables and queries), and modules. Each of these Container objects contains a collection of Document objects representing all the objects of the specified type in the current database. Each Document object contains only summary information about each object and does not provide access to the properties of the object or the data it contains. You use DAO Recordset objects to work with the data in a table or query, and you use members of the Forms or Reports collection to work with forms and reports themselves.

However, in Access, DAO is no longer the default programmatic way to interact with data and objects that contain data; therefore, Access has two new objects—CurrentData and

CurrentProject—that contain collections of AccessObject objects, which are used in place of the Container and Document objects available through DAO in previous versions.

Access uses the CurrentData object to store collections of AccessObject objects that are administered by the database engine, for example, tables and queries in .mdb-type databases, and database diagrams, stored procedures, tables, and views in .adp-type databases. Information about each collection of objects is stored in a collection where each object is represented as an AccessObject object. For example, information about tables is contained in the AllTables collection, and information about views is stored in the AllViews collection. To access the CurrentData object, you use the CurrentData property of the Application object. When code is running in an add-in or library database, you would use the CodeData object to refer to the objects managed by the add-in or library database. The CodeData property of the Application object returns the CodeData object.

> **Note**   AccessObject objects contain information about the objects that contain data, but do not provide access to the data itself.

You use the CurrentProject property of the Application object to get information about the Access objects in a database, such as data access pages, forms, macros, modules, and reports. The CurrentProject property of the Application object returns the CurrentProject object, which contains collections of AccessObject objects as well as information about the name, path, and connection of the database itself. For example, the AllForms collection contains information about all the forms in a database, and the AllReports collection contains information about all the reports in the database. When code is running in an add-in or library database, the CodeProject object contains the collections of AccessObject objects in the add-in or library database. The CodeProject property of the Application object returns the CodeProject object.

An AccessObject object exposes the following properties you can use to get information about an object: IsLoaded, Name, Parent, Properties, and Type. These properties are described in the following table.

AccessObject property	Description
IsLoaded	A Boolean value indicating whether the object is currently loaded. This property is True when an object is open in any view.
Name	A String value representing the name of the object.
Parent	Returns the parent object for the specified object. For example, the parent of an item in the AllForms collection is the AllForms collection object. The parent of the CurrentProject object is the Application object.
Properties	Returns an AccessObjectProperties collection, which contains all the custom properties associated with a particular AccessObject object. The Properties collection can store String or Long Integer values only.
Type	A Long Integer value representing one of the objects specified by the acObjectType intrinsic constants.

Note   Collections of AccessObject items are indexed beginning with a value of 0 for the first item in the collection, 1 for the second item, and so on.

The following sample shows how you can use the IsLoaded property to determine if a form, report, or data access page is currently loaded:

```
With CurrentProject
    Select Case intObjectType
        Case acForm
            IsObjectOpen = .AllForms(strObjName).IsLoaded
        Case acReport
            IsObjectOpen = .AllReports(strObjName).IsLoaded
        Case acDataAccessPage
            IsObjectOpen = .AllDataAccessPages(strObjName).IsLoaded
        Case Else
            Err.Raise ERR_INVALIDOBJTYPE
    End Select
End With
```

The intObjectType variable would be passed to a procedure as an argument of type acObjectType.

The next sample illustrates how to add custom properties to a form:

```
Sub AddCustomFormProperty(strFormName As String, _
                          strPropName As String, _
                          varPropValue As Variant)
    ' This procedure illustrates how to add custom
    ' properties to the Properties collection that
    ' is associated with an AccessObject object.

    With CurrentProject.AllForms(strFormName).Properties
        .Add strPropName, varPropValue
    End With
End Sub
```

The Printer Object and Printer Collection

Microsoft® Access contains a Printer object and a Printers collection that make it possible for you to control printer configuration without using Microsoft® Windows® api calls and the complex structure that PrtDevMode requires. This object makes it possible for you to change printer settings without opening the object in a design model, making custom printer settings in MDE/ADE files possible. You can make these changes even during print preview.

For example, to set printer properties for a Catalog report, you could use the following code:

```
Reports("Catalog").Printer.LeftMargin = 1440  'Set left margin to 1 inch
Reports("Catalog").Printer.Orientation = acPRORLandscape  'Set
orientation to landscape
Reports("Catalog").Printer.PaperSize = acPRPSLegal 'Set paper size to
legal
```

To cycle through the installed printers on the system, you can use the following:

```
Dim prt As Access.Printer
For Each prt In Application.Printers
    Debug.Print prt.DeviceName
Next
```

The AddItem and RemoveItem Objects

Microsoft® Access adds the methods AddItem and RemoveItem to the combo box and list box objects. These new methods make it possible for you to add and remove values from a combo box or list box programmatically. For multicolumn combo boxes, you use a semicolon-delimited string to add values to separate columns.

For example, to add values to a two-column combo box, use the format:

```
Combo1.AddItem "ALFKI;Alfred's Futterkiste"
```

The following string removes the first item in a combo box:

```
Combo1.RemoveItem 0
```

To remove an item where the bound column is ALFKI, you can use this format:

```
Combo1.RemoveItem "ALFKI"
```

The Save Model

Microsoft® Access speeds up the process of regularly saving your work. Until you compile your project, Access saves only the modules that you have modified since your last save. This makes it less of a chore to save often during active development. After you compile the project, Access will save the complete project each time. Until then, it is more efficient to save only the parts you have changed.

Working with the Screen Object

Other Microsoft® Office applications have properties that return a reference to active objects. For example, Microsoft® Word has the ActiveDocument property to determine which document currently has the focus. Microsoft® Excel has properties to return the active Workbook, Worksheet, Cell, Chart, and Window objects. Similarly, Microsoft® PowerPoint® has the ActivePresentation property to determine the active presentation.

In Microsoft® Access, you use the Screen object to work with the object or control that currently has the focus. The Screen object has properties that return a reference to the currently active control (on a form or report), data access page, datasheet, form, or report. These properties are useful in code that operates against an object and must know only the type of object. For example, the following line of code hides the currently active form:

```
Screen.ActiveForm.Visible = False
```

The next example shows how you can use the Screen object to determine which cell in a datasheet is selected:

```
MsgBox "The selected item is located at: Row " _
    & Screen.ActiveDatasheet.SelTop & ", Column " _
    & Screen.ActiveDatasheet.SelLeft
```

The Screen object also has properties you can use to work with the previously active control and the mouse pointer.

Note If you try to refer to an object by using properties of the Screen object and there is no object of that type currently active, an error occurs.

Working with the DoCmd Object

The DoCmd object makes it possible for you to carry out various Microsoft® Access commands by using Microsoft® Visual Basic® for Applications (VBA). These commands are called actions when they are used in Access macros and are called methods of the DoCmd object when they are carried out in code.

Note In other Microsoft® Office applications, the term "macro" is synonymous with a VBA procedure. In Access, macros are completely different from the VBA code you write in a procedure. For more information about Access macros, search the Microsoft® Access Help index for "macros, overview," and then open the topic "Macros: What they are and how they work."

Two of the most common tasks that require methods of the DoCmd object are opening and closing Access objects. To open an Access object, you use the DoCmd object's Open*Object* method, where *Object* represents the name of the object you want to open. For example, you use the OpenForm method to open a form, the OpenReport method to open a report, and the OpenQuery method to open a query. All of the Open*Object* methods take arguments that specify the object to open and how to display the object. For example, the following code opens the Customers form as read-only in Form view (acNormal) and specifies that only customers in the USA be shown:

```
DoCmd.OpenForm FormName:="Customers", View:=acNormal, _
    WhereCondition:="Country = 'USA'", DataMode:=acFormReadOnly
```

You can use the OpenReport method to open a report in Design view or Print Preview, or you can specify that the report be printed, as in the following example:

```
DoCmd.OpenReport ReportName:="CustomerPhoneList", _
    View:=acViewNormal, WhereCondition:="Country = 'USA'"
```

Note   When you use the acViewNormal constant in the view argument of the OpenReport method, the report is not displayed but is printed to the default printer.

You use the DoCmd object's Close method to close an Access object. You can use the optional arguments of the Close method to specify the object to close and whether to save any changes. The following example closes the Customers form without saving changes:

```
DoCmd.Close acForm, "Customers", acSaveNo
```

Note   All the arguments of the Close method are optional. If you use the method without specifying arguments, the method closes the currently active object.

You can use the DoCmd object's RunCommand method to run commands that appear on an Access menu or toolbar that do not have separate methods exposed in the Access object model. The RunCommand method uses a collection of enumerated constants to represent available menu and toolbar commands. For more information about the RunCommand method, search the Microsoft® Access Visual Basic® Reference Help index for "RunCommand method."

Working with the Modules Collection

The Modules collection contains a Module object representing each module that is currently opened for editing. The Module object might represent a standard or class module that is currently open in the Microsoft® Visual Basic® Editor or a module associated with a form or report that is open in Design view. You can use the methods and properties of a Module object to get information about the code contained in the module or to insert procedures or lines of code. The objects in this collection are typically used by code running in an add-in or wizard.

For more information about the Modules collection and Module objects, search the Microsoft® Access Visual Basic® Reference Help index for "Modules collection" or "Module object."

Working with the References Collection

The References collection contains Reference objects representing each reference in the References dialog box (Tools menu in the Microsoft® Visual Basic® Editor) to another project or object library. A new Microsoft® Access database contains four references by default. You can add or remove references by using the References dialog box or by using methods of the References collection in Microsoft® Visual Basic® for Applications (VBA) code.

For more information about the References collection and Reference objects, search the Microsoft® Access Visual Basic® Reference Help index for "References collection" or "Reference object."

Working with Reports, Forms, and Data Access Pages

Microsoft® Access provides three objects you can use to display data to the user: reports, forms, and data access pages. Although these objects have many similar features, they are used in different ways.

You use reports to display formatted data. The user cannot edit or add data to a report. Reports can be viewed in the database where they were created or printed. You can also save reports as snapshot files so they can be viewed outside an Access application. For more information about working with snapshot files, search the Microsoft® Access Help index for "report snapshots."

You can also use forms to display data to users. However, the real power of forms comes from their ability to collect data from users or let users add new records or edit existing records. Forms can also be printed or saved as reports or data access pages.

Note   Although Microsoft® Access hosts Microsoft® Visual Basic® for Applications (VBA) as it does with the other Microsoft® Office applications, it uses its own built-in forms package. UserForms are not available in Access.

Data access pages combine the features of forms and reports so that you can display data to users and let users interact with data through Microsoft® Internet Explorer version 5 or later. (You can also use other Web browsers to display data access pages, but users will not be able to work with the data directly.) Although you design data access pages by using Access, you save them to disk as separate files designed to be used in a Web browser, which means users can work with Access data from within an Access database or over an intranet or the Internet. Data access pages can contain data in an Access database (.mdb file) or Access project (.adp file).

Access forms, reports, and data access pages have numerous properties, methods, and events you can use to specify how the object will look and behave. A complete discussion of all properties, methods, and events is beyond the scope of this section. For information about a specific property, method, or event, search the Microsoft® Access Visual Basic® Reference Help index for the name of the item about which you want information.

You can use the Application object's CreateForm, CreateReport, and CreateDataAccessPage methods to programmatically create forms, reports, and data access pages. You can also add controls to these objects through VBA code, but unless you are building an add-in or a wizard, you typically create these objects by using the Access user interface and then display them from code. When you display an object, you can use various properties of the object to specify the records it will contain.

Working with PivotViews

Microsoft® Access adds two new views to the set of views that currently exist for tables, queries, stored procedures, and functions. The views are called PivotTable View and PivotChart View, and they make it easy to create flexible reports and to quickly publish your work to the Web using data access pages.

PivotView reports are powerful tools for presenting and analyzing data. They provide a means to view a single set of data in a variety of configurations in a manner similar to the capabilities provided by Microsoft® Excel. As with a query, a PivotView report can answer a question about a data set: Which customers provided the most sales for the first quarter of this year? In which country was a particular product most popular last year? How well did a particular sales representative do in Europe for the past two years?

If you are skilled at building queries, you can answer each of these questions with a separate query. The advantage of the PivotView report, however, is when you have defined the data set, you can "pivot" the data to answer all of these questions with a single data set. For most users, this is easier and more intuitive than building a query, especially when the PivotView report combines data from multiple tables and queries. In addition, because PivotTable data is cached in memory, PivotView reports provide extremely fast querying.

Referring to Open Objects

The Application object has properties that return collections of open Microsoft® Access objects. The Reports property returns a reference to the Reports collection that contains all currently open reports. The Forms property returns a reference to the Forms collection that contains all currently open forms. The DataAccessPages property returns a reference to the DataAccessPages collection that contains all currently open data access pages. You specify a member of a collection by using its name or its index value in the collection. You typically use the index value only when iterating through all the members of a collection because the index value of an item can change as items are added to or removed from the collection. For example, the following sample uses the form's name to reference the Open Customers form:

```
Dim rstCustomers As ADODB.Recordset

Set rstCustomers = Forms("Customers").Recordset
```

The next example closes and saves all open data access pages by looping through the DataAccessPages collection:

```
For intPageCount = DataAccessPages.Count - 1 To 0 Step -1
   DoCmd.Close acDataAccessPage, _
      DataAccessPages(intPageCount).Name, acSaveYes
Next intPageCount
```

The Forms, Reports, and DataAccessPages collections contain only open objects. To determine if an object is open, you can use the IsLoaded property of an item in the AllForms, AllReports, or AllDataAccessPages collections, or you can use the SysCmd method with the acSysCmdGetObjectState constant. You can also use the CurrentView property to determine if a form is open in Design, Form, or Datasheet view or if a data access page is open in Design or Page view. The following procedure uses the SysCmd method and the CurrentView property to determine if a form is open in Form or Datasheet view:

```
Function IsLoaded(ByVal strFormName As String) As Boolean
    ' Returns True if the specified form is open in Form view or Datasheet
view.

    Const OBJ_STATE_CLOSED = 0
    Const DESIGN_VIEW = 0

    If SysCmd(acSysCmdGetObjectState, acForm, strFormName) <>
OBJ_STATE_CLOSED Then
        If Forms(strFormName).CurrentView <> DESIGN_VIEW Then
            IsLoaded = True
        End If
    End If
End Function
```

The Data Behind Forms and Reports

Most of the forms you create will be designed to display or collect data. Forms can display data for viewing, editing, or input. Forms are also used to create dialog boxes that collect information from a user, but do not display data. Reports display static data only, and aren't used to edit or collect data.

The source of the data behind a form or report is specified by the object's RecordSource property. The RecordSource property can be a table, a query, or a Structured Query Language (SQL) statement. You can display subsets of the data contained in the object's RecordSource property by using the Filter property to filter the data or by using the wherecondition argument of the OpenForm or OpenReport method to specify a subset of data. When you have specified a record source for a form or report, you can use the field list (in form or report Design view) to drag fields from the object's source of data to the object.

If you set the RecordSource property by using Microsoft® Visual Basic® for Applications (VBA), you can use the name of an existing table or query, or a SQL statement. The easiest way to create a SQL statement to use in code, whether from within a Microsoft® Access module or another Microsoft® Office application, is to use the Access query design grid to create a query that displays the appropriate records. When the query contains the records you want, click SQL View on the View menu and copy the SQL string that defines your query. You can then paste the SQL string into your VBA code and replace any hard-coded criteria with variables that will contain the data you want to use as criteria.

The following figure shows a query created in the query design grid that selects all fields from the Customers table for the customer named B's Beverages.

Specifying Criteria in the Query Design Grid

The SQL view for this query contains the following SQL statement:

```
SELECT * FROM Customers WHERE CompanyName = "B's Beverages";
```

You can modify this SQL statement for use in the following VBA procedure so that it will display a single customer record for any company passed in the strCompanyName variable:

```
Option Explicit
Dim frmTempForm As Form

Sub ShowCustomerRecord(strCompanyName As String)
    Dim strSQL As String

    strSQL = "SELECT * FROM Customers WHERE CompanyName = " _
        & """" & strCompanyName & """"
    Set frmTempForm = New Form_Customers
    With frmTempForm
        .RecordSource = strSQL
        .Visible = True
    End With
End Sub
```

Specifying String Criteria by Using Variables in Code

When you specify criteria for a query, filter, or wherecondition argument from code, you typically use a variable. For example, you could specify the wherecondition argument of the OpenReport method as in the following:

```
DoCmd.OpenReport ReportName:="CustomerPhoneList", _
    WhereCondition:="CompanyName = " & "'" & strCompanyName & "'"
```

When the criteria used is a string, the variable can be surrounded with single quotation marks (`'`). However, if the value of the variable contains a single quotation mark, this technique will not work. For example, if you are searching for records that match the criteria `"CompanyName = 'B's Beverages'"`, you will encounter errors. If there is any chance that a variable will contain a value that itself contains a single quotation mark, you should surround the variable with two sets of double quotation marks (`"`), as shown in the following example:

```
DoCmd.OpenReport ReportName:="CustomerPhoneList", _
    WhereCondition:="CompanyName = " & """" & strCompanyName & """"
```

For more information about using quotation marks in strings, search the Microsoft® Access Visual Basic® Reference Help index for "quotation marks," and then open the topic "Quotation Marks in Strings."

When you are working with forms, you can also use the new Recordset property to specify the Recordset object that contains the records of the form or the subform. The following example illustrates how to change the source of data for a currently open form:

```
Sub ChangeRecordsetProperty()
    Dim frmNewRecords      As Form
    Dim rstNewRecordset    As New ADODB.Recordset


    Call ShowCustomerRecord("B's Beverages")
    Stop ' View Customers form containing 1 record.


    Set frmNewRecords = Forms(Forms.Count - 1)
    rstNewRecordset.Open "SELECT * FROM Customers", _
        CurrentProject.Connection, adOpenKeyset, adLockOptimistic
    Set frmNewRecords.Recordset = rstNewRecordset
    Stop ' View Customers form containing 91 records.
End Sub
```

The Recordset property of forms is new in Access. You use the Recordset property to specify or determine the Recordset object representing a form's source of data. The recordset represented by the Recordset property is a read-only recordset. If you must programmatically work with the data contained in the records displayed in a form, you must to use the Data Access Object (DAO) RecordsetClone property or the ActiveX Data Objects (ADO) Clone method to create a second recordset that you can manipulate with VBA code. The Recordset property can be accessed only by using VBA code and can be used to bind multiple forms to a single recordset or to synchronize multiple forms or multiple Recordset objects. When you change a form's Recordset property, you must use the Set statement, as illustrated in the preceding code sample.

Note   Changing a form's Recordset property might also change the RecordSource, RecordsetType, and RecordLocks properties. In addition, other data-related properties also might be overridden, for example, the Filter, FilterOn, OrderBy, and OrderByOn properties might all be affected when you change the Recordset property of a form.

Working with Controls on Forms and Reports

Although forms, reports, and data access pages are the objects you use to present or gather data from users, it is really the controls on these objects that do all the work. Access contains a wide variety of built-in controls that you can use on these objects.

Forms, reports, and data access pages all use controls to display information or to make it possible for the user to interact with the object or the data it contains. Forms and reports have a Controls property that returns a collection of all the controls on the object.

Controls Collections for Forms and Reports

You can refer to a control on a form or report as a member of the Controls collection or by using the name of the control itself. For example, the following lines of code illustrate three ways to return the RowSource property setting for a combo box control on a form. Because the Controls property is the default property of a Form object, you can refer to the control's name without explicitly specifying the Controls property, as shown in the second and third examples that follow:

```
strSource =
Forms("SalesTotals").Controls("cboSelectSalesPerson").RowSource
strSource = Forms("SalesTotals")!cboSelectSalesPerson.RowSource
strSource = Forms!SalesTotals!cboSelectSalesPerson.RowSource
```

Note   The **!** operator is used to refer to user-defined items, such as forms, reports, and controls on Access forms or reports.

You can also use the Controls property to work with all the controls on a form or report. For example, the following code loops through all the controls on a form and sets the Text property for each text box control to a zero-length string (""):

```
Sub ClearText(frmCurrent As Form)
    Dim ctlCurrent As Control
    For Each ctlCurrent In frmCurrent.Controls
        If ctlCurrent.ControlType = acTextBox Then
            ctlCurrent.Value = ""
        End If
    Next ctlCurrent
End Sub
```

You can pass the Form object to the ClearText procedure by using the Me property. The Me property returns an object representing the form, report, or class module where code is currently running. For example, you could call the ClearText procedure from a form by using the following syntax:

```
Call ClearText(Me)
```

Certain controls on forms and reports also have a Controls collection. For example, the option group control might contain a Controls collection representing option button, toggle button, check box, or label controls in the option group. The tab control has a Pages collection containing a Page object for each page in the tab control. Each Page object also has a Controls collection representing all the controls on a page in a tab control.

Subform and Subreport Controls

Forms and reports can also contain subform or subreport controls that contain another form or report. These controls make it possible for you to display related records from another form or report within a main form or report. A common example of this is a Customers form that contains a subform containing customer orders. You use the SourceObject property of the subform or subreport control to specify the form or report that will be displayed in the control.

The form or report in the subform or subreport control can share a common field, known as the linking field, with the records displayed in the main form or report. The linking field is used to synchronize the records between the subform or subreport and the main form or report. For example, if the record sources for an Orders subform and a Customers main form both contain a CustomerID field, this would be the common field that links the two forms. To specify the linking field, you use the LinkChildFields property of the subform or subreport control and LinkMasterFields property of the main form or report. However, the easiest way to create a linked subform or subreport is to open the main form or report in Design view, drag the appropriate form or report from the Database window to the main form or report, and then release the mouse button.

You use the Form property of a subform control to refer to controls on a subform. You use the Report property of a subreport control to refer to controls on a subreport. The following examples illustrate how to get the value of a control on a subform or subreport by using VBA. The first two lines show alternative ways to reference a control named Quantity on a subform. The last line shows how to use the RecordCount property to get the number of records contained in the recordset associated with a subreport control:

```
lngOrderQuantity =
Forms("CustomerOrders").Controls("SubForm1").Form!Quantity

lngOrderQuantity = Forms!CustomerOrders!SubForm1.Form!Quantity

lngNumProducts =
Reports!SuppliersAndProducts!SubReport1.Form.Recordset.RecordCount
```

List Box and Combo Box Controls on Forms

List box and combo box controls are very powerful and versatile tools for displaying information and making it possible for the user to interact with the data displayed on a form. These controls work differently in Access than list box and combo box controls in other Office applications, and it is important to understand these differences if you want to use these controls effectively.

If you are used to working with these controls in other applications, the most important difference is how you add items to and remove items from these controls. In other applications, these controls have AddItem and RemoveItem methods to add and remove items. These methods are not supported for Access list and combo box controls. Instead, you use combinations of RowSource and RowSourceType properties to specify the data that appears in a list box or combo box control. The relationship between the RowSource property setting and the RowSourceType property setting is illustrated in the following table.

RowSourceType property setting	RowSource property setting
Table/Query	Table name, query name, or SQL statement
Value List	Semicolon-delimited list of values
Field List	List of field names from a table, query, or SQL statement
User-defined function	No value specified

For more information about setting the RowSourceType and RowSource properties to fill a list box or combo box control, search the Microsoft® Access Visual Basic® Reference Help index for "RowSource property" or "RowSourceType property."

If you are creating list box or combo box controls through the Access user interface, you can take advantage of the List Box Wizard and the Combo Box Wizard to set the various properties required to display data in these controls. To use these wizards, make sure the Control Wizards tool in the toolbox is pressed in, then click the List Box or Combo Box tool in the toolbox, and then click the place on the form where you want the control to appear. Follow the instructions displayed by the wizard.

You can set the properties of a list box or combo box control without using the wizard by using the control's property sheet or VBA. You use the ControlSource property to bind a list box or combo box control to a field in the recordset specified in the form's RecordSource property. As mentioned earlier, you use the RowSource property in combination with the RowSourceType property to specify the source of data for the list box or combo box control.

The BoundColumn property specifies which column in the record source specified by the RowSource property will contain the value of the list box or combo box control. If a list box or combo box control does not have a ControlSource property setting, you can set the BoundColumn property to 0. When you do this, the Value property of the control will contain the row number of the selected row specified by the RowSource property. The row number of the selected row is the same as the value of the control's ListIndex property. The ColumnCount and ColumnWidths properties specify which columns are displayed in the control.

The following sample fills a combo box control with data from an SQL statement, specifies which column in the SQL statement specified by the RowSource property will contain the value for the control, and uses the ColumnWidths property to specify which columns are displayed in the control:

```
With Me!cboEmployees
    .RowSource = "SELECT EmployeeID, FirstName, " _
        & "LastName FROM Employees ORDER BY LastName"
    .RowSourceType = "Table/Query"
    .BoundColumn = 1
    .ColumnCount = 3
    .ColumnWidths = "0in;.5in;.5in"
    .ColumnHeads = False
    .ListRows = 5
End With
```

The preceding code fills a combo box with data from 3 fields (columns) from each record (row) in the Employees table, as specified by the RowSource property. The BoundColumn property is set to the first field in the Employees table, in this case, EmployeeID. When an item is selected from the combo box, the value of the EmployeeID field will be the control's value and is the value saved to the field specified by the ControlSource property. Note that the first column in the ColumnWidths property is set to 0 inches. This hides the bound column (EmployeeID) from the user when the combo box's drop-down list is displayed. The user sees only the FirstName and LastName fields, and these fields are displayed in .5-inch wide columns. Note also that the ColumnHeads property is set to False, meaning that the names of the FirstName and LastName fields are not shown in the control's drop-down list. And finally, the ListRows property is set to 5, specifying that the control's drop-down list will display only 5 records at a time.

Using a User-Defined Function to Fill a List Box or Combo Box Control

You can specify a user-defined function as the RowSourceType property setting for a list box or combo box control. The function you use for this property setting has to meet specific criteria in order to work correctly because the function is called repeatedly as Access fills the control with data. For more information about creating and using user-defined functions to fill a list box or combo box control, search the Microsoft® Access Visual Basic® Reference Help index for "RowSourceType property," then open the "RowSourceType, RowSource Properties" topic, and then use the See Also jump to open the "RowSourceType Property (User-Defined Function)—Code Argument Values" topic.

Adding New Values to a Combo Box Control

You use the LimitToList property to specify whether a user can add new values to a bound combo box from the user interface when the form is in Form view or Datasheet view. When this property is set to True (the default), the user can't add new items to the combo box. If the BoundColumn property is set to any column other than 1, Access will automatically set the LimitToList property to True. When this property is set to False, new values are added to the underlying record source specified by the RowSource property.

When the LimitToList property is set to True, any attempt to add a new item to a combo box control will cause the NotInList event to occur. You can add code to the NotInList event procedure to handle the attempt to add new data to the control. This event procedure uses the NewData and Response arguments to represent the new data the user has tried to enter and the response you want to provide in the attempt to add new data. Setting the Response argument to one of the following built-in constants specifies how you want to respond to the attempt to add data to the control: acDataErrAdded, acDataErrContinue, or acDataErrDisplay. For example, the following sample illustrates one way to add new data to a combo box control:

```
Private Sub CatégoryID_NotInList(NewData As String, _
                          Response As Integer)

    If MsgBox("Do you want to add '" _
        & NewData & "' to the items in this control?", _
        vbOKCancel, "Add New Item?") = vbOK Then

        ' Remove new data from combo box so control can be requeried
        ' after the AddNewData form is closed.
        DoCmd.RunCommand acCmdUndo

        ' Display form to collect data needed for the new record.
        DoCmd.OpenForm "AddNewData", acNormal, , , acAdd, acDialog, NewData

        ' Continue without displaying default error message.
        Response = acDataErrAdded
    Else
        Response = acDataErrContinue
    End If
End Sub
```

For more information about how to use the NotInList event procedure, search the Microsoft® Access Visual Basic® Reference Help index for "NotInList event."

Enabling Multiple Selections in a List Box Control

To make it possible for users to make multiple selections from a list box control, you set the MultiSelect property. When the MultiSelect property is set to Simple (2) or Extended (1), the Value property of the control is Null. You work with multiple selections in a list box control by using the Selected, ItemsSelected, and Column properties.

Working with Data Access Pages

Data access pages are HTML documents comprised of HTML code, HTML intrinsic controls, and Microsoft® ActiveX® controls. Data access pages rely on DHTML and are designed to work best with Microsoft® Internet Explorer version 5 or later. (You can also use other Web browsers to display data access pages, but users will not be able to work with the data directly.)

A data access page can be a simple HTML document or can include data-bound controls that let users use a Web browser to interact with data stored in a database. Microsoft® Access provides a WYSIWYG design environment for creating data access pages and a means for deploying those pages and any necessary supporting files to a Web server, network server, or local file system. In addition, you can view and use data access pages within Access itself.

You might be tempted to think of data access pages as HTML documents that combine the best features of forms and reports for display on the Web, but that would be a very narrow definition. Data access pages do support much of the functionality you are used to in Access forms and reports, but they also provide a completely new way to interact with data from within an Access database or on the Web. These objects make it possible for users to use a Web browser to work with data in an interactive manner and in a way that has never been possible before. Data access pages are similar to forms in that you can use them to view, edit, or delete existing records, and you can also use them to add new records to an underlying record source. They are similar to reports in that you can sort and filter records as well as group records according to criteria you specify. In addition, while a page is displayed, you can manipulate the records that are displayed and change how the records are displayed.

You can create data access pages from scratch in Access or you can base them on existing HTML pages created by using some other HTML authoring tool. Only those pages created or modified within the Access design environment will be visible in the Pages object list in the Database window. This means that if you edit an HTML document in Access, a link to that document is created, even if you later use another tool to make additional changes. In addition, because the data access pages that appear in the Database window are links to the files stored on disk, you can delete a page in the Database window without deleting the file from disk. Unlike other objects in an Access database, data access pages are stored on disk as .htm files that are separate from the Access database in which they are created.

Creating a data access page in Access is similar to creating a form or report. Data access pages have their own object list in the Database window, and when they are opened in Design view, they have a toolbox and property sheet. The toolbox contains tools for inserting the HTML intrinsic controls, such as the text box, label, list box, and command button controls. In addition, the toolbox contains tools for inserting controls that are useful only on data access pages, such as expand, bound HTML, and scrolling text controls. The toolbox also contains tools for inserting the Microsoft® Office Web Component controls on a data access page.

Note Because Access does not use the shared Microsoft® Office components related to Script objects or HTMLProject objects, you can't use these objects to work with scripts or the HTML code in data access pages through VBA code. To work with scripts or the HTML code in an Access DataAccessPage object, you use the Microsoft® Script Editor or a DataAccessPage object's Document property, which returns the Web browser's document object for an HTML page.

Creating, Saving, and Closing Data Access Pages

You will typically create data access pages in the data access page design environment in Access. However, there might be circumstances where you want to use VBA code to display a data access page within Access or to programmatically output a page to a separate location, such as a Web server on your local intranet.

You create a data access page programmatically by using the Application object's CreateDataAccessPage method. You can use the CreateDataAccessPage method to work with an existing HTML page as a data access page or to create a new, blank page. For example, the following code illustrates how to use this method to create a new page called BlankDAP.htm:

```
Application.CreateDataAccessPage FileName:="c:\WebPages\BlankDAP.htm" _
    CreateNewFileName:=True
```

The CreateDataAccessPage method creates a new blank page by default and adds a link to that page in the Pages object list in the Database window. If the file specified in the FileName argument already exists when the method is called and the CreateNewFileName argument is set to True (the default), an error occurs. If you set the method's CreateNewFileName argument to False, the FileName argument must contain the path and name of an existing file. If the file does not exist, an error occurs. If the FileName argument contains the path and file name of a file for which there is already a link in the Pages object list in the Database window, a new, uniquely named link is created that points to the same file on disk. If you provide a name but do not specify the path to a new file, the page is created in the current directory.

You can determine the path and file name for pages that appear in the Pages object list in the Database window by using the read-only FullName property of the AccessObject object that represents a particular data access page. For example, the following code prints the Name and FullName properties for each page in the current database:

```
Dim objDAP As AccessObject

For Each objDAP In CurrentProject.AllDataAccessPages
Debug.Print "The '" & objDAP.Name & _
    "' is located at: " & objDAP.FullName
Next objDAP
```

When you call the CreateDataAccessPage method, Access creates a temporary file on disk. To permanently save the page and create a pointer to it from the Pages object list in the Database window, you must use the Save method or the Close method of the DoCmd object.

The following code fragment illustrates how you could create a new data access page, work with the HTML in the page, and then create a link to the page and permanently save it to disk. The procedure also illustrates one way to use an error trap to handle files that already exist.

```
Function CreateDAP(strFileName As String) As Boolean
    ' This procedure illustrates how to create a data access
    ' page, work with the HTML in the page, and then save the page.
    ' The procedure also shows how to use an error trap to avoid
    ' the error that ocurrs if strFileName already exists.
    Dim dapNewPage As DataAccessPage

    Const DAP_EXISTS As Long = 2023

    On Error GoTo CreateDAP_Err
    ' Create the new page.
    Set dapNewPage = Application.CreateDataAccessPage(strFileName, True)

    ' Use the Document property to return the Internet Explorer 5
    ' document object, and then use the objects on the page to
    ' work with the HTML in the page.
    With dapNewPage.Document
        .All("HeadingText").innerText = "This page was created
programmatically!"
        .All("HeadingText").Style.display = ""
        .All("BeforeBodyText").innerText = "When you work " _
            & "with the HTML in a data access page, you " _
            & "must use the document property of the page " _
            & "to get to the HTML. "
        .All("BeforeBodyText").Style.display = ""
    End With

    ' Close the page and save all changes.
    DoCmd.Close acDataAccessPage, dapNewPage.Name, acSaveYes

    CreateDAP = True
```

```
CreateDAP_End:
   Exit Function
CreateDAP_Err:
   If Err = DAP_EXISTS Then
      ' The file specified in strFileName already exists,
      ' so replace it with this new page.
      If MsgBox("'" & strFileName & "' already exists. Do you want to " _
         & "replace it with a new, blank page?", vbYesNo, _
         "Replace existing page?") = vbYes Then
         Set dapNewPage = Application.CreateDataAccessPage(strFileName,
False)
         Resume Next
      Else
         CreateDAP = False
         Resume CreateDAP_End
      End If
   Else
      CreateDAP = False
      Resume CreateDAP_End
   End If
End Function
```

Note When you create a new data access page, the display property of the style object for the HeadingText and BeforeBodyText elements is set to None by default. The preceding example also illustrates how to change this setting so the text you insert is visible when the page is viewed.

The CreateDAP procedure uses the data access page's Document property to return the Internet Explorer 5 document object and then sets properties of elements in the page. This procedure also uses the innerText property of an HTML element to specify the text that appears in the element.

Opening and Working with Data Access Pages

Although data access pages are designed to be viewed in a browser, you can display data access pages in Access to let users view and work with data as they do with forms and reports.

To open an existing data access page for which a link exists in the Pages object list in the Database window, you use the DoCmd object's OpenDataAccessPage method. You use the View argument of the OpenDataAccessPage method to specify whether to view the page in Design view or Page view. The following example illustrates how to open the Employees page in Page view:

```
DoCmd.OpenDataAccessPage "Employees", acDataAccessPageBrowse
```

To determine whether a page is currently open in Page view or Design view, you use a DataAccessPage object's CurrentView property.

The DataAccessPages collection contains all currently open data access pages. You can access an open page as a member of this collection and gain access to the properties and methods of the page itself as well as any controls on the page. The following sample code opens the Employees page in Design view, applies a theme, adds some text to the main heading, and then displays the page to the user:

```
With DoCmd
    .Echo False
    .OpenDataAccessPage "Employees", acDataAccessPageDesign
    With DataAccessPages("Employees")
        .ApplyTheme "Blends"
        .Document.All("HeadingText").innerText = "Today is " _
            & Format(Date, "mmmm d, yyyy"
    End With
    .OpenDataAccessPage "Employees", acDataAccessPageBrowse
    .Echo True
End With
```

Note To save the changes you make to a data access page, you must make sure the page is in Design view, and then use the DoCmd object's Save method to save changes. If you programmatically make changes to a page while it is in Page view, those changes will be lost as soon as you call the Save method.

To get information about the pages in your database, including whether a page is currently open, you use the CurrentProject object's AllDataAccessPages collection. To specify or determine property settings for a page or controls on a page, you use the properties of a DataAccessPage object. The following sample uses both techniques to print information about data access pages to the Immediate window:

```
Sub DAPGetPageInfo()
    ' This procedure prints information about the data access pages
    ' in this database to the Immediate window.
    Dim objCurrentDAP      As AccessObject
    Dim strPageInfo        As String

    Const DAP_DESIGNVIEW   As Integer = 0
    Const DAP_PAGEVIEW     As Integer = 1

    Debug.Print "There are "; CurrentProject.AllDataAccessPages.Count _
        & " data access pages in this database."
```

```
For Each objCurrentDAP In CurrentProject.AllDataAccessPages
    Debug.Print objCurrentDAP.Name & ":"
    Debug.Print vbTab & "File name: " & objCurrentDAP.FullName
    If objCurrentDAP.IsLoaded <> True Then
        Debug.Print vbTab & "The '" & objCurrentDAP.Name _
            & "' page is not currently open."
    Else
        Select Case DataAccessPages(objCurrentDAP.Name).CurrentView
            Case DAP_DESIGNVIEW
                Debug.Print vbTab & "The '" & objCurrentDAP.Name _
                    & "' page is open in Design view."
            Case DAP_PAGEVIEW
                Debug.Print vbTab & "The '" & objCurrentDAP.Name _
                    & "' page is open in Page view."
        End Select
    End If
Next objCurrentDAP
End Sub
```

Note that the DataAccessPages collection contains DataAccessPage objects, whereas the AllDataAccessPages collection contains AccessObject objects.

When you work with data access pages inside Access, you can use VBA code in a form, for example, to specify or determine property settings of the page or controls on a page. In the next example, the SimplePageExample page is opened and the DataEntry property of the page's Data Source control is set to True so the page can be used only to enter new records:

```
Private Sub cmdSimpleDAPDataEntry_Click()
    With DoCmd
        .Echo False
        .OpenDataAccessPage "SimplePageExample", _
            acDataAccessPageBrowse
        DataAccessPages("SimplePageExample").Document _
            .All("MSODSC").DataEntry = True
        .Echo True
    End With
End Sub
```

Note The ActiveX control that binds controls on a page to an underlying data source is the Microsoft® Office Data Source control (MSODSC). This control is included in every data access page you create but is not visible on the page itself. In the preceding example, the DataEntry property of the MSODSC is set to True. As you can see, the control is created by using an id property setting of `"MSODSC"`, and you use this id property to specify that the control is a member of the all collection in the data access page's Document object.

Caution   Although the HTML underlying the MSODSC is available, you should never modify the HTML directly either in Access or in any HTML authoring tool. To set properties of the MSODSC, you must use its property sheet in the Microsoft® Script Editor or use Microsoft® Visual Basic® Scripting Edition (VBScript) code in the data access page itself.

To open the SimplePageExample page so that it displays all records, you would use the following code:

```
DoCmd.OpenDataAccessPage "SimplePageExample", acDataAccessPageBrowse
```

You can also use the Microsoft® Script Editor to add to a page script that runs when the page is displayed or in response to events that occur on the page. The script you add to a page is part of the page itself and can run when the page is displayed in Access or in a Web browser.

Using the Microsoft Script Editor with Data Access Pages

The Microsoft® Script Editor is an editor and debugger that you can use to work with the HTML code and script in a data access page. This section describes how to use the Script Editor with data access pages.

When you view a data access page in the Script Editor, you see color-coded HTML code and script in the page. In addition, depending on the controls you have placed on the page, you might also see icons representing some controls. For example, the Data Source control is displayed as an icon. You can see the HTML and XML code underlying a control's icon by right-clicking the icon in the Script Editor and clicking Always View As Text on the shortcut menu.

When you create a new data access page, the page contains a two-dimensional section, represented by a `<DIV>` tag in the HTML code that uses the CLASS attribute `MSOShowDesignGrid` and a default ID attribute of `SectionUnbound`. When you add data-bound controls to this section of the page, Access automatically changes the ID attribute to reflect the controls you are using. For example, if you drag the Customers table to this section, Access changes the ID attribute to `HeaderCustomers`. You can place controls anywhere within the two-dimensional section as you can on a form or report. Outside of this section, controls cannot be positioned in this manner.

When you create event procedures, the Script Editor does not insert the event procedure arguments when they are required. You must insert these yourself. For example, every event associated with the Data Source control requires a single dscEventInfo argument. If you double-click the Current event for the Data Source control (MSODSC) in the Script Editor's Script Outline window, the following script block is inserted in your page:

```
<SCRIPT Language=vbscript FOR=MSODSC EVENT=Current>

<!--

-->

</SCRIPT>
```

You must add the event's argument or arguments by adding parentheses and a name for the argument or arguments. It does not matter what name you use for each argument, and it does not matter if the argument is actually used in your script. You must supply all the arguments to the event, even if your code does not use them, or the code will not work. For example, here is the corrected event handler for the Data Source control's Current event:

```
<SCRIPT Language=vbscript FOR=MSODSC EVENT=Current(EventInfo)>
<!--
-->
</SCRIPT>
```

Security Considerations for Data Access Pages

Because data access pages are designed to work both within and outside Access databases, security issues pertaining to data access pages require special attention. Understanding these issues requires an understanding of database security as well as Internet Explorer security.

Access and XML

Moving information between applications and across the Web often has been difficult because of differences in data formats and proprietary structures. With Extensible Markup Language (XML), however, data, metadata, and presentation information can be moved, translated, and stored without difficulty. XML is a transport format, however, and does not make it possible for you to combine information from multiple files and query the result or create merged subsets easily.

Microsoft® Access provides the means for you to import data formatted in XML, and makes it possible for you, the developer, and the users of Access, either to load pre-existing tables with information contained within an XML file or to create the tables on Import. Then, you can use the many other features of Access to manipulate and query your data.

Access also provides an export mechanism for sharing data stored in Microsoft® Jet, linked through Microsoft® SQL Server™ and referenced by views or queries. Adding a TransferXML method to support XML export and import makes it possible for Access to expand its information sharing capabilities.

Working with Microsoft Excel Objects

The Microsoft® Excel object model contains several dozen objects that you can manipulate through Microsoft® Visual Basic® for Applications (VBA) code. Almost anything you can do with Excel from its user interface, you can do by manipulating its objects through VBA. In addition, you can do things through VBA that can't be done through the user interface.

When you use VBA to work with Excel objects, from either within Excel itself or another Office application, you have access to every part of Excel. The objects you will work with include cells, ranges, sheets, workbooks, charts, and more. In other words, every element in Excel can be represented by an object that you can manipulate through VBA.

There are four Excel objects you will work with more than any others: the Application object, the Workbook object, the Worksheet object, and the Range object.

In This Section

Understanding the Excel Application Object
> Use the Microsoft® Excel Application object to determine or specify application-level properties or execute application-level methods.

Understanding the Workbook Object
> Work with the Workbook object to use with a single Microsoft® Excel workbook, and use the Workbooks collection to work with all currently open Workbook objects.

Understanding the Worksheet Object
> Use a worksheet, containing a grid of cells, to work with data and hundreds of properties, methods, and events.

Understanding the Range Object
> Develop a full understanding of the Range object and how to use it effectively in Microsoft® Visual Basic® for Applications (VBA) procedures and harness the power of Microsoft® Excel.

Understanding the Excel Application Object

The Microsoft® Excel Application object is the top-level object in Excel's object model. You use the Application object to determine or specify application-level properties or execute application-level methods. The Application object is also the entry point into the rest of the Excel object model.

When you work with properties and methods of the Application object by using Microsoft® Visual Basic® for Applications (VBA) from within Excel, the Application object is available to you by default. This is known as an implicit reference to the object. If you work with Excel objects from another Office application, then you must create an object variable representing the Excel Application object. This is known as an explicit reference to the object. For example, the following two procedures return the name of the currently active Worksheet object. The ShowNameFromInsideXL procedure is designed to work from within Excel and uses an implicit reference to the Application object. In other words, it references the ActiveSheet property of the Application object without explicitly referencing the Application object itself. The ShowNameFromOutsideXL procedure is designed to be run from outside Excel and so must use an explicit reference to the Application object.

```
Sub ShowNameFromInsideXL()
    MsgBox "'" & ActiveSheet.Name & "' is the currently active worksheet."
End Sub


Sub ShowNameFromOutsideXL()
    Dim xlApp As Excel.Application

    Const XL_NOTRUNNING As Long = 429
```

```
    On Error GoTo ShowName_Err
    Set xlApp = GetObject(, "Excel.Application")
    MsgBox "'" & ActiveSheet.Name & "' is the currently active worksheet."
    xlApp.Quit
    Set xlApp = Nothing

ShowName_End:
    Exit Sub
ShowName_Err:
    If Err = XL_NOTRUNNING Then
        ' Excel is not currently running.
        Set xlApp = New Excel.Application
        xlApp.Workbooks.Add
        Resume Next
    Else
        MsgBox Err.Number & " - " & Err.Description
    End If
    Resume ShowName_End
End Sub
```

Shortcuts to Active Objects

As with other Microsoft® Office XP application object models, the Microsoft® Excel Application object exposes several properties you can use to work with a currently active Excel object. For example, you often will write Microsoft® Visual Basic® for Applications (VBA) procedures designed to work with information in the currently selected cell, or with the currently active worksheet. The Application object exposes the ActiveCell, ActiveChart, ActivePrinter, ActiveSheet, ActiveWindow, and ActiveWorkbook properties, which you can use to return a reference to the currently active cell, chart, printer, sheet, window, or workbook. The following examples illustrate various ways you might use some of these properties:

```
' ActiveWorkbook property example:
Function SaveBookAs(strFileName As String) As Boolean
    ActiveWorkbook.SaveAs ActiveWorkbook.Path & "\" & strFileName
End Function
```

```
' ActiveCell property example:
Function CustomFormatCell()
    With ActiveCell
        If IsNumeric(.Text) And .Formula < 0 Then
            With .Font
                .Bold = True
                .Italic = True
            End With
            .Borders.Color = 255
        End If
    End With
End Function
```

```
' ActiveSheet property example:
Function ChangeName(strNewName As String) As Boolean
    ActiveSheet.Name = strNewName
End Function
```

In addition to the ActiveWorkbook property, you can use the Application object's Workbooks and Worksheets properties to return equivalent Excel objects. The Workbooks property returns the Workbooks collection that contains all the currently open Workbook objects. The Worksheets property returns the Sheets collection associated with the currently active workbook. The following example uses the Workbooks property to determine if a workbook is already open, and if not, to open it:

```
Function OpenBook(strFilePath As String) As Boolean
    ' This procedure checks to see if the workbook
    ' specified in the strFilePath argument is open.
    ' If it is open, the workbook is activated. If it is
    ' not open, the procedure opens it.
    Dim wkbCurrent      As Excel.Workbook
    Dim strBookName     As String

    On Error GoTo OpenBook_Err

    ' Determine the name portion of the strFilePath argument.
    strBookName = NameFromPath(strFilePath)
    If Len(strBookName) = 0 Then Exit Function
    If Workbooks.Count > 0 Then
        For Each wkbCurrent In Workbooks
```

```
            If UCase$(wkbCurrent.Name) = UCase$(strBookName) Then
                wkbCurrent.Activate
                Exit Function
            End If
        Next wkbCurrent
    End If
    Workbooks.Open strBookName
    OpenBook = True

OpenBook_End:
    Exit Function
OpenBook_Err:
    OpenBook = False
    Resume OpenBook_End
End Function
```

Note In the preceding example, the OpenBook procedure calls a custom procedure named NameFromPath that returns the file name portion of the full path and file name passed to the OpenBook procedure in the strFilePath argument.

Understanding the Workbook Object

In the Microsoft® Excel object model, the Workbook object appears just below the Application object. The Workbook object represents an Excel .xls or .xla workbook file. You use the Workbook object to work with a single Excel workbook. You use the Workbooks collection to work with all currently open Workbook objects.

You can also use the Application object's ActiveWorkbook property to return a reference to the currently active workbook. The Workbooks collection has a Count property you can use to determine how many visible and hidden workbooks are open. By default, Excel typically has one hidden workbook named Personal.xls. The Personal.xls workbook is created by Excel as a place to store macros. If the hidden Personal.xls workbook is the only open workbook, the ActiveWorkbook property returns Nothing, but the Workbooks collection's Count property returns 1. The Workbooks collection's Count property will return 0 only when there are no hidden or visible open workbooks.

Creating, Saving, Opening, and Closing Workbook Objects

You create a new Workbook object by using the Workbooks collection's Add method. The Add method not only creates a new workbook, but also immediately opens the workbook as well. The Add method also returns an object variable that represents the new workbook just created. The new workbook will contain the number of worksheets specified in the Sheets In New Workbook dialog box on the General tab of the Options dialog box (Tools menu). You can also specify the number of sheets a new workbook will have by using the Application object's SheetsInNewWorkbook property.

You can save a new workbook by using the Workbook object's SaveAs method and specifying the name of the workbook you want to save. If a workbook by that name already exists, an error occurs. When a workbook has been saved by using the SaveAs method, additional changes are saved by using the Workbook object's Save method. You can also save a copy of an existing workbook with a different file name by using the SaveCopyAs method. You can supply a file name to be used with the SaveAs or SaveCopyAs method, or you can use the Application object's GetSaveAsFileName method to let the user supply the name to be used to save the workbook. If the user clicks Cancel in the Save As dialog box, the GetSaveAsFileName method returns False.

Before you save a new workbook by using the SaveAs method, the Workbook object's Name property setting is a value assigned by Excel, such as Book1.xls. After you save the workbook, the Name property contains the name you supplied in the Filename argument of the SaveAs method. The Name property is read-only; to change the name of a workbook, you must use the SaveAs method again, and pass a different value in the Filename argument.

> **Note**   A Workbook object's FullName property contains the object's path and file name, whereas the Path property contains only the saved path to the current workbook. Before a new workbook is saved, the FullName property has the same as the Name property, and the Path property has no value.

The Workbooks collection's Open method opens an existing workbook. When you open a workbook by using the Open method, it also becomes the active workbook. You can supply a file name to be used with the Open method, or you can use the Application object's GetOpenFileName method to let the user select the workbook to open. If the user clicks Cancel in the Open dialog box, the GetOpenFileName method returns False.

You use a Workbook object's Close method to close an open workbook. To specify whether pending changes to the workbook should be saved before the object is closed, you use the SaveChanges argument. If the SaveChanges argument is omitted, the user is prompted to save pending changes. You can also use the Close method of the Workbooks object to close all open workbooks. If there are unsaved changes to any open workbook when this method is used, the user is prompted to save changes. If the user clicks Cancel in this Save dialog box, an error occurs. You can suppress this Save dialog box by setting the Application object's DisplayAlerts property to False before executing the Close method. When you use the Workbooks object's Close method in this manner, any unsaved changes to open workbooks are lost. After the Close method has run, remember to set the DisplayAlerts property to True.

> **Note**   The Auto_Open and Auto_Close procedures are ignored when a workbook is opened or closed by using the Open or Close methods. You can force these procedures to run by using the Workbook object's RunAutoMacros method. The Microsoft® Visual Basic® for Applications (VBA) code in a workbook's Open and BeforeClose event procedures will be executed when the workbook is opened or closed by using the Open or Close methods.

The following example illustrates how to create a new workbook and specify the number of worksheets it will have:

```
Function CreateNewWorkbook(Optional strBookName As String = "", _
      Optional intNumSheets As Integer = 3) As Workbook
   ' This procedure creates a new workbook file and saves it by using the
path
   ' and name specified in the strBookName argument. You use the
intNumsheets
   ' argument to specify the number of worksheets in the workbook;
   ' the default is 3.
   Dim intOrigNumSheets      As Integer
   Dim wkbNew                As Excel.Workbook

   On Error GoTo CreateNew_Err

   intOrigNumSheets = Application.SheetsInNewWorkbook
   If intOrigNumSheets <> intNumSheets Then
      Application.SheetsInNewWorkbook = intNumSheets
   End If
   Set wkbNew = Workbooks.Add
   If Len(strBookName) = 0 Then strBookName =
Application.GetSaveAsFilename
   wkbNew.SaveAs strBookName
   Set CreateNewWorkbook = wkbNew
   Application.SheetsInNewWorkbook = intOrigNumSheets

CreateNew_End:
   Exit Function
CreateNew_Err:
   Set CreateNewWorkbook = Nothing
   wkbNew.Close False
   Set wkbNew = Nothing
   Resume CreateNew_End
End Function
```

Note A Workbook object's Saved property is a Boolean value indicating whether the workbook has been saved. The Saved property will be True for any new or opened workbook where no changes have been made and False for a workbook that has unsaved changes. You can set the Saved property to True. Doing this prevents the user from being prompted to save changes when the workbook closes but does not actually save any changes made since the last time the workbook was saved by using the Save method.

A Note About Working with Workbooks Through Automation

When you are using Automation to edit an Excel workbook, keep the following in mind.

Creating a new instance of Excel and opening a workbook results in an invisible instance of Excel and a hidden instance of the workbook. Therefore, if you edit the workbook and save it, the workbook is saved as hidden. The next time the user opens Excel manually, the workbook is invisible and the user has to click Unhide on the Window menu to view the workbook.

To avoid this behavior, your Automation code should unhide the workbook before editing it and saving it. Note that this does *not* mean Microsoft® Excel itself has to be visible.

Understanding the Worksheet Object

Most of the work you will do in Microsoft® Excel will be within the context of a worksheet. A worksheet contains a grid of cells you can use to work with data and hundreds of properties, methods, and events you can use to work with the data in a worksheet.

To work with the data contained in a worksheet, in a cell or within a range of cells, you use a Range object. The Worksheet and Range objects are the two most basic and most important components of any custom application you create within Excel.

The Workbook object's Worksheets property returns a collection of all the worksheets in the workbook. The Workbook object's Sheets property returns a collection of all the worksheets and chart sheets in the workbook.

Each Excel workbook contains one or more Worksheet objects and can contain one or more chart sheets as well. Charts in Excel are either embedded in a worksheet or contained on a chart sheet. You can have only one chart on a chart sheet, but you can have multiple charts on a worksheet. Each embedded chart on a worksheet is a member of the Worksheet object's ChartObjects collection. Worksheet objects are contained in the Worksheets collection, which you can access by using the Workbook object's Worksheets property. When you use Microsoft® Visual Basic® for Applications (VBA) to create a new workbook, you can specify how many worksheets it will contain by using the Application object's SheetsInNewWorkbook property.

Referring to a Worksheet Object

Because a Worksheet object exists as a member of a Worksheets collection, you refer to a worksheet by its name or its index value. In the following example, both object variables refer to the first worksheet in a workbook:

```
Sub ReferToWorksheetExample()
    ' This procedure illustrates how to programmatically refer to
    ' a worksheet.
    Dim wksSheetByIndex     As Excel.Worksheet
    Dim wksSheetByName      As Excel.Worksheet
    With ActiveWorkbook
        Set wksSheetByIndex = Worksheets(1)
        Set wksSheetByName = Worksheets("Main")
        If wksSheetByIndex.Index = wksSheetByName.Index Then
            MsgBox "The worksheet indexed as #" _
                & wksSheetByIndex.Index & vbCrLf _
                & "is the same as the worksheet named '" _
                & wksSheetByName.Name & "'", vbOKOnly, "Worksheets Match!"
        End If
    End With
End Sub
```

Note You can also use the Application object's ActiveSheet property to return a reference to the currently active worksheet in the currently active workbook.

You can use the Microsoft® Visual Basic® for Applications (VBA) Array function to work with multiple worksheets at the same time, as shown in the following example:

```
Sub ReferToMultipleSheetsExample()
    ' This procedure shows how to programmatically refer to
    ' multiple worksheets.
    Dim wksCurrent As Excel.Worksheet

    With ActiveWorkbook.Worksheets(Array("Employees", "Sheet2", "Sheet3"))
        .FillAcrossSheets (Worksheets("Employees").UsedRange)
    End With
    Stop
    ' The worksheets named "Sheet2" and "Sheet3" should now
    ' contain the same table that is found on the "Employees"
    ' sheet. Press F5 to clear the contents from these worksheets.
    For Each wksCurrent In ActiveWorkbook _
        .Worksheets(Array("Sheet2", "Sheet3"))
        wksCurrent.UsedRange.Clear
    Next wksCurrent
End Sub
```

You can specify or determine the name of a worksheet by using its Name property. To change the name of a new worksheet, you first add it to the Worksheets collection and then set the Name property to the name you want to use.

Adding, Deleting, Copying, and Moving a Worksheet Object

You can add one or more worksheets to the Worksheets collection by using the collection's Add method. The Add method returns the new Worksheet object. If you add multiple worksheets, the Add method returns the last worksheet added to the Worksheets collection. If the Before or After arguments of the Add method are omitted, the new worksheet is added before the currently active worksheet. The following example adds a new worksheet before the active worksheet in the current collection of worksheets:

```
Dim wksNewSheet As Excel.Worksheet


Set wksNewSheet = Worksheets.Add
With wksNewSheet
    ' Work with properties and methods of the
    ' new worksheet here.
End With
```

You use the Worksheet object's Delete method to delete a worksheet from the Worksheets collection. When you try to programmatically delete a worksheet, Microsoft® Excel will display a message (alert); to suppress the message, you must set the Application object's DisplayAlerts property to False, as illustrated in the following example:

```
Function DeleteWorksheet(strSheetName As String) As Boolean
    On Error Resume Next


    Application.DisplayAlerts = False
    ActiveWorkbook.Worksheets(strSheetName).Delete
    Application.DisplayAlerts = True
    ' Return True if no error occurred;
    ' otherwise return False.
    DeleteWorksheet = Not CBool(Err.Number)
End Function
```

Note   When you set the DisplayAlerts property to False, always set it back to True before your procedure has finished executing, as shown in the preceding example.

You can copy a worksheet by using the Worksheet object's Copy method. To copy a worksheet to the same workbook as the source worksheet, you must specify either the Before or After argument of the Copy method. You move a worksheet by using the Worksheet object's Move method. For example:

```
Worksheets("Sheet1").Copy After:=Worksheets("Sheet3")
Worksheets("Sheet1").Move After:=Worksheets("Sheet3")
```

The next example illustrates how to move a worksheet so that it is the last worksheet in a workbook:

```
Worksheets("Sheet1").Move After:=Worksheets(Worksheets.Count)
```

> **Note** When you use either the Copy or the Move method, if you do not specify the Before or After argument, Excel creates a new workbook and copies the specified worksheet to it.

Understanding the Range Object

In Microsoft® Excel, the Range object is the most powerful, dynamic, and often-used object. When you develop a full understanding of the Range object and how to use it effectively in Microsoft® Visual Basic® for Applications (VBA) procedures, you will be well on your way to harnessing the power of Excel.

The Excel Range object is somewhat unique in terms of objects. In most cases, an "object" is a thing with some clearly identifiable corollary in the Excel user interface. For example, a Workbook object is recognizable as an .xls file. In a workbook, the collection of Worksheet objects is represented in the user interface by separate tabbed sheets. But the Range object is different. A range can be a different thing in different circumstances. A Range object can be a single cell or a collection of cells. It can be a single object or a collection of objects. It can be a row or column, and it can represent a three-dimensional collection of cells that span multiple worksheets. In addition, unlike other objects that exist as objects and as members of a collection of objects, there is no Ranges collection containing all Range objects in a workbook or worksheet. It is probably easiest to think of the Range object as your handle to the thing you want to work with.

In This Section

The Range Property
> Use the Range property to return a Range object in many different circumstances.

The ActiveCell and Selection Properties
> Learn how the ActiveCell property returns a Range object representing the currently active cell and the Selection property returns a Range object representing all the cells within the current selection when a cell or group of cells is selected.

Using the CurrentRegion and UsedRange Properties
> Use the CurrentRegion and UsedRange properties to work with a range of cells whose size you have no control over.

Using the Cells Property
> Understand how the Cells property loops through a range of cells on a worksheet or refers to a range by using numeric row and column values.

Using the Offset Property

Use the Offset property to return a Range object with the same dimensions as a specified Range object but offset from the specified range.

Related Sections

Working with Microsoft Excel Objects

Use Microsoft® Visual Basic® for Applications (VBA) to work with Microsoft® Excel objects, from within either Excel itself or another Microsoft® Office XP application to gain access to every part of Excel.

Understanding the Excel Application Object

Use the Microsoft® Excel Application object to determine or specify application-level properties or execute application-level methods.

Understanding the Workbook Object

Work with the Workbook object to use with a single Microsoft® Excel workbook, and use the Workbooks collection to work with all currently open Workbook objects.

Understanding the Worksheet Object

Use a worksheet, containing a grid of cells, to work with data and hundreds of properties, methods, and events.

The Range Property

You will use the Range property to return a Range object in many different circumstances. The Application object, the Worksheet object, and the Range object all have a Range property. The Application object's Range property returns the same Range object as that returned by the Worksheet object. In other words, the Application object's Range property returns a reference to the specified cell or cells on the active worksheet. The Range property of the Range object has a subtle difference that is important to understand. Consider the following example:

```
Dim rng1 As Range
Dim rng2 As Range
Dim rng3 As Range


Set rng1 = Application.Range("B5")
Set rng2 = Worksheets("Sheet1").Range("B5")
Set rng3 = rng2.Range("B5")
```

The three Range objects do not all return a reference to the same cell. In this example, rng1 and rng2 both return a reference to cell B5. But rng3 returns a reference to cell C9. This difference occurs because the Range object's Range property returns a reference *relative* to the specified cell. In this case, the specified cell is B5. Therefore, the "B" means that the reference will be one column to the right of B5, and the "5" means the reference will be the fifth row below the row specified by B5. In other words, the Range object's Range property returns a reference to a cell that is n columns to the right and y rows down from the specified cell.

Typically, you will use the Range property to return a Range object, and then use the properties and methods of that Range object to work with the data in a cell or group of cells. The following table contains several examples illustrating usage of the Range property.

To	Use this code
Set the value of cell A1 on Sheet1 to 100	`Worksheets("Sheet1").Range("A1").Value = 100`
Set the value for a group of cells on the active worksheet	`Range("B2:B14").Value = 10000`
Set the formula for cell B15 on the active worksheet	`Range("B15").Formula = "=Sum(B2:B14)"`
Set the font to bold	`Range("B15").Font.Bold = True`
Set the font color to green	`Range("B15").Font.Color = RGB(0, 255, 0)`
Set an object variable to refer to a single cell	`Set rngCurrent = Range("A1")`
Set an object variable to refer to a group of cells	`Set rngCurrent = Range("A1:L1")`
Format all the cells in a named range	`Range("YTDSalesTotals").Font.Bold = True`
Set an object variable to a named range	`Set rngCurrent = Range("NovemberReturns")`
Set an object variable representing all the used cells on the Employees worksheet	`Set rngCurrent = Worksheets("Employees").UsedRange`
Set an object variable representing the group of related cells that surround the active cell	`Set rngCurrent = ActiveCell.CurrentRegion`
Set an object variable representing the first three columns in the active worksheet	`Set rngCurrent = Range("A:C")`
Set an object variable representing rows 3, 5, 7, and 9 of the active worksheet	`Set rngCurrent = Range("3:3, 5:5, 7:7, 9:9")`
Set an object variable representing multiple noncontiguous groups of cells on the active sheet	`Set rngCurrent = Range("A1:C4, D6:G12, I2:L7")`

To	Use this code
Remove the contents for all cells within a specified group of cells (B5:B10) while leaving the formatting intact	`Range("B5", "B10").ClearContents`

As you can see from the examples in the preceding table, the Cell argument of the Range property is either an A1-style string reference or a string representing a named range within the current workbook.

You will also use the Range property to return Range objects as arguments to other methods in the Microsoft® Excel object model. When you use the Range property in this way, make sure you fully qualify the Worksheet object to which the Range property applies. Failing to use fully qualified references to the Range property in arguments for Excel methods is one of the most common sources of error in range-related code.

The ActiveCell and Selection Properties

The ActiveCell property returns a Range object representing the currently active cell. When a single cell is selected, the ActiveCell property returns a Range object representing that single cell. When multiple cells are selected, the ActiveCell property represents the single active cell within the current selection. When a cell or group of cells is selected, the Selection property returns a Range object representing all the cells within the current selection.

To understand how the ActiveCell and Selection properties relate to one another, consider the case where a user selects cells A1 through F1 by clicking cell A1 and dragging until the selection extends over cell F1. In this case, the ActiveCell property returns a Range object that represents cell A1. The Selection property returns a Range object representing cells A1 through F1.

When you work with the Microsoft® Excel user interface, you typically select a cell or group of cells and then perform some action on the selected cell or cells, such as entering a value for a single cell or formatting a group of cells. When you use Microsoft® Visual Basic® for Applications (VBA) to work with cells, you are not required to make a selection before performing some action on a cell or group of cells. Instead, you only must return a Range object representing the cell or cells you want to work with. For example, to enter "January" as the value for cell A1 by using the user interface, you would select cell A1 and type January. The following sample performs the same action in VBA:

```
ActiveSheet.Range("A1").Value = "January"
```

Using VBA to work with a Range object in this manner does not change the selected cells on the current worksheet. However, you can make your VBA code act upon cells in the same way as a user working through the user interface by using the Range object's Select method to select a cell or range of cells and then using the Range object's Activate method to activate a cell within the current selection. For example, the following code selects cells A1 through A6 and then makes cell A3 the active cell:

```
With ActiveSheet
    .Range("A1:A6").Select
    .Range("A3").Activate
End With
```

When you use the Select method to select multiple cells, the first cell referenced will be the active cell. For example, in the preceding sample, after the Select method is executed, the ActiveCell property returns a reference to cell A1, even though cells A1 through A6 are selected. After the Activate method is executed in the next line of code, the ActiveCell property returns a reference to cell A3 while cells A1 through A6 remain selected. The next example illustrates how to return a Range object by using the ActiveCell property or the Selection property:

```
Dim rngActiveRange As Excel.Range


' Range object returned from the Selection property.
Set rngActiveRange = Selection
Call PrintRangeInfo(rngActiveRange)
' Range object returned from the ActiveCell property.
Set rngActiveRange = ActiveCell
Call PrintRangeInfo(rngActiveRange)
```

> **Note**   The PrintRangeInfo custom procedure called in the preceding example prints information about the cell or cells contained in the Range object passed in the argument to the procedure.

The Macro Recorder and the Selection Object

When you are learning to work with the Excel object model, it is often helpful to turn on the macro recorder and carry out the steps you want to accomplish and then examine the VBA code that results to see which objects, properties, and methods are used. You should be aware, however, that in many cases the macro recorder records your actions from the perspective of a user interacting with the user interface. This means that the Selection object, the Select method, and the Activate method are used over and over.

When you get a solid grasp on the most efficient way to work with Excel objects, you will find yourself rewriting or restructuring the VBA code written by the macro recorder to use the Range object instead.

Using the CurrentRegion and UsedRange Properties

There are many circumstances where you will write code to work against a range of cells, but at the time you write the code, you will not have information about the range. For example, you might not know the size or location of a range or the location of a cell in relation to another cell. You can use the CurrentRegion and UsedRange properties to work with a range of cells whose size you have no control over. You can use the Offset property to work with cells in relation to other cells where the cell location is unknown.

As shown in the following figure, the Range object's CurrentRegion property returns a Range object representing a range bounded by (but not including) any combination of blank rows and blank columns or the edges of the worksheet.

The Ranges Returned by the ActiveCell and CurrentRegion Properties

The CurrentRegion property can return many different ranges on a single worksheet. This property is useful for operations where you must know the dimensions of a group of related cells, but all you know for sure is the location of a cell or cells within the group. For example, when the active cell is inside a table of cells, you could use the following line of code to apply formatting to the entire table:

```
ActiveCell.CurrentRegion.AutoFormat xlRangeAutoFormatAccounting4
```

You could also use the CurrentRegion property to return a collection of cells. For example:

```
Dim rngCurrentCell As Excel.Range


For Each rngCurrentCell In ActiveCell.CurrentRegion.Cells
    ' Work with individual cells here.
Next rngCurrentCell
```

Every Worksheet object has a UsedRange property that returns a Range object representing the area of a worksheet that is being used. The UsedRange property represents the area described by the farthest upper-left and farthest lower-right nonempty cells in a worksheet and includes all cells in between. For example, imagine a worksheet with entries in only two cells: A1 and G55. The worksheet's UsedRange property would return a Range object containing 385 cells between and including A1 and G55.

You might use the UsedRange property together with the SpecialCells method to return a Range object representing all cells in a worksheet of a specified type. For example, the following code returns a Range object that includes all the cells in the active worksheet that contain a formula:

```
Dim rngFormulas As Excel.Range

Set rngFormulas = ActiveSheet.UsedRange.SpecialCells(xlCellTypeFormulas)
```

Using the Cells Property

You use the Cells property to loop through a range of cells in a worksheet or to refer to a range by using numeric row and column values. The Cells property returns a Range object representing all the cells, or a specified cell, in a worksheet. To work with a single cell, you use the Item property of the Range object returned by the Cells property to specify the index of a specific cell. The Item property accepts arguments specifying the row or the row and column index for a cell.

Because the Item property is the default property of the Range object, it is not necessary to explicitly reference it. For example, the following Set statements both return a reference to cell B5 on Sheet1:

```
Dim rng1 As Excel.Range
Dim rng2 As Excel.Range


Set rng1 = Worksheet("Sheet1").Cells.Item(5, 2)
Set rng2 = Worksheet("Sheet1").Cells(5, 2)
```

The row and column index arguments of the Item property return references to individual cells beginning with the first cell in the specified range. For example, the following message box displays "G11" because that is the first cell in the specified Range object:

```
MsgBox Range("G11:M30").Cells(1,1).Address
```

The following procedure illustrates how you would use the Cells property to loop through all the cells in a specified range. The OutOfBounds procedure looks for values that are greater than or less than a specified range of values and changes the font color for each cell with such a value:

```
Function OutOfBounds(rngToCheck As Excel.Range, _
                lngLowValue As Long, _
                lngHighValue As Long, _
                Optional lngHighlightColor As Long = 255) As Boolean
' This procedure illustrates how to use the Cells property
' to iterate through a collection of cells in a range.
' For each cell in the rngTocheck range, if the value of the
' cell is numeric and it falls outside the range of values
' specified by lngLowValue to lngHighValue, the cell font
' is changed to the value of lngHighlightColor (default is red).
```

```
    Dim rngTemp              As Excel.Range
    Dim lngRowCounter        As Long
    Dim lngColCounter        As Long


    ' Validate bounds parameters.
    If lngLowValue > lngHighValue Then
        Err.Raise vbObjectError + 512 + 1, _
            "OutOfBounds Procedure", _
            "Invalid bounds parameters submitted: " _
                & "Low value must be lower than high value."
        Exit Function
    End If


    ' Iterate through cells and determine if values
    ' are outside bounds parameters. If so, highlight value.
    For lngRowCounter = 1 To rngToCheck.Rows.Count
        For lngColCounter = 1 To rngToCheck.Columns.Count
            Set rngTemp = rngToCheck.Cells(lngRowCounter, lngColCounter)
            If IsNumeric(rngTemp.Value) Then
                If rngTemp.Value < lngLowValue Or rngTemp.Value >
lngHighValue Then
                    rngTemp.Font.Color = lngHighlightColor
                    OutOfBounds = True
                End If
            End If
        Next lngColCounter
    Next lngRowCounter
End Function
```

In addition, you can use a For Each…Next statement to loop through the range returned by the Cells property. The following code could be used in the OutOfBounds procedure to loop through cells in a range:

```
' Iterate through cells and determine if values
' are outside bounds parameters. If so, highlight value.
```

```
For Each rngTemp in rngToCheck.Cells
    If IsNumeric(rngTemp.Value) Then
        If rngTemp.Value < lngLowValue Or rngTemp.Value > lngHighValue Then
            rngTemp.Font.Color = lngHighlightColor
            OutOfBounds = True
        End If
    End If
Next rngTemp
```

Using the Offset Property

You can use the Offset property to return a Range object with the same dimensions as a specified Range object but offset from the specified range. For example, you could use the Offset property to create a new Range object adjacent to the active cell to contain calculated values based on the active cell.

The Offset property is useful in circumstances where you do not know the specific address of the cells you must work with, but you do know where the cell is located in relation to other cells you must work with. For example, you might have a command bar button in your custom application that fills the active cell with the average of the values in the two cells immediately to the left of the active cell:

```
ActiveCell.Value = (ActiveCell.Offset(0, -2) + ActiveCell.Offset(0, -
1)/2)
```

Working with Microsoft FrontPage Objects

Microsoft® FrontPage® is a powerful and popular application used to create, deploy, and manage Web sites. You also can use FrontPage to create individual Web pages or modify existing Web pages.

FrontPage supports the Microsoft® Visual Basic® Editor and Microsoft® Visual Basic® for Applications (VBA). In addition, to make it possible for you to work with the various parts of a FrontPage-based web or a Web page, FrontPage now exposes a complete object model that you can use either from within a FrontPage VBA project or from another application through Automation. The new VBA language elements replace the FrontPage 98 language elements. To ensure backward compatibility, the FrontPage 98 language elements are included as hidden elements in the latest version of FrontPage object model, but these language elements are not recommended for use in FrontPage.

> **Note** You can use the Object Browser and Microsoft FrontPage Visual Basic Reference Help to learn more about individual objects, properties, methods, and events.

Although all Office applications support VBA, it is used a bit differently in FrontPage and Microsoft® Outlook® than it is in the other Office applications. FrontPage and Outlook support a single VBA project that is associated with a running instance of the application. The other Office applications make it possible for you to associate a VBA project with each Office document. For example, you can have several workbooks open in Excel at one time, and each workbook can have its own VBA project that contains modules, class modules, and UserForms. In FrontPage, you can have several webs or Web pages open at one time, but there is only one VBA project. The FrontPage VBA project is stored in a file named Microsoft FrontPage.fpm.

In This Section

Understanding the FrontPage Object Model
  Learn how to use Microsoft® FrontPage® to work with Web sites.

Understanding the Page Object Model
  Write script to work with the HTML elements in a Web page through the DHTML document object model.

Understanding the FrontPage Object Model

Microsoft® FrontPage® is designed to work with Web sites. A Web site can exist on a local intranet or on a server on the World Wide Web. There are several different metaphors you can use when envisioning a Web site. For example, you can think of a Web site as a collection of windows showing different parts of the Web site in an open instance of FrontPage. Or, you might think of a Web site as a collection of files on disk, organized in folders, all of which are organized under one main folder that contains the entire web. Finally, you could think of a Web site as the relationship between pages that exists as a result of the navigation structure between the pages.

When you have one or more Web sites open in FrontPage, the Webs collection contains a Web object representing each open Web site. Each Web object has a WebWindow object that represents the main application window containing the web. The WebWindow object looks like a separate instance of FrontPage, for example, each WebWindow object has its own FrontPage icon on the Windows taskbar. Each WebWindow object has a PageWindows collection that contains a PageWindow object for each open Web page. In addition, each PageWindow object has a Document property that returns the DHTML document object for a Web page in the FrontPage web.

When you first open FrontPage, you see a blank Web page open in Page view. You can use the Normal, HTML, and Preview tabs along the bottom of the page to edit the page in different ways or to preview it in your Web browser. The FrontPage menu bar and toolbars appear above the page, and the FrontPage Views bar appears along the left side of the page. At this point, FrontPage contains a single blank document only. There is no open Web site, and as a result, the Webs collection object's Count property returns zero. In addition, the WebWindows collection contains a single WebWindow object, and the PageWindows collection contains one PageWindow object that contains the blank page.

Each of these objects and collections has methods and properties you can use to work with the object. For example, the PageWindow object has a Document property you can use to work with the HTML elements contained in the Web page and an IsDirty property you can use to determine if the page has been changed. In addition, the PageWindow object has an ApplyTheme method you can use to apply a FrontPage theme to the page, as well as Save and SaveAs methods you can use to save the page.

Webs based on FrontPage exist on disk as a collection of files organized in folders. The base for the web is the root folder in the directory structure. For example, if you created a web called MyPersonalWeb on your hard disk, the root folder for the web could be C:\MyWebs\MyPersonalWeb. All the directories that make up your Web site would be under the MyPersonalWeb folder. For example, when you use FrontPage to create a Web site based on the Personal Web template, FrontPage creates nine subfolders for the web that contain supporting files, such as images and style sheets.

The file structure of a web as it exists on disk also is available through the object model. Each folder in the web is represented by a WebFolder object. The RootFolder property returns the root WebFolder object in the web. The WebFolders collection contains a WebFolder object for each folder in the web. Each WebFolder object has, among others, a Folders property and a Files property. The Folders property returns a WebFolders collection for all the subfolders under a folder. The Files property returns a WebFiles collection that contains a WebFile object for each file in a folder.

The navigation structure of a Web site starts with a home page that can branch off to other pages in the Web site. In FrontPage, you can move programmatically through the navigation structure of a Web site by using NavigationNode objects. A NavigationNode object represents a node in the navigation structure of a Web site. The NavigationNodes collection contains all the NavigationNode objects in a Web site. You start navigation at the home page by using the HomeNavigationNode property, which returns the NavigationNode object for the Web site's home page. Each NavigationNode object has a Children property that returns the NavigationNodes collection representing all of the pages you can navigate to from a NavigationNode object. You use the Move method to move among NavigationNode objects in the NavigationNodes collection returned by the Children property. You use the Next and Prev properties to return the next or previous NavigationNode object.

Whether you use windows, files, or navigation nodes to move among objects in FrontPage will depend on what you are trying to accomplish.

> **Note**   You can get more information about the objects, methods, and properties in the FrontPage object model by using Microsoft FrontPage Visual Basic Reference Help.

Understanding the Application Object

The Application object is the top-level object in the Microsoft® FrontPage® object model. It represents FrontPage itself and provides access to all of the objects in the FrontPage object model. If you are automating FrontPage from another Microsoft® Office application, you should set a reference to the Microsoft FrontPage Page Object Reference library by clicking References on the Tools menu in the Microsoft® Visual Basic® Editor in the application from which you are working. Then, you can write code to create an instance of an Application object variable, as shown in the following example:

```
Dim fpApp As FrontPage.Application
Set fpApp = New FrontPage.Application
```

To create a FrontPage Application object without setting a reference to the FrontPage 4.0 Object Reference library, you can use the CreateObject function.

If you are writing Microsoft® Visual Basic® for Applications (VBA) code from within the FrontPage VBA project, you can refer to the Application object directly without creating an object variable.

From the Application object, you can reach any other object in the FrontPage object model. In addition, the properties, methods, and events of the Application object are also global properties that you can use to return currently active objects. A global property is a property that you can use to return an object without having to refer to the Application object or any top-level objects. The global properties that represent active objects in FrontPage are ActiveDocument, ActivePageWindow, ActiveWeb, and ActiveWebWindow. The following examples illustrate how you can work with these properties and the objects they represent:

```
' Apply the classic theme to the active document and specify
' vivid colors and active graphics.
ActiveDocument.ApplyTheme "classic", fpThemeVividColors +
fpThemeActiveGraphics


' Locate the HelpInformation.htm file in the currently active web.
Dim wflCurrentFile As WebFile

Set wflCurrentFile = ActiveWeb.LocateFile("HelpInformation.htm")
If Not wflCurrentFile Is Nothing Then
    With wflCurrentFile
        ' Code to work with found file here.
    End With
End If


' Check to see if the page in the active page window has changed and,
' if so, save it to disk.
With ActivePageWindow
    If .IsDirty Then
        .Refresh SaveChanges:=True
    End If
End With
```

```
' Display a message showing the window captions for all open
' documents in the active web window.
Dim pgeCurr          As PageWindow
Dim strCaptions      As String


If ActiveWebWindow.PageWindows.Count > 0 Then
    For Each pgeCurr In ActiveWebWindow.PageWindows
        strCaptions = strCaptions & pgeCurr.Caption & vbCrLf
    Next pgeCurr
    If Len(strCaptions) > 0 Then
        MsgBox "The following pages are currently open:" & vbCrLf &
strCaptions
    End If
End If
```

The Application object also exposes properties you can use to get information about the current machine, such as the user's name, the version of FrontPage, the language settings, the registry values, and so on. You can use the System property to return the System object, which provides information about the operating system and screen resolution. You also can use the ProfileString property of the System object to read and write FrontPage registry values.

In addition to getting information about the current machine, the Application object provides 10 application-level events you can use to run VBA code when the events occur.

Understanding the Page Object Model

When you write script to work with the HTML elements in a Web page, you are working with the page through the DHTML document object model. FrontPage exposes nearly all of the methods and properties of this object model through the FrontPage Page object model. To see the restrictions of the Page object model, search the Microsoft FrontPage Visual Basic Reference Help index for "object model," and then open the "Exploring the FrontPage Object Model" topic.

In FrontPage, you can use Microsoft® Visual Basic® for Applications (VBA) code to work with the HTML elements in a Web page. You use the Document property or the ActiveDocument property to return a DHTML document object. When you have the document object, you have access to all HTML elements contained in a Web page.

Working with Microsoft Outlook Objects

You can create custom Microsoft® Outlook® objects and manipulate those objects from within Outlook or from another application. You can manipulate Outlook objects by using Microsoft® Visual Basic® for Applications (VBA) code from within Outlook or another Microsoft® Office XP application by using Automation. The Outlook object model exposes Outlook objects, which you can use to gain programmatic access to Outlook functionality. Before you use VBA to access Outlook objects, methods, or properties from another application, you must first set a reference to the Microsoft Outlook object library by clicking References on the Tools menu in the Visual Basic Editor.

In This Section

Understanding the Application and NameSpace Objects
> Learn how to use the Application object's CreateItem method to create a new Microsoft® Outlook® item and access existing Outlook items by using the NameSpace object.

Working with Outlook Folders and Items
> Access folders for any built-in Microsoft® Outlook® item.

Understanding the Explorer and Inspector Objects
> Open the Explorer and Inspector objects programmatically, and display items for the user.

Understanding VBA in Outlook
> Associate a Microsoft® Visual Basic® for Applications (VBA) project as code behind an individual Microsoft® Office XP document.

Understanding Events in Outlook
> Work with application-level events associated with the application itself or top-level objects within the application or item-level events associated with a particular Microsoft® Outlook® item.

Understanding the Application and NameSpace Objects

When you manipulate Microsoft® Outlook® objects, you always start with the Application object. If you are using Microsoft® Visual Basic® for Applications (VBA) in Outlook, there is a reference to the Outlook object library set by default. If you are using Automation to work with Outlook objects from another application, you must first set a reference to the Outlook object library by using the References dialog box in the application you are working from. If you have set a reference to the Outlook object library, you create a new instance of an Outlook Application object by using the New keyword as follows:

```
Dim olApp As Outlook.Application

Set olApp = New Outlook.Application
```

If you have not set a reference to the Outlook object library, you must use the CreateObject function. There can only be one instance of Outlook available at one time. Therefore, when Outlook is not running, the New keyword (or the CreateObject function) creates a new, hidden, instance of Outlook. If an instance of Outlook is already running, then using the New keyword (or the CreateObject function) returns a reference to the running instance.

You use the Application object's CreateItem method to create a new Outlook item. You access existing Outlook items by using the NameSpace object.

All the sample procedures discussed in this section use global object variables to represent the Application object and the NameSpace object. Each procedure first checks to see if the Application object variable has been created and, if not, calls the InitializeOutlook procedure to create an instance of the global Application and NameSpace object variables. For example:

```
' Declare global Outlook Application and NameSpace variables.
' These are declared as global variables so that they need not
' be re-created for each procedure that uses them.
Public golApp          As Outlook.Application
Public gnspNameSpace   As Outlook.NameSpace


Function InitializeOutlook() As Boolean
    ' This function is used to initialize the global Application and
    ' NameSpace variables.

    On Error GoTo Init_Err

    Set golApp = New Outlook.Application      ' Application object.
    Set gnspNameSpace = golApp.GetNamespace("MAPI") ' Namespace object.

    InitializeOutlook = True


Init_End:
    Exit Function
Init_Err:
    InitializeOutlook = False
    Resume Init_End
End Function
```

You use an olItemType constant as the CreateItem method's single argument to specify whether you want to create a new appointment, contact, distribution list, journal entry, mail message, note, posting to a public folder, or task. The CreateItem method returns an object of the type specified in the olItemType constant; you can then use this object to set additional properties of the item. For example, the following procedure creates a new mail message and sets the recipients, attachments, subject, and message text by using the information passed to the procedure as arguments:

```
Function CreateMail(astrRecip As Variant, _
                    strSubject As String, _
                    strMessage As String, _
```

```
                     Optional astrAttachments As Variant) As Boolean
' This procedure illustrates how to create a new mail message
' and use the information passed as arguments to set message
' properties for the subject, text (Body property), attachments,
' and recipients.

Dim objNewMail          As Outlook.MailItem
Dim varRecip            As Variant
Dim varAttach           As Variant
Dim blnResolveSuccess   As Boolean


On Error GoTo CreateMail_Err


' Use the InitializeOutlook procedure to initialize global
' Application and NameSpace object variables, if necessary.
If golApp Is Nothing Then
    If InitializeOutlook = False Then
        MsgBox "Unable to initialize Outlook Application " _
            & "or NameSpace object variables!"
        Exit Function
    End If
End If


Set golApp = New Outlook.Application
Set objNewMail = golApp.CreateItem(olMailItem)
With objNewMail
    For Each varRecip In astrRecip
        .Recipients.Add varRecip
    Next varRecip
    blnResolveSuccess = .Recipients.ResolveAll
    For Each varAttach In astrAttachments
        .Attachments.Add varAttach
    Next varAttach
    .Subject = strSubject
    .Body = strMessage
    If blnResolveSuccess Then
        .Send
```

```
    Else
        MsgBox "Unable to resolve all recipients. Please check " _
            & "the names."
        .Display
    End If
End With


CreateMail = True


CreateMail_End:
    Exit Function
CreateMail_Err:
    CreateMail = False
    Resume CreateMail_End
End Function
```

The preceding procedure also illustrates how to use a MailItem object's Recipients and Attachments properties to return the respective collection objects and then add one or more recipients or attachments to a mail message.

You use the Application object's GetNameSpace method to instantiate an object variable representing a recognized data source. Currently, Outlook supports the "MAPI" message store as the only valid NameSpace object. To see an example of how to use the GetNameSpace method to create a NameSpace object variable, see the InitializeOutlook procedure earlier in this section.

If Outlook is not running when you create a NameSpace object variable, the user will be prompted for a profile if the user's mail services startup setting is set to Prompt for a profile to be used. Startup settings are on the Mail Services tab of the Options dialog box (Tools menu). You can use the NameSpace object's Logon method to specify a profile programmatically. Profiles are stored in the Windows registry under the \HKEY_CURRENT_USER\Software\Microsoft\Windows Messaging Subsystem\Profiles subkey.

Working with Outlook Folders and Items

You can think of the NameSpace object as the gateway to all existing Microsoft® Outlook® folders. By default, Outlook creates two top-level folders representing all public folders and all mailbox folders. Mailbox folders contain all Outlook built-in and custom folders. Each folder is a MAPIFolder object. MAPIFolder objects can contain subfolders (which are also MAPIFolder objects), as well as individual Outlook item objects, such as MailItem objects, ContactItem objects, JournalItem objects, and so on.

> **Note** In Outlook, an item is the object that holds information (similar to files in other applications). Items include mail messages, appointments, contacts, tasks, journal entries, and notes.

When you have created a NameSpace object variable, you can access the top-level folder for any built-in Outlook item by using the NameSpace object's GetDefaultFolder method. For example, the following code sample returns a reference to the ContactItems folder:

```
Dim fldContacts As Outlook.MAPIFolder
Set fldContacts = gnspNameSpace.GetDefaultFolder(olFolderContacts)
```

You can also return a reference to any folder by using the name of the folder. For example, the following procedure returns a reference to the folder in the current user's mailbox whose name is specified in the strFolderName argument:

```
Function GetFolderByName(strFolderName As String) As Outlook.MAPIFolder
    ' This procedure illustrates how to return a MAPIFolder
    ' object representing any folder in the mailbox folders
    ' collection whose name is specified by the strFolderName
    ' argument.
    Dim fldMain As Outlook.MAPIFolder

    On Error Resume Next

    ' Use the InitializeOutlook procedure to initialize global
    ' Application and NameSpace object variables, if necessary.
    If golApp Is Nothing Then
        If InitializeOutlook = False Then
            MsgBox "Unable to initialize Outlook Application " _
                & "or NameSpace object variables!"
            Exit Function
        End If
    End If


    Set fldMain =
gnspNameSpace.Folders(GetMailboxName()).Folders(strFolderName)
    If Err = 0 Then
        Set GetFolderByName = fldMain
    Else
        ' Note: The most likely cause of an error here is that
        ' the folder specified in strFolderName could not be found.
        Set GetFolderByName = Nothing
    End If
End Function
```

The NameSpace object has at least two top-level folders representing all public folders and the user's mailbox. The preceding procedure uses the GetMailboxName procedure to return the name of the mailbox folder.

When you return a reference to a folder in the user's mailbox, that folder might contain additional folders, individual Outlook items, or both.

```vba
Sub GetFolderInfo(fldFolder As Outlook.MAPIFolder)
    ' This procedure prints to the Immediate window information
    ' about items contained in a folder.
    Dim objItem         As Object
    Dim dteCreateDate   As Date
    Dim strSubject      As String
    Dim strItemType     As String
    Dim intCounter      As Integer

    On Error Resume Next

    If fldFolder.Folders.Count > 0 Then
        For Each objItem In fldFolder.Folders
            Call GetFolderInfo(objItem)
        Next objItem
    End If
    Debug.Print "Folder '" & fldFolder.Name & "' (Contains " _
        & fldFolder.Items.Count & " items):"
    For Each objItem In fldFolder.Items
        intCounter = intCounter + 1
        With objItem
            dteCreateDate = .CreationTime
            strSubject = .Subject
            strItemType = TypeName(objItem)
        End With
        Debug.Print vbTab & "Item #" & intCounter & " - " _
            & strItemType & " - created on " _
            & Format(dteCreateDate, "mmmm dd, yyyy hh:mm am/pm") _
            & vbCrLf & vbTab & vbTab & "Subject: '" _
            & strSubject & "'" & vbCrLf
    Next objItem
End Sub
```

The GetFolderInfo procedure examines a folder for subfolders and calls itself recursively until there are no subfolders remaining. It then prints information about the items contained in the folder or subfolder to the Immediate window. Note that the `objItem` object variable is declared by using the Object data type so that the procedure can work with any Outlook item.

To work with a single item or subset of items in a folder, you use the Restrict method, which returns a collection of objects that match the criteria specified in the method's single argument. For example, the following procedure uses the Restrict method to create a collection of Outlook ContactItem objects that match the name supplied in the strLastName argument:

```
Function GetItemFromName(strLastName As String, _
                    Optional strFirstName As String = "", _
                    Optional strCompany As String = "") As Boolean
  ' This procedure returns an Outlook ContactItem that matches the
  ' criteria specified in the arguments passed to the procedure.
  Dim fldFolder          As Outlook.MAPIFolder
  Dim objItemsCollection As Object
  Dim objItem            As Object
  Dim strCriteria        As String
  Dim objMatchingItem    As Object


  On Error GoTo GetItem_Err


  ' Use the InitializeOutlook procedure to initialize global
  ' Application and NameSpace object variables, if necessary.
  If golApp Is Nothing Then
    If InitializeOutlook = False Then
      MsgBox "Unable to initialize Outlook Application " _
        & "or NameSpace object variables!"
      Exit Function
    End If
  End If


  Set fldFolder = gnspNameSpace.GetDefaultFolder(olFolderContacts)


  If Len(strLastName) = 0 And Len(strFirstName) = 0 Then
    If Len(strCompany) > 0 Then
      strCriteria = "[Company] = '" & strCompany & "'"
    End If
```

```vba
    Else
        strCriteria = IIf(Len(strFirstName) = 0, _
            "[LastName] = '" & strLastName & "'", _
            "[LastName] = '" & strLastName & _
            "' AND [FirstName] = '" & strFirstName & "'")
    End If
    Set objItemsCollection = fldFolder.Items.Restrict(strCriteria)
    If objItemsCollection.Count > 0 Then
        If objItemsCollection.Count = 1 Then
            For Each objItem In objItemsCollection
                Set objMatchingItem = _
                    gnspNameSpace.GetItemFromID(objItem.EntryId)
                objMatchingItem.Display
                GetItemFromName = True
                Exit Function
            Next objItem
        Else
            GetItemFromName = False
            Exit Function
        End If
    End If


    GetItemFromName = True


GetItem_End:
    Exit Function
GetItem_Err:
    GetItemFromName = False
    Resume GetItem_End
End Function
```

When you are using the Restrict method, you use Outlook field names within brackets to specify criteria for a search. You can join multiple criteria by using operators such as And, Or, and Not. For example, the following sample returns all the mail items sent in the last seven days that are unread and marked as highly important:

```vba
Dim fldMail       As Outlook.MAPIFolder
Dim itmItems      As Outlook.Items
```

```
strCriteria = "[SentOn] > '" & (Date - 7) _
   & "' And [UnRead] = True And [Importance] = High"
```

```
Set fldMail = gnspNameSpace.GetDefaultFolder(olFolderInbox)
Set itmItems = fldMail.Items.Restrict(strCriteria)
```

This line illustrates how to return all the Outlook ContactItem items that contain a value in the Business Address field:

```
Set objContacts = fldContacts.Items.Restrict("[BusinessAddress] <> '" &
strZLS & "'")
```

The NorthwindContacts.dot sample file is a Microsoft® Word template that retrieves contacts from the Outlook Contacts folder and then displays the contacts in a UserForm. When the user selects a contact from the form, the contact name and address information is inserted in an address block in a letter.

> **Note**   The NorthwindContacts.dot sample file also illustrates how to collect contact information from a database so that the user can insert name and address information into a letter.

Understanding the Explorer and Inspector Objects

The Explorer object represents what you would recognize as the Microsoft® Outlook® user interface. For example, when you open Outlook, you are working in the Outlook Explorer object. A window that contains a specific Outlook item, such as a mail message or a contact, is an Outlook Inspector object.

You can open these objects programmatically and display items for the user. You can also use the ActiveExplorer and ActiveInspector methods of the Application object to return a programmatic reference to the Explorer or Inspector object that the user is currently working with.

If you want to use Microsoft® Visual Basic® for Applications (VBA) to add, remove, or manipulate command bars in Outlook, you start with a reference to the Explorer or Inspector object that contains the command bar you want to use and then use the object's CommandBars property to return a reference to the object's CommandBars collection. For example, the following code illustrates how to get a reference to the CommandBars collection for the active Explorer object:

```
Dim cbrExplorerBars As CommandBars
```

```
Set cbrExplorerBars = ActiveExplorer.CommandBars
```

> **Note**   You can use the GetExplorerInfo and GetInspectorInfo procedures to see sample code that uses the Explorer and Inspector objects to get information about what is displayed in the active Outlook Explorer and Inspector objects, including information about built-in and custom command bars. The following figure illustrates the kind of information you can get from an Explorer object.

Information Returned by the GetExplorerInfo Procedure

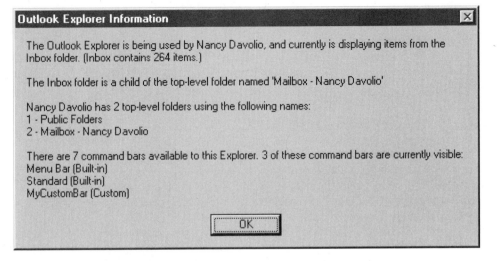

Understanding VBA in Outlook

Developers have wanted to use Microsoft® Visual Basic® for Applications (VBA) in Microsoft® Outlook® since Outlook was first released. Outlook supports both the VBA language and the Visual Basic Editor found in all other Office applications.

Outlook supports a single VBA project that is associated with a particular user and a running instance of the application. The other Microsoft® Office XP applications (except Microsoft® FrontPage®) let you associate a VBA project as code behind an individual Office document. Because Outlook has no document similar to the other Office applications, VBA code is associated only with the application.

> **Note** The closest thing to a "document" in Outlook is an Outlook item (for example, a mail message, an appointment item, or a task). As in previous versions of Outlook, you use Visual Basic Scripting Edition (VBScript) to write code behind an Outlook item.

The Outlook VBA project is stored in a file named VbaProject.OTM in the following locations:

- **Microsoft Windows.** If user profiles have been set up for multiple users, VbaProject.OTM is stored in the C:\Windows\Profiles*UserName*\Application Data\Microsoft\Outlook subfolder. If user profiles have not been set up, VbaProject.OTM is stored in the C:\Windows\Application Data\Microsoft\Outlook subfolder.

- **Microsoft Windows NT Workstation and Microsoft Windows NT Server.** The VbaProject.OTM file is stored in the C:\Winnt\Profiles*UserName*\Application Data\Microsoft\Outlook subfolder.

- **Microsoft Windows 2000.** The VbaProject.OTM file is stored in the C:\Documents and Settings*UserName*\Application Data\Microsoft\Outlook subfolder.

You use VBA in Outlook to customize the application by working with the objects, methods, properties, and events available through the Outlook object model. For example, you can add code to application-level events to process messages, add custom command bar controls to call custom VBA procedures, or create Component Object Model (COM) add-ins by using the Visual Basic Editor to debug the add-in as it is being developed and tested. You can access the Visual Basic Editor just as you do in any other Office application, by pointing to Macro on the Tools menu, and then clicking Visual Basic Editor.

Understanding Events in Outlook

There are two classes of events in Microsoft® Outlook®, and you work with each class differently. The first class of events supported in Outlook represents application-level events. Because these events are associated with the application itself, or with top-level objects within the application, such as folders or the Outlook Bar, you can use Microsoft® Visual Basic® for Applications (VBA) code to handle these events.

The second class represents item-level events that are associated with a particular Outlook item. For example, an Outlook MailItem object has events such as Open, Close, Forward, and Send. As in previous versions of Outlook, you use Visual Basic Scripting Edition (VBScript) code within the item itself to handle these item-level events.

Application-Level Events

When you create a new Microsoft® Visual Basic® for Applications (VBA) project in Microsoft® Word or Microsoft® Excel, the project contains, by default, a class module bound to the application's current document. For example, Word creates a module for the ThisDocument object and Excel creates a module for the ThisWorkbook object. In Microsoft® Outlook®, because you use VBA to work with the application, the VBA project contains a class module called ThisOutlookSession, which is pre-bound to the Outlook Application object. As a result, all application-level events are available to you in the Visual Basic Editor Procedures drop-down list when you click the Application object in the Object drop-down list.

There are six events associated with the Application object that you can use to run custom VBA procedures. For example, you could use the Startup event to call custom procedures to customize the Outlook workspace or to create or display custom command bars or command bar controls. You could use the NewMail event procedure to call custom procedures that implement your own rules for handling incoming mail. These events are somewhat self-explanatory, and you can get complete documentation for each event by searching the Microsoft Outlook Visual Basic Reference Help index for the name of the event.

Item-Level Events

Working with the event procedures exposed by Microsoft® Outlook® objects (other than the Application object) is identical to creating event procedures in the other Office applications. First, you must declare an object variable by using the WithEvents keyword in the ThisOutlookSession module (or in another class module) for each object you want to work with. Second, you must add the Microsoft® Visual Basic® for Applications (VBA) code to the event procedure that you want to run when the event occurs. Finally, you must initialize the object variables that you have created.

For example, the following VBA code illustrates how to create an object variable that represents the Outlook Bar in the ThisOutlookSession module:

```
Dim WithEvents obpOutlookBar As Outlook.OutlookBarPane
```

When you declare an object variable as shown in the previous example, the variable name appears in the Object drop-down list in the class module's Code window. When you select this variable from the Object list, you can select the object's available event procedures by using the Procedure drop-down list. For example, the OutlookBarPane object shown earlier exposes the BeforeGroupSwitch and BeforeNavigate events.

```
Private Sub opbOutlookBar_BeforeNavigate(ByVal Shortcut As
OutlookBarShortcut, _
    Cancel As Boolean)
  If Shortcut.Name <> "Inbox" Then
    Msgbox "Sorry, you only have permission to access the Inbox."
    Cancel = True
  End If
End Sub
```

Now you need to initialize the object variable. You can do this in two places: in the Application object's Startup event procedure, so that the variable is always available, or in a custom procedure you create for the purpose of initializing object variables. The following code shows how to initialize the object variable by using the Startup event procedure:

```
Private Sub Application_Startup()
    Set opbOutlookBar = Application.ActiveExplorer.Panes("OutlookBar")
End Sub
```

To determine how to instantiate an object variable, search the Microsoft Outlook Visual Basic Reference Help index for the name of the object you want to work with. For example, the Help topic for the OutlookBarPane object shows that the object is a member of the Panes collection and also that you use the string "OutlookBar" to identify the object within the collection.

Note You can get more information about the objects, methods, and properties in the Outlook object model by using Microsoft Outlook Visual Basic Reference Help.

Working with Microsoft PowerPoint Objects

As with other Microsoft® Office applications, you begin automating Microsoft® PowerPoint® by using the Application object. From the Application object, you can open an existing Presentation object or create a new presentation. Each Presentation object contains one or more Slide objects and each Slide object can contain Shape objects that represent text, graphics, tables, and other items found on a slide.

In This Section

Understanding the PowerPoint Application Object
> Use the Application object to get started writing Microsoft® Visual Basic® for Applications (VBA) code to work with PowerPoint.

Working with the Presentation Object
> Use a PowerPoint template, a presentation saved with a .pot extension that contains master slides and might contain regular slides, to apply a consistent look to an entire presentation.

Working with PowerPoint Slides
> Use the Slides collection returned by the Slides property of the Presentation object to add new slides to or access an existing slide in a presentation.

Working with Shapes on Slides
> Understand how to refer to a Shape object on a slide.

Understanding the PowerPoint Application Object

When you write Microsoft® Visual Basic® for Applications (VBA) code to work with Microsoft® PowerPoint®, you begin with the Application object. If you are writing VBA code within PowerPoint, the Application object is created for you. If you are automating PowerPoint from some other application, you first create a PowerPoint Application object variable and then create an instance of PowerPoint. Unlike the other Microsoft® Office applications (except Microsoft® Outlook®), there can be only one instance of PowerPoint running at a time. If an instance of PowerPoint is running and you use the New keyword or the CreateObject or GetObject function to instantiate a PowerPoint object variable, that object variable will point to the currently running instance of PowerPoint. This single instance of the Application object can contain any number of open Presentation objects.

Microsoft PowerPoint's Application object has properties you can use to access shared Office components such as command bars and the Office Assistant. In addition, the Application object has properties that return the currently active presentation or window, or information about the printer.

Information Returned by the Application object properties

```
┌─────────────────────────────────────────────┐
│ PowerPoint Application Object Information  ⊠ │
├─────────────────────────────────────────────┤
│                                             │
│  PowerPoint is currently visible and the following │
│  information is available from the Application object: │
│                                             │
│  Visible command bars:                      │
│  1 - Menu Bar (Built-in)                    │
│  2 - Standard (Built-in)                    │
│  3 - Formatting (Built-in)                  │
│  4 - Drawing (Built-in)                     │
│                                             │
│  Printer:                                   │
│  HP LaserJet 4Si                            │
│                                             │
│  Open Presentations:                        │
│  PowerPointTools.ppt (Template: fireball)   │
│  Presentation1 (Template: High Voltage) (Active) │
│                                             │
│  Loaded Application-Specific Add-ins: (0)   │
│  Loaded COM Add-ins: (1)                    │
│                                             │
│            ┌────────────────┐               │
│            │       OK       │               │
│            └────────────────┘               │
│                                             │
└─────────────────────────────────────────────┘
```

Working with the Presentation Object

When you are working with Microsoft® PowerPoint® objects through Microsoft® Visual Basic® for Applications (VBA), you typically work with a Presentation object and the slides it contains. You use a PowerPoint template—a presentation saved with a .pot extension that contains master slides and might contain regular slides—to apply a consistent look to an entire presentation.

Working with Open Presentations

You create a reference to an open presentation in two ways: by using the Application object's ActivePresentation property or by accessing a Presentation object as a member of the Presentations collection. There are three ways you can access a Presentation object through the Presentations collection:

- By using the presentation's file name.

- By using the Caption property setting of the Window object that contains the presentation.

- By using the presentation's index value. Microsoft® PowerPoint® presentations are indexed in the order in which they are opened.

The following examples illustrate the different ways to set a reference to an open presentation:

```
Dim prsPres As PowerPoint.Presentation
```

```
' Use the ActivePresentation property.
Set prsPres = ActivePresentation


' Use the presentation's file name.
Set prsPres = Presentations("PowerPointTools.ppt")


' Use the Caption property setting of the Window
' object that contains the presentation.
Set prsPres = Presentations("PowerPointTools")


' Use the presentation's index value in the collection.
Set prsPres = Presentations(1)
```

Working with Existing Presentations

You use the Presentations collection's Open method to open a presentation saved to disk and create a reference to that presentation at the same time. The following example opens the PowerPointTools.ppt presentation:

```
Dim ppApp       As PowerPoint.Application
Dim prsPres     As PowerPoint.Presentation


Set ppApp = New PowerPoint.Application
Set prsPres =
ppApp.Presentations.Open("c:\opg\Samples\CH05\PowerPointTools.ppt")
With prsPres
    ' Code to manipulate presentation and its
    ' contents goes here.
End With
```

Creating a New Presentation

There are two ways you can create a Microsoft® PowerPoint® presentation:

- By using the Open method of the Application object. You can use any file format recognized by PowerPoint in the Open method's FileName argument. For example, if the FileName argument specifies a Microsoft® Word document in outline view, the outline will be converted to a new presentation with a slide representing each paragraph that has the Heading 1 style in the document.

- By using the Presentations collection's Add method. For example:

```
Dim ppApp      As PowerPoint.Application
Dim prsPres    As PowerPoint.Presentation

Set ppApp = New PowerPoint.Application
With ppApp
    Set prsPres = .Presentations.Add(msoFalse)
    With prsPres
        ' Code here to add and format slides in
        ' the new presentation.
    End With
End With
```

> **Note** The WithWindow argument of the Add and Open methods accepts a Boolean value that specifies whether the Window object that contains the presentation will be visible. (The default is True.) Although the Auto List Members drop-down list for the Add method's WithWindow argument contains five enumerated constants, you should use only the msoTrue or msoFalse constants.

When you use Microsoft® Visual Basic® for Applications (VBA) to create a new presentation, it exists in memory, but will not be saved to disk until you use the Presentation object's SaveAs method. (Use the Save method to save changes to a presentation that has already been saved to disk.) The following procedure creates a new Presentation object and immediately saves the presentation by using the name supplied in the strPresName argument. It then returns the new Presentation object to the calling procedure.

```
Function PPTCreatePresentation(ppApp As PowerPoint.Application, _
                        strPresName As String) As
PowerPoint.Presentation
    ' This procedure illustrates how to use the SaveAs method to
    ' save a new presentation as soon as it is created.
    ' Note that in this example, the new Presentation object
    ' is not visible.

    On Error GoTo PPTCreate_Err

    Set PPTCreatePresentation = ppApp.Presentations.Add(msoFalse)
    If InStr(strPresName, "\") = 0 Then
        strPresName = "c:\" & strPresName
    End If
```

```
    PPTCreatePresentation.SaveAs strPresName
PPTCreate_End:
    Exit Function
PPTCreate_Err:
    Select Case Err
        Case Err <> 0
            Set PPTCreatePresentation = Nothing
    End Select
    Resume PPTCreate_End:
End Function
```

Formatting a Presentation

You use a Microsoft® PowerPoint® template to apply a consistent look to an entire presentation. A PowerPoint template is a presentation saved with a .pot extension that contains master slides and might contain regular slides. To see the difference, compare the master-slide-only templates found in C:\Program Files\Microsoft Office\Templates\Presentation Designs with the templates found in C:\Program Files\Microsoft Office\Templates\Presentations. Templates that contain slides typically include boilerplate text that you can replace with your own text to make a custom presentation.

Master slides specify the basic layout and formatting for the title slide in a presentation as well as regular slides, handouts, and notes. When you use the ApplyTemplate method, you specify the template that contains the master slides, which include the layout and formatting you want to apply to your presentation. For example, the following sample code applies the Fireball.pot template to the currently active presentation:

```
With ActivePresentation
    .ApplyTemplate FileName:="c:\program files\microsoft office\" _
        & "templates\presentation designs\fireball.pot"
End With
```

You can also use Microsoft® Visual Basic® for Applications (VBA) to create or manipulate master slides directly. Each Presentation object has a property that returns the available master slide that contains the formatting you want to use. You use the Presentation object's TitleMaster, SlideMaster, HandoutMaster, and NotesMaster properties to return a Slide object that represents the master slide you want to work with. Any changes you make to the layout or formatting of a master slide are applied to all slides of the specified type in the current presentation. For example, the following sample adds the CompanyLogo.bmp image to the background of the title master slide:

```
ActivePresentation.TitleMaster _
.Shapes.AddPicture(Filename:="c:\CompanyLogo.bmp", _
    Left:=100, Top:=200, Width:=400, Height:=300)
```

The master properties are useful when you want to apply changes to all slides based on a master, rather than applying changes one slide at a time. If you have an image or other formatting you want to appear on all slides in a presentation, make the change to the appropriate master slide.

Running a Slide Show from a Presentation

You use properties of the SlideShowSettings object to specify how you want a slide show to appear and which slides to include in the show. You use the SlideShowSettings object's Run method to start the slide show. You access the SlideShowSettings object by using the Presentation object's SlideShowSettings property. These objects and properties are most useful if you want to create and run a Microsoft® PowerPoint® presentation from another Microsoft® Office application. For example, the following code is from the PresentationView sample procedure, and it is used in Microsoft® Word to take a Word outline and display it as a PowerPoint presentation. The slide show runs automatically, and when it is finished, it returns the focus to the Word document from which the macro was run.

```
Set prsPres = ppApp.Presentations.Open(strOutlineFileName)
' Format the presentation and set the slide show timings.
With prsPres
    .ApplyTemplate strTemplate
    With .Slides.Range.SlideShowTransition
        .AdvanceTime = intShowSlide
        .AdvanceOnTime = msoTrue
    End With
    ' Run the slide show, showing each slide once,
    ' and then end the show and close the presentation.
    With .SlideShowSettings
        .AdvanceMode = ppSlideShowUseSlideTimings
        .ShowType = ppShowTypeSpeaker
        .StartingSlide = 1
        .EndingSlide = prsPres.Slides.Count
        Set objCurrentShow = .Run.View
        Do Until objCurrentShow.State = ppSlideShowDone
            DoEvents
        Loop
    End With
End With
```

Working with PowerPoint Slides

Every Microsoft® PowerPoint® presentation (with the exception of some templates) is a collection of slides. Each slide can contain text or graphics and might include animation effects. The Presentation object has a Slides property that returns the Slides collection. The Slides collection is used to add new slides to or access an existing slide in a presentation. Each slide is represented in the collection by a Slide object.

Working with the Slides Collection

You primarily use the Slides collection to add new slides to a presentation or to access a specific slide within a presentation. You use the Slides collection's Add method to add a new slide to a collection. You use arguments of the Add method to specify the location of the slide in the Slides collection and to specify the slide's layout. The following example shows how you would add a new blank slide to the end of the current Slides collection:

```
Dim sldNewSlide         As PowerPoint.Slide
Dim lngLastSlideAdded   As Long


With ActivePresentation
    Set sldNewSlide = .Slides.Add(.Slides.Count + 1, ppLayoutBlank)
    With sldNewSlide
        ' Add code to set properties of the slide here.
        lngLastSlideAdded = .SlideID
    End With
End With
```

You can add existing slides, or data that can be converted to slides, to a presentation by using the Slides collection's InsertFromFile method. For example, you could create a new presentation that used the opening and closing slides from a company presentation template and then used a Word outline to create the slides that make up the body of the presentation:

```
Dim ppApp      As New PowerPoint.Application
Dim prsPres    As PowerPoint.Presentation


With ppApp
    Set prsPres = .Presentations.Add
    With prsPres
        .ApplyTemplate "c:\corp\corpPresentations.pot"
        .Slides.InsertFromFile "c:\PPTOutline.doc", 1
    End With
End With
```

To locate a slide within the collection, you use the Slides collection's FindBySlideID method. Each slide in a PowerPoint presentation has a SlideID property that is a Long Integer value that uniquely identifies the slide regardless of its location in the Slides collection. When you add to or delete slides from a collection, a slide's index value might change, but its SlideID property will always be the same. The first code sample in this section illustrates how to save the SlideID property to a variable so that it might be used again to locate the slide. The following sample shows how to locate a slide by using the Long Integer value representing the SlideID property:

```
Function FindSlide(lngID As Long) As PowerPoint.Slide
    ' This procedure returns the slide whose SlideID property value
    ' matches lngID. If no match is found, the return value of the
    ' procedure is = Nothing.
    On Error Resume Next
    Set FindSlide = ActivePresentation.Slides.FindBySlideID(lngID)
End Function
```

Working with Slide Objects

By default, Microsoft® PowerPoint® names slides by using the convention Slide*n*, where *n* is a number representing the location of the slide at the time it was added to the Slides collection. You can specify your own name for a slide by setting the Slide object's Name property.

There are four ways to access a Slide object in the Slides collection:

- By using an index value representing the location of the slide in the Slides collection.

- By using the slide's name.

- By using the slide's SlideID property with the Slides collection's FindBySlideID method.

- By using the SlideIndex property of the SlideRange object from the PowerPoint Selection object to return the currently selected slide; however, using the SlideIndex property in this manner might return an error, if more than one slide is selected.

The following code sample illustrates three ways to return the third Slide object in the current presentation and a way to return the currently selected slide:

```
Dim sldCurrentSlide As PowerPoint.Slide
' Using the slide's index value.
Set sldCurrentSlide = ActivePresentation.Slides(3)

' Using the slide's name.
Set sldCurrentSlide = ActivePresentation.Slides("Slide3")

' Using the FindBySlideID method, where lngSlide3 contains the SlideID
' property for the third slide.
```

```
Set sldCurrentSlide = ActivePresentation.Slides.FindBySlideID(lngSlide3)
```

```
' Using the SlideIndex property to return the currently selected slide.
' This sample shows how to determine if a single slide is currently
selected.
If ActiveWindow.Selection.SlideRange.Count = 1 Then
    Set sldCurrentSlide = ActivePresentation _
        .Slides(ActiveWindow.Selection.SlideRange.SlideIndex)
End If
```

If you want to work with a group of Slide objects, perhaps to apply consistent formatting to the slides, you can use the Slides collection's Range method. The Range method returns a SlideRange object representing one or more Slide objects in a presentation.

If you use the Range method without an argument, the method returns a SlideRange object that contains all the Slide objects in a presentation.

You use the Range method's Index argument to specify one or more Slide objects to include in the SlideRange object returned by the method. If the argument is a single integer, the method returns a SlideRange object for the Slide object whose index value matches the integer. For example, the following sample returns a SlideRange object representing the third slide in the current presentation:

```
Dim sldCurrSlide As PowerPoint.SlideRange
Set sldCurrSlide = ActivePresentation.Slides.Range(3)
```

In addition to using the Index argument, you can also use the Microsoft® Visual Basic® for Applications (VBA) Array function as an argument to the Range method in order to return a SlideRange object containing multiple Slide objects. The Array function uses a comma-delimited list of values to be included in the array. When used as an argument to the Range method, the comma-delimited list should contain the index values or names of the slides you want to include in the SlideRange object returned by the method. The following sample shows how to use the Array function to return a SlideRange object containing the first four slides with even-numbered index values:

```
Dim sldCurrSlides As PowerPoint.SlideRange
Set sldCurrSlides = ActivePresentation.Slides.Range(Array(2,4,6,8))
```

The next sample illustrates how to use the Array function to return a SlideRange object that is a collection of specific named slides in a presentation:

```
Dim sldCurrSlides As PowerPoint.SlideRange

Set sldCurrSlides = ActivePresentation.Slides _
    .Range(Array("CostOfGoods", "SalesTotals", "Benefits", "Forecast"))
```

```
With sldCurrSlides
    ' Set properties common to all slides in this collection.
End With
```

Note You can also use the Array function as an argument to the Range method for a Shapes collection in order to return a collection of specified Shape objects as a ShapeRange object.

Working with Shapes on Slides

Just as a Microsoft® PowerPoint® presentation consists of a collection of slides, a PowerPoint slide typically consists of one or more Shape objects. Whether a slide contains a picture, a title, text, an OLE object, an AutoShape, a diagram, or other content, everything on the slide is a Shape object.

You can refer to a Shape object on a slide in two ways:

- By using the value of the shape's index in the collection of shapes on the slide. A shape will have an index value equal to its position in the Shapes collection at the time it was added to the collection.

- By using the name of the shape. You can specify the name of a Shape object by setting its Name property. By default, PowerPoint sets the name of a shape at the time it is added to a slide. The naming convention is *shapetype n*, where *shapetype* is the type of shape added and *n* is a number representing 1 plus the number of shapes on the slide when the current shape was added. For the first shape added to a slide, $n = 2$. To find out more about the types of shapes available in PowerPoint, search the Microsoft PowerPoint Visual Basic Reference Help index for "Shapes collection object."

To work with multiple shapes on a slide, you use the Range method of the Shapes collection. The Range method returns a ShapeRange object containing the shapes specified in the method's argument. If no Index argument is supplied, the Range method returns a ShapeRange object containing all the shapes on a slide. To specify multiple shapes, you can use the Microsoft® Visual Basic® for Applications (VBA) Array function.

Adding Shapes to Slides

Typically, you use the Add method of a collection object to add an item to the collection. For example, to add a slide to a Microsoft® PowerPoint® presentation, you use the Presentation object's Slides collection's Add method. However, adding shapes to a slide is a little different. The PowerPoint object model provides a different method for each shape you can add to a slide. For example, the following sample inserts a new slide at the end of the current presentation and uses two methods of the Shapes collection to add shapes to the slide. The AddTextEffect method is used to add a WordArt shape and the AddTextbox method is used to add a text box shape:

```
Sub AddTestSlideAndShapes()
    ' Illustrate how to add shapes to a slide and then
    ' center the shapes in relation to the slide and
    ' each other.
    Dim sldNewSlide        As PowerPoint.Slide
    Dim shpCurrShape       As PowerPoint.Shape
    Dim lngSlideHeight     As Long
    Dim lngSlideWidth      As Long

    With ActivePresentation
        ' Determine height and width of slide.
        With .PageSetup
            lngSlideHeight = .SlideHeight
            lngSlideWidth = .SlideWidth
        End With
        ' Add new slide to end of presentation.
        Set sldNewSlide = .Slides.Add(.Slides.Count + 1, ppLayoutBlank)
        With sldNewSlide
            ' Specify a background color for the slide.
            .ColorScheme = ActivePresentation.ColorSchemes(3)
            ' Add a WordArt shape by using the AddTextEffect method.
            Set shpCurrShape = .Shapes.AddTextEffect(msoTextEffect16, _
                "Familiar Quotations", "Tahoma", 42, msoFalse, msoFalse, 100, _
100)
            ' Locate the WordArt shape at the middle of the slide, near the
top.
            With shpCurrShape
                .Left = (lngSlideWidth - .Width) / 2
                .Top = (lngSlideHeight - .Height) / 8
            End With
            ' Add a Textbox shape to the slide and add text to the shape.
            Set shpCurrShape = .Shapes _
                .AddTextbox(msoTextOrientationHorizontal, 100, 100, 500, 500)
            With shpCurrShape
```

```
        With .TextFrame.TextRange
            .Text = "'If not now, when? If not us, who?'" _
                & vbCrLf & "'There is no time like the present.'" _
                & vbCrLf & "'Ask not what your country can do for you,
" _
                & "ask what you can do for your country.'"
            With .ParagraphFormat
                .Alignment = ppAlignLeft
                .Bullet = msoTrue
            End With
            With .Font
                .Bold = msoTrue
                .Name = "Tahoma"
                .Size = 24
            End With
        End With
        ' Shrink the Textbox to match the text it now contains.
        .Width = .TextFrame.TextRange.BoundWidth
        .Height = .TextFrame.TextRange.BoundHeight
        .Left = (lngSlideWidth - .Width) / 2
        .Top = (lngSlideHeight - .Height) / 2
      End With
    End With
  End With
End Sub
```

Positioning Shapes on Slides

When you add a shape to a slide, the method you use typically requires you to specify values to establish the dimensions of the shape. In some cases, as with the AddTextEffect method (illustrated in the AddTestSlideAndShapes procedure shown earlier in "Adding Shapes to Slides"), you specify values for the Left and Top properties of the shape (the height and width of the shape is determined by the text it contains). In other cases (as with the AddTextbox method, also illustrated in the AddTestSlideAndShapes procedure), you must specify values for the Shape object's Left, Top, Width, and Height properties.

The height and width of shapes are specified in pixels. The default slide size is 720 pixels wide and 540 pixels high. The center of a slide is 360 pixels from the left edge of the slide and 270 pixels from the top of the slide. You can center any shape horizontally by using the formula (*SlideWidth - ShapeWidth*) / 2. You can center any shape vertically by using the formula (*SlideHeight -*

ShapeHeight) / 2. You can programmatically specify or determine the height and width setting for the slides in a presentation by using the Presentation object's PageSetup property to return a PageSetup object, and then use the PageSetup object's SlideHeight and SlideWidth properties. This technique is also illustrated in the AddTestSlideAndShapes procedure shown earlier.

To position one or more shapes on a slide either in relation to the slide or to other shapes on the slide, you can use the Align or Distribute methods of a ShapeRange object.

Working with Text in a Shape

Much of what you do with shapes on slides involves adding or modifying text. In addition to the Textbox shape, many other Shape objects can contain text. For example, you can add text to many of the AutoShape Shape objects.

All shapes that support text have a TextFrame property you can use to return a TextFrame object. You can determine if a shape supports the use of a text frame by using the Shape object's HasTextFrame property. Each TextFrame object has a HasText property you can use to determine if the text frame contains text.

The TextFrame object has a TextRange property you use to return a TextRange object. You use the TextFrame object's Text property to specify or determine the text within a frame. You use the properties and methods of the TextRange object to work with the text associated with a Microsoft® PowerPoint® shape.

> **Note** Placeholder shapes contain default text that is visible from the PowerPoint user interface, but is not available programmatically. When you set the Text property of a Placeholder shape's TextRange object, the default text is replaced with the text you specify.

There is one Shape object that contains text but does not use the TextFrame or TextRange objects. The TextEffect property returns a TextEffectFormat object that contains the properties and methods used to work with WordArt shapes. You add WordArt shapes to a slide by using the Shapes collection's AddTextEffect method. The text of the WordArt shape and the location of the shape are specified in the arguments to the AddTextEffect method. You use the TextEffectFormat object's Text property to read or change the text in a WordArt shape. For example, the following code changes the text of an existing WordArt shape on the first slide of the current presentation:

```
With ActivePresentation
    strExistingText =   .Slides(1).TextEffect.Text
    If Len(strNewText) <= Len(strExistingText) Then
        .Slides(1).TextEffect.Text = strNewText
    End If
End With
```

Note that this code checks to make sure the new text is not longer than the existing text. This step is required because a WordArt shape does not automatically resize itself to accommodate new text. Alternatively, you could capture the properties of the existing WordArt shape, then delete it and replace it with a new WordArt shape that uses the same properties as the old shape.

Working with Microsoft Project Objects

With the Microsoft® Project 2000 object model, you can build powerful custom applications easily. Microsoft® Visual Basic® Applications Edition programming system extends the Visual Basic programming style to access Project project-planning software–supplied objects. In addition, the Visual Basic programming style is extended to access a Microsoft® Excel spreadsheet, Microsoft® Word word processing, the Microsoft® Access database management system, and the Microsoft® PowerPoint® presentation graphics program. This common macro language across applications makes it possible for access to schedule data stored in a project, as well as all the interface commands in the macro language found in Project.

In This Section

Understanding the Project Object Model
> Each Project object contains summary information, tasks, and resources. The Project object represents an individual project or a collection of projects.

Understanding the Project Application Object
> The Application object is the top of the hierarchy. All project objects are accessed through the Application object.

Understanding the Project Object Model

The Application object contains all Microsoft® Project objects. Each Project object contains summary information, tasks, and resources. The Project object represents an individual project or a collection of projects. In addition, Project objects are parent objects of Windows, Tasks, Resources, and Calendars collections.

Project objects can be referenced using the Application property ActiveProject, by referring to the project's index value or by naming the project:

```
Sub ProjectRefs()
MsgBox ActiveProject
MsgBox Projects(1).Name
MsgBox Projects("Project1").ProjectStart
End Sub
```

Project Object Properties

Fields in the project summary task record can be browsed or edited using Project object properties. The following examples return information from these fields. After running the macro, review the information on the Schedule tab in the Tools Options dialog box.

```
Sub ProjectProperties()
MsgBox ActiveProject.ActualCost
MsgBox ActiveProject.Author
```

```
MsgBox ActiveProject.AutoLinkTasks
ActiveProject.AutoLinkTasks = False
End Sub
```

Other properties are useful for returning active views, tables, and filters. Make sure to run the following procedure from a task or resource view:

```
Sub ProjectCurrentProperties()
MsgBox ActiveProject.CurrentView
MsgBox ActiveProject.CurrentTable
MsgBox ActiveProject.CurrentFilter
End Sub
```

Project Object Methods

The Tasks method returns a task or tasks in a Project object. To iterate through tasks try the following two routines:

```
Sub TaskDisplay()
Dim i As Integer
Dim t As Variant

For i = 1 To ActiveProject.Tasks.Count
MsgBox ActiveProject.Tasks(i).Name
Next i
For Each t In ActiveProject.Tasks
MsgBox t.Name
Next t
End Sub
```

The *Resources* method returns a resource or resources in a Project object:

```
Sub ResourceNameDisplay()
Dim r as Variant
For Each r in ActiveProject.Resources
MsgBox r.Name
Next r
End Sub
```

The TaskViewList, TaskTableList, TaskFilterList, ResourceViewList, ResourceTableList, and ResourceFilterList methods return available views, tables, and filters in a project. The following example displays a list of available task views:

```
Sub ListViews()
Dim strViewList As String
Dim i As Integer
NL = Chr$(13) & Chr$(10)
strViewList = "Task Views:" & NL

For i = 1 To ActiveProject.TaskViewList.Count
strViewList = strViewList & ActiveProject.TaskViewList(i) & NL
Next i


MsgBox strViewList
End Sub
```

Understanding the Project Application Object

The Application object is the top of the hierarchy. All Microsoft® Project objects are accessed through the Application object. Application object methods represent the common command functionality of the user interface. These methods are used for the basic Project commands. The Application object is the parent of the Cell, Project, Selection, and Window objects, as well as the Projects and Windows collections.

For example, to open a new project from a template file:

```
Sub Tester()
Application.FileOpen Name:="LANSUB.MPT"
End Sub
```

Using the Application object to refer to Project objects is optional when writing macros. This returns the same result as the previous example:

```
Sub Tester()
FileOpen Name:="LANSUB.MPT"
End Sub
```

To move the active cell, use one of the following options, SelectCellDown, SelectCellRight, SelectCellLeft, SelectCellUp, or SelectColumn.

```
Sub Tester()
For I = 1 To 10
SelectCellRight I
SelectCellDown I
SelectCellLeft I
SelectCellUp I
```

```
Next I
SelectColumn
End Sub
```

Application object properties describe the Project environment. These properties are used to manage settings in the Options and Leveling dialog boxes. Although not all properties are editable, many are:

```
Sub TitleBarExample()
MsgBox Application.ActiveWindow
Application.ActiveWindow.Caption = "CPM is Cool"
End Sub
```

Working with Microsoft Visio Objects

Microsoft® Visio® products provide a sophisticated toolset for information technology professionals who design, model, and manage complex enterprise-level systems.

Automation is a means by which a program written in Microsoft® Visual Basic® for Applications (VBA), or other computer languages that support automation, can incorporate the functionality of the Visio applications simply by using its objects. VBA is incorporated in Visio, so you are not required use a separate development environment to write your programs.

The way objects in an application are related to each other, along with each object's properties (data), methods (behavior), and events, is called the program's object model. In the Visio object model, most objects correspond to items you can see and select in the Visio user interface. For example, a Shape object represents a shape in a drawing.

In automation, the application that provides the objects (such as the Visio application) makes the objects accessible to other applications, and provides the properties and methods that control them.

The application that uses the objects (such as your program) creates instances of the objects and sets their properties or invokes their methods to make the objects serve the application.

In This Section

Understanding the Visio Object Model
> The Microsoft® Visio® object model represents the objects, properties, methods, and events that the Visio engine exposes through automation.

Understanding the Visio Application Object
> The Application object is a property of the Microsoft® Visio® global objects, so you can access any of the Application object's properties by referencing directly the Application property of the Visio global object.

Understanding the Visio Object Model

The Microsoft® Visio® object model represents the objects, properties, methods, and events that the Visio engine exposes through automation. More important, it describes how the objects are related to each other.

Most objects in the model correspond to items you can see and select in the Visio user interface. For example, a Shape object can represent anything on a Visio drawing page that you can select with the pointer tool—a shape, a group, a guide, or an object from another application that is linked, embedded, or imported into a Visio drawing.

Visio objects reside in an instance of the Visio application. Microsoft® Visual Basic® for Applications (VBA) code runs within an instance of Visio and accesses the objects it requires. An external program runs outside an instance of the Visio application, so it starts the Visio application or accesses an instance of Visio that is running, and then it accesses the Visio object it needs.

Some objects represent a collection of other objects. A collection contains zero or more objects of a specified type. For example, a Document object represents one open document in an instance of Visio; the Documents collection represents all of the documents that are open in the instance.

Using Visio Object Types

You can take advantage of the Visio type library to write code more effectively. By using Visio object types declared in the type library, you can declare variables as specific types, such as Visio.Page, which is illustrated in the following code:

```
Dim pagObj As Visio.Page
```

This example uses Visio to inform the program that it is referencing Visio object types in the Visio type library, and it uses Page to inform the program that the pagObj variable is a Page object. Here are a few more object types:

```
Dim docsObj As Visio.Documents   'A Documents collection
Dim docObj As Visio.Document     'A Document object
Dim shpsObj As Visio.Shapes      'A Shapes collection
Dim shpObj As Visio.Shape        'A Shape object
Dim mastObj As Visio.Master      'A Master object
```

Getting and Releasing Visio Objects

You get an object by declaring an object variable, navigating through the object model to get a reference to the object you want to control, and assigning the reference to the object variable. After you have a reference to an object, you can get and set the values of its properties or use methods that cause the object to perform actions.

The following are some guidelines for getting and releasing Visio objects:

- **Declare object variables** Declare a Visio object type as defined in the Visio type library. Use the Set statement to assign the reference to the object variable.

- **Access Visio objects through properties** Most Visio objects have properties whose values refer to other objects. You can use these properties to navigate up and down the layers of the object model to get to the object you want to control.

- **Refer to an object in a collection** A collection is an object that represents objects of a particular type. You can get a reference to a particular object in the collection. The Item property returns a reference to an object in the collection.

- **Iterate through a collection** A collection's Count property returns the number of objects in the collection. Most often, you will use the Count property to set the limit for an iteration loop.

- **Release an object** An object in a collection is released automatically when the program finishes running or when all object variables referring to that object go out of scope.

- **Use compound object references** You can concatenate Visio object references, properties, and methods in single statements as you can with Microsoft® Visual Basic® for Applications (VBA) objects. However, simple references are sometimes more efficient, even if they require more lines of code.

- **Restrict the scope and lifetime of object variables** You can prevent invalid references by restricting the scope and lifetime of an object variable. For example, when your program resumes execution after giving control to the user, you can release certain objects and retrieve them again to make sure that the objects still are available and your program has references to the objects in their current state.

Understanding the Visio Application Object

Unlike a stand-alone program, which must obtain a reference to the Microsoft® Visio® Application object by creating it or getting it, code in a Microsoft® Visual Basic® for Applications (VBA) project executes in a running instance of Visio. Therefore, you are not required to obtain a reference to the Application object. The Visio engine provides the global object, which represents the Visio instance. In addition, the Visio engine provides the ThisDocument object, which represents the Visio document associated with your project.

The global object represents the instance and provides more direct access to certain properties. The properties of the Visio global object are not prefixed with a reference to an object.

The Application object is a property of the Visio global objects, so you can access any of the Application object's properties by referencing the Application property of the Visio global object directly.

The following are three examples of code that get the first document in a Documents collection—all three use different syntax.

Example 1 creates an Application object. Typically, this code is used when writing an external program:

Example 1

```
Dim appVisio As Visio.Application
Dim docsObj As Visio.Documents
Dim docObj As Visio.Document
Set appVisio = CreateObject("visio.application")
Set docsObj = appVisio.Documents
Set docObj + docsObj.Item(1)
```

Example 2 uses the Application property of the Visio global object:

Example 2

```
Dim docsObj As Visio.Documents
Dim docObj As Visio.Document
Set docsObj = Application.Documents
Set docObj = docsObj.Item(1)
```

Example 3 directly accesses the Documents property of the Visio global object:

Example 3

```
Dim docObj As Visio.Document
Set dicObj + Documents.Item(1)
```

You might have noticed in examples 2 and 3 that `Application` and `Documents` are not preceded by an object. When you are referencing any property or method of the Visio global object, you are not required to declare a variable for the global object or reference it as the preceding object of a property—the global object is implied. The third example is the most direct method of accessing the Documents collection from a VBA Project.

The following are some of examples of code for commonly used properties of the Visio global object.

```
Set docObj = ActiveDocument
Set pagObj = ActivePage
Set WinObj = ActiveWindow
```

> **Note** The Visio global object is available only when you are writing code in the VBA project of a Visio document.

Working with Microsoft Word Objects

In Microsoft® Word, the fundamental working object is a document and everything is part of the document. When you are using VBA to work with Word, a Document object represents an open document, and all Document objects are contained in the Application object's Documents collection. Because each Document object is based on a template, each document has an AttachedTemplate property.

A document is a collection of characters arranged into words, words are arranged into sentences, sentences are arranged into paragraphs, and so on. Therefore, each Document object has a Characters collection, a Words collection, a Sentences collection, and a Paragraphs collection. Furthermore, each document has a Sections collection of one or more sections, and each section has a HeadersFooters collection that contains the headers and footers for the section. In addition, some or all of the text in the document might have certain formatting attributes set, and paragraphs might have built-in or custom styles applied.

In This Section

Understanding Application-Level Objects
> Learn about the Application object and other objects that affect Word.

The Document Object
> Create or open documents, and add them to the Documents collection.

Working with Document Content
> Work with objects contained in the Document object.

Understanding Application-Level Objects

Application-level objects are the Application object itself and its properties, methods, options (displayed in the Options dialog box), as well as the built-in dialog boxes in Word—in other words, these are objects that can affect more than one document at a time or are accessed and manipulated independent of the currently active Document object.

In This Section

Working with the Application Object
> Access all the other objects exposed by the application as well as properties and methods unique to the Application object itself.

Working with the Settings in the Options Dialog Box
> Learn how to use the Options, View, and Dialog options.

Working with Word Dialog Boxes
> Create your own custom dialog boxes by using the functionality of one of the Word built-in dialog boxes.

Modifying Built-in Commands
> Customize the behavior of Word by running your own VBA procedure in place of a built-in procedure.

Working with the Application Object

Every time you write VBA code in Word, or write code to automate Word from some other application, you begin with the Application object. From the Application object, you can access all the other objects exposed by the application as well as properties and methods unique to the Application object itself.

Note If you are working in Word, the Application object is created for you, and you can use the Application property to return a reference to the Word Application object. If you are automating Word from some other application, you must create a Word Application object variable and then create an instance of Word.

To access properties and methods of the Application object, you use the following syntax:

```
Application.PropertyName
Application.MethodName (arg1, arg2, argN)
```

You can access child objects of the Application object by using the following syntax:

```
Application.ObjectName
```

–or–

```
ObjectName
```

Note You do not have to use the Application property in this context because these objects are global.

Working with the Settings in the Options Dialog Box

The Options dialog box contains many settings that let you customize the way Word looks and behaves. You can view this dialog box by clicking Options on the Tools menu. To programmatically access the settings in this dialog box, you use the Options object or the View object of a Window object. You can also access these settings through the Dialog object that represents the tab in the Options dialog box that contains the setting you want to manipulate.

Using the Options Object

The Options object contains many properties that represent items in the Options dialog box. For example, the Options object's ReplaceSelection property setting is equivalent to the Typing replaces selection setting on the Edit tab of the Options dialog box. The easiest way to identify which properties of the Options object represent settings on a tab in the Options dialog box is to record a macro that changes a setting and then examine the property settings Word records. For example, the Print tab of the Options dialog box contains fourteen settings. Two settings (Print PostScript over text and Print data only for forms) apply only to the active document and are therefore properties of the Document object. The remaining settings represent properties of the Options object. A macro that records a change to a setting on the Print tab would create, in part, the following list of Options object properties:

```
With Options
    .UpdateFieldsAtPrint = False
    .UpdateLinksAtPrint = False
    .DefaultTray = "Use printer settings"
    .PrintBackground = True
```

```
    .PrintProperties = False
    .PrintFieldCodes = False
    .PrintComments = True
    .PrintHiddenText = True
    .PrintDrawingObjects = True
    .PrintDraft = False
    .PrintReverse = False
    .MapPaperSize = True
End With
```

If you change the settings of Options object properties, make sure you return each setting to its original value when you are finished. Many of these properties are global application-level settings, and you might be making changes that the user would not want persisted. The following example illustrates how to return Options object properties to their original settings when a procedure that changes those properties ends:

```
Sub PrintAllDocInfo()
    ' This procedure illustrates how to use the Options object
    ' to change certain settings, print a document, and then
    ' return the settings to their original state.
    Dim blnProps        As Boolean
    Dim blnFields       As Boolean
    Dim blnComments     As Boolean
    Dim blnHidden       As Boolean

    With Options
        ' Save the existing property settings.
        blnProps = .PrintProperties
        blnFields = .PrintFieldCodes
        blnComments = .PrintComments
        blnHidden = .PrintHiddenText
        ' Set properties to True and print document.
        .PrintProperties = True
        .PrintFieldCodes = True
        .PrintComments = True
        .PrintHiddenText = True
        Application.PrintOut
        ' Return properties to original settings.
        .PrintProperties = blnProps
```

```
        .PrintFieldCodes = blnFields
        .PrintComments = blnComments
        .PrintHiddenText = blnHidden
    End With
End Sub
```

Using the View Object and the Dialog Object

The View object lets you determine or specify all the attributes of a Window object. For example, you can run the following code sample from the Immediate window in the Microsoft® Visual Basic® Editor to determine whether hidden text is displayed in the current document:

```
? ActiveWindow.View.ShowHiddenText
```

Note that although many of the View object properties map directly to settings in the Options dialog box, they do not necessarily map to settings on the View tab of that dialog box.

You use the Dialogs collection to access a Dialog object that represents a tab in the Options dialog box. For example, if you execute the following code from the Immediate window, it prints the current setting for the Typing replaces selection check box on the Edit tab of the Options dialog box:

```
? CBool(Dialogs(wdDialogToolsOptionsEdit).ReplaceSelection)
```

Working with Word Dialog Boxes

You can create your own custom dialog boxes by using UserForms, but before you do, you should determine whether you could simply appropriate the functionality of one of Word's more than two hundred built-in dialog boxes.

From VBA, you access any of Word's built-in dialog boxes through the Dialogs collection. The Dialogs collection is a global object, so you can reference it without specifying the Application property. For example, you can run the following code from the Immediate window to return the number of dialog boxes in the Dialogs collection:

```
? Dialogs.Count
```

To work with a particular dialog box, you create an object variable declared As Dialog and use one of the wdWordDialog constants to specify the dialog box you want to reference. For example, the following code creates a reference to the Spelling and Grammar dialog box:

```
Dim dlgSpell As Dialog

Set dlgSpell = Dialogs(wdDialogToolsSpellingandGrammar)
```

When you instantiate a Dialog object variable in this way, you can easily determine or specify the various dialog box settings. When you refer to one of these settings in VBA, you can reference it as a property of the dialog box. For example, you can refer to the All setting on the View tab of the Options dialog box by using the ShowAll property:

```
MsgBox "The 'All' setting on the View tab is currently set to " _
    & CBool(Dialogs(wdDialogtoolsOptionsView).ShowAll)
```

Dialog box properties are typically set from the user interface by using check box controls, combo box controls, or text box controls. Check box controls contain the value 1 when they are selected and 0 when they are not selected. Combo box controls contain the index value of the item selected, beginning at 0 for the first item in the control. Text box controls contain a String value representing the text in the control.

You also have control over how a dialog box is displayed and when changes to settings take effect. When you display a dialog box from the Word user interface and change a setting, the change usually takes effect as soon as you click the dialog box's OK button, although some dialog box settings take effect immediately. When you use VBA to display a dialog box, you can control how the dialog box behaves by using either the Dialog object's Show method or its Display method. If you use the Show method, the dialog box behaves just as it does when Word displays it. The Display method simply displays the dialog box and you must use additional VBA code to take further action in response to any selections made in the dialog box by the user. Both methods also return a value representing whether the user clicked OK, Cancel, Close, or some other button in the dialog box.

Modifying Built-in Commands

One simple but very powerful method you can use to customize the way Microsoft® Word works is to run your own VBA procedure in place of a built-in procedure. Doing this lets you customize the behavior of Word in any way you can imagine.

There is no limit to the kinds of things you can do and the kinds of built-in behaviors you can change. You could save documents created by using your custom template to a different directory than documents created by using Normal.dot. You could modify the File New command to create custom document properties for every new document. You could display your own custom dialog box instead of the Word dialog box normally displayed in response to a menu command. You could also let the built-in command run and then detect whether a user made certain selections from a Word dialog box.

The first thing you have to do is figure out which procedure Word runs to perform a built-in action. This is easy to do for all built-in menu commands. If you press ALT+CTRL+PLUS SIGN (+) on the numeric keypad (not the PLUS SIGN on the keyboard) and then click the menu item you want to investigate, Word displays the Customize Keyboard dialog box, which shows the name of the built-in procedure in the Commands list. For example, in the following figure, you can see that Word runs the FileSaveAs procedure whenever a user clicks Save As on the File menu.

The Customize Keyboard Dialog Box

There are three ways you can substitute your own procedure for a built-in Word procedure:

- In any standard module, create a VBA procedure that uses the same name as the procedure you want to replace. For example, if you create a procedure named FileSaveAs, Word will run your procedure instead of the built-in FileSaveAs procedure whenever the built-in procedure would normally be called.

- Create a module and name it by using the name of the built-in command you want to replace. Then add a subroutine named Main() to the module and add your custom code to that procedure.

- Create a new procedure by using the Macros dialog box. To do this, point to Macro on the Tools menu, and then click Macros. In the Macros dialog box, click Word Commands in the Macros in list. The Macro name list will then display the hundreds of built-in Word procedures. You can learn something about what these procedures do by clicking a procedure name in the list and reading its description in the Description box at the bottom of the dialog box. When you locate the command you want to modify, click it and then use the Macros in list to select the template or document in which to save the procedure. Then click the Create button to create a new VBA procedure that uses the same name as the built-in command.

The Document Object

The Document object is just below the Application object in Word's object model and is at the heart of Word programming. When you open a new document from the user interface, you create a new Document object. Each document you create or open is added to the Documents collection, and the document that has the focus is called the active document.

In This Section

Working with the Document Object
    Create or open documents and add them to the Documents collection.

Opening, Creating, Saving, and Closing New Documents
    Create and manipulate new documents by using the Documents collection's methods.

Working with the Document Object

You can reference a Document object as a member of the Documents collection by using either its index value (where 1 is the first document in the collection) or its name. In addition, you can use the ActiveDocument property to return a reference to the document that currently has the focus. For example, if a document named Policies.doc is the only open document, the following three object variables will all point to Policies.doc:

```
Dim docOne      As Word.Document
Dim docTwo      As Word.Document
Dim docThree    As Word.Document


Set docOne = Documents(1)
Set docTwo = Documents("Policies.doc")
Set docThree = ActiveDocument
```

You will rarely refer to a document by using its index value in the Documents collection because this value can change for a given document as other documents are opened and closed. Typically, you will use the ActiveDocument property or a Document object variable created by using the Documents collection's Add method or Open method. The following example shows how you can use the ActiveDocument property to add an address to the document that currently has the focus:

```
Sub AddOPGAddress()
    With ActiveDocument
        .Envelope.Insert Address:="The MOD Team" _
            & vbCrLf & "One Microsoft Way" & vbCrLf _
            & "Redmond, WA 98052", ReturnAddress:= _
            "One Happy Customer" & vbCrLf & _
            "77 Pine Bough Lane" & vbCrLf & _
            "Any Town, USA 12345"
    End With
End Sub
```

The next example illustrates how to create an instance of a Document object variable by using the Documents collection's Open method. After the Document object variable is set, the code calls the procedure from the prior example to add an envelope and then the envelope and the document are printed. Finally, the document is closed and all changes are saved.

```
Dim docPolicy As Word.Document

Set docPolicy = Documents.Open("c:\my documents\policies.doc")
With docPolicy
    Call AddOPGAddress
    .Envelope.PrintOut
    .PrintOut
    .Close SaveChanges:=True
End With
```

> **Note** The document opened by using the Open method or the document created by using the Add method will also be the currently active document represented by the ActiveDocument property. If you want to make some other document the active document, use the Document object's Activate method.

Opening, Creating, Saving, and Closing New Documents

You use the Documents collection's Open method to open an existing document. The FileName argument can include the full path to the file or the file name alone. If the file specified in the FileName argument does not include the full path to the document, Word looks for the document in the current directory. If Word can't find the file by using the file path and file name specified in the FileName argument, an error occurs.

Instead of using a hard-coded path and file name, you can use the FileSearch object to make sure the file exists before trying to open it. You can also create a Dialog object that represents the File Open dialog box and use it to let the user select the file name to use as the FileName argument of the Open method.

You create a new document by using the Documents collection's Add method. The Add method can accept up to two optional arguments. You use the Template argument to specify the template on which to base the new document. If you leave this argument blank, the new document is based on the Normal.dot template. The NewTemplate argument is a Boolean value that specifies whether to create the new document as a template. The following example creates a new document based on the Normal.dot template:

```
Dim docNew As Word.Document

Set docNew = Documents.Add
With docNew
    ' Add code here to work with the new document.
End With
```

The method you use to save a document depends on whether the document is new or has already been saved. To save an existing document, you use the Document object's Save method. To save a new document, you use the Document object's SaveAs method and specify a file name in the method's FileName argument. If you use the Save method on a new document, Word displays the Save As dialog box to prompt the user to give the document a name.

You can also save a new document as soon as it is created by using the Add method and the SaveAs method together as follows:

```
Documents.Add.SaveAs FileName:="c:\my documents\fastsave.doc"
Set docNew = Documents("fastsave.doc")
```

If you use the Documents.Add.SaveAs syntax, you will not be able to set a Document object variable at the same time you use the Add method. Instead, you can refer to the newly created document by using the ActiveDocument property or by using the document's name in the Documents collection, as shown in the preceding example.

To close a document, you use the Document object's Close method. If there are changes to the document and you do not specify the SaveChanges argument, Word prompts the user to save changes. To prevent this prompt from appearing, use either the wdDoNotSaveChanges or the wdSaveChanges built-in constant in the Close method's SaveChanges argument. To close all open documents at once, use the Documents collection's Close method and either the wdDoNotSaveChanges or the wdSaveChanges constant in the SaveChanges argument.

Working with Document Content

When you have a document to work with, most of the tasks you'll want to perform with VBA will involve working with the text in the document or manipulating the objects contained in the document. Documents contain words, sentences, paragraphs, sections, headers and footers, tables, fields, controls, images, shapes, hyperlinks and more. All of these objects are available to you through VBA.

The starting point for much of what you do to the contents of a document will be to specify a part of the document and then to do something to it. This might involve, for example, adding or removing text or formatting words or characters. The two objects you will use to accomplish much of this work are the Range object and the Selection object.

In This Section

The Range Object
> Understand the Range object, including creating, defining, determining the location of, and working with text in a Range object.

The Selection Object
> Learn about the Selection object, including how to use its Type property to get information about the state of the current selection.

The Selection Object vs. the Range Object
> Compare and contrast the Selection and Range objects.

Working with Bookmarks
> Use bookmarks to mark a location in a document or as a container for text in a document.

The Find and Replacement Objects
> Loop through a document looking for some specific text, formatting, or style, and specify what you want to use to replace the item you found.

The Range Object

A Range object represents a contiguous area in a document, defined by a starting character position and an ending character position. The contiguous area can be as small as the insertion point or as large as the entire document. It can also be, but does not have to be, the area represented by the current selection. You can define a Range object that represents a different area than the current selection. You can also define multiple Range objects in a single document. The characters in a Range object include nonprinting characters, such as spaces, carriage returns, and paragraph marks.

> **Note**   The area represented by the current selection is contained in the Selection object.

A Range object is similar to a Word bookmark in that they both define a specific area within a document. However, unlike a bookmark, a Range object exists only so long as the code that creates it is running. In addition, when you insert text at the end of a range, Word automatically expands the range to include the new text. When you insert text at the end of a bookmark, Word does not expand the bookmark to include the new text.

Creating, Defining, and Redefining a Range

You typically create a Range object by declaring an object variable of type Range and then instantiating that variable by using either the Document object's Range method or the Range property of another object, such as a Character, Word, Sentence, or Selection object. For example, the following code creates two Range objects that both represent the second sentence in the active document.

```
Public Sub GetRangeExample()
    ' This example shows how the Range method and the Range
    ' property both return the same characters.
```

```
Dim rngRangeMethod        As Word.Range
Dim rngRangeProperty      As Word.Range

With ActiveDocument
    If .Sentences.Count >= 2 Then
        Set rngRangeMethod = .Range(.Sentences(2).Start, _
            .Sentences(2).End)
        Set rngRangeProperty = .Sentences(2)
    End If
End With


Debug.Print rngRangeMethod.Text
Debug.Print rngRangeProperty.Text
End Sub
```

When you use the Range method to specify a specific area of a document, you use the method's Start argument to specify the character position where the range should begin and you use the End argument to specify where the range should end. The first character in a document is at character position 0. The last character position is equal to the total number of characters in the document. You can determine the number of characters in a document by using the Characters collection's Count property. As shown in the preceding example, you can also use the Start and End properties of a Bookmark, Selection, or Range object to specify the Range method's Start and End arguments. You can set the Start and End arguments to the same number. In this case, you create a range that does not include any characters.

You can set or redefine the contents of a Range object by using the object's SetRange method. You can specify or redefine the start of a range by using the Range object's Start property or its MoveStart method. Likewise, you can specify or redefine the end of a range by using the Range object's End property or its MoveEnd method.

The following example begins by using the Content property to create a Range object that covers the entire contents of a document. It then changes the End property to specify that the end of the range will be at the end of the first sentence in the document. It then uses the SetRange method to redefine the range to cover the first paragraph in the document. Finally, it uses the MoveEnd method to extend the end of the range to the end of the second paragraph in the document. At each step in the example, the number of characters contained in the range is printed to the Immediate window.

```
Public Sub RedefineRangeExample1()
    ' This procedure illustrates how to use various properties
    ' and methods to redefine the contents of a Range object.
    ' See also the RedefineRangeExample2 procedure.
    Dim rngSample As Range
    Set rngSample = ActiveDocument.Content
```

```
With rngSample
    Debug.Print "The range now contains " & .Characters.Count _
        & " characters."
    .End = ActiveDocument.Sentences(1).End
    Debug.Print "The range now contains " & .Characters.Count _
        & " characters."
    .SetRange Start:=0, End:=ActiveDocument.Paragraphs(1).Range.End
    Debug.Print "The range now contains " & .Characters.Count _
        & " characters."
    .MoveEnd Unit:=wdParagraph, Count:=1
    Debug.Print "The range now contains " & .Characters.Count _
        & " characters."
End With
End Sub
```

You can also redefine a Range object by using the object's Find property to return a Find object. The following example illustrates the use of the Find property to locate text within the active document. If the text is found, the Range object is automatically redefined to contain the text that matched the search criteria.

```
With rngRangeText.Find
    .ClearFormatting
    If .Execute(FindText:=strTextToFind) Then
        Set RedefineRangeExample2 = rngRangeText
    Else
        Set RedefineRangeExample2 = Nothing
    End If
End With
```

Many Word objects have a Range property that returns a Range object. You use an object's Range property to return a Range object under circumstances where you must work with properties or methods of the Range object that are not available from the object itself. For example, the following code uses the Range property of a Paragraph object to return a Range object that is used to format the text in the first paragraph in a document:

```
Dim rngPara As Range

Set rngPara = ActiveDocument.Paragraphs(1).Range
```

```
With rngPara
    .Bold = True
    .ParagraphFormat.Alignment = wdAlignParagraphCenter
    .Font.Name = "Arial"
End With
```

After you identify the Range object, you can apply methods and properties of the object to modify the contents of the range or get information about the range. You use the Range object's StoryType property to determine where in the document the Range is located.

Working with Text in a Range Object

You use a Range object's Text property to specify or determine the text the range contains. For example, the following code first displays the text within a Range object, then changes it and displays the new text, and finally restores the original text:

```
Public Sub ChangeTextSample()
    ' This procedure illustrates how to use the Range object's Text
    ' property to copy and paste text into a document while
    ' maintaining the original paragraphs.
    '
    ' When the rngText variable is instantiated, it includes all of
    ' the text in the first paragraph in the active document plus the
    ' paragraph mark at the end of the paragraph. Note how the new
    ' text in the strNewText variable includes a paragraph mark
    ' (vbCrLf) to replace the mark removed when the orginal text was
    ' replaced.
    Dim rngText             As Range
    Dim strOriginalText     As String
    Dim strNewText          As String

    strNewText = "Now is the time to harness the power of VBA in Word." _
        & "This text is replacing the original text in the first " _
        & "paragraph. This is all done using only the Text property " _
        & "of the Range object!" _
        & vbCrLf
```

```
    Set rngText = ActiveDocument.Paragraphs(1).Range
    With rngText
        MsgBox .Text, vbOKOnly, "This is the original text."
        strOriginalText = .Text
        .Text = strNewText
        MsgBox .Text, vbOKOnly, "This is the new text inserted in paragraph
1."
        .Text = strOriginalText
        MsgBox "The original text is restored."
    End With
End Sub
```

In this example, the Range object's Text property is used to specify the text that appears in the document.

Determining Where the Range Is Located

You can use the Range object's StoryType property to determine where the range is located. Stories are distinct areas of a document that contain text. You can have up to 11 story type areas in a document, representing areas such as document text, headers, footers, footnotes, comments, and more. You use the StoryRanges property to return a StoryRanges collection. The StoryRanges collection contains Range objects representing each story in a document.

A new Word document contains a single story, called the Main Text story, which represents the text in the main part of the document. Even a blank document contains a character, a word, a sentence, and a paragraph.

You do not expressly add new stories to a document, but rather, Word adds them for you when you add text to a portion of the document represented by one of the 11 story types. For example, if you add footnotes, Word adds a Footnotes story. If you add comments, Word adds a Comments story to the document.

You use the Range property to return a Range object representing each story in a document. For example, the following code prints the text associated with the Main Text story and the Comments story:

```
Dim rngMainText        As Word.Range
Dim rngCommentsText    As Word.Range

Set rngMainText = ActiveDocument.StoryRanges(wdMainTextStory)
Set rngComments = ActiveDocument.StoryRanges(wdCommentsStory)
Debug.Print rngMainText.Text
Debug.Print rngComments.Text
```

Inserting Text in a Range

You use the Range object's InsertBefore or InsertAfter methods to add text to an existing Range object. In fact, there is an entire class of methods, with names that begin with "Insert," that you can use to manipulate a Range object.

It's useful to have a procedure that combines the Range object's InsertBefore and InsertAfter methods with the Text property. Having such a procedure creates a single place to handle much of the work you will do when manipulating text programmatically.

You can call the InsertTextInRange procedure when you must add text to a Range object. In other words, the procedure is useful when you want to programmatically make any changes to existing text in a Word document.

The InsertTextInRange procedure uses one required arguments and two optional argument. The strNewText argument contains the text you want to add to the Range object specified in the rngRange argument. The intInsertMode optional argument specifies how the new text will be added to the range. The values for this argument are one of three custom enumerated constants that specify whether to use the InsertBefore method, the InsertAfter method, or the Text property to replace the existing range text.

```
Public Function InsertTextInRange(strNewText As String, _
                        Optional rngRange As Word.Range, _
                        Optional intInsertMode As
opgTextInsertMode = _
                        Replace) As Boolean
' This procedure inserts text specified by the strNewText
' argument into the Range object specified by the rngRange
' argument. It calls the IsLastCharParagraph procedure to
' strip off trailing paragraph marks from the rngRange object.

    Call IsLastCharParagraph(rngRange, True)

    With rngRange
        Select Case intInsertMode
            Case 0 ' Insert before text in range.
                .InsertBefore strNewText
            Case 1 ' Insert after text in range.
                .InsertAfter strNewText
            Case 2 ' Replace text in range.
                .Text = strNewText
            Case Else
        End Select
```

```
        InsertTextInRange = True
    End With
End Function
```

Note The IsLastCharParagraph procedure is used to strip off any final paragraph marks before inserting text in the range. The IsLastCharParagraph procedure is discussed earlier.

Understanding Paragraph Marks

When you create a Range object that represents a Character, Word, or Sentence object, and that object falls at the end of a paragraph, the paragraph mark is automatically included within the range. The Range object also includes all additional subsequent empty paragraph marks. For example, in a document where the first paragraph consists of three sentences, the following code creates a Range object that represents the last sentence in the first paragraph:

```
Set rngCurrentSentence = ActiveDocument.Sentences(3)
```

Because the rngCurrentSentence Range object refers to the last sentence in the first paragraph, that paragraph mark (and any additional empty paragraph marks) will be included in the range. If you then set the Text property of this object to a text string that didn't end with a paragraph mark, the first and second paragraphs in the document would be deleted.

When you write VBA code that manipulates text in a Word document, you must account for the presence of a paragraph mark in your text. There are two basic techniques you can use to account for paragraph marks when you are cutting and pasting text in Range objects:

- Include a new paragraph mark (represented by the vbCrLf constant) in the text to be inserted in the document. This technique is illustrated in the ChangeTextSample procedure shown in "Working with Text in a Range Object".

- Exclude the final paragraph mark from a Range object. The following code sample shows how to change the contents of a Range object to exclude the final paragraph mark. The example uses the Chr$() function with character code 13 to represent a paragraph mark.

```
Function IsLastCharParagraph(ByRef rngTextRange As Word.Range, _
                    Optional blnTrimParaMark As Boolean = _
                    False) As Boolean
    ' This procedure accepts a character, word, sentence, or
    ' paragraph Range object as the first argument and returns True
    ' if the last character in the range is a paragraph mark, and
    ' False if it is not. The procedure also accepts an optional
    ' Boolean argument that specifies whether the Range object
    ' should be changed to eliminate the paragraph mark if it
    ' exists. When the blnTrimParaMark argument is True, this
    ' procedure calls itself recursively to strip off all trailing
    ' paragraph marks.
```

```
    Dim strLastChar As String

    strLastChar = Right$(rngTextRange.Text, 1)
    If InStr(strLastChar, Chr$(13)) = 0 Then
        IsLastCharParagraph = False
        Exit Function
    Else
        IsLastCharParagraph = True
        If Not blnTrimParaMark = True Then
            Exit Function
        Else
            Do
                rngTextRange.SetRange rngTextRange.Start, _
                    rngTextRange.Start + rngTextRange.Characters.Count - 1
                Call IsLastCharParagraph(rngTextRange, True)
            Loop While InStr(rngTextRange.Text, Chr$(13)) <> 0
        End If
    End If
End Function
```

In this example, the Count property of the Range object's Characters collection is used to redefine the Range object's end point.

The Selection Object

When you use the Word user interface to work with a document, you typically select (highlight) text and then do something to the text, such as formatting it, typing new text, or moving it to another location. The Selection object represents the currently selected text in a Word document. The Selection object is always present in a document; if no text is selected, it represents the insertion point. Unlike the Range object, there can only be one Selection object at a time. You can use the Selection object's Type property to get information about the state of the current selection. For example, if there is no current selection, the Selection object's Type property returns wdSelectionIP. The Type property will return one of nine different values represented by the wdSelectionType enumerated constants.

You access a Selection object by using the Selection property. This property is available from the Application, Window, and Pane objects. However, because the Selection property is global, you can refer to it without referencing another object first. For example, the following sample code illustrates how you use the Selection property to get information about the currently selected text:

```
Sub SelectionCurrentInfo()
    Dim strMessage As String
```

```
With Selection
    If .Characters.Count > 1 Then
        strMessage = "The Selection object in '" & ActiveDocument.Name _
            & "' contains " & .Characters.Count & " characters, " _
            & .Words.Count & " words, " & .Sentences.Count _
            & " sentences, and " & .Paragraphs.Count _
            & " paragraphs."
        MsgBox strMessage
    End If
End With
End Sub
```

The Selection Object vs. the Range Object

In many ways, the Selection object is similar to a Range object. The Selection object represents an arbitrary portion of a document. It has properties that represent characters, words, sentences, paragraphs, and other objects in a Word document. The main difference is that when you use the Range object, it's not necessary to first select the text. In addition, there can only be one Selection object at a time, but the number of Range objects you can create is unlimited.

The Selection object and the Range object have many common methods and properties, and it is easy to return a Range object from a Selection object or to create a Selection object from a Range object. However, most things you can do with a Selection object, you can do even faster with a Range object. There are two main reasons for this:

- The Range object typically requires fewer lines of code to accomplish a task.

- Manipulating a Range object does not incur the overhead associated with Word having to move or change the selection "highlight" in the active document.

In addition, you can do much more with a Range object than you can with a Selection object:

- You can manipulate a Range object without changing what the user has selected in the document. Practically speaking, you could save the original selection by using a Range object variable, manipulate the Selection object programmatically, and then use the saved Range object's Select method to display the original selection, but there is rarely a good reason to show the user that the selection is changing. Some WordBasic developers relied on changing the selection to indicate to the user that the code is still running (and the machine has not locked up). But this is not the right way to convey information to a user. An operation that takes a long time to execute should signal its progress by using a progress meter or by posting status messages to the status bar.

- You can maintain multiple Range objects in your code, and, where necessary, store those objects in a custom Collection object. You cannot do these two things by using only the Selection object.

When it comes to manipulating text, the Selection and Range objects have many methods and properties in common—for example, all the InsertName methods and the Text property discussed in "Working with Text in a Range Object". However, the Selection object has a unique set of methods for manipulating text. These are the TypeText, TypeParagraph, and TypeBackspace methods. You use these methods to enter or remove text and insert paragraph marks in a Selection object. To get the results you expect, there are a few things you must understand about the TypeName methods.

With the exception of the InsertParagraph and InsertFile methods, which remove selected text, the InsertName methods let you work with a selection without deleting existing text. In contrast, the TypeName methods might delete existing text, depending on the value of the Options object's ReplaceSelection property.

When the ReplaceSelection property is True, using any of the TypeName methods results in the currently selected text being replaced. When the ReplaceSelection property is False, the TypeText and TypeParagraph methods behave just as the InsertBefore method: The text or paragraph mark is inserted at the beginning of the current selection. When the ReplaceSelection property is False, the TypeBackspace method behaves the same as the Collapse method of a Range or Selection object when the wdCollapseStart constant is specified in the Direction argument. The Collapse method collapses a range or selection so that its starting point and ending point are the same.

Working with Bookmarks

In many ways, a Bookmark object is similar to a Selection or Range object in that it represents a contiguous area in a document. It has a starting position and an ending position, and it can be as small as the insertion point or as large as the entire document. However, a Bookmark object differs from a Selection or Range object because you can give the Bookmark object a name and it does not go away when your code stops running or when the document is closed. In addition, although bookmarks are normally hidden, you can make them visible by setting the View object's ShowBookmarks property to True.

You use bookmarks to mark a location in a document or as a container for text in a document. The following examples illustrate these uses:

- You could use bookmarks to mark areas in a document that will contain data supplied by the user or obtained from an outside data source. For example, a business letter template might have bookmarks marking the locations for name and address information. Your VBA code could obtain the data from the user or from a database and then insert it in the correct locations marked by bookmarks. When a location is marked, navigating to that location is as simple as navigating to the bookmark. You can determine if a document contains a specific bookmark by using the Bookmarks collection's Exists method. You display a location marked by a bookmark by using the Bookmark object's Select method. When a bookmark is selected, the Selection object and the Bookmark object represent the same location in the document.

- If you have a document that contains boilerplate text that you must modify in certain circumstances, you could use VBA code to insert different text in these specified locations depending on whether certain conditions were met. You can use a Bookmark object's Range property to create a Range object, and then use the Range object's InsertBefore method, InsertAfter method, or Text property to add or modify the text within a bookmark.

When you understand the subtleties associated with adding or changing text through VBA code, working with bookmarks can be a powerful way to enhance your custom applications created in Word.

You add a bookmark by using the Bookmarks collection's Add method. You specify where you want the bookmark to be located by specifying a Range or Selection object in the Add method's Range argument. When you use the InsertBefore method, the InsertAfter method, or the Text property, a Range object automatically expands to incorporate the new text. As you will see in the next few examples, a bookmark does not adjust itself as easily, but making a bookmark as dynamic as a range is a simple exercise.

When you use the Range object's InsertBefore method to add text to a bookmark, the text is added to the start of the bookmark and the bookmark expands to include the new text. For example, if you had a bookmark named CustomerAddress on the following text (the brackets appear when the ShowBookmarks property is set to True)

[Seattle, WA 12345]

you could add the street address to this bookmark by using the following VBA code:

```
Dim rngRange As Word.Range


Set rngRange = ActiveDocument.Bookmarks("CustomerAddress").Range
rngRange.InsertBefore "1234 Elm Drive #233" & vbCrLf
```

As you might expect, the bookmark expands to include the additional address information:

[1234 Elm Drive #233
Seattle, WA 12345]

Now suppose you want to use the InsertAfter method to add text to the end of a bookmark that contains the street address, and you want to add the city, state, and zip code information by using this code:

```
Dim rngRange As Word.Range


Set rngRange = ActiveDocument.Bookmarks("CustomerAddress").Range
rngRange.InsertAfter vbCrLf & "Seattle, WA 12345"
```

Note that when you use the InsertAfter method to add text to the end of a bookmark, the bookmark does not automatically expand to include the new text:

[1234 Elm Drive #233]
Seattle, WA 12345

This behavior could create problems if you were unaware of it. But now you are aware of it, and the solution is quite easy. The first part of the solution results from the benefits achieved when you use the Selection and Range objects together. The second part results from another aspect of bookmarks that you must know: When you add a bookmark to a document in which the bookmark already exists, the original bookmark is deleted (but not the text it contained) when the new bookmark is created.

The following sample code uses the InsertAfter method to add text to the end of the CustomerAddress bookmark. It then uses the Range object's Select method to create a Selection object covering all the text you want to bookmark. Finally, it uses the Bookmarks collection's Add method to add a new bookmark that has the same name as the original bookmark and then uses the Selection object's Range property to specify the location of the bookmark:

```
Dim rngRange As Word.Range


Set rngRange = ActiveDocument.Bookmarks("CustomerAddress").Range
With rngRange
    .InsertAfter vbCrLf & "Seattle, WA 12345"
    .Select
End With
ActiveDocument.Bookmarks.Add "CustomerAddress", Selection.Range
```

If you use the Range object's Text property to replace the entire contents of a bookmark, you run into a similar problem: The text in the bookmark is replaced, but in the process, the bookmark itself is deleted. The solution to this problem is the same solution we used for the InsertAfter method in the preceding example. You insert the new text, use the Range object's Select method to select the text, and then create a new bookmark that has the same name as the original bookmark.

The Find and Replacement Objects

Among the most frequently used commands in the Word user interface are the Find and Replace commands on the Edit menu. These commands let you specify the criteria for what you want to locate. They are both really the same thing, with the Replace command's functionality being just an extension of the Find command's functionality. In fact, you might have noticed that Find, Replace, and Go To appear on different tabs of the same dialog box—the Find and Replace dialog box.

Much of the VBA code you write in Word involves finding or replacing something in a document. There are several techniques you can use to locate text or other elements in a document, for example, using the GoTo method or the Select method. Typically, you use the Find object to loop through a document looking for some specific text, formatting, or style. To specify what you want to use to replace the item you found, you use the Replacement object, which you can access by using the Replacement property of the Find object.

The Find object is available from both the Selection object and the Range object; however, it behaves differently depending on whether it is used from the Selection object or the Range object. Searching for text by using the Find object is one of those situations where the Selection and Range objects can be used together to accomplish more than either object can its own.

The following list describes differences between the behavior of the Range object and the Selection object when you are searching for an item in a document:

- When you are using the Selection object, your search criteria are applied only against the currently selected text.

- When you are using the Selection object, if an item matching the search criteria is found, the selection changes to highlight the found item, as illustrated by the following example, which uses the Find object to search within the currently selected text:

```
With Selection.Find
    .ClearFormatting
    strFindText = InputBox("Enter the text you want to find.", _
        "Find Text")
    If Len(strFindText) = 0 Then Exit Sub
    .Text = strFindText
    If .Execute = True Then
        MsgBox "'" & Selection.Text & "'" _
            & " was found and is now highlighted."
    Else
        MsgBox "The text could not be located."
    End If
End With
```

- When you are using the Find object off of the Range object, the definition of the Range object changes when an item matching the search criteria is found. Failing to account for this change in the definition of the Range object can cause all kinds of debugging headaches. The following code sample illustrates how the Range object is redefined:

```
Dim rngText      As Word.Range
Dim strToFind    As String

Set rngText = ActiveDocument.Paragraphs(3).Range
With rngText.Find
    .ClearFormatting
    strToFind = InputBox("Enter the text you want to find.", _
        "Find Text")
    If Len(strToFind) = 0 Then Exit Sub
    .Text = strToFind
    If .Execute = True Then
        MsgBox "'" & strToFind & "'" & " was found. " _
            & "As a result, the Range object has been " _
            & "redefined and now covers the text: " _
            & rngText.Text
```

```
    Else
        MsgBox "The text could not be located."
    End If
End With
```

Regardless of whether you are using the Find object with the Range object or the Selection object, you must account for the changes that occur to the object when the search is successful. Because the object itself might point to different text each time the search is successful, you might have to account for this and you might also have to keep track of your original object so that you can return to it when the search has been completed.

Specifying and Clearing Search Criteria

You specify the criteria for a search by setting properties of the Find object. There are two ways to set these properties. You can set individual properties of the Find object and then use the Execute method without arguments. You can also set the properties of the Find object by using the arguments of the Execute method. The following two examples execute identical searches:

```
' Example 1: Using properties to specify search criteria.
With Selection.Find
    .ClearFormatting
    .Forward = True
    .Wrap = wdFindContinue
    .Text = strToFind
    .Execute
End With


' Example 2: Using Execute method arguments to specify search criteria.
With Selection.Find
    .ClearFormatting
    .Execute FindText:=strToFind, _
        Forward:=True, Wrap:=wdFindContinue
End With
```

The Find object's search criteria are cumulative, which means that unless you clear out the criteria from a previous search, new criteria are added to the criteria used in the previous search. You should get in the habit of always using the ClearFormatting method to remove formatting from the criteria from a previous search before specifying the criteria for a new search. The Find object and the Replacement object each has its own ClearFormatting method. When you are performing a find and replace operation, you must use the ClearFormatting method of both objects, as illustrated in the following example:

```
With Selection.Find
    .ClearFormatting
    .Text = strToFind
    With .Replacement
        .ClearFormatting
        .Text = strReplaceWith
    End With
    .Execute Replace:=wdReplaceAll
End With
```

Finding All Instances of the Search Criteria

When you use the Execute method as shown in the preceding examples, the search stops at the first item that matches the specified criteria. To locate all items that match the specified criteria, use the Execute method inside a loop, as shown in the following example:

```
Public Sub SearchAndReturnExample()
    ' This procedure shows how to use the Execute method inside
    ' a loop to locate multiple instances of specified text.
    Dim rngOriginalSelection    As Word.Range
    Dim colFoundItems           As New Collection
    Dim rngCurrent              As Word.Range
    Dim strSearchFor            As String
    Dim intFindCounter          As Integer

    If (Selection.Words.Count > 1) = True Or _
            (Selection.Type = wdSelectionIP) = True Then
        MsgBox "Please select a single word or part or a word. " _
            & "This procedure will search the active document for " _
            & "additional instances of the selected text."
            Exit Sub
    End If

    Set rngOriginalSelection = Selection.Range
    strSearchFor = Selection.Text

    ' Call custom procedure that moves the insertion point to the
    ' start of the document.
    Call GoToStartOfDoc
```

```
With Selection.Find
    .ClearFormatting
    .Forward = True
    .Wrap = wdFindContinue
    .Text = strSearchFor
    .Execute
    Do While .Found = True
        intFindCounter = intFindCounter + 1
        colFoundItems.Add Selection.Range, CStr(intFindCounter)
        .Execute
    Loop
End With

rngOriginalSelection.Select

If MsgBox("There are " & intFindCounter & " instances of '" _
        & rngOriginalSelection & "' in this document." & vbCrLf & vbCrLf _

        & "Would you like to loop through and display all instances?", _
        vbYesNo) = vbYes Then
    intFindCounter = 1
    For Each rngCurrent In colFoundItems
        rngCurrent.Select
        MsgBox "This is instance #" & intFindCounter
        intFindCounter = intFindCounter + 1
    Next rngCurrent
End If

    rngOriginalSelection.Select
End Sub
```

The preceding example also illustrates how to use a Collection object to store the matching items as Range objects. In this example, the user is given the option of viewing all matching items, but you could use the same technique to work with the found items as a group.

Replacing Text or Other Items

To replace one item with another, you must specify a setting for the Replace argument of the Execute method. You can specify the replacement item by using either the Text property of the

Replacement object or the ReplaceWith argument of the Execute method. To delete an item by using this technique, use a zero-length string ("") as the replacement item. The following example replaces all instances of the text specified by the strFind argument with the text specified in the strReplace argument:

```
Sub ReplaceText(strFind As String, _
                strReplace As String)
   Application.ScreenUpdating = False
   ActiveDocument.Content.Select
   With Selection.Find
      .ClearFormatting
      .Forward = True
      .Wrap = wdFindContinue
      .Execute FindText:=strFind, _
         Replace:=wdReplaceAll, ReplaceWith:=strReplace
   End With
End Sub
```

Restoring the User's Selection After a Search

In most cases, when you finish a search operation, you should return the selection (or the insertion point if there was no previous selection) to where it was when the search began. You do this by saving the state of the Selection object before you begin a search, and then restoring it when the search is completed, as shown in the following example:

```
Sub SimpleRestoreSelectionExample()
   Dim rngStartMarker      As Word.Range
   Dim strToFind           As String

   Set rngStartMarker = Selection.Range
   strToFind = InputBox("Enter the text to find.", "Find Text")
   With Selection.Find
      .ClearFormatting
      .Text = strToFind
      If .Execute = True Then
         MsgBox "'" & strToFind & "'" & " was found and is " _
            & "currently highlighted. Click OK to restore your " _
            & "original selection."
```

```
        Else
            MsgBox "'" & strToFind & "'" & " was not found."
        End If
    End With
    rngStartMarker.Select
End Sub
```

Working with Shared Office Components

Microsoft® Office includes a set of shared objects available in all Office applications that help you search for files, use the Office Assistant, manipulate command bars, read and write document properties, read and write script, and hook add-ins to your Office application. Because these objects are shared among all Office applications, it is easy to write code that uses these objects and that will run without modification from within any Office application or custom Office application.

You can use these objects to customize the appearance of your application, create custom toolbars and menu bars in code, perform custom file searches, or customize the Office Assistant to respond to the user's actions.

In This Section

Referencing Shared Office Components
Return a reference to a shared component object by using the appropriate properties.

Working with the FileSearch Object
Programmatically access the functionality of the Office File Open dialog box.

Working with the Office Assistant
Use the objects, methods, and properties of the Office Assistant object to programmatically control the Office Assistant.

Working with Command Bars
Write code to manipulate command bars that can be used in any Microsoft® Office application or custom application you develop.

Working with Document Properties
Use document properties to create, maintain, and track information about a Microsoft® Office document.

Working with Scripts
Access script, or insert script into a cell or range in a Microsoft® Excel worksheet, a Microsoft® PowerPoint® slide, a Microsoft® Word document, or Word Selection object.

Referencing Shared Office Components

Every Microsoft® Office application includes accessor properties that provide access to the shared Office components. For example, an Office application's Assistant property returns a reference to the Assistant object, the FileSearch property returns a reference to the FileSearch object, and the Scripts property returns a reference to the Scripts collection. From within any Office application, you can return a reference to a shared component object by using the appropriate accessor property; you do not have to use the New keyword to create an object variable that references the shared Office component.

> **Note** All Office applications, except Microsoft® Access, Microsoft® FrontPage®, and Microsoft® Outlook®, include a reference to the Microsoft Office XP object library by default. Before you can work with shared Office components in Access, FrontPage, or Outlook, you must first manually set a reference to the Microsoft Office XP object library.

As with any object model, before you can work with an object, you must either set an object variable to the object you want to work with or use the host application's accessor property. For example, the following code fragments illustrate using the accessor property (in these cases, the FileSearch, Assistant, and CommandBars accessor properties are used) to access various shared Office components.

```
With Application.FileSearch
    .NewSearch
    .LookIn = "C:\My Documents"
    .FileName = "*.doc"
    If .Execute() > 0 Then
        ' Work with found files here.
    End If
End With


Dim objAssistant As Assistant


Set objAssistant = Application.Assistant


With objAssistant
    .On = True
    .Visible = True
    .Animation = msoAnimationCharacterSuccessMajor
End With


Dim cbrCustomBar As CommandBar
```

```
Set cbrCustomBar = Application.CommandBars(strCBName)

With cbrCustomBar.Controls(strCtlName)
    .Enabled = Not .Enabled
End With
```

> **Note**   To set a reference to a shared Office component from outside an Office application, you must still use the accessor property of an Office application. For example, to set a reference to the FileSearch object from a Microsoft® Visual Basic® application, you could set a reference to the Microsoft® Word Application object and then use the Word FileSearch property to return a reference to the FileSearch object. For example:

```
Dim wdApp As Word.Application

Set wdApp = New Word.Application

With wdApp.FileSearch
```

Working with the FileSearch Object

The FileSearch object exposes a programmatic interface to all the functionality of the Office File Open dialog box, including the features found in the Advanced Find dialog box, which is available from the Open dialog box. You can use the objects, methods, and properties of the FileSearch object to search for files or collections of files based on criteria you supply.

> **Note**   If Microsoft Fast Find is enabled, the FileSearch object can use Fast Find indexes to speed up its searching capabilities.

In This Section

The Basics of File Searching
   Understand the methods and properties of file searching.

Using Advanced File-Searching Features
   Learn about some more complex file-searching features.

Creating Reusable File-Search Code
   Learn why the FileSearch object is a great candidate for encapsulation in a class module.

The Basics of File Searching

The following code fragment illustrates how to use an application's FileSearch property to return a reference to the FileSearch object. Because the FileSearch object is shared among all Microsoft® Office applications, this code will work without modification from within any Office application:

```
Function FindFile(strFileSpec As String)
    Dim fsoFileSearch As FileSearch
```

```
    Set fsoFileSearch = Application.FileSearch
    With fsoFileSearch
        .NewSearch
        .LookIn = "c:\"
        .FileName = strFileSpec
        .SearchSubFolders = False
        If .Execute() > 0 Then
            For Each varFile In .FoundFiles
                strFileList = strFileList & varFile & vbCrLf
            Next varFile
        End If
    End With
    MsgBox strFileList




End Function
```

The FileSearch object has two methods and several properties you can use to build custom file-searching functionality into your custom Office applications. The previous example uses the NewSearch method to clear any previous search criteria and the Execute method to carry out the search for the specified files. The Execute method returns the number of files found, and also supports optional parameters that make it possible for you specify the sort order, the sort type, and whether to use only saved Fast Find indexes to perform the search. You use the FoundFiles property to return a reference to the FoundFiles object that contains the names of all matching files found in your search.

> **Note**   You must use the NewSearch method to clear any search criteria from previous searches; otherwise, the new search criteria will be added to the existing search criteria.

You use the LookIn property to specify what directory to begin searching in and the SearchSubFolders property to specify whether the search should extend to subfolders of the directory specified in the LookIn property. The FileName property supports wildcard characters and a semicolon-delimited list of file names or file-type specifications.

For more information about using the methods and properties of the FileSearch object, search the Microsoft Office Visual Basic Reference Help index for "FileSearch object."

Using Advanced File-Searching Features

You get programmatic access to the advanced features of the FileSearch object by using its PropertyTests collection. These features correspond to the options available in the Advanced Find dialog box, which is available through the Office File Open dialog box.

The Advanced Find Dialog Box

The PropertyTests collection contains the criteria for a file search. Some of these criteria might have been specified by properties of the FileSearch object itself while others must be added to the PropertyTests collection by using its Add method.

In the following example, one of the file-search criteria added to the PropertyTests collection corresponds to the Contents setting in the Property box and another corresponds to the includes words setting in the Condition box in the preceding figure.

```
Set fsoFileSearch = Application.FileSearch
With fsoFileSearch
    .NewSearch
    .FileName = strFileName
    .LookIn = strLookIn
    .SearchSubFolders = blnSearchSubDir
    .PropertyTests.Add "Contents", msoConditionIncludes, strFindThisText
    If .Execute(msoSortByFileName, msoSortOrderAscending, True) > 0 Then
        For Each varFile In .FoundFiles
            cboFoundCombo.AddItem varFile
        Next varFile
```

```
Else
    cboFoundCombo.AddItem "No Matching Files Located!"
End If
cboFoundCombo.ListIndex = 0
End With
```

Creating Reusable File-Search Code

Searching for files is something you might do repeatedly in any number of different Office applications. This makes the FileSearch object a great candidate for encapsulation in a class module that could be used in any Microsoft® Office application that requires file-searching capabilities.

Dialog Box Used to Gather Custom Search Criteria

The Find Office Files dialog box is shown immediately after executing a search for files with an ".xls" extension in the "c:\my documents" directory. Code behind the Find Matching Files command button uses a global variable named objFileInfo to call the GetFileList method of the custom clsGetFileInfo class as follows:

```
Sub UpdateFileList()
    ' If the file-search specifications are valid, update
    ' the files contained in the form's combo box with a current
    ' list of matching files.
```

```
Dim varFoundFiles      As Variant
Dim varFile            As Variant


varFoundFiles = objFileInfo.GetFileList


If IsArray(varFoundFiles) Then
    With Me
        .cboMatchingFiles.Clear
        For Each varFile In varFoundFiles
            .cboMatchingFiles.AddItem varFile
        Next varFile
        .cboMatchingFiles.ListIndex = 0
        .lblFilesFound.Caption = CStr(objFileInfo.MatchingFilesFound) _
            & " Matching Files Found:"
    End With
Else
    MsgBox "No files matched the specification: '" & Me.txtFileSpec &
"'"

    End If
End Sub
```

The class contains several properties used to set the properties of the FileSearch object. It also exposes the GetFileList method that returns an array containing all files that match the specified criteria.

```
Public Function GetFileList() As Variant
    ' This function returns an array of files that match the criteria
    ' specified by the SearchPath and SearchName properties. If the
    ' SearchSubDirs property is set to True, the search includes
    ' subdirectories of SearchPath.

    Dim intFoundFiles      As Integer
    Dim astrFiles()        As String
    Dim fsoFileSearch      As FileSearch

    Set fsoFileSearch = Application.FileSearch
    With fsoFileSearch
        .NewSearch
        .LookIn = p_strPath
```

```
        .FileName = p_strName
        .FileType = msoFileTypeAllFiles
        .SearchSubFolders = p_blnSearchSubs

    If .Execute(p_intSortBy, p_intSortOrder) > 0 Then
        p_intFoundFiles = .FoundFiles.Count
        ReDim astrFiles(1 To .FoundFiles.Count)
            For intFoundFiles = 1 To .FoundFiles.Count
                astrFiles(intFoundFiles) = .FoundFiles(intFoundFiles)
            Next intFoundFiles
            GetFileList = astrFiles
    Else
        GetFileList = ""
    End If
  End With
End Function
```

Working with the Office Assistant

You can use the Office Assistant to animate characters that interact with your users, provide context-sensitive help, highlight parts of your user interface, collect information from users, or otherwise provide a "social" interface to your application that many users find interesting and fun to use. The Office Assistant character is drawn onscreen without an enclosing window that can interact with other elements of the application interface, pointing out controls or directing the user's attention to specific sections of a document.

You use the objects, methods, and properties of the Assistant object to programmatically control the Office Assistant, the Office Assistant balloon, and all the items inside the balloon.

In This Section

Microsoft Agent ActiveX Control vs. the Office Assistant
    Learn when to use features of the Agent that are available only through the control.

Programming the Office Assistant
    Make the Assistant visible, move it to different locations on the screen, specify the animation you want to run, and display Assistant balloons containing text and controls.

Working with Balloon Objects
    Use the Office Assistant Balloon object to enables the Assistant to communicate with and get feedback from users.

Using Balloon Controls
>Understand how to use Balloon controls.

Modeless Balloons and the Callback Property
>Create a modeless balloon, and set its Callback property.

Microsoft Agent ActiveX Control vs. the Office Assistant

The Office Assistant is based on the Microsoft Agent ActiveX control. Many of the Agent control's methods and properties are exposed through the Assistant's object model. You can use the Agent control in Microsoft® Office applications, on Web pages, or in any environment that supports Microsoft® ActiveX® controls.

There are some circumstances where you would use the Agent control instead of the Assistant object to provide Office Assistant services:

You want to use features of the Agent that are available only through the control—for example, the Agent's speech-recognition capabilities.

You want to use the Agent control in an Office application where the Assistant object is not available. For example, if you have an Access run-time application on a machine that does not have Office installed, you can use the Agent control to provide the full range of Assistant services without accessing the Assistant's object model.

You want to use the Agent to provide Assistant-like services on a Web page. The Agent control is added to HTML pages by using the <OBJECT> tag and is manipulated by using script.

Programming the Office Assistant

Programming the Assistant is a matter of setting an object variable to the Assistant object and then accessing the properties and methods you must have to make the assistant do what you want. You can make the Assistant visible, move it to different locations on the screen, specify the animation you want to run, and display Assistant balloons containing text and controls.

One important thing to remember when you programmatically manipulate the properties of the Assistant is that the user might have set various Assistant properties that you should preserve. Any time you manipulate the Assistant, you should save the properties that existed before you began and then restore those properties when you are finished. For example, if the user normally has the Assistant turned off and you programmatically turn it on to perform some task, you should make sure you turn it off when you are finished using it.

In previous versions of Microsoft® Office, the Assistant is either visible and available or not visible and unavailable, but the Assistant can never be completely turned off. In Office XP, the Assistant has an On property that affects whether the Assistant is available at all.

You use the Assistant's On and Visible properties to determine its initial state. When the On property is set to False, the Visible property is False and any attempt to programmatically manipulate the Assistant (except for a call to the Assistant's Help method) is ignored and no error is raised. When the On property is set to True, the Assistant will be either visible or hidden depending on the Visible property's setting.

Note When the On property's value is changed from False to True, the Visible property is set to True.

The following example demonstrates how to save the initial settings for the On and Visible properties, how to make the Assistant visible, and a simple animation technique:

```
Sub SimpleAnimation()
    ' This procedure shows simple Assistant animation
    ' techniques. It calls the Wait procedure between
    ' animations to give the animation time to complete.

    Dim blnAssistantVisible    As Boolean
    Dim blnAssistantOn         As Boolean

    With Application.Assistant
       blnAssistantOn = .On
       blnAssistantVisible = .Visible

       If Not blnAssistantOn Then
          .On = True
       ElseIf Not blnAssistantVisible Then
          .Visible = True
       End If
       .Animation = msoAnimationCheckingSomething
       Call Wait(5000)
       .Animation = msoAnimationEmptyTrash
       Call Wait(7000)
       .Animation = msoAnimationCharacterSuccessMajor
       Call Wait(5000)
       If (Not blnAssistantOn) Or (Not blnAssistantVisible) Then
          .On = blnAssistantOn
          .Visible = blnAssistantVisible
       End If
    End With
End Sub
```

Note The Wait procedure used in the previous example is a subroutine that uses a custom class object to wait the number of milliseconds specified in the procedure's argument. When you are stringing Assistant animations together, this procedure is required to give one animation time to finish before another animation begins.

The Assistant's FileName property specifies the animated character that is displayed when the Assistant is visible. Character files use an ".acs" extension, and several characters are supplied with Office. In addition, you can create your own character files by using the Microsoft Agent ActiveX control's character editor.

Characters you create should be stored in the host application's folder or in the C:\Windows\Application Data\Microsoft\Office\Actors subfolder; if multiple users work on the same machine and user profiles have been set up on the machine, store your characters in the host application's folder or in the C:\Windows\Profiles*UserName*\Application Data\Microsoft\Office\Actors subfolder. For more information about setting up user profiles, search the Microsoft® Windows® Help index for "user profiles."

You specify which character is displayed by setting the Assistant's FileName property to the name of the .acs file for the character you want to use. For example, the following procedure changes the character to the name of the character specified in the strCharName argument:

```
Function ChangeCharacter(strCharName As String) As Integer
    ' This procedure changes the existing Assistant
    ' character to the character specified in the
    ' strCharName argument. The procedure's return
    ' values are set by using constants defined in the
    ' Declarations section of this module.

    With Application.Assistant
        If UCase(.FileName) = UCase(strCharName) Then
            ChangeCharacter = ASST_CHAR_SAMECHAR
            Exit Function
        End If
        .FileName = strCharName
        ChangeCharacter = ASST_CHAR_CHANGED
    End With
End Function
```

Note If you are using a character supplied by Office, you are not required to include the full path to the .acs file you want to use. When you set the FileName property, Visual Basic for Applications (VBA) will look for the file in the host application's folder and then in the C:\Windows\Application Data\Microsoft\Office\Actors subfolder and, if it exists, in the C:\Windows\Profiles*UserName*\Application Data\Microsoft\Office\Actors subfolder. If your character files are located somewhere other than the three locations discussed here, you must set the FileName property by using the full path to the file. If the file cannot be found, a message is displayed. If the user clicks OK, the same file-search sequence is executed again. If the user clicks Cancel, the attempt to change the FileName property is ignored and no error occurs.

Working with Balloon Objects

The Assistant's Balloon object enables the Assistant to communicate with and get feedback from your users. Balloon objects are designed to make it possible for you create a simple interface for user interaction. They are not designed to replace complex dialog boxes.

Balloon objects can contain text that can be plain, underlined, or displayed in different colors. In addition, Balloon objects can contain labels or check boxes, certain icons, and bitmaps. Only one Balloon object can be visible at a time, but you can create multiple Balloon objects in code and use them when required.

You create a Balloon object by using the Assistant's NewBalloon property. When you have created the new Balloon object, you can set its properties and then display it by using the Balloon object's Show method. The following two simple procedures illustrate many of the features of Balloon objects discussed so far. The TestCreateSimpleBalloon procedure creates two formatted strings used to specify the balloon Heading and Text properties. The procedure then creates the balSimple Balloon object by calling the CreateSimpleBalloon procedure and passing in the heading and text strings. CreateSimpleBalloon sets several other "default" properties for this balloon and then returns the new Balloon object to the calling procedure where it is displayed by using the Show method.

```
Sub TestCreateSimpleBalloon()
    Dim balSimple          As Balloon
    Dim strMessage         As String
    Dim strHeading         As String
    Dim blnAssistVisible   As Boolean

    strHeading = "This is a simple balloon."
    strMessage = "When you have finished reading this message, click OK to
proceed." _
        & vbCrLf & "{cf 249}This text is red." & vbCrLf & "{cf 252}This
text is blue." _
        & vbCrLf & "{cf 0}This text has a {ul 1}word{ul 0} that is
underlined." _
        & vbCrLf & "This text is plain."
    blnAssistVisible = Application.Assistant.Visible

    Set balSimple = CreateSimpleBalloon(strMessage, strHeading)
```

```
    If Not blnAssistVisible Then
        Call ShowAssistant
    End If
    With balSimple
        .Show
    End With
    Application.Assistant.Visible = blnAssistVisible
End Sub


Function CreateSimpleBalloon(strText As String, _
                                strHeading As String) As Office.Balloon


    Dim balBalloon As Balloon

    With Application.Assistant
        Set balBalloon = .NewBalloon
        With balBalloon
            .BalloonType = msoBalloonTypeButtons
            .Button = msoButtonSetOK
            .Heading = strHeading
            .Icon = msoIconTip
            .Mode = msoModeModal
            .Text = strText
        End With
        Set CreateSimpleBalloon = balBalloon
    End With
End Function
```

Note that the strMessage variable contains a string that includes embedded brackets such as {cf 252}, {cf 0}, {ul 1}, and {ul 0}. You use the {cf *value*} brackets to specify the color of the text that follows the bracket. You use the {ul *value*} brackets to specify where text underlining begins and ends. For more information about specifying text color and underlining text in Balloon objects, search the Microsoft® Office Visual Basic Reference Help index for "Text property."

If you run the sample code, you will notice that the code stops executing while the Balloon object is displayed. This is because the balloon's Mode property specifies that the balloon is modal. In addition, you can display modeless Balloon objects.

Using Balloon Controls

You add labels or check box controls to a Balloon object by using the Balloon object's Labels or Checkboxes property, respectively. (Note that label controls in Balloon objects are similar to option button controls.) You specify the text associated with a label or check box by using the control's Text property. You specify a single control by using an index number between 1 and 5, which represents the number of the label or check box control in the balloon. For example, the following sample shows one way to use label controls in a Balloon object:

```
With balBalloon
    .Button = msoButtonSetNone
    .Heading = "Balloon Object Example One"
    .Labels(1).Text = "VBA is a powerful programming language."
    .Labels(2).Text = "Office is a great development environment."
    .Labels(3).Text = "The Assistant is cool!"
    .Labels(4).Text = "Balloon objects are easy to use."
    .Text = "Select one of the following "_
        & .Labels.Count & "Options:"


    ' Show the balloon.
    intRetVal = .Show


    ' Save the selection made by the user.
    If intRetVal > 0 Then
        strChoice = "{cf 4}" & .Labels(intRetVal).Text & "{cf 0}"
    Else
        strChoice = ""
    End If
End With


Set balBalloon = Assistant.NewBalloon
With balBalloon
    .Text = "You selected option " & CStr(intRetVal) & ": '" _
        & strChoice & "'"
    .Show
End With
```

Note that when the balloon is displaying label controls, you are not required to have OK or Cancel buttons, because the balloon is dismissed as soon as any label control is selected, and the user can select only one control at a time. This is not the case when you use check box controls. The user can select more than one check box before dismissing the balloon, so your code should account for multiple selections. The next example shows one way to display check box controls and then identify the selections made by the user:

```
With balBalloon
    .Button = msoButtonSetOK
    .Heading = "Balloon Object Example Two"
    .Checkboxes(1).Text = "VBA is a powerful programming language."
    .Checkboxes(2).Text = "Office is a great development environment."
    .Checkboxes(3).Text = "The Assistant is cool!"
    .Checkboxes(4).Text = "Balloon objects are easy to use."
    .Text = "How many of the following " _
        & .Checkboxes.Count & " statements do you agree with?"
    ' Save the selection made by the user.
    intRetVal = .Show
    ' Construct the string to display to the user based on the
    ' user's selections.
    For Each chkBox In .Checkboxes
        If chkBox.Checked = True Then
            strChoice = strChoice & "{cf 4}" & chkBox.Text & "{cf 0}" & "'
and '"
        End If
    Next chkBox
    ' Remove the trailing "' and '" from strChoice.
    If Len(strChoice) <> 0 Then
        strChoice = Left(strChoice, Len(strChoice) - 7)
    End If
End With

' Create new Balloon object and display the user's choices.
Set balBalloon = Assistant.NewBalloon
With balBalloon
    If intRetVal > 0 Or Len(strChoice) > 0 Then
        .Text = "You selected '" & strChoice & "'."
```

```
    Else
        .Text = "You didn't make a selection."
    End If
    .Show
End With
```

Modeless Balloons and the Callback Property

When you display a modeless balloon, the user is able to use your application while the balloon is displayed. You specify that a balloon is modeless by setting the Mode property to the built-in constant msoModeModeless.

When you create a modeless balloon you must also set its Button property to something other than msoButtonSetNone and its Callback property to the name of a procedure to call when the user clicks a button in the modeless balloon. The procedure named in the Callback property must accept three arguments: a Balloon object, a long integer representing the button selected (msoBalloonButtonType values or a number representing the button clicked when the BalloonType property is set to msoBalloonTypeButtons), and a long integer representing the Balloon object's Private property.

You use the Private property to assign a value to a Balloon object that uniquely identifies it to the procedure named in the Callback property. You could use this property in a single generic callback procedure that is called from multiple modeless balloons. For example, in the following code, the sample contains a five-step tour of a Northwind Company spreadsheet that uses a collection of modeless balloons representing each step in the tour. All five Balloon objects name the BalloonCallBackProc procedure in their Callback property setting. Each Balloon object uses a unique value in its Private property setting, and the BalloonCallBackProc procedure uses this value and the value of the button clicked by the user (lngBtnRetVal) to identify which balloon has called the procedure and which button was clicked. The Balloon objects that call this procedure all specify a Private property by using a module-level constant (BALLOON_ONE, BALLOON_TWO, and so on) that indicates in which step of the tour they are called. Each balloon has a Close button and either a Next button, a Back button, or both, depending on the balloon's location in the tour. This single procedure is designed to handle all selections made in all balloons:

```
Function BalloonCallBackProc(balBalloon As Balloon, _
                    lngBtnRetVal As Long, _
                    lngPrivateBalloonID As Long)


    ' This procedure is specified in the Callback property
    ' setting for all five balloons used in the Modeless
    ' Balloon Demo. These balloons are created in the AddBalloon
    ' procedure and stored in the mcolModelessBalloons collection.
```

```
Const BUTTON_BACK As Long = -5
Const BUTTON_NEXT As Long = -6

' Close current balloon.
balBalloon.Close

Select Case lngPrivateBalloonID + lngBtnRetVal
    Case BALLOON_ONE + BUTTON_NEXT
        ' User clicked first balloon, Next button.
        Call ShowModelessBalloon(CStr(BALLOON_TWO))
    Case BALLOON_TWO + BUTTON_NEXT
        Call ShowModelessBalloon(CStr(BALLOON_THREE))
    Case BALLOON_TWO + BUTTON_BACK
        Call ShowModelessBalloon(CStr(BALLOON_ONE))
    Case BALLOON_THREE + BUTTON_NEXT
        Call ShowModelessBalloon(CStr(BALLOON_FOUR))
    Case BALLOON_THREE + BUTTON_BACK
        Call ShowModelessBalloon(CStr(BALLOON_TWO))
    Case BALLOON_FOUR + BUTTON_NEXT
        Call ShowModelessBalloon(CStr(BALLOON_FIVE))
    Case BALLOON_FOUR + BUTTON_BACK
        Call ShowModelessBalloon(CStr(BALLOON_THREE))
    Case BALLOON_FIVE + BUTTON_BACK
        Call ShowModelessBalloon(CStr(BALLOON_FOUR))
    Case Else
        ' User clicked Close button.
        Set mcolModelessBalloons = Nothing
    End Select
End Function
```

This is just one example of the kinds of things you can do with modeless Balloon objects. You have a great deal of flexibility over what you can do with a balloon and a great deal of programmatic control over how your users interact with the balloons you create. You can use the Object Browser to get a complete listing of all the Balloon object's properties and methods. You can use the Microsoft® Office Visual Basic Reference Help index to get more information about these properties and methods.

Working with Command Bars

Microsoft® Office applications all share the same technology for creating menus and toolbars, and this technology is available to you through the command bars object model. In Office applications, there are three kinds of CommandBar objects: toolbars, menu bars, and pop-up menus. Pop-up menus are displayed in three ways: as menus that drop down from menu bars, as submenus that cascade off menu commands, and as shortcut menus. Shortcut menus (also called "right-click menus") are menus that appear when you right-click something.

Because the command bars object model is shared by all Office applications, you can write code to manipulate command bars that can be used in any Office application or custom application you develop. Everything you can do in a host application by using the Customize dialog box you also can do by using Microsoft® Visual Basic® for Applications (VBA) code. In addition, there are some things you can do only by using VBA code.

Understanding how to work with command bars in Office applications requires that you understand not only what they have in common across all applications (the command bars object model) but also how they differ within each application.

In This Section

Understanding Application-Specific Command Bar Information
> Learn how each Microsoft® Office application stores command bar information in a different location and, in some cases, implements command bars in a different way.

Manipulating Command Bars and Command Bar Controls with VBA Code
> Use objects, collections, properties, and methods to show, hide, and modify existing command bars and command bar controls, as well as create new ones.

Understanding Application-Specific Command Bar Information

Despite sharing a common object model, each Microsoft® Office application stores command bar information in a different location and, in some cases, implements command bars in a different way. The primary difference is how and where each Office application stores custom command bars.

> **Note** When you make changes to any of the built-in command bars in an Office application, information about those changes is stored in the Windows registry on a per-user basis. Information about the visibility and location of built-in and custom command bars is stored in the registry as well.

Each Office application stores its command bars either with the Office document that contains the command bars, or in an application-specific file. One important result of this is that command bars cannot be shared between Office documents of different types although they can be shared among documents of the same type. You cannot create a command bar in Microsoft® Word and then copy that command bar to a Microsoft® Access application and use it there.

With the exception of Access, all Office applications store command bar information in specific locations, the path to which depends on whether user profiles have been set up for multiple users on the computer where the command bars are created. For more information about setting up user profiles, search the Microsoft® Windows® Help index for "user profiles."

Microsoft Access Command Bars

The command bars you create in Microsoft® Access are stored with the database in which they are created. If you want to create command bars that are available to more than one database, you must create them in an add-in database and reference that database from each database application where you want the command bars to be available.

Built-in command bars and information about them, for example their visibility and location, is stored in the Windows registry.

The location of information about command bars in an Access database is not dependant upon whether user profiles have been set up for multiple users.

Microsoft Excel Command Bars

Microsoft® Excel makes it possible for you store command bars with an individual workbook or in the Excel workspace. Workspace command bars are saved in a file named Excel.xlb. If user profiles have been set up for multiple users, Excel.xlb is stored in the C:\Windows\Profiles*UserName*\Application Data\Microsoft\Excel subfolder. If user profiles have not been set up, Excel.xlb is stored in the C:\Windows\Application Data\Microsoft\Excel subfolder.

You can copy command bars from the workspace to a workbook by using the Attach Toolbars dialog box (click Attach on the Toolbars tab of the Customize dialog box). You cannot copy command bars to a workbook by using Microsoft® Visual Basic® for Applications (VBA) code. After you have copied a command bar to a workbook, you can delete it from the workspace by clicking Delete on the Toolbars tab of the Customize dialog box or by using the Delete method of the CommandBars collection.

> **Note**   When you open a workbook, Excel copies the workbook's custom command bars that do not already exist in the workspace to the workspace. These copied command bars are not deleted from the workspace when you close your workbook. If you want custom command bars to be available only when your workbook is open, you must programmatically delete them from the workspace when your workbook closes. When you delete a command bar in this fashion, you are removing only the workspace copy, not the workbook copy. The workbook copy will be copied again to the workspace the next time your custom application opens. If you do not delete the workspace copy and the workspace copy of the command bar is modified by the user, the workbook copy will not be recopied to the workspace when your workbook is reopened.

> **Note**   You cannot use VBA to copy a workspace command bar to a workbook or to delete a workbook command bar from a workbook. The only way to delete a custom command bar from a workbook is to use the Delete button in the Attach Toolbars dialog box.

Note If a control on the workspace copy of the command bar calls code that exists in a workbook and the workbook is not open when the control is used, the workbook is immediately opened and made visible.

Command bars that you create to distribute with a custom application should be stored in the application's workbook or template.

Microsoft FrontPage Command Bars

In Microsoft® FrontPage®, you can create custom command bars that will be available in the FrontPage workspace. In other words, custom command bars are generally available and are not linked to a specific FrontPage-based web. FrontPage command bars are saved in a file named CmdUI.PRF. If user profiles have been set up for multiple users, CmdUI.PRF is stored in the C:\Windows\Profiles*UserName*\Application Data\Microsoft\FrontPage\State subfolder. If user profiles have not been set up, CmdUI.PRF is stored in the C:\Windows\Application Data\Microsoft\FrontPage\State subfolder.

Microsoft Outlook Command Bars

In Microsoft® Outlook®, command bars are stored in the Outlook workspace in the Outcmd.dat file. If user profiles have been set up for multiple users, the Outcmd.dat file is stored in the C:\Windows\Profiles*UserName*\Application Data\Microsoft\Outlook subfolder. If user profiles have not been set up, the Outcmd.dat file is stored in the C:\Windows\Application Data\Microsoft\Outlook subfolder.

Microsoft PowerPoint Command Bars

In Microsoft® PowerPoint®, custom command bars are stored only in the application workspace in a file named PPT.pcb. If user profiles have been set up for multiple users, the PPT.pcb file is stored in the C:\Windows\Profiles*UserName*\Application Data\Microsoft\PowerPoint subfolder. If user profiles have not been set up, the PPT.pcb file is stored in the C:\Windows\Application Data\Microsoft\PowerPoint subfolder.

Note Command bars are not visible while a PowerPoint presentation is running. Therefore, changes you make to PowerPoint command bars are limited to those that are available in the design-time environment.

Microsoft Word Command Bars

When you create a command bar in Microsoft® Word, you have the option of storing that command bar in the Normal.dot template, in a separate template, or in the currently active document. If the command bar is stored with the Normal.dot template, it will be available to any document, even if the document is based on a different template. If the command bar is stored with the currently active document and that document is a template, the command bar will be available for any document created based on that template. If the command bar is stored with a document, it will be available only when that document is open.

In Word, custom command bars are stored in the Normal.dot file by default. If user profiles have been set up for multiple users, this file is stored in the C:\Windows\Profiles*UserName*\Application Data\Microsoft\Templates subfolder. If user profiles have not been set up, the Normal.dot file is stored in the C:\Windows\Application Data\Microsoft\Templates subfolder. Command bars created in other documents or in document templates are stored with that document or template.

When you create custom applications based on Word, it is typical to store your code in a custom document template so that the code is available to documents created based on your template. You should also store any custom command bars in the template on which your custom application documents are based. If you must have your command bars available to documents based on more than one template, you can store them in a global template or add-in.

> **Note** It is not a good practice to store your code or command bars in a user's Normal.dot file. Many users or system administrators protect the Normal.dot file from modifications to prevent the file from being infected by a virus or to keep the file from growing to an unreasonable size. Because you can never be sure that Normal.dot will be available for modifications, you should use your own custom template or add-in to distribute your code.

When you create custom command bars in Word by using the Customize dialog box, you specify where the command bar is stored by using the Save In box on the Commands tab of the Customize dialog box. When you create a custom command bar in Word by using Microsoft® Visual Basic® for Applications (VBA) code, you specify where it is stored by using the CustomizationContext property of the Application object.

Manipulating Command Bars and Command Bar Controls with VBA Code

The command bars object model exposes a wealth of objects, collections, properties, and methods that you can use to show, hide, and modify existing command bars and command bar controls, and create new ones. In addition, you can specify a Microsoft® Visual Basic® for Applications (VBA) procedure to run when a user clicks a command bar button or to respond to events triggered by a command bar or command bar control. The following sections provide a broad overview of the kinds of things you can do in your custom Microsoft® Office applications and how to accomplish them.

Note Many of the examples in this section refer to the "Menu Bar" CommandBar object. This is the name of the main menu bar in Microsoft® Word, Microsoft® PowerPoint®, and Microsoft® Access. The main menu bar in Microsoft® Excel is called "Worksheet Menu Bar." To experiment with sample code that refers to the "Menu Bar" CommandBar object in Excel, simply change the reference from "Menu Bar" to "Worksheet Menu Bar."

Getting Information About Command Bars and Controls

Each Microsoft® Office application contains dozens of built-in command bars and can contain as many custom command bars as you choose to add. Each command bar can be one of three types: menu bar, toolbar, or pop-up menu. All of these command bar types can contain additional command bars and any number of controls. To get a good understanding of the command bars object model, it is often best to start by examining the various command bars and controls in an existing application.

You can use the following procedure to print (to the Debug window) information about any command bar and its controls:

```
Function CBPrintCBarInfo(strCBarName As String) As Variant
    ' This procedure prints (to the Debug window) information
    ' about the command bar specified in the strCBarName argument
    ' and information about each control on that command bar.

    Dim cbrBar                      As CommandBar
    Dim ctlCBarControl              As CommandBarControl
    Const ERR_INVALID_CMDBARNAME    As Long = 5

    On Error GoTo CBPrintCBarInfo_Err

    Set cbrBar = Application.CommandBars(strCBarName)

    Debug.Print "CommandBar: " & cbrBar.Name & vbTab & "(" _
        & CBGetCBType(cbrBar) & ")" & vbTab & "(" _
        & IIf(cbrBar.BuiltIn, "Built-in", "Custom") & ")"
    For Each ctlCBarControl In cbrBar.Controls
        Debug.Print vbTab & ctlCBarControl.Caption & vbTab & "(" _
            & CBGetCBCtlType(ctlCBarControl) & ")"
    Next ctlCBarControl


CBPrintCBarInfo_End:
    Exit Function
CBPrintCBarInfo_Err:
    Select Case Err.Number
        Case ERR_INVALID_CMDBARNAME
            CBPrintCBarInfo = "'" & strCBarName & _
                "' is not a valid command bar name!"
        Case Else
            CBPrintCBarInfo = "Error: " & Err.Number _
                & " - " & Err.Description
    End Select
```

```
    Resume CBPrintCBarInfo_End
End Function
```

You call this procedure in the Visual Basic Editor's Immediate window by using the name of a command bar as the only argument. For example, if you execute the following command from the Immediate window:

```
? CBPrintCBarInfo("Web")
```

You will see a listing of all the controls and their control types on the Office Web built-in toolbar, as shown in the following figure.

Listing of Web Toolbar Controls

```
┌─────────────────────────────────────────────────┐
│ 📄 Immediate                            _ □ ✕   │
├─────────────────────────────────────────────────┤
│  ? CBPrintCBarInfo("Web")                     ▲ │
│ CommandBar: Web (Toolbar)     (Built-in)        │
│     &Back    (Button)                           │
│     &Forward    (Button)                        │
│     &Stop Current Jump   (Button)               │
│     &Refresh Current Page    (Button)           │
│     &Start Page (Button)                        │
│     Search the &Web (Button)                    │
│     Favorites    (Popup)                        │
│     &Go (Popup)                                 │
│     &Show Only Web Toolbar   (Button)        ▼  │
│     &Address:    (Combobox)                     │
│ ◄ │                                        ► │  │
└─────────────────────────────────────────────────┘
```

When a control type is shown as "Popup," as with the Favorites control above, the control itself is a command bar. You can get a listing of the controls on a pop-up menu command bar by calling the CBPrintCBarInfo procedure and passing in the name of the pop-up menu as the strCBarName argument. For example:

```
? CBPrintCBarInfo("Favorites")
```

Note that the CBPrintCBarInfo procedure calls two other custom procedures to get the command bar type and the control type. To get information about every command bar of any type in an application, you can use the PrintAllCBarInfo procedure.

> **Note** To refer to a member of the CommandBars collection, use the name of the CommandBar object or an index value that represents the object's location in the collection. The controls on a command bar are members of the CommandBar object's Controls collection. To refer to a control in the Controls collection, use the control's Caption property or an index value that represents the control's location within the collection. All collections are indexed beginning with 1.

Creating a Command Bar

You can create toolbars by using the Customize dialog box or by using Microsoft® Visual Basic® for Applications (VBA) code in any Microsoft® Office application. In Microsoft® Access, you also can create menu bars and pop-up menus by using the Customize dialog box. However, in all other Office applications, you must use VBA code to create menu bars or pop-up menus.

You create a custom command bar by using the CommandBars collection's Add method. The Add method creates a toolbar by default. To create a menu bar or pop-up menu, use the msoBarMenuBar or msoBarPopup constant in the Add method's Position argument. The following code sample illustrates how to create all three types of CommandBar objects:

```
Dim cbrCmdBar       As CommandBar
Dim strCBarName     As String


' Create a toolbar.
strCBarName = "MyNewToolbar"
Set cbrCmdBar = Application.CommandBars.Add(Name:=strCBarName)


' Create a menu bar.
strCBarName = "MyNewMenuBar"
Set cbrCmdBar = Application.CommandBars _
    .Add(Name:=strCBarName, Position:=msoBarMenuBar)


' Create a pop-up menu.
strCBarName = "MyNewPopupMenu"
Set cbrCmdBar = Application.CommandBars _
    .Add(Name:=strCBarName, Position:=msoBarPopup)
```

After you have created a command bar, you still must add any controls that you want and set the command bar's Visible property to True.

Hiding and Showing a Command Bar

You hide or show a toolbar by using the CommandBar object's Visible property. When you display a toolbar, you can specify where it will appear on the screen by using the Position property. For example, the following code sample takes three arguments: the name of a toolbar, a Boolean value indicating whether it should be visible or hidden, and a value matching an msoBarPosition constant specifying where on the screen the toolbar should be displayed. The sample code also illustrates how to use the CommandBar object's Type property to make sure the specified command bar is a toolbar:

```
Function CBToolbarShow(strCBarName As String, _
                       blnVisible As Boolean, _
                       Optional lngPosition As Long = msoBarTop) As
Boolean

    ' This procedure displays or hides the command bar specified in the
    ' strCBarName argument according to the value of the blnVisible
    ' argument. The optional lngPosition argument specifies where the
    ' command bar will appear on the screen.

    Dim cbrCmdBar As CommandBar

    On Error GoTo CBToolbarShow_Err

    Set cbrCmdBar = Application.CommandBars(strCBarName)

    ' Show only toolbars.
    If cbrCmdBar.Type > msoBarTypeNormal Then
        CBToolbarShow = False
        Exit Function
    End If
    ' If Position argument is invalid, set to the default
    ' msoBarTop position.
    If lngPosition < msoBarLeft Or lngPosition > msoBarMenuBar Then
        lngPosition = msoBarTop
    End If

    With cbrCmdBar
        .Visible = blnVisible
        .Position = lngPosition
    End With

    CBToolbarShow = True

CBToolbarShow_End:
    Exit Function
```

```
CBToolbarShow_Err:
   CBToolbarShow = False
   Resume CBToolbarShow_End
End Function
```

You display a custom menu bar by setting its Visible property to True and setting the existing menu bar's Visible property to False.

Copying a Command Bar

You must use Microsoft® Visual Basic® for Applications (VBA) code to copy an existing command bar. You create a copy of a command bar by creating a new command bar of the same type as the one you want to copy, and then use the CommandBarControl object's Copy method to copy each control from the original command bar to the new command bar. The following procedure illustrates how to use VBA to copy an existing command bar:

```
Function CBCopyCommandBar(strOrigCBName As String, _
                    strNewCBName As String, _
                    Optional blnShowBar As Boolean = False) As
Boolean

    ' This procedure copies the command bar named in the strOrigCBName
    ' argument to a new command bar specified in the strNewCBName
argument.

        Dim cbrOriginal        As CommandBar
        Dim cbrCopy            As CommandBar
        Dim ctlCBarControl     As CommandBarControl
        Dim lngBarType         As Long

        On Error GoTo CBCopy_Err

        Set cbrOriginal = CommandBars(strOrigCBName)

        lngBarType = cbrOriginal.Type
        Select Case lngBarType
            Case msoBarTypeMenuBar
                Set cbrCopy = CommandBars.Add(Name:=strNewCBName,
Position:=msoBarMenuBar)
```

```
        Case msoBarTypePopup
            Set cbrCopy = CommandBars.Add(Name:=strNewCBName,
    Position:=msoBarPopup)
        Case Else
            Set cbrCopy = CommandBars.Add(Name:=strNewCBName)
        End Select


    ' Copy controls to new command bar.
    For Each ctlCBarControl In cbrOriginal.Controls
        ctlCBarControl.Copy cbrCopy
    Next ctlCBarControl


    ' Show new command bar.
    If blnShowBar = True Then
        If cbrCopy.Type = msoBarTypePopup Then
            cbrCopy.ShowPopup
        Else
            cbrCopy.Visible = True
        End If
    End If
    CBCopyCommandBar = True
CBCopy_End:
    Exit Function
CBCopy_Err:
    CBCopyCommandBar = False
    Resume CBCopy_End
End Function
```

This procedure will not work if you pass in the name of an existing command bar in the strNewCBName argument, because that argument represents the name of the new command bar.

Note   If you copy a pop-up menu and set the blnShowBar argument to True, the pop-up menu will be displayed at the current location of the mouse pointer. For more information about displaying pop-up menus, search the Microsoft Office Visual Basic Reference Help index for "ShowPopup method."

Deleting a Command Bar

You can delete toolbars and menu bars from the Customize dialog box or by using Microsoft® Visual Basic® for Applications (VBA). You can delete pop-up menus only by using VBA. Use the

Delete method of the CommandBars collection to remove an existing command bar from the collection. The following procedure illustrates one way to delete a CommandBar object:

```
Function CBDeleteCommandBar(strCBarName As String) As Boolean
    On Error Resume Next
    Application.CommandBars(strCBarName).Delete
End Function
```

An error will occur if strCBarName is not the name of an existing command bar. The procedure uses the On Error Resume Next statement to ignore this error because, if an error occurs, it means there is nothing to delete. In addition, it could mean you tried to delete a built-in command bar, such as Standard, which cannot be deleted.

Preventing Users from Modifying Custom Command Bars

There might be circumstances when you want to make sure that users of your custom application cannot delete or disable your custom command bars by using the Customize dialog box. The easiest, but least secure, way to keep users from modifying your custom command bars is to disable the command bars and make sure they are visible only when absolutely necessary. You disable a command bar by setting its Enabled property to False. You hide a command bar by setting its Visible property to False. However, hiding a command bar does nothing to prevent users from getting to the bar through the Customize dialog box.

To completely restrict access to your custom command bars, you must restrict all access to the Customize dialog box. This dialog box can be accessed in three ways: by pointing to Toolbars on the View menu and then clicking Customize; by right-clicking any command bar and then clicking Customize on the shortcut menu; and by clicking Customize on the Tools menu.

All Microsoft® Office applications use the Toolbar List pop-up command bar to provide access to built-in and custom command bars. The Toolbar List command bar appears when you click Toolbars on the View menu or when you right-click any command bar. If you set the Enabled property of the Toolbar List command bar to False as shown in the following line of code, a user will not be able to open the Customize dialog box from either of these access points:

```
CommandBars("Toolbar List").Enabled = False
```

> **Note** Because of the way the Toolbar List command bar is constructed, you cannot disable any of its commands. The only way to disable commands on this command bar is to disable the entire command bar.

Because you also can open the Customize dialog box by clicking Customize on the Tools menu, you will have to disable this command as well to completely restrict access to your custom command bars. The following procedure illustrates how to disable all access to the Customize dialog box:

```
Sub AllowCommandBarCustomization(blnAllowEnabled As Boolean)
    ' This procedure allows or prevents access to the command bars
    ' Customize dialog box according to the value of the blnAllowEnabled
    ' argument.
    CommandBars("Tools").Controls("Customize...").Enabled =
blnAllowEnabled
    CommandBars("Toolbar List").Enabled = blnAllowEnabled
End Sub
```

Working with Personalized Menus

Personalized menus are a feature in Microsoft® Office XP that makes it possible for you see a collapsed subset of menu items that you use most often. You specify whether personalized menus are enabled by pointing to Toolbars on the View menu, clicking Customize, clicking the Options tab, and then selecting the Always show full menus commands first check box. Personalized menus are turned on by default.

Note The personalized menus feature does not apply to shortcut menus.

You can turn on personalized menus for all command bars in an application or for individual command bars only. You can use the CommandBars collection's AdaptiveMenus property to specify whether personalized menus are on or off for all command bars. You use a CommandBar object's AdaptiveMenu property to specify whether that object's menus are displayed as personalized menus.

You use a CommandBarControl object's Priority property to specify whether a control on a menu will be visible when personalized menus are on. When you add a custom CommandBarControl object to a command bar, it will be visible by default. If you set a control's Priority property to 1, the control will always be visible. If you set the Priority property to 0, the control will initially be visible but might be hidden by the host application if it is not used regularly. When a control is hidden, it is still available on the menu, but you must expand the menu to see it.

The CommandBarControl object's IsPriorityDropped property specifies whether a control is currently displayed. When this property is set to True, the control is hidden. Selecting a control that has its IsPriorityDropped property set to True changes the property setting to False, which makes the control visible the next time its menu is displayed.

The host application might change the IsPriorityDropped property setting if the control is not used again within a certain time period. For more information about how long a control remains visible, search the Microsoft Office Visual Basic Reference Help index for "IsPriorityDropped property."

The following procedure turns personalized menus on or off for all command bars or a single command bar according to the value of the blnState argument:

```vba
Function SetPersonalizedMenuState(blnState As Boolean, _
                        Optional cbrBar As CommandBar = Nothing)
    ' This procedure sets the AdaptiveMenus property to the value of the
    ' blnState argument. If a CommandBar object is supplied in the cbrBar
    ' argument, the AdaptiveMenu property for that command bar is set to
    ' the value of the blnState argument.
    On Error Resume Next
    If cbrBar Is Nothing Then
        Application.CommandBars.AdaptiveMenus = blnState
    Else
        cbrBar.AdaptiveMenu = blnState
    End If
End Function
```

The following procedure changes the setting of the Priority property for a menu item:

```vba
Function PromoteMenuItem(cbrBar As CommandBar, _
                    strItemCaption As String)
    ' This procedure changes the Priority property setting for the
    ' cbrBar command bar control whose Caption property setting
    ' matches the value of the strItemCaption argument.
    Dim ctlMenuItem As CommandBarControl

    On Error Resume Next
    If cbrBar.AdaptiveMenu = False Then Exit Function
    Set ctlMenuItem = cbrBar.Controls(strItemCaption)
    With ctlMenuItem
        If .Priority <> 1 Then
            .Priority = 1
        End If
    End With
End Function
```

Working with Images on Command Bar Buttons

Every built-in command bar button has an image associated with it. You can use these images on your own command bar buttons as long as you know the FaceId property value of the built-in button that contains the image. The values for the FaceId property range from zero (no image) to the total number of button images used in the host application (typically a few thousand). One easy way to browse the available button images is to build a toolbar, add some buttons, and assign

FaceId property values to those buttons. The buttons display the image associated with the specified FaceId property value. For example, to see button images with values from 200 to 299, you would call CBShowButtonFaceIDs from the Immediate window in this way:

```
? CBShowButtonFaceIDs(200, 299)
```

And the button images would display as shown in the following figure.

A Collection of Built-in Toolbar Icons

You can see the value of the FaceId property for any image on the command bar by resting your mouse pointer on the image until the value appears in the button's ToolTip.

Another way to copy the image from one command bar button to another is to use the FindControl method of the CommandBars collection to determine the value of the FaceId property for the image you want to copy. Then, you can use the CommandBarControl object's CopyFace and PasteFace methods to copy the image to a new control. The following sample code illustrates how to use these methods to paste the icon associated with an existing command bar button to a new command bar button.

```
Private Sub CBCopyIconDemo()
    ' This procedure demonstrates how to copy the image associated
    ' with a known toolbar button to a new toolbar button. This example
    ' copies the image associated with the "Contents and Index" control
    ' on the Help menu to a new command bar control.

    Dim cbrNew              As CommandBar
    Dim ctlNew              As CommandBarControl
    Const ERR_CMDBAR_EXISTS As Long = 5

    On Error Resume Next
    Set cbrNew = CommandBars.Add("TestCopyFaceIcon")
    If Err = ERR_CMDBAR_EXISTS Then
        Call CBDeleteCommandBar("TestCopyFaceIcon")
        Set cbrNew = CommandBars.Add("TestCopyFaceIcon")
    ElseIf Err <> 0 Then
        Exit Sub
```

```
End If
On Error GoTo 0
Set ctlNew = cbrNew.Controls.Add(msoControlButton)
Call CBCopyControlFace("Help", "Contents and Index")

With ctlNew
    .PasteFace
End With
cbrNew.Visible = True
End Sub
```

This procedure calls two other custom procedures. The CBDeleteCommandbar procedure was discussed in the previous section and is used to delete the command bar if it already exists. The CBCopyControlFace procedure copies the image of the specified control to the Clipboard:

```
Function CBCopyControlFace(strCBarName As String, _
                  strCtlCaption As String)


    ' This procedure uses the CopyFace method to copy the image associated
    ' with the control specified in the strCtlCaption argument to the
Clipboard.

    Dim ctlCBarControl As CommandBarControl

    Set ctlCBarControl = CommandBars.FindControl(msoControlButton, _
        CBGetControlID(strCBarName, strCtlCaption))
    ctlCBarControl.CopyFace
End Function
```

The CBCopyControlFace procedure uses the CBGetControlID procedure as the Id argument for the FindControl method. CBGetControlID returns the Id property for the specified control by using the following line:

```
CBGetControlID = Application.CommandBars(strCBarName) _
    .Controls(strControlCaption).ID
```

The CommandBar object also supports a FindControl method that searches for the specified control only on the CommandBar object itself.

To see these procedures working together, place the insertion point (cursor) anywhere in the CBCopyIconDemo procedure and use the F8 key to step through the code. Try changing the command bar name and control name to copy different images to the new control.

Working with Command Bar Controls

Each CommandBar object has a CommandBarControls collection, which contains all the controls on the command bar. You use the Controls property of a CommandBar object to refer to a control on a command bar. If the control is of the type msoControlPopup, it also will have a Controls collection representing each control on the pop-up menu. Pop-up menu controls represent menus and submenus and can be nested several layers deep, as shown in the second example below.

In this example, the code returns a reference to the New button on the Standard toolbar:

```
Dim ctlCBarControl As CommandBarControl
```

```
Set ctlCBarControl = Application.CommandBars("Standard").Controls("New")
```

Here the code returns a reference to the Macros... control on the Macro pop-up menu on the Tools menu on the "Menu Bar" main menu bar:

```
Dim ctlCBarControl As CommandBarControl
```

```
Set ctlCBarControl = Application.CommandBars("Menu
Bar").Controls("Tools") _
    .Controls("Macro").Controls("Macros...")
```

Note   The "Menu Bar" CommandBar object refers to the main menu bar in Microsoft® Word, Microsoft® PowerPoint®, and Microsoft® Access. The main menu bar in Microsoft® Excel is called "Worksheet Menu Bar." To experiment with sample code that refers to the "Menu Bar" CommandBar object in Excel, simply change the reference from "Menu Bar" to "Worksheet Menu Bar."

Because each pop-up menu control is actually a CommandBar object itself, you also can refer to them directly as members of the CommandBars collection. For example, the following line of code returns a reference to the same control as the previous example:

```
Set ctlCBarControl = Application.CommandBars("Macro") _
    .Controls("Macros...")
```

When you have a reference to a control on a command bar, you can access all available properties and methods of that control.

Note   When you refer to a command bar control by using the control's Caption property, you must be sure to specify the caption exactly as it appears on the menu. For example, in the previous code sample, the reference to the control caption "Macros..." requires the ellipsis (...) so it matches how the caption appears on the menu.

Adding Controls to a Command Bar

To add a control to a command bar, use the Add method of the Controls collection, specifying which type of control you want to create. You can add controls of the following type: button (msoControlButton), text box (msoControlEdit), drop-down list box (msoControlDropdown), combo box (msoControlComboBox), or pop-up menu (msoControlPopup).

The following example adds a new menu to the "Menu Bar" command bar and then adds three controls to the menu:

```
Private Sub CBAddMenuDemo()
    ' Illustrates adding a new menu and filling it with controls. Also
    ' illustrates deleting a menu control from a menu bar.
    '
    ' In Microsoft Excel, the main menu bar is named "Worksheet Menu Bar"
    ' rather than "Menu Bar".

    Dim strCBarName     As String
    Dim strMenuName     As String
    Dim cbrMenu         As CommandBarControl

    strCBarName = "Menu Bar"
    strMenuName = "Custom Menu Demo"

    Set cbrMenu = CBAddMenu(strCBarName, strMenuName)

    ' Note: The following use of the MsgBox function in
    ' the OnAction property setting will work only with
    ' command bars in Microsoft Access. In the other Office
    ' applications, you call built-in VBA functions for the
    ' OnAction property setting. To call a built-in VBA
    ' function from a command bar control in the other Office
    ' applications, you must create a custom procedure that
    ' uses the VBA function and call that custom procedure in
    ' the OnAction property setting.
    Call CBAddMenuControl(cbrMenu, "Item 1", _
        "=MsgBox('You selected Menu1 Control 1.')")
    Call CBAddMenuControl(cbrMenu, "Item 2", _
        "=MsgBox('You selected Menu1 Control 2.')")
    Call CBAddMenuControl(cbrMenu, "Item 3", _
        "=MsgBox('You selected Menu1 Control 3.')")
```

```
' The menu should now appear to the right of the
' Help menu on the menu bar. To see how to delete
' a menu from a menu bar, press F8 to step through
' the remaining code.
Stop
Call CBDeleteCBControl(strCBarName, strMenuName)
End Sub
```

Note that the CBAddMenuDemo procedure calls three other procedures: CBAddMenu, CBAddMenuControl, and CBDeleteCBControl. CBAddMenu returns the new pop-up menu as a CommandBarControl object. In addition, if the command bar specified by the strCBarName argument does not exist, CBAddMenu creates it. CBAddMenuControl adds a button control to the menu created by CBAddMenu and sets the control's OnAction property to the code to run when the button is clicked. CBDeleteCBControl just removes the menu created in the CBAddMenu procedure. CBAddMenu and CBAddMenuControl are shown below:

```
Function CBAddMenu(strCBarName As String, _
                strMenuName As String) As CommandBarControl


    ' Add the menu named in strMenuName to the
    ' command bar named in strCBarName.

    Dim cbrBar              As CommandBar
    Dim ctlCBarControl      As CommandBarControl

    On Error Resume Next
    Set cbrBar = CommandBars(strCBarName)
    If Err <> 0 Then
        Set cbrBar = CommandBars.Add(strCBarName)
        Err = 0
    End If

    With cbrBar
        Set ctlCBarControl = .Controls.Add(msoControlPopup)
        ctlCBarControl.Caption = strMenuName
    End With
    Set CBAddMenu = ctlCBarControl
End Function
```

```
Function CBAddMenuControl(cbrMenu As CommandBarControl, _
                         strCaption As String, _
                         strOnAction As String) As Boolean

    ' Add a button control to the menu specified in cbrMenu and set
    ' its Caption and OnAction properties to the values specified in
    ' the strCaption and strOnAction arguments.

    Dim ctlCBarControl As CommandBarControl

    With cbrMenu
        Set ctlCBarControl = .Controls.Add(msoControlButton)
        With ctlCBarControl
            .Caption = strCaption
            .OnAction = strOnAction
            .Tag = .Caption
        End With
    End With
End Function
```

You normally set the OnAction property to the name of a procedure to run when the button is clicked. In the example above, however, the OnAction property is set by using a string that contains the built-in VBA MsgBox function and the text to display in the message box. When multiple command bar controls use the same OnAction property setting, you can use the ActionControl property and the Parameter property to determine which command bar button is calling the procedure. In addition, you can use Microsoft® Visual Basic® for Applications (VBA) code that executes in response to CommandBar and CommandBarControl events.

You can add any built-in command bar control to a command bar by using the Id property of the built-in control. The following procedure illustrates a technique to add a built-in control to a command bar.

```
Function CBAddBuiltInControl(cbrDestBar As CommandBar, _
                            strCBarSource As String, _
                            strCtlCaption As String) As Boolean

    ' This procedure adds the built-in control specified in
    ' strCtlCaption from the strCBarSource command bar to the
    ' command bar specified by cbrDestBar.
```

```
On Error GoTo CBAddBuiltInControl_Err

If CBDoesCBExist(strCBarSource) <> True Then
    CBAddBuiltInControl = False
    Exit Function
End If

cbrDestBar.Controls.Add ID:=CBGetControlID(strCBarSource,
strCtlCaption)
    CBAddBuiltInControl = True

CBAddBuiltInControl_End:
    Exit Function
CBAddBuiltInControl_Err:
    CBAddBuiltInControl = False
    Resume CBAddBuiltInControl_End
End Function
```

> **Note** When you specify a control's Id property, you also specify the action the control will take when it is selected and, if applicable, the image that appears on the face of the control. To add a control's image without its built-in action, you specify only the FaceId property.

Showing and Enabling Command Bar Controls

You specify whether a command bar control appears on a command bar by using its Visible property. You specify whether a command bar control appears enabled or disabled (grayed out) by using its Enabled property. For example, the following two lines of code could be used to toggle the Visible and Enabled properties of the named controls:

```
Application.CommandBars("Menu Bar").Controls("Edit").Enabled = _
    Not Application.CommandBars("Menu Bar").Controls("Edit").Enabled

Application.CommandBars("Formatting").Controls("Font").Visible = _
    Not Application.CommandBars("Formatting").Controls("Font").Visible
```

> **Note** The "Menu Bar" CommandBar object refers to the main menu bar in Microsoft® Word, Microsoft® PowerPoint®, and Microsoft® Access. The main menu bar in Microsoft® Excel is called "Worksheet Menu Bar." To experiment with sample code that refers to the "Menu Bar" CommandBar object in Excel, simply change the reference from "Menu Bar" to "Worksheet Menu Bar."

When a command bar control's Enabled property is False, the control appears on the command bar but is disabled and cannot be manipulated.

Visually Indicating the State of a Command Bar Control

Many menu commands or toolbar buttons are used to toggle the state of some part of an application from one condition to another. For example, in Microsoft® Office applications, the Bold button and the Align Left button will appear pressed in or not pressed in, depending on the formatting applied to text at the current selection. You can achieve this same effect with your custom command bar button controls by setting the State property to one of the msoButtonState constants.

Note The State property is read-only for built-in command bar controls.

The following procedure shows how to explicit set the State property of a custom command bar button control:

```
Function CBCtlSetState(strCBarName As String, _
                       strCtlCaption As String) As Boolean


    ' Set the State property of the strCtlCaption control
    ' on the strCBarName command bar. The State property is
    ' read-only for built-in controls, so if strCtlCaption
    ' is a built-in control, return False and exit the procedure.


    Dim ctlCBarControl As CommandBarControl


    On Error Resume Next


    Set ctlCBarControl = _
Application.CommandBars(strCBarName).Controls(strCtlCaption)


    If ctlCBarControl.BuiltIn = True Then
        CBCtlSetState = False
        Exit Function
    End If
```

```
If ctlCBarControl.Type <> msoControlButton Then
   CBCtlSetState = False
   Exit Function
End If


CtlCBarControl. State =
If C.State = MsoButtonDown Then
     C.State = MsoButtonUp
   Else If C.State = MsoButtonUp Then
     C.State = MsoButtonDown
   Else
     'State is mixed, leave it
End If


If Err = 0 Then
   CBCtlSetState = True
Else
   CBCtlSetState = False
End If
End Function
```

Working with Command Bar Events

You can use command bar event procedures to run your own code in response to an event. In addition, you can use these event procedures to substitute your own code for the default behavior of a built-in control. The CommandBars collection and the CommandBarButton and CommandBarComboBox objects expose the following event procedures that you can use to run code in response to an event:

- The CommandBars collection supports the OnUpdate event, which is triggered in response to changes made to a Microsoft® Office document that might affect the state of any visible command bar or command bar control. For example, the OnUpdate event occurs when a user changes the selection in an Office document. You can use this event to change the availability or state of command bars or command bar controls in response to actions taken by the user.

    Note   The OnUpdate event can be triggered repeatedly in many different contexts. Any code you add to this event that does a lot of processing or performs a number of actions might affect the performance of your application.

- The CommandBarButton control exposes a Click event that is triggered when a user clicks a command bar button. You can use this event to run code when the user clicks a command bar button.

- The CommandBarComboBox control exposes a Change event that is triggered when a user makes a selection from a combo box control. You can use this method to take an action depending on what selection the user makes from a combo box control on a command bar.

To expose these events, you must first declare an object variable in a class module by using the WithEvents keyword. The following code, entered in the Declarations section of a class module, creates object variables representing the CommandBars collection, three command bar buttons, and a combo box control on a custom toolbar:

```
Public WithEvents colCBars       As Office.CommandBars
Public WithEvents cmdBold        As Office.CommandBarButton
Public WithEvents cmdItalic      As Office.CommandBarButton
Public WithEvents cmdUnderline   As Office.CommandBarButton
Public WithEvents cboFontSize    As Office.CommandBarComboBox
```

When you use the WithEvents keyword to declare an object variable in a class module, the object appears in the Object box in the Code window, and when you select it, the object's events are available in the Procedure box. For example, if the clsCBarEvents class module contained the previous code, you could select the colCBars, cmdBold, cmdItalic, cmdUnderline, and cboFontSize objects from the Object drop-down list and each object's event procedure template would be added to your class module as follows:

```
Private Sub colCBars_OnUpdate()
    ' Insert code you want to run in response to selection changes in an
    ' Office document.
End Sub


Private Sub cmdBold_Click (ByVal Ctrl As Office.CommandBarButton, _
                    CancelDefault As Boolean)
    ' Insert code you want to run in response to this event.
End Sub


Private Sub cmdItalic_Click (ByVal Ctrl As Office.CommandBarButton, _
                    CancelDefault As Boolean)
    ' Insert code you want to run in response to this event.
End Sub


Private Sub cmdUnderline_Click (ByVal Ctrl As Office.CommandBarButton, _
                    CancelDefault As Boolean)
    ' Insert code you want to run in response to this event.
End Sub
```

```
Private Sub cboFontSize_Change (ByVal Ctrl As Office.CommandBarComboBox)
    ' Insert code you want to run when a selection is made in a combo box.
End Sub
```

You add to the event procedures the code that you want to run when the event occurs.

> **Note**   If you set the variable for a command bar control object to a built-in command button, you can set the Click event's CancelDefault argument to True to prevent the button's default behavior from occurring. This behavior is useful if you are developing an add-in and want code to run instead of, or in addition to, the application code that runs when a built-in button is clicked.

After you have added code to the event procedures, you create an instance of the class in a standard or class module and use the Set statement to link the control events to specific command bar controls. In the following example, the InitEvents procedure is used in a standard module to link clsCBarEvents object variables to specific command bar controls on the Formatting Example toolbar:

```
Option Explicit
Dim clsCBClass As New clsCBEvents


Sub InitEvents()
  Dim cbrBar As Office.CommandBar


  Set cbrBar = CommandBars("Formatting Example")
  With cbrBar
    Set clsCBClass.cmdBold = .Controls("Bold")
    Set clsCBClass.cmdItalic = .Controls("Italic")
    Set clsCBClass.cmdUnderline = .Controls("Underline")
    Set clsCBClass.cboFontSize = .Controls("Set Font Size")
  End With
  Set clsCBClass.colCBars = CommandBars
End Sub
```

When the InitEvents procedure runs, the code you placed in the command bar's and command bar controls' event procedures will run whenever the related event occurs.

Working with Document Properties

Every file created by a Microsoft® Office XP application supports a set of built-in document properties. In addition, you can add your own custom properties to an Office document either manually or through code. You can use document properties to create, maintain, and track information about an Office document such as when it was created, who the author is, where it is stored, and so on. In addition, when you save an Office document as an HTML file, all of the document properties are written to the HTML file within <XML> tag pairs. This makes it possible for you to use document properties to track or index files according to properties you specify, regardless of what format you use to save the file.

Note   Office uses the term "document" to represent any file created by using an Office application.

You can view and set built-in and custom document properties by clicking Properties on the File menu. (In Microsoft® Access, click Database Properties on the File menu.)

In This Section

Document Properties in Microsoft Access, Microsoft FrontPage, and Microsoft Outlook
   Understand document properties in Microsoft® Office XP applications.

Working with the HTMLProject Object
   Determine the current state of an Office document, access individual HTMLProjectItem objects, and save current projects and documents.

Document Properties in Microsoft Access, Microsoft FrontPage, and Microsoft Outlook

Microsoft® Access does not use the DocumentProperties collection to store the built-in and custom properties displayed in its Database Properties dialog box. You can access these properties by using Data Access Objects (DAO) in an .mdb-type database and in a SQL database. For more information about database properties, search the Microsoft Access Visual Basic Reference Help index for "database properties."

The Document Properties Dialog Box

Microsoft® FrontPage® also does not use the DocumentProperties collection to store the built-in and custom properties displayed in its Page Properties dialog box (File menu). In FrontPage, built-in and custom properties are stored in the MetaTags and Properties collections of a WebFile object.

Microsoft® Outlook® does not provide a Document Properties dialog box from the File menu as the other Microsoft® Office applications do.

You access the DocumentProperties collection by using the BuiltInDocumentProperties and CustomDocumentProperties properties of an Office document. For an example that prints all built-in and custom document properties for an Office document to the Immediate window, see the PrintAllDocProperties procedure in the modDocumentPropertiesCode module in the ExcelExamples.xls file.

Note   The BuiltInDocumentProperties property returns a collection that contains properties that might apply only to certain Office applications. If you try to return the value of these properties in the wrong context, an error occurs. The sample code shows how to trap this error and continue to identify all the properties that are valid in a given context.

The following code sample shows how to determine the value of a built-in document property. The GetBuiltInProperty procedure accepts an Office document object (Workbook, Document, or Presentation) and a property name and returns the value of the built-in property, if available:

```vba
Function GetBuiltInProperty(objDoc As Object, _
                        strPropname As String) As Variant


    ' This procedure returns the value of the built-in document
    ' property specified in the strPropName argument for the Office
    ' document object specified in the objDoc argument.


    Dim prpDocProp      As DocumentProperty
    Dim varValue        As Variant


    Const ERR_BADPROPERTY       As Long = 5
    Const ERR_BADDOCOBJ         As Long = 438
    Const ERR_BADCONTEXT        As Long = -2147467259


    On Error GoTo GetBuiltInProp_Err

    Set prpDocProp = objDoc.BuiltInDocumentProperties(strPropname)
    With prpDocProp
        varValue = .Value
        If Len(varValue) <> 0 Then
            GetBuiltInProperty = varValue
        Else
            GetBuiltInProperty = "Property does not currently have a value
set."
        End If
    End With


GetBuiltInProp_End:
    Exit Function
GetBuiltInProp_Err:
    Select Case Err.Number
        Case ERR_BADDOCOBJ
            GetBuiltInProperty = "Object does not support
BuiltInProperties."
```

```
      Case ERR_BADPROPERTY
         GetBuiltInProperty = "Property not in collection."
      Case ERR_BADCONTEXT
         GetBuiltInProperty = "Value not available in this context."
      Case Else
   End Select
   Resume GetBuiltInProp_End:
End Function
```

> **Note**   For a complete list of built-in document properties, search the Microsoft Office Visual Basic Reference Help index for "DocumentProperty object."

You can determine the value of an existing custom document property by using the same techniques as those illustrated in the previous code example. The only difference is that you would use the Office document's CustomDocumentProperties collection to return the DocumentProperty object you were interested in.

You use the Add method of the CustomDocumentProperties collection to add a custom DocumentProperty object to the DocumentProperties collection. When you add a custom property, you specify its name, data type, and value. You can also link a custom property to a value in the Office document itself. When you add linked properties, the value of the custom property changes when the value in the document changes. For example, if you add a custom property linked to a named range in a Microsoft® Excel spreadsheet, the property will always contain the current value of the data in the named range.

The following procedure illustrates how to add both static and linked custom properties to the DocumentProperties collection. It is essentially a wrapper around the Add method of the DocumentProperties collection that includes parameter validation and deletes any existing custom property before adding a property that uses the same name.

```
Function AddCustomDocumentProperty(strPropName As String, _
                        lngPropType As Long, _
                        Optional varPropValue As Variant = "", _
                        Optional blnLinkToContent As Boolean =
False, _

                        Optional varLinkSource As Variant = "")
   _

                        As Long


   ' This procedure adds the custom property specified in the strPropName
   ' argument. If the blnLinkToContent argument is True, the custom
   ' property is linked to the location specified by varLinkSource.
   ' The procedure first checks for missing or inconsistent input
parameters.
```

```
    ' For example, a value must be provided unless the property is linked,
and
    ' when you are using linked properties, the source of the link must be
provided.

    Dim prpDocProp As DocumentProperty

    ' Validate data supplied in arguments to this procedure.
    If blnLinkToContent = False And Len(varPropValue) = 0 Then
        ' No value supplied for custom property.
        AddCustomDocumentProperty = ERR_CUSTOM_LINKTOCONTENT_VALUE
        Exit Function
    ElseIf blnLinkToContent = True And Len(varLinkSource) = 0 Then
        ' No source provided for LinkToContent scenario.
        AddCustomDocumentProperty = ERR_CUSTOM_LINKTOCONTENT_LINKSOURCE
        Exit Function
    ElseIf lngPropType < msoPropertyTypeNumber Or _
            lngPropType > msoPropertyTypeFloat Then
        ' Invalid value for data type specifier. Must be one of the
        ' msoDocProperties enumerated constants.
        AddCustomDocumentProperty = ERR_CUSTOM_INVALID_DATATYPE
        Exit Function
    ElseIf Len(strPropName) = 0 Then
        ' No name supplied for new custom property.
        AddCustomDocumentProperty = ERR_CUSTOM_INVALID_PROPNAME
        Exit Function
    End If

    Call DeleteIfExisting(strPropName)

    Select Case blnLinkToContent
        Case True
            Set prpDocProp = ActiveWorkbook.CustomDocumentProperties _
                .Add(Name:=strPropName, LinkToContent:=blnLinkToContent, _
                Type:=lngPropType, LinkSource:=varLinkSource)
            ActiveWorkbook.Save
        Case False
```

```
        Set prpDocProp = ActiveWorkbook.CustomDocumentProperties. _
            Add(Name:=strPropName, LinkToContent:=blnLinkToContent, _
            Type:=lngPropType, Value:=varPropValue)
    End Select
End Function
```

Note   When you programmatically add a custom property to the DocumentProperties collection and the property is linked to a value in the underlying Office document, you must use the document's Save method, as illustrated previously, before the property value will be reflected correctly for the new DocumentProperty object.

Working with the HTMLProject Object

The HTMLProject object is the top-level object representing the HTML code in a Microsoft® Office document. It is the equivalent of the top-level project branch in the Microsoft Script Editor Project Explorer when it contains an Office document. The HTMLProject object has properties you can use to determine the current state of an Office document and to access individual HTMLProjectItem objects, and methods you can use to save the current project or document.

For example, you can tell if a document is currently opened in the Microsoft Script Editor and if the HTML code that exists in the Script Editor is the same as what is contained in the document. If the HTML code is out of sync, you can programmatically synchronize the HTML code before manipulating the document's contents. You can add HTML to a document programmatically or load it from a file saved on disk. In addition, you can use the objects contained within the HTMLProject object and their properties and methods to manipulate the HTML code or add script to the HTML code.

Note   The HTMLProject object is not available in Microsoft® Access, Microsoft® FrontPage®, or Microsoft® Outlook®. To manipulate the HTML code in an Access DataAccessPage object, you use the object's Document property. To work with the HTML code in a page in FrontPage, you use the HTML tab in the FrontPage design environment.

The HTMLProject object's HTMLProjectItems property returns a collection of all of the HTMLProjectItem objects in the project. The default number of HTMLProjectItem objects in an Office application will depend on the kind of Office document you are working with. The following table shows the default number of HTMLProjectItem objects in a new Office document.

Application	Default number of HTMLProjectItem objects
Microsoft® Excel	5 items (Book, Tab, Sheet1, Sheet2, Sheet3)
Microsoft® PowerPoint®	2 items (SlideMaster, Slide1)
Microsoft® Word	1 item (Document Web Page)

You reference an HTMLProject object by using the HTMLProject property of an Office document. For example, the following code illustrates how to return a reference to the top-level HTMLProject object in each Office application:

```
' Create Word reference:
Dim prjWord As Word.HTMLProjectItem
Set prjWord = ActiveDocument.HTMLProject


' Create PowerPoint reference:
Dim prjPPT As PowerPoint.HTMLProjectItem
Set prjPPT = ActivePresentation.HTMLProject
' Create Excel reference:
Dim prjXL As Excel.HTMLProjectItem
Set prjXL = ActiveWorkbook.HTMLProject
```

When you have created a reference to the HTMLProject object, you then use the
HTMLProjectItems property to access individual HTMLProjectItem objects. In the following
example, the IsHTMLProjectDirty procedure can be used to determine if the HTMLProject object
in an Office document is "dirty" (contains changes). You use the blnRefreshProject argument to
specify whether to refresh, or synchronize, the HTML code with the source Office document.

```
Function IsHTMLProjectDirty(objOffDoc As Object, _
                        blnRefreshProject As Boolean) As Boolean
    ' This procedure determines if the HTMLProject object
    ' in the document represented by the objOffDoc argument
    ' is dirty and, if so, refreshes the project according
    ' to the value of the blnRefreshProject argument.

    Dim prjProject As HTMLProject

    On Error GoTo IsHTMLDirty_Err

    Set prjProject = objOffDoc.HTMLProject
    With prjProject
        ' The Office document will be locked as soon as any
        ' changes are made to the HTML code in the document.
        If .State = msoHTMLProjectStateDocumentLocked Then
            IsHTMLProjectDirty = True
            If blnRefreshProject = True Then
                ' Merge the changes to the HTML code with the
                ' underlying Office document.
                .RefreshDocument
            End If
```

```
        Else
            IsHTMLProjectDirty = False
        End If
    End With


IsHTMLDirty_End:
    Exit Function
IsHTMLDirty_Err:
    Select Case Err
        Case Is > 0
            IsHTMLProjectDirty = False
            Resume IsHTMLDirty_End
    End Select
End Function
```

You could use the preceding procedure to determine the state of any Office document by using the ActiveWorkbook, ActivePresentation, or ActiveDocument property in the first argument.

When you have a reference to an HTMLProjectItem object, you can work directly with the HTML code in the document by using the object's Text property. For example, you can run the following code from the Immediate window to print all of the HTML code in a Word document:

```
? ActiveDocument.HTMLProject.HTMLProjectItems(1).Text
```

You can change the HTML code in an Office document by using the LoadFromFile method or by setting the Text property to the HTML code you want to use. The following example illustrates how to replace the HTML code in a Word document with the HTML code contained in a file on disk:

```
ActiveDocument.HTMLProject.HTMLProjectItems(1).LoadFromFile =
"c:\MyHTMLFile.htm"
```

Often, you will want to leave the existing HTML code in a document unchanged, but you will want to insert additional HTML code or script to give the document additional functionality when viewed in a Web browser. In the following example, the AddHTMLAndScriptExample procedure inserts within the first section of a Word document HTML code that includes formatted text, a command button, and script that executes when the command button is clicked. The formatted text and command button are contained in text returned by the GetText procedure and the script that executes when the command button is clicked is returned by the GetScript procedure. The InsertHTMLText procedure inserts the HTML code and script in an existing document just after the location specified by the procedure's second argument.

```
Sub AddHTMLAndScriptExample(objOffDoc As Object)
    Dim itmPrjItem      As HTMLProjectItem
    Dim strNewText      As String
    Dim strNewScript    As String
```

```
Dim strNewHTML        As String

strNewText = GetText()
strNewScript = GetScript()

Set itmPrjItem = objOffDoc.HTMLProject.HTMLProjectItems(1)

With itmPrjItem
    strNewHTML = .Text
    Call InsertHTMLText(strNewHTML, "<div class=Section1>", strNewText

        & vbCrLf & strNewScript)
    .Text = strNewHTML
End With
End Sub
```

Working with Scripts

You can use the Scripts collection and the Script object to programmatically access script, or insert script into a cell or range in a Microsoft® Excel worksheet, a Microsoft® PowerPoint® slide, or a Microsoft® Word document or Word Selection object. In addition, if you use a Microsoft® Office application to open an HTML page, any script contained in that page will be available through the Scripts collection.

Every Script object that is inserted in an Office document includes a Shape object of the type msoScriptAnchor. In Excel and PowerPoint, these shapes are added to the Worksheet or Slide object's Shapes collection. In Word, these shapes are added to a document's InLineShapes collection.

If you want to write script in a document you create in an Office application, use the Microsoft Script Editor. On the other hand, if you want to add script to an Office document programmatically, from an add-in for example, use the objects, properties, and methods of the script object model discussed here.

In This Section

Understanding Script Object Properties
    Learn how to access Script objects and add them to documents.

Adding and Removing Script from a Document
    Add script to and remove script from a document by using the Scripts collection's Add and Delete methods.

Understanding Script Object Properties

The Scripts collection contains all the Script objects in a Microsoft® Office document. A Script object represents a <SCRIPT> tag pair, its attribute settings, and all the text contained between the tag pair. An Office document or an HTML page can contain several script blocks and each script block can contain any number of procedures. For example, the following HTML code contains three script blocks. The first block initializes an array representing the days of the week, the second block contains a procedure that executes when the page loads, and the third block contains the WriteDay and WriteDate procedures that create a part of the text that is displayed on the page itself.

```
<HTML>
<HEAD>
<TITLE>Developing Office Developer Applications</TITLE>
<SCRIPT LANGUAGE="VBSCRIPT" ID="scrDayArray">
<!--
    Option Explicit
    Dim arrDays(6)
    Dim strDay

    arrDays(0) = "Sunday"
    arrDays(1) = "Monday"
    arrDays(2) = "Tuesday"
    arrDays(3) = "Wednesday"
    arrDays(4) = "Thursday"
    arrDays(5) = "Friday"
    arrDays(6) = "Saturday"
-->
</SCRIPT>
<SCRIPT LANGUAGE="VBSCRIPT" ID="scrShowDay">
<!--
    Option Explicit
    Function ShowDayMessage()
        Dim intDay
        Dim strDayOfWeek

        intDay = WeekDay(Date())
        strDayOfWeek = arrDays(intDay - 1)
        MsgBox "Today is " & strDayOfWeek
```

```
        Call WriteDay(strDayOfWeek)
        Call WriteDate()
    End Function
-->
</SCRIPT>
</HEAD>

<BODY ONLOAD="ShowDayMessage()">
<H2>Developer Office Developer VBA and Workflow Solutions:</H2>
<H3>Shared Office Components</H3>
<HR>

<DIV ID=DayText>
<!-- Day and date text is inserted here. -->
</DIV>

<SCRIPT LANGUAGE="VBSCRIPT" ID="scrWriteDay">
<!--
    Option Explicit
    Function WriteDay(strDay)
        DayText.innerText = "Today is " & strDay
    End Function

    Function WriteDate()
        Dim strDay
        Dim strNum

        strDay = Day(Date())
        If Len(strDay) = 2 Then
            If left(strDay, 1) = 1 Then
                strNum = 0
            Else
                strNum = Right(strDay, 1)
            End If
        Else
            strNum = strDay
        End If
```

```
    Select Case CInt(strNum)
        Case 1
            strDay = strDay & "st"
        Case 2
            strDay = strDay & "nd"
        Case 3
            strDay = strDay & "rd"
        Case else
            strDay = strDay & "th"
    End Select

    DayText.innerText = DayText.innerText & _
        ", the " & strDay & " day of the month."
  End Function
-->
</SCRIPT>
</BODY>
</HTML>
```

Listing of Various Script Properties

```
Immediate                                                    [x]
? ActiveDocument.Scripts.Count
 3
? ActiveDocument.Scripts(1).Id
scrDayArray
? ActiveDocument.Scripts("scrDayArray").Language
 2
? Activedocument.Scripts("scrDayArray").Location
 1
? Activedocument.Scripts("scrDayArray").ScriptText

<!--
    Option Explicit
    Dim arrDays(6)
    Dim strDay

    arrDays(0) = "Sunday"
    arrDays(1) = "Monday"
    arrDays(2) = "Tuesday"
    arrDays(3) = "Wednesday"
    arrDays(4) = "Thursday"
    arrDays(5) = "Friday"
    arrDays(6) = "Saturday"
-->
```

You access a Script object within the Scripts collection by using either the index for the object within the collection, or the value of the object's ID attribute. If a <SCRIPT> tag has an ID attribute, the value of that attribute becomes the value of the Script object's Id property. If the <SCRIPT> tag does not have an ID attribute setting, an index value is the only way to locate the Script object within the Scripts collection.

When a document that contains script is opened in an Office application, script blocks are added to the Scripts collection in the order in which they appear in the document. When you add a Script object to a document, the new object is added at the end of the collection of Script objects, regardless of the value of the object's Location property. However, when the document is closed and reopened, that same script will appear in the Scripts collection in the order in which it appears in the document.

Because a Script object's index position within the Scripts collection can change between the time the object is added and the time the document is saved and reopened, it is never a good idea to try to locate a specific Script object within the Scripts collection by using its index position in the collection. Instead, you should make a habit of specifying an Id property value when creating a Script object and using that Id property value to locate the Script object within the Scripts collection. It is useful to use the index when you are looping through all the Script objects in a document, however.

Note If a <SCRIPT> tag in a document uses the same ID attribute as another <SCRIPT> tag, the Scripts collection will contain only the first Script object that uses the duplicate ID attribute. Any other tags that use the same ID attribute will not be included in the collection.

The Script object's Location property returns a long integer representing an msoScriptLocation constant that specifies whether the script is located in the <HEAD> element or the <BODY> element of the HTML code. If you do not specify a value for this argument, the default location is within the <BODY> element. Similarly, the Language property returns a long integer representing an msoScriptLanguage constant that specifies the LANGUAGE attribute of the <SCRIPT> tag. If you do not specify a value, the default is Microsoft® Visual Basic® Scripting Edition (VBScript), except in Microsoft® Access, where it is Microsoft® JScript®.

Note The Script object's ScriptText property returns everything between the <SCRIPT> tags, but not the <SCRIPT> tags themselves. You must account for this when you are using the Script object's Add method to programmatically add your own script to a document.

Adding and Removing Script from a Document

You add script to a document by using the Scripts collection's Add method. The Add method uses optional arguments that make it possible for you specify the script's location, language, ID attribute, additional <SCRIPT> tag attributes, and the script to be contained within the <SCRIPT> tags. The Add method also automatically generates HTML comment tags (<!— and —>) around your script, so browsers that do not recognize script can ignore it. If you use the Add method without specifying any of the method's arguments, you create an empty <SCRIPT> tag pair that looks similar to this:

```
<SCRIPT ID="" LANGUAGE="VBScript">
<!--


-->
</SCRIPT>
```

You use the Anchor argument of the Add method to specify where the Script object should be located in a document.

- In Microsoft® Word, if you do not specify a value for the Anchor argument, the Script object is inserted at the current location of the insertion point (cursor). In addition, you can add a Script object to a Selection object or an InLineShape object. When you specify a Selection object in the Anchor argument, the Script object is inserted at the end of the Selection object. When you specify an InLineShape object in the Anchor argument, the Script object is inserted before the paragraph marker for the paragraph that is the anchor point for the shape. You cannot add a Script object to a Range object in Word.

- In Microsoft® Excel, if you do not specify a value for the Anchor argument, the Script object is inserted in the currently active cell. You can also add a Script object to a Range object by specifying the Range object in the Anchor argument. You cannot add a Script object to a Shape object in Excel. If you do specify a Shape object in the Anchor argument, the argument is ignored and the Script object is inserted in the currently active cell.

- In Microsoft® PowerPoint®, you can only add a Script object to a Slide object. If you specify a Shape object in the Anchor argument, the argument is ignored and the Script is inserted in the specified Slide object.

    Note To see the Shape objects that are inserted when script is added to an Office document, point to Macro on the Tools menu, and then click Show All Script. The Show All Script is not on the menu by default; you must add it from the Customize dialog box on the Tools menu.

The following procedure uses the Scripts collection's Add method to add a <SCRIPT> tag pair and some Microsoft® Visual Basic ® Scripting Edition (VBScript) code to the <HEAD> element of the current Word document:

```
Function AddScriptToDocumentDemo()
    ' This procedure illustrates how to use the Scripts collection
    ' to add VBScript code to an Office document.
    Dim strScriptCode As String
    Dim scrArrayScript As Script

    On Error Resume Next

    Set scrArrayScript = ActiveDocument.Scripts("scrDayArray")
    If Err = 0 Then
        ' The script is already in the document so no
        ' need to add it again.
        Exit Function
    End If

    strScriptCode = vbTab & "Option Explicit" & vbCrLf & vbTab _
        & "Dim arrDays(6)" & vbCrLf & vbTab _
        & "arrDays(0) = " & """"Sunday"""" & vbCrLf & vbTab _
        & "arrDays(1) = " & """"Monday"""" & vbCrLf & vbTab _
        & "arrDays(2) = " & """"Tuesday"""" & vbCrLf & vbTab _
        & "arrDays(3) = " & """"Wednesday"""" & vbCrLf & vbTab _
        & "arrDays(4) = " & """"Thursday"""" & vbCrLf & vbTab _
        & "arrDays(5) = " & """"Friday"""" & vbCrLf & vbTab _
        & "arrDays(6) = " & """"Saturday""""
```

```
With Application.ActiveDocument
    .Scripts.Add Location:=msoScriptLocationInHead, _
        Language:=msoScriptLanguageVisualBasic, ID:="scrDayArray", _
        ScriptText:=strScriptCode
End With
End Function
```

You can remove all the script and <SCRIPT> tags from a document by using the Scripts collection's Delete method. You remove a single script from the Scripts collection by using the Script object's Delete method.

Getting the Most Out of Visual Basic for Applications

As a developer, your goal is to write code that's fast, efficient, easy to read and maintain, and if possible, reusable. To do so, you must have a solid working knowledge of Microsoft® Visual Basic® for Applications (VBA)—what features the language includes and what you can do with it.

As you develop applications, you'll find that there are a number of operations that you must perform repeatedly—parsing a file path, for example, or returning all the files in a directory. Rather than rewriting these routines every time you require them, you can begin building an arsenal of procedures that solve common problems. This section gives you a head start by providing functions that perform some often-required operations on strings, numbers, dates and times, files, and arrays. It also explains the key aspects of each procedure and covers fundamental VBA programming issues so that you can continue to expand your code arsenal yourself. You can use these procedures not only in VBA code but also in Visual Basic Scripting Edition (VBScript) code in HTML documents.

In This Section

Working with Strings
   Understand how to get information from strings.

Working with Numbers
   Learn how to use numeric values and data types in Microsoft® Visual Basic® for Applications (VBA).

Working with Dates and Times
   Manipulate date values in Microsoft® Visual Basic® for Applications (VBA), and understand how VBA stores date values internally.

Working with Files
   Understand the Microsoft Scripting Runtime object library, and work with drives, folders, and files as objects.

Understanding Arrays
> Use arrays when you must store a number of values of the same type, but you don't want to create individual variables to store them all.

Tips for Defining Procedures in VBA
> Define a Function or Sub procedure, and use the options available to you to make your code more extensible or more flexible.

Optimizing VBA Code
> Understand how to streamline your Microsoft® Visual Basic® for Applications (VBA) code to streamline your memory requirements.

Working with Strings

Data structures composed of a sequence of alphanumeric characters, strings are basic in concept, but getting the information you require from them can be a different story.

In This Section

Comparing Strings
> Compare strings to determine whether they contain equivalent characters and how they differ if they do not match.

Calculating String Length
> Determine the length of a string using the Len function to parse its contents.

Searching a String
> Search strings to find out whether they contain a particular character or group of characters by using the InStr or InStrRev functions.

Returning Portions of a String
> Learn how to parse the string to be able to work with part of a string's contents.

Working with Strings as Arrays
> Quickly turn once-lengthy string-manipulation procedures into just a few lines of code.

Finding and Replacing Text Within a String
> Find and replace all occurrences of a substring within a string using the Replace function.

Converting Text in a String from One Case to Another
> Use the Microsoft® Visual Basic® for Applications (VBA) StrConv function to convert text in a string from one case to another.

Working with String Variables
> Understand how to dimension a variable, assign a value to it, and output that variable as part of a string.

Comparing Strings

You can compare strings to determine whether they contain equivalent characters and how they differ if they do not match. When you compare two strings, you're actually comparing the ANSI value of each character to the value of the corresponding character in the other string. You can specify whether you want to make comparisons case-sensitive or whether you want to ignore the case and simply compare the strings' characters.

Specifying the String-Comparison Setting for a Module

The Option Compare statement determines how strings are compared within a module. There are three settings for the Option Compare statement:

- Option Compare Binary Strng comparisons are case-sensitive. Option Compare Binary is the default string-comparison setting for all the Microsoft® Office applications except Microsoft® Access, for which Option Compare Database is the default.

- Option Compare Text Strng comparisons are case-insensitive. To make case-insensitive string comparison the default method for a module, add this statement to the module's Declarations section.

- Option Compare Database Strng comparisons depend on the sort order for the specified locale; the default sort order is case-insensitive. The Option Compare Database setting is available only for Access databases. Note that when you create a new module in Access, the Option Compare Database statement is automatically inserted in the module's Declarations section. If you delete the Option Compare Database statement, the default string-comparison setting for the module is Option Compare Binary.

    Note If you're writing code in Access that you might want to export to another Microsoft® Visual Basic® for Applications (VBA) host application, you should explicitly specify string comparisons as binary or text-based in the line that performs the comparison. Because the Option Compare Database setting is available only in Access, the code will not compile when you import it into another application unless you remove this setting. If you have explicitly specified the string-comparison method for each line that performs comparisons, you can export the code and be confident that string comparisons will continue to work as expected after you remove the Option Compare Database setting.

    Tip To change the sort order for a database, click Options on the Tools menu, click the General tab, and then change the New Database Sort Order setting. After you change this setting, any new database you create will perform text comparisons based on the new sort order; changing this option has no effect on existing databases.

Comparing Strings by Using Comparison Operators

Because you're actually comparing ANSI values when you compare two strings, you can use the same comparison operators that you would use with numeric expressions—greater than (>), less than (<), equal to (=), and so on. In addition to these numeric comparison operators, you can use the Like operator, which is specifically for use in comparing strings, including strings that contain wildcard characters.

Using Comparison Operators

When you use comparison operators such as the greater than (>) and less than (<) operators to compare two strings, the result you get depends on the string-comparison setting for the module. Consider the following example:

```
"vba" > "VBA"
```

If the string-comparison setting is Option Compare Binary, the comparison returns True.

When Microsoft® Visual Basic® for Applications (VBA) performs a binary text comparison, it compares the binary values for each corresponding position in the string until it finds two that differ. In this example, the lowercase letter "v" corresponds to the ANSI value 118, while the uppercase letter "V" corresponds to the ANSI value 86. Because 118 is greater than 86, the comparison returns True.

If the string-comparison setting is Option Compare Text, "vba" > "VBA" returns False, because the strings are equivalent apart from case.

In a Microsoft® Access database, if the string-comparison setting is Option Compare Database and the New Database Sort Order option is set to General (the default setting), the string comparison is case-insensitive and the example returns False.

Using the Like Operator

You can perform wildcard string comparisons by using the Like operator. The following table shows the wildcard characters supported by VBA.

Wildcard	Represents	Example
*	Any number of characters	t* matches any word beginning with "t."
?	Any single character	t??t matches any four-letter word beginning and ending with "t."
#	Any single digit (0–9)	1#3 matches any three-digit number beginning with "1" and ending with "3."
[charlist]	Any single character in charlist	[a-z] matches any letter that falls between "a" and "z" (case-sensitivity depends on Option Compare setting).

Wildcard	Represents	Example
[!charlist]	Any single character not in charlist	[!A-Z] excludes the uppercase alphabetic characters (case-sensitivity depends on Option Compare setting).

You can use the Like operator to perform data validation or wildcard searches. For example, suppose you want to ensure that a user has entered a telephone number in the format *nnn-nnn-nnnn*. You can use the Like operator to check that the entry is valid, as the following procedure does:

```
Function ValidPhone(strPhone As String) As Boolean
    ' This procedure checks that the passed-in value is
    ' a valid, properly formatted telephone number.

    ValidPhone = strPhone Like "###-###-####"
End Function
```

This procedure compares characters in a string to make sure that certain positions contain numeric characters. To return True, all characters must be digits between 0 and 9 or hyphens, and the hyphens must be present at the correct position in the string.

Overriding the Default String-Comparison Setting

To perform a string comparison within a procedure and override the string-comparison setting for the module, you can use the StrComp function. The StrComp function takes two strings as arguments, along with a compare argument, which you can use to specify the type of comparison. The possible settings for the compare argument are vbBinaryCompare, vbTextCompare, and (in Microsoft® Access) vbDatabaseCompare. If you omit this argument, the StrComp function uses the module's default comparison method.

The following table lists the possible return values for the StrComp function.

If	Then StrComp returns
string1 < string2	-1
string1 = string2	0
string1 > string2	1
string1 Or string2 Is Null	Null

For example, running the following code from the Immediate window prints "1", indicating that the ANSI value of the first character in the first string is greater than the ANSI value of the first character in the second string:

```
? StrComp("vba", "VBA", vbBinaryCompare)
```

On the other hand, if you specify text-based string comparison, this code prints "0", indicating that the two strings are identical:

```
? StrComp("vba", "VBA", vbTextCompare)
```

Other Microsoft® Visual Basic® for Applications (VBA) string functions that perform string comparison also provide a compare argument that you can use to override the default string-comparison setting for that function call. For example, the InStr and InStrRev functions both have a compare argument.

Calculating String Length

Often you must know the length of a string to parse its contents. You can use the Len function to calculate the length of a string:

```
Dim lngLen As Long
lngLen = Len(strText)
```

When Microsoft® Visual Basic® for Applications (VBA) stores a string in memory, it always stores the length of the string in a long integer at the beginning of the string. The Len function retrieves this value and is therefore quite fast.

The Len function is useful when you must determine whether a string is a zero-length string (""). Rather than comparing the string in question to a zero-length string to determine whether they're equivalent, you can simply check whether the length of the string is equal to 0. For example:

```
If Len(strText) > 0 Then
    ' Perform some operation here.
End If
```

Searching a String

When you must know whether a string contains a particular character or group of characters, you can search the string by using one of two functions. The traditional candidate for this job is the InStr function, which you can use to find one string within another. The InStr function compares two strings, and if the second string is contained within the first, it returns the position at which the substring begins. If the InStr function doesn't find the substring, it returns 0.

The InStr function takes an optional argument, the start argument, in which you can specify the position to begin searching. If you omit this argument, the InStr function starts searching at the first character in the string.

The newest version of Microsoft® Visual Basic® for Applications (VBA) includes a function called InStrRev, which behaves in the same way as the InStr function, except that it begins searching at the end of the string rather than at the beginning. As with the InStr function, you can specify a starting position for the InStrRev function; it will search backward through the string beginning at that point. If you know that the substring you're looking for probably falls at the end of the string, the InStrRev function might be a better option. For example, the InStrRev function makes it easier to parse a file path and return just the file name.

Note Both the InStr and InStrRev functions return the same value when they locate the same substring. Although the InStrRev function begins searching at the right side of the string, it counts characters from the left side, as does the InStr function. For example, calling either the InStr or InStrRev function to search the string "C:\Temp" for the substring "C:\" returns 1. However, if the substring appears more than when, and you haven't specified a value for the start argument, the InStr function returns the position of the first instance and the InStrRev function returns the position of the last instance.

The following procedure counts the occurrences of a particular character or group of characters in a string. To call the procedure, you pass in the string, the substring that you're looking for, and a constant indicating whether the search should be case-sensitive. The CountOccurrences procedure uses the InStr function to search for the specified text and return the value of the position at which it first occurs; for example, if it's the third character in the string, the InStr function returns 3. The procedure increments the counter variable, which keeps track of the number of occurrences found, and then sets the starting position for the next call to the InStr function. The new starting position is the position at which the search text was found, plus the length of the search string. By setting the start position in this manner, you ensure that you don't locate the same substring twice when you're searching for text that's more than one character in length.

The possible constant values are specified by the built-in enumerated constants in vbCompareMethod, which groups the three VBA string-comparison constants (vbBinaryCompare, vbDatabaseCompare, and vbTextCompare). If you declare an argument as type vbCompareMethod, VBA lists the constants in that grouping when you call the procedure. This is a convenient way to remember what values an argument takes. In addition, you can define your own enumerated constants and use them as data types.

```
Function CountOccurrences(strText As String, _
                          strFind As String, _
                          Optional lngCompare As VbCompareMethod) As Long


    ' Count occurrences of a particular character or characters.
    ' If lngCompare argument is omitted, procedure performs binary
comparison.

    Dim lngPos      As Long
    Dim lngTemp     As Long
    Dim lngCount    As Long


    ' Specify a starting position. We don't need it the first
    ' time through the loop, but we'll need it on subsequent passes.
    lngPos = 1
    ' Execute the loop at least once.
    Do
        ' Store position at which strFind first occurs.
```

```
    lngPos = InStr(lngPos, strText, strFind, lngCompare)
    ' Store position in a temporary variable.
    lngTemp = lngPos
    ' Check that strFind has been found.
    If lngPos > 0 Then
        ' Increment counter variable.
        lngCount = lngCount + 1
        ' Define a new starting position.
        lngPos = lngPos + Len(strFind)
    End If
' Loop until last occurrence has been found.
Loop Until lngPos = 0
' Return the number of occurrences found.
CountOccurrences = lngCount
End Function
```

Calling this function from the Immediate window as follows returns "3":

```
? CountOccurrences("This is a test", "t", vbTextCompare)
```

Returning Portions of a String

To work with part of a string's contents, you must parse the string. You can use the InStr or InStrRev function to find the position at which to begin parsing the string. When you've located that position, you can use the Left, Right, and Mid functions to do the job. The Left and Right functions return a specified number of characters from either the left or right portion of the string. The Mid function is the most flexible of the parsing functions—you can specify a starting point anywhere within the string, followed by the number of characters you want to return.

> **Note** Some of the Microsoft® Visual Basic® for Applications (VBA) string functions come in two varieties, one that returns a string, and one that returns a string-type Variant value. The names of the functions that return a string include a dollar sign ("$"); for example, Chr$, Format$, LCase$, Left$, LTrim$, Mid$, Right$, RTrim$, Space$, Trim$, and UCase$. The functions that return a string-type Variant value have no dollar sign; for example, Chr, Format, LCase, Left, LTrim, Mid, Right, RTrim, Space, Trim, and UCase. The string-returning functions are faster; however, you'll get an error if you call them with a value that is Null. The functions that return a string-type Variant value handle Null values without an error. Code examples in this section use the string-returning functions where appropriate.

The following procedure parses a file path and returns one of the following portions: the path (everything but the file name), the file name, the drive letter, or the file extension. You specify which part of the string you want to return by passing a constant to the lngPart argument. The lngPart argument is defined as type opgParsePath, which contains custom enumerated constants declared in the modPublicDefs module in VBA.mdb.

Note that this procedure uses the InStrRev function to find the last path separator, or backslash (\), in the string. If you used the InStr function, you'd have to write a loop to make sure that you'd found the last one. With the InStrRev function, you know that the first backslash you find is actually the last one in the string, and the characters to the right of it must be the file name.

```
Function ParsePath(strPath As String, _
                   lngPart As opgParsePath) As String


    ' This procedure takes a file path and returns
    ' the path (everything but the file name), the drive letter,
    ' or the file extension,
    ' depending on which constant was passed in.


    Dim lngPos          As Long
    Dim strPart         As String
    Dim blnIncludesFile As Boolean


    ' Check that this is a file path.
    ' Find the last path separator.
    lngPos = InStrRev(strPath, "\")
    ' Determine whether portion of string after last backslash
    ' contains a period.
    blnIncludesFile = InStrRev(strPath, ".") > lngPos


    If lngPos > 0 Then
       Select Case lngPart
          ' Return file name.
          Case opgParsePath.FILE_ONLY
             If blnIncludesFile Then
                strPart = Right$(strPath, Len(strPath) - lngPos)
             Else
                strPart = ""
             End If
          ' Return path.
          Case opgParsePath.PATH_ONLY
             If blnIncludesFile Then
                strPart = Left$(strPath, lngPos)
```

```
        Else
            strPart = strPath
        End If
    ' Return drive.
    Case opgParsePath.DRIVE_ONLY
        strPart = Left$(strPath, 3)
    ' Return file extension.
    Case opgParsePath.FILEEXT_ONLY
        If blnIncludesFile Then
            ' Take three characters after period.
            strPart = Mid(strPath, InStrRev(strPath, ".") + 1, 3)
        Else
            strPart = ""
        End If
    Case Else
        strPart = ""
    End Select
End If
ParsePath = strPart

ParsePath_End:
    Exit Function
End Function
```

Calling this function as follows from the Immediate window returns "Test.txt":

```
? ParsePath("C:\Temp\Test.txt", opgParsePath.FILE_ONLY)
```

Working with Strings as Arrays

It might be hard to believe, but some of the most exciting features in Microsoft® Visual Basic® for Applications (VBA) in Microsoft® Office XP are the functions for working with strings as arrays. These functions can turn once-lengthy string-manipulation procedures into just a few lines of code. And in many cases, they're faster than using loops and string-parsing techniques to work with the contents of a very large string.

The Split Function

The Split function takes a string and converts it into an array of strings. By default, it divides the string into elements by using the space character as a delimiter, so that if you pass in a sentence, each element of the array contains a word. For example, if you pass this string to the Split function

```
"This is a test"
```

you'll get an array that contains the following four elements:

```
"This"
```

```
"is"
```

```
"a"
```

```
"test"
```

You can specify that the Split function split the string based on a different delimiter by passing in the delimiter argument.

When you've split a string into an array, it's easy to work with the individual elements. The Split function sizes the array for you, so you don't have to worry about maintaining the array's size.

The following example uses the Split function to count the number of words in a string. The procedure takes a string and returns a long integer indicating the number of words found. Because the string is divided into elements at the space between each word, each element of the resulting array represents a word. To determine the number of words, you simply must determine the number of elements in the array. You can do this by subtracting the lower bound from the upper bound and adding 1.

```
Function CountWords(strText As String) As Long
    ' This procedure counts the number of words in a string.

    Dim astrWords() As String

    astrWords = Split(strText)
    ' Count number of elements in array -- this will be the
    ' number of words.
    CountWords = UBound(astrWords) - LBound(astrWords) + 1
End Function
```

The Join Function

After you've finished processing an array that's been split, you can use the Join function to concatenate the elements of the array together into a single string again. The Join function takes an array of strings and returns a concatenated string. By default it adds a space between each element of the string, but you can specify a different delimiter.

The following procedure uses the Split and Join functions together to trim extra space characters from a string. It splits the passed-in string into an array. Wherever there is more than one space within the string, the corresponding array element is a zero-length string. By finding and removing these zero-length string elements, you can remove the extra white space from the string.

To remove zero-length string elements from the array, the procedure must copy the non-zero-length string elements into a second array. The procedure then uses the Join function to concatenate the second array into a whole string.

Because the second array isn't created by the Split function, you must size it manually. It's easy to do, however—you can size it initially to be the same size as the first array, then resize it after you've copied in the non-zero-length string elements.

```vba
Function TrimSpace(strInput As String) As String
    ' This procedure trims extra space from any part of
    ' a string.

    Dim astrInput()    As String
    Dim astrText()     As String
    Dim strElement     As String
    Dim lngCount       As Long
    Dim lngIncr        As Long

    ' Split passed-in string.
    astrInput = Split(strInput)

    ' Resize second array to be same size.
    ReDim astrText(UBound(astrInput))

    ' Initialize counter variable for second array.
    lngIncr = LBound(astrInput)
    ' Loop through split array, looking for
    ' non-zero-length strings.
    For lngCount = LBound(astrInput) To UBound(astrInput)
        strElement = astrInput(lngCount)
        If Len(strElement) > 0 Then
            ' Store in second array.
            astrText(lngIncr) = strElement
            lngIncr = lngIncr + 1
        End If
    Next
    ' Resize new array.
    ReDim Preserve astrText(LBound(astrText) To lngIncr - 1)
```

```
    ' Join new array to return string.
    TrimSpace = Join(astrText)
End Function
```

To test the TrimSpace procedure, try calling it from the Immediate window with a string such as the following:

```
? TrimSpace("  This  is  a  test  ")
```

> **Tip**   To see the elements in each array while the code is running, step through the procedure, and use the Locals window to view the values contained in each variable.

The Filter Function

The Filter function searches a string array for all elements that match a given text string. The Filter function takes three arguments: a string array, a string containing the text to find, and a constant specifying the string-comparison method. It returns a string array containing all the matches that it finds.

You can use the Filter function to determine whether a particular element exists in an array. An example, the ConvertToProperCase procedure, appears in Converting Strings.

When working with the Filter function, you might notice that it returns a particular element even if only part of the element matches the search text. In other words, if your search text is the letter "e," and the array you're searching contains the element "test," the array returned by the Filter function will contain the element "test."

Given this behavior, you might be tempted to use the Filter function to rewrite the CountOccurrences procedure shown earlier in this section. Before doing so, bear in mind that the CountOccurrences procedure counts every occurrence of a particular character in a string, even if there is more than one occurrence in a word. When you are using the Filter function, on the other hand, you can count an occurrence only once per element, even if the character occurs twice within a single element in the array.

Replacing Text Within a String

Microsoft® Visual Basic® for Applications (VBA) provides another function, the Replace function, which makes it easy to find and replace all occurrences of a substring within a string. The Replace function takes up to six arguments: the string to be searched, the text to find within the string, the replacement text, what character to start at, how many occurrences to replace, and a constant indicating the string-comparison method. You don't even have to write a loop to use the Replace function—it automatically replaces all the appropriate text for you with one call.

For example, suppose you want to change the criteria for an SQL statement based on some condition in your application. Rather than re-creating the SQL statement, you can use the Replace function to replace just the criteria portion of the string, as in the following code fragment:

```
strSQL = "SELECT * FROM Products WHERE ProductName Like 'M*' ORDER BY
ProductName;"
strFind = "'M*'"
strReplace = "'T*'"


Debug.Print Replace(strSQL, strFind, strReplace)
```

Running this code fragment prints this string to the Immediate window:

```
SELECT * FROM Products WHERE ProductName Like 'T*' ORDER BY ProductName;
```

Wildcard Search and Replace

The Replace function greatly simplifies string search-and-replace operations, but it doesn't make it possible for you to perform wildcard searches. Here's another place where the Split and Join functions come in handy.

The ReplaceWord procedure shown below takes three mandatory arguments: a string to be searched, the word to find within the string, and the replacement text. When you call this procedure, you can include wildcard characters in the string that you pass for the strFind argument. For example, you might call the ReplaceWord procedure from the Immediate window with these parameters:

```
? ReplaceWord("There will be a test today", "t*t", "party")
```

The procedure splits the strText argument into an array, then uses the Like operator to compare each element of the array to strFind, replacing the elements that match the wildcard specification.

```
Function ReplaceWord(strText As String, _
                     strFind As String, _
                     strReplace As String) As String


    ' This function searches a string for a word and replaces it.
    ' You can use a wildcard mask to specify the search string.


    Dim astrText()    As String
    Dim lngCount      As Long


    ' Split the string at specified delimiter.
    astrText = Split(strText)


    ' Loop through array, performing comparison
    ' against wildcard mask.
    For lngCount = LBound(astrText) To UBound(astrText)
```

```
      If astrText(lngCount) Like strFind Then
         ' If array element satisfies wildcard search,
         ' replace it.
         astrText(lngCount) = strReplace
      End If
   Next
   ' Join string, using same delimiter.
   ReplaceWord = Join(astrText)
End Function
```

Converting Text in a String from One Case to Another

To convert text in a string from one case to another, you can use the Microsoft® Visual Basic® for Applications (VBA) StrConv function. The StrConv function converts a string to lowercase, uppercase, or proper case (initial capital letters). It takes a string and a constant that specifies how to convert the string. For example, the following code fragment converts a string to proper case:

```
Debug.Print StrConv("washington, oregon, and california", vbProperCase)
```

Running this code prints the following text to the Immediate window:

```
Washington, Oregon, And California
```

> **Note** The StrConv function performs other string conversions as well. For example, it converts a string from Unicode to ANSI, or vice versa. For more information about the StrConv function, search the Visual Basic Reference Help index for "StrConv function."

Most likely, you'll be about three-fourths satisfied with this result—you probably want "washington," "oregon," and "california" to be capitalized, but not "and." The word "and" is a minor word that isn't capitalized according to grammatical convention, unless it's the first word in the sentence. Unfortunately, VBA doesn't know which words to convert and which to leave alone, so it converts everything. You must manually write code to handle the cases you don't want capitalized.

If you want VBA to omit the minor words, you can define those words in a file or a table, and perform a comparison against the file or table when you convert each word. The following procedure, ConvertToProperCase, does just that—it takes a string, splits it into individual words, compares each word against a list in a text file, and converts all non-minor words to proper case.

The ConvertToProperCase procedure calls another procedure, the GetMinorWords procedure. This procedure reads a text file containing a list of minor words and returns an array of strings containing each word in the text file. The ConvertToProperCase procedure then uses the Filter function to compare each word in the string to be converted against the list of words contained in the array of minor words. If a word doesn't appear in the list, then it's converted to proper case. If it does appear, it's converted to lowercase.

```vba
Function ConvertToProperCase(strText As String) As String
    ' This function takes a string and converts it to proper
    ' case, except for any minor words.

    Dim astrText()      As String
    Dim astrWords()     As String
    Dim astrMatches()   As String
    Dim lngCount        As Long

    ' Return array containing minor words.
    astrWords = GetMinorWords

    ' Split string into array.
    astrText = Split(strText)

    ' Check each word in passed-in string against array
    ' of minor words.
    For lngCount = LBound(astrText) To UBound(astrText)
        ' Filter function returns array containing matches found.
        ' If no matches are found, upper bound of array is less than
        ' lower bound. Store result returned by Filter function in a
        ' String array, then compare upper bound with lower bound.
        astrMatches = Filter(astrWords, astrText(lngCount))
        If UBound(astrMatches) < Lbound(astrMatches) Then
            ' If word in string does not match any word in array
            ' of minor words, convert word to proper case.
            astrText(lngCount) = StrConv(astrText(lngCount), vbProperCase)
        Else
            ' If it does match, convert it to lowercase.
            astrText(lngCount) = StrConv(astrText(lngCount), vbLowerCase)
        End If
    Next

    ' Join the string.
    ConvertToProperCase = Join(astrText)
End Function
```

The ConvertToProperCase procedure calls the GetMinorWords procedure, which opens the text file that contains the list of minor words, gets a string containing all the words in the list, splits the string into an array, and returns the array. GetMinorWords calls another procedure, the GetLikelyDelimiter procedure, which finds the first likely delimiter character in the text file.

Note To call the ConvertToProperCase procedure, you must set a reference to the Microsoft Scripting Runtime object library.

Working with String Variables

Almost any application uses strings that contain variables in some form or another; you dimension a variable, assign a value to it, and output that variable as part of a string. If you must output a string that contains multiple variables, it can often be a painstaking process adding all of the quote characters and concatenation operators in the right places.

For example, the following code contains several string variables:

```
Dim Fname As String, Lname As String
Dim varAge As Variant, varDate as Variant

Fname = "John"
Lname = "Doe"
varAge = 42
varDate = "August 15"

TextBox1.Text = Fname & Lname & " will be " & varAge & _
    " od on " & varDate & " of this year."
```

In the preceding example, it would be easy to leave out a quotation mark character or space or to misplace a concatenation character. The result would be a compile-time error, and finding your mistake could prove especially difficult in a long string.

The String Editor add-in, included in Microsoft® Office XP Developer, greatly simplifies the process of formatting complex strings such as SQL statements or scripts. Using the String Editor, you can simply enter your string as straight text, then mark any string variables within the string. On completion, the String Editor will automatically format the string for you, inserting all of the necessary quotes and other formatting characters.

To insert a formatted string into your code

1. Select an insertion point in the Code Editor where you want to add a string.

2. From the **Add-Ins** menu, select **String Editor**.

    Note The String Editor menu item is only available when the VBA String Editor add-in is loaded.

3. Type the string into the String Editor. For example:

```
Fname Lname will be varAge od on varDate of this year.
```

4. For each variable within the string, select the variable, and click the **Toggle String** button on the **String Editor** toolbar.

   Each selection will be marked as a variable and color-coded blue in the String Editor.

5. Click the **Update** button to insert the formatted string into your code with all of the necessary formatting characters.

The following table shows some examples of the formatting applied by the String Editor.

In the String Editor	Resulting code
The dog is happy.	"The dog is happy."
The dog is happy.	"The dog is " & vbNewLine & "happy."
The strAnimal is happy.	"The " & strAnimal & " is happy."
The dog is happy.	vbTab & "The dog is happy."
"The dog is happy"	Chr$(34) & "The dog is happy" & Chr$(34)

Working with Numbers

Almost every procedure you write in Microsoft® Visual Basic® for Applications (VBA) uses numeric values in some way. For optimal performance and efficiency, and for accuracy in calculations, it is important to understand the different numeric data types and when to use which.

In This Section

The Integer, Long, and Byte Data Types
Understand the three data types in Microsoft® Visual Basic® for Applications (VBA) that can represent integers—the Integer, Long, and Byte data types.

The Boolean Data Type
Use the Boolean data type to specify True or False.

The Floating-Point Data Types
Specify extremely small or large numbers using the Single and Double data types.

The Currency and Decimal Data Types
Use these scaled integer data types when you cannot afford rounding errors and you do not require as many decimal places as the floating-point data types provide.

Conversion, Rounding, and Truncation
Learn about the functions that help you covert, round, and truncate decimals.

Formatting Numeric Values
Format numbers using the following Microsoft® Visual Basic® for Applications (VBA) functions: FormatNumber, FormatCurrency, FormatPercent, and Format.

Using the Mod Operator
Determine whether two numbers divide evenly or how close they come to dividing evenly using the Mod operator, which divides two numbers and returns the remainder.

Performing Calculations on Numeric Arrays
Understand how to perform mathematical functions on a variable set of numbers.

The Integer, Long, and Byte Data Types

Three data types in Microsoft® Visual Basic® for Applications (VBA) can represent integers, or whole numbers: the Integer, Long, and Byte data types. Of these, the Integer and Long types are the ones you are most likely to use regularly.

The Integer and Long data types can both hold positive or negative values. The difference between them is their size: Integer variables can hold values between -32,768 and 32,767, while Long variables can range from -2,147,483,648 to 2,147,483,647. Traditionally, VBA programmers have used integers to hold small numbers, because they required less memory. In recent versions, however, VBA converts all integer values to type Long, even if they are declared as type Integer. Therefore, there is no longer a performance advantage to using Integer variables; in fact, Long variables might be slightly faster because VBA does not have to convert them.

The Byte data type can hold positive values from 0 to 255. A Byte variable requires only a single byte of memory, so it is very efficient. You can use a Byte variable to hold an Integer value if you know that value will never be greater than 255. However, the Byte data type is typically used for working with strings. For some string operations, converting the string to an array of bytes can significantly enhance performance.

The Boolean Data Type

The Boolean data type is a special case of an integer data type. The Boolean data type can contain True or False; internally, Microsoft® Visual Basic® for Applications (VBA) stores the value of True as -1, and the value of False as 0.

You can use the CBool function to convert any numeric value to a Boolean value. When another numeric data type is converted to a Boolean value, any nonzero value is equivalent to True, and zero (0) is equivalent to False. For example, `CBool(7)` returns True, and `CBool(5 + 2 - 7)` returns False, because it evaluates to `CBool(0)`.

The following procedure determines whether a number is even. The procedure uses the Mod operator to determine whether a number can be divided by 2 with no remainder. If a number is even, dividing by 2 leaves no remainder; if it is odd, dividing by 2 leaves a remainder of 1:

```
Function IsEven(lngNum As Long) As Boolean
   ' Determines whether a number is even or odd.


   If lngNum Mod 2 = 0 Then
      IsEven = True
   Else
      IsEven = False
   End If
End Function
```

Another way to write this procedure is to convert the result of an expression to a Boolean value and then use the Not keyword to toggle its value, as shown in the following example. If the lngNum argument is odd, then it must be nonzero; converting lngNum to a Boolean value yields True. Because the procedure must return False if the value is odd, using the Not keyword to toggle the Boolean value gives the correct result.

```
Function IsEven(lngNum As Long) As Boolean
   ' Determines whether a number is even or odd.


   IsEven = Not CBool(lngNum Mod 2)
End Function
```

Note that the revised IsEven procedure condenses a five-line If…Then statement into a single line of code. If you are using an If…Then statement to set a value to True under one condition and to False under another, as the IsEven procedure does, you can condense the If…Then statement by modifying its condition to return True or False. However, the revised procedure might be somewhat harder to understand.

The Floating-Point Data Types

Microsoft® Visual Basic® for Applications (VBA) provides two floating-point data types, Single and Double. The Single data type requires 4 bytes of memory and can store negative values between -3.402823 x 1038 and -1.401298 x 10-45 and positive values between 1.401298 x 10-45 and 3.402823 x 1038. The Double data type requires 8 bytes of memory and can store negative values between -1.79769313486232 x 10308 and -4.94065645841247 x 10-324 and positive values between 4.94065645841247 x 10-324 and 1.79769313486232 x 10308.

The Single and Double data types are very precise—that is, they make it possible for you to specify extremely small or large numbers. However, these data types are not very accurate because they use floating-point mathematics. Floating-point mathematics has an inherent limitation in that it uses binary digits to represent decimals. Not all the numbers within the range available to the Single or Double data type can be represented exactly in binary form, so they are rounded. Also, some numbers cannot be represented exactly with any finite number of digits—pi, for example, or the decimal resulting from 1/3.

Because of these limitations to floating-point mathematics, you might encounter rounding errors when you perform operations on floating-point numbers. Compared to the size of the value you are working with, the rounding error will be very small. If you do not require absolute accuracy and can afford relatively small rounding errors, the floating-point data types are ideal for representing very small or very large values. On the other hand, if your values must be accurate—for example, if you are working with money values—you should consider one of the scaled integer data types.

The Currency and Decimal Data Types

The two scaled integer data types, Currency and Decimal, provide a high level of accuracy. These are also referred to as fixed-point data types. They are not as precise as the floating-point data types—that is, they cannot represent numbers as large or as small. However, if you cannot afford rounding errors, and you do not require as many decimal places as the floating-point data types provide, you can use the scaled integer data types. Internally, the scaled integer types represent decimal values as integers by multiplying them by a factor of 10.

The Currency data type uses 8 bytes of memory and can represent numbers with fifteen digits to the left of the decimal point and four to the right, in the range of -922,337,203,685,477.5808 to 922,337,203,685,477.5807.

The Decimal data type uses 12 bytes of memory and can have between 0 and 28 decimal places. The Decimal data type is a Variant subtype; to use the Decimal data type, you must declare a variable of type Variant, and then convert it by using the CDec function.

The following example shows how to convert a Variant variable to a Decimal variable. It also demonstrates how using the Decimal data type can minimize the rounding errors inherent in the floating-point data types.

```
Sub DoubleVsDecimal()
    ' This procedure demonstrates how using the
    ' Decimal data type can minimize rounding errors.

    Dim dblNum      As Double
    Dim varNum      As Variant
    Dim lngCount    As Long

    ' Increment values in loop.
    For lngCount = 1 To 100000
        dblNum = dblNum + 0.00001
        ' Convert value to Decimal using CDec.
```

```
        varNum = varNum + CDec(0.00001)
    Next

    Debug.Print "Result using Double: " & dblNum
    Debug.Print "Result using Decimal: " & varNum
End Sub
```

The procedure prints these results to the Immediate window:

```
Result using Double: 0.999999999998084
Result using Decimal: 1
```

A Note About Division

Any time you use the floating-point division operator (/), you are performing floating-point division, and your return value will be of type Double. This is true whether your dividend and divisor are integer, floating-point, or fixed-point values. It is true whether or not your result has a decimal portion.

For example, running the following code from the Immediate window prints "Double":

```
? TypeName(2.34/5.9)
```

So does this code, even though the result is an integer:

```
? TypeName(9/3)
```

Because all floating-point division returns a floating-point value, you cannot be certain that your result is accurate to every decimal place, even if you are performing division on Decimal or Currency values. There will always be an inherent possibility of rounding errors, although they are likely to be small.

If you are dividing integers, or if you do not care about the decimal portion of the result, you can use the integer division operator (\). Integer division is faster than floating-point division, and the result is always an Integer or Long value, either of which requires less memory than a Double value. For example, running this code from the Immediate window prints "Integer":

```
? TypeName(9\3)
```

Conversion, Rounding, and Truncation

When you convert a decimal value to an integer value, Microsoft® Visual Basic® for Applications (VBA) rounds the number to an integer value. How it rounds depends on the value of the digit immediately to the right of the decimal place—digits less than 5 are rounded down, while digits greater than 5 are rounded up. If the digit is 5, then it is rounded down if the digit immediately to the left of the decimal place is even, and up if it is odd. When the digit to be rounded is a 5, the result is always an even integer.

For example, running the following line of code from the Immediate window prints "8," because VBA rounds down when the number immediately to the left of the decimal is even:

```
? CLng(8.5)
```

However, this code prints "10," because 9 is odd:

```
? CLng(9.5)
```

If you want to discard the decimal portion of a number, and return the integer portion, you can use either the Int or Fix function. These functions simply truncate without rounding. For example, `Int(8.5)` returns 8, and `Int(9.5)` returns 9. The Int and Fix functions behave identically unless you are working with negative numbers. The Int function rounds to the lower negative integer, while the Fix function rounds to the higher one.

For example, the following code evaluates to "-8":

```
? Fix(-8.2)
```

Using the Int function, on the other hand, yields "-9":

```
? Int(-8.2)
```

> **Note**   The Int and Fix functions always return a Double value. You might want to convert the result to a Long value before performing further operations with it.

VBA includes a new rounding function called Round, which you can use to round a floating-point or fixed-point decimal to a specified number of places. For example, the following code rounds the number 1.2345 to 1.234:

```
? Round(1.2345, 3)
```

Although the Round function is useful for returning a number with a specified number of decimal places, you cannot always predict how it will round when the rounding digit is a 5. How VBA rounds a number depends on the internal binary representation of that number. If you want to write a rounding function that will round decimal values according to predictable rules, you should write your own.

Formatting Numeric Values

Microsoft® Visual Basic® for Applications (VBA) provides several functions that you can use to format numbers, including the FormatNumber, FormatCurrency, FormatPercent, and Format functions. Each of these functions returns a number formatted as a string.

The FormatNumber function formats a number with the comma as the thousands separator. You can specify the number of decimal places you want to appear. For example, calling the following code from the Immediate window prints "8,012.36":

```
? FormatNumber(8012.36)
```

The FormatCurrency function formats a number with a dollar sign, including two decimal places by default. Calling this code from the Immediate window prints "$10,456.45":

```
? FormatCurrency(10456.45)
```

The FormatPercent function formats a number as a percentage, including two decimal places by default. For example, calling this code from the Immediate window prints "80.00%":

```
? FormatPercent(4/5)
```

If you must have finer control over the formatting of a number, you can use the Format function to specify a custom format. For example, to display leading zeros before a number, you can create a custom format that includes placeholders for each digit. If a digit is absent, a zero appears in that position. The following procedure shows an example that returns a formatted string complete with leading zeros:

```
Function FormatLeadingZeros(lngNum As Long) As String
    ' Formats number with leading zeros.

    FormatLeadingZeros = Format$(lngNum, "00000")
End Function
```

For more information about creating custom formats, search the Visual Basic Reference Help index for "Format function."

Using the Mod Operator

The Mod operator divides two numbers and returns the remainder. It is useful when you must determine whether two numbers divide evenly, or how close they come to dividing evenly. The Mod operator always returns an Integer or Long value, even when you divide floating-point or fixed-point numbers.

For example, the IsFactor procedure takes two arguments, a number and a potential factor, and returns True if the second argument is indeed a factor of the first. The procedure uses the Mod operator to determine whether one value divides evenly into the other.

```
Function IsFactor(lngNum As Long, _
                lngFactor As Long) As Boolean

    ' Determines whether one number is a factor of another number.

    IsFactor = Not CBool(lngNum Mod lngFactor)
End Function
```

Performing Calculations on Numeric Arrays

Many mathematical functions operate on a variable set of numbers. For example, you can take the median, or middle value, of a set of any size. Because you will not know how many numbers the set will contain while you are writing code to find the median, you cannot create a procedure with a set number of arguments. Instead, you can use a dynamic array to store an indeterminate number of values and perform an operation on them.

The following procedure takes a parameter array and returns the median of the values in the array. A parameter array encompasses a variable number of arguments that are passed to a procedure as an array. The ParamArray keyword specifies a parameter array, which must be defined as type Variant.

The Median procedure calls another procedure, IsNumericArray, which determines whether the array contains any non-numeric elements before the Median procedure attempts to find the median. It then calls the QuickSortArray procedure, which sorts the array. Finally, it determines whether the array contains an even or odd number of elements. If the number of elements is odd, the middle element in the sorted array is the median. If the number of elements is even, the median is the average of the two midmost elements.

```
Function Median(ParamArray avarValues() As Variant) As Double
    ' Return the median of a set of numbers.

    Dim lngCount        As Long
    Dim varTemp         As Variant

    ' Store array in temporary variable.
    varTemp = avarValues()

    ' Check whether array is numeric.
    If IsNumericArray(varTemp) Then
        ' Determine how many elements are in array.
        lngCount = UBound(varTemp) - LBound(varTemp) + 1
        ' Sort the array.
        QuickSortArray varTemp
        ' Determine whether array contains an odd or even number of
elements.
        If IsEven(lngCount) Then
            ' If even, need to find the two middle elements and
            ' return the average of their values.
            ' Remember we're working with a zero-based array!
            Median = (varTemp(lngCount / 2 - 1) + varTemp(lngCount / 2)) / 2
        Else
            ' If odd, need to find the middle element.
            Median = varTemp(Int(lngCount / 2))
        End If
    Else
        ' Return -1 if array isn't numeric.
        Median = -1
    End If
End Function
```

To test the Median procedure, try calling it with an even set of numbers, then with an odd set of numbers, as follows:

```
? Median(45, 67, 23, 89, 52, 101)
```

To make sure it is working properly, you can check it against the Excel Median worksheet function. Note that the Excel Median function can take no more than 30 arguments, while the procedure shown here can take any number of arguments.

You could also modify this procedure to take an array, rather than a parameter array. The parameter array is somewhat easier to test in isolation, but a procedure that takes an array might be more practical for use within your code. For example, you might have a procedure that fills an array with numeric data from a data source, which you then can pass to the Median procedure to determine the median of the set of numbers, without having to pass each value as an argument to the procedure.

The strategy shown here for finding the median also works for other operations that take an indeterminate number of values, such as finding the average or standard deviation, or performing other statistical calculations.

Working with Dates and Times

Microsoft® Visual Basic® for Applications (VBA) provides a data type for storing date and time values, the Date data type. Convenient as the Date data type is, manipulating date values in VBA can still be tricky. To easily work with dates, you must understand how VBA stores date values internally.

In This Section

The Date Data Type
Store date and time values by using the Date data type.

Getting the Current Date and Time
Three functions in Microsoft® Visual Basic® for Applications (VBA) can tell you exactly when it is: the Now, Date, and Time functions.

Formatting a Date
Use predefined formats to format a date, or create a custom format for a date.

Date Delimiters
Understand how to indicate to Microsoft® Visual Basic® for Applications (VBA) that a value is a date.

Assembling a Date
Break down dates into component parts—day, month, and year—to perform a calculation on one element, and then reassemble the date.

Getting Part of a Date
Get information about a date, such as what quarter or week it falls in or what day of the week it is.

Adding and Subtracting Dates
 Learn how to add and subtract intervals to given dates.

Calculating Elapsed Time
 Use functions to calculate the time that has elapsed between two dates, and present that time in the desired format.

The Date Data Type

Microsoft® Visual Basic® for Applications (VBA) provides the Date data type to store date and time values. The Date data type is an 8-byte floating-point value, so internally it is the same as the Double data type. The Date data type can store dates between January 1, 100, and January 1, 9999.

VBA stores the date value in the integer portion of the Date data type, and the time value in the decimal portion. The integer portion represents the number of days since December 30, 1899, which is the starting point for the Date data type. Any dates before this one are stored as negative numbers; all dates after are stored as positive values. If you convert a date value representing December 30, 1899, to a double, you'll find that this date is represented by zero.

The decimal portion of a date represents the amount of time that has passed since midnight. For example, if the decimal portion of a date value is .75, three-quarters of the day has passed, and the time is now 6 P.M.

Because the integer portion of a date represents number of days, you can add and subtract days from one date to get another date.

Getting the Current Date and Time

Three functions in Microsoft® Visual Basic® for Applications (VBA) can tell you exactly when it is: the Now, Date, and Time functions. The Now function returns both the date and time portions of a Date variable. For example, calling the Now function from the Immediate window returns a value such as this one:

```
2/23/98 6:16:47 PM
```

The Date function returns the current date. You can use it if you do not have to know the time. The Time function returns the current time, without the date.

Formatting a Date

You can use predefined formats to format a date by calling the FormatDateTime function, or you can create a custom format for a date by using the Format function.

The following procedure formats a date by using both built-in and custom formats:

```
Sub DateFormats(Optional dteDate As Date)
    ' This procedure formats a date using both built-in
    ' and custom formats.
```

```
' If dteDate argument has not been passed, then
' dteDate is initialized to 0 (or December 30, 1899,
' the date equivalent of 0).
If CLng(dteDate) = 0 Then
   ' Use today's date.
   dteDate = Now
End If


' Print date in built-in and custom formats.
Debug.Print FormatDateTime(dteDate, vbGeneralDate)
Debug.Print FormatDateTime(dteDate, vbLongDate)
Debug.Print FormatDateTime(dteDate, vbShortDate)
Debug.Print FormatDateTime(dteDate, vbLongTime)
Debug.Print FormatDateTime(dteDate, vbShortTime)
Debug.Print Format$(dteDate, "ddd, mmm d, yyyy")
Debug.Print Format$(dteDate, "mmm d, H:MM am/pm")
End Sub
```

Date Delimiters

When you work with date literals in your code, you must indicate to Microsoft® Visual Basic® for Applications (VBA) that a value is a date. If you do not, VBA might think you are performing subtraction or floating-point division.

For example, if you run the following fragment, the value that VBA assigns to the Date variable is not April 5, 1998, but 4 divided by 5 divided by 98. Because you are assigning it to a Date variable, VBA converts the number to a date, and prints "12:11:45 AM" to the Immediate window:

```
Dim dteDate As Date
dteDate = 4 / 5 / 98
Debug.Print dteDate
```

To avoid this problem, you must include delimiters around the date. The preferred date delimiter for VBA is the number sign (#). In addition, you can use double quotation marks, as you would for a string, but doing so requires VBA to perform an extra step to convert the string to a date. If you rewrite the fragment as follows to include the date delimiter, VBA prints "4/5/98" to the Immediate window:

```
Dim dteDate As Date
dteDate = #4/5/98#
Debug.Print dteDate
```

Assembling a Date

To work with a date in code, you sometimes must break it down into its component parts—that is, its day, month, and year. When you have done this, you can perform a calculation on one element, and then reassemble the date. To break a date into components, you can use the Day, Month, and Year functions. Each of these functions takes a date and returns the day, month, or year portion, respectively, as an Integer value. For example, Year(#2/23/98#) returns "1998."

To reassemble a date, you can use the DateSerial function. This function takes three integer arguments: a year, a month, and a day value. It returns a Date value that contains the reassembled date.

Often you can break apart a date, perform a calculation on it, and reassemble it all in one step. For example, to find the first day of the month, given any date, you can write a function similar to the following one:

```
Function FirstOfMonth(Optional dteDate As Date) As Date


    ' This function calculates the first day of a month, given a date.
    ' If no date is passed in, the function uses the current date.


    If CLng(dteDate) = 0 Then
        dteDate = Date
    End If


    ' Find the first day of this month.
    FirstOfMonth = DateSerial(Year(dteDate), Month(dteDate), 1)
End Function
```

The FirstOfMonth procedure takes a date or, if the calling procedure does not pass one, uses the current date. It breaks the date into its component year and month, and then reassembles the date using 1 for the day argument. Calling this procedure with the dteDate argument #2/23/98# returns "2/1/98".

The following procedure uses the same strategy to return the last day of a month, given a date:

```
Function LastOfMonth(Optional dteDate As Date) As Date


    ' This function calculates the last day of a month, given a date.
    ' If no date is passed in, the function uses the current date.


    If CLng(dteDate) = 0 Then
        dteDate = Date
    End If
```

```
' Find the first day of the next month, then subtract one day.
LastOfMonth = DateSerial(Year(dteDate), Month(dteDate) + 1, 1) - 1
End Function
```

Microsoft® Visual Basic® for Applications (VBA) also provides functions that you can use to disassemble and reassemble a time value in the same manner. The Hour, Minute, and Second functions return portions of a time value; the TimeSerial function takes an hour, minute, and second value and returns a complete time value.

Getting Part of a Date

The previous section showed how to return the year, month, and day from a date. You can get other information about a date as well, such as what quarter or week it falls in, or what day of the week it is.

The Weekday function takes a date and returns a constant indicating on what day of the week it falls. The following procedure takes a date and returns True if the date falls on a workday—that is, Monday through Friday—and False if it falls on a weekend.

```
Function IsWorkday(Optional dteDate As Date) As Boolean
    ' This function determines whether a date
    ' falls on a weekday.

    ' If no date passed in, use today's date.
    If CLng(dteDate) = 0 Then
        dteDate = Date
    End If

    ' Determine where in week the date falls.
    Select Case Weekday(dteDate)
        Case vbMonday To vbFriday
            IsWorkday = True
        Case Else
            IsWorkday = False
    End Select
End Function
```

In addition to the individual functions that return part of a date—Year, Month, Day, and Weekday—Microsoft® Visual Basic® for Applications (VBA) includes the DatePart function, which can return any part of a date. Although it might seem redundant, the DatePart function gives you slightly more control over the values you return, because it gives you the option to specify the first day of the week and the first day of the year. For this reason, it can be useful when you are writing code that might run on systems in other countries. In addition, the DatePart function is the only way to return information about what quarter a date falls into.

Adding and Subtracting Dates

To add an interval to a given date, you must use the DateAdd function, unless you are adding days to a date. As mentioned earlier, because the integer portion of a Date variable represents the number of days that have passed since December 30, 1899, adding integers to a Date variable is equivalent to adding days.

By using the DateAdd function, you can add any interval to a given date: years, months, days, weeks, quarters. The following procedure finds the anniversary of a given date; that is, the next date on which it occurs. If the anniversary has already occurred this year, the procedure returns the date of the anniversary in the next year.

```
Function Anniversary(dteDate As Date) As Date
    ' This function finds the next anniversary of a date.
    ' If the date has already passed for this year, it returns
    ' the date on which the anniversary occurs in the following year.
    Dim dteThisYear As Date

    ' Find corresponding date this year.
    dteThisYear = DateSerial(Year(Date), Month(dteDate), Day(dteDate))
    ' Determine whether it's already passed.
    If dteThisYear < Date Then
        Anniversary = DateAdd("yyyy", 1, dteThisYear)
    Else
        Anniversary = dteThisYear
    End If
End Function
```

To find the interval between two dates, you can use the DateDiff function. The interval returned can be any of several units of time: days, weeks, months, years, hours, and so on.

The following example uses the DateDiff function to return the day number for a particular day of the year. The procedure determines the last day of the last year by using the DateSerial function, and then subtracts that date from the date that was passed in to the procedure.

```
Function DayOfYear(Optional dteDate As Date) As Long

    ' This function takes a date as an argument and returns
    ' the day number for that year. If the dteDate argument is
    ' omitted, the function uses the current date.
```

```
' If dteDate argument has not been passed, dteDate is
' initialized to 0 (or December 30, 1899, the date
' equivalent of 0).
If CLng(dteDate) = 0 Then
   ' Use today's date.
   dteDate = Date
End If


' Calculate the number of days that have passed since
' December 31 of the previous year.
DayOfYear = Abs(DateDiff("d", dteDate, _
   DateSerial(Year(dteDate) - 1, 12, 31)))
End Function
```

Calling this procedure with the value of #2/23/98# returns "54."

Calculating Elapsed Time

You can use the DateAdd and DateDiff functions to calculate the time that has elapsed between two dates, and then, with a little additional work, present that time in the desired format. For example, the following procedure calculates a person's age in years, taking into account whether his or her birthday has already occurred in the current year.

Using the DateDiff function to determine the number of years between today and a birthdate does not always give a valid result because the DateDiff function rounds to the next year. If a person's birthday has not yet occurred, using the DateDiff function will make the person one year older than he or she actually is.

To remedy this situation, the procedure checks to see whether the birthday has already occurred this year, and if it has not, it subtracts 1 to return the correct age.

```
Function CalcAge(dteBirthdate As Date) As Long

   Dim lngAge As Long

   ' Make sure passed-in value is a date.
   If Not IsDate(dteBirthdate) Then
      dteBirthdate = Date
   End If

   ' Make sure birthdate is not in the future.
   ' If it is, use today's date.
```

```
    If dteBirthdate > Date Then
        dteBirthdate = Date
    End If


    ' Calculate the difference in years between today and birthdate.
    lngAge = DateDiff("yyyy", dteBirthdate, Date)
    ' If birthdate has not occurred this year, subtract 1 from age.
    If DateSerial(Year(Date), Month(dteBirthdate), Day(dteBirthdate)) >
Date Then
        lngAge = lngAge - 1
    End If
    CalcAge = lngAge
End Function
```

Working with Files

With the advent of the Scripting Runtime object library, you can work with drives, folders, and files as objects.

In This Section

The Microsoft Scripting Runtime Object Library
    Understand the Scripting Runtime Object Library, and learn how to set a reference to it.

Returning Files from the File System
    Use the FileSystemObject to work with drives, folders, and files in the file system.

Setting File Attributes
    Use the File object and Folder object to read or set file or folder attributes.

Logging Errors to a Text File
    Use objects to write to a text file, return an object that refers to a new or existing file, and use methods to open it for input or output.

The Dictionary Object
    Understand the features of the Dictionary object—the Exists method, the CompareMode property, the Key property, and the RemoveAll method.

The Microsoft Scripting Runtime Object Library

When you install the Office XP applications, one of the object libraries installed on your system is the Scripting Runtime object library. This object library contains objects that are useful from either Microsoft® Visual Basic® for Applications (VBA) or script, so it is provided as a separate library.

The objects in the Scripting Runtime library provide easy access to the file system, and make reading and writing to a text file much simpler than it is in previous versions.

By default, no reference is set to this library, so you must set a reference before you can use it. If Microsoft Scripting Runtime does not appear in the References dialog box (Tools menu), you should be able to find it in the Windows system directory as Scrrun.dll.

The top-level objects in the Scripting Runtime object library are the Dictionary object and the FileSystemObject object. To use the Dictionary object, you create an object variable of type Dictionary, then set it to a new instance of a Dictionary object:

```
Dim dctDict As Dictionary

Set dctDict = New Dictionary
```

To use the other objects in the Scripting Runtime library in code, you must first create a variable of type FileSystemObject, and then use the New keyword to create a new instance of the FileSystemObject, as shown in the following code fragment:

```
Dim fsoSysObj As FileSystemObject

Set fsoSysObj = New FileSystemObject
```

You can then use the variable that refers to the FileSystemObject to work with the Drive, Folder, File, and TextStream objects.

The following table describes the objects contained in the Scripting Runtime library.

Object	Collection	Description
Dictionary		Top-level object. Similar to the VBA Collection object. Use this to store data key item pairs.
Drive	Drives	Refers to a drive or collection of drives on the system.
File	Files	Refers to a file or collection of files in the file system.
FileSystemObject		Top-level object. Use this object to access drives, folders, and files in the file system.
Folder	Folders	Refers to a folder or collection of folders in the file system.
TextStream		Refers to a stream of text that is read from, written to, or appended to a text file.

Returning Files from the File System

When you have created a new instance of the FileSystemObject, you can use it to work with drives, folders, and files in the file system.

The following procedure returns the files in a particular folder to a Dictionary object. The GetFiles procedure takes three arguments: the path to the directory, a Dictionary object, and an optional Boolean argument that specifies whether the procedure should be called recursively. It returns a Boolean value indicating whether the procedure was successful.

The procedure first uses the GetFolder method to return a reference to a Folder object. It then loops through the Files collection of that folder and adds the path and file name for each file to the Dictionary object. If the blnRecursive argument is set to True, the GetFiles procedure is called recursively to return the files in each subfolder.

```
Function GetFiles(strPath As String, _
                dctDict As ScriptingDictionary, _
                Optional blnRecursive As Boolean) As Boolean


    ' This procedure returns all the files in a directory into
    ' a Dictionary object. If called recursively, it also returns
    ' all files in subfolders.


    Dim fsoSysObj      As FileSystemObject
    Dim fdrFolder      As Folder
    Dim fdrSubFolder   As Folder
    Dim filFile        As File


    ' Return new FileSystemObject.
    Set fsoSysObj = New FileSystemObject


    On Error Resume Next
    ' Get folder.
    Set fdrFolder = fsoSysObj.GetFolder(strPath)
    If Err <> 0 Then
        ' Incorrect path.
        GetFiles = False
        GoTo GetFiles_End
    End If
    On Error GoTo 0
```

```
' Loop through Files collection, adding to dictionary.
For Each filFile In fdrFolder.Files
    dctDict.Add filFile.Path, filFile.Name
Next filFile


' If Recursive flag is true, call recursively.
If blnRecursive Then
    For Each fdrSubFolder In fdrFolder.SubFolders
        GetFiles fdrSubFolder.Path, dctDict, True
    Next fdrSubFolder
End If
' Return True if no error occurred.
GetFiles = True


GetFiles_End:
    Exit Function
End Function
```

You can use the following procedure to test the GetFiles procedure. This procedure creates a new Dictionary object and passes it to the GetFiles procedure.

```
Sub TestGetFiles()
    ' Call to test GetFiles function.

    Dim dctDict As ScriptingDictionary
    Dim varItem As Variant

    ' Create new dictionary.
    Set dctDict = New Dictionary
    ' Call recursively, return files into Dictionary object.
    If GetFiles(GetTempDir, dctDict, True) Then
        ' Print items in dictionary.
        For Each varItem In dctDict
            Debug.Print varItem
        Next
    End If
End Sub
```

You can also use the Office FileSearch object to find a file or group of files. The FileSearch object has certain advantages in that you can search subfolders, search for a particular file type, or search the contents of a file by simply setting a few properties.

On the other hand, the Microsoft Scripting Runtime object library makes it possible for you to work with individual files or folders as objects that have their own methods and properties.

Setting File Attributes

The File object and Folder object provide an Attributes property that you can use to read or set a file or folder's attributes, as shown in the following example.

The ChangeFileAttributes procedure takes four arguments: the path to a folder, an optional constant that specifies the attributes to set, an optional constant that specifies the attributes to remove, and an optional argument that specifies that the procedure should be called recursively. You can specify many attributes by using any logical combination of the file attributes.

If the folder path passed in is valid, the procedure returns a Folder object. It then checks to see if the lngSetAttr argument was provided. If so, it loops through all the files in the folder, appending the new attribute or attributes to each file's existing attributes. It does the same for the lngRemoveAttr argument, except in this case it removes the specified attributes if they exist for files in the collection.

Note   The following code does not handle the case of setting the attributes to Normal or zero (0). If you want to set the attribute to Normal, you must use lngRemoveAttr for all the attributes.

Finally, the procedure checks whether the blnRecursive argument has been set to True. If so, it calls the procedure for each file in each subfolder of the strPath argument.

```
Function ChangeFileAttributes(strPath As String, _
                    Optional lngSetAttr As FileAttribute, _
                    Optional lngRemoveAttr As FileAttribute, _
                    Optional blnRecursive As Boolean) As Boolean


   ' This function takes a directory path, a value specifying file
   ' attributes to be set, a value specifying file attributes to be
   ' removed, and a flag that indicates whether it should be called
   ' recursively. It returns True unless an error occurs.

   Dim fsoSysObj      As FileSystemObject
   Dim fdrFolder      As Folder
   Dim fdrSubFolder   As Folder
   Dim filFile        As File
```

```vba
' Return new FileSystemObject.
Set fsoSysObj = New FileSystemObject

On Error Resume Next
' Get folder.
Set fdrFolder = fsoSysObj.GetFolder(strPath)
If Err <> 0 Then
    ' Incorrect path.
    ChangeFileAttributes = False
    GoTo ChangeFileAttributes_End
End If
On Error GoTo 0

' If caller passed in attribute to set, set for all.
If lngSetAttr Then
    For Each filFile In fdrFolder.Files
        filFile.Attributes = filFile.Attributes Or lngSetAttr
    Next
End If

' If caller passed in attribute to remove, remove for all.
If lngRemoveAttr Then
    For Each filFile In fdrFolder.Files
        filFile.Attributes = filFile.Attributes - lngRemoveAttr
    Next
End If

' If caller has set blnRecursive argument to True, then call
' function recursively.
If blnRecursive Then
    ' Loop through subfolders.
    For Each fdrSubFolder In fdrFolder.SubFolders
        ' Call function with subfolder path.
        ChangeFileAttributes fdrSubFolder.Path, lngSetAttr, _
lngRemoveAttr, True
    Next
End If
```

```
    ChangeFileAttributes = True


ChangeFileAttributes_End:
    Exit Function
End Function
```

Logging Errors to a Text File

The Scripting Runtime object library simplifies the code required to read from and write to a text file. To use the new objects to write to a text file, you return a file object that refers to a new or existing file, and then use the OpenAsTextStream method to open it for input or output. The OpenAsTextStream method has an IOMode argument, which you can set to indicate whether you want to read from the file, write to it, or append to it.

The OpenAsTextStream method returns a TextStream object, which is the object you use to work with the text in the file. To read a line, for example, you can use the TextStream object's ReadLine method; to write a line, you can use the WriteLine method. When you're finished working with the file, you can use the Close method to close it.

The following procedure logs an error to a text file. It takes two arguments: an ErrObject argument, which is a reference to the Err object that contains the current error, and an optional strProcName argument, which specifies the procedure in which the error occurred.

The LogError procedure writes to a text file in the Microsoft® Windows® Temp folder. To determine where the Windows Temp folder is, it calls another procedure, the GetTempDir procedure. This procedure makes a call to the Windows application programming interface (API) to determine the Temp folder. Windows cannot boot without a designated Temp folder, so you can be certain that the Temp folder will always be available.

The LogError procedure is meant to be used to log multiple errors. The first time the procedure is called, no log file exists, so it must create one. On each subsequent call, the procedure must open the existing log file. The simplest way to do this is to look for the name of the file that you're expecting, and if it is not there, handle the error and create the file.

Unfortunately, when the procedure is first called and the error occurs, the existing information in the Err object is cleared and the information for the new error takes its place. Because there is only one Err object available in Microsoft® Visual Basic® for Applications (VBA), the error information that you passed to the procedure is lost when a new error occurs. Therefore, the first thing that the procedure does is to store the error number and description of the error in variables.

When the procedure has a reference to the text file (APP_ERROR_LOG), it opens it for appending, and then writes the error information to the file line by line.

```
Sub LogError(errX As ErrObject, _
            Optional strProcName As String)
```

```vba
' This procedure logs errors to a text file. It is used in
' this section to log synchronization errors.
'
' Arguments:
' errX: A variable that refers to the VBA Err object.

Dim fsoSysObj    As FileSystemObject
Dim filFile      As File
Dim txsStream    As TextStream
Dim lngErrNum    As Long
Dim strPath      As String
Dim strErrText   As String


Set fsoSysObj = New FileSystemObject

' Store error information.
lngErrNum = errX.Number
strErrText = errX.Description
' Clear error.
errX.Clear
' Return Windows Temp folder.
strPath = GetTempDir
If Len(strPath) = 0 Then
    GoTo LogError_End
End If


On Error Resume Next
' See if file already exists.
Set filFile = fsoSysObj.GetFile(strPath & APP_ERROR_LOG)
' If not, then create it.
If Err <> 0 Then
    Set filFile = fsoSysObj.CreateTextFile(strPath & APP_ERROR_LOG)
End If
On Error GoTo 0


' Open file as text stream for reading.
Set txsStream = filFile.OpenAsTextStream(ForAppending)
```

```
    ' Write error information and close.
    With txsStream
        .WriteLine lngErrNum
        .WriteLine strErrText
        If Len(strProcName) > 0 Then .WriteLine strProcName
        .WriteLine Now
        .WriteBlankLines 1
        .Close
    End With


LogError_End:
    Exit Sub
End Sub
```

To try the LogError procedure, you can call the following procedure. This procedure suspends error handling, then uses the Raise method of the Err object to force an error. It then passes the Err object to the LogError procedure, along with the name of the procedure that caused the error.

```
Sub TestLogError()
    ' This procedure tests the LogError function.


    On Error Resume Next
    ' Raise an error.
    Err.Raise 11
    ' Log it.
    LogError Err, "TestLogError"
End Sub
```

The Dictionary Object

The Dictionary object is a data structure that can contain sets of pairs, where each pair consists of an item, which can be any data type, and a key, which is a unique String value that identifies the item. The Dictionary object is similar in some ways to the VBA Collection object; however, the Dictionary object offers certain features that the Collection object lacks, including:

- The Exists method. You can use this method to determine whether a particular key, and its corresponding item, exist in a Dictionary object. The Exists method makes it simpler and more efficient to search a Dictionary object than to search a Collection object.

- The CompareMode property. Setting this property specifies the text-comparison mode for the Dictionary object, so that you can search for a key in either a case-sensitive or case-insensitive manner. By default, it is set to BinaryCompare, which means that the Exists method will return True only if it finds a binary match. There is no way to specify a text-comparison mode for a key that retrieves an item from a Collection object.

- The Key property. This property enables you to return the key for a particular item in the dictionary. An item in a Collection object also has a key, which you can use to retrieve that item; however, there is no way to retrieve the key itself.

- The RemoveAll method. This method removes all items in the Dictionary object. A Collection object, on the other hand, has no method for removing all items at once, although setting the Collection object to Nothing has the same effect.

The primary advantage of the Dictionary object over the Collection object is the fact that it is easier to search a Dictionary object for a given item. Despite this advantage, the Dictionary object does not replace the Collection object entirely. The Collection object is useful in some situations where the Dictionary object is not. For example, if you're creating a custom object model, you can use a Collection object to store a reference to a custom collection, but you cannot use a Dictionary object to do this.

For more information about the Dictionary object, see the VBScript documentation on the Microsoft Scripting Technologies Web site at http://msdn.microsoft.com/scripting/default.htm.

Understanding Arrays

Arrays make it possible for you to refer to a series of variables by the same name and to use a number (an index) to tell them apart. This helps you create smaller and simpler code in many situations, because you can set up loops that deal efficiently with any number of cases by using the index number. Arrays are useful when you must store a number of values of the same type, but you do not know how many, or you do not want to create individual variables to store them all.

For example, suppose you must store a numeric value for every day of the year. You could declare 365 separate numeric variables, but that would be a lot of work. Instead, you can create an array to store all the data in one variable. The array itself is a single variable with multiple elements; each element can contain one piece of data.

You can use loops, together with a couple of special functions for working with arrays, to assign values to or retrieve values from the various elements of an array.

In This Section

Creating Arrays
> Understand how to create two types of arrays in Microsoft® Visual Basic® for Applications (VBA)—fixed-size arrays and dynamic arrays.

Arrays and Variants
> Learn how a Variant variable can store an array.

Assigning One Array to Another
> Assign one array to another if two dynamic arrays have the same data type.

Returning an Array from a Function
Call a procedure that returns an array and assign it to another array.

Passing an Array to a Procedure
Declare an array in one procedure, and then pass that array to another procedure to be modified.

Sorting Arrays
Understand how to sort an array, which is an iterative process that requires a complex algorithm.

Using the Filter Function to Search String Arrays
Search a string array if you simply must know whether an item exists in the array by using the Filter function.

Using a Binary Search Function to Search Numeric Arrays
Learn how the binary-search algorithm performs efficient searching on a sorted array—whether numeric or string.

Searching a Dictionary
Use object programming constructs, such as For Each…Next and With…End With statements, to work with the Dictionary object.

Creating Arrays

You can create two types of arrays in Microsoft® Visual Basic® for Applications (VBA)—fixed-size arrays and dynamic arrays. A fixed-size array has a fixed number of elements, and is useful only when you know exactly how many elements your array will have while you're writing the code. Most of the time you'll create dynamic arrays.

Arrays can be of any data type. The data type for an array specifies the data type for each element of the array; for example, each element of an array of type Long can contain a Long value. The following code fragment declares an array variable of type Long:

```
Dim alngNum() As Long
```

> **Note**   You do not have to include the parentheses when you refer to an array variable, except when you declare it, resize it, or refer to an individual element. However, you might want to include the parentheses everywhere to make it clear that the variable is an array.

When you have declared a dynamic array variable, you can resize the array by using the ReDim statement. To resize the array, you provide a value for the upper bound, and optionally, for the lower bound. The upper and lower bound of an array refer to the beginning and ending indexes for the array.

You must specify the upper bound for the array when you resize it. The lower bound is optional, but it is a good idea to include it, so that it is obvious to you what the lower bound of the array is:

```
' This array contains 100 elements.
ReDim alngNum(0 To 99)
```

If you do not include the lower bound, it is determined by the Option Base setting for the module. By default, the Option Base setting for a module is 0. You can set it to 1 by entering `Option Base 1` in the Declarations section of the module.

If you are using the ReDim statement on an array that contains values, those values might be lost when the array is resized. To ensure that any values in the array are maintained, you can use the Preserve keyword with the ReDim statement, as follows:

```
ReDim Preserve alngNum(0 To 364)
```

Resizing an array with the Preserve keyword can be slow, so you want to do it as infrequently as possible. A good way to minimize use of the Preserve keyword in your code is to estimate the amount of data you require to store and size the array accordingly. If an error occurs because you have not made the array large enough, you can resize it within the error handler as many times as necessary. When you're through working with the array, if it is larger than you require, you can resize it to make it just large enough to contain the data it currently has.

Arrays and Variants

A Variant variable can store an array. For example, the following code fragment assigns an array of type String to a Variant variable:

```
Dim astrItems(0 To 9)    As String
Dim varItems             As Variant

varItems = astrItems
```

When a static array is initialized, or when a dynamic array is redimensioned, each element is initialized according to its type. In other words, String type elements are initialized to zero-length strings, Integer and Long type elements are initialized to zero (0), and Variant type elements are initialized to Empty. The point is that in the preceding example, it is not necessary to fill the array to work with it. By simply declaring an array of ten elements as type String, we've created an array containing ten zero-length strings.

An array of type Variant can store any data type in any of its elements. For example, a Variant type array can have one element of type String, one element of type Long, and another of type Date. It can even store a Variant variable that contains another array.

A Variant type array can also store an array of objects. If you know that an array will store only objects, you can declare it as type Object rather than as type Variant. And if you know that an array of objects will contain only one type of object, you can declare the array as that object type.

> **Tip** You might want to consider using a Collection or Dictionary object to store groups of objects in a single variable, rather than creating an array of objects. The advantage to using an array over a Collection or Dictionary object is that it is easy to sort. But if you're storing objects, you probably do not care about the sort order. Because a Collection or Dictionary object resizes itself automatically, you do not have to worry about keeping track of its size, as you do with an array.

Assigning One Array to Another

If two dynamic arrays have the same data type, you can assign one array to another. Assigning one array to another of the same type is quick because the first array is simply pointed to the memory location that stores the second array.

For example, the following code fragment assigns one string array to another:

```
Dim astr1() As String
Dim astr2(0 To 9) As String


astr1 = astr2
```

> **Note**   This type of assignment works only for arrays of the same type. The two arrays must both be dynamic arrays, and they must be declared as the exact same type: if one is type String, the other must be type String. It cannot be type Variant or any other data type. If you want to assign one array's elements to an array of a different type, you must create a loop and assign each element one at a time.

Returning an Array from a Function

The previous example assigned one array variable to another. Based on this example, you might guess that you can also call a procedure that returns an array and assign that to another array, as in the following code fragment:

```
Dim astr1() As String


astr1 = ReturnArray
```

To return an array, a procedure must have a return value type of the array's data type, or of type Variant. The advantage to declaring a procedure to return a typed array versus a Variant value is that you are not required to use the IsArray function to ensure that the procedure indeed returned an array. If a procedure returns a value of type Variant, you might want to check its contents before performing array operations.

The ReturnArray procedure prompts the user for input and creates an array of the resulting values, resizing the array as required. Note that to return an array from a procedure, you simply assign the array to the name of the procedure.

```
Function ReturnArray() As String()
    ' This function fills an array with user input, then
    ' returns the array.

    Dim astrItems()     As String
    Dim strInput        As String
```

```vba
Dim strMsg          As String
Dim lngIndex        As Long

On Error GoTo ReturnArray_Err

strMsg = "Enter a value or press Cancel to end:"

lngIndex = 0

' Prompt user for first item to add to array.
strInput = InputBox(strMsg)
If Len(strInput) > 0 Then
   ' Estimate size of array.
   ReDim astrItems(0 To 2)
   astrItems(lngIndex) = strInput
   lngIndex = lngIndex + 1
Else
   ' If user cancels without adding item,
   ' don't resize array.
   ReturnArray = astrItems
   GoTo ReturnArray_End
End If

' Prompt user for additional items and add to array.
Do
   strInput = InputBox(strMsg)
   If Len(strInput) > 0 Then
      astrItems(lngIndex) = strInput
      lngIndex = lngIndex + 1
   End If
' Loop until user cancels.
Loop Until Len(strInput) = 0

' Resize to current value of lngIndex - 1.
ReDim Preserve astrItems(0 To lngIndex - 1)
ReturnArray = astrItems
```

```
ReturnArray_End:
    Exit Function


ReturnArray_Err:
    ' If upper bound is exceeded, enlarge array.
    If Err = ERR_SUBSCRIPT Then ' Subscript out of range
        ' Double the size of the array.
        ReDim Preserve astrItems(lngIndex * 2)
        Resume
    Else
        MsgBox "An unexpected error has occurred!", vbExclamation
        Resume ReturnArray_End
    End If
End Function
```

When you call a procedure that returns an array, you must take into account the case in which the returned array does not contain any elements. For example, in the preceding ReturnArray procedure, if you cancel the input box the first time that it appears, the array returned by the procedure contains no elements. The calling procedure must check for this condition. The best way to do this is to define a procedure such as the following one, which takes an array and checks the upper bound. If the array contains no elements, checking the upper bound causes a trappable error.

```
Function IsArrayEmpty(varArray As Variant) As Boolean
    ' Determines whether an array contains any elements.
    ' Returns False if it does contain elements, True
    ' if it does not.

    Dim lngUBound As Long

    On Error Resume Next
    ' If the array is empty, an error occurs when you
    ' check the array's bounds.
    lngUBound = UBound(varArray)
    If Err.Number <> 0 Then
        IsArrayEmpty = True
    Else
        IsArrayEmpty = False
    End If
End Function
```

Note The VBA Split and Filter functions can also return an array that contains no elements. Checking the upper or lower bounds on an array returned by either of these procedures does not cause an error, however. When the Split or Filter function returns an array containing no elements, the lower bound of that array is 0, and the upper bound is -1. Therefore, to determine whether the returned array contains any elements, you can check for the condition where the upper bound of the array is less than the lower bound.

Passing an Array to a Procedure

You can declare an array in one procedure, and then pass the array to another procedure to be modified. The procedure that modifies the array does not have to return an array. Arrays are passed by reference, meaning that one procedure passes to the other a pointer to the array's location in memory. When the second procedure modifies the array, it modifies it at that same memory location. Therefore, when execution returns to the first procedure, the array variable refers to the modified array.

Sorting Arrays

Sorting an array is an iterative process that requires a fairly sophisticated algorithm. An example of a common sorting algorithm, the QuickSort algorithm. The QuickSort algorithm is explained in thorough detail in the *Visual Basic Language Developer's Handbook* by Ken Getz and Mike Gilbert (Sybex, 2000)—a good place to start if you're looking for more information about sorting arrays.

In brief, the QuickSort algorithm works by using a divide-and-sort strategy. It first finds the middle element in the array, then works its way from the rightmost element to the middle, and from the leftmost element to the middle, comparing elements on both sides of the middle value and swapping their values if necessary. When this part of the sort is complete, the values on the right side are all greater than those on the left, but they're not necessarily in order. The procedure then looks at the values on the left side by using the same strategy—finding a middle value and swapping elements on both sides. It does this until all the elements on the left side have been sorted, and then it tackles the right side. The procedure calls itself recursively and continues executing until the entire array has been sorted.

Using the Filter Function to Search String Arrays

The Filter function makes it easy to search a string array if you simply must know whether an item exists in the array. The Filter function takes a string array and a string containing the search text. It returns a one-dimensional array containing all the elements that match the search text.

One potential disadvantage of using the Filter function to search an array is that it does not return the index of the elements of the array that match the search text. In other words, the Filter function tells you whether an element exists in an array, but it does not tell you where.

Another potential problem with using the Filter function to search an array is that there is no way to specify whether the search text should match the entire element or whether it only must match a part of it. For example, if you use the Filter function to search for an element matching the letter "e," the Filter function returns not only those elements containing only "e," but also any elements containing larger words that include "e."

The following procedure augments the capabilities of the Filter function to search an array and returns only elements that match exactly. The FilterExactMatch procedure takes two arguments: a string array to search and a string to find. It uses the Filter function to return an array containing all elements that match the search string, either partially or entirely. It then checks each element in the filtered array to verify that it matches the search string exactly. If the element does match exactly, it is copied to a third string array. The function returns this third array, which contains only exact matches.

```
Function FilterExactMatch(astrItems() As String, _
                          strSearch As String) As String()


    ' This function searches a string array for elements
    ' that exactly match the search string.


    Dim astrFilter()    As String
    Dim astrTemp()      As String
    Dim lngUpper        As Long
    Dim lngLower        As Long
    Dim lngIndex        As Long
    Dim lngCount        As Long


    ' Filter array for search string.
    astrFilter = Filter(astrItems, strSearch)


    ' Store upper and lower bounds of resulting array.
    lngUpper = UBound(astrFilter)
    lngLower = LBound(astrFilter)


    ' Resize temporary array to be same size.
    ReDim astrTemp(lngLower To lngUpper)


    ' Loop through each element in filtered array.
    For lngIndex = lngLower To lngUpper
        ' Check that element matches search string exactly.
```

```
        If astrFilter(lngIndex) = strSearch Then
            ' Store elements that match exactly in another array.
            astrTemp(lngCount) = strSearch
            lngCount = lngCount + 1
        End If
    Next lngIndex


    ' Resize array containing exact matches.
    ReDim Preserve astrTemp(lngLower To lngCount - 1)
    ' Return array containing exact matches.
    FilterExactMatch = astrTemp
End Function
```

Using a Binary Search Function to Search Numeric Arrays

The Filter function works well for searching string arrays, but it is inefficient for numeric arrays. To use the Filter function for a numeric array, you have to convert all of the numeric elements to strings, an extra step that impairs performance. Then you must perform string-comparison operations, when numeric comparisons are much faster.

Although it is more involved, the binary-search algorithm performs efficient searching on a sorted array—whether numeric or string. The binary-search algorithm divides a set of values in half, and determines whether the value being sought lies in the first half or the second half. Whichever half contains the value is kept, and the other half is discarded. The remaining half is then again divided in half, and the process repeats until the algorithm either arrives at the sought value or determines that it is not in the set. Note that the array must be sorted for this algorithm to work.

For an in-depth discussion of the binary-search algorithm, see the *Visual Basic Language Developer's Handbook* by Ken Getz and Mike Gilbert (Sybex, 2000).

Searching a Dictionary

Strictly speaking, a Dictionary object is not an array, but it is similar. Both are data structures that can store multiple values. The Dictionary object has certain advantages over an array: you can use object programming constructs such as For Each…Next and With…End With statements to work with it, and you do not have to worry about sizing it, as you do an array.

If you use a Dictionary object instead of an array to store a set of data, you can check whether a particular item exists in the dictionary by calling the Exists method of the Dictionary object and passing it the key for the item you want. However, the Exists method does not provide any information regarding where the item is within the dictionary or how many times it occurs.

An advantage of using the Exists method with a Dictionary object, rather than using the Filter function with an array, is that the Exists method returns a Boolean value, while the Filter function returns another array. If you are not required to know how many times the search item occurs, using the Dictionary object might simplify your code.

Tips for Defining Procedures in VBA

When you are defining a Function or Sub procedure, you have options available to you that can make your code more extensible or more flexible. The following sections discuss how to extend your procedures by using optional arguments, using parameter arrays to pass a variable number of arguments, and passing arguments by value and by reference.

In This Section

Using Optional Arguments
   Add functionality without updating all the code that calls those procedures by adding optional arguments to user-defined procedures.

Using Parameter Arrays
   Pass an array of arguments to a procedure by using a parameter array.

Passing Arguments by Value or by Reference
   Understand the difference between passing arguments by value and passing arguments by reference when you define a procedure.

Using Optional Arguments

Optional arguments are arguments that are not required for a procedure to be compiled and run. Many built-in functions and methods take optional arguments. Adding optional arguments to user-defined procedures is a way to add functionality without updating all the code that calls those procedures. In addition, if you declare arguments that are not always required as optional, you can minimize resource use by passing only those arguments that are necessary for a given procedure call.

To define an optional argument in a user-defined procedure, use the Optional keyword. You can have as many optional arguments as you want, but when you denote one argument as optional, any arguments that follow it in the argument list must be optional also, as shown in the following procedure definition:

```
Function SomeProc(strRequired1 As String, _
                  strRequired2 As String, _
                  Optional lngOpt1 As Long, _
                  Optional blnOpt2 As Boolean)
```

Within the body of the procedure, you must have a way to check whether the optional argument was passed in. In many cases, if an optional argument has not been passed in, you might want it to have a default value. If the calling procedure does not provide a value for an optional argument, the optional argument is automatically initialized in the same way it would be if it were a variable—string arguments are initialized to a zero-length string, numeric arguments to zero (0), Boolean arguments to False, and so on.

You can override this default initialization by providing a different default value for the optional argument in the procedure definition. The value you provide becomes the default value when the calling procedure fails to pass a value for the optional argument. The following procedure definition sets the default value for an argument of type Long to 1 and for an argument of type Boolean to True:

```
Function SomeProc(strRequired1 As String, _
                  strRequired2 As String, _
                  Optional lngOpt1 As Long=1, _
                  Optional blnOpt2 As Boolean=True)
```

As you can see, an argument of any data type except Variant always will have a value, and it might not be possible to determine within the procedure whether the value was passed in or whether it is the default value. If you must know whether the argument was passed in, define the optional argument as type Variant. Then, use the IsMissing function within the procedure to determine whether the argument has been passed in, as shown in the following procedure:

```
Sub TestIsMissing(varTest As Variant)
    If IsMissing(varTest) Then
        Debug.Print "Missing"
    Else
        Debug.Print varTest
    End If
End Sub
```

The IsMissing function works only with the Variant data type; because any other data type always will have a default initialization value, the IsMissing function will return False regardless of whether a value has been passed for the argument.

Using Parameter Arrays

You can pass an array of arguments to a procedure by using a parameter array. The advantage to using a parameter array is you are not required to know at design time how many arguments will be passed to a procedure—you can pass a variable number of arguments when you call it.

To define a parameter array, use the ParamArray keyword followed by an array of type Variant, as shown in the following procedure definition:

```
Function SomeProc(ParamArray avarItems() As Variant)
```

A parameter array always must be an array of type Variant, and it always must be the last argument in the argument list.

To call a procedure that includes a parameter array, pass in a set of any number of arguments, as shown here:

```
? SomeProc("red", "yellow", "blue", "green", "orange")
```

Within the body of the procedure, you can work with the parameter array as you would with any other array.

Passing Arguments by Value or by Reference

When you define a procedure, you have two choices regarding how arguments are passed to it: by reference or by value. When a variable is passed to a procedure by reference, Microsoft® Visual Basic® for Applications (VBA) actually passes the variable's address in memory to the procedure, which can modify it directly. When execution returns to the calling procedure, the variable contains the modified value.

When an argument is passed by value, VBA passes a copy of the variable to the procedure. Then, the procedure modifies the copy, and the original value of the variable remains intact; when execution returns to the calling procedure, the variable contains the same value that it had before being passed.

By default, VBA passes arguments by reference. To pass an argument by value, precede the argument with the ByVal keyword in the procedure definition, as shown here:

```
Function SomeProc(strText As String, _
                ByVal lngX As Long) As Boolean
```

If you want to denote explicitly that an argument is passed by reference, you can preface the argument with the ByRef keyword in the argument list.

Passing by reference can be useful as long as you understand how it works. For example, you must pass arrays by reference; you will get a syntax error if you try to pass an array by value. Because arrays are passed by reference, you can pass an array to another procedure to be modified, and then you can continue working with the modified array in the calling procedure.

Optimizing VBA Code

There are many tips for optimizing your Microsoft® Visual Basic® for Applications (VBA) code, such as streamlining your code to conserve memory resources, creating object variables when you must refer to an object more than once within a procedure, minimizing concatenation operations, and so on.

In This Section

Declaring Variables
Streamline your memory requirements and speed up performance when you are using variables.

Mathematical Operations
Learn how to speed up operations on numbers.

String Operations
> Understand how to enhance the performance of string operations.

Loops
> Determine how to save resources when you are executing loops.

Declaring Variables

The following points provide suggestions for ways to streamline your memory requirements and speed up performance when you are using variables:

- To conserve memory resources, always declare all your variables with specific data types. When you declare a variable without a specific data type, Microsoft® Visual Basic® for Applications (VBA) creates a variable of type Variant, which requires more memory than any of the other data types.

- Be aware of how much memory each data type requires and what range of values it can store. Always use a smaller data type if possible, except in the case where using a smaller data type will force an implicit conversion. For example, because variables of type Integer are converted to variables of type Long, it makes sense to declare variables that will store integer values as type Long instead of as type Integer.

- Avoid using floating-point data types unless you must have them. Although it is larger, the Currency data type is faster than the Single data type, because the Currency data type does not use the floating-point processor.

- If you refer to an object more than once within a procedure, create an object variable and assign to it a reference to the object. Because the object variable stores the object's location in memory, VBA will not have to look up the location again.

- Declare object variables as specific types rather than as type Object, so you can take advantage of early binding.

Mathematical Operations

The following points provide suggestions for ways to speed up operations on numbers:

- When performing division on integers, use the integer division operator (\) rather than the floating-point division operator (/), which always returns a value of type Double regardless of the types of the numbers being divided.

- Keep in mind that any time you use a Single or Double value in an arithmetic expression with integer values, the integers are converted to Single or Double values, and the final result is a Single or Double value. If you are performing several operations on a number that is the result of an arithmetic operation, you might want to explicitly convert the number to a smaller data type.

String Operations

The following points provide suggestions for ways to enhance the performance of string operations:

- Minimize concatenation operations when you can. You can use the Mid function on the left side of the equal sign to replace characters within the string, rather than concatenating them together. The drawback to using the Mid function is that the replacement string must be the same length as the substring you are replacing.

```
Dim strText As String

strText = "this is a test"
Mid(strText, 11, 4) = "tent"
Debug.Print strText
```

- Microsoft® Visual Basic® for Applications (VBA) provides a number of intrinsic string constants that you can use to replace function calls. For example, you can use the vbCrLf constant to represent a carriage return/linefeed combination within a string, rather than using Chr(13) & Chr(10).

- String-comparison operations are slow. Sometimes, you can avoid them by converting a character in the string to an ANSI value. For example, the following code checks whether the first character in a string is a space:

```
If Asc(strText) = 32 Then
```

The previous code is faster than the following:

```
If Left(strText, 1) = " " Then
```

Loops

The following points provide suggestions for ways to save resources when you are executing loops:

- Analyze your loops to see whether you are repeating memory-intensive operations needlessly. For example, are there any variables that you can set outside the loop, rather than within it? Are you performing a conversion procedure each time through the loop that could be done outside the loop?

- Consider whether you must loop only until a certain condition is met. If so, you might be able to exit the loop early. For example, suppose you are performing data validation on a string that should not contain numeric characters. If you have a loop that checks each character in a string to determine whether the string contains any numeric characters, you can exit the loop as soon as you find the first numeric character.

- If you must refer to an element of an array within a loop, create a temporary variable that stores the element's value rather than referring to it within the array. Retrieving values from an array is slower than reading a variable of the same type.

Add-ins, Templates, Wizards, and Libraries

Creating a Microsoft® Office XP application is about enhancing and extending powerful applications that you and other users already have on your desktops. You can take advantage of the features in Microsoft® Word, Microsoft® Excel, Microsoft® PowerPoint®, Microsoft® Access, Microsoft® FrontPage®, and Microsoft® Outlook®, as well as all the time and resources Microsoft has invested in developing and testing these applications, to build an application quickly and easily that meets users' requirements without requiring a lot of training and support.

One way to provide users with a custom application is to build an add-in. An add-in extends an application by adding functionality that is not in the core product itself. If you are a frequent user of Excel or Access, you might already be familiar with some of the add-ins that these applications include. For example, the Linked Table Manager in Access is an add-in that was built in Microsoft® Visual Basic® for Applications (VBA).

You can create two different types of add-ins: Component Object Model (COM) add-ins and application-specific add-ins. COM add-ins can work in more than one of the Office XP applications.

The other type of add-in you can create is an application-specific add-in. You can create application-specific add-ins in Office XP, as well as in previous versions of Office. An application-specific add-in works in only one application.

Another way to distribute a custom Office application is to create a template. A template provides the user with a basis for creating a new document. For example, a Word template might include the basic layout for a report that an employee can use to create a new document with the same layout and simply fill in the new information.

In addition to the add-ins and templates mentioned earlier, you also can create two specialized kinds of add-ins: wizards and code libraries. Wizards are add-ins, and they help users through a complex process step-by-step. Code libraries are add-ins in which you can store frequently used procedures and generic code. By setting a reference to a code library, you can call procedures stored within that library from your current VBA project.

In This Section

What Is a COM Add-in?
> Extend the functionality of your Microsoft® Office-based applications without adding complexity for the user.

Building COM Add-ins for the Visual Basic Editor
> Customize your development environment and work with components in a Microsoft® Visual Basic® for Applications (VBA) project from code.

Building COM Add-ins for Office Applications
> By building COM add-ins, you can extend the functionality of your Microsoft® Office-based applications without adding complexity for the user.

Building Application-Specific Add-ins

> Add functionality to Microsoft® Office XP applications by creating application-specific add-ins.

Creating Templates

> Learn how to give users a framework within which to complete common tasks by using templates.

Creating Wizards

> Understand how to create a wizard to walk users through a series of steps to create a new document, spreadsheet, presentation, database, or Web application and to deliver an application is that is easy to use.

What Is a COM Add-in?

A COM add-in is a dynamic-link library (DLL) that is specially registered for loading by the Microsoft® Office XP applications. You can build COM add-ins with any of the Office applications in Office XP Developer. In addition, you can create COM add-ins with Microsoft® Visual Basic® or Microsoft® Visual C++®. For more information about these tools, see the Microsoft Developer Network (MSDN®) Web site at http://msdn.microsoft.com.

> **Note**   A COM add-in also can be a Microsoft® ActiveX® .exe file for Visual Basic. However, DLLs generally provide better performance than .exe files.

COM add-ins use the Component Object Model that makes it possible for you to create a single add-in that is available to one or many of the Office applications—Microsoft® Word, Microsoft® Excel, Microsoft® Access, Microsoft® PowerPoint®, Microsoft® Outlook®, Microsoft® FrontPage®, or even the Visual Basic Editor. By developing COM add-ins, you can extend the functionality of your Office-based applications without adding complexity for users.

COM Add-ins vs. Application-Specific Add-ins

In the previous and current versions of Microsoft® Word, Microsoft® Excel, Microsoft® Access, and Microsoft® PowerPoint®, you can use Microsoft® Visual Basic® for Applications (VBA) to create add-ins specific to each of those applications. For example, you can create an add-in for Word that builds a custom report from a selected database and another add-in for Excel that performs a similar task. You save the Word add-in as a Word template file (*.dot), and the Excel add-in as an Excel add-in file (*.xla). Despite the fact that the add-ins share common code, you have to create separate add-ins to add functionality to both applications.

> **Note**   Microsoft® Outlook® and Microsoft® FrontPage® do not provide any way to create application-specific add-ins by using VBA.

A COM add-in, on the other hand, can share some add-in functionality and code across applications. The COM Add-in project contains a component for each application in which it will run and is registered for each application. Usually, a COM add-in contains some code that is common across all applications and some that is specific to each application. For example, if you build a COM add-in to create a custom report in Word or Excel from a database, the code that accesses the database and retrieves a set of data can be shared. When you have retrieved the data, you must work with the Word object model to write the data to Word and with the Excel object model to write the data to Excel.

The following table lists both types of add-ins and their file extensions.

Add-ins	File extensions	Available to
Word add-ins (application-specific)	.dot, .wll, .wiz	Word only
Excel add-ins (application-specific)	.xla, .xll	Excel only
PowerPoint add-ins (application-specific)	.ppa, .pwz	PowerPoint only
Access add-ins (application-specific)	.mda, .mde	Access only
Exchange Client extensions (application-specific)	.dll	Outlook and Microsoft® Exchange clients only
COM add-ins	.dll	Word, Excel, Access, PowerPoint, Outlook, and FrontPage

COM add-ins and application-specific add-ins also differ in terms of how the user views and installs available add-ins. In all Microsoft® Office XP applications, the COM Add-Ins dialog box displays the available COM add-ins.

Viewing the List of Available COM Add-ins

By default, there is no menu item or toolbar button to display the COM Add-ins dialog box, but you can easily display it.

To add a menu item or toolbar button for the COM Add-ins dialog box

1. In the Microsoft® Office XP application, click **Customize** on the **Tools** menu.

2. Click the **Commands** tab.

3. In the **Categories** list, click **Tools**.

4. In the **Commands** list, click **COM Add-ins**. You might have to scroll through the list to find it.

5. Drag the **COM Add-ins** command to a toolbar or a menu.

6. Close the **Customize** dialog box.

> **Note** In Microsoft® Outlook®, you can access the **COM Add-Ins** dialog box if you click **Options** on the **Tools** menu, click the **Other** tab, and then click **Advanced Options**. In the **Advanced Options** dialog box, click **COM Add-Ins**.

When you click the COM Add-Ins toolbar button or menu item, the COM Add-Ins dialog box appears, showing the list of available COM add-ins. You can load (connect) or unload (disconnect) an add-in by selecting the check box next to it. Loading a COM add-in loads it into memory, so you can work with it. Unloading an add-in removes it from memory; you cannot use the add-in until you load it again.

You can add a new COM add-in to the list by clicking Add and locating the add-in. Clicking Add and selecting an add-in that does not appear in the list registers the add-in DLL if it is not registered already and adds the add-in to the list of available COM add-ins for an Office XP application.

To remove a COM add-in from the list, select it, and click Remove. Removing an add-in deletes the registry key that contains the name and load behavior of the add-in. The registry contains information about a COM add-in in two places. As with any other DLL, the add-in's DLL is registered as a unique object on the system. Additionally, information about the add-in is placed in another section of the registry to notify Office applications that the add-in exists. This section is deleted when you remove an add-in from the list. The DLL itself remains registered, and if you add the add-in to the list again, the add-in's informational section is re-created in the registry.

> **Note** You can add only DLLs that are COM add-ins to the list of available add-ins in the COM Add-Ins dialog box. Moreover, only add-ins registered for the application you are working in can be registered. For example, if you are working in Microsoft® Access, you cannot add a COM add-in that is registered only for Microsoft® Word and Microsoft® Excel. In addition, you can create COM add-ins for the Microsoft® Visual Basic® Editor. Loading and unloading a COM add-in for the Visual Basic Editor is slightly different from doing so for COM add-ins in the host application's user interface.

Viewing Available Application-Specific Add-ins

Application-specific add-ins appears in various dialog boxes depending on which application you are using. In Microsoft® Word, this is the Templates and Add-Ins dialog box; in Microsoft® Excel and Microsoft® PowerPoint®, it is the Add-Ins dialog box; in Microsoft® Access, it is the Add-In Manager.

Each dialog box has buttons to add or remove add-ins from the list of application-specific add-ins, and a check box to indicate whether the add-in is loaded. As with COM add-ins, the application-specific add-in must be loaded into memory before it can be used.

Building COM Add-ins for the Visual Basic Editor

By creating COM add-ins for the Microsoft® Visual Basic® Editor, you can customize your development environment and work with components in a Visual Basic for Applications (VBA) project from code. For example, you can build a code wizard that walks a programmer through a series of steps and then builds a procedure, or you can build a code analyzer that determines how many times and from where a procedure is called.

When you create a COM add-in for the Visual Basic Editor, it appears in all instances of the Visual Basic Editor. You cannot, for example, create a COM add-in that appears only in the Visual Basic Editor in Microsoft® Word; it will also appear in the Visual Basic Editor in Microsoft® Access,

Microsoft® Excel, Microsoft® PowerPoint®, Microsoft® FrontPage®, and any other VBA host applications on the computer where the COM add-in DLL is registered.

Note also that you can create multiple add-ins in a single DLL. Each add-in designer in the Add-in project represents a separate add-in. For example, you can create a single DLL that contains a suite of add-ins for developers, and the developers can load just the add-ins they want to use.

To control the Visual Basic Editor from the code inside an add-in, you use the Microsoft Visual Basic for Applications Extensibility library. This object library contains objects that represent the parts of a VBA project, such as the VBProject object and the VBComponent object. The top-level object in the VBA Extensibility library object model is the VBE object, which represents the Visual Basic Editor itself. For more information about the object model, use the Object Browser.

> **Note** Do not confuse the VBA Extensibility library with the IDTExtensibility2 library. Although their names are similar, the VBA Extensibility library provides objects that you can use to work with the Visual Basic Editor from an add-in while it is running, and the IDTExtensibility2 library provides events that are triggered when the add-in is connected or disconnected. In addition, do not confuse the VBA Extensibility library with the Microsoft Visual Basic 6.0 Extensibility library, which is used for creating add-ins in Microsoft Visual Basic.

Creating COM Add-ins in Office Developer

You can create your own COM add-ins in Microsoft® Visual Basic® for Applications (VBA) with Microsoft® Office XP Developer. You do not require external development tools, such as Microsoft® Visual C++® or Microsoft® Visual Basic®, to create COM add-ins.

You can use Add-In Designers to create COM add-ins for use in VBA or any Office application. For example, you might create an add-in tool to format and print code that could be shared with other developers, or you might create an add-in for Microsoft® Excel to calculate tax rates that could be shared with Office users.

COM add-ins created with Office Developer are packaged as dynamic link libraries (DLL files) and are registered so that they can be loaded by Office XP applications.

To add an Add-In Designer to your project

1. From the **File** menu, select **New Project**.

2. In the **New Project** dialog box, select **Add-In Project**.

3. An Add-In Designer will be added to your project.

The Add-In Designer provides several properties that can be set to define the attributes of your add-in, including Name, Description, and Load Behavior. It also provides several events that can be used to add code, such as OnConnection, OnStartupComplete, and OnDisconnection.

The actual code for your COM add-in depends on what you want the add-in to do, as well as which application the add-in is for. Each of the applications that can use COM add-ins exposes its extensibility structure using its object model; you can view the object model for your particular application in the Object Browser.

To package the COM add-in as a DLL in VBA

After you have written and debugged your code, you can make your add-in into a DLL.

- From the **File** menu, select **Make** *projectname***.dll**.

    Note This will create the COM add-in, add the appropriate registry entries, and make the COM add-in available for use in your Office host.

Creating a COM Add-in for the Visual Basic Editor

For the most part, creating a COM add-in for the Microsoft® Visual Basic® Editor is similar to creating one for a Microsoft® Office XP application. COM add-ins for the Visual Basic Editor also includes the add-in designer or a class module that implements the IDTExtensibility2 library.

One key difference to note is that the initial load behavior setting for a COM add-in for the Visual Basic Editor differs from that of a COM add-in for an Office application. A COM add-in for the Visual Basic Editor can have one of two initial load behaviors: None, meaning that the add-in is not loaded until the user loads it, or startup, meaning that the add-in is loaded when the user opens the Visual Basic Editor.

To create a COM add-in using Visual Basic for Applications in the Visual Basic Editor

1. Create a new Add-in project, select **Visual Basic for Applications IDE** in the **Application** box, and then select **VBE 6.0** in the **Application Version** box. Set the initial load behavior for the add-in to either **None** or **Startup**.

2. Set a reference to the **Microsoft Visual Basic for Applications Extensibility 5.3** library in file Vbe6ext.olb.

    Note If the object library does not appear in the list of available references, you can browse for it in C:\Program Files\Common Files\Microsoft Shared\VBA\VBA6, the default installation directory. The name of the library as it appears in the Object Browser is VBIDE.

3. The **OnConnection** event procedure passes in the Application argument, which contains a reference to the instance of the Visual Basic Editor in which the add-in is running. You can use this object to work with all other objects in the VBA Extensibility library. Create a public module-level object variable of type **VBIDE.VBE**, and assign the object referenced by the Application argument to this variable.

4. Within the OnConnection event procedure, you can optionally include code to hook the add-in's form up to a command bar control in the Visual Basic Editor. You can work with the Visual Basic Editor's command bars by using the **CommandBars** property of the **VBE** object.

5. Build any forms or other components to be included in the project.

6. Place a breakpoint in the **OnConnection** event procedure, and then select **Run Project** from the **Run** menu.

7. In a Visual Basic for Applications (VBA) host application, such as Microsoft® Excel, open the Visual Basic Editor, select **Add-In Manager** on the **Add-Ins** menu, and select your add-in from the list. Select the **Loaded/Unloaded** check box to load the add-in, if it is not set to load on startup.

8. Debug the add-in. When you have debugged it to your satisfaction, chose Stop Project from the Run menu, end the running project, and make the add-in's DLL by clicking **Make** *projectname*.**dll** on the **File** menu.

> **Note** To test and debug the add-in, you must open another instance of the Visual Basic Editor to see it. The add-in does not appear in the instance of the editor that you are using to create it.

You can use the same strategies to distribute COM add-ins for the Visual Basic Editor as you use to distribute COM add-ins for the Office XP applications.

Working with the Microsoft Visual Basic for Applications Extensibility Library

The Microsoft® Visual Basic® for Applications (VBA) extensibility library provides objects that you can use to work with the Visual Basic Editor and any VBA projects that it contains. From an add-in created in Visual Basic 6.0, you can return a reference to the VBE object, the top-level object in the VBA Extensibility library, through the Application argument of the OnConnection event procedure. This argument provides a reference to the instance of the Visual Basic Editor in which the add-in is running.

The VBProject object refers to a VBA project that is open in the Visual Basic Editor. A VBProject object has a VBComponents collection, which in turn contains VBComponent objects. A VBComponent object represents a component in the project, such as a standard module, class module, or form. Because a VBComponent object can represent any of these objects, you can use its Type property to determine which type of module you are currently working with.

For example, suppose you have a variable named vbeCurrent, of type VBIDE.VBE, which represents the instance of the Visual Basic Editor in which the add-in will run. The following code fragment prints the names and types of all components in the active project to the Immediate window:

```
Dim vbcComp As VBIDE.VBComponent

For Each vbcComp In vbeCurrent.ActiveVBProject.VBComponents
    Debug.Print vbcComp.Name, vbcComp.Type
Next vbcComp
```

A VBComponent object has a CodeModule property that returns a CodeModule object, which refers to the code module associated with that component. You can use the methods and properties of the CodeModule object to manipulate the code in that module on a line-by-line basis. For example, you can insert lines by using the InsertLines method, or perform find and replace operations by using the Find and Replace methods.

To work with command bars in the Visual Basic Editor, use the CommandBars property of the VBE object to return a reference to the CommandBars collection.

For more information about working with the VBA Extensibility library, search the Visual Basic Reference Help index for "VBProject object."

Building COM Add-ins for Office Applications

Because Microsoft® Office XP applications support the Component Object Model (COM) add-in architecture, you can use the same tools and installation file formats (a Microsoft® ActiveX® .dll or .exe) to develop add-ins for all Office applications. By building COM add-ins, you can extend the functionality of your Office-based applications without adding complexity for the user.

You can also create add-ins for Office Developer and for the Microsoft® Visual Basic® Editor. You can make such add-ins available to or from any application that supports Visual Basic for Applications (VBA), including applications other than Office.

In This Section

Working with Add-in Designers
> Create and register your COM add-in with an add-in designer.

Specifying Load Behavior
> Load (connect) the add-in, and make it available to the user; or unload (disconnect) the add-in, so it cannot be run.

Writing Code in the Add-in Designer
> Begin writing code in the designer's class module when you have specified general information for a COM add-in in the add-in designer.

Hooking a COM Add-in Up to a Command Bar Control
> Integrate your COM add-in (if it has a user interface) with the host application in some way, so the user can interact with it.

Debugging a COM Add-in
> Load and use the COM add-in from within a Microsoft® Office XP application to test and debug it.

Making the DLL
> Turn your COM add-in into a DLL when you have finished debugging it.

Distributing COM Add-ins
> Install all the files necessary to distributing your COM add-in to other users on each user's system and register the add-in.

COM Add-ins and Security
> Specify security settings for Microsoft® Office XP applications in the Office XP Security dialog box.

Working with Add-in Designers

An add-in designer is a file included with the template project that helps you create and register your COM add-in. You can create a COM add-in without including an add-in designer, but the add-in designer simplifies the process of creating and registering the add-in. You can use an add-in designer to specify important information for your COM add-in: its name and description, the application in which it is to run, and how it loads in that application.

Similar to forms in a Visual Basic project, an add-in designer (shown in the following figure) has a user interface component and an associated class module. The user interface component is never visible to the user when the add-in is running, however; it is visible only to the developer at design time. You can think of the add-in designer as a sort of dialog box where you specify settings for an add-in.

The Add-in Designer (Example)

The class module contains the events that occur when the add-in is loaded or unloaded. You can use these events to integrate the add-in into the application.

When you create the add-in DLL, Visual Basic 6.0 uses the information you have given to the add-in designer to properly register the DLL as a COM add-in. Visual Basic 6.0 writes the add-in's name, description, and initial load behavior setting to the registry. The add-in's host application reads these registry entries and loads the add-in accordingly.

Creating COM Add-ins for Multiple Applications

Each add-in designer in your project creates an add-in that can run in only one application. To create a COM add-in that is available to more than one application, you create a new add-in designer for each application that you want to use the add-in and then customize the add-in designer for each application.

For example, suppose that you want to create an add-in for Microsoft® Word and Microsoft® PowerPoint® that creates an organizational chart from a table in a database and inserts the chart into the document or slide. You would begin by making sure there is an add-in designer for Word and one for PowerPoint.

To create a new Add-in project

1. From the **File** menu in Microsoft® Visual Basic® Editor, click **New Project**, and then click **Add-in Project**. The first add-in designer in the Add-in project appears.

2. Change the add-in designer's **Name** property setting in the **Properties** window. It might be helpful to indicate in the name of the add-in designer which designer goes with which application. For example, the add-in designer for Microsoft® Excel in the Image Gallery project is named dsrImageExcel.

3. Enter the appropriate information in the **General** and **Advanced** tabs of the add-in designer. Select the application that you want the add-in designer to work with on the **General** tab. For details, see "Configuring an Add-in Designer."

4. To add code to the add-in designer, open the **View** menu, and click **Code**.

To add another add-in designer to the Add-in project

1. Open the **Insert** menu, and click **Components**.

2. On the **Designers** tab, select **Addin class,** and click **OK**.

3. Open the **Insert** menu, and click **Addin Class**.

To make a DLL file for the Add-in project

1. Save the Add-in project.

2. Open the **File** menu, and click **Make *projectname*.DLL** (the default is AddInProject1.DLL).

3. In the **Make Project** dialog box, select the desired DLL name and location.

4. Click the **Options** button to open the **Project Properties** dialog box if you want to assign a specific version number, add version information, or specify a DLL base address. After you have entered the information, click **OK** to close the Project Properties dialog box.

5. Click **OK** on the **Make Project** dialog box to make the DLL file.

Configuring an Add-in Designer

To create your add-in, you first must fill out the options on the General tab of the add-in designer. The following table explains each option.

Option	Description
Addin Display Name	The name that will appear in the COM Add-ins dialog box in a Microsoft® Office XP application. The name you supply should be descriptive to the user. If the name is to come from a resource file specified in the Satellite DLL Name box on the Advanced tab, it must begin with a number sign (#), followed by an integer specifying a resource ID within the file.
Addin Description	Descriptive text for a COM add-in, available from Microsoft® Visual Basic® for Applications (VBA) in the Description property of the COMAddIn object. If the description is to come from a resource file specified in the Satellite DLL Name box on the Advanced tab, it must begin with a number sign (#), followed by an integer specifying a resource ID within the file.
Application	The application in which the add-in will run. This list displays applications that support COM add-ins.
Application Version	The version of the application in which the add-in will run.
Initial Load Behavior	The way that the add-in loads in the application. The list of possible settings comes from the registry. Common used behaviors include Startup and On Demand.
Addin is command-line safe (does not put up any UI)	Does not apply to COM add-ins running in Office XP applications.

The Advanced tab of the add-in designer makes it possible for you to specify a file containing localized resource information for the add-in and to specify additional registry data. The following table describes the options available on the Advanced tab.

Option	Description
Satellite DLL Name	The name of a file containing localized (translated) resources for an add-in; the file must be located in the same directory as the add-in's registered DLL.
Registry Key for Additional Add-in Data	The registry subkey to which additional data is to be written.
Add-in Specific Data	The names and values to be stored in the registry subkey. Only String and DWORD type values are permitted.

Working with Host Application Object Models

There are a few things to keep in mind as you add forms and other components to your COM add-in. First, your COM add-in is similar to a separate application running inside a Microsoft® Office XP application. Therefore, you must set references to any object libraries you want to work with from within the COM Add-in project. If your add-in will be run in more than one application, you can use the OnConnection event procedure to determine which application your add-in is currently running in and then selectively run code that works with that application's objects.

To figure out which application the add-in is currently running, use the object supplied by the Application argument of the OnConnection event procedure. Assign this object variable to a global object variable. In the code that interacts with the host application, check to see which application you are working with, and use that application's object model to perform the task.

A DLL is loaded into memory only once, but each application that accesses the DLL gets its own copy of the DLL's data, stored in a separate space in memory. Therefore, you can use global variables in a COM add-in without worrying about data being shared between two applications that are using the COM add-in at the same time. For example, the Image Gallery sample add-in can run simultaneously in Microsoft® Word, Microsoft® Excel, and Microsoft® PowerPoint®. When Word loads the add-in, the OnConnection event occurs and a reference to the Word Application object is stored in a global variable of type Object. If Excel then loads the add-in, the OnConnection event occurs and a reference to the Excel Application object is stored in a global variable of type Object but in a different space in memory. Within the code for the add-in, you can use the If TypeOf…End If construct to check to which application's Application object the variable points.

```
' Global object variable, declared in modSharedCode module.
Public gobjAppInstance As Object


Private Sub cmdInsert_Click()
    ' Insert selected image.
    ' Check which object variable has been initialized.
    If TypeOf gobjAppInstance Is Word.Application Then
        ' Insert into Word.
        Word.Selection.InlineShapes.AddPicture FileName:= _
            img(mlngSel).Tag, LinkToFile:=False, _
            SaveWithDocument:=True
    ElseIf TypeOf gobjAppInstance Is Excel.Application Then
        gobjAppInstance.ActiveSheet.Pictures.Insert img(mlngSel).Tag
    ElseIf TypeOf gobjAppInstance Is Powerpoint.Application Then
        gobjAppInstance.ActiveWindow.Selection.SlideRange.Shapes.AddPicture
```

```
            FileName:=img(mlngSel).Tag, LinkToFile:=msoFalse, _
            SaveWithDocument:=msoCTrue, Left:=100, Top:=100
    End If
End Sub
```

Specifying Load Behavior

When a COM add-in has been properly registered, it is available to whatever applications are specified in the add-in designers that the project contains. The registered COM add-in display name appears in the COM Add-in dialog box; if it does not, click Add to browse for the add-in and add it to the list.

Selecting the check box next to an add-in in the COM Add-ins dialog box loads (connects) the add-in and makes it available to the user; clearing the check box unloads (disconnects) the add-in, and it cannot be run.

As the developer, you specify the default setting for when a COM add-in should be loaded. You do this in the Initial Load Behavior list in the add-in designer.

Note Users can change this setting later by using the Add-in Manager.

You can specify that an add-in be loaded in one of the following ways:

- Only when the user loads it in the COM Add-ins dialog box, or when Microsoft® Visual Basic® for Applications (VBA) code loads it by setting the Connect property of the corresponding COMAddIn object.

- Every time the application starts.

- The first time the application starts, so that it can create a toolbar button or menu item for itself. After that, the add-in is loaded only when the user requests it by clicking the menu item or button.

The following table describes the different settings for the Initial Load Behavior setting.

Initial Load Behavior setting	Behavior
None	The COM add-in is not loaded when the application boots. It can be loaded in the COM Add-ins dialog box or by setting the Connect property of the corresponding COMAddIn object.
Startup	The add-in is loaded when the application boots. When the add-in is loaded, it remains loaded until it is explicitly unloaded.
Load on Demand [1]	The add-in is not loaded until the user clicks the button or menu item that loads the add-in, or until a procedure sets its Connect property to True. In most cases, you will not set the initial load behavior to Load on Demand directly; you will set it to Load at Next Startup Only, and it will be set automatically to Load on Demand on subsequent boots of the host application.

Initial Load Behavior setting	Behavior
Load at Next Startup Only [1]	After the COM add-in has been registered, it loads as soon as the user runs the host application for the first time. The next time the user boots the application, the add-in is loaded on demand—that is, it does not load until the user clicks the button or menu item associated with the add-in, or through the COM Add-in dialog box.
Command line/Startup	Add-in loads either when specifically invoked from a command-line parameter, when Visual Basic starts.
Command line	Add-in loads only when specifically invoked from a command-line parameter.

[1] Not available to add-ins developed using VBA.

Writing Code in the Add-in Designer

After you have specified general information for a COM add-in in the add-in designer, you can begin writing code in the designer's class module. To view the add-in designer's class module, right-click the add-in designer in the Project Explorer, and then click View Code on the shortcut menu.

Code that is in the add-in designer handles the add-in's integration with the host application. For example, code that runs when the add-in is loaded or unloaded resides in the add-in designer's module. If the add-in contains forms, the add-in designer might contain code to display the forms.

Implementing the IDTExtensibility2 Library

A COM add-in has events that you can use to run code when the add-in is loaded or unloaded, or when the host application has finished starting up or is beginning to shut down. To use these events, you must implement the IDTExtensibility2 library, which provides a programming interface for integrating COM add-ins with their host applications. When you implement the IDTExtensibility2 library within a class module, the library makes a set of new events available to the module. You must have these events to control your COM add-in.

Using the Add-in project in Microsoft® Visual Basic® for Applications (VBA) implements the IDTExtensibility2 library for you in the add-in designer's class module. If you are creating the COM add-in from scratch in Visual Basic 6.0, use the following procedure:

To manually implement the IDTExtensibility2 library in Visual Basic 6.0

1. Set a reference to the library by clicking **References** on the **Project** menu and then selecting the check box next to **Microsoft Add-in Designer**. If this library does not appear in the list, you can add it by clicking **Browse** and finding the file Msaddndr.dll. By default, this file is located in the C:\Program Files\Common Files \Designer subfolder.

2. In the Declarations section of the add-in designer's class module, add the following code:

```
Implements IDTExtensibility2
```

3. In the Code window, click **IDTExtensibility2** in the **Object** box. This adds the template for the procedure to the **OnConnection** event.

4. Create event procedure templates for the four remaining event procedures by clicking them in the **Procedure** dialog box in the **Code Window**.

5. Add code or a comment to each of the five event procedures.

> **Note** You must include the event-procedure template for each event provided by the IDTExtensibility2 interface. If you omit any of the event procedures, your project will not compile. If you are not adding code to an event-procedure template, it is a good idea to add a comment; a single apostrophe (') is sufficient.

Working with the IDTExtensibility2 Event Procedures

The IDTExtensibility2 library provides five events that you can use to manipulate your add-in and the host application: OnConnection, OnDisconnection, OnAddInsUpdate, OnStartupComplete, and OnBeginShutdown. The following sections describe each of these event procedures.

The OnConnection Event

The OnConnection event occurs when the COM add-in is loaded (connected). An add-in can be loaded in one of the following ways:

- The user starts the host application and the add-in's load behavior is specified to load when the application starts.

- The user loads the add-in in the COM Add-ins dialog box.

- The Connect property of the corresponding COMAddIn object is set to True. For more information about the COMAddIn object, search the Microsoft® Office Visual Basic Reference Help index for "COMAddIn object."

The OnConnection event procedure takes four arguments, described in the following table.

Argument	Type	Description
Application	Object	Provides a reference to the application in which the COM add-in is currently running.
ConnectMode	Custom Long	A constant that specifies how the add-in was loaded.
AddInInst	Object	A COMAddIn object that refers to the instance of the class module in which code is currently running. You can use this argument to return the programmatic identifier for the add-in.

Argument	Type	Description
Custom()	Variant	An array of Variant type values that provides additional data. The numeric value of the first element in this array indicates how the host application was started: from the user interface (1), by embedding a document created in the host application in another application (2), or through Automation (3).

The constants for the ConnectMode argument are grouped in the ext_ConnectMode enumeration. These constants are described in the following table.

Constant	Description
ext_cm_AfterStartup	Add-in was loaded after the application started, or by setting the Connect property of the corresponding COMAddIn object to True.
ext_cm_External	Does not apply to building COM add-ins for Microsoft® Office XP applications.
ext_cm_Startup	Add-in was loaded on startup.

If you are building a COM add-in that will run in more than one host application, you might find that you call the same code from each add-in designer's OnConnection event. For example, you might create a new command bar button in the OnConnection event procedure in the same way within each add-in designer. If so, it is more efficient to create a public procedure in a standard module and call it from within the OnConnection event procedure for each add-in designer than to include the same code in each add-in designer.

The following example shows the OnConnection event procedure. The OnConnection event procedure calls the CreateAddInCommandBarButton procedure in the modSharedCode module. This procedure creates a new command bar button and returns a reference to it. The OnConnection event procedure then assigns this reference to a private event-ready variable of type CommandBarButton.

```
' Event-ready variable declared in add-in designer's module.
Private WithEvents p_ctlBtnEvents   As Office.CommandBarButton


Private Sub IDTExtensibility2_OnConnection(ByVal Application As Object, _
    ByVal ConnectMode As AddInDesignerObjects.ext_ConnectMode, _
    ByVal AddInInst As Object, _
    custom() As Variant)
```

```vba
    ' Call shared code to create new command bar button
    ' and return a reference to it. Assign reference to
    ' event-ready CommandBarButton object declared with
    ' WithEvents within this module.

    Set p_ctlBtnEvents = CreateAddInCommandBarButton(Application, _
        ConnectMode, AddInInst)
End Sub


' Public function in modSharedCode module.
Public Function CreateAddInCommandBarButton(ByVal Application As Object, _
    ByVal ConnectMode As AddInDesignerObjects.ext_ConnectMode, _
    ByVal AddInInst As Object) As Office.CommandBarButton

    ' This procedure assigns a reference to the Application
    ' object passed to the OnConnection event to a global
    ' object variable. It then creates a new command bar
    ' button and returns a reference to the button to the
    ' OnConnection event procedure. The advantage to putting
    ' this code in a public module is that if you have more
    ' than one add-in designer in the project, you can call
    ' this procedure from each of them rather than duplicating
    ' the code.


    Dim cbrMenu            As Office.CommandBar
    Dim ctlBtnAddIn        As Office.CommandBarButton


    On Error GoTo CreateAddInCommandBarButton_Err

    ' Return reference to Application object and store it
    ' in public variable so that other procedures in add-in
    ' can use it.
    Set gobjAppInstance = Application
```

```
' Return reference to command bar.
Set cbrMenu = gobjAppInstance.CommandBars(CBR_NAME)


' Add button to call add-in from command bar, if it doesn't
' already exist.
' Constants are declared at module level.
' Look for button on command bar.
Set ctlBtnAddIn = cbrMenu.FindControl(Tag:=CTL_KEY)
If ctlBtnAddIn Is Nothing Then
    ' Add new button.
    Set ctlBtnAddIn = cbrMenu.Controls.Add(Type:=msoControlButton, _
        Parameter:=CTL_KEY)
    ' Set button's Caption, Tag, Style, and OnAction properties.
    With ctlBtnAddIn
        .Caption = CTL_CAPTION
        .Tag = CTL_KEY
        .Style = msoButtonCaption
        ' Use AddInInst argument to return reference
        ' to this add-in.
        .OnAction = PROG_ID_START & AddInInst.ProgId _
            & PROG_ID_END
    End With
End If


' Return reference to new commandbar button.
Set CreateAddInCommandBarButton = ctlBtnAddIn

CreateAddInCommandBarButton_End:
    Exit Function


CreateAddInCommandBarButton_Err:
    ' Call generic error handler for add-in.
    AddInErr Err
    Resume CreateAddInCommandBarButton_End
End Function
```

The CreateAddInCommandBarButton procedure first performs a critical step: it assigns the object passed to the procedure in the Application argument to a public module-level object variable. This object variable persists as long as the COM add-in is loaded, so any other procedures in the module can determine in what application the add-in is currently running.

A public module-level variable declared in a standard module in a COM add-in remains in existence from the time the add-in is loaded to the time it is unloaded.

This procedure also contains code that creates a new menu item on the Tools menu of the host application the first time the add-in is loaded. Before creating the new menu item, the procedure checks to see whether the item already exists. If the item does exist, the procedure returns a reference to the existing menu item rather than creating a new one. The OnConnection event procedure then assigns the reference returned by the CreateAddInCommandBarButton procedure to a variable (p_ctlBtnEvents) that has been declared by using the WithEvents keyword, so that the menu item's Click event procedure will be triggered when the user clicks the new menu item.

The OnDisconnection Event

The OnDisconnection event occurs when the COM add-in is unloaded. You can use the OnDisconnection event procedure to run code that restores any changes made to the application by the add-in and to perform general clean-up operations.

An add-in can be unloaded in one of the following ways:

- The user clears the check box next to the add-in in the COM Add-ins dialog box.

- The host application closes. If the add-in is loaded when the application closes, it is unloaded. If the add-in's load behavior is set to Startup, it is reloaded when the application starts again.

- The Connect property of the corresponding COMAddIn object is set to False.

The OnDisconnection event procedure takes two arguments, described in the following table.

Argument	Type	Description
RemoveMode	Custom Long	A constant that specifies how the add-in was unloaded.
custom()	Variant	An array of Variant type values that provides additional data. The numeric value of the first element in this array indicates how the host application was started: from the user interface (1); by embedding a document created in the host application in another application (2); or through Automation (3).

The following table lists the available constants for the RemoveMode method, which are grouped in the ext_DisconnectionMode enumeration.

Constant	Description
ext_dm_HostShutdown	Add-in was unloaded when the application was closed.
ext_dm_UserClosed	Add-in was unloaded when the user cleared the corresponding check box in the COM Add-ins dialog box or when the Connect property of the corresponding COMAddIn object was set to False.

The following code shows the OnDisconnection event procedure that calls the RemoveAddInCommandBarButton procedure located in the modSharedCode module. If the user unloads the add-in, the add-in's menu command is deleted; otherwise, it is maintained for the next time the user starts the application:

```
Private Sub IDTExtensibility2_OnDisconnection(ByVal _
    RemoveMode As AddInDesignerObjects.ext_DisconnectMode, _
    custom() As Variant)

    ' Call common procedure to disconnect add-in.
    RemoveAddInCommandBarButton RemoveMode
End Sub


Function RemoveAddInCommandBarButton(ByVal _
    RemoveMode As AddInDesignerObjects.ext_DisconnectMode)

    ' This procedure removes the command bar button for
    ' the add-in if the user disconnected it.

    On Error GoTo RemoveAddInCommandBarButton_Err

    ' If user unloaded add-in, remove button. Otherwise,
    ' add-in is being unloaded because application is
    ' closing; in that case, leave button as is.
    If RemoveMode = ext_dm_UserClosed Then
        On Error Resume Next
        ' Delete custom command bar button.
        gobjAppInstance.CommandBars(CBR_NAME).Controls(CTL_NAME).Delete
        On Error GoTo RemoveAddInCommandBarButton_Err
    End If
```

```
RemoveAddInCommandBarButton_End:
    Exit Function


RemoveAddInCommandBarButton_Err:
    AddInErr Err
    Resume RemoveAddInCommandBarButton_End
End Function
```

The OnStartupComplete Event

The OnStartupComplete event occurs when the host application completes its startup routines, in the case where the COM add-in loads at startup. If the add-in is not loaded when the application loads, the OnStartupComplete event does not occur—even when the user loads the add-in in the COM Add-ins dialog box. When this event does occur, it occurs after the OnConnection event.

You can use the OnStartupComplete event procedure to run code that interacts with the application and that should not be run until the application has finished loading. For example, if you want to display a form that gives users a choice of documents to create when they start the application, you can put that code in the OnStartupComplete event procedure.

The OnBeginShutdown Event

The OnBeginShutdown event occurs when the host application begins its shutdown routines, in the case where the application closes while the COM add-in is still loaded. If the add-in is not loaded when the application closes, the OnBeginShutdown event does not occur. When this event does occur, it occurs before the OnDisconnection event.

You can use the OnBeginShutdown event procedure to run code when the user closes the application. For example, you can run code that saves form data to a file.

The OnAddInsUpdate Event

The OnAddInsUpdate event occurs when the set of loaded COM add-ins changes. When an add-in is loaded or unloaded, the OnAddInsUpdate event occurs in any other loaded add-ins. For example, if add-ins A and B both are loaded currently, and then add-in C is loaded, the OnAddInsUpdate event occurs in add-ins A and B. If C is unloaded, the OnAddInsUpdate event occurs again in add-ins A and B.

If you have an add-in that depends on another add-in, you can use the OnAddInsUpdate event procedure in the dependent add-in to determine whether the other add-in has been loaded or unloaded.

Note The OnStartupComplete, OnBeginShutdown, and OnAddInsUpdate event procedures each provide only a single argument, the Custom() argument, which is an empty array of Variant type values. This argument is ignored in COM add-ins for Office XP applications.

Hooking a COM Add-in Up to a Command Bar Control

If your COM add-in has a user interface, it must be integrated with the host application in some way, so the user can interact with it. For example, the user interface for your COM add-in most likely includes a form. At some point, code in the add-in must be run to display the form.

One way to integrate your add-in with an application's user interface is to include code in the OnStartupComplete event procedure that creates a new command bar control (toolbar button or menu item) in the host application. When your add-in is loaded, the user can click the button or menu item to work with the add-in. You can use the OnConnection event procedure, but it does not guarantee that the command bar object has been loaded.

Similarly, you can add code to unload your add-in in the OnBeginShutdown event procedure or the OnDisconnection event procedure.

The critical aspect of integrating an add-in through a command bar control is the process of setting up the event sink. You must create a command bar control that is event-ready, so its Click event is triggered when the user clicks the control. You can use the WithEvents keyword to create an event-ready command bar control.

If you set the load behavior for your add-in to Load at Next Startup Only, you also must set the OnAction property for the command bar control. If you do not set the OnAction property, the add-in will load the first time the application starts. The next time you start the application, however, the load behavior for the add-in will be set to Load on Demand, and the command bar control that you have created for the add-in will not load the add-in unless the OnAction property has been set.

Even if your add-in is not demand-loaded, it is a good idea to set this property in your code, in case you later change the load behavior for the add-in. The syntax for setting the OnAction property for a COM add-in is:

```
ctlButton.OnAction = "!<ProgID>"
```

where *ctlButton* is the CommandBarButton object and *ProgID* is the programmatic identifier for the add-in. The programmatic identifier is the sub key that is created for the add-in in the Microsoft® Windows® registry. Each add-in designer or class module that implements the IDTExtensibility2 library in the COM Add-in project adds its own programmatic identifier to the registry, beneath the AddIns sub key for the host application in which it will run. The programmatic identifier for a COM add-in consists of the name of the project followed by the name of the add-in designer or class module. For example, the programmatic identifier for the ImageGallery add-in for Microsoft® Word is ImageGallery.dsrImageWord.

To return the programmatic identifier for an add-in, you can use the AddInInst argument that is passed to the OnConnection event procedure. This argument provides a reference to the add-in designer or class module in which code is running currently. The AddInInst argument is an object of type COMAddIn, which has a ProgId property that returns the programmatic identifier. Note that you must concatenate the !< and > delimiters before and after the programmatic identifier string to properly set the OnAction property.

Note If your add-in will run in Word, you also must set the Tag property for the CommandBarButton object to a unique String value. This makes sure the command bar button will respond to the Click event and load the add-in for each new document window that the user opens. Because the Tag property provides you with additional information about the control, it is a good idea to set the Tag property for a command bar button that loads a COM add-in in any host application.

Creating a Command Bar Control

In some cases, you might want to provide access to your add-in through a menu command.

To create a command bar control that displays the add-in's form

1. In the add-in designer's module, use the **WithEvents** keyword to declare a module-level variable of type **CommandBarButton**. This creates an event-ready **CommandBarButton** object.

2. In the same module, create the **Click** event procedure template for the **CommandBarButton** object by clicking the name of the object variable in the **Object** box and then clicking **Click** in the **Procedure** dialog box.

3. Write code within the event-procedure template to open the form when the **Click** event occurs.

4. In the **OnConnection** event procedure, check to see whether the command bar control already exists, and return a reference to it if it does. If it does not exist, create the new command bar control, and return a reference to it. You must check whether the command bar control exists, so you do not create a new control each time your code runs.

5. When you create the new command bar control, set the **Tag** property for the **CommandBarButton** object to a unique string. This is necessary only for COM add-ins running in Microsoft® Word, but it is recommended for COM add-ins running in any host application.

6. When you create the new command bar control, set the **OnAction** property for the command bar control if the COM add-in is to be demand-loaded. If you fail to set the **OnAction** property, the command bar button will load the add-in the first time the application starts, but it will not load the add-in when the application is closed and reopened.

7. Within the **OnConnection** event procedure, assign the reference to the command bar control to the event-ready **CommandBarButton** object variable.

8. Add code to the **OnDisconnection** event to remove the command bar control when the add-in is unloaded.

   Note The add-in designer in the COM add-in template project includes code that performs all these steps to create a menu item on the **Tools** menu. By default, the template project has a reference set to the Microsoft® Office XP object library, so you can work with Office command bars.

Debugging a COM Add-in

When you are developing a COM add-in in Microsoft® Visual Basic® for Applications (VBA), you can debug the add-in by putting the project into run mode. With the project in run mode, you can load and use the COM add-in from within a Microsoft® Office XP application to test and debug it by using any of the Visual Basic debugging tools.

To debug a COM add-in in the Visual Basic Editor

1.   Open the Add-in project in **Visual Basic Editor**.

2.   Place any desired breakpoints, **Stop** statements, or watches in the code.

3.   On the **Run** menu, click **Run Project**. This compiles your project, alerting you to any compilation errors, and then puts the project into run mode.

4.   Open the intended host application for the COM add-in. If you have set the add-in's load behavior to **Startup** or **Load at Next Startup Only**, the add-in loads as soon as you start the application. If the add-in's load behavior is set to **None** or **Load on Demand**, open the COM Add-ins dialog box, and select the check box next to your add-in to load it.

When the add-in loads, the OnConnection event occurs. You can now enter break mode in the Add-in project in the Visual Basic Editor and debug the code.

Making the DLL

After debugging your COM add-in to your satisfaction, you can package it as a DLL. If you created your COM add-in using Microsoft® Office XP Developer, it is already a .dll. However, if you created it in Microsoft® Visual Basic® Editor, you must create the .dll. To create the .dll in Visual Basic, click Make projectname.dll on the File menu. The Make Project dialog box appears; note that you can enter a name for the DLL that is different from the suggested name. The process of making the DLL registers it on the local machine.

When you make the DLL in the Visual Basic Editor, the information in the add-in designer is used to add a sub key to the Windows registry, indicating which applications can host the add-in. The COM add-in then appears in the COM Add-ins dialog box in those applications for which it is registered.

Add-in Registration

Before you can use a COM add-in in a Microsoft® Office XP application, the add-in DLL must be registered, just as any other DLL on the computer. The DLL's class ID is registered beneath the \HKEY_CLASSES_ROOT subtree in the registry. The DLL can be registered on a user's computer by using a setup program, such as those created by the Packaging Wizard or by running the Regsvr32.exe command-line utility that is included with Microsoft® Windows®. Adding a COM add-in by using the COM Add-ins dialog box also registers the DLL—if it was created with Microsoft® Visual Basic® 6.0.

Registering the DLL beneath the \HKEY_CLASSES_ROOT subtree informs the operating system of its presence, but additional information must be added to the registry for the add-in to be available to an Office XP application. This is the information that you can specify in the add-in designer—the add-in's name, description, target application, target application version, and initial load behavior. The add-in designer makes sure this application-specific information is written to the correct place in the registry at the same time that the add-in DLL is registered. The COM Add-ins dialog box displays the information contained in the subkey for the corresponding Office XP application.

This subkey must be added to the following registry subkey, where *appname* is the name of the application in which the add-in will run:

\HKEY_CURRENT_USER\SOFTWARE\Microsoft\Office*appname*\AddIns

The new subkey itself must be the programmatic identifier of the COM add-in, which consists of the name of the project followed by the name of the class module or add-in designer. For example, the registry subkey for the Image Gallery add-in for Microsoft® Word would be ImageGallery.dsrImageWord.

The following table describes the entries that you can add beneath this subkey. Only the LoadBehavior entry is required; the others are optional.

Name	Type	Value
Description	String	Name to appear in COM Add-ins dialog box
FriendlyName	String	String returned by Description property
LoadBehavior	DWORD	Integer indicating load behavior: 0 (None), 3 (Startup), 9 (Load on Demand), or 16 (Load At Next Startup Only)

Distributing COM Add-ins

If you are planning to distribute your COM add-in to other users, you must install all the necessary files on each user's system and register the add-in. How you do this depends on the environment in which you are developing the add-in.

Distributing COM Add-ins Created with Office Developer

If you are developing in Microsoft® Office XP Developer, the easiest way to distribute a COM add-in is to create a setup program for the add-in. The user can install and register the add-in by running the setup program.

Before you can create the setup program, you must compile the COM Add-in Project to a DLL.

To create the setup program, run the Packaging Wizard on the Add-in project, which was compiled to DLL. The Packaging Wizard will create a setup program that installs and registers the add-in DLL and any other necessary files but not the code.

Distributing COM Add-ins Created with Visual Basic 6.0

If you are developing in Microsoft® Visual Basic® 6.0, the easiest way to distribute a COM add-in is to include the add-in designer in the Add-in project and then create a setup program for the add-in. The user can install and register the add-in by running the setup program.

To create the setup program, run the Visual Basic 6.0 Package and Deployment Wizard on the Add-in project. When the user runs the setup program, all the files required for the add-in to run will be copied to the user's computer and registered.

For more information about using the Visual Basic 6.0 Package and Deployment Wizard, see the documentation included with Visual Basic 6.0.

COM Add-ins and Security

You can specify security settings for Microsoft® Office XP applications in the Office XP Security dialog box, available by pointing to Macro on the Tools menu and then clicking Security. The Security Level tab includes a check box, Trust all installed add-ins and templates. If this box is selected, Office XP applications will load all COM add-ins, application-specific add-ins, and templates in trusted folders without checking to see whether they have valid digital signatures from trusted sources.

If this check box is not selected, the Office XP application checks to see whether the add-in or template has been signed digitally by a trusted source before loading it. If it has, the add-in will be loaded under any security level. If it has not been signed, if it has not been signed by a trusted source, or if the signature has been invalidated, the add-in will not load under high security. Under medium security, users will be warned that the add-in might not be safe. Under low security, the add-in will load and run without prompting the user.

To digitally sign a COM add-in DLL, you must obtain a digital certificate from a certificate authority, and you must run the Signcode.exe utility included with the Microsoft Internet Client Software Development Kit (SDK) on the COM add-in DLL. A digital certificate identifies the developer of a component as a trusted source. For more information about digitally signing a DLL, search the Microsoft Developer Network (MSDN®) Web site, at http://msdn.microsoft.com/, for "digital signing."

You can use the COMAddIn object and the COMAddIns collection to control COM add-ins from Microsoft® Visual Basic® for Applications (VBA) code that is running within the host application. For example, you can load an add-in programmatically when a user clicks a button to access a particular feature; or, you can load an add-in from VBA when you open an application through Automation.

The Office XP object library supplies the COMAddIn object and the COMAddIns collection. The Application object for each Office XP application—Microsoft® Word, Microsoft® Excel, Microsoft® PowerPoint®, Microsoft® Access, Microsoft® FrontPage®, and Microsoft® Outlook®—has a COMAddIns property, which returns a reference to the COMAddIns collection. For any application, the COMAddIns collection contains only those COM add-ins that are registered for that application. The COMAddIns collection in Excel, for example, contains no information about COMAddIn objects in Word.

The Connect property of a COMAddIn object sets or returns the load status of the add-in. Setting this property to True loads the add-in, while setting it to False unloads it.

The ProgId property returns the name of the registry subkey that stores information about the COM add-in. The registry subkey takes its name from the COM add-in's programmatic identifier, which consists of the name of the Add-in project followed by the name of the add-in designer or class module that is actually supplying the add-in for a particular application. For example, when it is properly registered, the Image Gallery sample add-in for Excel has the following value for its ProgId property:

```
ImageGallery.dsrImageExcel
```

The name of the Add-in project is ImageGallery, and the name of the add-in designer for the Excel version of the add-in is dsrImageExcel.

You can use an add-in's ProgId property value to return a reference to the add-in from the COMAddIns collection, as shown in the following code fragment, which prints the current value of the Excel Image Gallery COM add-in's Connect property:

```
Debug.Print
Excel.Application.COMAddIns("ImageGallery.dsrImageExcel").Connect
```

You can use the COMAddIn object and COMAddIns collection to get information about available COM add-ins from code running in an Office XP application. You can also use it to load and unload add-ins from code running in the add-in host application, or from code that is performing an Automation operation on the host application from another application.

If you are concerned about the performance of your application, you might want to load an add-in only at certain times. You can control this by loading and unloading it through VBA code.

The following code uses Automation to launch Word from another application, such as Excel, and load the Image Gallery add-in. To run this code from another application, remember to first set a reference to the Word object library.

```
Function LoadWordWithImageGallery() As Boolean
    ' Loads Word and connects Image Gallery add-in.
    ' If Image Gallery add-in is not available, procedure
    ' fails silently and returns False.

    Dim wdApp        As Word.Application
    Dim cmAddIn      As Office.COMAddIn
```

```
' Create instance of Word and make visible.
Set wdApp = New Word.Application
wdApp.Visible = True


' Return reference to COM add-in, checking for error
' in case it doesn't exist.
On Error Resume Next
' Set reference to COM add-in by using its ProgId property value.
Set cmAddIn = wdApp.COMAddIns("ImageGallery.dsrImageWord")
If Err.Number = 0 Then
    ' Connect add-in.
    cmAddIn.Connect = True
    ' Perform other operations here.
    ' .
    ' .
    ' .

    LoadWordWithAddIn = True
Else
    ' Return False if error occurred.
    LoadWordWithAddIn = False
End If


' Enter break mode here to verify that add-in is loaded.
Stop


' Quit Word.
wdApp.Quit
Set wdApp = Nothing
End Function
```

Building Application-Specific Add-ins

For some solutions, creating an application-specific add-in is easier and more convenient than building a COM add-in.

In This Section

Word Add-ins
    Add functionality to a Microsoft® Word solution by creating a Word-specific add-in.

Excel Add-ins
> Build a Microsoft® Excel add-in to add tools or commands to a user's Excel environment.

PowerPoint Add-ins
> Build a Microsoft® PowerPoint® add-in to provide additional functionality to users while they are developing or running a PowerPoint slide presentation.

Access Add-ins
> Build add-ins for Microsoft® Access to help users manage and analyze their databases.

Adding and Removing Command Bars for Word, Excel, and PowerPoint Add-ins
> Include code to display or to create the command bar and control when the add-in loads and to hide or to remove the command bar and control when it unloads.

Controlling Word, Excel, and PowerPoint Add-ins from Code
> Use Microsoft® Word, Microsoft® Excel, and Microsoft® PowerPoint® AddIn objects and the AddIns collections to control the behavior of application-specific add-ins from Microsoft® Visual Basic® for Applications (VBA).

Securing an Access, Excel, PowerPoint, or Word Add-in's VBA Project,
> Protect your code and prevent users from changing it by setting a password for the add-in Microsoft® Visual Basic® for Applications (VBA) project.

Word Add-ins

You can add functionality to a Microsoft® Word solution by creating a Word-specific add-in (also sometimes referred to as a global template). Add-ins are good for adding generic functionality to the Word environment. For example, you might create a Word add-in that contains common tools for working with Word documents. The user can use any of these tools with his or her documents by clicking the toolbars and menu commands that the add-in provides.

To see a list of currently available Word add-ins, click Templates and Add-Ins on the Tools menu. The currently loaded add-ins appear checked in the Global templates and add-ins list in the Templates and Add-Ins dialog box.

Although Word add-ins and Word templates both have the .dot file extension, they contribute functionality to a Word document in different ways. An add-in is a supplemental program that adds custom commands or custom features to an application. A template is a special kind of document that provides boilerplate text, custom styles, and macros for shaping a final document.

Creating a Word Add-in

You should create an add-in when:

- Your solution does not require boilerplate text or custom styles.

- You want to make some functionality available to any document the user creates, through toolbar buttons, menu commands, or macros.

To create a Word add-in

1. Create a Microsoft® Word document. Then, from the **File** menu, select **Save As**, and select **Word Document Template** in the **Save as Type** box.

2. From the **Tools** menu, select **Macro**, and then select **Visual Basic Editor**.

3. From the **File** menu, select **New Project**, and then select **Add-In Project**.

4. Specify the new add-in, and add code that creates a new toolbar with buttons that call your code when they are clicked.

5. From the **Debug** menu, select **Compile** *ProjectName*.

6. If you want, you can protect the project from viewing, as described in Securing an Access, Excel, PowerPoint, or Word Add-in's VBA Project.

7. Save the template as type Document Template with the .dot extension.

To change the default path for templates

1. In Word, from the **Tools** menu, select **Options**.

2. In the **Options** dialog box, select the **File Locations** tab.

3. From the **File types** list, select **User templates**, and then click **Modify**.

    Note   If you want the add-in to load automatically when you start Word, save the add-in to the **Word Startup** folder. In addition, you can modify the default location for workgroup templates in the **Options** dialog box. Workgroup templates are templates that you share on a network with other users.

Loading a Word Add-in

You can load an add-in manually, automatically, or programmatically.

To load a Microsoft® Word add-in manually, select Templates and Add-Ins from the Tools menu, and then select the check box next to the template's name in the Global templates and add-ins list.

   Note   If the add-in does not appear in the list, click Add to locate it. When an add-in is loaded, it is available to each new document that is created until you clear the check box in the Global templates and add-ins list in the Templates and Add-Ins dialog box.

To load a Word add-in automatically, save the template file in the Word Startup folder on your computer.

To load a Word add-in programmatically, you can try one of the two following methods.

*   Call the Add method of the AddIns collection and pass in the add-in file name. By default, the Add method adds the add-in to the AddIns collection, if it is not there already, and loads the add-in. If the add-in is in the AddIns collection, it will appear in the Global templates and add-ins list in the Templates and Add-Ins dialog box. To add the add-in to the collection without loading it, pass in False for the optional Install argument.1.

- Set the Installed property of the corresponding AddIn object to True. When you try to set this property, an error will occur if the add-in has not been added to the collection already.

If an error occurs in a loaded add-in, you cannot debug the add-in code while it is loaded or view or modify its project. To view or change the code that is in the add-in project, open it directly in Word.

Running Code when a Word Add-in Is Loaded or Unloaded

To run code automatically when an add-in is loaded, create a Sub procedure named AutoExec in a standard module in the Add-In project. Any code within this procedure runs when the add-in is loaded. To run code when an add-in is unloaded, add a Sub procedure named AutoExit. If you close and reopen Microsoft® Word while an add-in is loaded, the AutoExec procedure runs when you reopen Word.

Note The Document_Open event procedure does not run when a document is loaded as an add-in. It runs only when the document is opened directly in Word.

Excel Add-ins

You can build a Microsoft® Excel add-in to add tools or commands to a user's Excel environment. To load an Excel add-in, click Add-Ins on the Tools menu, and select the add-in from the list, or browse to find it if it does not appear in the list.

When the add-in has been loaded, any toolbars or menu items that it includes appear in Excel. An add-in remains loaded until the user unloads it or until Excel is closed, so tools in the add-in are available to all open workbooks. When the user closes Excel, the add-in is unloaded. It will be reloaded when Excel is opened only if the add-in is saved to the XLStart folder.

Several characteristics distinguish an Excel add-in from a typical workbook file:

- An add-in has the file extension .xla to indicate that it is an add-in.

- When you save a workbook as an Excel add-in, the workbook window is made invisible and cannot be viewed. You can use the invisible workbook and worksheets for storing calculations or data that your add-in requires while it is running.

- Users cannot use the SHIFT key to bypass events that are built into the add-in. This feature makes sure any event procedures you have written in the add-in will run at the proper time.

- Excel messages (alerts) are not displayed by code running in an add-in. In a standard workbook file, messages appear to verify that the user wants to perform an operation that might result in data loss, such as deleting a worksheet or closing an unsaved workbook file. In an add-in, you can perform such operations without the messages being displayed.

Creating an Excel Add-in

You create a Microsoft® Excel add-in by creating a workbook, adding code and custom toolbars and menu items to it, and saving it as an Excel add-in file.

To create an Excel add-in

1. Create a new workbook, add code to it, and create any custom toolbars or menu bars.

2. On the **File** menu, click **Properties**. In the *DocumentName* **Properties** dialog box, click the **Summary** tab, and then use the **Title** box to specify the name for your add-in, as you want it to appear in the **Add-Ins** dialog box.

3. Compile the Add-In project by clicking **Compile Project** on the **Debug** menu in the Visual Basic Editor.

4. If you want, you can protect the project from viewing as described in Securing an Access, Excel, PowerPoint, or Word Add-in's VBA Project.

5. Save the add-in workbook as type Excel add-in, which has the extension .xla.

    Note   When you are creating an Excel add-in, pay close attention to the context in which your code is running. When you want to return a reference to the add-in workbook, use the **ThisWorkbook** property, or refer to the workbook by name. To refer to the workbook that is open in Excel currently, use the **ActiveWorkbook** property, or refer to the workbook by name.

When you have saved the add-in, you can reopen it in Excel to make changes to the project. The saved add-in no longer has a visible workbook associated with it, but when you open it, its project is available in the Microsoft® Visual Basic® Editor.

Saving the add-in workbook as an Excel add-in sets the IsAddIn property of the corresponding Workbook object to True.

You can debug an Excel add-in while it is loaded. When you load an add-in, its project appears in the Solution Explorer in the Visual Basic Editor. If the project is protected, you must enter the correct password to view its code.

Loading an Excel Add-in

You can load a Microsoft® Excel add-in in one of three ways:

*   **Manually**   Select the check box next to the name of the add-in in the Add-Ins dialog box on the Tools menu.

*   **Automatically when Excel starts**   Save the add-in to the ..\ \Excel\XLStart subfolder. You can change the location of the XLStart subfolder on the General tab of the Options dialog box (Tools menu).

*   **Programmatically**   Use the Add method of the AddIns collection to add the add-in to the list of available add-ins, and then set the Installed property of the corresponding AddIn object to True.

For example, the following procedure loads an add-in by first checking whether it is in the AddIns collection and adding it if it is not. Then, the procedure sets the add-in's Installed property to True. To call this procedure, pass in the path and file name of the add-in that you want to add:

```
Function Load_XL_AddIn(strFilePath As String) As Boolean
    ' Checks whether add-in is in collection, and
    ' then loads it. To call this procedure, pass
    ' in add-in's path and file name.

    Dim addXL           As Excel.AddIn
    Dim strAddInName    As String

    On Error Resume Next
    ' Call ParsePath function to return file name only.
    strAddInName = ParsePath(strFilePath, FILE_ONLY)
    ' Remove extension from file name to get add-in name.
    strAddInName = Left(strAddInName, Len(strAddInName) - 4)
    ' Attempt to return reference to add-in.
    Set addXL = Excel.AddIns(strAddInName)
    If Err <> 0 Then
        Err.Clear
        ' If add-in is not in collection, add it.
        Set addXL = Excel.AddIns.Add(strFilePath)
        If Err <> 0 Then
            ' If error occurs, exit procedure.
            Load_XL_AddIn = False
            GoTo Load_XL_AddIn_End
        End If
    End If
    ' Load add-in.
    If Not addXL.Installed Then addXL.Installed = True
    Load_XL_AddIn = True

Load_XL_AddIn_End:
    Exit Function
End Function
```

Running Code Automatically when an Excel Add-in Is Loaded or Unloaded

To run code automatically when a Microsoft® Excel add-in is loaded, you have two choices:

- **Create a Sub procedure named Auto_Open in a standard module in the Add-In project.** Any code within this procedure runs when the add-in is loaded. To run code when an add-in is unloaded, add a procedure named Auto_Close.

  –or–

- **Add code to the add-in workbook's Open event procedure.** The code in this procedure also runs when an add-in is loaded, and it runs before the Auto_Open procedure runs.

Keep in mind that if you want an add-in to load automatically when Excel starts up, you must save it in the ...\Microsoft\Excel\XLStart subfolder. If the add-in is not saved in this folder, it is not loaded when Excel starts.

PowerPoint Add-ins

Microsoft® PowerPoint® add-ins are similar to Microsoft® Excel add-ins. You build a PowerPoint add-in to provide additional functionality to users while they are developing or running a PowerPoint slide presentation. In most cases, the user works with your add-in by clicking a toolbar button or menu item that you have included with the add-in.

Creating a PowerPoint Add-in

To create a Microsoft® PowerPoint® add-in, you create a new presentation and add code and custom toolbars. Then, you save your presentation as both a presentation file (.ppt) and a PowerPoint add-in (.ppa).

To create a PowerPoint add-in

1. Create a new presentation and add code to its Microsoft® Visual Basic® for Applications (VBA) project, and create any custom toolbars or menu bars.

2. When you have tested and debugged the code, compile the project by clicking **Compile VBAProject** on the **Debug** menu.

3. If you want, you can protect the project from viewing as described in Securing an Access, Excel, PowerPoint, or Word Add-in's VBA Project.

4. Save the project as a PowerPoint presentation, with the extension .ppt, and then save the project as a PowerPoint add-in, which has the extension .ppa. By default, PowerPoint add-ins are saved to the same folder as Excel add-ins—..\Microsoft\Addins subfolder. This folder is where PowerPoint looks for add-ins when you browse for a new add-in in the **Add-Ins** dialog box (**Tools** menu).

   Note   When you save the project as a PowerPoint add-in, you can no longer view the VBA project, not even in break mode, nor can you view the slides associated with it.

Therefore, you also should save your PowerPoint add-in as a standard presentation, in case you must make changes to it and resave it as an add-in.

Loading a PowerPoint Add-in

You can load a Microsoft® PowerPoint® add-in in any of the following ways:

- **Manually** Click Add-Ins on the Tools menu. The Available Add-Ins list displays the available add-ins; you can add add-ins to the list by clicking Add New and locating the add-in file. Any add-in that is loaded currently has an "x" next to its name. To unload an add-in, select it, and click Unload. You can use an add-in only when it is loaded.

- **Automatically when PowerPoint starts** Set the AutoLoad property of the AddIn object to True in the Microsoft® Visual Basic® Editor The next time you start PowerPoint, the add-in is loaded, and the Loaded property is set to True.

- **Programmatically** Set the Loaded property of the corresponding AddIn object to True.

Running Code Automatically when a PowerPoint Add-in Is Loaded or Unloaded

To run code automatically when an add-in is loaded, create a Sub procedure named Auto_Open in a standard module in the Add-In project. Any code within this procedure runs when the add-in is loaded. To run code when an add-in is unloaded, add a procedure named Auto_Close.

If you close Microsoft® PowerPoint® while an add-in is loaded, the Auto_Open procedure will run when you reopen PowerPoint, because the add-in is reloaded on startup.

Access Add-ins

You can build add-ins for Microsoft® Access to help users manage and analyze their databases. Access includes several add-ins, which are written in Microsoft® Visual Basic® for Applications (VBA). For example, the Linked Table Manager is an add-in that handles the updating of linked tables when the database containing the source tables is moved or renamed. The wizards included with Access are also add-ins.

Access add-ins have the file extension .mda or .mde. A user can open an .mda file and look at the code, unless you have secured the modules by using either user-level security or project-level security. When you create an .mde file, however, all VBA source code is removed. The .mde contains only compiled VBA code, which cannot be viewed by the user. Creating an .mde file is therefore the best way to secure your code, if you are concerned about protecting your source code. For more information about .mda and .mde files, search the Microsoft Access Help index for "MDE files."

When you write code that will run in an Access add-in, use caution when referring to the current database. If you want to refer to the add-in database in which code is currently running, use the CodeProject or CodeData object to return a reference to this database. If you want to refer to the database that is currently open in Access, use the CurrentProject or CurrentData object.

Creating Menu Add-ins for Access

The simplest Microsoft® Access add-in is a menu add-in. A menu add-in calls a procedure in another database, perhaps a database that is serving as a code library. For example, a simple menu add-in might call a procedure that generates a report containing information about the various objects in the current database, such as the date they were created and their descriptions. Menu add-ins appear when you point to Add-Ins on the Tools menu.

To create a menu add-in

1. Add a subkey to the registry that specifies the name of the file containing the procedure and the name of the procedure itself. Menu add-ins are listed beneath the following subkey in the registry:

    \HKEY_LOCAL_MACHINE\SOFTWARE\Microsoft\Office\Access\Addins\Menu add-ins

2. To specify the command that should appear on the **Add-Ins** submenu of the **Tools** menu, create a new subkey beneath the Add-In's subkey. For example, naming this subkey **&Analyze Database Objects** would result in a command named <u>A</u>**nalyze Database Objects** on the **Add-Ins** submenu.

3. To hook up the menu command to the add-in, add two entries (in this case, **String** values) beneath the command's subkey, one named **Expression** and one named **Library**. Set the value of the **Library** entry to the path and file name of the database that contains the procedure that provides an entry point to the add-in. Set the value of the **Expression** entry to the name of the procedure itself. For example, if the procedure is named **AnalyzeDatabaseObjects** and it resides in a database named **CodeLib.mda**, you would set these entries as follows:

    Expression: "=AnalyzeDatabaseObjects()"

    Library: "C:\Windows\Application Data\Microsoft\AddIns\CodeLib.mda"

After you have added these keys, the new add-in command will appear on the Add-Ins submenu of the Tools menu the next time you open Access.

> **Note**   If you must distribute your Access menu add-in to users, create an installable add-in, so the add-in is properly registered on users' machines.

Creating Installable Add-ins for Access

You can create add-ins that the user can load (install) or unload (uninstall) by using the Add-In Manager. The Add-In Manager can load the following types of add-ins:

*   Menu add-ins, such as those described in Creating Menu Add-ins for Access.

*   Object wizards, which help the user create a new table, query, form, data access page, or report. Microsoft® Access includes a number of built-in object wizards, which are available in the New Table, New Query, New Form, New Data Access Page, and New Report dialog boxes. An object wizard that you create also will appear in one of these dialog boxes.

*   Control wizards, which help the user to add either an Access control or a Microsoft® ActiveX® control to a form, report, or data access page. A control wizard runs only if the

Control Wizards tool in the toolbox is depressed. When this button is depressed, clicking a control in the toolbox and dropping it onto a form, report, or data access page launches the wizard that is associated with that control.

- Builders, which help the user to set a property for an object in the database—usually through a dialog box. When a builder is available for a particular property, the Build button (the small button with the ellipsis [...]) appears next to that property's name in the property sheet.

To load or unload one of these add-ins, the Add-In Manager relies on the presence of a table within the add-in, called the USysRegInfo table. The USysRegInfo table provides information that the Add-In Manager writes to the registry. Access uses this registry information to launch the add-in in response to an action taken by the user.

Note The USysRegInfo table is a system table and usually is hidden. To view system tables, click Options on the Tools menu, click the View tab, and then select the System objects check box.

You must create the USysRegInfo table; it is not created for you automatically when you create a new .mda file. The USysRegInfo table must contain the four fields described in the following table.

Field	Field type	Description
Subkey	Text	The name of the subkey that contains the registry information for the add-in
Type	Number	The type of value to create beneath the subkey: subkey (0), String (1), or DWORD (4)
ValName	Text	The name of the registry entry to be created
Value	Text	The value to be stored in the registry entry defined by the ValName field

Each record in the USysRegInfo table describes a subkey or value that is to be added to the registry for a particular add-in. The table can contain information for multiple add-ins.

For each add-in, the USysRegInfo table must contain a minimum of three records: one to create the subkey for the add-in, one to add the Library entry, and one to add the Expression entry. Note that these are the same values required to create a menu add-in, as described in the previous section. You can add other records to store additional values in the registry. For example, you might add a record that creates a registry entry that indicates where a bitmap file required by the add-in is stored.

In the Subkey field, you can use the HKEY_CURRENT_ACCESS_PROFILE*AddInType**AddInName* string to create the new registry entry. The Add-In Manager uses this string to determine the location on the user's machine of Access-specific information in the registry, so Access can create the entry for the add-in in the appropriate place. If the user started Access with the /profile command-line option, this string makes sure the registry entry is created beneath the specified Access user profile; otherwise, the entry is created under the \HKEY_LOCAL_MACHINE\SOFTWARE\Microsoft\Office\2002\Access\AddInType subkey in the registry. For more information about starting Access from the command line with the /profile option, search the Microsoft Access Help index for "user profiles."

Note A user profile that you use to start Access from the command line is not the same thing as a user profile that is defined for logging on to the operating system. An Access user profile applies only to Access, and only when you start Access from the command line. A user profile defined for the operating system applies to every application on the system and is used to maintain system data for individual users.

You can also use the HKEY_LOCAL_MACHINE\SOFTWARE\Microsoft\Office\2002\Access*AddInType* string to specify that the registry entries for the add-in always should be created under this registry subtree and that Access user profiles are to be ignored. Note that in this case you must include the full registry path to the add-in's subkey.

Sample USysRegInfo Table

Subkey	Type	ValName	Value
HKEY_CURRENT_ACCESS_PROFILE \Menu Add-ins\&Create Procedures Table	0		
HKEY_CURRENT_ACCESS_PROFILE \Menu Add-ins\&Create Procedures Table	1	Library	|ACCDIR\ProcTable.mda
HKEY_CURRENT_ACCESS_PROFILE \Menu Add-ins\&Create Procedures Table	1	Expression	=AddProcsToTable()

Adding and Removing Command Bars for Word, Excel, and PowerPoint Add-ins

If the user runs tools in your add-in by clicking a command bar control (toolbar button or menu item), you can include code to display or to create the command bar and control when the add-in loads and to hide or to remove the command bar and control when it unloads. Although it might seem to be more effort, creating and destroying the command bar from within your code gives you greater control over when the command bar is displayed than only storing the command bar in the add-in file.

To create the command bar when the add-in is loaded, add code to the procedure that runs when the add-in is loaded: AutoExec for Microsoft® Word, or Auto_Open for Microsoft® Excel and Microsoft® PowerPoint®.

Note These code examples do not show error handling. For example, the procedures do not handle the case when another add-in might have a command bar with the same name.

First, check whether the command bar already exists. If it does not, create it and add a button that runs a Sub procedure, as shown in the following example:

```
Private Const CBR_INSERT As String = "Insert Info Wizard"
Private Const CTL_INSERT As String = "Insert Info"
```

```
Sub AutoExec()
    Dim cbrWiz      As CommandBar
    Dim ctlInsert   As CommandBarButton
    On Error Resume Next
    ' Determine whether command bar already exists.
    Set cbrWiz = CommandBars(CBR_INSERT)
    ' If command bar does not exist, create it.
    If cbrWiz Is Nothing Then
        Err.Clear
        Set cbrWiz = CommandBars.Add(CBR_INSERT)
        ' Make command bar visible.
        cbrWiz.Visible = True
        ' Add button control.
        Set ctlInsert = cbrWiz.Controls.Add
        With ctlInsert
            .Style = msoButtonCaption
            .Caption = CTL_INSERT
            .Tag = CTL_INSERT
            ' Specify procedure that will run when button is clicked.
            .OnAction = "ShowForm"
        End With
...Else
        ' Make sure the existing commandbar is visible
        cbrWiz.Visible = True
    End If
End Sub
```

To delete the command bar when the add-in is unloaded, add code to the procedure that runs when the add-in is unloaded: AutoExit for Word, or Auto_Close for Excel and PowerPoint. The following procedure deletes the command bar created in the previous example:

```
Sub AutoExit()
    On Error Resume Next
    ' Delete command bar, if it exists.
    CommandBars(CBR_INSERT).Delete
End Sub
```

Controlling Word, Excel, and PowerPoint Add-ins from Code

Microsoft® Word, Microsoft® Excel, and Microsoft® PowerPoint® all have an AddIns collection that contains AddIn objects that correspond to application-specific add-ins. You can use these AddIn objects and the AddIns collections to control the behavior of application-specific add-ins from Microsoft® Visual Basic® for Applications (VBA).

Note that the AddIns collection and the COMAddIns collection are two separate collections. Both are returned by a property of the Application object: the AddIns property for application-specific add-ins, and the COMAddIns property for COM add-ins. However, the Microsoft® Office XP object library provides the COMAddIns collection, while the AddIns collection is part of the host application's object model.

Although the AddIn objects and the AddIns collections for Word, Excel, and PowerPoint are similar, they each have different properties and methods. For example, each AddIn object has a read/write property that you can set to load or unload the add-in. In Word and Excel, this is the Installed property; in PowerPoint, it is the Loaded property.

The following code displays information about PowerPoint add-ins in a message box:

```
Sub DisplayPptAddins()
    ' This procedure displays information about add-ins currently
    ' registered and/or loaded in PowerPoint. To determine which
    ' add-ins are registered, VBA looks for add-ins in the registry.

    Dim lngNumAddIns      As Long
    Dim addPpt            As AddIn

    ' Used to build the dialog box.
    Dim strPrompt         As String
    Dim strRegistered     As String
    Dim strLoaded         As String
    Dim strTitle          As String

    ' Get the total number of add-ins.
    lngNumAddIns = PowerPoint.AddIns.Count
```

```vba
    Select Case lngNumAddIns
      Case 0
        ' No add-ins registered.
        strTitle = "No add-ins"
        strPrompt = "You currently have no PowerPoint" _
         & " add-ins registered."
      Case 1
        ' One add-in registered.
        strTitle = "One add-in Registered"
        strPrompt = addPpt.FullName
      Case Is > 1
        ' Set up the title for the dialog box.
        strTitle = lngNumAddIns & " add-ins Registered"

        ' Determine which add-ins are loaded and/or registered.
        strLoaded = "Loaded: " & vbCrLf
        strRegistered = vbCrLf & "Registered: " & vbCrLf

        ' Loop through the AddIns collection.
        For Each addPpt In PowerPoint.AddIns
            ' Check Loaded property.
          If addPpt.Loaded = msoTrue Then
              strLoaded = strLoaded & addPpt.FullName _
                & vbCrLf
          Else
              strRegistered = strRegistered & _
                & addPpt.FullName & vbCrLf
          End If
        Next addPpt
        ' Combine the loaded add-ins list with registered
        ' add-ins list.
        strPrompt = strLoaded & strRegistered
    End Select

    ' Display the dialog box.
    MsgBox strPrompt, vbInformation, strTitle
End Sub
```

For more information about using the AddIn object and AddIns collection, search the VBA host application's (Word, Excel, or PowerPoint) Visual Basic Reference Help index for "AddIn Object" and "AddIns collection."

Securing an Access, Excel, PowerPoint, or Word Add-in's VBA Project

If you want to protect your code and prevent users from changing it, you can set a password for the add-in's Microsoft® Visual Basic® for Applications (VBA) project.

To set the project password

1.   Click **VBAProject Properties** on the **Tools** menu in the **Visual Basic Editor**.

2.   On the **Protection** tab, select the **Lock** project for viewing check box.

3.   Enter a password, and confirm it.

Creating Templates

In some cases, your application might require you to give users a framework within which to complete common tasks. A template can provide such a framework. Within a template, you can include boilerplate text and graphics, custom styles, toolbars and menu items, macros, and Microsoft® Visual Basic® for Application (VBA) code.

In This Section

Word Templates
   Create custom word-processing applications, and take advantage of the power of Microsoft® Word to create nicely formatted invoicing, reporting, and form letter applications easily.

Excel Templates
   Use a Microsoft® Excel template when you want to distribute a custom spreadsheet application that has an Excel user interface component.

PowerPoint Templates
   Use a Microsoft® PowerPoint® template when you must have a custom application for building presentations.

Access Templates
   Create default templates for the forms and reports stored in a database, so when you create a new form or report, it is based automatically on the default template.

Word Templates

Microsoft® Word is ideal for creating custom word-processing applications. You can take advantage of the power of Word to create nicely formatted invoicing, reporting, form letter applications, and so on.

Every Word document has an associated Microsoft® Visual Basic® for Applications (VBA) project. However, code you write in one document is not available easily to other documents. If you are creating an application in Word, it makes sense to create a custom document template and distribute that template to your users. That way, a number of different documents can call the code in the template. The same holds true for custom styles, toolbars, and recorded macros.

To further illustrate the advantages of packaging code in a template, consider the New event for a Word Document object. This event occurs when you create a new document from a template. The Document_New event procedure itself must reside in the template project; there is no reason to use it in a regular Word document (.doc file), because you cannot create a new document from another document.

The Normal Template

The Normal template (Normal.dot) is loaded automatically when you start Microsoft® Word. By default, new documents are based on the Normal template. Even if you attach another template to a document, any styles, text, AutoText entries, command bars, recorded macros, or code included in the Normal template are available to any document open in Word. If you look at the Project Explorer in the Microsoft® Visual Basic® Editor, you will see that the Normal template always appears.

Although you can customize the Normal template, it is not always the best way to distribute an application to users, because replacing their own Normal template might inconvenience them. They will lose any custom settings or macros they might have created. Moreover, many users and system administrators restrict access to the Normal template, so you might not be able to replace or modify it anyway.

A better way to distribute applications is to create either a custom document template or an add-in (global template) that can be loaded in addition to the Normal template. Which one should you use? If you want to build an application that makes it possible for users to create new documents based on an existing document and that can include text and custom styles, use a custom document template. If you want to add toolbars, menu commands, or macros that are available to every document the user opens, create an add-in. After an add-in is loaded, it is available to every document the user opens until the add-in is unloaded.

Custom Document Templates

One way to build an application in Microsoft® Word is to create a custom template on which a user bases new documents. The template that is attached to a document is specified in the Document template box in the Templates and Add-ins dialog box (Tools menu). A document can have only one document template. Even when a document template is attached to a document, however, the Normal template remains loaded.

You should create a custom document template when:

- Your application requires that some boilerplate text or fields be included in the document when it is created.

- You want to make custom styles available to each document the user creates.

- Your application includes custom toolbars or menus the user can use while working with documents based on the template.

- You want to call Microsoft® Visual Basic® for Applications (VBA) procedures in the template from code running in a document that is based on the template.

Custom document templates are good for ensuring that all users have a consistent set of styles and tools for working on a particular project. For example, if your team is writing a book, you can create a document template the writers use as the basis for each section.

Creating a Custom Document Template

To create a custom document template, click New on the File menu, select General Templates from the templates menu, then click the General tab, click Blank Document, and then select Template under the Create New section.

> **Note**   By default, custom command bars are saved in Normal.dot. To save a command bar with a custom document template, create the command bar by clicking Customize on the Tools menu, clicking the Toolbars tab, and then clicking New. In the New Toolbar dialog box, click the document template's name in the Make toolbar available to list.

Creating a New Document Based on a Word Template

To create a new document based on your custom template, click New on the File menu to open the New dialog box. Your template should appear on the General tab or on one of the other tabs if you saved it in a subfolder of the Templates folder. Click the template, and then click OK.

In addition, you can attach a custom template to an existing document. Doing so will not add any text that is in the template to your document, but any code, styles, and toolbars in the template will be available to your document. On the Tools menu, click Templates and Add-ins, and then click Attach to find and attach your document template.

If you look at the VBA project for a document that has a custom document template attached, you will see that three projects appear in the Project Explorer in the Visual Basic Editor: the document's project, the custom template's project, and the Normal template's project. You can write code in any of these projects. In addition, you can call a procedure in the Normal template or in the custom template from a procedure in the document's project.

> **Note**   When you create a document based on a template, that template appears in the document's References folder in the Project Explorer. If you open the References dialog box by clicking References on the Tools menu, you will see that the template appears selected in the list of available references. Attaching a template to a Word document sets a reference to the template's VBA project, making the code that is in that template available to any procedure in the document.

Word Document Templates vs. Word Add-ins (Global Templates)

Microsoft® Word add-ins and document templates both have the same file extension, the .dot extension. In fact, you can use a template as an add-in or an add-in as a template.

The best way to use a Word template is as the basis for new documents. For example, you might create an invoicing template that employees could use to create customer invoices. When users create a new document based on the template, some of the information is available to them already—the name of your company, the date, and so on. All they must do is enter the customer name and the items purchased.

An add-in, on the other hand, provides custom tools that employees can use to work with all of their Word documents, similar to the custom features provided in the UsefulTools.dot add-in. When you load an add-in, it remains loaded for each document opened in Word until you explicitly unload it.

The following table summarizes the similarities and differences between Word templates and add-ins:

Custom document template	Add-in
A document template has the .dot file extension.	An add-in has the .dot file extension.
You can attach only one template to a document. (The Normal template always is loaded whether or not there is an attached template.)	You can load multiple add-ins at the same time.
A template is attached to a document at the time the document is created or after the document is created by clicking the Attach button in the Templates and Add-ins dialog box (Tools menu) and selecting the template.	An add-in is loaded by selecting the corresponding check box in the Global templates and add-ins list in the Templates and Add-ins dialog box.
A template can be used by any document, but it must be attached to each individual document.	When loaded, an add-in is available to all documents.
A template adds toolbar buttons, menu items, macros, styles, or boilerplate text to a specific document.	An add-in adds toolbar buttons, menu items, or macros to the Word environment. It does not display any boilerplate text or contain any custom styles.
The attached template can be accessed from VBA by using the AttachedTemplate property of a Document object. Templates are available in the Templates collection. The Templates collection contains the Normal template, the attached template (if any), and any loaded add-ins.	Add-ins in the Global templates and add-ins list, whether loaded or not, can be accessed from VBA through the Word AddIns collection. In addition, add-ins can be accessed through the Templates collection.

Custom document template	Add-in
A reference to the template's VBA project is set automatically when you attach a template to a document. Therefore, you can call procedures in the template's project from the document's project.	No reference is set to an add-ins' VBA project when it is loaded. Therefore, although you can call procedures in the add-in project through toolbars, menu items, or macros, you cannot call directly a procedure in an add-ins' project from code running in a document unless you explicitly set a reference to the add-ins' project.

Excel Templates

Microsoft® Excel templates differ from Microsoft® Word templates in that when you create a new workbook based on a template, your workbook is really a copy of that template. In Word, creating a document based on a template loads two Microsoft® Visual Basic® for Applications (VBA) projects—one for the template and one for the document.

Use an Excel template when you want to distribute a custom spreadsheet application that has an Excel user interface component. For example, you might create a reporting template that is formatted in a standardized fashion, with embedded graphics, so any reports users create with the template have the same look.

To create a new Excel template, create a new workbook and add the elements you want to include in the template, such as code, custom dialog boxes, custom worksheet and chart layouts, toolbars, and recorded macros. Save the template file in the C:\Windows\Application Data\Microsoft\Templates folder with the .xlt extension; if user profiles are being used, save the template in the C:\Windows\Profiles*UserName*\Application Data\Microsoft\Templates folder.

Excel includes sample templates that you can install to familiarize yourself with how templates work and to get ideas for creating your own templates.

PowerPoint Templates

As with a Microsoft® Excel template, when you create a new Microsoft® PowerPoint® presentation based on a template, the new presentation is a copy of the template. Only one Microsoft® Visual Basic® for Applications (VBA) project is loaded for the new presentation, but it includes all the components you have defined in the presentation template.

Use a PowerPoint template when you must have a custom application for building presentations. A presentation template makes it easy for your users to build attractive slide presentations and saves them time laying out the presentation or looking for the right graphics. You can include content in the template, such as information about departmental contacts, for example, or placeholders for quarterly sales information in a financial presentation. In addition, you can include instructions that guide the user in completing the presentation.

PowerPoint includes a number of custom templates you can use and modify. The templates that appear on the Design Templates tab of the General Templates menu contain only formatted backgrounds. The templates that appear on the Presentations tab also contain text and placeholders for information, navigation buttons, and instructions for completing the presentation.

To create a PowerPoint template, create a new presentation, add any text, graphics, buttons, toolbars, custom dialog boxes, and code, and save the presentation in the C:\Windows\Application Data\Microsoft\Templates folder; if user profiles are being used, save the template in the C:\Windows\Profiles\UserName\Application Data\Microsoft\Templates folder.

To create a new presentation based on your custom template, run PowerPoint, and click New on the File menu. Select your template in the New Presentation dialog box, and then click OK.

Access Templates

Templates in Microsoft® Access are different from templates for any other Microsoft® Office XP application. Instead of creating a template for a database (.mdb) file, you can create default templates for the forms and reports stored in a database. This means, when you create a new form or report, it is based on the default template automatically. You can create a template for a form or a report in one of two ways:

- Create the form or report that you want to be the template, and save it with the name Normal to replace the default template.

  –or–

- Create the form or report that you want to be the template, and save it with whatever name you want. On the Tools menu, click Options, click the Forms/Reports tab, and then type the name of your template in the Form Template or Report Template box.

    Note Access saves the settings for the Form Template and Report Template options in your Access workgroup information file, not in your user database (the .mdb file). When you change an option setting, the change applies to any database you open or create. To see the name of the template that is used currently for new forms or reports, click Options on the Tools menu, and then click the Forms/Reports tab.

To use your templates in other databases, copy or export the templates to them. If your templates are not in a database, Access uses the Normal template for any new forms and reports you create. However, the names of your templates appear in the Form Template and Report Template options in every database in your database system, even if the templates are not in every database.

Creating Wizards

A wizard is a template or add-in that walks a user through a series of steps to create a new document, spreadsheet, presentation, database, Web application, or some object within any of those applications. Typically, when users launch a wizard, they are presented with a series of information-gathering forms, and when they have entered all the necessary information in a form, the wizard creates the new component or completes a task.

The advantages of using a wizard to deliver an application are that it is easy to use and that you can include detailed instructions on each frame of the wizard. For example, Microsoft® Word includes a Letter wizard that gathers information from the user and then creates a new letter based on that information. The wizard saves the user from having to lay the letter out correctly, as well as from having to think about where the information is placed in the final document. The Word letter templates provide the same result as the Letter wizard, but the user has to figure out where each bit of information in the letter goes and navigate around the document to insert it.

In This Section

Common Characteristics of Wizards
> Understand how the way you choose to create a wizard depends on the level of complexity of your wizard, which application or applications you want it to run, and how you want to distribute it to your users.

Word Wizards
> Create an application-specific wizard for Microsoft® Word, or use wizards that Word includes optionally.

Excel Wizards
> Understand that a Microsoft® Excel wizard is a template or add-in.

PowerPoint Wizards
> Use the Auto Content wizard, which automatically generates a presentation with generic content based on information the user entered in the wizard.

Access Wizards
> Create a table, query, form, or report wizard that can be integrated into the Microsoft® Access user interface.

Common Characteristics of Wizards

You can create a wizard by using any of the following:

- A Microsoft® Word, Microsoft® Excel, or Microsoft® PowerPoint® template

- A Word, Excel, PowerPoint, or Microsoft® Access application-specific add-in

- A COM add-in for Microsoft® Office XP applications or for the Microsoft® Visual Basic® Editor

What you choose depends on the level of complexity of your wizard, which application or applications in which you want it to run, and how you want to distribute it to your users. A template or application-specific add-in is the simplest application. A COM add-in might be more complex, because the add-in DLL and any dependent files must be properly registered on the user's computer.

Some other common characteristics of wizards include:

- A form or set of forms that gathers information from the user and that appears when the user launches the wizard

- Navigation buttons (such as the standard Next, Previous, Cancel, and Finish buttons) that make it possible for the user to move back and forth between pages

- The ability to launch the wizard either from a command bar control or by creating a new document based on the wizard

- An optional special file extension

As you can see, wizards do not significantly differ from add-ins or templates.

> **Tip** Rather than creating a new form for each page of your wizard, you can create a multi-page control on a form, with a unique control layout on each page. Then, when the user clicks the Next or Previous button, move the focus to the appropriate page. This way, you are not required to re-create the form background and buttons for each page of the wizard. Also, you do not have to manage the opening and closing of multiple forms.

Word Wizards

Microsoft® Word includes several wizards that are installed optionally; the Letter wizard, the Memo wizard, and the Résumé wizard are a few examples. These files have the extension .wiz, but they are Word templates. You can open them in Word and view their VBA projects.

To create an application-specific wizard for Word, first create a Word template that contains any boilerplate text, plus the wizard forms and code. The wizard should include code that displays a form as soon as the user launches the wizard.

Next, determine how users will launch the wizard. If they will launch the wizard from a command bar control, you can add the control programmatically from code running in a Word add-in.

To design a wizard that is launched from a command bar control

1. Add the **AutoExec** procedure to a standard module in the wizard's project, and include the code to create the control in that procedure.

2. In the code that creates the control, set the control's **OnAction** property to the name of a procedure in the wizard project that displays the starting form for your wizard.

3. Add the **AutoExit** procedure, and include code to remove the control when the wizard is unloaded, so the user does not see the control unless the wizard is loaded.

4. Load your wizard as an add-in.

If the user will launch the wizard by creating a new document, you are not required to have a command bar control, nor the AutoExec nor AutoExit procedures.

To design a wizard that is launched by creating a new document

1. In the wizard's VBA project, open the **ThisDocument** module.

2. Create the Document_New event procedure by clicking **Document** in the **Object** box and **New** in the **Procedure** box.

3. Within this event procedure, call the procedure that displays the wizard's starting form.

4. Copy the wizard template to the C:\Windows\Application Data\Microsoft\Templates folder, or if user profiles are being used, to the C:\Windows\Profiles*UserName*\Application Data\Microsoft\Templates folder, and change the file's extension to .wiz. Confirm this change when Windows prompts you to do so.

When users create a new document by clicking New on the File menu, they will see your wizard displayed in the New dialog box. Clicking the wizard and then clicking OK creates a new document and runs the Document_NewEvent procedure, which displays the wizard's starting form.

Excel Wizards

A Microsoft® Excel wizard is a template or add-in. No special file format indicates that an Excel file is a wizard. To create an Excel wizard, follow the guidelines discussed in Excel Templates and Excel Add-ins.

PowerPoint Wizards

Microsoft® PowerPoint® includes the Auto Content wizard, which automatically generates a presentation with generic content based on information that the user entered in the wizard. Unfortunately, you cannot view the Microsoft® Visual Basic® for Applications (VBA) project associated with the Auto Content wizard, because it is saved as a PowerPoint add-in.

The presentations created by the Auto Content wizard are based on the presentation templates included with PowerPoint. You could create a new presentation based on one of these templates and achieve the same result. Again, the advantage to using the wizard is that it enters some of the information into the presentation for you.

To create a custom PowerPoint wizard, follow the instructions for building a PowerPoint add-in described in PowerPoint Add-ins. Remember to save your presentation as a .ppt file in case you must re-create the add-in.

If you want the user to be able to create a new presentation based on your wizard, copy the wizard to the C:\Windows\Application Data\Microsoft\Templates folder, or if user profiles are being used, to the C:\Windows\Profiles*UserName*\Application Data\Microsoft\Templates folder, and change its extension to .pwz. When users click New on the File menu in PowerPoint, they can click your wizard in the New Presentation dialog box, and then click OK to launch the wizard and create a new presentation.

Access Wizards

A Microsoft® Access wizard is an add-in that can be integrated into the Access user interface. You can create a table, query, form, or report wizard, which appears in the list of options in the New Table, New Query, New Form, or New Report dialog box. For example, you can design a wizard to help users build complex queries, such as update queries.

In addition, you can create control wizards, which are launched when users create new controls on a form or report. Users can disable control wizards by toggling the state of the Control Wizards tool in the toolbox.

You can add a USysRegInfo table to a wizard database and use the Add-in Manager to install wizards. The registry subkeys you must create to register a wizard, however, are different from those you create to register an add-in.

CHAPTER 3

Developing Workflow Applications for Exchange Server

Generally, the term "workflow" is used to describe applications that are modeled as business processes. Typical workflow applications include forms routing/approval, document review/publishing, and issue tracking. While you can implement such applications in nearly any programming language or development environment, you can simplify the task with the use of a workflow engine and specialized workflow modeling tools.

- Modeling tools make it possible for the overall design, or "flow," of a business process to be specified in a simple, high-level representation called a process definition. You can modify or extend the process definition easily without rewriting all of the low-level application code.

- The workflow engine executes and manages individual instances of a process definition, also known as process instances.

To develop a workflow application

1. Plan your application before starting. Numerous considerations make application development much easier if they are addressed from the start—for example, security and schema. For more information, see "Workflow Applications Architecture for Exchange Server" and "Planning a Workflow Process for Exchange Server."

2. Create the workflow process for your application. For more information, see "Building a Workflow Process for Exchange Server."

3. Add script to your application if desired to provide customized functionality. For more information, see "Scripting in the Workflow Designer for Exchange Server."

4. Create the user interface with a separate program that has read/write capabilities with Exchange 2000 Server or SharePoint Portal Server. For more information, see "Developing the User Interface for Exchange Workflow."

5. Activate your workflow. For more information, see "Enabling a Workflow Process for Exchange Server."

6. Test your workflow application. For more information, see "Testing Your Workflow for Exchange Server."

Workflow Applications Architecture for Exchange Server

A workflow application consists of forms and documents that a user manipulates and tools on the server that manage those documents according to a set of rules. The application architecture is comprised of a presentation layer and a business logic layer.

Presentation Layer

A workflow application includes forms or documents with which the user interacts directly. This layer is called the front-end layer, or presentation logic, of the application. It could be a Microsoft® Word document, a Microsoft® Outlook® form, or some other presentation layer that you design. These all work, because workflows are triggered by any save or post in the workflow folder, and the Microsoft® Exchange 2000 Server Web Store provides heterogeneous document storage. Whatever you use as your presentation layer is up to you and has no relation to the functionality addressed by CDO Workflow objects. This layer is independent of CDO Workflow objects and usually runs on a client computer.

Business Logic Layer

You use CDO Workflow Objects to design and run workflow applications. These applications contain the business rules that govern your document approval and routing processes. While the presentation layer usually runs on a separate client computer, the business rules run on the server with the Web Store, where the target documents are stored. Your business logic or workflow layer operates in a separate process from the Web Store process. You can create the workflow process using any language, such as Microsoft® Visual Basic®, and create event sinks, or you can use the Workflow Designer for Exchange 2000 Server in the Microsoft development environment.

In This Section

Workflow Applications
> Workflow processes are used to enforce business rules, such as who sees an item, the sequence of events an item goes through, the routing of an item, or even when an item can be created or deleted.

Exchange Server and Public Folders
> Behind the scenes, the Workflow Designer uses Collaboration Data Objects (CDO) Workflow Objects for Exchange. CDO is a set of COM components that integrates seamlessly with the Microsoft® ActiveX® Data Objects (ADO) 2.5 component.

Application User Interface
> An important task in developing any application is designing the user interface.

Workflow Scripting
> The built-in functionality of workflow events can be enhanced using Microsoft® Visual Basic® Scripting Edition (VBScript).

Workflow Applications

Workflow processes are used to enforce business rules, such as who sees an item, the sequence of events an item goes through, the routing of an item, or even when an item can be created or deleted. The Workflow Designer for Exchange 2000 Server creates workflow processes specifically for Exchange folders. When workflow is applied to a folder, all items in that folder must conform to the information flow created by the workflow process.

A workflow process is made up of a series of tasks and events, the order in which they must occur, and the script that is executed for each event or transition. In its simplest form, a workflow process automates and enforces the order of tasks. For example, a user can create a new item in a folder and assign it to another user. This user can resolve the item and assign it to the original user who then can close the issue.

The Workflow Designer for Exchange Server uses a graphical user interface (GUI) to represent the workflow process as a diagram that can be edited. The conceptual model for a workflow process in the Workflow Designer for Exchange Server includes states, events, and transitions.

Workflow component	Description
State	A state defines the current status of an item in the workflow process, such as Resolved. For more information, see "Adding and Modifying States in a Workflow."
Event	An event defines the operations that can be performed on an item, such as Create. In addition, workflow events can be used to trigger scripts. For more information, see "Choosing Workflow Events."
Transition	A transition moves an item from one state to another. Change is an example of an event that can be used to cause a transition. When creating a transition, in addition to selecting the event, you also must specify the next state. For more information, see "Order of Workflow Events."

When a new workflow process is created, the developer must name the empty process. Create and Delete events are added to this empty workflow process automatically. The Create event appears in the workflow process diagram as the starting block and the Delete event appears as the ending block. States, events, and transitions can be added to enhance the workflow process.

In the following diagram of a workflow process, the rectangles represent states, the arrows represent transitions, and the squares represent the starting block (create) and the ending block (delete). The lines with bends in them (transition within), labeled Edit, represent events that do not cause state changes.

Workflow Process

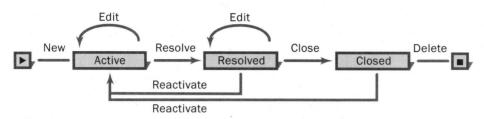

The following is an example of how the diagram looks as an actual workflow process in the Development Environment. Notice that the events, labeled Edit earlier, have transitions within the same state. These special transitions signify that an event does occur, but there is no advance in the workflow state.

Workflow Diagram

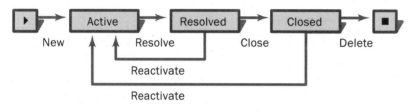

Workflow Events

There are seven types of events that can be used in your workflow process. Each state can be assigned only one Enter, Exit, and Create event but can be assigned multiple Delete, Change, Expiry, and Receive events.

The following table lists the available workflow events and descriptions of when they are triggered:

Event	Description
Create	Triggered when a new item is created in the folder.
Enter	Triggered when transitioning into a given state. The Enter event also starts the clock ticking for the Expiry action.
Exit	Triggered when transitioning out of a given state.
Delete	Triggered when an item is deleted.
Change	Triggered when an item is changed. The Change event can be used to create a state transition.
Receive	Triggered when an e-mail item, which is an update to an existing item participating in the workflow process, is received in the folder. The Receive event can be used to create a state transition.

Event	Description
Expiry	Triggered when the time defined for the Enter event has elapsed. Expiry is a time-based event. The time between the Enter event and the Expiry event is designated in days, hours, or minutes. Fifteen minutes is the minimum duration.

Change, Expiry, and Receive events can be used to create state transitions. A single state can have multiple transitions; for example, from a state called CreateOrder, you can have up to three transitions to a state called OrderCanceled; one created with Change, a second with Receive, and a third with Expiry. In the following example, the transition event-type icons are displayed on the diagram.

Workflow Diagram with Transitions

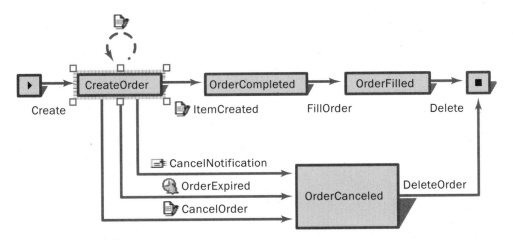

As you can see in the previous illustration, the CreateOrder state has three Change events; one on the CreateOrder itself and two used to create state transitions. From CreateOrder, there are three transitions to the OrderCanceled state; one made with the Change event, a second with Expiry, and the third with Receive. The transition created with the Change event could be used to cancel the order if a field in the item is marked as canceled. The transition using the Expiry event could be used to cancel an item if it remains in the CreateOrder state for a certain length of time. The third transition, made using the Receive event, could be used if an e-mail notification is sent canceling the order.

Event Order

Workflow events are evaluated in a particular order by the workflow engine in Microsoft® Exchange 2000 Server. For each item in the workflow-enabled folder, the workflow engine evaluates the workflow process to find a match of current state, next state, and condition equaling True.

When an item is created in the workflow-enabled folder, the workflow engine matches Create events first and, if the condition evaluates to True, executes the associated event script procedure.

Next, the workflow engine matches Enter events and, if the condition evaluates to True, executes the associated event script procedure.

For existing items in the workflow-enabled folder, the workflow engine looks first for a Change event to match the current state and next state fields. When it finds a Change event, it looks for an Exit event. If it finds an Exit event, it executes the Exit event before proceeding with the Change event. After executing the Exit event, it executes the Change event and then looks for an Enter event. If it finds a matching Enter event and the condition evaluates to True, the associated event script procedure executes.

Note If your workflow process logic never permits the condition or the primary Change event to evaluate to False, none of the other Change events for the state will ever be executed.

Exchange Server and Public Folders

Workflow Designer for Microsoft® Exchange 2000 Server makes it possible for developers to create and to modify workflow processes for Exchange folders. Behind the scenes, the Workflow Designer uses Collaboration Data Objects (CDO) Workflow Objects for Microsoft Exchange. CDO is a set of COM components that integrates seamlessly with the Microsoft® ActiveX® Data Objects (ADO) 2.5 component.

When you create a workflow process, the Workflow Designer creates a set of rules for the selected folder and its association with an event sink. The set of rules is called a process definition, the association is called an event registration, and the event sink is the CDO Workflow Event Sink.

The CDO Workflow Event Sink is the interface between the Exchange 2000 Web Store process and the workflow engine. It is registered automatically as a COM+ application package when you install Exchange.

The association between your folder and the event sink makes it possible for the Exchange Web store to notify the event sink when an event occurs in your folder. The event sink in turn calls the workflow engine to handle the work item's transition.

The workflow engine controls the state changes to documents in your workflow folder. It runs in response to certain system and Web store events and encapsulates the logic for advancing the state of your workflow documents. This makes it possible for you to control the status of documents you are tracking or guiding.

The engine relies on a table of events, called the action table, to evaluate and execute transitions for documents saved in the workflow-enabled folder. The Workflow Designer for Exchange Server creates the action table for you based on the states and events which you create in the workflow diagram.

When you define a workflow process using the Workflow Designer, the events you create determine how the system will respond. When you add script to these events, you can customize the response further.

The Workflow Designer for Exchange Server makes it possible to create a workflow process. It performs many basic tasks for you, such as creating the action table and adding events and scripts based on values you enter in the designer. However, creating a full-blown application requires you to understand CDO Workflow Objects and how to use the ADO 2.5 component for Exchange.

To find more information about workflow and Exchange 2000 Server, refer to the Microsoft® Developer Network (MSDN®) Library at http://msdn.microsoft.com/library/default.asp. The MSDN Library contains the Exchange 2000 Server SDK, which includes in-depth information about the following Microsoft Exchange 2000 Server (Platform SDK) topics:

- Concepts and Architecture
- Programming Tasks
- Reference

Application User Interface

An important task in developing any application is designing the user interface. A poorly designed user interface can contribute to confusion, errors, and frustration for the user. A well-designed user interface can make the application intuitive and increase user efficiency.

Your user interface could be a Microsoft® Word document, a Microsoft® Outlook® form, or another presentation layer you design. These all work, because workflows are triggered by any save or post in the workflow folder, and the Microsoft® Exchange 2000 Server Web Store provides heterogeneous document storage. Whatever you use as your user interface is up to you and has no relation to the functionality addressed by CDO Workflow objects. Typically, the user interface is independent of CDO Workflow objects and runs on a client computer or in the browser.

Workflow Scripting

The built-in functionality of workflow events can be enhanced using Microsoft® Visual Basic® Scripting Edition (VBScript). Scripts associated with a workflow events are entered on the Script Editor.

A single transition, such as moving from one state to another, can trigger several different events that must occur in a particular sequence. You can control the flow of your script with conditional statements and looping statements. Using conditional statements, you can write Microsoft® Visual Basic® Scripting Edition (VBScript) code that makes decisions and repeats actions.

For each event in your workflow process, you can specify a conditional statement to evaluate whether a condition is True or False and, depending on the result, to specify one or more statements to run. Usually, the condition is an expression that uses a comparison operator to compare one value or variable with another.

For instance, if you must validate that a certain user was updating an item, you could write a function that evaluates the sender property of the WorkflowSession object. If this function returns True, then the event script procedure is fired.

Sales Tracking Scenario

You have a sales tracking workflow process, and you want to notify the stock room when an order is marked as completed. You can use script on the Change event to evaluate the contents of the completed field. When this field is set to Yes to indicate the order is completed, an event script procedure that sends a message to the stock room is triggered. If the condition returns False, the event is stopped, and the event script is not executed.

The following illustration shows a state called Active that has a Change event used to create a transition to a state called Resolved. When an item in the folder is changed, the condition is evaluated. If the condition is set to False or if a function called by the statement returns False, the transition does not occur, and the event script associated with Change—in this case, a call to a procedure called SendMail—is not executed.

Change Event

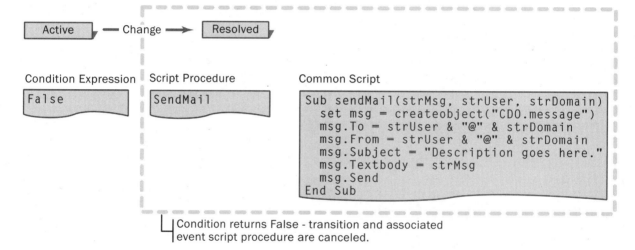

Condition returns False - transition and associated event script procedure are canceled.

In many applications, particularly document-approval applications, you might want to make it possible for editing updates that do not advance the workflow state. In such a case, you can add a Transition-Within Change event.

For example, the following illustration portrays a portion of an order entry workflow process. As an order is updated, the Change event is triggered many times before the order is filled. A Change event called UpdateItem has been added to the OrderCompleted state (shown on the left). There is another Change event on this state called CompleteOrder (shown on the right).

The CompleteOrder event calls a function that evaluates a field called OrderCompleted. Each time the order is updated, both change events are triggered. However, the CompleteOrder transition does not occur until the OrderCompleted field is set to True by the user.

Multiple Change Events

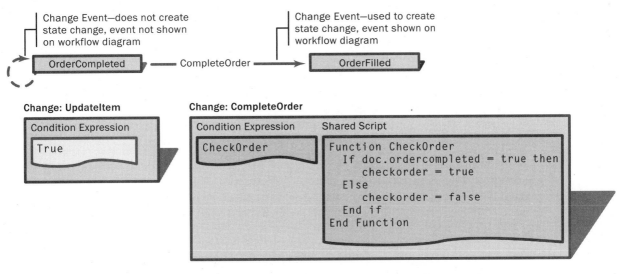

Note   The CheckOrder function shown in the illustration is not complete syntactically.

Planning a Workflow Process for Exchange Server

As with all development, planning is the key to creating successful applications. The Workflow Designer for Exchange 2000 Server automates many of the activities required to create a workflow process for Exchange 2000 Server or SharePoint Portal Server. However, it is important you understand the related technologies and dependencies.

When the workflow process is created, issues, such as how the application will look (the user interface) and how the users will interact with objects, must be considered. These elements must be created outside of the Workflow Designer.

In addition, because a workflow application depends on security and permissions from Exchange 2000 Server and from the operating system, these permissions and privileges must be reviewed carefully before beginning development.

In This Section

Development Steps
   An overview of workflow process development methods.

Permissions Checklist
   List of issues related to developer and user permissions.

Development Steps

The following guidelines are designed to help you design a workflow process using the Workflow Designer in the Microsoft Development Environment.

To design a workflow process

1. Identify the business processes associated with the information you are tracking in your folder. For example, you might have a folder that contains information about employee issues and resolutions. The business process to track this information might be defined as a system for initiating, commenting, and resolving employee issues.

2. Identify the steps in your business process, and determine the events and conditions, such as routing and mail services, you want to associate with each step. For example, when an issue is entered and set to Active, a message can be sent to the manager indicating there is a new, Active issue. When the issue is resolved, the employee who entered the issue could receive e-mail indicating the issue resolution.

3. Create a new workflow process in the Workflow Designer, and add states and events. The steps you identified in Step 2 become the states when you determine the events and conditions required for your business process—for example, Active, Resolved, and Closed.

4. Add script as required to the workflow events associated with an event. For example, you can write a script that directs the Close event to trigger the sending of e-mail to the employee who entered the issue.

Permissions Checklist

Before beginning development of a workflow process, you must set both developer and user permissions.

For the Developer

The first set of permissions requirements for workflow are those enforced at design-time, that is, when you are using the Workflow Designer. They determine who can write and save workflow processes on a given server. These development issues are managed through the Microsoft® Exchange 2000 Server Active Directory Users and Computers and Components Services consoles.

The permissions settings include:

*   **Workflow Event Sink Identity.** By default, the Workflow Event Sink is set to run under the account of the interactive user, the user currently logged onto the Exchange Server. As long as the Administrator is logged onto the server, workflow functions appropriately. However, if a non-administrative user is logged onto the server, you might start to see NetConnect errors in the Application Log. Therefore, it is suggested that you change the Identity to a particular Administrative user.

*   **Are you a folder owner?** Only folder owners can modify application-design elements, such as schema, forms, views, and workflow, of a folder. If you are not a folder owner, it will not

be possible for you to use the Workflow Designer. Folder owner permissions can be granted from Exchange 2000 System Manager or from Microsoft® Outlook®. If you create a folder, you automatically become a folder owner.

- **Has the server administrator granted you permissions to register workflows?** Not every folder owner has permissions to write workflows. Users also must have permissions to register the CDO Workflow Event Sink. The server administrator determines who has permissions to register the event sink by managing membership in the Can Register Workflow role. Only users and groups listed in this role can register workflows on a particular server.

  For procedural information, refer to Installing COM+ Applications in Exchange Management Console Help.

- **What kinds of activities are you going to require in your workflow script?** By default, workflow processes run in Restricted mode, which means script procedures associated with workflow actions are limited to modifying properties of the document undergoing workflow, sending notification mail, and writing to the AuditTrail. The server administrator determines who has permissions to run scripts requiring Privileged mode by managing membership in the Privileged Workflow Authors role. If your workflow processes must perform more complex script driven operations, then either you or the group in which you are registered must be a member of the Privileged Workflow Authors role.

  Note　In addition, you must set the Run as Privileged property in the process definition.

  For procedural information, refer to Installing COM+ Applications in Exchange Management Console Help.

The following is an example of the Exchange 2000 Server Active Directory Users and Computers and Components Services consoles.

Component Services

For the User

The second set of permission requirements apply to the items undergoing workflow at run time. The typical requirements for any Exchange application include:

- **Does the user have write permissions?** Users who modify, edit, or approve items undergoing workflow must have write permissions to those items. Permissions can be assigned at the folder-level or item-level programmatically or by using Microsoft® Outlook® or Microsoft® Exchange 2000 System Manager.

- **Does the user have read permissions?** Users who must open the contents of items, follow a URL to an item, or view the workflow items in a window must have read permissions to the items.

Building a Workflow Process for Exchange Server

The Workflow Designer for Exchange Server makes it possible for you to build, modify, and add script to workflow processes for Microsoft® Exchange 2000 public folders or SharePoint Portal Server folder. A workflow process is made up of a series of tasks and events, the order in which they must occur, and (optionally) the script that is executed for each event. In its simplest form, a workflow process automates and enforces the order of tasks.

Before you can build a workflow process, you must:

- Have or create a public folder in Microsoft Exchange 2000 Server or SharePoint Portal Server.

- Have appropriate permissions on the Exchange 2000 Server or SharePoint Portal Server.

- Plan the business processes you want to track.

In This Section

Understanding the Workflow Process
> A workflow process is a series of tasks or events, the order in which they must be performed, permissions defining who can perform them, and code that can be run when they are performed.

Configuring the Exchange Server for Workflow Development
> Before you can create a public workflow project, you must first configure the Exchange Server for workflow applications.

Creating the Exchange Folder for the Project
> Before you can create a workflow project, you must have a public folder in Microsoft® Exchange 2000 Server or SharePoint Portal Server.

Creating the Project and Workflow Process for Exchange Server
> When you create a workflow process, you can modify it by adding, deleting, or rearranging its components or adding scripts to automate processes.

Setting the Project Properties for Exchange Server
> The Project Properties are workflow-related properties for all Microsoft® Exchange folders or SharePoint Portal Server folders.

Using the Workflow Design Surface
> The Workflow Design Surface is used to lay out and to design the workflow process.

Adding and Modifying States in a Workflow
> After creating a workflow process and adding states, you can add additional events to these states, such as Enter or Exit.

Adding and Modifying Transitions in Workflow
> After creating a workflow process and adding states, you can add transitions, such as Change or Receive, to connect the new state to existing states in your diagram.

Copying a Workflow Process for Exchange Server
    When you have created a workflow process, you might want to copy it to the current folder and then modify it or copy it to another folder.

Deleting a Workflow Process for Exchange Server
    If you have delete permissions on the folder, you can remove a workflow process. When a workflow process has been deleted, you cannot undo the delete to recover it.

Viewing and Printing the Workflow
    After you have created a workflow process, you can view it and print it.

Testing Your Workflow for Exchange Server
    After adding a workflow process and a user interface, you can test the workflow process.

Understanding the Workflow Process

A workflow process is a series of tasks or events, the order in which they must be performed, and code that runs when they are performed. The workflow process is applied to items in the selected folder. Multiple workflow processes can be defined for a single folder. However, only one process can be designated as the default process.

> **Note**   You can have workflow process per item if you have set the Ad Hoc workflow property on the default workflow process and have associated workflow for that item.

In the Workflow Designer for Exchange Server, a diagram representing the workflow process is displayed on the Workflow Designer Design Surface. The following diagram shows a graphical representation of your workflow process, including the states, the transitions between the states, and the events associated with the states.

Workflow Designer Design Surface

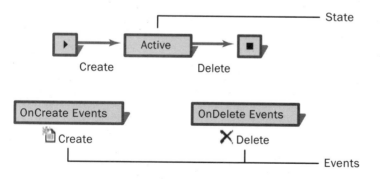

In the previous illustration, there exists only one state, Active. The Item Create and Item Delete events are added automatically. These events make it possible for the user to create and to delete items in the folder. When an item is created, it is set to Active.

Using the workflow toolbox, you can add additional workflow states, such as Resolved and Closed. Then, you can add the corresponding transitions, such as Resolve and Close, to link the states. In addition, you can modify the workflow process to handle non-linear workflow. For example, after an item is closed, a user might want to reopen it to adjust an amount or correct an error. This requires adding an additional state, called Reopened, along with adding the appropriate events, including two transitions, Reopen and Reresolve. The following diagram illustrates these changes.

Example Workflow

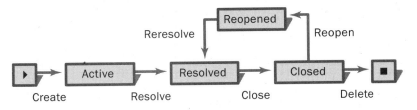

Workflow Components

A workflow process is comprised of workflow states, events, and (optionally) scripts.

When you create a workflow state, you create a defined step or condition in the workflow process, such as Active, Resolve, or Closed.

Each state can have multiple events. Some events, such as Change, Receive, and Expiry, are used to create a transition from one state to another. Other events, including Enter, Exit, Create, and Delete, typically are used to trigger Microsoft® Visual Basic® Scripting Edition (VBScript) association with the workflow process.

Scripts use events as triggers and add them to the Script Editor as validation functions and sub procedures. In addition, you can create common scripts that are used by multiple procedures.

Default Workflow Process

When you select the New Workflow Process option, a new empty workflow process is created. A default name is given to the workflow process, Process1, which can be renamed at the time of creation or in the Properties window. If the Properties window is not displayed, use the View, Properties Window option.

The initial workflow process is enhanced with states, transitions, and events.

In addition to transitions, such as Change, Receive, and Expiry, you might add Enter and Exit events to trigger script. For example, if you want to evaluate the current value in an item before it is changed, you use the Enter event to run a script as soon as a state is entered. Otherwise, when an item enters the Resolved state, the current date, current time, and value in the item's Resolved By field are sent to the manager indicating the item is resolved.

Configuring the Exchange Server for Workflow Development

To configure the Exchange Server for workflow applications, the user account that is used to run workflow applications has to be part of these two COM+ roles:

- Can Register Workflow

- Privileged Workflow Authors

To add the user to the two COM+ roles

1. From the **Start** menu, point to **Programs**, point to **Administrative Tools**, and then point to **Component Services**.

2. In the **Component Services** dialog box, open the **Component Services** node, then **Computers**, then **My Computer**, then **COM+ Applications**, then **Workflow Event Sink**, and finally open **Roles**.

   There are two workflow roles there—**Can Register Workflow** and **Privileged Workflow Authors**.

3. Add the user to both of these roles by right clicking and adding the user.

   The user account also must be a member of the Exchange Domain Servers group.

4. From the **Start** menu, point to **Programs**, point to **Administrative Tools**, and then point to **Active Directory Users and Computers**.

5. In the **Domain Users** folder, right-click the user name, and select **Properties**.

6. Select the **Member Of** tab, and click **Add**.

7. Find the **Exchange Domain Servers** group, and add the user.

   To have workflow applications run under this user's account:

8. From the **Start** menu, point to **Programs**, point to **Administrative Tools**, and then point to **Component Services**.

9. In the **Component Services** dialog box, open the **Component Services** node, then **Computers**, then **My Computer**, and finally open **COM+ Applications**.

10. Right-click **Workflow Event Sink**, and then select **Properties**.

11. Select the **Identity** tab, and then select this user.

12. Add the user, and enter required password.

You might have to shut down and restart the application for the changes to take place.

Creating the Exchange Folder for the Project

Before you can create a workflow project, you must have a public folder in Microsoft® Exchange 2000 Server. For example, you could add a folder called Expense Reports to Public Folders.

To add a public folder using Microsoft Outlook

1. Start Microsoft® Outlook®, and display the folder list if it is not shown already by selecting **Folder List** from the **View** menu.

2. Expand the **Public Folders** node, and then expand **All Public Folders**.

3. Right-click **All Public Folders**, and select **New Folder**.

4. Enter a name for the new folder, such as Expense Reports.

5. Navigate to the folder by selecting the folder you just created on the **Public Folders** node.

Sometimes it is not convenient to setup Outlook simply to create folders. You also can use Outlook Web Access by using Microsoft® Internet Explorer to navigate to the Exchange Server.

To add a public folder using Microsoft Internet Explorer

1. Start Internet Explorer.

2. In the **Address Bar**, type http://*server name*/Public to display Microsoft Outlook Web Access.

3. The public folders will be displayed in the **Folder List** on the left.

4. Right-click the **Public Folders** node, and select the **New Folder** option. The currently logged on user will be set as the folder owner automatically. If you create a subfolder under an existing folder, both the currently logged in user and the owner of the main folder will have owner permissions on the subfolder.

When you have a folder created, it is a good idea to create a Network Place for the folder or at least for the http://MyServer/Public location. To do so, double-click the My Network Places icon on the Microsoft® Windows® 2000 desktop, double-click the Add Network Place icon, and follow the wizard.

Creating the Project and Workflow Process for Exchange Server

When you create a new workflow project, a new solution is created, and the project is added to this solution. Workflow Designer for Exchange Server also generates automatically a new empty workflow process, containing only starting and ending shapes.

Each solution can contain multiple projects of various types, including one or more workflow projects for Exchange Server or Microsoft® SQL Server™ and Dashboard projects.

Each Exchange Workflow project is based on a single public folder and might contain one or more workflow processes.

The solution file (*.sln) is stored by default.

Note To add workflow to a folder, you must have Owner permissions on the folder and be a member of the Can Author Workflow role on the Exchange Server or SharePoint Portal Server where the folder is located.

To create a project and workflow process

1. Open **Microsoft Office XP Developer, Microsoft Development Environment**.

2. From the **File** menu, select **New**, and then select **Project**.

3. The **New Project** dialog box is displayed; select **Office Developer Projects**. Under **Templates**: three project icons are displayed, Exchange Workflow, SQL Workflow and Dashboard project.

4. Select the **Exchange Workflow Project** icon.

5. In the **New Project** dialog box, enter a name for the new project and a folder location in the form of a URL, for example http://myserver/public/myfolder. The folder location will default to the last folder opened.

   Note You cannot browse to an http location unless you have created a network place.

6. Click **OK**.

   Caution Each Exchange folder location can contain only one Exchange Workflow Project. Each project can contain multiple workflow processes.

An empty workflow process is created, and the workflow diagram is displayed on the **Design Surface**.

Setting the Project Properties for Exchange Server

Project Properties are workflow-related properties for the selected Microsoft® Exchange 2000 Server public folder or SharePoint Portal Server folder. All the properties appear and are editable in the Property Grid and in the Project Property Page. The Property Page provides longer descriptions for each property. It is launched using the Properties Page button near the top of the Properties window.

In the Properties Grid, Boolean properties are set with True/False drop-down boxes and the Default Workflow Process and (Name) properties are editable text boxes. Selecting the (Custom) property displays the "..." button that will launch the Property Pages.

In This Section

Displaying the Project Properties
> The Workflow Project represents a Microsoft® Exchange folder or SharePoint Portal Server folder; therefore, the properties for the folder are the same as for the project.

Setting the Security Mode
> The security mode regulates the types of scripts that can be executed from within your workflow process.

Setting the Default Workflow Process for Exchange Server
> When workflow is activated for a folder, items in the folder use the default workflow process unless another workflow process is specified explicitly for use by your application.

Enabling a Workflow Process for Exchange Server
> When you have specified a default workflow process for an Exchange folder or SharePoint Portal Server folder, you must activate workflow to apply the workflow process to items in the folder.

Displaying the Project Properties

In the Properties Grid, the check boxes are represented as Boolean (True/False) dropdown boxes, and the Default Workflow Process is a text box, with a "…" button that will launch the Property Pages.

To display the Project Properties Pages

1. Open the **Development Environment**. Open an existing solution, or use **File, New** to create a workflow project. The solution, along with any of its projects and existing workflow processes, is displayed in the **Solution Explorer**.

2. From the **View** menu, select **Property Pages**. You also can right-click the project in the **Solution Explorer**, and select **Properties** from the context menu.

To display the Properties Grid

1. Open the **Development Environment**. Open an existing solution or use **File, New** to create a workflow project. The solution, along with any of its projects and existing workflow processes is displayed in the **Solution Explorer**.

2. The **Properties Grid** will be displayed below the **Solution Explorer**. If it is not, from the **View** menu, select **Properties Window**, or press **F4**.

Setting the Security Mode

A workflow process can run in either privileged or restricted mode. The Security Mode (PrivilegedContext property) regulates the types of scripts that can be executed from within your workflow process. The default is for a workflow process to run in privileged mode (PrivilegedContext = True).

Note To run a workflow process in privileged mode, you must be a member of the Privileged Workflow Authors role, which is set under Component Services.

To set the security mode

1. Open the **Development Environment**. Open an existing solution, or use **File, New** to create a workflow project. The solution, along with any of its projects and existing workflow processes, is displayed in the **Solution Explorer**.

2. Select a workflow process from the **Solution Explorer**.

3. In the **Properties Grid**, the **PrivilegedContext** property is set to True by default.

–or-

1. From the **View** menu, select **Property Pages**. You also can right-click the workflow process in the **Solution Explorer**, and select **Properties** from the context menu.

2. To specify privileged mode, select the **Run workflow script in privileged author context** check box. To specify restricted mode, clear the **Run workflow script in privileged author context** check box.

    Caution If you select **Run workflow script in privileged author context** and you do not have the required permissions, the workflow process will not run. If this option is not selected and you have scripts that require privileged mode to execute, errors will be returned at run time.

3. Click **OK**.

    Note When the workflow process runs, membership in the Privileged Workflow Authors role is evaluated for the last person who modifies and saves a workflow process.

Setting the Default Workflow Process for Exchange Server

The Default Workflow Process (DefaultWorkflow property) specifies the default workflow process to be applied to a workflow-enabled folder. When workflow is enabled for a folder, items in the folder use the default workflow process unless another workflow process is specified explicitly for use by your application.

To set the default workflow process

1. Open the **Development Environment**. Open an existing solution, or use **File, New** to create a workflow project. The solution, along with any of its projects and existing workflow processes, is displayed in the **Solution Explorer**.

2. Select the workflow project from the **Solution Explorer**.

3. From the **View** menu, select **Property Pages**. You also can right-click the project in the **Solution Explorer** and select **Properties** from the context menu.

4. In the **Default Workflow Process:** text box, enter the name of the workflow process you want to set as the default, or select the "**...**" to browse for other available workflow processes. When browsing for the desired workflow process, the filter will only filter for *.wfd or *wef files. In addition, the name of the default workflow process can be entered into the **Property Grid**, in the **DefaultWorkflow** property field.

If the selected workflow process is not in the current folder, a URL including the location and name of the process will be entered in the text box. It is important to note that external default workflow process will not be displayed in the Solution Explorer; it is displayed only in the **Properties Grid**.

> **Note** The default workflow process must reside on the same server as the Microsoft® Exchange 2000 Server project folder.

> **Note** To use a workflow process other than the default, the **Ad-hoc workflow allowed on documents** option must be selected on the **Property Page** or set to **True** on the **Properties Grid**.

Enabling a Workflow Process for Exchange Server

When you have specified a default workflow process (WorkflowEnabled property) for a Microsoft® Exchange 2000 Server folder or SharePoint Portal Server folder, you must activate workflow to apply the workflow process to items in the folder.

To enable a workflow process

1. Open the **Development Environment**. Open an existing solution, or use **File, New** to create a workflow project. The solution, along with any of its projects and existing workflow processes, is displayed in the **Solution Explorer**.

2. Select the workflow project from the **Solution Explorer**.

3. From the **View** menu, select **Property Pages**. You also can right-click the project in the **Solution Explorer**, and select **Properties** from the context menu.

4. To enable workflow, select the **Workflow enabled on this folder** check box, or in the **Property Grid** set the **WorkflowEnabled** property to **True**.

5. Click **OK**.

> **Caution** Before deleting a workflow-enabled folder, deactivate workflow for the folder.

Using the Workflow Design Surface

The Workflow Design Surface is used to lay out and to design the workflow process. You can enhance or modify your workflow process using this Workflow Design Surface, the tools in the Workflow toolbox, and the properties in the Properties window. Drag icons from the toolbox to the design surface to create workflow states, transitions, and comments.

When you double click a state or transition, the Script Editor is displayed with the associated event script. You also can right-click and select View Code from the Context menu.

Note   Not all objects in the workflow diagram can have script associated with them.

The Workflow Design Surface and toolbox are used to do the following:

- Adding a State

- Renaming a State

- Deleting a State

- Adding and Modifying Events for States

- Adding and Modifying Transitions in Workflow

Adding and Modifying States in a Workflow

The Add New Workflow Process option only creates an empty workflow process, so you must create states, transitions, and events using the Workflow Design toolbox on the design surface.

For each step an item must go through in your process, you add a state to your workflow. Then, you create appropriate transitions to connect your states and designate the flow of your business rules. You enhance the workflow process by adding appropriate events to your states and using these events as triggers for the script you write.

The Workflow Design Surface and toolbox are used to add and modify states in the following ways:

- Adding a State

- Renaming a State

- Setting a State Caption

- Deleting a State

Adding a State

The State tool, in the Workflow toolbox, is used to place state shapes on the Workflow Design Surface. A state shape represents state operations performed by the workflow.

There are three ways to add a state shape. You can double-click the State tool, drag the State Shape tool onto the design surface, or single-click the tool and single-click the design surface.

If you plan to add multiple states, you can turn on Sticky mode. Press CTRL and click the State Shape tool, and then click multiple times the design surface to add states. Press ESC to turn off Sticky mode.

Note   When Sticky mode is turned on, you can select any of the workflow tools, and add objects to the diagram.

To add a workflow state

1. Open the **Development Environment**. Open an existing solution, or use **File, New** to create a workflow project. The solution, along with any of its projects and existing workflow processes, is displayed in the **Solution Explorer**.

2. Select the workflow process from the **Solution Explorer**.

3. From the **View** menu, select **Open**, or double-click the workflow process.

   Note   You can view the **Toolbox** by selecting **Toolbox** from the **View** menu.

4. Select the **State** tool, and click the design surface. The **State** shape will be created at the location of the click. **Properties**, such as name and caption, can be set for the state shape in the **Property Page** or **Properties Grid**.

5. To connect this new state with existing states, you must create a new workflow transition.

   Note   To add one shape in the diagram window multiple times, press and hold CTRL as you choose the shape in the Toolbox. Click in the diagram to place the shape, enter a name if desired, and then click again to add another shape. Choose the Pointer in the Toolbox to stop adding shapes on the design surface.

Renaming a State

State names must be unique. They must be comprised of letters, numbers, and underscores. No spaces or extended characters are supported. State names are used to identify uniquely the state and do not ever have to be shown to the user. They are used to create associated event procedures, such as State1_OnEnter. For many applications, it is only important that the workflow author/administrator understand the meanings of the state names. As long as a workflow process is in development, you can change the names without repercussions. However, when a workflow process is in production, if you change the name, you potentially are changing the workflow logic.

Caution   If you have a workflow process that is in production, do not rename states without changing items to a state value represented on the diagram.

To rename a state

- On the Workflow Design Surface, select the state, and enter a new name for the state in the **Properties Grid**. Names must consist of letter, numbers, and underscores.

Setting a State Caption

State captions also must be unique. However, captions support extended characters, such as spaces and non-English characters.

To set a state caption

- On the Workflow Design Surface, select the state, and enter a new caption value directly in the state itself or in the **Caption** property in the **Properties Grid**.

Deleting a State

If you no longer require a state in the process, you can remove it. Any associated transitions, actions, and script will be removed.

To delete a state

1. Make sure none of the existing items in the folder are in the state you want to delete. If existing items do use the state, you must move them to another state.

   Caution If you delete without changing existing rows to a different state, those items cannot be modified.

2. Make sure the state following the one you want to delete has another event entering it. If it does not, add another state or event to connect that state to the diagram.

3. On the Workflow Design Surface, right-click the state, and choose **Delete**.

   The state and all of its associated events are removed from the design surface and deleted from the workflow.

   Note Any transitions entering or leaving the state will get deleted also.

Adding and Modifying Transitions in Workflow

After creating a workflow process and adding states, you can add transitions, such as Change, Receive, or Expiry, to connect the new state to existing states in your diagram. In addition, workflow events can be used to trigger scripts, adding automation to your workflow process.

The Workflow Design Surface and toolbox are used to add and modify transitions in the following ways:

- Adding a Transition
- Changing the Transition Type
- Renaming an Event
- Setting a Transition Caption

Adding a Transition

1. Open the **Development Environment**. Open an existing solution, or use **File, New** to create a workflow project. The solution, along with any of its projects and existing workflow processes, is displayed in the **Solution Explorer**.

2. Select the workflow process from the **Solution Explorer**.

3. From the **View** menu, select **Open**, or double-click the workflow process.

4. Select the **Transition** tool, click the shape at the start of the transition, and then drag to the shape at the end of the transition. The transition is created between the two shapes. **Properties**, such as name, caption, and type of transition event, can be set in the **Property Page** or **Properties Grid**. By default, the transition will be a Change transition type. This means a change to an item will cause the transition.

    If you have multiple states to connect, you can turn on Sticky mode. Press CTRL and click the transition shape, and then drag to create transitions between the states. Press ESC to turn off Sticky mode.

    Note   To add one transition into the diagram window multiple times, press and hold CTRL as you choose the shape in the Toolbox. Click in the diagram to place the shape, enter a name if desired, and then click again to add another shape. Choose the Pointer in the Toolbox to stop adding shapes on the design surface.

    Caution   If you drag one transition directly over another transition, it might appear that they have merged into one transition; however, both transitions still exist.

Changing the Transition Type

By default, transitions are created with a transition type of Change. The transition type is displayed in the Properties Grid and the Property Page of the selected transition.

The icon associated with each transition gives a visual clue as to the current transition type.

To change the transition type

- On the Workflow Design Surface, select a transition, right-click to display the **Property Page**, and from the **Type** drop-down box, select **Change**, **Expiry**, or **Receive**. In addition, you can change the type using the **Type** property in the **Properties Grid**.

Renaming an Event

Transition names do not have to be shown to the user. For many applications, it is only important that the workflow author/administrator understand the meanings of the transition names.

As long as a workflow process is in development, you can change the names without repercussions. However, when a workflow process is in production, if you change the name, you potentially are changing the workflow logic.

Caution If you have a workflow process that is in production, do not rename transitions without changing items to a transition value represented on the diagram.

To rename a transition

- On the Workflow Design Surface, select the transition, and enter a new name for the transition in the **(Name)** property in the **Properties Grid**.

Setting a Transition Caption

Transition captions also must be unique. However, captions support extended characters such as spaces and non-English characters.

To change a transition caption

- On the Workflow Design Surface, select the transition, and enter a new caption for the transition in the **Caption** property in the **Properties Grid**.

Copying a Workflow Process for Exchange Server

When you have created a workflow process, you might want to copy it to the current folder and then modify it or copy it to another folder.

Workflow processes can be saved as a Workflow Process Definition (*.wfd), or as File System Format (*.wef). The first option, which is the default, is the native format that is saved to the Microsoft® Exchange 2000 Server folder or SharePoint Portal Server folder. The second option will save the workflow process, properties, and common script out in File System Format (meaning binary format). This will make it possible for copies of workflow to be distributed easily to users who do not have access to the same Exchange server.

Note To save a workflow process, it must be opened on the design surface.

To copy a workflow process

1. Open the **Development Environment**. Open an existing solution, or use **File, New** to create a workflow project. The solution, along with any of its projects and existing workflow processes, is displayed in the **Solution Explorer**.

2. Double-click a workflow process in the **Solution Explorer** to display the workflow design on the Design Surface.

3. From the **File** menu, select **Save Copy of <name>.wfd As…**.

4. A dialog displaying the current Exchange folder is shown; select the destination folder for the copy, enter a name for the copy, and then click **OK**.

   Note You must have Owner permissions and be a member of the Can Register Workflow role to save the copy to the Exchange folder.

Deleting a Workflow Process for Exchange Server

If you are the folder owner or have delete permissions on the folder, you can remove a workflow process. When a workflow process has been deleted, you cannot undo the delete to recover it.

To delete a workflow process

1. Open the **Development Environment**. You are prompted to select a folder. The folder you select is displayed with any existing workflow processes.

2. Select the workflow process in the **Solution Explorer**.

3. From the **Edit** menu, select **Delete**.

4. A dialog box displays a message confirming that you want to permanently delete the workflow. Click **Yes**.

> **Caution** Before deleting a workflow-enabled folder, deactivate workflow for the folder.

Viewing and Printing the Workflow

After you have created a workflow process, you can view it and print it.

To open an existing workflow process

1. Open the **Development Environment**. Open an existing solution, or use **File, New** to create a workflow project. The solution, along with any of its projects and existing workflow processes, is displayed in the **Solution Explorer**.

2. Double click the workflow process from the **Solution Explorer**.

Use the **Workflow Design Surface** to do the following:

- Change the look of the diagram.

- Zoom or crop the diagram.

- Print the workflow diagram.

Changing the Look of the Diagram

If you want to change the look of the diagram, you can rearrange the state shapes and transition lines.

To rearrange states

- Drag each state to the desired location in the diagram.

After rearranging the states, the diagram might become cluttered with overlapping lines or irregular spacing.

To arrange the diagram

- From the **Format** menu, select **Arrange Diagram**, and then select **Horizontal** or **Vertical**. In addition, you can right-click the design surface.

  Horizontal will arrange the diagram from left to right, according to the algorithm. **Vertical** will arrange the diagram from top to bottom, according to the algorithm.

To re-order the diagram

- From the **Format** menu, select **Order**, and then select **Bring to Front** or **Send to Back**. In addition, you can right-click the design surface.

Zooming the Diagram

If you want to zoom in to see more detail or zoom out to see the full diagram, you can enlarge the entire diagram or shrink it to fit the Design Surface, so all the items are visible on the design surface.

To zoom to a specific size

1. From the **View** menu, select **Zoom**, or right-click the design surface.

2. In the **Zoom** dialog box, select the zoom size between 10% and 400%

Printing the Workflow Diagram

If you want to keep a hard copy of your workflow diagram for reference, you can print it. The printer prints the entire diagram, even if you have zoomed in or cropped your view by resizing the diagram pane.

To print the diagram

1. Select the workflow process from the **Solution Explorer**, and open the workflow.

2. From the **File** menu, choose **Print**.

3. In the **Print** dialog box, click **Print**.

     Note This does not print the script.

Testing Your Workflow for Exchange Server

After adding a workflow process and a user interface, you can test the workflow process. Even without any script, the workflow states you have designated, along with permissible transitions and events, are enforced when you enter data into your user interface. For more information about user interfaces, see "Developing the User Interface for Exchange Workflow."

Note Before you can test your workflow, you must have it workflow enabled in the folder. For more information, see "Enabling a Workflow Process for Exchange Server."

To test a workflow process

1. Use the user interface you created, either a Microsoft® Outlook® form or a Web form, to post the form to the workflow enabled exchange folder.

2. If you have designed a workflow process that sends notification mail on the OnCreate or OnChange event, an e-mail message is then sent to you.

3. If workflow is not performing as expected, return to your workflow diagram and make sure you have saved your workflow. In addition, make sure you have created the necessary transitions and added appropriate events for your states.

Developing the User Interface for Exchange Workflow

Workflows are triggered by any save or post in the workflow folder, and the Exchange Web Storage System provides heterogeneous document storage. Whatever you use as your user interface is up to you and has no relation to the functionality addressed by CDO Workflow objects. Typically, the user interface is independent of CDO Workflow objects and runs on a client computer.

Designing a user interface is best approached as an iterative process—you rarely will come up with a perfect design on the first pass. The following topics introduce you to the process of designing an interface using Microsoft® Outlook® and introduce the tools you must have to create a great application for your users.

The workflow will work with any form, and any front end, even a standard Outlook message form. In most applications, you will have a custom front end, with custom fields for your application. You can access these fields through script in your workflow.

Because the workflow is triggered only by saves, you might want a button in your form to trigger a workflow transition and then save the workflow item. In addition, you might want to create custom views of your form for different states in your workflow.

In This Section

User Interface Considerations
> The user interface is perhaps the most important part of an application; it is certainly the most visible.

Outlook Forms
> A form is an easy way to distribute and collect information electronically.

User Interface Considerations

The user interface is perhaps the most important part of an application; it is certainly the most visible. To users, the interface is the application; they might not even be aware of the code that is executing behind the scenes. No matter how much time and effort you put into writing and optimizing your code, the usability of your application depends on the interface.

When you design an application, a number of decisions must be made regarding the interface. Should you use the single-document or multiple-document style? How many different forms will you require? How much assistance must you provide?

Before you begin designing the user interface, you must think about the purpose of the application you designed in Planning a Workflow Process for Exchange Server. The design for a primary application that will be in constant use should be different from one that is used only occasionally for short periods. An application with the primary purpose of displaying information has different requirements than one used to gather information.

The intended audience also should influence your design. An application aimed at less-experienced users demands simplicity in its design, while one for experienced users can be more complex. Other applications used by your target audience might influence their expectations for an application's behavior. If you plan to distribute internationally, language and culture must be considered part of your design.

In addition, you can refer to the Microsoft® Developer Network (MSDN®) Library at www.msdn.microsoft.com for additional information about designing a user interface and working with Web pages.

Outlook Forms

Microsoft® Outlook® forms make it possible for your users to access your workflow application when you post it to the public folder in Outlook. Outlook provides built-in forms such as the New Message form to compose messages and the New Contact form to enter information for a contact. If you have sent an e-mail message or created an appointment, you have used a form. Every Outlook item is based on a form.

You use the Outlook Forms design environment to create custom forms either from an item (based on a built-in form) or from a Microsoft® Office XP file. Use a built-in form to leverage functionality from the item associated with it—for example, to include automatic name checking in a custom form, create it from a form based on a mail message. To modify a form, you can add and remove fields, controls, options, and tabs. You can use an Office file to incorporate functionality from another Office program, such as Microsoft® Excel or Microsoft® Word, into a custom form. A form can be saved as a file (for use as a template or in another program) or in a forms library (to make the form available to others).

In This Section

Creating an Outlook Form

     To create the user interface for a workflow, you might want to create two different views of the Post form in Microsoft® Outlook®.

Publishing the Outlook Form

     To make the form available to the workflow, you must publish it.

Creating an Outlook Form

To create the user interface for a workflow, you might want to create two different views of the Post form in Microsoft® Outlook®:

- **Edit Compose Page view**. This view is used by the person inputting data. You are shown this view automatically when you are designing a form. The text boxes on the form can provide values to the script used in the workflow.

To create the Edit Compose Page view of the Outlook form

1. In **Outlook**, open the public folder to which you want to add the workflow.

2. From the **Tools** menu, choose **Design**, and then choose **Design a Form**.

3. In the **Design Form** dialog box, choose **Post**. Click **OK**.

4. In the form, resize the message area to create space for the expense report fields.

5. Display the form **Control Toolbox**.

6. Add the desired controls to the form. Resize the form if necessary.

7. To modify the control properties, right click the control, and select **Properties**.

     Note   You can also use the Field Chooser to add predefined fields to the form. If the Field Chooser is not displayed, select Field Chooser from the Form menu.

Publishing the Outlook Form

To make the form available to the workflow, you must publish it. In addition, you can specify it as the default form for the folder. You must have editor, publishing editor, or owner permissions to add forms to a public folder.

     Caution   Do not enable workflow on a folder before publishing the form. If you do, you might get a permissions error even though you are the owner of the folder.

To publish the form and specify it as the default form for the folder

1. From the **Tools** menu, choose **Design**, and then choose **Publish Form As**.

2. In the **Publish Form As** dialog box, enter a name for the form, and then click **Publish**.

Note The name you provide is the name that the user sees when choosing a form to post in the folder. For example, for an expense report example, you can name it "Expense Report."

3. Close the form, and select **No** when prompted to save your changes (because the form is published already, you are not required to save your changes).

4. In the **Folder** list, right-click the folder to which you want to add workflow, and choose **Properties**.

5. In the **When posting to this folder, use** dialog box, select the form you created, and click **OK**.

Your form will appear when a user decides to post to that folder.

Help Files in Workflow Application

Adding online Help to your Microsoft® Exchange workflow application can reduce the amount of time required to train and support users of your applications.

The following table provides suggestions for the types of Help topics you might want to make available to users.

User tasks	Provide information about
Changing workflow states	What workflow events are, how to use the events and transitions available in the application, and which permissions are associated with the events.
Using the custom Microsoft® Outlook® form	How to complete the form, what fields are required, what the user can expect to happen when the form is posted to the folder.

By using the tools provided with HTML Help Workshop or your favorite HTML editor, you can author topics for a Help system by using the same tools and technologies used to create Web pages—including hyperlinks, Microsoft® ActiveX® controls, scripting, and Dynamic HTML (DHTML) support.

The more complicated your workflow application is, the more help users might require to use the application. Whenever possible, you should provide information about any potential problems or issues that users might see.

Scripting in the Workflow Designer for Exchange Server

When creating workflow processes with the Workflow Designer for Exchange 2000 Server, you are not required to write any scripts to make a workflow process run. However, to add functionality to your workflow process, you can add Microsoft® Visual Basic® Scripting Edition (VBScript) to your workflow events.

In This Section

Creating Script Procedures
  Create the script in the script editor to use procedures or functions in your workflow process.

Workflow Process Security Mode
  The workflow process security mode controls the types of actions that can be executed by your workflow scripts.

Choosing Workflow Events
  Determine the appropriate event to use to trigger a procedure.

Debugging Script in the Workflow Designer for Exchange Server
  The Workflow Designer for Exchange 2000 Server relies on server-side script that cannot display user information. As a result, you cannot use typical debugging options. The options available to you depend on your access to the server on which the scripts are running.

Script Examples for Exchange Server
  The examples in this section are available for use in your workflow scripting.

Creating Script Procedures

To use procedures or functions in your workflow process, you create the script in the script editor.

You are not required to write any scripts to make your workflow process run. The only required script, a validation procedure that returns True making it possible for workflow events to occur, is added automatically when you create a workflow process or add an event.

Each workflow event has two associated script functions—a validation script procedure and an event script procedure. When a workflow event is triggered, the workflow engine invokes the script engine and executes the validation function. If this validation function returns True, the associated event and event script procedure are executed.

To access the Script Editor and add script

1. In the **Solution Explorer**, select the workflow process you are enhancing with script.

2. From the **View** menu, select **Code**, or double click the transition in the **Design Surface** where you want to add code.

3. Create a procedure, including Sub and End Sub tags, or a function, including Function and End Function tags.

Workflow Process Security Mode

The workflow process security mode controls the types of events that can be executed by your workflow scripts. At design time, the security mode for the workflow process is not verified. You can create any script procedure and save it as part of your workflow process. However, when a workflow process executes script at run time, the security mode property of the process definition is evaluated to determine whether it is running in privileged or restricted mode.

Privileged Mode

In privileged mode, any type of script procedure can be executed. Script executes under the same Microsoft® Windows® 2000 security context as the workflow engine itself—typically, the Workflow System Account defined by the server administrator. For example, script running in privileged mode can delete a Microsoft® Exchange 2000 folder and all the items in it or change the permissions for users.

Additionally, when running in privileged mode, your script procedures are able to create COM objects, making it possible for you to integrate with other business applications that provide COM components.

Restricted Mode

Restricted mode script executes under a security context with few or no permissions (anonymous). The workflow engine permits only the following events in restricted mode: modifying properties of the item undergoing workflow, sending notification e-mail, and writing to the AuditTrail Provider.

If your workflow process is running in restricted mode and it attempts to execute a procedure that is not permitted, an error is displayed, and the procedure is canceled.

For more information about the security mode of workflow processes, see "Mode Property" in the Exchange 2000 Server SDK reference section of the Microsoft® Developer Network (MSDN®) Online Exchange Server Developer Center at http://msdn.microsoft.com/exchange/.

Choosing Workflow Events

Sometimes the most difficult aspect of programming is determining the appropriate event to use to trigger a procedure. In a workflow process, events govern workflow activities and are used to trigger script. There are seven workflow actions to choose from: Create, Delete, Enter, Exit, Change, Receive, and Expiry.

Each workflow event has a validation function. If this validation returns False, then the event is canceled, and any script associated with the event is not triggered. If the validation returns True, then the event is committed, and the associated script is executed.

When writing script for workflow events, you must be familiar with the available events and the order in which they are executed. In addition, it is critical to understand how these events loop and the consequences of changing the names of script procedures.

Understanding the order of workflow events is important, because it affects how and when your script runs. For example, if you have two script procedures that are meant to execute in a certain order, it is important you add them to the appropriate events, so the procedures are triggered in the correct sequence.

The workflow engine determines the order in which workflow events are triggered. The workflow engine evaluates the different event types in a particular order. For instance, if you have a Change event and an Exit event for a state and both associated conditions are True, the workflow engine executes the Exit event before proceeding with the Change event.

Order of Workflow Events

A state change is a transition from one state to another. In a workflow process, Change, Receive, and Expiry events can be used to create transitions.

States and transition are displayed on the workflow design surface, but the event order is not displayed.

To view the order

1. Select the state on the workflow design surface.

2. From the **View** menu, select **Property Pages**.

3. In the **Property Pages** dialog box, select the **Transitions** tab.

   If you have more than one event for the state, the order can be adjusted by highlighting a transition and using the up and down arrows. Additional transitions also can be added on the **Property Pages Transitions** tab.

Whenever Change, Receive, or Expiry events are used, you have the following event order:

Action Causes State Change

Exit (current state) $\Rightarrow$ *Transition Action* $\Rightarrow$ Enter (next state)

When the action is not used to make a state change, the Enter action re-enters the current state.

Action Does Not Cause State Change

Exit (current state) $\Rightarrow$ *Transition Action* $\Rightarrow$ Enter (current state)

Workflow Events

This section provides detailed information about each of the five events. Included are the event order, the activities the event permits or denies, and any special rules that apply to the event, such as how many times it can be added to a state or a workflow process.

This topic contains the following sections:

- Create: occurs when an item is created/saved to the folder.

- Delete: occurs when an item is deleted from the folder.

- Change: occurs when the item is changed/edited.

- Receive: occurs when a response is received in the folder for the item in the workflow.

- Expiry: occurs when a specified amount of time elapses from the moment the enter event is fired in the state.

Create

On the workflow design surface, Create is displayed as a transition from the starting block to the state containing the Create event. Select the starting block, and access the property pages to view all of the Create events for the workflow process.

Order of Events

- Create $\Rightarrow$ Enter

Limitations and Special Cases

- To permit creation of items in a workflow-enabled folder, there must be at least one Create event included in your workflow process. If a workflow process does not have a Create event or the condition for the Create event returns False, items cannot be created.

Delete

On the workflow design surface, Delete is displayed as a transition from the state containing the Delete event to the ending block. Select the ending block, and access the property pages to display all of the Delete events for the workflow process.

Order of Events

- Exit $\Rightarrow$ Delete

Limitations and Special Cases

- To permit deletion of items in a workflow-enabled folder, there must be at least one Delete event included in your workflow process. If a state does not have a Delete event or the condition for the Delete event returns False, items currently in that state cannot be deleted.

Change

Change events are displayed on the workflow design surface when they are used to create a state change. To see all the Change events for a state, select the state on the workflow design surface, and access the property pages.

Order of Events if Change Causes a State Change

- Exit (current state) $\Rightarrow$ Change (next state) $\Rightarrow$ Enter (next state)

Order of Events if not a State Change

- Exit (current state) $\Rightarrow$ Change (current state) $\Rightarrow$ Enter (current state)

Limitations and Special Cases

- To permit edits or updates of items in a workflow-enabled folder, there must be at least one Change event included in your workflow process. If a state does not have a Change event or the condition for the Change event returns False, items currently in that state cannot be edited or changed in any way.

- Each state can have multiple Change events.

- If you have multiple Change events in a state, adjust the event order, so the transitions are evaluated in the order appropriate for your workflow process. A Change event that does not cause a state change always should be evaluated last.

Receive

Receive events are displayed on the workflow design surface when they are used to create a state change. To see all the Receive events for a state, select the state on the workflow design surface, and access the property pages.

Order of Events if Receive Causes a State Change

- Exit (current state) $\Rightarrow$ Receive (next state) $\Rightarrow$ Enter (next state)

Order of Events if not a State Change

- Exit (current state) $\Rightarrow$ Receive (current state) $\Rightarrow$ Enter (current state)

Limitations and Special Cases

- To make it possible for the workflow to respond to e-mail, you must add a Receive events to the state. The Receive event does not execute every time e-mail is received in the workflow-enabled folder. The Receive event is triggered only when you send an e-mail message through script and the recipient replies. When the reply reaches the folder, the Receive event is triggered.

- Each state can have multiple Receive events.

- If you have multiple Receive events in a state, adjust the event order, so the transitions are evaluated in the order appropriate for your workflow process. A Receive event that does not cause a state change always should be evaluated last.

Expiry

Expiry events are displayed on the workflow design surface when they are used to create a state change. To see all the Expiry events for a state, select the state on the workflow design surface, and access the property pages.

Order of Events if Expiry Causes a State Change

- Exit (current state) $\Rightarrow$ Expiry (next state) $\Rightarrow$ Enter (next state)

Order of Events if not a State Change

- Exit (current state) $\Rightarrow$ Expiry (current state) $\Rightarrow$ Enter (current state)

Limitations and Special Cases

- The Expiry event is executed after a designated amount of time has passed. The State Expires option of the Enter event sets the expiration time.

  The expiration time is an integer multiple of the base frequency which is initialized to be 15 minutes. If an item enters a state with an Expiry event, the expiration time begins to count down at the next 15-minute interval. Therefore, if an item with a 15-minute expiration time enters a state at 2:10 and the interval occurs at 2:15, the item expiration time starts count down at 2:15, and the item would expire 15 minutes later at 2:30.

- Each state can have multiple Expiry events.

- If you have multiple Expiry events in a state, adjust the event order, so the transitions are evaluated in the order appropriate for your workflow process. An Expiry event that does not cause a state change always should be evaluated last.

Debugging Script in the Workflow Designer for Exchange Server

The Workflow Designer for Exchange Server relies on server-side script that cannot display user information. As a result, you cannot use typical debugging options, such as the MSGBOX function. There are, however, several different strategies for debugging server-side workflow scripts. The options available to you depend on your access to the server on which the scripts are running.

- **If you are an administrator with physical access to the server console**   You can use the Microsoft Script Debugger on the server console. You can enable script debugging for your application folder within the Workflow Designer. On the Project Property Page, select the Script debugging enabled for this folder check box. For more information, search for "Microsoft Script Debugger" in the Exchange Server Programmer's Reference at http://msdn.microsoft.com/exchange/.

- **If you have access to the Microsoft® Windows NT® event logs on the server through the Event Viewer program**   You can use the default Workflow AuditTrail Provider to log messages to the event log.

  The following line of script will write the string "Document check executed properly." to the AuditTrail Provider:

  ```
  WorkflowSession.AddAuditEntry "Document check executed properly."
  ```

  For more information, search for "AuditTrail" on the Microsoft® Developer Network (MSDN®) Library online at http://msdn.microsoft.com/library/default.asp.

- **If you do not have access to either the server console or the server event logs** But, you are running in privileged mode, see "Workflow Process Security Mode." One way of tracking the occurrence of state changes is to create a script in the Script Editor to write a message to a file. If you are running in restricted mode, you can track the state changes using a procedure that sends e-mail. In either case, you call the script in the event procedure of the event you are monitoring.

Script Examples for Exchange Server

In each example, the "Example Script" section provides the code for the function or procedure that should be placed in the Script Editor, which is available from the View menu and then by selecting Code.

The following examples are available for use in your workflow scripting:

In This Section

Creating and Sending an E-mail
: Illustrates the use of the GetnewWorkflowMessage method.

Creating and Posting a Message
: Creates and posts a message in your workflow-enabled folder in response to workflow events.

Evaluating the Current User
: Describes a CheckUser function, which determines the user who initiated a state change.

Writing Messages to File
: Creates a text file and adds text to the file in response to workflow events.

Function Returning the HTTP URL of a File in the Store
: Sends an e-mail message containing a link to an HTTP URL of the message in the store.

Expire Item and Send Notification
: Sends e-mail to the item owner indicating that an item that has been awaiting attention/action has now expired.

Set Permissions
: Specifies what user (using the user's SMTP e-mail address) should have author access to the item. You must call ClearPermissions prior to setting permissions.

Clear Permissions
: Changes the permissions for the person who submitted the form change to read-only after an item is submitted.

Creating and Sending an E-mail

This example illustrates the use of the GetNewWorkflowMessage method. This is a member method of the WorkflowSession intrinsic object. You do not have to create the WorkflowSession object, because the workflow engine passes it to the script host. GetNewWorkflowMessage returns a WorkflowMessage object. As a result, the script can use the IWorkflowMessage interface to set the "From," "To," "Subject," and "TextBody" fields, as well as send the message.

Example Script

```
Sub SendMail(MySubject)
    Set WFMsg = WorkflowSession.GetNewWorkflowMessage()
    With WFMsg
        .From = WorkflowSession.Sender
        .To = WorkflowSession.Sender
        .Subject = MySubject
        .TextBody = WorkflowSession.StateFrom & " -> " &
WorkflowSession.StateTo
        .SendWorkflowMessage 0 'cdowfNoTracking
    End With
End Sub
```

Creating and Posting a Message

The following example describes a PostMsg procedure, which creates and posts a message in your workflow-enabled folder in response to workflow events.

Example Script

```
'// Name      : PostMsg
'// Purpose   : Posts a message in the designated folder for the user who
initiated the action.
'// Prereq    : none
'// Inputs    : strSubject, subject for the post. StrDomain, domain where
folder is located, strFolder location of the folder where item will be
posted
'// Return    : Item posted in designated folder.


Sub PostMsg(strSubject, strDomain, strFolder)
    MyURL = "file://./backofficestorage/" & strDomain & "/Public Folders/"
& strFolder
    Set MyMsg = CreateObject("CDO.Message")
    MyMsg.Subject = strSubject
    MyMsg.TextBody = "This is a Text Body"
    MyMsg.From = WorkflowSession.Sender
    MyMsg.DataSource.SaveTo MyURL & "/" & strSubject, Nothing
End Sub
```

Evaluating the Current User

The following example describes a CheckUser function, which determines the user who initiated a state change. The function uses two common string functions, instr and Left, to capture the user's name.

To use this example, create the CheckUser function in the Script Editor.

Example Script

```
'// Name      : CheckUser
'// Purpose   : checks the sender of the WorkflowSession object
'// Prereq    : none
'// Inputs    : strUSer user to be checked
'// Return    : Returns TRUE if the user indicated is the sender


Function CheckUser (strUser)
  User =  left(workflowsession.sender,instr(workflowsession.sender,"@")-
1)
  If User <> strUser then
     checkuser = FALSE
  else
     checkuser = TRUE
  end if
end function
```

Writing Messages to File

The following example describes a WriteFile procedure, which creates a text file and adds text to the file in response to workflow events.

Example Script

```
'// Name      : WriteFile
'// Purpose   : Creates a file and appends a line of text to the file.
'// Prereq    : none
'// Inputs    : strFileName, filename and extension;strFileText, any text
string you wish to dislay in the message body.
'// Return    : Creates a file, appends text to the file.
```

```
Sub WriteFile (strFilename,strFileText)
   Set fso = CreateObject("Scripting.FileSystemObject")
   Set f = fso.CreateTextFile(strFilename)
   f.writeline(strFileText)
   f.close
   set fso = Nothing
end sub
```

Function Returning the HTTP URL of a File in the Store

The following example describes a Sendmail with a link to a file procedure, which sends an e-mail message containing a link to an HTTP URL of the message in the store.

Example Script

```
set oMapper = CreateObject("Exoledb.UrlMapper.1")

Dim fileURL
Dim filePath
Dim httpURL
Dim iPos
Dim iPathLength
Dim serverName
Dim path
Dim address

fileURL = WorkflowSession.Fields("DAV:href").Value
filePath = oMapper.ExoledbFileUrlToFilePath(fileURL)
httpURL = oMapper.FilePathToHttpUrls(filePath)

iPathLength = Len(httpURL(0))   ' get full length of http url

'extract the server name out of the the full domain
iPos = InStr(httpURL(0), ".") - 1
serverName = Left(httpURL(0), iPos)
```

```
'parse out the domain information
iPos = InStr(8, httpURL(0), "/") - 1
iPathLength = iPathLength - iPos
path = Right(httpURL(0), iPathLength)

'recreate the http url withouth the domain information
address = serverName & path
```

Expire Item and Send Notification

The following example sends e-mail to the item owner indicating that an item that has been awaiting attention/action has now expired. The item is returned to the Draft state. This example was designed for an expense report approval process.

```
Sub ExpireExpenseReport()

    Dim strSubject
    Dim strBody

    strSubject = "Action Required: Expense Report Approval Request"

    strOutlookURL = GetPathAndSubject
    strBody = "There is an expense report waiting for your approval." _
        & vbCRLF & vbCRLF
    strBody = "View the expense report by clicking here. _
        <outlook://public folders/All public Folders/" _
        & strOutlookURL & ">" & vbCRLF & vbCRLF
    strBody = "-------------------------------------" & vbCRLF
    strBody = "Submitted: " & CTXT(Date) & "   " & CTXT(Time) & vbCRLF
    strBody = "Expense ending state: " & WorkflowSession.StateTo

    strSMTPAddress = WorkflowSession.Fields("ApprovalAuthority").Value

    SendMessage strSMTPAddress, strSubject, strBody

End Sub
```

Set Permissions

The parameter specifies what user (using the user's SMTP e-mail address) should have author access to the item. You must call ClearPermissions prior to setting permissions.

```
Sub SetPermissions (strSMTPAddress)
    WorkflowSession.ItemAuthors.Add strSMTPAddress, 0
End Sub
```

Clear Permissions

The following example changes the permissions for the person who submitted the form change to read-only after an item is submitted.

```
Sub ClearPermissions()
    WorkflowSession.ItemAuthors.Clear
End Sub
```

CHAPTER 4

Developing Workflow Applications for SQL Server

Generally, the term "workflow" is used to describe applications that are modeled as business processes. Typical workflow applications include forms routing/approval, document review/publishing, and issue tracking. While you can implement such applications in nearly any programming language or development environment, you can simplify the task with the use of a workflow engine and specialized workflow modeling tools.

Modeling tools make it possible for the overall design, or "flow," of a business process to be specified in a simple, high-level representation. You can modify or extend the process definition easily without rewriting all of the low-level application code.

With the Workflow Designer for SQL Server development tools, you can create an application that enforces business rules and includes integrated row-level security features. You also have the power of Microsoft® Access available to help design and manage the Microsoft® SQL Server™ database schema and to create data access pages for the Web site user interface.

To develop a workflow application

1. Plan your application before starting. Numerous considerations make application development much easier if they are addressed from the start—for example, security and schema. For more information, see "Planning Workflow Applications for SQL Server."

2. Create a SQL Server database, and then open it in the Workflow Designer to register it as an application.

3. Design the workflow process for your application. For more information, see "Building Workflow Applications for SQL Server."

4. Add script to your application, if desired, to provide customized functionality. For more information, see "Scripting Workflow Events for SQL Server."

5. Define database roles using SQL Server Enterprise Manager, and restrict particular activities to certain roles as required. For more information, see "Setting up Accounts, Logins, Roles, and Users."

6. Create the Web site user interface with a separate program that has read/write capabilities with SQL Server. Access data access pages are some of the fastest and most powerful tools you can use. For more information, see "Developing the User Interface for SQL Server."

7. Save your application as a template to make it available for distribution. For more information, see "Creating Templates."

8. Manage and maintain your workflow applications, templates, and database users with the Workflow Manager for SQL Server.

Workflow Applications Architecture for SQL Server

Workflow applications are designed to automate business processes that control items within a database. In addition to a database, the application architecture includes the presentation layer, which is a user interface such as a Web site, and the business logic layer, which consists of the tables and stored procedures that specify the business processes and security for the database.

Presentation Layer

A workflow application includes a user interface that is used to interact with the database. This interface is called the form, presentation layer, or front-end layer of the application. If you use Microsoft® Access to create the form using data access pages, you can take advantage of the built-in functionality of the Microsoft Office Developer Workflow Toolbar control. Any application package or language that works with Microsoft® SQL Server™ can be used to create the presentation layer, but the workflow toolbar can be used only with data access pages.

Business Logic Layer

Workflow applications use triggers and stored procedures to enable your business processes and enforce business rules. While the presentation layer runs on a separate client computer, the business rules run on the server where the database exists. When you install Workflow Designer for SQL Server, several extended stored procedures are added to the Master database and a new database is created, modSystem, where the Workflow Designer keeps internal information and stored procedures. When you begin adding workflow to a database, the Workflow Designer registers the database by adding information to modSystem and by adding a number of stored procedures, tables, and views to your database.

The Workflow Application Architecture

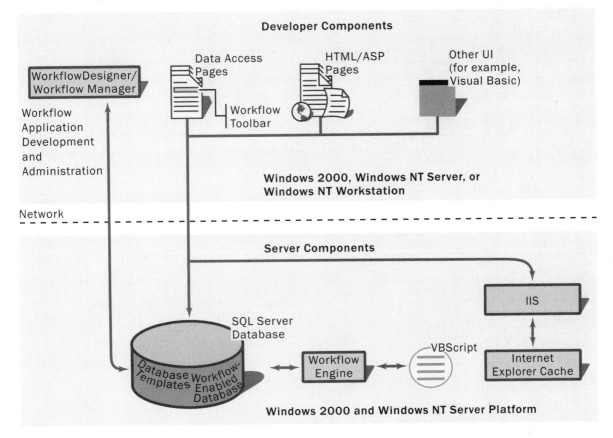

Workflow Applications

Workflow applications improve efficiency by automating business processes and enforcing business rules, such as who sees a database record, the sequence of events an item goes through, the routing of an item, or even when a record can be created or deleted. Using the Workflow Designer for SQL Server, you can create an application that provides the security, user information, and workflow control required to implement a business process successfully.

A workflow application includes databases and a user interface that is created separately (using data access pages, for example), but the central component is the workflow process. A workflow process is made up of a series of states (indicating what tasks must be done) and events, the order in which the states must occur, and the script that is executed for each event or transition. In its simplest form, a workflow process enforces the order of tasks. For example, a user can create a new item in a database and assign it to another user. This user can resolve the item and assign it to the original user, who then can close the issue.

The Workflow Designer for SQL Server uses a graphical user interface (GUI) to represent the workflow process as a diagram. The conceptual model for a workflow process in the Workflow Designer for SQL Server includes states, events, and transitions.

Workflow component	Description
State	A state defines the current status of an item in the workflow process, such as Active, Resolved, or Closed. For more information, see "Adding and Modifying States in a Workflow."
Event	An event defines the operations that can be performed on an item, such as Create, Delete, or Change. In addition, workflow events can be used to trigger scripts. For more information, see "Scripting Workflow Events for SQL Server."
Transition	A transition moves an item from one state to another. For example, onChange is an event that can be used to cause a transition when an item is changed. To create a transition, you select the event and specify the next state. For more information, see "Scripting Workflow Events for SQL Server."

When you create a workflow application, consider the following components; they will help ensure successful implementation:

- Application Design
- System Configuration
- Security Configuration

Application Design

As with any other database application, the success of your workflow application is going to depend on the strength of your data model, including the relationship of user tables and the design of the workflow process. In addition to the basic database schema, you must consider how the application interface will look to your users and how users will interact with data and database objects.

System Configuration

Before starting development, consider all of the computer configurations required to run and manage the application. Think about the configuration of your server, of the development computer, and of the end user's computer. The Workflow Designer has very specific software-configuration requirements that should be reviewed carefully.

Security Configuration

Security considerations and limitations must be analyzed thoroughly. Because the Workflow Designer builds on and over other programs, the permissions and privileges set up on other systems have a strong impact on workflow application development and deployment on a server. These programs and components include:

- Microsoft® Windows® 2000, Microsoft® Windows NT® Server, Windows NT Workstation, Windows NT File System (NTFS)
- Microsoft® SQL Server™ and Microsoft® SQL Server™ 2000 Desktop Engine
- Microsoft® Exchange
- Microsoft® Internet Explorer
- Active Directory

Within the Workflow Designer itself, you have the ability to set up row-level permissions.

When implementing security within a workflow application, you will have the ability to set up database roles and assign users to those roles. This security model is portable and lends itself to creating templates based on existing applications.

SQL Server Workflow Databases

The Workflow Designer primarily uses two databases in Microsoft® SQL Server™ for the storage and retrieval of workflow information for each application:

- The modSystem database, which stores the tables and information to support all workflow applications. If you are using Named Instances, each instance will have its own modSystem database to manage workflow applications on that instance.
- Your workflow-enabled database, which stores information about the specific workflow application created for it. The objects added to your database include the tables, views, and stored procedures required to run the workflow application.

In addition, the Workflow Designer uses several extended stored procedures that were added to the Master database during installation.

> **Caution** You should not directly modify any tables in the modSystem database, because you can break the current functionality in the workflow application and impair forward compatibility with future versions of Microsoft® Office XP Developer. The Workflow Designer handles maintenance of the modSystem database. In addition, you should not modify any of the objects that the Workflow Designer creates in your workflow-enabled databases.

The modSystem Database

Each installation of Workflow Designer server components includes a single SQL Server database that acts as the registry for all the workflow applications on the server. This database, named modSystem, is a repository for templates and other internal components, such as the workflow application User Directory, and for metadata about all workflow applications created on the server. The modSystem tables are maintained by the Workflow Designer, so when changes are made to a workflow application, the modSystem tables are updated accordingly.

The Workflow-Enabled Database

A workflow application includes a SQL Server database containing objects, such as tables, stored procedures, and views that were created for the business process, as well as the database objects created by the Workflow Designer to enforce rules and events on data processing. The objects in a workflow-enabled database fall into two categories: internal workflow objects and user-defined objects.

- **Internal workflow objects** store information about the schema or structure of the workflow application. This includes information about the database tables used by the application and the relationships between columns in those tables.

- **User-defined objects** are defined by the database developer and are organized hierarchically. Every workflow application has at least one main user table that is the top-level or root of the hierarchy. In addition, a workflow application might have one or more detail tables and lookup tables that contain related information. For example, an Issue Tracking application might have a main table that stores issues, a detail table that stores multiple comments related to each issue, and a lookup table that stores a list of countries where issues might have originated. Most simple applications have only a single main user table, however more complex applications might require two or more main tables and numerous detail and lookup tables.

Workflow Web Sites

A Web-based user interface for your workflow application can be created using any program or language that works with Microsoft® SQL Server™, but the Workflow Designer for SQL Server is designed to take advantage of the functionality found in data access pages created using Microsoft® Access. The workflow application's capabilities are embedded in both the database and the Web pages that make up the user interface.

As an example, look at the Issue Tracking workflow sample that is included with Microsoft® Office XP Developer. It presents a Web page to the user that makes possible the entry of new issues (for example, customer complaints). As an issue progresses though different workflow states, the user's Web page changes to reflect appropriate events (for example, when an issue is resolved, it can be closed).

The logic that controls workflow is contained in the workflow application database, as is the data presented on the Web page. The presentation of the data is managed by the Web page itself.

The Workflow Designer will create some basic Web page files for you when you start to work on a database. If you are extending an existing database to take advantage of the workflow engine, then the registration process that takes place when you start adding workflow to the database will create the Web page files at the URL you specify in the opening dialog. If you are creating an instance of a template, the Web pages that were part of the original instance of the application are included.

For example, when you create an instance of a workflow application from the Issue Tracking sample template, the Web site consists of Access data access pages. Each Web page contains a form with controls connected to the database. The view and filter options for the application are based on a grid control.

Workflow Web Sites Created from Templates

New Workflow Web sites are created with the following properties:

- Web security options are inherited from the parent Web. For tightest security, disable anonymous and clear-text on the root Web before creating any applications.

- The access permissions and content control settings are inherited from the parent Web.

- The workflow application Web does not inherit Microsoft® FrontPage® permissions from the parent Web. Explicit permissions are set granting application owners FrontPage admin permissions, and all other users are granted FrontPage user permissions.

- The workflow application Web is created as an Internet Information Services (IIS) application root, so it can host an ASP application.

- Default document settings are inherited from the parent Web.

- Developers - always use default.htm or default.asp as the default document.

- Administrators - configure IIS so default.htm and default.asp are recognized as default documents; otherwise, workflow applications might not work properly.

Workflow Templates

A template is a copy of an existing workflow application. A template contains the entire application, including the database schema, permissions, roles, workflow rules, and Web files that make up the application, so it can be transferred easily from one server to another server that has Workflow Services for SQL Server installed. You can create an instance of a complete workflow application from a template onto your server, and you can create your own templates from existing applications. You can reuse and customize existing templates to save development time. Microsoft® Office XP Developer offers two template wizards: one for creating a template from an existing application and one for creating an instance of an application from a template.

- The SQL Server Workflow Template Creation wizard creates a template that incorporates all aspects of a workflow application.

- SQL Server Workflow Template Instantiation wizard creates a new application from a template.

When you create a template using the wizards, the template is added automatically to the modSystem database for the instance of the server you are using. In addition, you can export it to a .tpl file if you want to distribute it or use it on another server.

If you are using SQL Server Named Instances on your server and you want to use a template on multiple instances, you can use the Workflow Manager for SQL Server to export the template to or import the template from another instance.

Templates make it easy to share the workflow applications that you create. For example, an expense-reporting application created for your main office could be distributed easily as a template to branch offices. Each branch could modify it as required after creating an instance of the workflow application.

Planning Workflow Applications for SQL Server

Planning is the key to developing successful workflow applications. Naturally, the database that stores the items to which you want to apply workflow is the centerpiece of your plan. This topic assumes you have created a database already and you are ready to add workflow to it. Based on the function of the database, you can identify the states that each item must pass through and the states that an item might pass through optionally or conditionally. Using the Workflow Designer for SQL Server, you can script events to control how items move from state to state through the workflow process.

In addition to the workflow process, you must develop a user interface and determine the various roles the application must have to control user interaction with data and database objects.

Workflow applications depend on the security and permissions provided by Microsoft® SQL Server™ and the operating system; these permissions and privileges must be reviewed carefully before beginning application development.

In This Section

Workflow Application Development Guidelines
> Review the design considerations for the database schema, scripting, and other aspects affecting a workflow application.

Security Permissions Model
> Workflow Designer for SQL Server leverages Microsoft® Windows® 2000 and Microsoft® SQL Server™ security for its own security model. You can manage users and groups through the Windows 2000 Active Directory.

Database Tools and Technologies
> Consider the features and capabilities of database tools Microsoft® Jet, Microsoft® SQL Server™ 2000 Desktop Engine, and Microsoft® SQL Server™.

The Workflow Engine Model
    Understand how the workflow engine enforces the workflow process definition and executes
    workflow events.

Workflow Application Development Guidelines

The following design guidelines can help you to avoid problems and implement features during the
design process. Review them completely before developing your workflow application.

In This Section

Database Schema Design Guidelines
    Familiarize yourself with the schema limitations that must be considered before you develop a
    database to which you plan to add workflow.

Workflow Scripting Guidelines
    Consider these guidelines and restrictions before you add script to your workflow process.

Data Access Page (User Interface) Guidelines
    Develop an effective user interface for your workflow application.

Database Schema Design Guidelines

When basing a workflow application on an existing database, remember:

- Before registering an existing database as a workflow application, make a backup copy of the
  database.

- Do not attempt design changes on a production database. Move or copy your database to a test
  environment, and perform all workflow implementation and schema changes there. After you
  are sure the workflow application is functioning as expected, deploy it to your production
  server.

When creating a database that you plan to incorporate into a workflow application, there are
certain schema limitations with which you should be familiar before you start development. These
restrictions also should be reviewed carefully if you plan to add workflow to an existing
Microsoft® SQL Server™ database.

General Guidelines

- SQL Server makes it possible to use the following data types in single column primary keys:
  datetime, smalldatetime, float, real, decimal, money, smallmoney, int, smallint, tinyint,
  timestamp, nvarchar, nchar, varchar, char, varbinary, binary, and uniqueidentifier.

- SQL Server does not make it possible to use the following data types in primary/unique keys:
  text, ntext, image, and bit.

- Table relationships are supported in Workflow Designer table hierarchies if they are based on primary key/foreign key relationships where those keys are any keys supported by SQL Server (including multi-column keys).

- Row-level security only can be implemented on a main table if it has a single column primary/unique key and that column is of type tinyint, smallint, or int.

- When you add a main table to a table hierarchy in the Workflow Designer, views are created for that main table and any related detail tables. If these tables already have permissions set on them, you must set the permissions on the associated views manually. Workflow Designer for SQL Server does not replicate existing table permissions to the newly created views.

  Note   Unrelated and lookup tables do not have views created for them.

- If you create a view in your database after the database has been enabled for workflow, you must apply permissions manually on the newly created view. If this view is to form the basis for a data access page, you must grant select privileges on the primary key and insert and delete privileges on the other columns to the roles that will be using the data access page.

- When naming objects, do not use spaces or special characters such as: " / \ [ ] : ; | = , + * ? < >. Also, avoid using SQL Server keywords, because the name will be interpreted as a keyword and not a database name.

Workflow Schema Guidelines

You only can enable workflow on tables with a single-column primary key or unique key. You cannot enable workflow on tables with concatenated keys (more than one column making up the primary key).

Row-Level Permissions Schema Guidelines

- To enable row-level permissions, a table should have an integer-compatible column that can be used as a row identifier by the code that enforces row permissions. Integer compatible types are int, smallint, tinyint, numeric, and decimal.

  Workflow Designer for SQL Server looks first for an int primary key and then for an identity column. The rowID column is provided by the modGetPermissionsJoinColumn stored procedure.

Workflow Scripting Guidelines

You can add script to your workflow events to enhance the workflow process. When scripting, the following guidelines and restrictions should be considered:

- By default, an error raised from a validation or event procedure causes the event's transaction to be rolled back. If you want to prevent this, trap the error using On Error Resume Next, and provide your own error handling.

- Make sure your script has error handling for cases where user directory information is not available—for example, to handle gracefully cases where a user's e-mail address or manager is blank or Null. This could happen when the required information is not available in the master Microsoft® Windows NT® domain or Microsoft® Exchange directory.

- You can link multiple workflow processes together by inserting, updating, or deleting rows in other workflow-enabled tables from your workflow script. This can be used to create parallel workflow processes.

- The validation procedure for an Expiry (OnExpire) event should return True if the time has expired; otherwise, False.

- Do not perform updates from within a validation procedure. This introduces unexpected side effects from the validation procedure, even when the validation returns False.

- You cannot display messages directly to the user interface from workflow script (for example, by use of a message box), because the script runs on the server.

- You can test and debug workflow by writing to the Logger object file.

Data Access Page (User Interface) Guidelines

When developing a data access page user interface for your workflow application, consider the following issues:

- When creating a data access page for a main or detail table, always bind (set the record source) to the base view and not to the table itself, because row-level permissions can be set only on views. You must specify a unique base table in the properties of the data access page for the view to be updateable.

- If your workflow application uses row-level permissions, it is up to the workflow application developer to provide a user interface that exposes this feature. The Issue Tracking sample provides HTML pages that can be used as examples.

Security Permissions Model

Workflow Designer for SQL Server leverages Microsoft® Windows® 2000 and Microsoft® SQL Server™ security for its own security model. You can manage users and groups through the Windows 2000 Active Directory. You can control access to databases through roles you assign and permissions you specify in SQL Server Enterprise Manager. You also can control the permissions a user has by specifying roles and permissions in the Workflow Designer. To make it possible for users to access your application, you must add them as users to the operating system. You can make user management more efficient by specifying groups and controlling users by the group they are in.

When working in SQL Server, the user passes through two stages of security: authentication and permissions validation. The authentication stage identifies the user using a login account and verifies only the ability to connect with SQL Server. If authentication is successful, the user connects to SQL Server. The user then requires permissions to access databases on the server, which is done by using an account in each database, mapped to the user login. The permissions validation stage controls the activities made available for the user to perform in the SQL Server database.

Workflow Designer for SQL Server uses SQL Server role-based security leveraged from Windows 2000 group domain accounts. Users are added and removed or their roles changed when a workflow application administrator deploys the workflow application or when the administrator adds or removes users from the Windows groups mapped to the roles.

Security rules that define what information can be viewed or updated by users belonging to each role are contained in the modSystem database. These rules can be modified using the security features available in SQL Server Enterprise Manager.

Workflow Designer for SQL Server leverages the database-, table-, and column-level security that SQL Server provides. Enabling row-level permissions and workflow event security extends the SQL Server security model. In addition, the workflow application can implement NTFS permissions on the Web site.

Database Role Security

As part of securing a database, you can create roles that you use to assign a common set of permissions to multiple users.

Organizing users by defining roles makes it easier to manage a secure workflow application. With this strategy, rather than assigning permissions to each user for each object in your workflow application, you assign permissions to a few roles and then add users to the appropriate role. When using the workflow application, users are granted permissions based on any roles to which they belong.

For example, in the Issue Tracking sample, the IssueTracking database is secured using an Authors role for users who are creating and modifying issues and a Readers role for users who have read-only permissions in the application. The Authors role has the least restrictive set of permissions, and the Readers role has the most restrictive set of permissions. When you create a user account for a new employee, you add that account to the appropriate role. Then, the employee has the permissions associated with that role.

The use of roles also works well when you create a template based on your application. Rather than having to change permissions for each user, the template contains information about each role and the permissions assigned to these roles. Then, when creating an application based on this template, users of the new workflow application can be assigned to the existing roles.

Workflow Security

Workflow permissions are role based also. When you create a workflow event, you can specify which roles are permitted to execute it. At run time, the engine verifies if the current user is a member of any of the roles with execute permissions for the event.

Role membership information is cached in each workflow application every time users are synchronized. This information is used to resolve mapping between the user Security Accounts

Manager (SAM) account name and application roles. In Windows 9x, workflow applications use the SAM account information cached during network login to verify execute permissions.

All workflow code runs under the context of the user account you configure for the workflow engine. The permissions you grant this account on the server depend on the workflow application's requirements and the sensitivity of other data on this computer.

Database Tools and Technologies

Workflow Designer for SQL Server uses Microsoft® SQL Server™ as the data store. SQL Server can support hundreds to thousands of simultaneous users. However, if you are building either a single-user application or a multi-user application for a small team, you can store the data in a Microsoft® SQL Server™ 2000 Desktop Engine database. The desktop engine is available on the Microsoft® Office XP CD-ROM.

A desktop engine database is compatible with SQL Server, but a desktop engine database cannot support as many users. Best performance with the desktop engine is achieved with five or fewer users. The advantage of using the desktop engine is that you can create a SQL Server database from within Microsoft® Access without having SQL Server on your computer. The desktop engine is a good tool for prototyping and designing an enterprise application that you can migrate to SQL Server, because you can run a desktop engine database under SQL Server without modification.

Note To create a workflow application using Workflow Designer for SQL Server, you must use either SQL Server or Microsoft® SQL Server™ 2000 Desktop Engine. Access .mdb databases are not supported. To use Access to design and modify your SQL Server database, you create an Access data project.

Client/Server Applications

In previous versions of Access, the only way to create a client/server application was to create an .mdb file with linked tables that used an ODBC driver to link to a database server, such as SQL Server. This kind of client/server application also required Access to load the Microsoft® Jet database engine to open the database and the linked tables, which created additional memory overhead.

Although Access continues to support client/server applications that use linked tables, it also supports a new file format and data access architecture that makes it possible for you to create a client application that connects to a SQL Server through OLE DB without loading the Jet database engine. To do this, you create an Access project file that is saved by using an .adp extension.

An Access project can store forms, reports, data access pages, macros, and Microsoft® Visual Basic® for Applications (VBA) modules locally in your client application file and use the OLE DB connection to display and work with the tables, views, relationships, and stored procedures that are stored on SQL Server. You create the forms, reports, macros, and VBA modules in an Access project by using most of the same tools and wizards you use to create these objects in Access databases. This makes it possible for you to develop client/server applications quickly that work directly against a SQL Server database.

Access also makes it possible for you to create new SQL Server databases and provides a variety of visual tools to create and modify the design of tables, views, stored procedures, triggers, and database diagrams on your database server. The tables, views, and stored procedures you create, as well as SQL SELECT statements, are all valid data sources for Access forms, reports, and data access pages.

In addition to providing you with the ability to create and design client/server applications from scratch, Access also includes the Upsizing wizard, which makes it possible for you to convert an existing Access database to a client/server application by creating a new SQL Server database linked to an Access client application.

With the addition of Workflow Designer for SQL Server, you can add workflow and security features, as well as the ability to create a template of your database application.

Relational Database Design

Regardless of which data store you choose, designing the database structure is likely to be the most challenging part of building the relational database application. To understand how the tables in the database should be structured and how they should relate to one another, you must understand the data. Although it is not difficult to modify the data model while you are developing the application, it is much more challenging after your customers are using the application. Therefore, it is important to put as much effort as necessary into the process of designing the data model before you begin writing code.

One way to start is to think of all the questions this database must answer. The answers become the columns (or fields) in your tables. How many corporate customers do we have by country? This could require the following columns: customer, country.

In addition to determining the columns in your tables, you must set up the relationships between tables. Sometimes, you have what appears to be a straightforward one-to-many relationship that turns out to be much more complex.

The following example illustrates some of the issues you must consider when designing a relational database.

Note   PK = Primary Key, FK = Foreign Key

Relational Database Design Example: Phase I

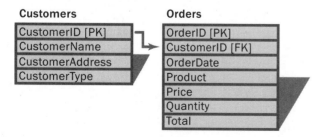

The simple one-to-many design of a Customers table with a single relationship to the Orders table has several limitations. For example, all the product information would have to be re-entered on each order. That would slow down the order entry process and could cause problems as products are added or changed.

Relational Database Design Example: Phase II

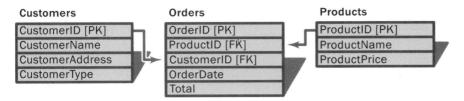

Adding a Products table to relate product information to the Order table is better, but there is still a major limitation. You can place only one order per order number. Therefore, another table is required to handle the order details.

Relational Database Design Example: Phase III

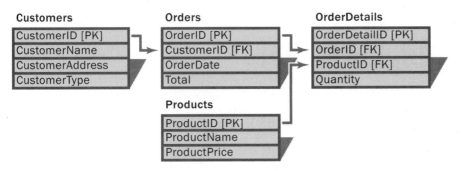

Adding an OrderDetails table and relating the Products table to this new table handles the relationship better. You can maintain and update the products separately, and each order can have one or many order details. Notice that total is still stored in the Orders table. This column could be updated using code, after the order total was calculated for good record keeping.

The design of your database itself enforces certain rules on the way users can enter data. For example, a user cannot violate a table's primary key by adding a duplicate record. In addition, you can establish custom validation rules using triggers that prevent users from entering invalid data.

The Workflow Designer for SQL Server automatically tracks foreign-key constraints when you add a main table to the table hierarchy and creates a tree of detail and lookup tables. If you have other related tables for which there are no foreign-key constraints, you can add those as lookup tables manually using the Workflow Designer for SQL Server.

Data Retrieval, Analysis, and Presentation

After you have designed the data-storage and data-entry components of your application, you should begin thinking about how to present and summarize the data in a format that makes sense to users. Although generally not as difficult as database design, determining what data users want to see and building reports to display the data in a usable format can be a challenging task.

Preplanning your reports also can lead you to rethink or enhance your database design. Sometimes, the lack of a certain column required for grouping or sorting does not become obvious until the reports are being designed.

Here are some questions to ask yourself as you design the reporting component of an application:

- Must the report be linked dynamically to the data source, or can it be a static report? If the report must display the most current data, it should be linked dynamically to the data source. On the other hand, if the data is not updated frequently or if the report must be re-created regularly because the structure of the underlying data source changes, you can create a static report.

- Must users interact with the data in the report, or can the report be read-only? If users must perform calculations on the data or manipulate the data to display it in novel ways, you might want to create the report in Microsoft® Excel or use Access data access pages to create it in a Web page.

- Must users be able to view the report from a Web page or from within one of the Office applications?

The Workflow Engine Model

The workflow process is a series of states and events, the order in which they must be performed, permissions defining who can perform them, and script that is executed for each event. The workflow engine is a component in the Workflow Designer for SQL Server infrastructure that makes workflow possible.

The workflow engine is used to enforce the workflow definition and execute workflow events. When a user table is enabled for workflow, workflow-related insert, update, and delete triggers are created for that table. Any change made to an item in the table will execute the corresponding workflow trigger that in turn calls a stored procedure, which invokes the workflow engine.

The Workflow Engine Functions

The workflow engine has three functions. First, it verifies whether a change is valid for the current workflow state. For example, if there is no Delete event defined for the current state, the engine does not make it possible for users to delete an item in that state.

Second, it checks if the current user has permissions to execute the workflow event. For example, if the event is a transition from Active to Resolved, the engine checks if the current user is permitted to execute this particular event.

Third, if the event is valid and the user has execute permissions, then the workflow engine evaluates the validation script. If the validation returns True, then it executes the event. If the event completes successfully, then the engine invocation returns success, and the trigger commits the change. If an error occurs while executing the validation or event scripts, then the engine reports the error to the trigger. The trigger raises a Microsoft® SQL Server™ error and rolls back the change.

Workflow Designer for SQL Server provides three table-level options that control the way the workflow engine works. The options can be set in the Properties Pages of each workflow process, and are stored in the modObjects table.

- **Enable workflow processing (EnableWorkflow property)**   Controls whether workflow is enforced for a given table. If set to True (default), the engine is called for each data change. Changing this property to False disables workflow processing, which makes it possible for database updates to be made that do not conform to the workflow rules. Use this setting if you want to suspend workflow processing while you make corrections to data in the table.

- **Make deleted rows available to script (MakeDeletedRowsAvailable property)**   Controls whether original values (stored in the DELETED table inside the trigger) are made available at run time. If set to True, the data values in a row prior to a user update, delete, or insert are available to workflow script using the Session object. Then, your script can compare values in the updated row with their original values to perform validation or other processing. Set this property to False (default) to improve performance if you do not require deleted rows in your script.

- **Run workflow in a separate process (SeparateProcess property)**   Controls whether the workflow engine is run in the same Microsoft® Windows® process as SQL Server. Running in a separate process isolates the workflow code from the server and yields more robust workflow applications. Running the workflow engine in the same process as SQL Server provides better performance, but errors in your workflow script could interfere with SQL Server.

  It is recommended you run the workflow engine in a separate process until you have fully debugged and tested your workflow process. The default is to run in a separate process.

  Note   All workflow code runs under the context of the user account you configure for the workflow engine. The permissions granted to this account on the server depend on the workflow application's requirements and the sensitivity of other data on this computer.

Schema Requirements for Workflow

Every workflow-enabled table has a status column that holds the workflow state that moves each item through the workflow process. This status column is an integer data type and has a foreign-key constraint with a keyword lookup table that stores the names of the workflow states. When you enable workflow on a table, the Workflow Designer adds this column, called modStateID, and the associated lookup table.

Building Workflow Applications for SQL Server

The Workflow Designer for SQL Server included with Microsoft® Office XP Developer makes it possible for you to build workflow-organizing applications based on a Microsoft® SQL Server™ database and a Web site user interface. The easiest method for developing the application is to create a workflow process using Workflow Designer for SQL Server and a user interface using Microsoft® Access, which makes it possible for you to incorporate the Office Developer Workflow Toolbar control into your data access pages. Using Access, it is easy to design and manage the SQL Server database schema and to create data access pages for the Web site user interface.

In This Section

Understanding the Workflow Application

The typical development life cycle involves planning, developing, testing, and distribution. While the workflow application follows this basic cycle, it provides flexibility in the development phase.

Creating Workflow Applications based on Templates

Put a copy of a complete workflow application on your server as easily as opening a template.

Creating Workflow Applications from Databases

Add workflow to an existing database.

Understanding the Workflow Process

Design, build, and utilize a workflow process—the graphic representation of states and events that is the center of a workflow application.

Setting up a Table Hierarchy

Identify the main tables to be used in your application, along with associated detail and lookup tables.

Understanding the Workflow Application

A workflow project includes one or more workflow processes and database tables. The project becomes an application when you create a user interface form that works with the database (using data access pages, for example). In the Solution Explorer of the Workflow Designer for SQL Server, you can see folders under each project that display your tables and workflow processes. There is no user interface folder, because the Web pages must be created using a separate application outside of the Workflow Designer environment, such as Microsoft® Access.

There are two ways to start a workflow project—you can create an instance of a template, which creates and registers the required database, or you can add workflow to an existing database.

- **Start from a template**   You can create an instance of an application from a template and then customize it to suit your requirements.

    Templates make distribution of complete workflow applications, including database schema and Web pages, a simple matter. For example, an expense-reporting workflow application created for your main office could be saved easily as a template and distributed to branch officers. Then, each branch can create an instance of the application as-is or modify it as required.

    Each template contains all of the information required to create a complete workflow application, including the database schema, workflow rules, and Web pages.

Note   To create an instance of a template, you must be using a version of Microsoft® SQL Server™ that is the same as or later than the version in which the template was created.

- **Start from a database**   You can create a new SQL Server database and a new Web site, or you can use an existing database and Web site and add workflow features to them.

  A workflow application must be based on a SQL Server database. You can create that database using SQL Server Enterprise Manager or Access. The easiest method is by using an Access data project (.adp). This type of Access file provides efficient, native-mode access to a SQL Server database through the OLE DB component architecture. Before you can use an Access database, you must use the Upsizing wizard in Access to convert the .mdb file to an Access project for a SQL Server database (.adp).

  An Access project is different from an Access database, because it contains only the presentation layer of an application, such as the code-based or HTML-based database objects—forms, reports, data access pages, macros, and modules. An Access project does not contain any data or data definition-based objects—tables, views, database diagrams, or stored procedures (which also can contain application code). Instead, these database objects are stored in the SQL Server database.

A typical procedure for creating a workflow application involves the following steps:

1. Planning your workflow. Identify the states and events that are required to complete the business process, and consider the security and database schema requirements.

2. Connecting to your database in the Workflow Designer. This registers the database and creates a basic Web site at the URL you specify.

3. Defining the table hierarchy. Identify the main table and any detail and lookup tables that must be added to the project.

4. Adding a workflow process to the project.

5. Defining database roles and assigning them to workflow events.

6. Creating the Web site user interface.

Creating Workflow Applications Based on Templates

You can use a template as a baseline for creating new applications. Create an instance of a workflow application from a template, and then modify that instance of the application in any way you want. When the workflow application has been modified, you can save it as a new template that includes all of your changes. This new template can be distributed and used to create new instances of the modified application.

To create a workflow application based on a template

1. Start the **SQL Server Workflow Template Instantiation wizard** by clicking **Instantiate Template** on the **Templates** tab of the Workflow Manager for SQL Server.

2. Select a server, and click **Connect** to display the templates on that server. If you do not see the server in the list, click **Refresh**, and check the list again.

   Note To appear in the templates list, a template must have been imported or exported to your server through the **Workflow Manager for SQL Server**. If you copied a template file to the server but did not use the **Workflow Manager**, it will not show up on the list.

3. Select a template, and click **Next**.

4. Specify identity and location of the new application, and then click **Next**.

   Note Although you can include spaces in your database name and Web URL, it is recommended you avoid including spaces in these object names. If you start the name with an underscore, it will be ignored by some components of the system.

5. Select which SQL Logins can access the database, and then assign roles to each.

   If the login you want is not in the list, click **New SQL Login**, and create a new one in the **New Microsoft SQL Server Login** dialog box by entering the **User name** in the format *<domain\username>* and clicking **OK**.

   Note The group or user must have a valid Microsoft® Windows® account. If a user does not have a valid account, creation of the workflow application will fail.

6. Indicate whether you want the wizard to create a Workflow Project (.spw) file for the application, and then click **Next**.

   Note If you do not create a **Workflow Project** file now, you must create one later if you want to modify the workflow application. You can create one by opening the database in the **Workflow Designer**.

7. Click **Finish**.

   Note The wizard uses the information you supplied and the information in the template to create a new Microsoft® SQL Server™ database and a Web site on the server you specified. This process might take a few minutes.

Creating Workflow Applications from Databases

A workflow application must be based on a Microsoft® SQL Server™ database. You can create that database using SQL Server Enterprise Manager or Microsoft® Access.

To add workflow to an existing database

1. From the **Start** button, point to **Programs**, point to **Microsoft Office XP Developer**, and then click **Microsoft Development Environment**.

2. Open the **File** menu, point to **New**, and click **Project**. The **New Project** dialog box is displayed.

3. Under **Project Types**, select **Office Developer Projects**.

4. Under **Templates**, select the **SQL Server Workflow Project** icon.

5. Enter a project file name and location path for the project (or accept the defaults), and click **OK**.

6. Select the server and the database on which you want to enable workflow. A default Web URL is created. You can change the URL if you would prefer a different location for your Web-based user interface.

7. Click **OK**. The database is registered with the server and the **Workflow Designer**, and is ready for you to add a workflow process.

8. Select the project node in the **Solution Explorer**.

9. Open the **Project** menu, and click **Add New Item**. The **Add New Item** dialog box is displayed.

10. Double-click the **Add a Workflow Process** icon.

11. Select the table you want to add workflow to from the list, and then click **OK**. The table and all dependant tables are added to the **Tables** folder, and the new workflow is added to the **Workflow Processes** folder. **Item Created** and **Item Deleted** shapes are added to the design surface.

12. Build your workflow by adding states and transitions from the toolbox to the design surface.

Using Access to Create SQL Server Databases

In Microsoft® Access, you can create an Access data project (ADP) that connects to a database residing in Microsoft® SQL Server™. When you are in an ADP, the Access database window shows information about views, database diagrams, and stored procedures that are available in the SQL Server database.

> **Note** If you have an existing Access database you want to use for a workflow application, you must use the Access Upsizing wizard to convert it to a SQL Server database. Then, you can use the Workflow Designer to add workflow and row-level security to your application.

To create a SQL Server database using Access

1. Open **Access**.

2. Select **Project (New Data)** from the **New File** window.

3. Give your project a name, click **Create**, and follow the steps in the wizard.

Note To complete the wizard, you must specify a SQL Server. If you do not have Database Creator permissions on that SQL Server, the wizard will not be able to connect and create a database.

4. When the wizard finishes, you can add tables to complete the design of your schema in the **Access Database** window.

Creating SQL Server Database Tables

After creating a database, you can add tables for storing your data. You can create them in your Microsoft® Access project as described in the following, or you can create them directly in the SQL Server Enterprise Manager.

To create SQL Server database tables in Access

1. In **Access**, with the database open, select **Tables** in the **Objects** list, and then double click **Create table in Design view**.

2. Create your columns.

    Note To enter data in a SQL Server table, you must set a primary key. Be sure to clear the **Allow Nulls** option.

3. Click **Save**, type a name for the table, and then close the table designer.

    Note For additional information about using Access, refer to the Access online Help.

Understanding the Workflow Process for SQL Server

A workflow process is made up of a series of states and events, the order in which they must occur, and (optionally) the script that is executed for each event. In its simplest form, a workflow process enforces the order of tasks. The workflow process is the center of a workflow project, which also includes the database table hierarchy. When you add a user interface to a workflow project, you create a complete workflow application.

Before you can build a workflow process, you must have a Microsoft® SQL Server™ database and have database owner (dbo) permissions. In addition, you must have a solid plan for the business processes you want to track, including the tables involved, the roles involved, and when the events are permissible.

For a basic issue tracking project, you might want to specify the states that you want to require and prevent an item from moving to the next state until the previous one is done. For example, before moving from Active to Closed, an issue must go through the state Resolved. This would require a basic linear-workflow diagram.

Basic states and events identified for issue tracking

New   Resolve   Close   Delete

If your workflow application is more complex, you can add alternate possible states and transitions to your workflow process. For example, after an issue has been closed, perhaps a user in the manager role must be able to reopen it. This requires adding an additional state, called Reopened, and the appropriate events, including two transitions, Reopen and Reresolve.

When you add the first state to the workflow process, the Workflow Designer adds a new column called ModStateID to your database table. Each state that you add to the workflow diagram has a state number assigned to it. When the item moves to another state, the ModStateID number changes to that of the new state.

After you have opened your database in the Workflow Designer, begin creating your workflow process by following these steps:

1. Select the main table that is governed by the workflow. For more information, see "Adding Workflow Processes to Databases."

2. Add states, events, and transitions to the workflow diagram. For more information, see "Designing Workflow Processes for SQL Server."

3. Place restrictions on who can perform certain events if desired. For more information, see "Controlling Permissions for Events."

4. Test your workflow process. For more information, see "Testing Workflow Processes for SQL Server."

5. Start using the workflow. For information on how a record starts the workflow process and how records move from one state to the next, see "Starting the Workflow for SQL Server."

Adding Workflow Processes to Databases

After you have registered your database in the Workflow Designer, you add a workflow process by choosing a main table that is governed by the workflow.

To add a workflow process to a database

1. Open your database in **Microsoft Office XP Developer**.

2. Select the project node in the **Solution Explorer**.

3. Open the **Project** menu, and click **Add New Item**. The **Add New Item** dialog box is displayed.

4. Double-click the **Add a Workflow Process** icon.

5. Select the table that you want to add workflow to from the list, and then click **OK**. The table and any other tables that share primary key or foreign key relationships with that table are

added to the **Tables** folder in the **Solution Explorer**, and the new workflow is added to the **Workflow Processes** folder.

6.   Build your workflow by adding states and transitions from the toolbox to the design surface.

Item Created and Item Deleted shapes are added to the design surface automatically when you add a workflow process to a table. The Item Created shape appears in the workflow process diagram as the starting block, and the Item Deleted shape appears as the ending block. Between these points, you add states, events, and transitions to design your workflow process.

If you save the workflow at this point, it starts being enforced as it is. However, because it has no valid states or events that make it possible for additions, changes, or deletions to be performed, nothing can be done with the table. To make it possible for work to be done on the table while the workflow is still incomplete, select the workflow process in the Solution Explorer, and set the EnableWorkflow property to False.

Designing Workflow Processes for SQL Server

To design a workflow process for a table in your workflow project, first analyze the steps that each item must follow and any constraints that control the process. For each step, you add an associated state to the workflow. Keep in mind that script can be added to each state and transition that validates conditions, controls the process, triggers other events, and so on.

When you selected a table for workflow, the Workflow Designer added Item Created and Item Deleted shapes to the design surface automatically. The Item Created shape appears in the workflow process diagram as the starting block, and the Item Deleted shape appears as the ending block. Between these points, you now add states, events, and transitions to design the workflow process.

To design a workflow process

1.   Drag the **State** shape from the **Workflow Toolbox** to the design surface.

2.   Change the caption on the state to a name that identifies the state clearly, such as Active or Opened.

3.   Click the **Transition** shape in the **Workflow Toolbox**, and then drag from the **Item Created** shape to the state you added. A transition arrow appears that points from the first object to the second.

4.   Add the remaining states and transitions to complete your workflow diagram.

     If you want to make it possible for a record to be edited without changing states, click the **Transition Within** shape in the **Workflow** toolbox, and then click the appropriate state.

5.   Add any desired script to the workflow process. Three script blocks are called when an item moves from one state to the next: previousstate_OnExit, OnChange, and nextstate_OnEnter.

     For example, you might want to trigger the sending of e-mail to the person who opened an issue when the ResolvedState_OnEnter script block is called.

6.   Test your workflow.

Controlling Permissions for Events

By default, it is possible for all users to perform all events. However, you might want to restrict who can perform certain events. Permissions can be added to your workflow transitions to make sure only designated roles can execute them. For example, in an expense reporting application, you might want only users assigned to the Manager role to be able to set an expense report to Approved.

To restrict user permissions for specific events

1. In the **Solution Explorer**, open the **Workflow Processes** folder.

2. Double-click the workflow process for which you want to set permissions. The workflow diagram is displayed on the design surface.

3. In the workflow diagram, select the transition for which you want to set permissions.

4. Open the **View** menu, and click **Property Pages**.

5. Select the **Permissions** tab, and specify the roles that have permissions for the event.

   To remove permissions from a transition, clear the check box next to the role.

6. Click **OK**.

Initiating Workflow for a Record

Workflow begins when a record is inserted into the workflow-enabled database, and you invoke the workflow process every time you save a record. To enter or save a record, you first must enter a valid state ID value into the modStateID column of that row.

Workflow is governed by the state ID number in the modStateID column. The modStateID column was added to the workflow-enabled table when the table was first registered for workflow. Each state in the workflow process has a state ID number that was assigned at design time automatically. This number is entered in the modStateID column, where it serves as the basis for determining what events are valid currently for each record. To set a value in the modStateID column, you can use the Office Developer Workflow Toolbar control in a data access page user interface, or you can write your own code to do it.

If you are using the Workflow Toolbar control in your user interface, it initializes the modStateID column to the value of the first state chosen by the user when the user saves the record for the first time, and it dynamically makes all permissible options available to the user each time the record is opened. If there is more than one possible state at the beginning of your workflow diagram, the user can to choose which state is the appropriate one for the new item.

If you are not using the Workflow Toolbar in your user interface, you must write code that accomplishes the same thing. To determine which events are valid currently for a record, compare the modStateID value in that record with the view called *<tablename>*WorkflowView in that database, which details all the events that are possible from each state according to the workflow diagram.

For an example of code that sets the initial modStateID for a record, look at the script in Walkthrough: Creating a Workflow Application for SQL Server with a Visual Basic Interface.

Moving from One State to the Next

If you have created your user interface using data access pages and the Office Developer Workflow Toolbar control, then users are presented with controls that make it possible for them to move to a subsequent valid state, and only to a valid state, every time they save a record.

Each time the user saves the record, the modStateID value is changed to that of the selected state, and the events associated with the transition from the current state to the next state are triggered. If there is more than one possible state to which to move, the user must choose the correct state based on business rules.

If you are not using the Workflow Toolbar in your user interface, you must include code that checks the *<tablename>*WorkflowView view for the next valid states, based on the record's current modStateID value, and presents those states as options to the user. Then, your code must change the record's modStateID to that of the next selected state. You can find the modStateID for each state in the *<tablename>*StateLookup table.

For an example of code that presents users with a record's next allowable states, look at the script in Walkthrough: Creating a Workflow Application for SQL Server with a Visual Basic Interface.

Testing Workflow Processes for SQL Server

After adding a workflow process to a table, you can test the workflow directly in the SQL Server Enterprise Manager. Even without any script, the workflow states, transitions, and events are enforced when you enter data into your table.

To test a workflow process

1. Find the modStateID for each state by opening the *<tablename>*StateLookup table in **Enterprise Manager** and noting the ID number beside each state name. You must know the modStateID to be able to move to a particular state in the workflow process when you are working directly in the tables.

2. Open the view for the workflow-enabled table in the **SQL Server Enterprise Manager**, and enter a new record.

    Change from one state to another by changing the ModStateID value. Try to change the status of your record from the first state to the last state. Unless you have added a transition event that makes this transition possible, you are notified that this is not a valid event. In addition, you are not able to delete the record while it is in a state that has no transition to the **Item Deleted** shape.

3. If workflow is not performing as expected, return to your workflow diagram and make sure you have saved your workflow and refreshed the database. In addition, make sure you have added the required transitions to your diagram and that the EnableWorkflow property for that workflow process is set to **True**. To check the workflow properties, open the **Properties**

window in the **Workflow Designer**, and then select the workflow process in the **Solution Explorer**.

Setting Up a Table Hierarchy

The Workflow Designer for SQL Server uses a hierarchy of tables to manage core features and services in a workflow-enabled database. The hierarchy consists of main, detail, and lookup tables. This hierarchical structure makes it possible for detail and lookup tables to inherit permissions and properties from the parent main table.

The hierarchy is displayed under the Tables folder of the Solution Explorer in the Workflow Designer for SQL Server. When you designate a table as a main table, all tables that have primary key or foreign key relationships with it also are included in the table hierarchy as either detail or lookup tables.

When you add a main table to the hierarchy, the Workflow Designer creates a view of the main table and sets access permissions for the Public role. Public permissions are required for data access page interaction.

When you add workflow to your application, Workflow Designer for SQL Server creates lookup tables that support the workflow and adds them to the table hierarchy. For example, when you add workflow to a table, a *<tablename>*StateLookup table is created and displayed in the Solution Explorer.

Defining Hierarchy Schema

Your workflow project typically includes a combination of main tables, detail tables, and lookup tables. As you develop your project, you can specify additional main tables as needed to enhance your workflow.

There are three types of tables that are displayed in the hierarchy: main, detail, and lookup tables.

Main tables are the root of data hierarchies. Main tables can be enabled for row-level permissions and workflow in a workflow application. For example, the Issues table in the Issue Tracking sample is a main table. It has workflow and row-level permissions enabled, and it contains information about each issue entered in the database.

Detail tables are child tables of main tables. The parent column for detail tables holds its parent table ID in the modObjects table in the modSystem database. Detail tables can hold multiple entities for one row in the parent table. They can be enabled for workflow. For example, the Comments table in the Issue Tracking sample is a detail table that holds comments associated with each issue in the Issues table.

Lookup tables are child tables of main or detail tables. Lookup tables have a many-to-one relationship with other tables in the project. For any column in a main or detail table that contains a defined set of keywords, the keywords can be stored in a lookup table, and the corresponding keyword lookup IDs stored in the main or detail table columns. In addition, the Workflow Designer uses lookup tables to manage core features. For example, the IssuesStateLookup table in the Issue Tracking sample is a lookup table that stores all the states of the workflow process for the Issues table.

Table Hierarchy Requirements

There are guidelines that must be followed when defining a table hierarchy. Although you can have multiple levels of detail tables under a main table, a detail table can appear under only one main table. Lookup tables can appear under multiple main tables.

A main table cannot be a detail table in a different hierarchy at the same time. In addition, a child table cannot have more than one parent. In other words, hierarchies cannot embed other hierarchies, and they cannot share common tables. Hierarchies define a partition over user tables.

Detail tables can have their own child tables with column entries in the modColumns table pointing to the detail tables. This makes consistent representation for data hierarchies possible. It also makes it possible for each main table to have more than one detail table and hierarchies of any depth.

You can apply table-level permissions uniformly to all the tables in the hierarchy. However, users can change the permissions on each table. Because detail tables are similar to rows (or sets of rows) in the virtual schema of the hierarchy, setting table permissions amounts to setting permissions on columns or groups of columns.

You can define main-detail dependencies in a hierarchy by associating one row from the main table with one row from the detail table. Such a relationship can be based on a primary key/foreign key constraint, but this is not a requirement. For example, you can associate the City column in a Customer table with a list of postal codes in a detail table. If many customers live in the same city, they will get the same list of postal codes. This is a many-to-many relationship and is valid in project hierarchies.

A workflow application can have other primary key/foreign key relationships defined between its tables. For example, two main tables, Customer and Orders, can have a one-to-many relationship defined on the customer ID row. Those relationships are valid in a workflow application, but they have no role in Workflow Designer for SQL Server-specific functions. In the example, the Customers and Orders tables can have their own workflow tables with no implicit dependencies on each other. The row-level permissions set on the Customers table will not be propagated to the Orders table and vice versa. The primary key/foreign key relationship, however, can be used in the data access pages designer to build hierarchical reports based on Customers and Orders.

The relationships created by the hierarchical arrangement of the tables are stored in two tables: modObjects and modColumns. The modObjects table stores information about user-defined tables and their relationships, as well as SQL views, user views, triggers, and stored procedures. The modColumns table stores entries for selected columns in a workflow application that require additional properties.

Creating a Table Hierarchy

The table hierarchy in the Workflow Designer for SQL Server is the set of all the tables that are used in the workflow application and the relationships between those tables. The hierarchy is displayed graphically under the Tables folder of the Solution Explorer. You create a table hierarchy by adding a main table to the workflow project.

Main tables are database tables that contain the primary information for your workflow application. These are typically tables to which you want to add workflow and row-level security. There can be multiple main tables in a database.

To create a table hierarchy

1. Open your database in **Microsoft® Office XP Developer**.

2. Select the **Project** node in the **Solution Explorer**.

3. Open the **Project** menu, and click **Add New Item**.

4. Double-click the **Add Main Table** icon in the **Add New Item** dialog box.

5. Select the table to which you want to add workflow from the list. All tables that have primary key or foreign key relationships with the designated main table are included automatically in the table hierarchy as either detail or lookup tables.

To view a table hierarchy

1. Expand the **Tables** folder in the **Solution Explorer**.

2. To see the detail or lookup tables associated with the main tables, expand the main table.

Adding Detail and Lookup Tables

When you add a main table to the table hierarchy, all related detail and lookup tables are added automatically to the hierarchy. However, if you make schema changes to your database, new related tables are not added to the hierarchy automatically. Add these tables to the hierarchy manually if you must have them for workflow.

> **Note** To add a table to the hierarchy, the table must exist already in the database.

To add a detail or lookup table to the table hierarchy

1. Open your database in **Microsoft® Office XP Developer**.

2. Select the **Project** node in the **Solution Explorer**.

3. Open the **Project** menu, and click **Add New Item**.

4. Double-click the **Add a Detail Table** or **Add a Lookup Table** icon in the **Add New Item** dialog box.

5. Select the detail or lookup table from the list.

   > **Note** If the table you select is not related to the main table, the **OK** button is made unavailable.

6. Click **OK**.

Removing User Tables

If you no longer want to include a table in the table hierarchy, you can remove it. When Workflow Designer for SQL Server removes a table from the hierarchy, the table remains in the database but is no longer available to the workflow application.

If the table you try to remove has a workflow process based on it, you receive a message prompting you to delete the dependent objects before you remove the table. When you delete a workflow process, it is deleted from the database and not simply removed from the application in the way tables are.

To remove a table from the hierarchy

1. In the **Solution Explorer**, expand the **Tables** folder. To see the detail or lookup tables, expand the main table nodes.

2. Select a table, and then on the **Edit** menu, click **Remove**.

3. If there are dependent objects, such as detail and lookup tables or workflow processes, you are asked to verify that you want to remove all of these objects.

Defining Table Security

Workflow application security is defined primarily using Microsoft® Windows® and Microsoft® SQL Server™. To add table and column permissions to your project, you can use the security features available in the SQL Server Enterprise Manager.

The Workflow Designer for SQL Server respects permissions on existing tables. However, when a main table has a primary key, select permissions are granted to Public on all the columns that make up the primary key. This is required for data access pages and any other clients using Microsoft® Data Access Components (MDAC) to be able to send updates into the base table.

After a table has been added to a workflow project, any subsequent permissions changes set by the user are preserved.

Table Permissions

Table permissions must be set through SQL Server Enterprise Manager or by using OSQL, a command line utility that is available with Microsoft® SQL Server™ 2000 Desktop Engine.

When a table is added to the table hierarchy, the permissions you want enforced on the selected table should be set on the view that is created on top of that table. The view will be named *<tablename>*View.

Existing table permissions are not replicated for the newly created view. If the table already has permissions, you must set them up again on the view.

For more information about setting table permissions, see the documentation for the application you are using to add the permissions.

Row-Level Permissions

Row-level permissions can be set only for main tables. When you enable row-level permissions for your application, a user can specify which roles have select, insert, update, and delete permissions on a per-row basis.

Detail tables automatically inherit permissions from the main table. Rows in detail tables automatically inherit permissions from the related row in the parent table. For example, in an order entry project, if only users in the "OrderClerk" role can enter and view a customer order, the same would hold true for the related OrderDetails table.

When row-level permissions are enabled for a user table, they are enforced in the view that is created for that table. Therefore, users should access the table only through this view.

To enforce access through the view, Workflow Designer for SQL Server modifies the permissions on the base table. The changes prevent users from retrieving data directly from the table. At the same time the changes enable data access pages to send updates, inserts, and deletes to the table.

The Workflow Designer for SQL Server only modifies the base table permissions if the table has a primary key when row-level permissions are enabled. The primary key is required by data access pages to update the table.

Modifications Made to Base Table Permissions

When you enable row-level permissions for a main table, the following changes are made to the base table and to its associated detail tables.

- Revoke select permissions on the table.

- Grant select permissions to Public on all the columns of the primary key. This is required to enable updating and deleting rows from data access pages.

- Grant insert permissions to Public on the table. This is required to enable inserting rows from data access pages.

- Grant update permissions to Public on the table. This is required to enable updating rows from data access pages. Row-level security is enforced by the Update trigger.

- Grant delete permissions to Public on the table. This is required to enable deleting rows from data access pages. Row-level security is enforced by the Delete trigger.

Row-Level Permissions Issues

When implementing row-level permissions, consider the following issues.

- When the "Enable row permissions" option is selected for a main table, it applies to all its detail tables as well. Therefore, row permissions are enforced in all views that the Workflow Designer creates for the detail tables. In addition, the changes listed earlier are applied to the detail table permissions.

- Any changes made to base table permissions after the "Enable row permissions" option is selected are preserved.

- When the "Enable row permissions" option is cleared, all row-level permissions associated with the table are deleted. No changes are made to table permissions. Therefore, when you disable row permissions, all roles that had access to some rows in the table can now access all the rows in the table.

- Workflow Designer always grants select permissions to Public on the base view created for each table.

Enabling Row-Level Permissions

To implement row-level permissions for any specified main table in a workflow application, you first must enable this feature for that table. Then, you must add row-level permissions functionality to your user interface.

To enable row-level permissions for your application

1. In the **Solution Explorer**, expand the **Tables** folder.

2. Select a main table that you want to enable row-level permissions on.

3. In the **Properties** grid, set the **RowPermissions** property to **True**.

Developing a User Interface for SQL Server

You can develop the user interface for your application in any tool that can connect to and use a Microsoft® SQL Server™ database. However, the easiest user interface to integrate with Workflow Designer for SQL Server is a Web site created using Microsoft® Access data access pages. Data access pages also make it possible for you to take advantage of the built-in functionality of the Office Developer Workflow Toolbar control.

Although you can use any Web development program to create your Web-based user interface, many of the procedures later in this documentation assume Access data access pages are used to create the Web site.

If you are using a template to create your workflow application, a Web site is created for you when you use the SQL Server Workflow Template Instantiation wizard. You can use this Web site as the basis of your new application's user interface.

In This Section

User Interface Considerations
    Design your user interface to use the Workflow Designer's features.

Row-Level Permissions and the Workflow User Interface
> Create a user interface where each workflow user can define quickly and easily row-level permissions that determine which roles can see items entered by that user.

Creating User Interfaces
> Make it possible for users to work easily with data in your workflow application by providing a powerful user interface.

Help Files in Workflow Applications
> Implement help for your application as HTML files on your application's Web site.

User Information for Workflow Applications
> Maintain security specific to your workflow applications on the server by means of the Workflow Application User Directory

Using Alternative User Interfaces
> Create a user interface for your workflow application using any tool that provides database access.

User Interface Considerations

You must create a user interface using a program outside of the Workflow Designer for SQL Server, such as Microsoft® Access. To use the Workflow Designer's features fully, your user interface must interact with the database and the Workflow Services for SQL Server.

Web Security Considerations

Because Workflow Designer uses Microsoft® FrontPage® Server extensions, when deploying to an existing Web site, owners must have FrontPage administrator permissions on the Web site.

When connecting to a database from your Web pages, it is recommended you use views rather than tables, because row-level permissions can be set on views. For example, in the Issue Tracking sample, the Web pages use IssuesView rather than the Issues table.

Web Server Security

If you want to take advantage of Microsoft® Windows® 2000 security features for data access and sharing while you are creating a Web site, it is important to use the NTFS file system partitioning on the server containing the Web site.

There are several reasons to consider using NTFS:

- NTFS makes it possible for you to configure the Access Control List (ACL) to grant or deny various forms of access to user and group accounts.

    Note An ACL is a list of user accounts, user groups, and their privileges associated with a particular resource, such as a directory or file. For example, a file could have a list of user accounts and user groups that can access it and information about what level of access they are granted to the file, such as read, write, or execute. ACLs are another core feature of the Windows 2000 security model and make it possible for flexible and precise access control to resources on the hard disk. Each directory and file has its own ACL that defines who can do what and where. Each ACL even has an ACL that specifies who can view and change the ACL itself.

- NTFS is more efficient with hard drive space.

- NTFS makes it possible for you to assign a variety of protections to files and directories, specifying which groups or individual accounts can access these resources in which ways. By using the inherited permissions feature and by assigning permissions to groups rather than to individual accounts, you can simplify the chore of maintaining appropriate protections.

Row-Level Permissions and the Workflow User Interface

You can create a user interface where each workflow user can quickly and easily define row-level permissions that determine which roles can see items entered by that user. This is a helpful security feature when sharing information within a team.

To use row-level security in your workflow application, first enable row-level permissions on your main table view. Then, on your data access page, you can create the user interface to make it possible for users to interact with this feature.

Row-level security in a workflow application is managed through the use of SQL Server stored procedures. The Workflow Designer creates three stored procedures used for enforcing row-level security in a workflow application:

- modGrantRowPermissions

- modEnumRowPermissions

- modDropRowPermissions

The Issue Tracking sample provides an example of one way to create a user interface to manage row-level permissions. To see how it is done in the sample, use Microsoft® FrontPage® to open the Issue Tracking Web site and look at the ItemPermissions.htm page. The ItemPermissions.htm page provides a means for the user to enable and set row-level permissions for each database role. The list of roles is generated based on the roles defined in that database. The list of roles on this page was created to provide convenient permissions combinations.

When the user has selected an option, the program permissions are dropped using the modDropRowPermissions stored procedure and added using the modGrantRowPermissions stored procedure.

Consider the following when implementing row-level permissions:

- By default, there are no row-level permissions defined for user tables, and all rows are available to all users with permissions to access the workflow application.

- When row-level permissions are granted, the database owner continues to have access to all rows regardless of membership in specific roles.

- Users must at least have select permissions to see a record.

- When assigning row-level permissions, users should specify at least one role with select, delete, grant, and update permissions. Otherwise, only the database owner is able to interact fully with the row.

- To see an example of how to check the permissions for a specific row, examine the CheckWriteState function located on the gridview.htm page in the Issue Tracking sample.

- The modEnumRowPermissions stored procedure returns the role name and rights for a row. It can be used to validate users or to display different pages depending on the current user's permissions.

Creating User Interfaces

To make it possible for users to work with data in your workflow application, you must provide a user interface. You create the user interface with a separate program, not with the Workflow Designer. Although you can use any type of user interface that has read/write capabilities on a Microsoft® SQL Server™ database, the topics in this section deal with how to use the data access pages in Microsoft® Access to create a Web-based user interface.

You can explore an example of a user interface by creating an instance of the Issue Tracking sample template supplied with Microsoft® Office XP Developer.

To create a Web-based user interface for a workflow application

1. Create an Access Data Project. For details, see "Using Access to Create SQL Server Databases."

2. Create your workflow application. The Workflow Designer prompts you for a Web site address when you register your database.

3. Create the data access pages required to display your data. Typically, a summary view of all workflow items are contained on one page, while a second page makes it possible for you to view and edit detail information for a selected item. The Issue Tracking sample provides an example.

4. Add the necessary database fields to each data access page, and format the user interface as desired.

5. Add the **Office Developer Workflow Toolbar** control to your pages.

6. Save the data access pages to the Web site address you specified when you registered the database.

7. Create Web pages that provide help to users.

Creating Webs Using FrontPage

A Web site is a location where all the Web pages required for a user interface are stored. A Web is created for you at the site you designate when you enable workflow on a database and when you create an instance of an application from a template. You can modify these Web pages or create your own using Microsoft® FrontPage®.

In addition, you can create a new Web by importing an existing Web from your local computer, network, or the World Wide Web or by converting a folder to a Web. You can find more information on these topics in the FrontPage Help system.

To create a Web site

1. Open **FrontPage**, and, from the File menu, point to **New**, and then point to **Web**.

2. Click **Empty Web**.

3. In **Options**, specify a location for the new Web site in the following format:
   http://<*ServerName*>/<*WebName*>

4. Click **OK**.

5. After the **Creating New Web** dialog box is displayed, you can close **FrontPage** and use **Access** to create the data access pages.

After creating the Web site on the server, you can create your data access pages and save them to this Web site.

Creating Data Access Pages

After you have enabled workflow on your database and have the tables and views required for data entry, you can create the data access pages using the Page editor in Microsoft® Access.

To create a new data access page

1. Open your Access Data Project in **Access**.

2. In the **Objects** list, click **Pages**.

3. Double-click **Create Data Access Page By Using Wizard**.

4. From the **Tables/Queries** list, scroll down to the **Views**, and select the view for the table that will be accessed using the Web page.

5. From the **Available Fields** list, add the columns you want to display on the Web page to the **Selected Fields** list. Click **Next**.

   Note   For the workflow toolbar to function, you must include the column that stores the modStateID.

6. Click **Next** to accept the default grouping levels.

7. Click **Next** to accept the default sort order by.

8. Give your Web page a title. Leave the option selected to modify the page's design. Click **Finish**.

9. With the data access page open in design view, open the **View** menu, and click **Properties**.

10. Select the **Data** tab.

11. In the **UniqueTable** property, select the name of the base table associated with the view.

12. Save your Web page to the site you designated when you first enabled workflow on the database.

Using the Office Developer Workflow Toolbar Control

You can add the Office Developer Workflow Toolbar control to your data access page user interface to make workflow tasks easier to perform. The toolbar shows the workflow events that are available for each record in the workflow application. This toolbar is generated dynamically based on the workflow process on the server.

The Workflow Toolbar control has properties, methods, and events that make it possible for you to display or hide toolbar options and use these features independently or together. The language property of the toolbar will conform automatically to that specified for the data access page.

To use the Workflow Toolbar control in your user interface, consider the following requirements:

- For the toolbar to display the workflow events on the data access page, the UniqueTable property must be set to the base table that contains the workflow process.

- You must include a field bound to the workflow state column (modStateID) on the data access page in either the first section or the section specified in the toolbar's RecordSource property. This field can be hidden.

Adding the Workflow Toolbar Control to Data Access Pages

After you have created your Web-based user interface using data access pages, add the Office Developer Workflow Toolbar control to make workflow tasks easier to perform.

To add the Workflow Toolbar control to a data access page

1. Open your Access Data Project in **Access**.

2. Open your data access page in **Design** view.

3. Click the data access page design surface where you would like to insert the toolbar.

    Tip The top portion of the page below the title often works well.

4. From the **Insert** menu, select **ActiveX Control**, and double-click **Microsoft Office Developer Workflow Toolbar**.

The toolbar control is added to the page and automatically binds to the workflow rules by inspecting the UniqueTable property on the data source control.

5. Save the data access page.

6. On the **File** menu, click **Web Page Preview** to see the toolbar.

Adding Script to Data Access Pages Using the Microsoft Script Editor

You can customize your data access page user interface with any form of scripting that is supported by the browser.

To add script to a data access page using the Microsoft Script Editor

1. Open your Access Data Project in **Access**.

2. Open your data access page in **Design** view.

3. On the **Tools** menu, point to **Macro**, and then click **Microsoft Script Editor**.

4. Write your script in the **Microsoft Script Editor**.

> **Note**   For additional information, see the online Help available from the **Help** button in the **Microsoft Script Editor**.

Creating a State Lookup Control on Data Access Pages

To create a list of available states from a lookup column, use the Dropdown List control. Bind the control to the modStateID column, which contains an integer used to enforce workflow rules. You can then display the names of the available states in your list (for example, Active, Resolved, or Closed).

To add lookup column support to your Web page using the Dropdown List control

1. In **Access**, open your data access page in **Design** view.

2. Delete the label for the **modStateID** column on your page.

3. Select the text box that links to the modStateID.

4. Open the **View** menu, and click **Properties**.

5. On the **Format** tab, change the value of the **Visibility** property to **hidden**, and close the properties window.

6. From the **Toolbox**, drag the **Dropdown List** control to the form.

7. When the wizard appears, accept the **I want the combo box to look up the values in a table or query** option, and click **Next**.

8. Select the **<Tablename>StateLookup** table, and click **Next**.

9. Add both the **ID** and **Name** fields to the **Selected Fields** list box, and click **Next**.

10. Make sure the **Hide key column (recommended)** check box is selected, so the state lookup ID number is hidden on the Web page. Adjust the state name column as required to display the values, and click **Next**.

11. Change the value of the label from **Name** to a caption appropriate for your application, and click **Finish**.

12. Select the **Dropdown List** control on the data access page design surface.

13. Open the **View** menu, and click **Properties**.

14. On the **Data** tab, in the **ControlSource** field, select **modStateID**.

15. Make sure the value of the **ListBoundField** property is set to **ID** and the **ListDisplayField** is set to **Name**.

Help Files in Workflow Applications

You can implement help for your application as HTML files on your application's Web site.

For an example of help information, see the HTML Help files associated with the Issue Tracking sample. You can find the Help folder in the Issue Tracking Web site that is created when you create an instance of the Issue Tracking sample template. You can copy these files directly, or you can customize them using any HTML editor.

The following table provides suggestions for the types of Help topics you might want to make available to users.

User tasks	Provide information about
Selecting workflow states	What each state means in the business process.
Changing workflow states	What workflow events are, how to use the events and transitions available in the application, and which application roles and permissions are associated with the events.
Using row-level permissions	How to use row-level permissions, how to set row-level permissions in an application, and what permissions are available.

The more complicated your workflow application is, the more help users might require to use the application. Whenever possible, you should provide information about any potential problems or issues that users might see.

User Information for Workflow Applications

To implement security specific to your workflow applications on the server or Microsoft® SQL Server™ Named Instance, the Workflow Services for SQL Server maintains the workflow application User Directory, which exists as the modUserList table in the modSystem database. It stores information about the Microsoft® Windows® 2000 domain users and groups who have access to the server and the workflow applications. It can include details such as e-mail addresses, telephone numbers, and managers.

The user directory also stores additional data for each user that is useful for scripting e-mail notifications and other functionality in your workflow. Rather than keep separate stores of duplicate information, you can set the user information to be synchronized automatically from your Microsoft® Exchange Server directory or Windows Active Directory, or you can synchronize manually through the Workflow Manager for SQL Server.

When you enable workflow on your database, the Workflow Designer creates a view in the database based on the modUserList table. This modUserList view can be used to make user information available in your application user interface, if desired.

The user information supplied in the user directory makes it possible for you to implement features such as:

- **Sending e-mail notifications to a valid user or group.** Use script to notify specific users or groups automatically when events are triggered in the application.

- **Displaying the full name of the person associated with a security account.** Stored user information can be queried by the application to display full names of the valid users instead of only their Windows account names.

- **Escalating issues to a manager.** Look up a user's manager in the user directory, and send e-mail or assign the issue to the manager.

The User Directory

The workflow application User Directory stores information that identifies users for your workflow applications. The information is stored and maintained separately for each server or Microsoft® SQL Server™ Named Instance and not for each workflow application on the server. To be stored in this directory, the user also must be identified as a Microsoft® Windows® 2000 user and have a SQL Server login with a role in your workflow application. In addition, Windows groups can be included as members in the user directory.

Contents

The user directory stores the following information about users:

- Windows 2000 user name (for example, "MyDomain\Bobk")

- First name

- Last name

- E-mail address

- Exchange Distinguished Name (uniquely identifies the user's Microsoft® Exchange mailbox)

- Manager

- Telephone number

- Company

- Department

Maintenance

The Workflow Manager for SQL Server provides several synchronization options for populating and maintaining the list of users who have access to workflow applications. You can choose to synchronize with an existing list of users, or you can maintain the directory manually. In addition, you can choose to synchronize once to populate the directory initially and then maintain the information manually thereafter.

Options

You can choose to keep the workflow application User Directory current in one of the following three ways:

- Synchronize with the Windows 2000 Active Directory.

- Synchronize with Exchange Server. If you are using Exchange Server to synchronize user information and a user has information in the Exchange Global Address List, then the additional information from Exchange is combined with the Windows user information in the user directory. If a Windows account has multiple Exchange mailboxes, the synchronization process automatically selects the first entry returned by Exchange. If you want to select a different mailbox, you can do so in the Workflow Manager for SQL Server.

- Maintain the directory manually. The server administrator can enter user information using the User Information tab in the Workflow Manager, but cannot add or delete users.

Permissions Required

Any member of the modAppOwners group can synchronize the user directory. However, only members of the SQL Server system administrators role can configure synchronization. Configuration includes enabling synchronization with Exchange or Active Directory, designating the Exchange server name, setting up the synchronization schedule, and changing user information manually.

Note If you make any changes to the membership of database roles in your workflow application, you must synchronize the user directory for role permissions to work properly.

Architecture

The workflow application User Directory, stored in a table in the modSystem database, contains information for all workflow users on that server or SQL Server Named Instance. In each workflow application, two objects work together to store the user information for that particular workflow application: modUserList and modUserRoles.

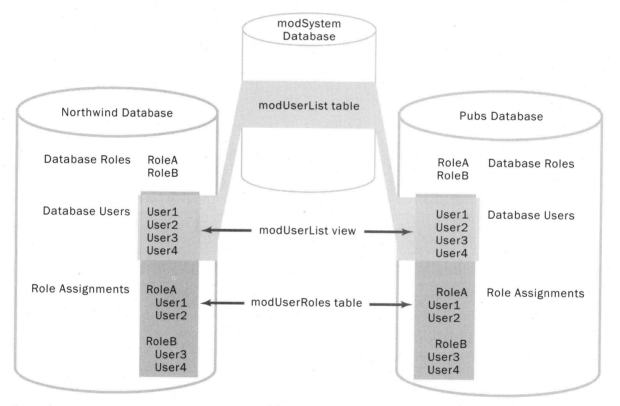

- **The modUserList table** is stored in the modSystem database. It contains information for all project users on a SQL Server.

- **A modUserRoles table** is stored in each workflow-enabled database. It associates users with the roles to which they belong. The user's SAMAccountName is tied to a RoleName in the workflow application.

- **A modUserList view** is stored in each workflow-enabled database. It displays the user information for users of the particular workflow application. This view is based on the modUserList table in the modSystem database, and its recordset is limited using the relationship between SAMAccountName in modUserRoles to SAMAccountName in modUserList.

> **Note** If you create a workflow application without a template, you must synchronize manually the first time to set up the initial user list. When creating a database from scratch or registering an existing database as a workflow application, the modUserList view and modUserRoles table do not have any data until the first time the user directory is synchronized manually. When creating a workflow application based on a template, the user directory is synchronized automatically upon completion of the Template wizard.

Maintaining the User Directory for Workflow Applications

For a user to be able to access your workflow application, you must add the user to your workflow application even if the user will not be writing to the database. You might want to have a user in the directory but not make it possible for them to see or modify data, in which case you can add them to a role that has no permissions on any database objects.

To keep the user directory current, the administrator designates a synchronization schedule. The user directory can be scheduled to synchronize on a regular basis to update the modUserList table with information for all of the users who have access to workflow applications.

Users in the User Directory

To have access to your applications, a user must be listed in the User Directory or be part of a group listed in the directory on the server or named instance that manages the workflow application.

> **Note** If you are using SQL Server Named Instances on your server, you must install the Workflow Services for SQL Server on each named instance. The Workflow Manager for SQL Server provided with the services only manages a single server or instance of a server at a time.

Synchronizing the User Directory

To add users to the workflow application User Directory initially, the application administrator must synchronize the user directory with Microsoft® Exchange server or the Active Directory. The administrator also must synchronize whenever user information changes to keep the directory current.

To synchronize the user directory

1. Open the **Workflow Manager for SQL Server**.

2. In the **Server** list, select a server, and click **Refresh**.

3. On the **User Information** tab, click **Synchronize Now**.

Note If buttons are disabled, click **Refresh**. If the buttons are disabled still, you do not have appropriate permissions to synchronize the user directory.

Populating Controls with User Information

To make user directory information available in your Web pages, you can create links to a view of the user directory from within the application. You cannot create an actual relationship link between the information in the user directory and a table in your database. The user directory information in your workflow application is stored in a view called modUserList.

You can use these controls on a Web page to show user information:

Control	Source property
combo-box	rowsource
list-box control	rowsource
drop-down list	ListRowSource

Make sure you set the source property to the modUserList view, specify the SAMAccountName column in the modUserList view as the primary key, and specify the data type as nvarchar with a character length of 64.

The following is an example of how the row source for your list control might appear:

```
SELECT SAMAccountName, CN FROM modUserList WHERE (NOT (CN IS NULL))
```

Using Alternative User Interfaces

You can create a user interface for your workflow application using any tool that provides database access. For example, you could develop a Microsoft® Visual Basic® application that connects to the Microsoft® SQL Server™ database. Any interface with read/write capabilities can be used with your database.

Setting Up Accounts, Logins, Roles, and Users

Workflow Designer for SQL Server integrates the security environment in Microsoft® Windows® 2000 and in Microsoft® SQL Server™. The security environment is stored, managed, and enforced through a hierarchical system of users. To simplify the administration of many users, Windows and SQL Server use groups and roles.

A group is an administrative unit within the Active Directory Services of Windows that contains Windows users or other groups. A role is an administrative unit within SQL Server that contains SQL Server logins, Windows domain accounts, groups, or other roles.

Arranging users into groups and roles makes it easier to grant or deny permissions to many users at one time. The security settings defined for a group are applied to all members of that group. When a group is a member of a higher-level group, all members of the group inherit the security settings of the higher-level group, in addition to the security settings defined for the group itself.

With this security strategy, rather than assigning permissions to each user for each object in your workflow application, you assign permissions to a few roles in the projects. These roles are associated with SQL Server logins and Windows accounts. Then, you can add users and groups to the appropriate roles. Users automatically inherit the permissions associated with any roles to which they belong.

> **Note** To simplify user administration, it is recommended you create an Active Directory group for each of your project's roles and add that group to the project, rather than adding each user individually. Then, you can add or remove users from workflow applications by managing the membership of the groups. You also can use the same groups to set permissions on other network resources, such as file shares and printers.

Security

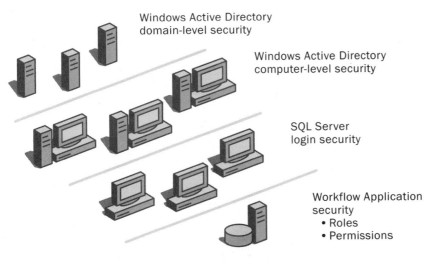

Windows Active Directory
domain-level security

Windows Active Directory
computer-level security

SQL Server
login security

Workflow Application
security
- Roles
- Permissions

Employees often must belong to security groups that do not fall within the strict organizational plan of the company. For example, administrative staff exists in every branch of the company and requires security permissions regardless of their organizational branch. To support this broader model, the security system in Windows and SQL Server makes it possible for groups to be defined across a hierarchy as well. For example, an administrative staff member can belong to an Administrative group, a department group, and a corporate group.

In This Section

Security Categories in Workflow Designer for SQL Server
    Understand the types of users and roles, their responsibilities, and permissions.

Windows 2000 and SQL Server Security
Create groups of accounts in Microsoft® Windows® 2000 and Microsoft® SQL Server™ that simplify managing the security features.

Creating Database Roles
Define a set of roles based on job functions, and assign to each role the permissions that apply to that job.

Creating Workflow Application Users
Add users to each workflow application.

Assigning Users to Database Roles
Add users and groups to the database roles in your application.

Defining Permissions for Database Roles
Specify which permissions are assigned to each role in the application.

Security Categories in Workflow Designer for SQL Server

There are three security categories for Workflow Designer for SQL Server users:

* Server administrator

* Workflow application owner and workflow application developer

  Because of the complementary duties of owners and developers, the positions are generally combined into a single category. Typically, the category is referred to as owner, because, while it is possible to be an owner without being a developer, to be a developer you also must be an owner.

* Workflow application user

Each of these categories is associated with specific responsibilities and permissions in Microsoft® Windows® 2000, Microsoft® SQL Server™, Microsoft® FrontPage®, and the workflow application that makes it possible for them to carry out those responsibilities. In some cases, the duties of the server administrator and the workflow application owner might overlap.

Server Administrator

Typically, the server administrator is responsible for the following activities:

* Creating Windows groups and users

* Creating SQL Server user logins and roles

* Assigning Windows groups and users to SQL Server roles

* Optionally assigning SQL Server database owner permissions (db_owner) to developers to make it possible for workflow application development to be done on existing SQL Server databases

- Setting up and executing workflow application User Directory synchronization
- Editing user information

Workflow Application Owner

The workflow application owner must be a member of the modAppOwners group. Generally, this role is responsible for the following activities:

- Creating SQL Server roles
- Assigning existing users to SQL Server roles
- Executing workflow application User Directory synchronization
- Defining role permissions for workflow events, database roles, and row-level security

Workflow Application Developer

The workflow application developer must be a member of the modAppOwners group. Usually, this role is responsible for the following activities:

- Creating and registering new workflow applications
- Creating new database templates
- Importing and exporting templates

Workflow Application User

A user who accesses the workflow application through a client browser has few responsibilities requiring special permissions. Instead, the workflow application user is typically assigned to a Windows group domain account associated with a database role. The user's privileges when using the application depend on the role to which the user belongs.

Note It is recommended you use group accounts to simplify server administration.

Permissions by Security Category

The permissions associated with these security categories are as follows:

Security Category	Windows 2000 account	SQL Server role	FrontPage permissions
Server administrator	System administrator	Sysadmin dbo in modSystem database	System administrator
Workflow application owner	modAppOwners group	modAppOwners database role dbo for the workflow applications they create db_owner permissions (required to register existing SQL Server databases as workflow applications)	FrontPage administrator group
Workflow application user	User or group account	SQL Server user or group login associated with Windows 2000 accounts	none

When Workflow Services for SQL Server are installed, setup creates a group called modAppOwners and sets all required Distributed Component Object Model (DCOM) permissions that make it possible for members of modAppOwners to create workflow applications.

Setup also creates a SQL Server login for the Windows modAppOwners group called <*servername*>\modAppOwners. This login is added to the database creators (db_creator) role on the server and db_user on the master and modSystem databases. These permissions make it possible for application owners to create workflow applications based on templates, create new SQL Server databases, and enable workflow on existing databases.

In addition, the modAppOwners Windows group is added to the FrontPage Administrator group, so members can create Web sites for workflow applications.

Permissions Defined by the Server Administrator

To grant a developer the appropriate permissions, the server administrator must add the developer to the Windows modAppOwners group using the Windows 2000 Server User Manager.

If the developer wants to enable workflow on an existing database, then the administrator must make the developer a database owner (db_owner) on this database. The person who creates a database is automatically the db_owner.

In addition, if the members of the modAppOwners group typically will be performing administrative tasks, such as creating new SQL Server logins, the server administrator should grant the modAppOwners group system administrator privileges on the SQL Server. This is not the default.

Permissions Defined by the Workflow Application Owner

As a member of the modAppOwners group, the workflow application owner can create SQL Server roles appropriate for a workflow application, add project users or groups to these roles, and set permissions on these roles as required by the workflow application. To create the roles, SQL Server logins and Windows 2000 accounts must exist already.

When developing the project, modAppOwners members can set permissions for workflow events within the Workflow Designer for SQL Server.

Row-level permissions can be set using stored procedures: modGrantRowPermissions, modDropRowPermissions, and modEnumRowPermissions. See the Issue Tracking sample application for an example of how to handle row-level permissions using these stored procedures.

Permissions Defined by Workflow Application Users

If row-level permissions are enabled in the workflow application, users can specify permissions for individual database records based on project roles. If a record is assigned to a user, that user can select specific roles to have read-only or write permissions for the issue.

Windows 2000 and SQL Server Security

Existing Microsoft® Windows® 2000 accounts (Active Directory Users or Groups) must be granted permissions to connect to Microsoft® SQL Server™ before they can access a database. If all members of a Windows group require connections to SQL Server, you can grant login permissions for the group as a whole.

Managing group permissions is easier than managing permissions for individual users. If you do not want a group to be granted permissions collectively, you can grant permissions to connect to SQL Server for each individual user.

Active Directory Users and Groups

In Windows 2000, users are individuals who have an account that provides specific privileges to access information and resources. Granting permissions to users to develop, manage, and use workflow applications is dependent upon the integration of Windows 2000 domain accounts and SQL Server roles. If a number of users all have the same permissions, they can be treated as a single unit, called a group, which can be assigned permissions that apply to all members of the group. Individuals can be added to or removed from groups as desired.

There are two types of Windows groups: global and local.

Global groups contain user accounts from the Windows 2000 Server domain in which they are created. Global groups cannot contain groups or users from other domains and cannot be created on a computer running Windows 2000 Professional.

Local groups can contain user accounts and global groups from the domain in which they are created and any trusted domain. Local groups cannot contain other local groups.

In addition, Windows 2000 has predefined, built-in local groups, such as Administrators, Users, and Guests. By default, these built-in groups always are available on any Windows 2000 computer, unless they are removed explicitly.

To grant access to SQL Server to a Windows local or global group, specify the domain or computer name on which the group is defined, followed by a backslash, and then the group name. For example, to grant access to the Windows 2000 group SQL_Users, in the Windows 2000 domain LONDON, specify LONDON\SQL_Users as the group name.

However, to grant access to a Windows built-in local group, specify BUILTIN, instead of the domain or computer name. To grant access to the built-in Windows local group Administrators, specify BUILTIN\Administrators as the group name to add to SQL Server.

Note You must have appropriate permissions on the server to create Windows groups or users or to create SQL Server users or roles.

For additional information about Windows accounts, see your Windows documentation.

SQL Server Logins

SQL Server logins are the account identifiers that control access to any SQL Server system. SQL Server will not complete a connection unless it has first verified that the login you specified is valid. This verification of the login is called authentication.

A member of the SQL Server sysadmin fixed-server role first must specify to SQL Server all the Windows accounts or groups that can connect to SQL Server. Your access to SQL Server is controlled by your Windows account or group, which is authenticated when you log on to the Windows operating system on the client.

When connecting, the SQL Server client software requests a Windows trusted connection to SQL Server. Windows will not open a trusted connection unless the client has logged on successfully using a valid Windows account. The properties of a trusted connection include the Windows group and user accounts of the client that opened the connection.

SQL Server gets the user account information from the trusted connection properties and matches them against the Windows accounts defined as valid SQL Server logins. If SQL Server finds a match, it accepts the connection. You are identified in SQL Server by your Windows group or user account.

Database Roles

Using database roles, you can collect users into a single unit to which you can apply permissions. Permissions granted to, denied to, or revoked from a role also apply to any members of the role.

SQL Server roles exist within a database and cannot span more than one database. Because roles are unique to each database, you can reuse a role name, such as "Reviewer" in each database that you create.

To assign users and groups to database roles, the users and groups must have valid Windows domain accounts and SQL Server logins.

Note If you make any changes to the membership of database roles in your workflow application, you must synchronize the user directory for role permissions to work properly.

The advantages of using database roles include:

- Users can belong to more than one database role at a time.

- Roles can contain Windows accounts and other SQL Server users and roles.

- A scalable model is provided for setting up the right level of security within a database.

It is easy to manage permissions in a database if you define a set of roles based on job functions and assign each role the permissions that apply to that job. Then, you can move users between roles rather than having to manage the permissions for each individual user.

Note The owner of a role determines who can be added or removed from the role. The owner is either the user explicitly specified as the owner when the role is created or the user who created the role when no owner is specified. If you make any changes to the membership of database roles in your workflow application, you must synchronize the user directory for role permissions to work properly.

Database roles are created for a particular database. In SQL Server 7.0 and SQL Server 2000, users can belong to multiple roles. Because users can belong to more than one database role at a time, it is no longer required for users to assume temporarily the identity (and permissions) of other users through aliases.

Note If you plan to make a template based on a workflow application, you should use role-based permissions for everything, because the set of database users will be different for each instance of a project based on the template.

Database User Accounts

While a SQL Server login makes it possible for a user to access SQL Server, a database user account is required for the user to access a specific database. Then, these user accounts can be associated with the roles defined in your workflow application.

A user account can be a member of any number of roles within the same workflow application. For example, a user can be a member of the admin role and the authors role for the same database, with each role granting different permissions.

The effective permissions on an object granted to a member of more than one role are the cumulative permissions of the roles, although denied permissions in one role has precedence over the same permissions granted in another role. For example, the admin role might grant access to a table while the authors role denies access to the same table. A member of both roles is denied access to the table, because denied access is the most restrictive.

Creating User and Group Accounts

You must have system administrator permissions on the server to create user and group accounts on a Microsoft® Windows® 2000 Server. Before creating Microsoft® SQL Server™ logins and database roles, you should create the appropriate Windows accounts for users and groups that will be working with the workflow applications.

To make managing workflow application users easier, it is recommended you create group accounts corresponding to the database roles in your application. It is easier to manage only the group account rather than managing SQL Server logins and database role membership for many users.

Naming Rules

A user or group name cannot be identical to any other user or group name on the domain or computer being administered. It can contain up to 20 uppercase or lowercase characters except for the following:

```
"  /  \  [  ]  :  ;  |  =  ,  + *  ? < >
```

A user or group name cannot consist solely of periods (.) and spaces.

For additional information on naming conventions for Windows accounts, see your Windows documentation.

Creating a New Windows 2000 User Account

Because Microsoft® SQL Server™ uses Microsoft® Windows® 2000 user authentication, your SQL Server users must have valid Windows accounts. Before creating SQL Server logins, use the following steps to create Windows user accounts. In addition, before you can add users to Windows groups, each user must have a valid Windows domain account.

To create a new user account

1. From the **Start** menu, point to **Programs**, then **Administrative Tools**, and then click **Computer Management**.

2. Expand **Local Users and Groups**, select **Users**, and choose **New User** from the **Action** menu.

3. In the **New User** dialog box, enter the appropriate information:

    - In **Username**, enter the user's alias. Typically, this is based on the user's full name.

    - In **Full Name**, enter the user's complete name.

    - In **Description**, enter a description of the user or the user account.

    - In both **Password** and **Confirm Password**, enter a password of up to 14 characters.

    - Specify additional options: Select or clear the check boxes for **User Must Change Password at Next Logon**, **User Cannot Change Password**, **Password Never Expires**, and **Account Disabled**.

4.   Click **Create**.

To add another user account, repeat steps 2 through 4.

Creating a New Local Group Account

A local group name cannot be identical to any other group or user name on the domain or computer being administered. It can contain up to 255 uppercase or lowercase characters except for the backslash character (\).

You can add user accounts and global groups from the local domain and from trusted domains.

To create a new local group

1.   From the **Start** menu, point to **Programs**, then **Administrative Tools**, and then click **Computer Management**.

2.   Expand **Local Users and Groups**, select **Groups**, and choose **New Group** from the **Action** menu.

3.   In the **New Group** dialog box, enter a name for the group and, if desired, a description.

4.   To add members, click **Add**. The **Select Users or Groups** dialog box opens.

5.   Select names from the **Name** list, and click **Add**. The names appear in the field below the **Add** button.

6.   Click **OK**. The newly added members are displayed in the **Members** list.

7.   To remove members from the new group, select one or more names in **Members**, and click **Remove**.

8.   Click **Create** to create the new group.

Creating a New Global Group Account

You can add a new global group to a machine running Microsoft® Windows® 2000 Server that is set up as the domain controller. The New Global Group option is unavailable when Low Speed Connection is selected or when you administer a computer running Windows 2000 Professional or a Windows 2000 Server that is not a domain controller.

   Note   You must have domain administrator privileges to create a global group.

To create a new global group

1.   From the **Start** menu, point to **Programs**, then **Administrative Tools**, and then click **Active Directory Users and Groups**.

2.   In the tree-view, select **User**.

3.   From the **Action** menu, choose **New**, and choose **Group**.

4.   In the **Group Name** box, type a group name.

5. In the **Description** box, type a description for the group.

6. To add members, select one or more user accounts in **Not Members**, and click **Add**.

7. To remove members from the new group, select one or more user accounts in **Members**, and click **Remove**.

Creating SQL Server Logins

Users gain access to Microsoft® SQL Server™ databases through a login that establishes their permission to connect (authentication). Because SQL Server uses Microsoft® Windows® 2000 authentication, each SQL Server login must be associated with a valid Windows account. Then, each SQL login based on the Windows user or group account can be granted permissions to connect to SQL Server.

Note SQL Server 7.0 and SQL Server 2000 no longer manage groups independently from the operating system. The groups from earlier versions of SQL Server have been replaced with roles, which are more powerful. However, you can manage SQL Server security at the level of an entire Windows group.

If you have system administrator privileges on SQL Server, you can create and modify SQL Server logins using the following methods:

* Creating SQL Server logins with Enterprise Manager

* Creating SQL Server logins with the SQL Server Workflow Template Instantiation wizard

You can add logins to SQL Server when you create an instance of a workflow application from a template using the wizard. However, this functionality succeeds only when the person creating the application has system administrator privileges on the SQL Server and if the SQL Server logins already have valid Windows accounts. A member of modAppOwners does not have the ability to create SQL Server logins unless the server administrator also gives the modAppOwners group system administrator privileges on the SQL Server.

Naming Rules

A user or group name cannot be identical to any other user or group name of the domain or computer being administered. It can contain up to 20 uppercase or lowercase characters except for the following:

" / \ [ ] : ; | = , + * ? < >

A user or group name cannot consist solely of periods (.) and spaces.

For additional information about naming conventions for SQL Server logins, see the *SQL Server Books Online*.

Creating SQL Server Logins with Enterprise Manager

By default, SQL Server Enterprise Manager is installed by SQL Server Setup as part of the server software on computers running Microsoft® Windows® 2000 and as part of the client software on computers running Windows 2000, Windows 98, and Windows ME.

To grant access to SQL Server to a Windows 2000 user or group account

1. Open the **SQL Server Enterprise Manager**, expand a server group, and then expand a server.

2. Expand **Security**, right-click **Logins**, and click **New Login**.

3. Select **Windows Authentication**.

4. In the **Name** field, enter the Windows account (in the form DOMAIN\User) to grant access to SQL Server.

5. Click **OK**.

Creating SQL Server Logins with the SQL Server Workflow Template Instantiation Wizard

If you are using a template created by a different team or at a different location, it is likely that you must add SQL Server logins for individuals who will be using the new application. Therefore, the wizard makes it possible for you to create SQL Server logins, assign these logins as database users, and designate roles for them.

To create SQL Server logins using the Workflow Template Instantiation wizard

1. Open the **Workflow Manager for SQL Server**, select a server, and click **Refresh**.

2. On the **Templates** tab, click **Instantiate Template**.

3. Select a template, and proceed through the wizard.

4. On the **Identify Roles** page, click **New SQL login**.

5. In the **Name** field, enter the Windows account (in the form DOMAIN\User) to grant access to SQL Server. Optionally, select a server from the **List names from Domain** field, and select the **Show all users** check box. Double-click under the list of **Available names** to populate the **User name** dialog box.

6. When you have the user name entered, click **OK**.

7. Now, you can add SQL logins to the **Database users** list using the **Add** button.

8. To designate a role for the login, select a SQL Server login from the list of database users, and select roles under **Roles for selected user**.

9. Proceed through the wizard, and click **Finish**.

The wizard then creates your SQL Server user accounts.

Creating Database Roles

To manage the permissions in your project database easily, it is recommended you define a set of roles based on job functions and assign each role the permissions that apply to that job. You create database roles with SQL Server Enterprise Manager.

To create a SQL Server database role

1. From the **Start** menu, point to **Programs**, then **Microsoft SQL Server**, and then click **Enterprise Manager**.

2. Expand a server group, and then expand a server.

3. Expand the databases group, and then expand a particular database.

4. Right-click **Roles**, and click **New Database Role**.

5. Enter a name for the role.

6. If you wish to assign users to this role, select **Add**.

7. Click **OK**.

Repeat these steps as required to create your database roles.

Creating Workflow Application Users

When you have created the Microsoft® Windows® 2000 accounts, Microsoft® SQL Server™ logins, and database roles for your users, then you can assign the users to your workflow application. While the SQL Server login makes it possible for the users to connect to the SQL Server system, a database user account is required to access individual databases. These user accounts are created within each workflow application and are unique to each application.

You create workflow application database users with SQL Server Enterprise Manager.

To create a workflow application user

1. From the **Start** menu, point to **Programs**, then **Microsoft SQL Server**, and then click **Enterprise Manager**.

2. Expand a server group, and then expand a server.

3. Expand the databases group, and then expand a particular database.

4. Right-click **User**, and click **New Database User**.

5. Select a login name from the list.

6. If you wish to designate role membership, enable the roles for the user.

7. You can select properties on a specific role if you want to add other roles to this role or view and modify the permissions for this role.

8. Click **OK**.

Repeat these steps as required to create additional database users.

Assigning Users to Database Roles

When you add a new user account to your database or you must change the permissions of an existing user, you can add the user to a workflow application database role rather than applying permissions directly to the account.

To assign a user to a database role

1. From the **Start** menu, point to **Programs**, then **Microsoft SQL Server**, and then click **Enterprise Manager**.

2. Expand a server group, and then expand a server.

3. Expand **Databases**, and then expand the database in which the role exists.

4. Click **Roles**.

5. In the details pane, right-click the role to which you want to add the user, and select **Properties**.

6. Click **Add**. Then, click a user or users to add. Only users in the current database can be added to the role.

   Note   When you add a Microsoft® Windows® 2000 login that does not have a user account in the database to a Microsoft® SQL Server™ database role, SQL Server creates a user account in the database automatically.

7. Click **OK** to close the **Add Role Members** dialog box.

8. Click **OK** to close the **Database Role Properties** dialog box.

Repeat these steps as required to add users to other database roles.

Defining Permissions for Database Roles

When users connect to a workflow application, the activities they can perform are determined by the permissions granted to their security accounts, Microsoft® Windows® 2000 groups, or role hierarchies to which their security accounts belong. The user must have the appropriate permissions to perform any activity that involves changing the database definition or accessing data.

To define role permissions

1. From the **Start** menu, point to **Programs**, then **Microsoft SQL Server**, and then click **Enterprise Manager**.

2. Expand a server group, and then expand a server.

3. Expand **Databases**, and then expand the database in which the role exists.

4. Click **Roles**.

5. In the details pane, right-click the role to which you want to assign permissions, and select **Properties**.

6. Click **Permissions**. If required, select **List all objects**. Objects are listed in rows, and permissions are listed in columns.

7. Enable and disable permissions on objects by selecting or clearing the appropriate boxes.

    Note If using row-level permissions for a table, you cannot grant **select** permissions on the entire table. You must grant **select** permissions only to the primary key column. Therefore, you must use a stored procedure to grant column permissions (permissions on a single column rather than an entire table).

Scripting Workflow Events for SQL Server

The built-in functionality of workflow events can be enhanced using Microsoft® Visual Basic® Scripting Edition (VBScript). Because the script within a workflow process is executed on the server, the compatibility of VBScript with Web browsers is not a consideration.

Within each event, you can add script to fulfill the requirements of your workflow application. To extend the capabilities of your workflow beyond the scripting language, you can invoke stored procedures from within your script. For example, you can call a stored procedure that uses the Microsoft® ActiveX® Data Objects (ADO) connection and Session object to work with data.

Scripting in the Workflow Designer is done in an editor called the Code Editor that features statement completion, drag-and-drop support, color-coding, Microsoft® IntelliMouse® support, script verification, and other enhancements.

When writing script for a workflow process, you must be familiar with the available events and the order in which they are executed. In addition, it is critical to understand how these events loop and the consequences of changing the names of script procedures.

Script Procedures

A single action, such as moving from one state in the workflow process to another, can trigger several different events, which occur in a particular sequence. For each of the workflow events, there are two associated script procedures—a validation script procedure and an event script procedure. Each is available as a separate script block in the Code Editor. For example, you can write four script procedures associated with states: OnEnter, OnEnterValidate, OnExit, and OnExitValidate. The validation script procedure must return a value of True for the associated event and event script procedure to be executed.

Workflow Events

There are six events: OnCreate, OnDelete, OnEnter, OnExit, OnChange, and OnExpire. These events serve two purposes—they represent valid events in your workflow process, and they are used to trigger scripts. All the events except OnExpire are triggered when records are saved.

For example, if you want to design a workflow process where a new record can be set to a state named New or a state named Review, each of these states must include a transition from the Item Created shape, which contains an OnCreate event by default. Similarly, if you want to make it possible for a record to be deleted regardless of its current state, you must add a transition to the Item Deleted shape, which includes the OnDelete event, to each state in your workflow process.

OnExpire events are regulated by the SQL Server Agent and are executed at a designated time defined by that agent. All the other events are triggered by user interaction with the data.

Note Any event can be used to generate a state change using script.

For each of these events, there is a validation script procedure and an event script procedure. The validation script procedure must return a value of True for the event script procedure to be executed. In addition, during transitions, all validation script procedures that are defined must return True before any event script procedure is executed.

For example, take the case of a state transition from Open to Resolved. If you have OnExit and OnEnter events defined for Open and Resolved respectively, the validation script procedures for OnExit of Open, OnChange between Open and Resolved, and finally OnEnter of Resolved must all return True for the corresponding event script procedures to be executed. Only after True is returned for all of the validation script procedures, will the event script procedures occur in the same order: OnExit of Open, OnChange between Open and Resolved, and finally OnEnter of Resolved.

Note OnEnter and OnExit are events that fire each time a state is entered or exited regardless of the transition that caused the entry or exit.

By default, each validation script procedure returns True. For example:

```
Function State1_OnEnterValidate()
    State1_OnEnterValidate = True
End Function
```

You can modify the validation script procedure to make it conditional. For example:

```
Function State1_OnEnterValidate()
    If CheckValue = 1 then
        State1_OnEnterValidate = True
    End if
End Function
```

If the CheckValue variable is not equal to one, the event script procedure will not be executed. In validation script procedures, CheckValue can be a variable, an item from the Session object, or a call to a function.

The following example uses the Session.Item object to look at a date field called DateModified. If it is equal to today's date, then the validation script returns a value of True.

```
Function State1_OnEnterValidate()
    If session.item("DateModified") = now Then
        State1_OnEnterValidate = True
    Else
        State1_OnEnterValidate = False
    End If
End Function
```

Order of Events

For each of the three transition events—OnCreate, OnChange, and OnDelete—additional events are executed in a certain order (for more detailed information, see "Order of Workflow Events").

OnCreate

- OnCreate ⇒ OnEnter

The OnCreate event executes when the user inserts a record in the database, followed by OnEnter of the designated first workflow state.

OnChange

- OnExit (State A) ⇒ OnChange (State A to State B) ⇒ OnEnter (State B)

When the user initiates a transition from one state to another or from a state back to the same state, three events are triggered: OnExit from the first state, OnChange for the transition, and OnEnter of the next state.

OnDelete

- OnExit (State B) ⇒ OnDelete

When a user deletes a record from the database, the OnExit event of the final state executes, followed by OnDelete.

Loop Suppression

If you make a transition from one state to another, the associated OnExit, OnChange, and OnEnter events will be evaluated. Because you might have code within the OnEnter event of the next state to evaluate and transition it to yet another state, looping could occur. Because looping indefinitely can cause Microsoft® SQL Server™ to hang or crash, Workflow Designer for SQL Server implements loop suppression by caching all the states the record has transitioned to during the current transaction context. When it is detected that you have been in a state previously, the transition to the state is made possible, but the loop is broken, because any subsequent OnExit, OnChange, and OnEnter events are not executed.

For example, if you have a workflow process that enforces the following transitions:

State A $\Rightarrow$ State B $\Rightarrow$ State C

- An issue in State A is moved to State B.

- The OnEnter event of State B triggers code that evaluates a condition and moves to State C.

- The OnEnter event of State C triggers code that evaluates a condition and moves back to State A.

- The OnEnter event of State A triggers code that evaluates a condition and moves to State B. At this point, you have looped back to your starting point.

- Although you entered State B previously during the transaction context, the entry is made possible, and the OnEnter event is executed. The OnEnter of State B evaluates and moves to State C again.

The loop is broken here. The OnExit of State B, OnChange from B to C, and OnEnter State C are not executed.

So, you loop completely through the events, and only the first event is executed twice.

Names of Script Procedures

Script procedure names in the Code Editor follow the convention of combining the Name property of the workflow object with the name of the event by means of an underscore. The validation script procedures append Validate to the end of the name. For example, the event script procedure for the OnExit event of a state named State1 is named State1_OnExit. The validation script procedure is named State1_OnExitValidate.

Scripting Events in the Workflow Designer for SQL Server

To add script to a workflow process for SQL Server, first decide which event you want to use as the trigger for the script.

> **Note** If your script updates any rows, you must have an OnChange event on the state. You are not required to script the OnChange event, but it must exist to support any updates. If you do not want to leave the state when performing the updates, add a Transition Within to the state.

To add code to workflow events

1. On the workflow process diagram, double-click the event icon for the event to which you want to add code. This opens the **Code Editor** and enters the **Sub/End Sub** tags for you.

2. Enter the code for the event script procedure.

3. If you want a validation script to run before the event is permitted, select the object name from the **Object** list at the top of the **Code Editor** window and the <eventname>Validate event from the **Event** list, and then add the script between the **Function/End Function** tags.

4. If desired, add any additional functions or procedures associated with the workflow script.

5. Click **Verify Script** on the **Tools** menu.

When to Use Which Event

To help you decide when to use one of the several types of events available in a workflow process, the events are divided into four categories:

- **Row events** facilitate changes to the rows storing information about an item. These events are used to trigger code and to designate permissible user interaction, such as creating a new record and deleting a record.

- **State entry or exit events** occur immediately on entering or on leaving a state.

- **Transition events** occur when moving from one state to another or from a state back to the same state.

- **Expiry events** automate changes based on the time-out conditions you specify.

You can use the following table to determine which of the events to use:

To execute script for this action	Use this event
A row is inserted into the database	OnCreate
A row is deleted from the database	OnDelete
A row is updated in the database	OnChange
A state is entered	OnEnter
A state is exited	OnExit
The record moves between states	OnChange
Specifying a condition for an automatic state change	OnExpire

Script Procedure Names

Script procedure names are based on the Name property of each state or transition, combined with the name of the event that triggers the script. These procedure names are added to the Code Editor when you double-click an event icon on the workflow process diagram. In addition, you can construct them by selecting a state or transition name from the Object list at the top of the Code Editor and then selecting an event from the Event list.

For example, if you add a transition from a state with Name property New to a state with Name property Review and you name the transition NewReview, then the validation script procedure for that transition is named NewReview_OnChangeValidate.

- NewReview refers to the Name property of the transition with which the event is associated.

- OnChange means this is an OnChange event triggered when a record that is in the state New is set to the state Review.

- Validate means this is a validation script procedure.

States have OnEnter and OnExit events associated with them. The script procedure for the OnEnter event of the state named Review is Review_OnEnter, and the validation script procedure is named Review_OnEnterValidate. Similarly, the OnExit script procedures are named Review_OnExit and Review_OnExitValidate.

A transition between states, and a Transition Within on a single state, has an OnChange event associated with it by default. The script procedure for the OnChange event of the transition named Change1 is Change1_OnChange, and the validation script procedure is named Change1_OnChangeValidate.

A transition from the Item Created shape to a state has an OnCreate event associated with it, rather than OnChange. The script procedure for the OnCreate event of the transition named Create1 is Create1_OnCreate, and the validation script procedure is named Create1_OnCreateValidate.

A transition from a state to the Item Deleted shape has an OnDelete event associated with it, rather than OnChange. The script procedure for the OnDelete event of the transition named Delete1 is Delete1_OnDelete, and the validation script procedure is named Delete1_OnDeleteValidate.

A transition that has the Type property set to Expiry has an OnExpire event associated with it, rather than OnChange. The script procedure for the OnExpire event of the transition named Expiry1 is Expire1_OnExpire, and the validation script procedure is named Expire1_OnExpireValidate.

Control of Row Changes Based on State

If you want the workflow process to make it possible for rows to be added, updated, or deleted from the table, you must supply the appropriate transition events.

Note   You are not required to add script; you only must add the transitions.

To make it possible for rows to be:	Add:
Inserted in a state	A transition from the Item Created shape to the state
Deleted in a state	A transition from the state to the Item Deleted shape
Modified in a state	A Transition Within to the state

OnEnter and OnExit Events

You can add script to a state that executes immediately before a record enters or after it exits that state, regardless of which transition the record follows. These events often are used to execute validation and e-mail notification scripts.

To add script that executes when a record moves into a state

- Double-click the **OnEnter** icon on that state in the workflow process diagram. The **Code Editor** opens with **OnEnter** event procedure tags added.

To add script that executes when a record leaves a state

- Double-click the **OnExit** icon on that state in the workflow process diagram. The **Code Editor** opens with **OnExit** event procedure tags added.

OnExpire Events

You can automate events by scripting an OnExpire event to evaluate a condition and, when that condition is met, perform an action—such as a transition or e-mail notification.

The SQL Server Agent monitors the OnExpire event. The agent runs stored procedures on the server to execute time-out events based on a predefined schedule. You can set up the agent to run hourly, daily, or weekly—based on the requirements of your workflow application.

After you add the Expiry transition to your workflow process, an administrator can set the SQL Server Agent time-out information in the Workflow Manager for SQL Server. Open the Workflow Manager and, on the Tools menu, click WorkflowTimeout Job.

Adding Transition Events

As an item makes a transition from state to state, you might want to specify conditions that determine whether the transition can occur or cause other commands to be executed.

To add a transition event

1. Add the states that you want to transition between to the workflow process diagram. For details, see "Designing Workflow Processes."

2. Click on the **Transition** tool in the **Workflow Toolbox**.

3. Click on the state from which you want the transition to start, and drag to the destination state. While you drag, a dotted line will stretch from the state to the cursor.

Automating Changes and Events

You can automate events by scripting an OnExpire event to evaluate a condition and, when that condition is met, perform an action—such as a transition or e-mail notification.

To add an OnExpire event

1. In the workflow process diagram, select the transition that you want to function as an **Expiry** transition.

2. Set the **Type** property of the transition to **Expiry**.

3. Double-click the **Expiry** transition in the workflow process diagram. If, for example, the transition is named Expire1, the **Code Editor** will open with **Sub Expire1_OnExpire/End Sub** event procedure tags added for the **OnExpire** event.

4. Select the name of the **Expiry** transition from the **Object** list at the top of the **Code Editor** window, and select **OnExpireValidate** from the **Event** list to add validation procedure tags to the script.

5. Enter your code to validate the time-out conditions and the script you want to execute on time-out.

6. Open the **Workflow Manager for SQL Server**.

7. On the **Tools** menu, click **WorkflowTimeout Job**.

8. Edit the timeout properties as desired. For details, refer to the Microsoft® SQL Server™ documentation.

Data Manipulation Using Workflow Script

The Session.Item object can be used to return values from the current record of a table, or to set values in a table. You specify the name of the column for which you want to retrieve or set a value. When setting values, you must run a Session.Item.Updatebatch method to commit the update.

If you change a value and then want to compare the new value with the original value, you can use the Session.OriginalItem object. However, you must have the MakeDeletedRowsAvailable property of the workflow process set to True to persist modified values. For more information, see "The Workflow Engine Model."

Session.Item is used in the Finding a Manager in the User Directory example to specify the name of the field that contains the SAMAccountName.

Following are three examples that use the Session object:

Getting a Value

```
Function GetValue(strFieldName)
'strFieldName is the name of the column that contains the data you are
returning
    GetValue = session.item(strFieldName)
End Function
```

Setting a Value

```
Sub SetValue(strFieldName)
'strFieldName is the name of the column that contains the data to which
you are appending the date
    Session.item(strFieldName) = session.item(strFieldName)& ' ' &  date
    Sesssion.item.updatebatch
End sub
```

Checking a Value

```
Function CheckValue(strFieldName)
'strFieldName is the name of the column that contains the data you are
comparing
    If session.item(strFieldName) <> session.originalitem(strFieldName)
then
        'Do something
    End if
End function
```

Retrieval of User Information by Workflow Script

You can use the Session object in workflow script to retrieve information from the workflow application User Directory. For example, use Session.UserList to access information such as the user's e-mail address or manager.

For example, in the Finding a Manager in the User Directory example, the function uses the current user's SAM Account Name to locate the name and e-mail address of the manager for that user. The script finds the manager by first locating the user in the user directory using the SAM Account Name

```
    ulist.Find strUL_SAM & "='" & Session.Item(strItem) & "'"
```

and then by identifying that user's manager.

```
    strManagerSID = ulist(strUL_MGR)
```

After the function has located the manager, it looks up the e-mail address for that manager and returns that information.

For example script showing functions that return user information from the user directory, see "Script Examples for SQL Server."

Lookup of Role Membership Based On SAMAccountName

The modIsMemberofRole function calls a stored procedure named modGetExecutePermissions to check the permissions for a specified user and role. If the designated user is a member of the specified role, then the function returns True.

You can call the modIsMemberofRole function in the validation script procedure for an OnCreate event to make sure only users in a certain role can create new records. For example, if you have a transition from the Item Created shape to a state named Active and there are no other script or permissions issues, anyone could create a new record and set the state to Active. However, for example, if you create a state called Override and only want users in the Manager role to be able to create a new record and immediately set the state to Override, you add a transition from the Item Created shape to the Override state. Then, you add script to the OnCreateValidation script procedure that checks role membership. The following is an example of such a function.

Calling the Function

Enter this code into the Code Editor, in a validation or event script procedure for the event that you want to trigger the script. It calls the function script that follows.

```
'// modIsMemberofRole(strSAMAccountName, strRoleName)
'// ------------------------------------------------------------
    ret = modIsMemberofRole (session.user,"Readers") 'session.user
returns the SAMAccountName of the current user
    call logger.printstring("Member of readers role: " & ret & chr(13) &
chr(10)) 'modWFE.log file in Windows directory
'// ------------------------------------------------------------
```

Function Script

Enter this code into the Code Editor wherever you usually store functions.

> **Note**   The modIsMemberofRole script requires the modCallSP function. For a copy of the modCallSP script, see "Calling a Stored Procedure."

```
'// ------------------------------------------------------------
'// Name      : modIsMemberofRole
'// Purpose   : returns whether a SAM Account Name is a member of a role
'//
'// Prereq    : function modCallSP
'// Inputs    : strSAMAccountName -  SAM Account Name
'//           : strRoleName - Role Name
'//
'// Return    : True/False
```

```
'// ------------------------------------------------------------
Function modIsMemberofRole(strSAMAccountName, strRoleName)

    '// declaration
    dim paramlist(2)

    '// initialization
    paramlist(1) = strSAMAccountName
    paramlist(2) = strRoleName

    ModIsMemberofRole = modCallSP("modIsMember", True, 2, paramlist)

End Function
'// ------------------------------------------------------------
```

Error Handling for Workflow Script

If any error occurs in the workflow script, by default, the entire transaction is rolled back. If you want to override the default behavior, you must add script that traps, evaluates, and clears the error, so the change is committed despite the errors.

When the error is cleared, your script can return information to the client to inform users of possible errors. You can create your own error message table that the client can use to populate message boxes or status lines.

In a custom user interface, you can control and modify error messages, including errors from workflow execution. To do this, you must use ADO to make it possible for your client applications to access and manipulate data from a database server through an OLE DB provider. After you execute a database update in ADO, the Connection object holds the errors returned by this operation in the Errors collection.

ADO supports key features for building client/server and Web-based applications. Its primary benefits are ease of use, high speed, low memory overhead, and a small disk footprint. ADO also features Remote Data Service (RDS), by which you can move data from a server to a client application or Web page, manipulate the data on the client, and return updates to the server in a single round trip.

To learn more about ADO, see the ADO Overview in Microsoft® Access documentation.

Testing and Debugging in the Workflow Designer for SQL Server

Debugging server-side script can be a challenge. Usually with Microsoft® Visual Basic® Scripting Edition (VBScript), you can use functions, such as msgbox, to determine the status of script variables during debugging. Because server script cannot display user information, you cannot take advantage of such features. To overcome this, Workflow Designer for SQL Server provides the Logger object.

The Logger object has two methods, PrintString and PrintObject, that append output to the Workflow Log (modwfe.log), which can be found in the Microsoft® Windows® directory on the server. You can use these methods to print out debugging information.

> **Note** Because the modwfe.log file is stored on the server, developers wanting to use the Logger object must have access to the file. The server administrator can share the file or directory to make it possible for you to access the log file. Members of the modAppOwners group do not have permissions to this file by default.

For example, the following script uses the PrintString method of the Logger object to print the value of a variable. The string is appended to the Modwfe.log file found in the Windows system directory.

```
dim strManager
strManager = "mymanager"
logger.printstring("The value for variable strManager is " & strManager)
```

To test that your workflow is functioning as you expect, you can print a string to the log whenever you trigger an event by adding code to the Code Editor such as:

```
Sub State1_OnEnter()
    logger.printstring("You have entered State1")
End Sub
```

The sample script Sending Mail Using SMTP can also be used to test that events are firing as expected.

For additional tips on debugging, visit the Microsoft® Office XP Developer Web site at http://www.microsoft.com/office/developer. Look in the Technical Resources area for articles about writing and debugging workflow script and using server-side Microsoft® ActiveX® controls and Visual Basic to debug complex scripts.

Creating Templates

A template is a complete copy of a workflow application that contains all of the information required to create another instance of the application, including the database schema, Web pages, and database roles.

Templates make it easy for you to distribute your applications to other servers that have Workflow Services for SQL Server installed. For example, an expense reporting application created for your main office could be distributed as a template to branch offices. Each branch could create instances of the application and use it as-is or modify it to meet the branch's special requirements.

The template created for a workflow application can incorporate a broad scope of possible contents. When you create an instance of a workflow application template, new objects are added to several areas of your server. You can see a new workflow process in the Solution Explorer, a new database in the SQL Server Enterprise Manager, and a new Web site in the Web server directory. In addition, there might be Help documents and other files saved in the template.

Templates also provide a quick way to create several customized applications based on your original schema. You can create an instance of an existing application, modify it to suit your requirements, and then save your changes as a new template.

Template Contents

A template created for a workflow application incorporates a broad range of contents. When you use the SQL Server Workflow Template Creation wizard to create a workflow application template, you incorporate the workflow process, the database, and the Web site.

To complete the Template Creation wizard, you provide a template name and description, select any data you want to exclude from the database tables in the template, and specify whether existing database users should be excluded from the template.

Then, the wizard invokes a server COM object (the template management object) to create a copy of the database, truncate the selected tables, remove the database users if desired, and to store a copy or backup of this database into a template components table created for the template. The Web site (as registered in the modApplications table in the modSystem database) is enumerated, and every file is stored as a template component along with a relative URL to restore it to its original relative location on deployment. The template is added to the modTemplates table in modSystem, so it appears in the list of installable templates on the server.

Database

To truncate user tables and remove database users, a temporary copy of the workflow-enabled database is created on the server. This database is created in the environment's temp directory. The COM template manager object runs under the context of the user who invokes it. To succeed at creating the template, you must be a member of the modAppOwners group.

Template Information

The template name, title, description, and version information is stored in a new row in the modTemplates table in the modSystem database. If you overwrite an existing template with another that has the same name and version, then the old row in the modTemplates table is deleted, along with its associated template components table.

In addition to this information, the template stores Microsoft® SQL Server™ configuration information. When you create a template, the configuration of the server where the template is made is stored in the template. If you deploy the template to a server with different configuration settings, a message will warn you of possible issues.

Creating a Template for a Workflow Application for SQL Server

Templates make it easy to share and distribute the workflow applications you create. Each template contains all of the information required to create a complete instance of the workflow application, including the workflow process, the database, and the Web site.

To save a workflow application as a template

1. Open the **Workflow Manager for SQL Server**.

2. On the **Workflow Applications** tab, click **Create Template**.

3. Click **Next**, select **Workflow Project**, and specify the server that hosts the database for the application you want to include in the template.

4. Click **Connect**, and select the application you want to save as a template.

5. Specify a name and title for the new template, and enter version information and a description if desired. After completing the wizard, you can view this information in the **Workflow Manager** on the **Templates** tab.

6. Specify any additional files you want to include in the template.

    For example, you might want to include a Help file or other non-database or Web-related files that support your application but are not part of the database, workflow, or Web site.

7. Specify what data from tables you want included in the template. By default, all data in the tables is included in the template. If you clear the check box next to a table, then table schema is still stored in the template, but the data is removed.

    Note   For each main table selected to be included in the template, all associated detail and lookup tables are included also. You cannot include the data from a main table and exclude the data from a lookup table that is related to the main table or one of its detail tables.

8. Click **Next** to accept the default option that excludes current users of the application from the template. To include existing users in the template, select the **Include current users in the template** option.

    Tip   Include the users only if this template will be used to create new applications for the same users as those specified for the selected application. For security reasons, you should exclude the users if you plan on providing this template to a different set of users.

9. Select one or both of the options for saving the template.

    - **Save Template on Server** puts the template directly on the target server, so an instance of it can be created without having to be imported from a file first. Select the server where you want to save the template from the server list. If you do not see the server in the list, click **Refresh**. After you have selected the server, click **Connect** to make sure the server is running. If the server is running, you will get a **Connection Successful** message.

    - **Save Template to File** creates a .tpl file that can be distributed to other servers that have **Workflow Services for SQL Server** installed.

10. Click **Finish**. The wizard backs up the database, truncates any specified tables, removes database users if desired, and stores the backed-up database information in the modTemplates table. It also enumerates all of the files in your Web site and stores them in the table.

    Note   This process might take a few minutes.

Saving a Template to a Server

To distribute your workflow application to others, you can create a template and either save it to a file or save it directly to a server. By saving it to a file, you can distribute the template to different servers or to a named instance on the same server. If you want to store the database and the Web site on two different servers, you can specify each location when you create an instance of the template.

Note   Be sure that the target server or named instance has Workflow Services for SQL Server installed.

To save a template to a server

1. Open the **Workflow Manager for SQL Server**, and click the **Templates** tab.

2. Select the task you would like to perform.

    - To save a template file from another server to your current server or named instance, click **Import from File**. Browse to the location of the file, and click **Open**.

    - To save a template file to a different server or named instance, select a template from the list, and click **Export to File**. Browse to the location where you want to save the file, enter a file name, and click **Save**.

Testing a Template

Before distributing your workflow application template, test it to make sure it creates an instance properly on the target system. Consider testing the installation of the template on the server as well as the functionality of the Web site.

After determining that the application installs and works correctly, you can distribute the template file (*.tpl) for use on any server that has Workflow Services for SQL Server installed.

To test your template

1. If you have not already done so, import the template using the **Workflow Manager**, so the template is registered in the modTemplates table on your server.

2. In the **Workflow Manager**, select the server in the **Server** box, and click **Refresh**.

3. Select the **Templates** tab, and verify the template is included in the list of available templates.

4. Select the template, and click **Instantiate Template** to start the wizard.

5. Use the wizard to create an instance of the workflow application. Designate where you want to install the database and the Web site.

6. Use the **SQL Server Enterprise Manager** to verify that the database exists in the Microsoft® SQL Server™ data folder. Use the **Internet Services Manager** to verify that the Web site exists on the Web server.

7. Open the Web site for the application from a client computer. Verify that the application works correctly.

8. To test the permissions you have created, log in using Microsoft® Windows® group accounts that belong to the different database roles used in the workflow application. Then, access the Web site, and test the functionality.

Developing a Digital Dashboard Using Web Parts

A Digital Dashboard is a container that provides a customized display of information consolidated from various information sources. Every Digital Dashboard is a web page containing one or more Web Parts, which are individual objects that contain data or script that presents information to the user.

The Microsoft® Office XP Developer environment makes it possible for you to create and customize Digital Dashboards and Web Parts.

In This Section

Understanding the Digital Dashboard
> A Digital Dashboard provides a flexible means of assembling, in one place, the information from a variety of sources, based on the requirements of the dashboard user.

Web Parts
> To make a dashboard functional, you must add Web Parts to it. A Web Part is a self-contained script or Web page. You can use Microsoft® Office XP Developer to add new Web Parts, or you can import pre-existing Web Parts from a catalog.

Understanding the Digital Dashboard

A Digital Dashboard is an Active Server Page (ASP) that references one or more Web Parts. Each Web Part is a self-contained module of Extensible Markup Language (XML), HTML, or script (Microsoft® JScript® or Microsoft® Visual Basic® Scripting Edition (VBScript)) and is designed to retrieve and render the information you want to include in the dashboard. When the user loads the dashboard, the dashboard retrieves the Web Parts that it is configured to display.

If you set the appropriate permissions while creating a Digital Dashboard, you can design it so users can exercise considerable control over the dashboard's content. For example, you can set dashboard properties that make it possible for your user to add, remove, or configure Web Parts at run time.

The Web Parts that make up a Digital Dashboard are easy to build. Your users can create relatively simple Web Parts. You can create more complex Web Parts using the development environment.

Why Digital Dashboards?

The advent of the World Wide Web has provided information workers with easy access to large volumes of data. However, the resulting information overload has resulted in a situation in which it remains difficult for workers to locate and assimilate easily the specific information they require. The result of this information overload can be lost information, mistaken priorities, trends that go unnoticed, and duplication of work.

A Digital Dashboard addresses this problem by providing a consolidated view of the specific information you require. Digital Dashboards combat information overload by:

- **Helping employees focus on business priorities.** A Digital Dashboard consolidates information from multiple sources. In addition, the Digital Dashboard framework is designed to be modular, so you can design and incorporate into the dashboard the information that represents your priorities.

- **Delivering information in the office or on the move.** Knowledge workers can use a Digital Dashboard no matter where they are. Information from different sources, including favorite Web sites and shared public folders, can be synchronized for offline viewing and analysis.

Creating a Digital Dashboard Project

You can use the Microsoft® Office XP Developer environment to create a Digital Dashboard project. When you create a Digital Dashboard, Office Developer creates a dashboard project and adds an HTML Web part to the project.

To create a dashboard

1. From the **Start** menu, select **Microsoft Office XP Developer**, and then select **Microsoft Development Environment**.

2. From the **File** menu, select **New**, and then select **Project**.

3. The **New Project** dialog box is displayed. Select **Office Developer Projects**.

4. Under **Templates:**, select the **Dashboard Project** icon.

5. In the **Folder** location box, do one of the following:

    - Type the URL to the Microsoft® Exchange 2000 Server or SharePoint Portal Server public folder location where you want to create your application. Typically, this URL will be in the form http://*ServerName*/Public.

      –or–

    - Click the **Browse** button to specify a folder location by using the **Select Folder** dialog box.

6. In the **Folder Name** dialog box, type the name for the folder that will contain your dashboard. This will be part of the URL used to open your dashboard. For example, if you enter

MyApplication, the URL to your application will look like
http://MyServer/Public/MyApplication.

7.   Click **OK**.

Modifying Basic Dashboard Properties

Each Digital Dashboard and Web Part exposes a standard set of properties that affect the
appearance and behavior of the dashboard. When you select the project or Web Part node in
Solution Explorer, the Properties window displays the properties for the selected item.

To set the properties on a Digital Dashboard

1.   In **Solution Explorer**, select the dashboard project or Web Part node.

2.   In the **Properties** window, specify the appropriate property values.

You can invoke the Properties window using View, Properties or by hitting F4. By default the
Properties window is displayed, unless you close it.

Security

When deploying Digital Dashboards, one of the most common issues that administrators face is
how to configure dashboards to supply information tailored to the roles of various users in the
organization. For example, an executive must have access to information that is very different from
what a salesperson or a shop foreman requires. Some Web Parts designed for executives should be
unavailable to a majority of users, but at the same time, there are Web Parts that everyone must
have, such as a Web Part that displays company announcements.

When a user or administrator modifies the properties of a dashboard or Web Part, the dashboard
factory writes those settings back to the store. For this reason, security is an essential
consideration.

A Digital Dashboard is an intranet application that is integrated fully with Microsoft® Windows®
2000 Internet and file system security. You configure Digital Dashboard security by setting Access
Control Lists (ACLs) on the underlying store. This makes it possible for you to control security for
individuals and groups in addition to Web Parts and dashboards. Integration between the stores and
Active Directory makes it possible for you to link group and user permissions to the core company
directory.

Deploying an Exchange Server Dashboard

The Exchange Server Digital Dashboard provides a scalable platform for deploying Digital
Dashboards. Microsoft® Exchange 2000 Server makes it possible for administrators to secure
dashboards and provides the ability for users to personalize shared dashboards.

To deploy an exchange dashboard

1. From the **Development Environment**, in the **Solution Explorer**, select the dashboard that you want to deploy.

2. From the **File** menu, select **File Save Copy As**.

3. In the **File Save As** dialog box, for the location, specify the server to which you want to deploy.

Secure Dashboards

As an administrator of an Exchange Server Digital Dashboard, you can control the extent to which users can modify their Digital Dashboards and Web Parts. The amount of control you give users often depends on the types of dashboards you deploy in your organization; for example, you probably want to give users full control of their personal dashboards, but you make it possible for users to modify only limited properties on a team dashboard or a dashboard that displays company news.

Here are some of the options that are available to you:

*   **Complete lock down.** In this scenario, you set Access Control Lists (ACLs) to restrict all write permissions to the administrator group only. Users cannot add or remove Web Parts or modify dashboard properties. When you deploy a Digital Dashboard that is locked down completely, links to the Layout and Settings pages do not appear in the user interface. The link to the Content page is present; however, on the Content·page, users only can see a list of Web Parts. They cannot import or delete Web Parts or modify their properties.

*   **Users can view Web Parts in a dashboard based on role.** In this scenario, you use read ACLs to limit access to certain Web parts in a given dashboard. This way, you can create a dashboard with a large number of Web Parts and control which users can see specific Web Parts in their dashboards. For example, the executives in your company would see a different set of Web Parts than the salespeople. If a user does not have permission to access a specific Web Part, that Web Part does not appear in the list of Web Parts on the Content page.

*   **Users can customize Web Parts but cannot import or delete them.** In this scenario, you use ACLs that control whether users can insert or delete rows in the Exchange Server catalog database. The Web Parts on the dashboard are locked down, but users can still customize the look and feel of the Web Parts and the dashboard.

*   **Users have full control.** In this scenario, you use ACLs to give users full control over a dashboard. Users can import and delete Web Parts and modify the look and feel of the dashboard by setting Web Part and dashboard properties.

Opening the SharePoint Portal Server Portal

As an organization creates more and more information, the need for workers to manage the information they possess becomes crucial. In addition, people in a group or organization can experience difficulty simply working together with the information at hand. Data stores, such as file shares, can be very large and store many different types of files, making it hard for anyone to find anything. Documents can get lost or versions of the same document misplaced. On occasion, people also might overwrite each other's documents accidentally.

Employees might find that the server infrastructure limits searches across multiple and different data stores; or, if a data store is accessible, they might be able to perform only limited text searches. Even after performing a search, there might be little or no organizational structure directing them to the information they require. Microsoft® SharePoint Portal Server combines document management and search technologies to help people write, review, manage, and locate information in the workspace, on an intranet portal, and on the Web.

To open the SharePoint Portal Server portal for the first time

1. From the **Start** menu, select **Microsoft Office XP Developer**, and then select **Microsoft Development Environment**.

2. From the **File** menu, select **New**, and then select **Project**.

3. The **New Project** dialog box is displayed. Select **Office Developer Projects**. Under **Templates:** up to three project icons are displayed, **Exchange Workflow Project**, **SQL Server Workflow Project**, and **Dashboard Project**.

4. Select the **Dashboard Project** icon.

5. In the Location drop-down text box, enter http://<*SharePointPortalServername*>/<*workspacename*>.

6. In the Name text box, enter **Portal**.

   > **Note** You must name the project **Portal**, otherwise you will not be able to open the SharePoint Portal Server portal.

7. Click **OK**.

This will add a Portal.ddp project file to the Portal folder. In addition, it will add a solution file to your client machine in My Documents\Office Developer Projects\PortalX\Portal.sln.

Now that you have a project and solution file for your workspace, you can open it.

To open the SharePoint Portal Server portal

1. From the **Start** menu, select **Microsoft Office XP Developer**, and then select **Microsoft Development Environment**.

2. From the **File** menu, select **Open**, and then select the project.

Web Parts

At the heart of the Digital Dashboard are Web Parts. Web Parts are reusable components that contain Web-based content, such as Extensible Markup Language (XML) code, HTML pages, or script, and that support a set of standard properties that determine how the Web Parts are rendered in a Digital Dashboard. Because Web Parts adhere to a common standard, you can store them in libraries that you use to assemble all of the Digital Dashboards for your organization.

Many dashboard and Web Part properties are user-specific, but administrators can control the extent to which a user can modify Web Parts or dashboards. For example, you can lock down the Web Parts in a given dashboard, making it impossible for users to remove them.

In This Section

Web Part Properties

The Web Part properties fall into four categories: basic, appearance, content, and execution. The basic properties define basic metadata for a Web Part. The appearance properties define how a Web Part appears on a dashboard. The content properties describe the content that the Web Part renders. The execution properties specify how the Web Part runs on the dashboard.

Ways to Add Web Parts to Your Dashboard

After you create a dashboard, you can tailor its functionality by adding Web Parts. Web Parts determine the content of a Digital Dashboard and can display any type of information or Web format that you would like to implement.

Types of Web Parts

You can build Web Parts from three places: Microsoft® Office XP Developer, the dashboard itself, or the Web Part Builder add-in for Microsoft® Visual InterDev®.

Guidelines for Building Good Web Parts

Good Web Parts deliver targeted information tailored to specific users in a manner that is appropriate for a Digital Dashboard. The look and feel of your Web Parts should be appealing to users and appropriate for a Digital Dashboard.

How a Digital Dashboard Factory Interprets Web Parts

A Digital Dashboard factory initializes Web Parts, gets content, and displays the content on the dashboard.

Web Part Properties

Web Parts that you create in Microsoft® Office XP Developer belong to the content class urn:schemas-microsoft-com:office:Webpart:.

Schema properties specify how a Web Part looks, the location from which it obtains content, how it runs, whether the user can customize its properties, and so on. All property names belong to the content class urn:schemas-microsoft-com:office:Webpart:.

When creating Web Parts in Office Developer, the property values that you specify for the Web Parts are the global defaults, that is, those used by default by everyone accessing the dashboard. However, dashboards can store user-specific property values for each user, so different users can have different values for these properties. Properties that are not user specific are metadata properties stored on the server.

The Web Part properties fall into four categories: basic, appearance, content, and execution. The basic properties define basic metadata for a Web Part. The appearance properties define how a Web Part appears on a dashboard. The content properties describe the content that the Web Part renders. The execution properties specify how the Web Part runs on the dashboard.

Web part properties fall into the following categories:

- **Basic metadata**   This includes title, description, and date that the Web Part was last modified, and so on.

- **Content**   The content of a Web Part can include Extensible Markup Language (XML) or HTML, or it can include Microsoft® Visual Basic® Scripting Edition (VBScript) or Microsoft® JScript® that retrieves and renders the Web Part data.

- **Appearance**   This includes the height, width, and so on of the Web Part.

- **Execution**   This includes whether and how often Web Part content is refreshed and whether the Web Part is isolated from other Web Parts on the dashboard.

Basic Properties

Property Name	User Specific	Description
Description	No	Description of the Web Part
LastModified	Yes	Date and time the Web Part was last modified (in Greenwich mean time)
Title	Yes	Title of the Web Part
Namespace	No	Namespace for the Web Part

Appearance Properties

Property Name	User Specific	Description
AllowMinimize	No	Indicates whether the user can minimize the Web Part
AllowRemove	No	Indicates whether a user can remove the Web Part from the dashboard
DetailLink	No	URL to a detail page for the Web Part, which is often a full-page user interface for the Web Part

Property Name	User Specific	Description
FrameState	Yes	Indicates the frame state of a Web Part (normal or minimized)
HasFrame	No	Is TRUE if you want the Web Part to include a frame with title and buttons
Height	Yes	Fixed height for the Web Part in the dashboard
IsIncluded	Yes	Indicates whether the Web Part should be included in the dashboard
IsVisible	Yes	Makes a Web Part visible or invisible in the dashboard view
PartOrder	Yes	The order of the Web Part relative to other Web Parts in the same zone
Width	Yes	Specifies a fixed width for the Web Part in the dashboard view
Zone	Yes	The area of the dashboard in which the Web Part is located

Content Properties

Property Name	User Specific	Description
ContentLink	No	URL to use instead of the embedded content
ContentType	No	Indicates the type of embedded content the Web Part contains (HTML, VBScript, JScript, XML, and so on)—read-only properties

Execution Properties

Property Name	User Specific	Description
CacheBehavior	No	Controls whether and how a dashboard factory should cache content—settings are None, All Users, or Each User
CacheTimeout	No	How long a dashboard factory should keep cached results
CustomizationLink	No	URL to a page that makes it possible for the user to customize the operation of the Web Part
MasterPartLink	No	URL to a master version of the Web Part
PartStorage	Yes	Element for storing Web Part state and customization information
RequiresIsolation	No	Indicates whether to isolate the Web Part from other Web Parts

Property Name	User Specific	Description
XSL	No	Embedded XSL style sheet to use on the Web Part's content before rendering the content to a dashboard
XSLLink	No	URL to an XSL style sheet to use on the Web Part's content before rendering the content to a dashboard

Ways to Add Web Parts to Your Dashboard

After you create a dashboard, you can tailor its functionality by adding Web Parts. Web Parts determine the content of a Digital Dashboard and can display any type of information or Web format that you would like to implement. A sample of Web Parts is provided with Microsoft® Office XP Developer. In addition, you can create your own Web Parts.

Adding Web Parts by Using Office Developer Digital Dashboard Projects

A Web Part is a reusable component that can contain any kind of Web-based information.

To add Web Parts to a dashboard project, use the Add New Item command. Using this command, you can add a Microsoft® JScript®, Microsoft® Visual Basic® Scripting Edition (VBScript), Extensible Markup Language (XML), or HTML Web Part to the dashboard project.

Use the Add Existing Item command to add an existing file to the dashboard. If the item you add is already a Web Part, then its property values are preserved and affect the appearance and behavior of the dashboard. If the added file is not a Web Part, then it is copied into the dashboard project.

To add a new Web Part to a dashboard

1. In the **Solution Explorer**, select the dashboard project.

2. From the **Project** menu, select **Add New Item**.

3. Select a part type (for example, HTML), and click **Open**.

To add an existing Web Part to a dashboard

1. In the **Solution Explorer**, select the dashboard project.

2. From the **Project** menu, select **Add Existing Item**.

3. Select the **Web Part** you want to add, and click **OK**.

> **Note**   Web parts can have extensions of .htm, .html, .xml, .js, .vbs or .dwp.

Types of Web Parts

Web Parts can contain embedded content, which includes HTML, scripts, Microsoft® ActiveX® controls, or Extensible Markup Language (XML), or they can contain links pointing to any type of Web-based content in any location.

The type of Web Part you build depends on the Web Part's purpose and the location and amount of content the Web Part will display. For example, if you are creating a Web Part that displays static content, such as a greeting, then you can embed the content in the Web Part itself. If you are creating a Web Part that pulls content from another source, such as your Web server, a database, or the Internet, then you can add a link that points to the source of the content.

Web Parts with Embedded Content

To create a Web Part that contains embedded content, you use the Content property in the Web Part schema.

In the Microsoft® Office XP Developer dashboard project, you can edit your Web Parts in the Code editor.

To edit your Web Parts in the Code editor

1. In the **Solution Explorer**, select the Web Part.

2. Double-click the Web Part to open the **Code editor**.

Web Parts with Linked Content

When you create a Web Part with linked content, you use the ContentLink property to add a link that points to any type of Web content. Types of content include HTML, Microsoft® Visual Basic® Scripting Edition (VBScript), Microsoft® JScript®, or Extensible Markup Language (XML). To make it possible for the dashboard factory to interpret linked content correctly, you should use the ContentType property in conjunction with ContentLink.

By default, content from ContentLink is read directly into the page and included in the dashboard's document object model. In most cases, however, you might want the Web Part to provide a window around the Web page to which you are linking. If so, set the RequiresIsolation property to TRUE to place the Web Part in an IFrame. For additional information about RequiresIsolation, see Guidelines for Building Good Web Parts.

Web Parts with XML Content

To create a Web Part that contains Extensible Markup Language (XML) content, you can use one of four pairs of properties.

Properties	Description
ContentLink and XSL	The ContentLink property contains a URL that points to an XML document. The XSL property contains an embedded style sheet the dashboard factory uses to transform the XML into HTML.
ContentLink and XSLLink	The ContentLink property contains a URL that points to an XML document. The XSLLink property contains a URL pointing to a style sheet that the dashboard factory uses to transform the XML content into HTML.
Content and XSL	The Content property contains embedded XML content. The XSL property contains an embedded style sheet the dashboard factory uses to transform the XML to HTML.
Content and XSLLink	The Content property contains embedded XML content. The XSLLink property contains a URL pointing to a style sheet that the dashboard factory uses to transform the XML to HTML.

XML and XSL Encoding Limitations

The following are a few XML and XSL encoding limitations that exist for the Digital Dashboard.

- Be sure to set the value of the ContentType property to 3, or XML, if your Web Part retrieves XML content through a URL in the ContentLink property. Otherwise, the dashboard factory will not render the XML correctly. If you use the ContentLink property but do not define the ContentType property correctly, the dashboard will temporarily convert that content into a string, causing an XSL error when transforming XML that does not use UTF-16 encoding.

- You cannot specify an encoding type for Web Parts that store an XSL link in the XSL property, because the dashboard factory passes the XSL through a string.

Guidelines for Building Good Web Parts

Good Web Parts deliver targeted information tailored to specific users in a manner that is appropriate for a Digital Dashboard. The look and feel of your Web Parts should be appealing to users and appropriate for a Digital Dashboard. The functionality of a Web Part should not interfere with other Web Parts on a dashboard. Isolating your Web Parts and using token replacement for all scripts and variables makes sure your Web Parts will run on a dashboard without causing naming and script collisions.

Informative and Customizable Web Parts

The purpose of a Digital Dashboard is to help reduce information overload by delivering tailored information to users in a manner they can assimilate easily. While it might be tempting to create complex Web Parts that deliver large amounts of constantly changing information, Web Parts such as these might not serve their purpose. Above all, a good Web Part must display information in a manner appropriate to a Digital Dashboard.

Before you begin building Web Parts, think about the requirements of your users. Often, the best Web Parts are ones that users can customize. For example, a Web Part that shows the contents of a Microsoft® Outlook® folder must display a view that each user can customize using the Outlook View control, or a Web Part that displays a stock ticker must be customizable, so it shows only the stocks each user selects.

Customizable Web Parts have three requirements: a way for the user to provide customization information, a location for storing that information, and a method of retrieving it. To provide an interface that makes it possible for users to customize a Web Part, you use the CustomizationLink property in the Web Part schema. You can store customization information on the client, on the server, or in the Web Part itself using the PartStorage property.

The CustomizationLink Property

When specified, the CustomizationLink property contains a URL for a page that makes it possible for users to customize the content of the Web Part. You can do this inline in the Web Part's content, or you can supply a URL in CustomizationLink. For example, the dashboard might place a small Edit button on the right side of the Web Part's title bar. When the user clicks the button, the view navigates to this URL, making it possible for the user to customize the content of the Web Part. Note that this is likely a per-user customization of content and does not affect the properties of the Web Part item in the Exchange Web store. In your customization pages, you often want to provide a Submit button that applies the user's changes and takes the user back to the dashboard. You can offer this by using Microsoft® Visual Basic® Scripting Edition (VBScript) to back up one page (window.history.back method).

This URL can point to anywhere, but it typically points to the site that is supplying the content for the Web Part. In addition, it can point to another Web Part or even the same Web Part, passing a parameter indicating customization.

The PartStorage Property

The best place to store customization information related to a Web Part is in the PartStorage property, which you can access through the Digital Dashboard Services Component. For more information about the Digital Dashboard Services Component, see the Digital Dashboard Services Component reference documentation.

In the following example, the script in an HTML Web Part tracks the user's name and address, so it can be retrieved the next time the users accesses the dashboard. The dashboard stores these values in custom properties using the State Management service of the Digital Dashboard Services Component. The Web Part specifies the namespace and name for each property, in addition to the value for each property. Later, the Web Part can retrieve this state information through the Properties collection.

The following is the content of the Web Part. Note that the Web Part uses the string 'This_WPQ_Part' to reference itself. For more information on the string '_WPQ_Part', see the "Part Discovery Service" section of the Digital Dashboard Services Component reference documentation.

```
<TABLE border=0 cellPadding=1 cellSpacing=1 style="HEIGHT: 228px; WIDTH:
415px" width="75%">
  <TR>
    <TD>Name:</TD>
    <TD><INPUT id=txtName name=text1 style="HEIGHT: 22px; WIDTH:
278px"></TD></TR>

</TABLE>
</P>
<INPUT id=load type=button value="Remember Me" LANGUAGE=javascript
onclick="load_onclick();">
<INPUT id=save type=button value="Place Order" LANGUAGE=javascript
onclick="save_onclick();">
<SCRIPT LANGUAGE=javascript>
function save_onclick() {
this_WPQ_Part.Properties ("urn:Custinfo#CustName", txtName.value, 0);
this_WPQ_Part.Properties ("urn:Custinfo#CustName ", txtAddress1.value,
0);
this_WPQ_Part.Properties ("urn:Custinfo#Address2", txtAddress2.value, 0);
this_WPQ_Part.Properties ("urn:Custinfo#City", txtCity.value, 0);
this_WPQ_Part.Properties ("urn:Custinfo#State", txtState.value, 0);
this_WPQ_Part.Properties ("urn:Custinfo#Zip", txtZip.value,
0);this_WPQ_Part.Save()
}
function load_onclick() {
txtName.value = this_WPQ_Part.Properties("CustName");
txtAddress1.value = this_WPQ_Part.Properties ("urn:Custinfo#Address1");
txtAddress2.value = this_WPQ_Part.Properties ("urn:Custinfo#Address2");
txtCity.value = this_WPQ_Part.Properties ("urn:Custinfo#City");
```

```
txtState.value = this_WPQ_Part.Properties ("urn:Custinfo#State");
txtZip.value = this_WPQ_Part.Properties ("urn:Custinfo#Zip");
}
</SCRIPT>
```

Cookies

When you create a customizable Web Part, the customization generally takes place inline in the dashboard. However, you also must make sure that other pages are supported.

For example, a Web Part that shows the contents of a Microsoft® Outlook® folder using the Outlook View control must be capable of showing the contents of any folder that the user chooses at run time. To do this, the Web Part must have information about which folder to display and possibly the name of a stored view to use. You can provide this type of functionality using client-side cookies.

The Web Part displays a user interface that makes it possible for a user to change the current folder or view. When the user changes the view, the Web Part uses client-side script to write a cookie containing the configuration information. When the user refreshes the dashboard or returns to it in another session, the Web Part uses the client-side script to read the cookie value and reapply the configuration information.

You can access cookies through the document object model (DOM). The code for this is document.cookie.

Although writing client-side cookies is the easiest way to store and retrieve user settings, these setting are confined to the client computer. A user cannot log onto another computer in the network and view the customized Web Part. If your Web Part includes embedded script that runs on the server, then that embedded script can access cookies passed by Microsoft® Internet Explorer through the Request.Cookies collection in Active Server Pages (ASP).

Cookies and Non-Isolated Content

Typical Web sites use cookies to identify the client between page requests. When a client accesses a page, the page drops a cookie associated with the site's domain that indicates the user has been validated. When the user requests another page from that domain, Microsoft® Internet Explorer passes the cookie value in the HTTP headers and the server then can determine which user is making the request.

A Digital Dashboard presents a new twist on this, because if a Web Part is not isolated, the request for content comes from the dashboard server and not the client computer.

For example, say you create a Web Part that displays the MSN home page (http://www.msn.com/). Users must be able to customize the page, and Internet Explorer must be able to determine the identity of the client. To accomplish this, the following process occurs:

1. The process begins when the client requests a dashboard for the first time. Internet Explorer sends a URL Get request to the server hosting the dashboard Active Server Pages (ASP). The dashboard ASP receives no cookies from Internet Explorer, because no cookies have been dropped that are associated with the domain of the dashboard ASP.

2. The dashboard factory renders Web Parts, one of which contains a **ContentLink** URL pointing to the MSN home page. The dashboard factory requests this URL, but because there are no cookies to forward, it does not send any cookies with the request.

3. Because the dashboard factory has not passed any cookies in the request, the MSN site returns a generic version of the home page to the dashboard factory.

4. To customize the Web Part, the user clicks the **Customize** button in the title bar of the Web Part. The hyperlink associated with this button points to the URL specified in the **CustomizationLink** property, but the dashboard factory also adds two query string parameters—ReturnURL and PartNamespace. ReturnURL is set to the dashboard.asp (the URL of the dashboard), and PartNamespace is set to the value in the **Namespace** property of the Web Part. The dashboard factory appends these to any existing query string parameters defined in **CustomizationLink** or adds a query string if no other query string parameters are defined.

   Note If the results of the **ContentLink** URL query is a login screen, that page will not have the correct information for the ReturnURL and PartNamespace parameters. To correct this, the dashboard factory uses a simple case insensitive string replace operation to search for two tokens—_OfficeDashReturnURL_ and _OfficeDashPartNamespace_— and to replace them with the appropriate values. For example, a Web site that supplies a login screen might return the following HTML:

```
<form
action="http://www.SomeService.com/login.asp?ReturnURL=_OfficeDashRetu
rnURL_&Partnamespace=_OfficeDashPartNamespace_"  method="POST">
<!-- Login form UI -->
</form>
```

5. After the user customizes the MSN home page, the site performs an HTTP redirect (Response.Redirect in ASP) back to the return URL. The site also includes three query string parameters in the redirection response: Partnamespace, UserTicket, and Expires.

   • Partnamespace can contain the same value passed to the site, or the site might modify it. This will be used to qualify the cookie name that the dashboard will eventually drop on the client computer and will be used to determine when to forward the cookie back to the site in future content requests.

   • UserTicket is an opaque string value, which contains any value the site adds. The dashboard factory does not use it. This value will be passed back to the site as the cookie value in future content requests making it possible for the site to determine the identity of the client.

   • Expires is a string specifying the cookie expiration date, and this is in the same format you use when specifying a cookie expiration date in ASP or client-side script, for example

"December 31, 2001." If this parameter is not included, the dashboard factory does not give the cookie an expiration value, which means the cookie will be deleted when the user closes the browser.

6.   When the client browser receives the redirect, it requests the redirect URL, which contains the query string parameters mentioned previously. The dashboard factory now receives these parameters.

What happens next will depend on whether the factory page itself is the return URL, or if the factory delegates this to another specialized page. If it is the former, the factory will go through its rendering processing first, but it will make sure to forward the UserTicket cookie back to any ContentLink that has the same namespace value as the PartNamespace return parameter. In addition, it will include a new cookie in the returned page. The cookie's name will be <PartNamespace>:UserTicket, and its value will be the value returned in the UserTicket parameter.

If the factory uses a specialized page to handle the ReturnURL, that page first returns the cookie described previously and then redirects back to the main dashboard ASP.

1.   Because the Web site has returned the UserTicket cookie value, the dashboard can forward this cookie value when requesting the URL in **ContentLink**. The algorithm for this is as follows:

- When requesting a ContentLink URL

- If any cookies exist whose name starts with Currentwebpart.Namespace

- Forward the cookie in the HTTP_COOKIE header under the name "UserTicket"

  Note   The cookie name the site receives is just UserTicket without the namespace. This makes it easier to locate.

2.   The MSN site retrieves the UserTicket cookie and any other cookies that the Web Part's client-side script might have dropped under the same namespace. The MSN site uses this ticket value to look up the user's personal settings and information and to generate specific content for that user.

Internet Explorer receives the cookie and stores it for future requests.

Web Parts that Maintain a Consistent Look and Feel

A good Web Part must have a look and feel that is consistent with other Web Parts on the dashboard. The dashboard defines a set of style classes that Web Parts inherit to make sure they render with a similar look and feel. The dashboard itself also uses these styles. Do not use linked or embedded style sheets that contain these styles, because they can overwrite the style of the entire dashboard. The following table describes the style classes that the dashboard defines.

Style Class	Description
BODY	Specifies default text formatting and any other global styles
P	Default text formatting
H1, H2, H3, H4, H5, H6	Headings within a Web Part
TH	Table header cells
TH.Filled	Table header cells filled with a background color
TD	Table cells within a Web Part
TD.Filled	Table cells filled with a background color
a:link	Hyperlink
a:hover	Hyperlink when mouse is over it
a:active	Hyperlink when it has been activated
a:visited	Visited hyperlink
LI	List items
INPUT	Input controls
TEXTAREA	Text areas
SELECT	Select (drop-down list) controls
OPTION	Options within a select
B, STRONG	Bold text
I, EM	Italic text
U	Underline text

The Isolation of Web Parts from Other Web Parts

Because the Web Parts you build are included in the Document Object Model of the Digital Dashboard along with other Web Parts, there is a high possibility of script collisions. Anytime you create a Web Part that contains client-side script, you must isolate that Web Part from the other Web Parts on the page. Any of the following cause an error in the dashboard:

- Functions that have the same name in multiple Web Parts
- Objects that have the same names in multiple Web Parts
- Variables that have the same name in multiple Web Parts

When you isolate a Web Part, script functions and event sinks in that Web Part run as though they are the only scripts on the page—function names do not conflict with function names in other Web Parts, and event sinks do not conflict with other event sinks on the page. In addition, HTML IDs in the isolated Web Part do not conflict with HTML IDs in other Web Parts on the dashboard, and any ID referenced in a script uniquely identifies an element in the content of that Web Part.

If you are building a Web Part that will not be isolated, that Web Part's module-level variables and procedures will be part of the same page as the dashboard's variables and procedures. The variables and procedures the dashboard uses have a ddv_ prefix to reduce the likelihood of duplicate variable or procedure names, but it is a good idea to prefix your variables and procedures with the replacement token "_WPQ_" to avoid name collisions with other non-isolated Web Parts. Do not include <HTML>, <HEAD>, or <BODY> tags in your source code, because your code will be inserted into a page that already contains these tags. It is good practice to wrap your code inside procedures whenever possible and limit variable declarations to the procedural level. This eliminates unnecessary variables and reduces the potential for namespace collisions.

The Isolation of Web Parts into Frames

To fully isolate a Web Part from the other Web Parts on a dashboard, use the **RequiresIsolation** property. This places the Web Part in an **IFrame**. When you use **RequiresIsolation**, the request for the content comes from the client computer (instead of the server), so the Web Part can pass cookies and prompt for basic authentication. The request for content for an isolated Web Part occurs asynchronously from the rest of the Web Parts on the page. This can be useful for Web Parts with linked content that loads slowly. The downside of using **RequiresIsolation** is that it makes the Digital Dashboard Services Component inaccessible because of security considerations.

String Replacements that Avoid Name Collisions

If you do not want to isolate a particular Web Part but are concerned about name collisions with HTML elements or scripting functions on the dashboard, you can use the Digital Dashboard Globally Unique Identifier (GUID) service to make sure the function names and HTML IDs in your Web Part are unique.

To use the service, add the prefix "_WPQ_" to the HTML IDs and function names in your Web Part. The dashboard then performs a string search-and-replace function, converting the string to the ID of the Web Part, which makes the HTML IDs and function names for your Web Part unique within the assembled page.

Token Replacements

To make it easier for Web Parts to function in a variety of environments, dashboard factories perform token replacements.

> **Note** Tokens are case-insensitive—you can use any combination of upper- and lower-case characters.

Token	Properties	Replacement
WPID	Content, ContentLink, CustomizationLink, DetailLink	Unique ID of this Web Part instance. Format can vary between data stores.
WPQ	Content	Unique ID of this Web Part instance with respect to other Web Parts in the same dashboard. This can be used to qualify HTML IDs and script function names to avoid name collision. Does not vary between data stores.
DashboardID	Content, ContentLink, CustomizationLink, DetailLink	Unique ID of this dashboard.
LogonUser	Content, ContentLink, MasterPartLink	Value retrieved from ASP function Request.ServerVariables("LOGON_USER"). This value typically contains the client's Microsoft® Windows® 2000 user name (for example, adventureworks\kimy). It can be used for user identification within an intranet. This makes it possible for a URL in ContentLink that points to an intranet site to identify the client without having to be set up to delegate Windows 2000 credentials.

Portable Web Parts

To be truly reusable, a Web Part must be able to be used in any Digital Dashboard. This means that Web Parts should not be dependent on other Web Parts, network connectivity, or computer configurations. To guarantee portability, follow these rules:

- **Do not create Web Parts that use the DOM of a specific dashboard.** Dashboard implementations can vary, and if you tie a Web Part to the document object model (DOM) of a particular Digital Dashboard, that Web Part might not function properly when used in a different dashboard.

- **Do not create dependencies between Web Parts.** Because users can customize their dashboards by adding and removing Web Parts, creating a Web Part whose functionality is tied to another Web Part on the dashboard is not a good practice. Your Web Part will not function properly if a user removes the Web Part on which it depends. Use the Digital Dashboard Services Component for communication between Web Parts. By using the discovery and notification functionality of the Digital Dashboard Services Component, Web Parts can interact without being dependent on one another. In addition, the Digital Dashboard Services Component makes it possible for you to capture Microsoft® Internet Explorer events without causing collisions.

- **Use common schemas for communication between Web Parts.** The most powerful element of the Digital Dashboard is that any Web Part can communicate with any other Web Part provided they use a common language to share collaborative data. For example, a Contacts Web Part can share information with a Phone Book Web Part. However, if Contacts sends out the name Smith, John and the corresponding entry in Phone Book is John Smith, the user will not get the right phone number. You can solve this problem by using common schemas. Microsoft® Exchange 2000 Server defines a number of common schemas for collaborative data, such as contacts, tasks, mail, and calendar items that are excellent for sharing these types of data.

- **Define Content.** If the dashboard cannot access ContentLink for some reason, it will try to display Content. If you define the ContentLink, you can present the user with a useful message or alternative content if the ContentLink you specified does not exist or is unavailable.

How a Digital Dashboard Factory Interprets Web Parts

A Digital Dashboard factory initializes Web Parts, gets content, and displays the content on the dashboard.

The initialization process begins when a user requests a dashboard.

The dashboard factory first checks the AutoUpdate property (from the Dashboard schema) for a value. If AutoUpdate contains a value of 1, or always, the dashboard factory checks for a value in the MasterPartLink property. If that property contains a value, the dashboard factory uses that value to get the master Web Part.

Note   If this operation fails, the dashboard factory uses the last found version of the master Web Part.

If MasterPartLink does not contain a value, the dashboard factory uses the current instance of the Web Part.

Next, the dashboard factory checks to determine whether the nonuser–specific properties of the Web Part differ from those of the master Web Part. If the properties differ, the dashboard factory updates the nonuser–specific properties to match those of the master Web Part.

After the initialization process is complete, the dashboard factory gets the content for the Web Part and renders it to the dashboard.

To render the dashboard

1. The dashboard factory checks to determine whether the **RequiresIsolation** property contains a value of TRUE. If so, the dashboard factory renders the isolated Web Part.

2. If the value in **RequiresIsolation** is FALSE, the dashboard factory checks for a value in the **ContentLink** property. If this property is defined, the dashboard factory receives content from the link. If **ContentLink** is not defined, the dashboard factory receives embedded content from the **Content** property.

3. Next, the dashboard factory checks the value in the **ContentType** property to determine whether the content runs on the server. If it does, the dashboard factory executes the content as script.

   Note If this operation fails, the Web Part displays a standard error message.

4. After checking for a value in **ContentType**, the dashboard factory checks for a value in the **XSLLink** property. If **XSLLink** contains a value, the dashboard factory gets the XSL from the link. If that property does not contain a value (or if the operation fails), the dashboard factory checks for a value in the **XSL** property.

5. The dashboard factory transforms XML content to HTML.

6. The dashboard factory performs the necessary token string replacements and displays the content of the Web Part in the dashboard.

Debugging and Error Handling

All code contains errors of one kind or another, and how you deal with errors might be the most important part of a well-designed application. There are two categories of errors: those you can prevent, which are called development errors, and those you cannot prevent but can trap, which are called run-time errors.

Development errors are either syntax errors or logic errors. Syntax errors occur from typographical errors, missing punctuation, or improper use of a language element—for example, forgetting to properly terminate an If…Then…Else statement. Logic errors are more commonly referred to as "bugs." These errors occur when code executes without causing an error but does not produce the results intended. You eliminate development errors by "debugging" your code. Many tools exist that can help you debug script and Microsoft® Visual Basic® for Applications (VBA) code.

Run-time errors are errors that occur while the application is running. These are errors where otherwise correct code fails because of invalid data or system conditions that prevent the code from executing (for example, lack of available memory or disk space). You handle run-time errors by writing error handlers and by writing procedures that can validate program or environmental conditions in appropriate circumstances.

Successfully debugging code is more of an art than a science. The best results come from writing understandable, maintainable code and using the available debugging tools. When it comes to successful debugging, there is no substitute for patience, diligence, and a willingness to test relentlessly, using all the tools at your disposal.

Writing good error handlers is a matter of anticipating problems or conditions that are beyond your immediate control and that will prevent your code from executing correctly at run time. Writing a good error handler should be an integral part of the planning and design of a good procedure. It requires a thorough understanding of how the procedure works and how the procedure fits into the overall application. And, of course, writing good procedures is an essential part of building solid Microsoft® Office XP applications.

In This Section

Writing Error-Free Code
> When you write Microsoft® Visual Basic® for Applications (VBA) code, or script in an HTML page, it is not a question of "if" the code will contain errors but "when" those errors will be introduced and how many there will be.

Debugging Code
> Microsoft® Visual Basic® for Applications (VBA) provides several debugging tools that help analyze how code operates and help locate errors in your code.

Handling Errors

When an error occurs in a procedure that does not have error handling enabled, Microsoft® Visual Basic® for Applications (VBA) responds by displaying an error message and terminating the application.

Writing Error-Free Code

When you write Microsoft® Visual Basic® for Applications (VBA) code, or script in an HTML page, it is not a question of "if" the code will contain errors but "when" those errors will be introduced and how many there will be. No matter how careful you are or how much experience you have, errors will occur. There are some things you can do to make sure errors are kept to a minimum.

The best way to reduce errors and minimize the amount of debugging you must do is to follow the guidelines discussed in Writing Solid Code. If you have written maintainable code, you also have written code that is going to be much easier to debug.

Make sure you use the Option Explicit statement in every module. The Option Explicit statement forces you to declare all variables before you use them in code. This simple step eliminates undeclared variables, which cause some of the most common, and often difficult to detect, errors in code. When you are writing Visual Basic Scripting Edition (VBScript) code, insert `Option Explicit` as the first line after the first <SCRIPT> tag on the HTML page.

Avoid using the Variant data type unless you are declaring a variable and you truly do not know what kind of data it might contain at run time. Variants are slow, they take up a lot of memory, and using them when not absolutely necessary can create hard-to-find bugs in your code.

Always declare variables as a group at the beginning of each procedure, and always declare each variable on a separate line. This will prevent you from inadvertently declaring a Variant variable. For example, the following line creates two Variant variables and one String variable, which is not what the developer intended:

```
Dim strFirstName, strLastName, strCompanyName As String
```

When you are creating VBA object variables, explicitly reference the object the variable represents rather than declaring the variable by using a Variant or Object data type. For example:

```
Dim xlSheet        As Excel.Worksheet
Dim cboUserNames   As ComboBox
```

When you are creating procedures that accept arguments that must fall within a specified range of data, validate the data before using it in the procedure. If an argument uses a value that represents a built-in enumerated constant, you will not have to validate the argument if you declare its data type by using the name of the enumerated constant class. If a procedure uses optional arguments, make sure that you supply the default value for each argument and make sure that the data supplied falls within the desired range. For example, the following procedure shows how to validate the data in an argument. If the data is invalid, the Raise method of the Err object is used to pass error information back to the calling procedure.

```
Function ErrorExample3(strTextToCheck As String) As Boolean

    ' This procedure illustrates using the Err.Raise method
    ' along with the vbObjectError constant to define and
    ' raise a custom error and return that error to the
    ' calling procedure. The CUSTOM_ERROR constant is defined
    ' in the Declarations section of the module by using the
    ' vbObjectError constant.

    Dim strTemp                  As String
    Const CUSTOM_ERR_DESC        As String = "The argument passed to " &
"ErrorExample3" _

                                 & " is invalid - a zero-length string is
not" _

                                 & " permitted."

    If Len(strTextToCheck) = 0 Then
        Err.Raise CUSTOM_ERROR, "ErrorExample3", CUSTOM_ERR_DESC
        ErrorExample3 = False
    Else
        ' Continue processing successful case here.
        ErrorExample3 = True
        strTextToCheck = "This procedure executed successfully!"
    End If
End Function
```

> **Note** When debugging, you can also use the Assert method of the Debug object to test the validity of the supplied data.

Test each procedure as soon as it is written to make sure that it does what it is supposed to do and, if necessary, validates data submitted in arguments. If your application uses data supplied by the user, make sure you test for unexpected input values. For example, if you expect a user to enter a numeric value in a text box control, what happens if the user enters text in that control instead?

Make sure you know that your code actually works. When an error occurs in a procedure, you know that your code does not work given the input data that caused the error. But it does not follow that if an error does not occur, you are safe to assume that your code does work. While debugging your code, use assertions to test for conditions that should exist at specific points in your code. For example, you can use assertions to test the validity of inputs to procedures.

When you locate a problem in your code, make sure you understand its nature and extent (errors in code are not always what they appear to be) and then fix it immediately. Avoid flagging errors or questionable code with the intent of coming back and fixing them later. You might never get back to it and what must be done will never be clearer in your mind than when you are creating the procedure.

When you do make a change to your code, use a comment to document the change. Consider commenting out old code but leaving it in a procedure until you are certain the new code works correctly.

Be aware that changing code in one place can introduce additional bugs somewhere else. When debugging code, never make more than one change to a procedure without retesting it and all related procedures after each change.

Debugging Code

Microsoft® Visual Basic® for Applications (VBA) provides several debugging tools that help analyze how code operates and help locate errors in your code. There is no magic to properly debugging your code and no correct series of steps that always leads to the discovery of errors. Instead, there are some very powerful tools that let you closely examine what is happening in your code so that you can figure out where and when things are going wrong.

You might want to know exactly where an error occurs in a series of nested procedure calls or when a variable is being changed from one value to another. The tool that works best will depend on what you are trying to accomplish.

For more information about debugging VBA code in general, search the Visual Basic for Applications Reference Help index for "debugging" and "debugging code."

In This Section

VBA Debugging Tools
   Microsoft® Visual Basic® for Applications (VBA) and the Visual Basic Editor contain many tools you can use to help debug your code.

Script Debugging Tools
   The Microsoft Script Debugger provides a comprehensive debugging environment for working with both client- and server-side script in HTML pages and Active Server Pages (ASP).

Additional Debugging Techniques
   These techniques in conjunction with the debugging tools give you an even more powerful arsenal for finding and fixing errors in your code.

VBA Debugging Tools

Microsoft® Visual Basic® for Applications (VBA) and the Visual Basic Editor contain many tools you can use to help debug your code. Some of the tools are available when you are actually writing your code; these are known as design-time tools. Other tools are used when your code is running; these are known as run-time tools, and they let you break into, examine, and step through running code to determine what is happening. Experienced Office developers use all of these tools at one time or another in the development process.

For more information about any of the specific debugging tools, search the Visual Basic for Applications Reference Help index for the name of the tool.

Design-Time Tools

The Visual Basic Editor has several features that can help you debug your code. You specify whether these features are turned on by clicking Options on the Tools menu, clicking the Editor tab, and then selecting the features you want under Code Settings. Turning on all these settings can make it easier to debug code. The Require Variable Declaration option is probably the most important because, when it is selected, the Option Explicit statement is inserted in the first line of any module you create, including those for forms, reports, and Microsoft® Office documents. The Option Explicit statement forces you to declare every variable you use and prevents one of the most common sources of hard-to-find bugs: misspelled variable names.

The Auto Syntax Check option specifies whether the Visual Basic Editor will check each line of code for errors as soon as you have finished writing the code. If this option is not selected, the Visual Basic Editor still will check the syntax of all your code before you can compile or run it.

The Auto Data Tips option specifies whether you can view the data contained in a variable while in break mode by resting the mouse pointer on the variable name.

The Options dialog box contains another important set of options that can make debugging easier. On the General tab, there is an Error Trapping section where you can specify what will happen when an error occurs in your code.

You will want to select different options in the Error Trapping section depending on where you are in the debugging process. The default setting is Break on Unhandled Errors. This setting makes it easier to debug error handlers because you can step through the code as it enters the error handler in all circumstances.

Generally, you will want to select the Break on Unhandled Errors option. However, when you are debugging code in class modules, you will want to select the Break in Class Module option so that you can identify the offending line of code in the class module. Otherwise, an error in a class module will cause code to break in the procedure that called the class module rather than in the class module itself. If your application has no class modules, selecting Break in Class Module has the same effect as selecting Break on Unhandled Errors.

For more information about the options available in the Options dialog box, click the tab that contains the option you are interested in, and then click the Help button.

Viewing Code after Errors in Microsoft Access

In previous versions of Microsoft® Access, you could prevent users from entering break mode when errors occurred by clearing the Allow Viewing Code After Error check box in the Startup dialog box (Tools menu). This setting did not actually secure code modules, but the option to view code was disabled when errors were encountered so that code could not be viewed easily. Because of changes in how Microsoft® Visual Basic® for Applications (VBA) is integrated into Access, the option to view code when errors are encountered is no longer available. However, you can prevent all unauthorized users from viewing your code under any circumstances by locking your application's VBA project.

Run-Time Tools

The Microsoft® Visual Basic® for Applications (VBA) run-time debugging tools are designed to give you a snapshot of what is happening in your code at any point. You use these tools together to let you take a closer look at what your code is doing at any point in time. The following table contains a list of all the tools available to you and a short description of when they are useful.

Tool	Description
Breakpoints	Breakpoints let you stop program execution on any line of executable code. When execution has stopped, you can use one or more of the other available tools to investigate your code. A breakpoint will stop your code on the line of code that will be executed next. When your code encounters a breakpoint, it is in break mode and remains in break mode until you press F5 to continue execution.
Step modes	You can use the four step modes to start execution of a subroutine or to continue execution after it has stopped at a breakpoint. The four available modes are Step Into, Step Over, Step Out, and Run To Cursor. Using any of these modes to step through code does not take the code out of break mode.
Watch expressions	Watch expressions let you monitor the value of any variable, property, object, or expression as your code executes. They also let you specify that your code should enter break mode upon some condition; for example, if an expression is true or if the value of a variable changes. If you do not have to continually monitor a value, you can use the Quick Watch dialog box to quickly check the value of a variable or expression.
Immediate window	This window is an extremely versatile tool that you should be using constantly to debug and test your code. All Debug.Print statements are output to the Immediate window. When your code is in break mode, the Immediate window has the same scope as the procedure in which the breakpoint is located. This makes it possible for you to test and change the value of variables. In addition, you can use the Immediate window to call procedures and test them by using different data without having to run your application from the beginning.
Locals window	This extremely powerful and often overlooked tool provides a snapshot view of the values of all variables, constants, objects, and properties of objects currently in scope when code is in break mode.

Tool	Description
Call stack	This stack contains a list of all active procedures when code is in break mode. This list can help you trace the execution of your code and highlight the possible location of errors in currently active procedures.

For more information about any of the debugging tools, search the Visual Basic for Applications Reference Help index for the name of the specific tool.

Script Debugging Tools

The Microsoft Script Debugger provides a comprehensive debugging environment for working with both client- and server-side script in HTML pages and Active Server Pages (ASP). The Script Debugger works with Microsoft® Visual Basic® Scripting Edition (VBScript) and Microsoft® JScript®. It provides all of the run-time debugging tools provided by VBA, with the exception of watch expressions. However, you cannot use the Print method of the Debug object to output information to the Script Debugger's Immediate window.

The Microsoft Script Debugger and its supporting documentation are available from the Microsoft Scripting Technologies Web site at http://msdn.microsoft.com/scripting/.

You can debug the script you add to a Microsoft® Office document by using the debugging capabilities of the Microsoft Script Editor.

To enable script debugging in the Script Editor, click Options on the Tools menu, and then click Debugger in the hierarchical view of options. Select the Just-In-Time debugger and Attach to programs running on this machine check boxes. When these options have been selected, errors in script will generate a message box that gives you the option of opening the Script Editor's debugger.

You can use the Script Editor to set breakpoints in your script. These breakpoints work just as they do when you are debugging VBA code in the Visual Basic Editor. The Script Editor also has the following debugging windows that you can use to work with script: Immediate, Locals, Watch, Threads, and Call Stack. These windows give you views into your running script in the same way that they let you debug VBA code when they are used in the Visual Basic Editor. There is one difference you must be aware of however. In the Script Editor, the script debugger is not as tightly integrated with the host application as the VBA debugger is in Office applications. This means that the Immediate and Watch windows in the Script Editor are not active unless your script is stopped at a breakpoint. In other words, you cannot set up a Watch variable in the Script Editor and watch its value change as your script executes.

You should remember to close the script debugger each time you are finished debugging or each time you return to running your script. This is because each time you open the debugger, a new instance of the Script Editor is created. If you do not close these instances, you can end up with several open windows on your desktop. To avoid opening and closing the script debugger, you can create a debug log file to record errors that occur on a page while a script is running. You can also open a separate window to display the logged error information.

Additional Debugging Techniques

The techniques discussed here can be used in conjunction with the tools discussed in the previous sections to give you an even more powerful arsenal for finding and fixing errors in your code.

Understanding Conditional Compilation

You can use conditional compilation to selectively include blocks of debugging code by testing for the value of a conditional compilation constant. If the constant is True, the debugging code is included. To do this, you specify a conditional compilation constant by using the #Const directive. You then test for the value of this constant within a procedure by using the #If...Then...#Else directive within a procedure. For example, the following procedure uses the value of the FLAG_DEBUG conditional compilation constant to determine if the conditional constant is set to True. If the constant is set to True, the Assert method of the Debug object is used to test the validity of the procedure's input parameters. For example:

```
Sub OutputString(strMessage As String, _
                Optional intOutputType As Integer = 0)

   Dim intFileNum As Integer

   #If FLAG_DEBUG = True Then
      ' Test validity of strMessage.
      Debug.Assert Len(strMessage) > 0

      ' Test validity of intOutputType.
      Debug.Assert intOutputType >= 0 and intOutputType <= 3
      Stop
   #End If

   Select Case intOutputType
      Case 0
      .

      .

      .

End Sub
```

Using conditional compilation is really a shortcut for commenting out entire blocks of code depending on a global setting. Without the ability to use the constant as a flag to direct program flow, you would have to litter your code with commented-out calls to alternative procedures. If you always use conditional compilation constants to test alternative procedures, then you have an easy way to turn on and off calls to the designated procedures and an easy way to find the code that you ultimately decide to remove. The cost of using this technique is that you must give a great deal of thought to how your code is constructed and called. Although this might mean a little more work, it results in manageable, maintainable, and reusable code.

Using Assertions

It is easy to tell when code is broken because an error occurs. It is often harder to tell that your code is using or creating invalid data. Just because a procedure runs without generating an error does not mean that there are no bugs in that procedure.

You use assertions to test for certain conditions in your code. Using an assertion is similar to making a statement about some condition in your code. If the statement is true, nothing happens. If the statement is false, your code enters break mode with the line containing the false statement highlighted. Using assertions to test the validity of expressions or variables in your code is similar to adding custom rules to Microsoft® Visual Basic® for Applications (VBA) itself that will cause the code to stop executing if one of the rules is violated.

The VBA Debug object has an Assert method that you can use to test the truth of a condition or statement in your code. Using the Assert method is similar to setting a watch expression that will break when some statement is true. If you are using the Assert method, the break will occur when the statement asserted is false.

Although the Assert method is a valuable tool for debugging and testing your code, it is not very useful in a distributed application because it forces execution to stop when an assertion is false. Eventually you will remove the Debug.Assert statements and replace them with error handlers. After your code has been debugged and thoroughly tested, you can remove the assertions by searching your project for Debug.Assert and deleting those lines from your final code.

Creating Custom Assertions

In some circumstances, you might not want to break into your code each time an assertion fails. For example, you might want to log assertion information to a file and use an error handler to handle any errors that result from the bad data. With a little bit of planning, you can create code to use while debugging that will let you handle assertions according to a flag you pass to a general routine. For example, the following procedure accepts arguments representing an assertion expression to test, the text of the assertion expression, the calling procedure's name, and a flag indicating how to display or log a failed assertion:

```
Function CustomAssertError(varExpression As Variant, _
                       strExpression As String, _
                       strCallingProc As String, _
                       Optional intOutputType As Integer = 0) As
Boolean
```

```vba
    Dim intFileNum        As Integer
    Dim strErrorMessage   As String
    Const DEBUG_LOGFILE   As String = "c:\CustomAssertLog.txt"

#If FLAG_DEBUG = True Then
    If varExpression = False Then
        strErrorMessage = "ASSERTION FAILURE! " & Now() & vbCrLf _
            & "The expression: " & vbCrLf & "'" & strExpression & "'" _
            & vbCrLf & "Called from: " & vbCrLf & "'" & strCallingProc _
            & "'" & vbCrLf & "failed!"

        Select Case intOutputType
            Case 0
                ' Display in message box.
                MsgBox strErrorMessage
            Case 1
                ' Write to Debug window.
                Debug.Print strErrorMessage
            Case 2
                ' Write to text file on disk.
                intFileNum = FreeFile
                Open DEBUG_LOGFILE For Append As #intFileNum
                Write #intFileNum, strErrorMessage
                Close #intFileNum
            Case Else
                Stop
        End Select
    End If
#End If
End Function
```

Handling Errors

When an error occurs in a procedure that does not have error handling enabled, Microsoft® Visual Basic® for Applications (VBA) responds by displaying an error message and terminating the application. While this behavior might be acceptable when you are writing and debugging code, it is never acceptable when your users are running your application.

A hallmark of the well-written application is its ability to anticipate and handle any error that might occur. In the best of cases, you have designed the error handler to anticipate the error and recover from it quickly and transparently to the user. No developer, no matter how diligent or experienced, will anticipate every error that can occur. In the worst case, the well-designed error handler will gracefully terminate the application and perhaps record information about the error to an error log.

You are not required to have an error handler in every procedure you write, and every error handler you write does not have to operate the same way. The key to effective error handling is knowing when to trap an error and what to do with it.

Whether you are handling errors in VBA or in script behind an HTML page, there are two basic tools you can use. One is the On Error statement, which you use to "enable" error handling in a procedure. The other is the Err object, which contains information about an error that has already occurred.

When a run-time error occurs, your error handler might be able to fix the error directly or give the user a chance to fix the error. If your error handler is unable to fix the error so that the code can continue to execute, it should make it possible for the program to fail gracefully.

When execution has passed to the error-handling routine, your code must determine which error has occurred and either fix the error or raise the error back to the calling procedure. If an error occurs within an error handler, VBA will handle the error (because error handling is no longer enabled), unless you call another procedure to handle such errors. You might consider writing a generic error-handling routine that can be used to handle errors generated within error handlers. VBA can have only one error handler active at a time in any procedure, but it can have more than one error handler active within the current procedure stack.

Basic Error Handling

Effective error-handling code can be quite simple or very sophisticated. It can create an error trap or handle errors in-line. It might display a message to the user or log information about the error to a file. But no matter how an error handler is implemented, the basic components of every error handler are the same. An error handler consists of code that does all of the following:

- Specifies what to do if an error occurs

- Handles the error that has occurred

- Specifies how program execution is to continue

The On Error statement is used to specify the first component. The Resume statement is used to specify the third component. The second component represents the code you write to handle any errors that occur.

The basic format for how an error trap is included in a procedure is as follows (the use of italics indicates the location of placeholders for elements you would specify in a real procedure):

```
Function ProcedureName(ArgumentList) As DataType
    ' Procedure comments.
    ' Declare local variables and constants.


    On Error GoTo ProcedureName_Err
    ' Procedure code.
    .

    ProcedureName = True (or some other return value)
ProcedureName_End:
    ' Cleanup code that closes open files and sets object variables =
Nothing.
    Exit Function
ProcedureName_Err:
    ProcedureName = False
    Select Case Err.Number
        Case AnticipatedError#1
            ' Handle error #1.
        Case AnticipatedError#2
            ' Handle error #2.
        Case UnAnticipatedErrors
            ' Handle unanticipated error.
        Case Else
            ' Handle unforseen circumstances.
    End Select
    Resume ProcedureName_End
End Function
```

Another common error-handling technique is to attempt an operation that you know will generate a specific error if some condition is not met. In this case you can use in-line error handling to attempt the operation and then test for the presence of the known error. For example, when you are using Automation to access the objects in another Office application, there are times when you will want to use an existing instance of the application. Only if there is no existing instance do you want to create a new instance. The following code fragment shows how to use in-line error handling to create a new instance of Microsoft® Excel only if there is no instance currently open:

```
On Error Resume Next
Set xlApp = GetObject(, "Excel.Application")
```

```
If Err = ERR_EXCEL_NOTRUNNING Then
    Set xlApp = CreateObject("Excel.Application")
End If
On Error GoTo ProcedureName_Err
```

Note that the On Error Resume Next statement is used to turn on in-line error handling. A test for the anticipated error comes immediately after the code that might cause the error. (In this example, a constant was created that contained the value of the anticipated error.) Finally, the procedure's regular error trap is re-enabled to handle any additional errors.

In some cases, you know an error might occur but you do not intend to handle it at all; instead, you plan to ignore it. For example, if your application tries to delete its custom command bar when it terminates, you will want to ignore errors that occur if the user has already deleted the command bar:

```
Private Sub Workbook_BeforeClose(Cancel As Boolean)
    ' Remove the custom command bar created when
    ' this application started. Ignore any error
    ' generated if it has already been deleted.


    On Error Resume Next


    CommandBars("CustomAppCmdbar").Delete
End Sub
```

Automating Error Handling

In an ideal world, all of the code that you write would run error-free. The reality is that, no matter how carefully you write your code, errors can and will occur. For that reason, it is a good idea to add error-handling routines to all of your procedures.

The VBA Error Handler add-in makes it easy to add error handlers to your procedures without typing in repetitive code. It inserts standardized error handling templates into your code; you simply fill in any procedure-specific code. You can choose to add error handlers to a single procedure, to all of the procedures within a module, or to all procedures in your project at once.

To add error handlers to your code

1. From the **Add-Ins** menu, select **VBA Error Handler**.

    Note The **VBA Error Handler** menu item is only available when the **VBA Error Handler** add-in is loaded.

2. Make a selection from the **Add Error Handlers To** group to determine whether error handlers will be added to the current procedure, all procedures in the current module, or all procedures in the current project.

3. Verify that the desired template is selected in the **Error Handling Template** box.

4. Type the name and initials for the **Author** if desired. With the default template, this information appears as part of the error handler. This information is stored in the registry for future use. If you do not enter information, the name and initials default to the registered user of the product.

5. Click **OK**.

The VBA Error Handler uses template files (.eht) to control the format of error handling blocks. You can edit the standard template (Errorhandler.eht) or create your own templates using Notepad or another text editor.

To update existing error handlers in your code

*   In the **VBA Error Handler** add-in, select the **Update existing error handlers** option.

When selected, this option updates all existing error handlers within the scope selected in the Add Error Handlers To group so they match the currently selected template.

> **Note**   If the Error Handler finds "On Error Goto <label>" within a procedure in existing code, no modifications are made to that code. If the Error Handler finds "On Error Goto <0>" or "On Error Resume Next" within a procedure, the code is modified to match the information specified in the template. The following comment is placed directly before the exiting On Error code:

```
' TODO: Turn normal error handler on when this condition is finished
```

Getting Information about an Error

You cannot handle an error until you know something about it. Where you get information about an error depends on what caused it. The two main sources of information about errors are the VBA Err object and the Microsoft® ActiveX® Data Objects (ADO) Error object. The VBA Err object provides information about VBA errors. The ADO Error Object and Errors Collection provide information about data-provider errors that occur when ADO objects are being used to access data. Errors that occur in ADO itself, as opposed to the data provider, are reported to The VBA Err Object.

The VBA Err Object

When an error occurs, Microsoft® Visual Basic® for Applications (VBA) uses the Err object to store information about that error. The Err object can only contain information about one error at a time. Each time an error occurs, any existing information in the Err object is replaced with information about the new error.

The properties of the Err object contain information such as the error number, description, and source. The Err object's Raise method is used to generate errors, and its Clear method is used to remove any existing error information.

For more information about the VBA Err object, search the Visual Basic for Applications Reference Help index for "Err object."

The ADO Error Object and Errors Collection

Any operation involving ADO objects can generate one or more errors from the data provider. Each error resulting from an ADO operation creates an Error object that is added to the Connection object's Errors collection. If another ADO operation generates one or more errors, the Errors collection is cleared, and a new set of Error objects is placed in the Errors collection.

When an ADO error occurs, the VBA Err object contains the error number for the first object in the Errors collection. The values of the Number and Description properties of the first Error object in the Errors collection should match the values of the Number and Description properties of the VBA Err object.

> **Note** If there is no valid Connection object, the VBA Err object is the only source for information about ADO errors. Some ADO methods can also generate warnings that are returned as members of the Errors collection but will not affect a program's execution.

For more information about the ADO Error object and Errors collection, search the ADO Help index for "Error object" and "Errors collection."

Returning Information about an Error

There are two ways of returning information about an error. The traditional Microsoft® Visual Basic® for Applications (VBA) style is to raise the error in a procedure, either by leaving out an error handler so that the VBA error is returned to the calling procedure or by using the Raise method of the Err object. The other way to return error information uses the Windows application programming interface (API) style, where an error value is assigned to one of the procedure's parameters.

If you use the API style of returning error information, the calling procedure must use in-line error handling to identify whether an error has occurred. If you use the traditional VBA style, the calling procedure can use either in-line error handling or an error handler. Neither way is inherently better than the other. The important point to remember is to adopt a style that works for you and to use it consistently.

Error Handling in Class Modules

You use class modules to create custom objects. When an error occurs in your class module, you do not want the error message to be raised in your class module, but rather you want to define a custom error and raise that error in the class module and send the error back to the calling procedure.

You can define custom errors by creating custom error numbers and assigning custom error descriptions. You then use the Raise method of the Err object to raise the custom error. You can use error numbers for your own errors in the range vbObjectError + 512 to vbObjectError + 65536.

You can assign custom error values and associated error descriptions by using module-level constants in your class module. Then, use those values when raising errors to be returned to the calling procedure.

In this example, a class module, clsMailMessage, defines a custom object used to add a simple mail-messaging component to any Office application. Constants are used to define custom error numbers and descriptions, as shown in the following example.

```
' Custom error constants:
Private Const CUSTOM_ERR_SOURCE        As String = "clsMailMessage Object"
Private Const CUSTOM_ERR_ERRNUMBASE    As Long = vbObjectError + 512


' Invalid MailType custom errors:
Private Const CUSTOM_ERR_INVALID_MAILTYPE _
    As Long = CUSTOM_ERR_ERRNUMBASE + 1
Private Const CUSTOM_ERR_INVALID_MAILTYPE_DESC _
    As String = "MailItem Type argument must be 1 (olTo), 2 (olCC), or 3
(olBCC)."


' Unable to initialize Outlook errors:
Private Const CUSTOM_ERR_OUTLOOKINIT_FAILED _
    As Long = CUSTOM_ERR_ERRNUMBASE + 2
Private Const CUSTOM_ERR_OUTLOOKINIT_FAILED_DESC _
    As String = "Could not initialize Microsoft Outlook."


' Unable to send mail errors:
Private Const CUSTOM_ERR_SENDMAIL_FAILED _
    As Long = CUSTOM_ERR_ERRNUMBASE + 3
Private Const CUSTOM_ERR_SENDMAIL_FAILED_DESC _
    As String = "Unable to send mail message."
```

Procedures within the class module use these values as arguments to the Raise method of the Err object to raise custom errors. For example, the following procedure raises a custom error if an invalid value is passed to the procedure in the *intType* argument:

```
Public Function MailAddRecipient(strName As String, _
                          Optional intType As Integer = olTo) As
Boolean
```

```
    ' This procedure adds a recipient name and MailItem object type
specifier
    ' to the p_strRecipients() array. This array is used in the CreateMail
    ' function to add recipients to the MailItem object's Recipients
collection.

    Static intToCntr As Integer

    ' Validate intType argument.
    If intType > 3 Or intType < 1 Then
        ' Raise error: Type argument must be olTo (or 1),
        ' olCC (or 2), or olBCC (or 3) only.
        Err.Raise Number:=CUSTOM_ERR_INVALID_MAILTYPE, _
            Source:=CUSTOM_ERR_SOURCE, _
            Description:=CUSTOM_ERR_INVALID_MAILTYPE_DESC
        MailAddRecipient = False
        Exit Function
    End If

    ReDim Preserve p_strRecipients(1, intToCntr)

    p_strRecipients(0, intToCntr) = strName
    p_strRecipients(1, intToCntr) = intType

    intToCntr = intToCntr + 1
End Function
```

Note   You cannot use the Raise method to return an error to the calling procedure if you have error handling turned on in the procedure where the error occurs. If error handling is on, you must use the Raise method again within the class module error handler.

Handling Script Errors

You have limited run-time error-handling options with script behind an HTML page, and the conditions that generate errors can differ depending on the scripting language you use. For example, in Microsoft® Visual Basic® Scripting Edition (VBScript), dividing by zero results in a run-time error. In Microsoft® JScript®, it does not.

In VBScript, you are limited to basic in-line error handling using the On Error Resume Next statement. You can suppress default error messages, but you cannot specify your own error-handling code to run when an error occurs. After you have trapped and handled an error, you use the Clear method of the Err object to clear out the error information.

In JScript, you can handle errors by using the window object's onerror event handler. The onerror event passes three arguments to the specified error-handling function: the error message itself, the URL representing the source of the error, and a number representing the line where the error occurred.

There are also special circumstances you should keep in mind when writing script and script-error handlers.

Script in an HTML page is not interpreted until the script is executed, which occurs at the earliest when an HTML page is loaded. This means that the language interpreter will not catch any syntax errors until the page is actually loaded.

Subtle logic errors can result from the required use of Variant variables with different data subtypes. For example, the statement "10" = 10 evaluates to True.

Script in the <HEAD> portion of the page is interpreted before script in the <BODY> portion of the page. A run-time error can occur if script in the <HEAD> portion of a page references elements within the <BODY> portion of a page and the script executes before the page is completely loaded.

Web pages consist of a number of different components that might be downloaded at different times. Because of this, you cannot always be sure that an element of your page referenced in script is going to be available when the script executes. For example, if you use framesets, objects, images, linked style sheets, applets, or plug-ins, you must verify that the component is available before performing operations that depend on the component.

Handling VBScript Run-Time Errors

Although Microsoft® Visual Basic® Scripting Edition (VBScript) provides the Err object, and that object exposes the same methods and properties available in the VBA Err object, writing error handlers using VBScript is not the same as in Visual Basic for Applications (VBA). The primary limitation is due to the limited functionality of the On Error statement in VBScript. In VBScript, you cannot branch to an error handler by using the familiar On Error GoTo ErrorHandler syntax. You can only enable error handling in VBScript by using the On Error Resume Next syntax.

The following code excerpt shows the error-handler portion of a script. The script performs simple division and then immediately checks to see if an error occurred and responds accordingly:

```
intResult = intNumerator/intDenominator


' Check for errors as a result of the division.
```

```
If Err <> 0 Then
    Select Case Err.Number
        Case DIVIDE_BY_ZERO
            If Len(txtDenominator.Value) = 0 Then
                strErrorResultText = "Missing!"
            Else
                strErrorResultText = "'" & txtDenominator.Value & "'"
            End If
            strErrorMessage = "Error: " & Err.Number & _
                vbCrLf & vbCrLf & "The value you entered in the " _
                & "text box was: " & strErrorResultText
            txtDenominator.Focus
        Case Else
            strErrorMessage = "Error: " & Err.Number & _
                vbCrLf & vbCrLf & "Unrecognized error!"
    End Select
    MsgBox strErrorMessage, CRITICAL_ERROR + MSGBOX_OKONLY, _
        "Error Type = " & Err.Description
End If
```

Handling JScript Run-Time Errors

In Microsoft® JScript®, you can use the window object's onerror event to trap an error and respond accordingly. The onerror event is triggered when an error occurs anywhere on an HTML page. The onerror event passes three arguments to the function specified by the `window.onerror = functionname;` line. The arguments are the error message itself, the URL representing the source of the error, and a number representing the line where the error occurred. For example:

```
<SCRIPT LANGUAGE = "JScript">
    function BadFunction(){
        This.badcode.willnot.work = 1000
    }

    function ForceError(msg, url, lno) {
        alert("Error Occurred! Handled by Generic Error Handler" + "\n" +
            "Error: " + msg + "\n" + "URL: " + url + "\n" +
            "Line Number: " + lno);
```

```
    return true;
}


window.onerror = ForceError;
</SCRIPT>
```

Note   Returning True in the error-handler procedure forces the default message box not to appear. For more information about scripting HTML and ASP pages by using VBScript or JScript, see the Microsoft Scripting Technologies Web.

Logging Errors

Logging errors is the process of recording information about an error. You can use error-logging techniques to help debug your application. And even though you hope that most bugs are removed from your code before you deploy your application to your users, you might consider using error-logging techniques in "finished" applications as well.

One powerful option to consider is to create your own error-logging object class that you can use in any application by simply adding the class module that contains the error-logging code to your project.

Localizing Your Application

Localization involves the process of adapting your application for the countries or parts of the world in which it will be used. In addition to translating the strings in a user interface, localization might involve changing the software itself where necessary. For example, you might have to move control buttons to adapt to increased string lengths after translation, or so that the user interface will make sense grammatically in another language.

Most localization efforts run into a variety of difficulties that result in higher than necessary costs for localizing a product and a product that is more difficult to use than it should be. Often, these issues can be tackled at the source, by designing and writing software that takes into consideration some basic localizability guidelines. Establishing and implementing localization guidelines might increase the quality, accuracy and user-friendliness of the international product version. Moreover, it could significantly reduce the cost of localizing your application into different languages.

In This Section

Localization Guidelines for Your User Interface
These suggestions provide some guidance in facilitating localization in regard to your user interface.

Localization Guidelines for Language and Terminology
These suggestions provide some language and terminology to consider when localizing your application.

Localization Guidelines for Your Code
Suggestions that might help you increase efficiency and reduce costs by writing code with localization in mind.

Localizing Your Access Runtime Application
Information about creating an application that uses the Access Runtime in different languages.

Localization Guidelines for Your User Interface

When delivering your product in foreign languages, it is important to consider how the user interface will appear to users around the world. While there are no hard-fast rules, the following suggestions provide some guidance in facilitating localization in regard to your user interface:

- **Consider differences in length for text strings**   Many languages use different amounts of space to convey the same meaning, therefore, when creating your application, you should consider the different lengths of the text strings for the language your application will be in. An average of 30% more space should be added for any text. Depending on the language and the phrase, the localized string might even require twice as much space.

- **Use generic images and icons**   Bitmaps that are culturally neutral and that do not contain anything that must be localized are ideal.

- **Use text that can wrap**   With labels for such controls as radio buttons and check boxes, it is important that you set the appropriate property that makes it possible for the text to wrap. Localization vendors often cannot change the properties of radio button and check box labels. If you do not make it possible for the text to wrap and the translation does not fit on one line, the localizer's only alternative is to omit some of the text.

- **Add one extra line per variable**   When variables are used in UI strings, localization usually requires extra space. As a rule of thumb, one line per variable should be added to the text box so that there is enough space for the localized text. For example, the translation of a sentence that does not contain variables might require the entire first line of a text box. Where there is a variable inside of the sentence, the inserted text for the variable would extend the sentence into the second line. Allocate enough space for this spillover so that it will still be readable.

- **Avoid hiding or overlapping controls**   UI controls such as buttons or drop-down lists should not be placed on top of other controls. Sizing and hotkey issues with hidden controls usually are found through testing, which might not be done during localization. In this case, the UI is not localizable because the button size cannot be extended to the length required for the translation without rearranging the button positions. Rearranging button positions can be costly and makes the UI inconsistent among languages.

- **Avoid hard coding localizable string elements**   Because localization vendors often don't work with the source code, hard coded strings are usually only found through testing. For example, there might be a string in a resource file without a period at the end of a sentence because the period is added in the code. Because they don't see the code, translators might assume that this is a mistake and end the translation with a period. The result would be localized versions that have two periods at the end of the sentence. It is best to avoid hard coding all localizable string elements to save time for localization, build and test teams.

- **Avoid using controls within a sentence**   You might want to place a UI control within a sentence. For example, you might want to give users a drop-down menu to make a choice within a sentence. This practice is not recommended, because to localize a sentence that includes UI controls, the localizer often has to either change the position of the controls (if possible) or be content with an improper sentence structure. Also, the UI controls are often drop-down combo boxes that are comprised of multiple controls. Moving and aligning these can be error-prone.

- **Avoid placing button text into a string variable**   Text on a button should never be dynamically linked onto the button from a string variable but should be placed on the button itself as a property of the button. Button sizes usually have to be adjusted to fit the length of the translation on it. Localizers have no way of telling which strings in the string table end up on which button at run time.

- **Remove unused strings**   Unused strings and dialog boxes should be removed from the source, so localizers do not waste time localizing them.

Localization Guidelines for Language and Terminology

How does your writing style affect localization? The following list of suggestions provides some language and terminology guidelines that should ease localizing your application.

- **Use clear, concise, and grammatically correct language**   Ambiguous words, obtuse or highly technical sentences, and grammatical mistakes increase translation time and costs. Consider how a non-native speaker might interpret and translate a phrase before writing it.

- **Be consistent**   Automated translation tools can significantly cut down on localization vendor's costs. But automatic translation tools only work if standard phrases are being used. Many localization vendors are paid per word. Consider the amount of money that can be saved if one standard phrase can be easily, or automatically translated into multiple languages. For example, the following messages could be standardized into one consistent message:

Message	Standardized version of message
Not enough memory	There is not enough memory available.
There is not enough memory available	There is not enough memory available.
Insufficient Memory!	There is not enough memory available.

- **Use descriptors**   Inserting a descriptor before a term can clarify the meaning of the sentence and, more importantly, helps the localizer to decide whether the term should be localized. For example, "Must specify InfID when detect is set to No" could be better stated as "When the option Detect is set to No, you must specify the parameter InfID."

- **Avoid colloquial words and phrases**   Colloquial words and phrases are very hard to translate and might be offensive in certain cultures. A product might be friendlier to other cultures if colloquial terms and scenarios are avoided.

- **Avoid compound nouns**   In the English language, it is possible to compound several nouns without adding a preposition or a sub clause. This is usually not possible in other languages, which presents the translator with the dilemma of figuring out which nouns belong together. Inserting prepositions when writing in English would clarify the meaning immediately. For example, "Site Server LDAP Service directory server" should be changed to "Directory server for the LDAP Service of the Site Server."

- **Abbreviations and acronyms**   When using abbreviations and acronyms, ensure that the abbreviations and acronyms have meanings that are understood by most users. You should always define abbreviations and acronyms that might not be obvious in all languages.

- **Punctuation and spacing**   Different languages often have different punctuation and spacing rules. Consider these differences when writing strings in code. For example, "17.5 MB" in English is localized to "17,5 MB" in German. Thus, if this string is constructed at run time, the localizer cannot change the point to a comma. For similar reasons, apply these considerations to numbers, dates, or any other information that might have different formats in other languages.

Localization Guideline for Your Code

When writing code, it might be useful to think about how your code will be localized into other languages. The following suggestions might help you increase efficiency and reduce costs by writing code with localization in mind.

- **Use unique variable names**   If the same variable name is used for different variables, for example, if the sequence of the variables is hard coded, the word order in the translated sentence might be wrong because word order differs from language to language.

Example code	Better code
Set created on %s at %s	Set created on %1 at %2
Backup of %s on %s at %s	Backup of %1 on %2 at %3
Printing %s of %s on %s	Printing %1 of %2 on %3

- **Use dynamic or maximum buffer sizes**   Length restrictions for strings are potential build breakers. For example, if a string goes into a boot sector of a fixed byte size and the assembly code grows, there is no space for a longer translated string, which could crash the application. This problem is not likely to occur if buffers are dynamic or make it possible for maximum buffer sizes.

- **Avoid composite strings**   The strings shown in the following table cannot be localized unless the localizer knows what the type of object or item the variables stand for. Even then, localization might be difficult, because the value of the variable might require a different syntax; the article "the" has variations in another language (in German: "der, die, das, dem, den, des," the same as in English where you have "a" or "an"); the adjectives might change according to the gender of the word; or other factors. Using composite strings increases the chances of mistranslation. These localization problems can be eliminated by writing out each message as a separate string instead of using variables.

Examples of composite strings
Are you sure you want to delete the selected %s?
%s drive letter or drive path for %s.
Are you sure you want to delete %s's profile?
Cannot %s to Removable, CD-ROM or unknown types of drives.
A %s error has occurred %sing one of the %s sectors on this drive.

- **Avoid strings that contain a preposition and a variable**   Strings that contain a preposition and a variable are difficult to localize because, in some languages, different prepositions are used in different contexts.

Example code	Better code
At %s	Time: %s
At %s	Date: %s
At %s	Location: %s

- **Avoid using compounded variables**   In the following example, to translate the preposition "on" correctly, you might have to ask the developer what the variables stand for.

Example String	Explanation from developer
%I:%M%p on %A, %B %d, %Y	%A Full weekday name
	%B Full month name
	%d Day of month as decimal number (01 - 31)
	%I Hour in 12-hour format (01 - 12)
	%M Minute as decimal number (00 - 59)
	%p Current locale's A.M./P.M. indicator for 12-hour clock
	%Y Year with century, as decimal number

- **Avoid dividing sentences across multiple strings**   When a sentence is broken up into several strings, the strings do not necessarily appear consecutively in the localizer's string table. It is very time-consuming to piece strings together to form a correct sentence. In addition, because translation is not a word-by-word matter but the sentence structures differ from language to language, there will not be a one-to-one match in the glossary, which in turn might cause erroneous automated translations.

Example of divided sentences (to be translated from English to German)
• "When this box is checked, Windows NT does not" "automatically display the user name of the last person" "to log on in the Authentication dialog box."

Example of divided sentences (translated from English to German)
• "Wenn dieses Kontrollkästchen aktiviert ist, zeigt" "Windows NT nicht automatisch den Namen des" "Benutzers an, der sich zuletzt in dem Dialogfeld" "Authentifizierung" angemeldet hat."

Example of divided sentences (translated back literally from German to English)
• "When this control box checked is, plays" "Windows NT not automatically the name of" "the user, who him/herself last in the dialog box" "Authentication" logged has."

Localizing Your Access Runtime Application

If you would like to create an Access Runtime application in different languages, the Access Runtime is available in all the languages in which Microsoft Access is localized. To create an application that uses the Access Runtime in another language, you must have a copy of Microsoft Office or Access in that language. The Access Runtime files are stored on the Office XP CD.

To package an Access Runtime application with a different language

1. From an Office application, open the **Visual Basic Editor** (ALT + F11).

2. From the **Add-Ins** menu, select **Packaging Wizard**.

    Note   If the **Packaging Wizard** is not listed on the **Add-Ins** menu, you must load it into the **Add-Ins** menu through the **Add-In Manager**, located on the **Add-Ins** menu.

3. Select an ADP, ADE, MDB, MDE, MDA, or MDW application as the main file for your application.

4. Continue stepping through the wizard and set the necessary options for your file until you get to the **Access Runtime** screen.

5. On the **Access Runtime** screen, the **Access Runtime** checkbox is automatically checked, along with the default options. Clear the check box for any features you do not want to include in your package.

6. In the **Which language version of Access Runtime do you want to use?** field, select the language you want to use in your application.

7. Complete the **Packaging Wizard** and set the necessary options for your file.

8. If the Packaging Wizard finds the correct language version of the Access Runtime at the location specified in the registry, then it is copied into the package and the wizard continues on to the next step.

    If the Packaging Wizard cannot find the correct language version of the Access Runtime, then a dialog box appears asking you to **Create New** version or **Browse** for an existing version in a different location.

    If the language you selected does not match the language of the CD image or the location is incorrect, a second dialog box appears asking you to select another location. Click OK to return to the Browse dialog box and select the location of the Office CD in the language you selected in the wizard.

Deploying Your Application

When it is time to deploy your Microsoft® Office application to users, you have many alternatives, ranging from copying a file to a common share on a network server to building a full-fledged setup package using the Packaging Wizard. How you choose to deploy your application depends largely on what type of application you have created.

The following sections outline different ways to deploy various types of Office Developer applications.

In This Section

The Packaging Process
    Background information about creating setup program packages.

Creating a Setup Package Using the Packaging Wizard
    Using the Packaging Wizard to create setup programs for your applications.

Deploying Office Templates and Application-Specific Add-ins
    Special considerations for deploying Office templates and application-specific add-ins to special folders on users' computers.

Deploying COM Add-ins
    Special considerations for deploying COM Add-ins.

Deploying Outlook and FrontPage Applications
    Special considerations when deploying applications using Microsoft® Outlook® or Microsoft® FrontPage®.

Deploying Microsoft Access Applications using the Access Runtime
    Information about how to deploy the Access Runtime with your application.

The Packaging Process

Packaging is the act of creating a package that can install your application onto the user's computer. A *package* consists of one or more .cab files that contain your compressed project files and any other files the user must have to install in order to run your application. These files might include setup programs, secondary .cab files, or other required files.

You can freely distribute any redistributable application or component that you create with Microsoft® Office Developer. Note that because Microsoft® FrontPage® and Microsoft® Outlook® only support projects that are based on user profiles, the Packaging Wizard cannot package applications using these products. You can, however, package and deploy any stand-alone project, such as Add-in projects, created in the Microsoft® Visual Basic® for Applications (VBA) environment regardless of the application used. In addition, the Packaging Wizard cannot package workflow applications for Microsoft® Exchange Server or Digital Dashboard projects.

In addition to document, spreadsheet, workbook, or other Office files, your application might require other files you have created, such as DLLs, Microsoft® ActiveX® controls (.ocx files), or bitmaps (.bmp files). You can also include the Microsoft Access Runtime and Graph9.exe with your packaged application if required. The Packaging Wizard makes it easy to package and distribute all of these files. For more information about the Access Runtime, see Deploying Microsoft Access Applications using the Access Runtime.

> **Note**   You also might be able to distribute other ActiveX controls, .exe files, and DLLs that you have purchased. Consult the manufacturer's license agreement for each of the files you plan to distribute to determine whether or not you have the right to distribute the file with your application.

In addition, you can use the Packaging Wizard to add dependency files. Dependency files list the run-time components that must be distributed with your application's project files.

These are the steps in the packaging process:

- **Determine the files you must distribute**.   The wizard must determine the project files and dependent files for your application before it can create the package. *Project files* are the files included in the application itself—for example, the .vbo file and its contents. *Dependent files* are run-time files or components your application requires to run. Dependency information is stored in various .dep files corresponding to the components in your project.

- **If necessary, create dependency files for your application's components**.   If you determined in the previous step that your application requires any dependency files, you should create these files prior to creating the package. You can then include these files as part of the package. For more information, see Including Dependency Files in Setup Packages.

- **Determine where to install files on the user's computer**.   Program and setup files are usually installed into a subdirectory of the Program Files directory, while system and dependent files are usually installed into the \Windows\System or \Winnt\System32 directory. Your setup program must take this into account and determine where to install each file.

- **Create your package**.   The wizard creates the package and the setup program (setup1.exe) for it, referencing all necessary files. The end result of this step is one or more .cab files and any necessary setup files.

Creating a Setup Package Using the Packaging Wizard

The Packaging Wizard makes it easy for you to build and deploy setup programs for your Microsoft® Office XP Developer applications. The wizard guides you through the steps of creating a setup program that contains all of the information required for installation.

Note The Packaging Wizard targets applications that create redistributable applications. Because Microsoft® FrontPage® and Microsoft® Outlook® only support projects that are based on user profiles, the Packaging Wizard cannot package applications using these products. However, you can package stand-alone projects, such as Add-in projects, created in the Microsoft® Visual Basic® for Applications (VBA) environment from within these applications.

You can create multiple packages for an application to facilitate the packaging of your application in multiple ways, for example, different packages can be used for each language you deploy your application in.

Note If your application is a template or application-specific add-in, creating a setup package with the Packaging Wizard might not be your best option because the wizard does not provide a way to install the template or add-in to the special folders reserved for these on the user's computer.

To create a setup package

1. Open the **Visual Basic Editor** (Alt+F11) from the Office application in which you created the application.

2. From the **Add-Ins** menu, click **Packaging Wizard**.

    Note If the Packaging Wizard is not listed on the **Add-Ins** menu, you must load it using the **Add-In Manager**, located in the **Add-Ins** menu.

3. On the **Identify Application and Package** screen select the package you would like to build for the selected main file. For details, see Identifying Application and Setup Package Information.

4. On the **Application Information** screen, enter the appropriate information about your application. In the **Setup Language** field, select the language you want the Setup program to use.

5. On the **Dependencies** screen, verify that all required files to be included in the package are selected. Add any additional files you want in your package. For details, see Including Dependency Files in Setup Packages.

6. The next few screens that appear depend on the type of application you are packaging. Provide application-specific information in the wizard screens. For details about specific applications, see:

    *   "Deploying Office Templates and Application-Specific Add-ins"

    *   "Deploying COM Add-ins"

    *   "Deploying Microsoft Access Applications using the Access Runtime"

    *   "Deploying Outlook and FrontPage Applications "

7. On the **Modify Installation Locations** screen, click **Next** to select the default installation locations or change the locations. For details, see Changing Default Installation Locations for Setup Packages.

8. On the **Define Start Menu Shortcuts** screen, click **Next** to accept the default shortcut. For details about customizing your Start menu shortcuts, see Defining Start Menu Shortcuts.

9. On the **Run On Complete** screen, select the **Run this command when installation is finished** check box to have a file launched when setup is complete. Select or enter the file name (or any command that can be run from the **Run** dialog box on the **Start** menu) in the field.

    Note The file you choose to run on complete must be added to the package if it will not be on the user's computer.

10. On the **Build the Application Package** screen, select the **Build the setup program** option to create the package now, or select the **Save the package script without building** option to save the package definition for building later.

11. Click **Finish** to close the Packaging Wizard. The wizard will begin packaging your application.

12. In the **Browse For Folder** dialog box, select a folder where you want to save your packaged application.

    Note To save to a network location, you can copy and paste the network path into the folder field.

13. If your package contains the Access Runtime components, you will be prompted to save the Access Runtime files to a local folder and to insert the Microsoft Office CD (not the Office Developer CD). For details, see Locating Access Runtime Files.

When the Packing Wizard finishes creating your package, you can find the Setup program in the folder you selected in the last step of the wizard. You can then test your Setup program.

To create the package again, open the Packaging Wizard, select the main file for the application, and then select the package you want to create. If you do not want to change any of the settings, click Finish to create the package.

To modify your package, open the Packaging Wizard, select the main file for the application, and then select the package you want to modify. Continue through the wizard, making any changes you want. When the changes are made, click Finish to create the package with the new settings. Note that the Packaging Wizard saves the package settings.

Identifying Application and Setup Package Information

To create a setup package for your application, you must identify the main file and a package script that will be used to define the how the application will be setup.

The Main file should point to the file that contains references to other files in the application. When browsing to find the main file, the dialog box identifies the types of files that are typically the main file. For example, for an application using Access, the main file should be the .mbd file and for an application using Word, the main file should be the .doc file.

In the Package Name field of the Packaging Wizard, you can select a package to use when creating the application setup program. You can use different packages for the same main file. The package stores information about installing the application.

The Packaging Wizard saves the setup information in a script file, so you can reuse the installation information to create the applications.

To create new packages

- In the **Packaging Wizard**, on the **Identify Application and Package** screen click **New** to create a new package, **Copy** to create a new copy of an existing package, or **Rename** to give an existing package a new name. Enter a name in the dialog box and click **OK**.

Including Dependency Files in Setup Packages

A dependency file contains information about the run-time requirements of an application or component—for example, which files are required, how they are to be registered, and where on the user's computer they should be installed.

For example, say you have created a Microsoft® Access database that uses a Microsoft® Excel workbook that is late-bound in code. To package this application, you would first create the workbook, and then you would package the application in Access, including the Access Runtime. When creating the package in the Packaging Wizard, include the Excel file in your package.

> **Note** Office Developer provides royalty-free run-time distribution licenses that make it possible for you to distribute copies of your application, including the Microsoft Access Runtime licensing key and the Microsoft Graph 9 run-time executable file. These are necessary to run Office applications on a computer that does not have Microsoft Office.

The Packaging Wizard will inform you if dependency information is missing for a component in your project.

> **Note** For some third-party projects, you might want to manually search for dependency files when using the Packaging Wizard.

To include a dependency file for your application

1. On the **Dependencies** screen in the **Packaging Wizard**, click **Add File** to browse for files you want to include in the package.

2. Select files in the list and click **Scan** to search for dependencies on the selected files to verify that all related files are included in the package.

3. In the list of found files, verify the files that should be included in your package. Clear the check box for any files that should not be included.

4. Work through the wizard until you have set the necessary options for your file, and then click **Finish**.

Changing Default Installation Locations for Setup Packages

When you create a setup package with the Packaging Wizard, you can specify where the application should be installed on a user's computers by choosing from a list of installation locations.

You can also identify whether a file should be shared with other applications or not. A shared file can be used by other applications. Designating it as a shared file ensures that the file is left on the user's computer when other applications using the shared file are uninstalled.

> **Note**   When you build a setup package with the Packaging Wizard, a new folder will be created in the user's C:\Program Files folder. By default, the folder is given the name you provided for the application on the Application Information screen. This folder is added even if you are not installing the application itself to the Program Files folder and is used to store information for uninstalling the application.

To modify the installation location for a particular file

1. In the **Packaging Wizard**, on the **Modify Installation Locations** screen, click the **Installation Location** field and use the drop-down menu to select a path location.

Installation location options	Example
$(AppPath)	C:\Program Files*ApplicationName*
$(WinPath)	C:\Windows
$(WinSysPath)	C:\Windows\System
$(WinSysPathSysFile)	C:\Windows\System32
$(CommonFiles)	C:\Program Files\Common Files
$(CommonFilesSys)	C:\Program Files\Common Files\System
$(ProgramFiles)	C:\Program Files
$(MSDAOPath)	C:\Program Files\Common Files\Microsoft Shared\DAO
$(Font)	C:\Windows\Fonts

2. Add subfolder information to an installation location by clicking in the **Installation Location** field at the end of the token and typing a backslash followed by the subfolder name, for example, $(ProgramFiles)\My Subfolder.

3. In the **Shared** field, use the drop-down menu to select whether the file should be shared with other applications. To share the file, select **True**. To not share the file, select **False**.

4. Click **Next**, or if you have established the necessary options for your setup package, then click **Finish** to package your application and close the Packaging Wizard.

Defining Start Menu Shortcuts

In the Packaging Wizard, you can either accept the default shortcuts or customize the Start menu groups and group items that should be created on the user's computer during installation of your application. You can create groups and items for your application within the Programs subdirectory of the Start menu.

In addition to creating new Start menu groups and items, you can edit the properties for an existing item, or you can remove groups and items.

To customize the Start Menu shortcut

1. Select the item you wish to modify in the **Start Menu Shortcuts** window, and click the appropriate command button.

To	Click
Add a new folder to the Start menu structure	New Folder
Add a new shortcut icon within a Start menu folder	New Shortcut
Remove the selected item from the Start menu structure	Remove
Define the properties for the selected item and to associate a shortcut with an application or command	Properties

2. To associate a shortcut icon with an application, select the shortcut icon and click **Properties**.

3. In the **Start Menu Item Properties** window you can edit properties, including the Name, description, command line, and icon for the application.

4. Click **Next**, or, if you have established the necessary options for your setup package, then click **Finish** to package your application and close the Packaging Wizard.

Testing Your Setup Package

After you have completed the packaging process and produced distribution media for your application, you must test your setup package.

Be sure to test your setup package on a computer that does not have the application files or any of the Microsoft® ActiveX® controls required by your application. You should also test your setup package on all applicable operating systems.

To test your floppy disk-based or CD-based setup package

1. Save your setup package created using the Packaging Wizard to a disk or CD.

2. Insert the first disk or the CD in the appropriate drive.

3.   Double-click **Setup.exe** from the disk drive.

4.   When the installation finishes, run the installed program to be sure it behaves as expected.

To test your network drive-based setup program

1.   From another computer on the same network as the distribution server, connect to the server and directory containing your distribution files.

2.   In the distribution directory, double-click the **Setup.exe** file.

3.   When the installation finishes, run the installed program to be sure it behaves as expected.

Deploying Office Templates and Application-Specific Add-ins

The Packaging Wizard is a good tool for building setup programs for many Microsoft® Office applications. However, Office templates and application-specific add-ins (versus COM add-ins) are exceptions, because they should be installed to special folders on a user's computer. The Packaging Wizard does not have the functionality to install to these special folders.

On a computer running Microsoft® Windows® without user profiles enabled, Office templates and add-ins should be installed to the following folders, respectively:

> C:\Windows\Application Data\Microsoft\Templates
> C:\Windows\Application Data\Microsoft\Addins

Otherwise, if user profiles are used, Office templates and add-ins should be installed to these folders:

> If your operating system is Windows 98, Windows Me, or Microsoft® Windows NT® 4:
>
> C:*WindowsFolder*\Profiles*UserName*\Application Data\Microsoft\Templates
> C:*WindowsFolder*\Profiles*UserName*\Application Data\Microsoft\Addins
>
> If your operating system is Windows 2000 or later:
>
> C:\Documents and Settings*UserName*\Application Data\Microsoft\Templates
> C:\Documents and Settings*UserName*\Application Data\Microsoft\Addins

Although it is not absolutely necessary to install a template or add-in to one of these folders, there are some advantages to doing so:

*   If a Microsoft® Word, Microsoft® Excel, or Microsoft® PowerPoint® custom template is stored on users' computers, it must be installed to the Templates folder in order for it to appear in the New dialog box (File menu).

*   Because the Templates and AddIns folders are the default folders for templates and add-ins, installing them there makes it easier for users to locate a template or add-in. For example, Excel add-ins (.xla files) that are installed in the AddIns folder automatically appear in the list

of available add-ins in the Add-ins dialog box (Tools menu), so that users do not have to browse to find the correct file.

- The Templates and AddIns folders are trusted folders, meaning that an add-in or template in one of these folders does not have to be digitally signed by a trusted source in order to run code when security is set to High. These folders are trusted by default, but it's possible to override this setting by clearing the Trust all installed add-ins and templates check box on the Trusted Sources tab of the Security dialog box.

  To open the Security dialog box in an Office application, point to Macro on the Tools menu, and then click Security. If you change the default folder for templates and add-ins, the new folder that you specify will be trusted.

There are simple ways to deploy templates and add-ins to the Templates and AddIns folders. You can use one of these strategies, or you can create your own simple custom installation program. For more information, see Deploying Application-Specific Add-ins.

What are User Profiles?

Microsoft Windows offers a user profiles feature. A user profile is an account maintained by the operating system that keeps track of a particular user's files and system configuration.

In Microsoft® Windows NT® Workstation, Windows NT Server, and Windows 2000, user profiles are automatically turned on all the time. Whenever a new user logs in, a user profile is created for that user. On Windows NT, the profile is created under the C:\Winnt\Profiles\UserName folder. On Windows 2000, it is created under C:\Documents and Settings\UserName. In other versions of Microsoft Windows, user profiles are optional.

When you log on to a computer as a user who has a user profile, Windows checks the data it has stored for that user profile, and loads with those settings in place. Additionally, it maintains a folder for files created under that user profile, the C:\Windows\Profiles\UserName folder.

Under any of the previously mentioned operating systems, the system can be secured so that each user has access only to the files, applications, and system configuration defined for his or her user profile. For example, files that are installed by a user who has administrative privileges might not be available to another user who does not share those privileges.

Deploying Custom Office Templates

When you create a new document in Microsoft Word, Microsoft Excel, or Microsoft PowerPoint, the New dialog box (File menu) displays a list of templates that you can choose from to create a new document. The dialog box can display three types of templates: built-in templates that are included with Microsoft Office; user-created templates, which are stored on users' computers; and workgroup templates, which are stored on a network share. Only templates from certain folders are displayed, however, so if you create a new template, you must save it to the correct location in order for it to be displayed in the dialog box. The following table indicates where the dialog box looks for each type of template.

Type of template	Default location	Notes
Built-in	C:\Program Files \Microsoft Office\Templates \LanguageID	The language ID is a number indicating the product language. For U.S. English, this is 1033. User-created templates saved here will not appear in the New dialog box.
User-created	C:\Windows\Application Data \Microsoft\Templates -or- C:\Windows\Profiles\UserName \Application Data\Microsoft \Templates -or- C:\Documents and Settings \UserName\Application Data \Microsoft\Templates -or- C:\Winnt\Profiles\UserName \Application Data \Microsoft\Templates	You can change this location in Word or Excel in the Options dialog box (Tools menu). In order to appear in the New dialog box, user-created templates must be stored in the location that is specified in the Options dialog box.
Workgroup	Not specified	You can specify a location for workgroup templates in the Options dialog box in Word, or from VBA code in Excel or Word. When you set this option, templates in the specified location appear in the New dialog box.

As you can see, you have two options for installing a custom template: You can install it locally on users' computers, or you can copy it to a shared folder on a network server.

Local Installation of a Custom Template

To install a custom template locally onto users' computers, you have a couple of options:

- You can e-mail the template to users or instruct users to copy it from a network share, with instructions for where to copy the template to on the users' computers.

- You can create a custom installation program to copy the template to the correct folder.

Deployment of a Workgroup Template to a Network Share

If you must deploy a custom template to multiple users, a good way to do this is to copy the template to a shared folder on a network server, so that it is available to everyone who has access to the share.

When you have copied the template to the shared folder, you must make sure that every user has specified this path for workgroup templates. Word and Excel both provide an option to specify a path for workgroup templates. You or users can set this option to point to the shared folder for each user's application.

There are several ways to set the workgroup templates option:

- You can instruct each user to set it.

- You can write code to set the option and run the code on all users' computers.

- For custom Word templates, if the Normal.dot file is under administrative control, you can set the option there. In this scenario, the Normal.dot file is probably read-only, so users cannot modify the setting.

In Word, you can modify the workgroup templates option through Microsoft Visual Basic for Applications (VBA) code by setting the DefaultFilePath property of the Options object, passing in the wdWorkgroupTemplatesPath constant for the *path* argument, as shown in the following code fragment:

```
Options.DefaultFilePath(wdWorkgroupTemplatesPath) =
"\\Server\Share\WorkgroupTemplates"
```

In Excel, you can modify the workgroup templates option through VBA code by setting the NetworkTemplatesPath property of the Application object:

```
Application.NetworkTemplatesPath = "\\Server\Share\WorkgroupTemplates"
```

For example, if you have Visual Basic, you can write a simple program that launches Word or Excel through Automation to set this option, and then compile the program into an .exe file and distribute it to all of the users through e-mail. When the users run the program, it will set the workgroup templates option correctly for them.

Storing a workgroup template on a common network share is a good idea from a maintenance standpoint, because you can modify the template without having to redistribute the template to every user. However, if you must deploy the template to users who do not have access to a common network share, you can build a custom installation program to deploy a template.

Deploying Office Application-Specific Add-ins

The AddIns folder under C:\Windows\Application Data\Microsoft, C:\Windows\Profiles*UserName*\Application Data\Microsoft, C:\Winnt\Profiles*UserName*\Application Data\Microsoft, or C:\Documents and Settings*UserName*\Application Data\Microsoft is the default folder for Microsoft® Word, Microsoft® Excel, Microsoft® PowerPoint®, and Microsoft® Access application-specific add-ins. The simplest way to deploy an application-specific add-in, of course, is to e-mail the add-in to users or to post it on a network share with instructions for copying it to the correct folder. There is nothing wrong with this approach; however, you cannot guarantee that users will copy the add-in correctly, especially if the add-in has any dependent files that might have to be installed to a different folder. If you must have more control over the installation process, you can create a custom setup program to install the application correctly.

Building such a setup program is relatively simple. Although you can build a setup program from any Microsoft® Visual Basic® for Applications (VBA) host application, Visual Basic is optimal because you can create an executable (.exe) file.

The most difficult aspect of building a custom setup program is determining the path to the Templates and AddIns folders on users' computers. To determine the location of the Templates and AddIns folders, you must call three Microsoft® Windows® application programming interface (API) functions. These functions are SHGetSpecialFolderLocation, SHGetPathFromIDList, and SHGetMalloc.

Deploying COM Add-ins

If you have built a COM add-in using Microsoft® Office XP Developer, you can create an installation program for it using the Packaging Wizard. The installation program must deploy the COM add-in dynamic-link library (DLL) as well as any files on which it is dependent, such as type libraries that might not be on users' computers.

A COM add-in DLL created with the COM Add-in designer in Office Developer or Visual Basic is a self-registering DLL, meaning that it will register itself properly when the setup program runs. When the DLL has registered itself, the COM add-in will appear in the list of available COM add-ins in the COM Add-ins dialog box. Therefore, it does not matter where you install the DLL. However, for the sake of consistency, you might want to choose one folder for installing all COM add-ins, such as the AddIns folder under C:\Windows\Application Data\Microsoft, C:\Windows\Profiles*UserName*\Application Data\Microsoft, C:\Winnt\Profiles*UserName*\Application Data\Microsoft, or C:\Documents and Settings*UserName*\Application Data\Microsoft.

Deploying Outlook and FrontPage Applications

Microsoft® Outlook® and Microsoft® FrontPage® differ from the other Microsoft® Office applications in the way that they store Microsoft® Visual Basic® for Applications (VBA) code. Whereas each Microsoft® Excel, Microsoft® Word, Microsoft® Access, or Microsoft® PowerPoint® file that you create contains its own VBA project, which is saved with that file, Outlook and FrontPage each provide only a single VBA project where all VBA code is stored and this VBA project is saved as a separate file. For Outlook, this file is named VbaProject.otm; for FrontPage, it is named FrontPage.fpm.

To deploy an Outlook or FrontPage application, you can develop the application locally on your development workstation and then when you distribute the VbaProject.otm or FrontPage.fpm file to users, replace the version of the file on the user's computer. However, each time you or another developer distributes an application in this manner, you'll be replacing the user's existing VbaProject.otm or FrontPage.fpm file, which might very well break existing applications.

A better strategy for building an Outlook or FrontPage application is to create a COM add-in. The COM add-in runs independently of the VBA project and of other COM add-ins, so your application will not affect the user's other applications. For information about creating COM Add-ins, see "Add-ins, Templates, Wizards, and Libraries."

Deploying Microsoft Access Applications using the Access Runtime

If you build an Access database (.mdb) as the front-end application, you can deploy the database to users who do not have Access on their workstations by distributing it together with the run-time version of Access. The Access Runtime is a version of Access for which certain features have been disabled, including the ability to create and modify databases.

Using the Packaging Wizard, you can create an installation program to distribute the Access Runtime to your users. When you purchase Office Developer, you are licensed to distribute the Access Runtime to as many workstations as you want.

When you choose an Access database as your main file in the Packaging Wizard, the wizard displays the Access Runtime screen where you can include the Access Runtime in your application.

To include the Access Runtime in a package using the Packaging Wizard

1. In the **Packaging Wizard**, select the **Access** file (.mdb or .adp) as the main file.

2. Follow the instructions in the wizard.

3. On the **Access Runtime** screen, select the **Yes, include the Access Runtime** option.

4. If you want to include the system components required to run an Access Runtime application in your package, select the **Include System Files** option. It is recommended that you include these files if you are unsure whether your users will have the required files on their computers.

5. If you want to include Internet Explorer 5.1 in your package, click the **Install Internet Explorer 5.1** option. This option is recommended if your application requires this version of Internet Explorer.

6. In the **Which language version of Access Runtime do you want to use** field, select the language for the setup program. You must have access to Access Runtime files for the language you select. These are available on the Microsoft Office XP installation CD. For details, see Locating Localized Versions of the Access Runtime Files.

7. On the **Access Runtime Properties** screen, select the additional data components you want to include in your package. You should include the **Microsoft Data Engine (MSDE)** if your package requires a local SQL Server store.

8. Continue with the **Packaging Wizard** to complete your package. The Packaging Wizard will begin building your package.

9. In the **Where would you like to save your packaged application** dialog box, select a folder where you want to save your packaged application.

    Note   To save to a network location, you can copy and past the network path into the path field.

The Packaging Wizard will search for the Access Runtime files for the language you selected in the Access Runtime screen. If the wizard cannot locate a copy of the correct files on your computer, a dialog box will appear asking you to provide the Office XP CD to copy the files to your computer.

For information about locating the correct Access Runtime files, see Locating Access Runtime Files.

Developing Access Runtime Applications

Developing Microsoft Access Runtime applications for distribution is similar to developing standard Microsoft® Access applications. You have great flexibility in choosing a strategy for developing your application. For example, you can create your application's tables and queries, then its forms and reports, then its macros and modules. Or you can develop your application feature by feature, creating a variety of objects as you go along. To manipulate the objects you create, you can use macros, Visual Basic for Applications code, or a combination of both.

For more information about Access Runtime applications, see:

* "The Development Process"

* "Simulating the Microsoft Access Runtime Environment"

* "Differences Between Full Microsoft Access and the Runtime Environment"

- "The Access Runtime Licensing Key"

- "Security for Your Application"

- "Locating Access Runtime Files"

The Development Process

Regardless of your strategy, there are several basic steps that you should follow when developing a Microsoft Access Runtime application for distribution.

1. Using full Microsoft Access, create and debug your application's tables, queries, forms, reports, macros, and modules. Forms will be a particularly important part of your run-time application.

2. Create help files and other documentation that will accompany your application. For more information, see Adding Help to Your Office Application.

3. Run your application using the /runtime command-line option, and debug any run-time environment errors. For details, see Simulating the Microsoft Access Runtime Environment.

4. Create your application's custom Setup program using the Packaging Wizard.

5. Install your application and test it on a computer that does not have Microsoft Access installed. For more information, see Testing your Setup Package.

6. Package your application and any printed documentation, and distribute it to your distribution sites.

Access Runtime applications have the same system requirements as Microsoft Access or Microsoft® Office.

Simulating the Microsoft Access Runtime Environment

Because some standard Microsoft Access features are hidden or disabled in the run-time environment, you should make sure your application works correctly in the run-time environment before distributing it.

If you have the Microsoft Office Developer tools installed, you can test and debug your application in Access by using the Access /runtime startup command-line option to turn off full Access features and simulate the environment in which users will run your application. Your application will look and behave as if your Microsoft Windows registry contains the run-time licensing key. However, the /runtime option does not secure your application. Any user who wants to could either remove the /runtime option from the shortcut or start Microsoft Access directly to access the design of your application's objects.

Also, for this method to work, your application must have a startup form that provides access to all the objects you want available (a main switchboard form), because you cannot display the

Database window in run-time mode. For more information about the behavior of the run-time environment, see "Differences Between Full Microsoft Access and the Run-Time Environment."

You can specify the /runtime command-line option by clicking **Run** on the **Start** menu or by creating a shortcut.

To create a shortcut to start your application with the /runtime option

1. Create a shortcut to start **Microsoft Access**.

2. Right-click the shortcut, click **Properties**, and then click the **Shortcut** tab.

3. In the **Target** box, following the path to MSAccess.exe, type the path to the database you want to open, and then type **/runtime**. If the path contains spaces, enclose it in quotation marks.

   For example, the following command line starts Microsoft Access and then opens the Developer Applications sample application in run-time mode.

   ```
   "C:\Program Files\Microsoft Office\Office\MSAccess.exe" "C:\Program
   Files\Microsoft Office\Office\Samples\Solutions.mdb" /runtime
   ```

   Note If you are working on a network that supports universal naming convention (UNC) paths (\\ServerName\SharedFolder), you can specify the location of the database without specifying a mapped drive letter. For example, you can copy your database to a shared network folder and define the shortcut's command line to open the database from that location by using the UNC path.

Differences Between Full Microsoft Access and the Run-Time Environment

Users of your application work in an environment that combines the built-in features of Microsoft Access with the objects that you create. Unlike applications created with Microsoft® Visual Basic® or Microsoft® Visual C++®, applications created with Microsoft Access are not compiled into a single executable file. Access applications work by running your application's database file (.mdb) in the Access Runtime environment with user profiles, which are stored in the Windows registry.

While an Access application is running, it might not be apparent which elements of the environment your application supplies and which elements the run-time environment supplies. Because your application has its own look and feel, it might not even be apparent that Microsoft Access is running. Although Microsoft Access Runtime applications are identical in most respects to full Microsoft Access applications, there are some differences that can affect how you design and develop them:

- The Database, Macro, and Visual Basic Environment windows are hidden, and all Design views are hidden, including the Filter windows.

- Built-in toolbars are no supported, but you can add custom toolbars to your application.

- Your application uses its own Help file.

- Some windows, menus (including shortcut menus), and commands are hidden or disabled.

- Visual Basic error handling is required. Errors that are not handled by your code will shut down the application without warning. For this reason, the use of macros is not recommended.

- Certain keystrokes and key combinations are disabled.

  Note If your application uses dynamic data exchange (DDE), you can specify either Microsoft Access or the application name specified by the AppDDEName user profile setting as a valid DDE application name. The run-time environment will respond to both.

The Access Runtime Licensing Key

When your application is installed on a user's computer, an entry that causes Microsoft Access to open in the run-time environment is made in the software licensing section of the Windows registry. The setup program you created with the Packaging Wizard automatically makes the necessary modifications.

When Access or your run-time application starts, it checks the licensing key to determine whether to open the database in full Access or in the run-time environment. If the application opens in the run-time environment, certain Access features are disabled and/or hidden from the user.

If no licensing key is present in the Windows registry, your run-time application will not run.

Security for Your Application

When you distribute your run-time application to users who have Microsoft Access on their computer, you should take several precautions to protect your database. The following recommendations will prevent users from making modifications to your objects and code or inadvertently causing problems with your application.

- Specify the /runtime option on all command lines that you use to start your application. This forces your application to open in the run-time environment, even if a user has full Microsoft Access on their computer.

- Use the Security Wizard that is provided with Access to secure all the objects in your database. To make sure that your database is completely secure, do not use the default workgroup defined by the Access workgroup information (.mdw) file that was created when you installed Access. You should create your own workgroup information file and give it a unique workgroup ID.

- Use customized menus and toolbars in your application. Make sure that you do not include any toolbar buttons or menu commands that would give users access to object Design views or the Macro or Module windows.

- Set the AllowBypassKey property to False to disable the SHIFT key. This prevents users from bypassing the startup properties or the AutoExec macro. To set the AllowBypassKey property by using a macro or Visual Basic, you must create the property with the CreateProperty method and append it to the Properties collection of the Database object.

- Set any database startup properties that could potentially give users access to the Database window or any Design view. These properties include Use Access Special Keys (AllowSpecialKeys), Allow Viewing Code After Error (AllowBreakIntoCode), Display Database Window (ShowStartupDBWindow), and Allow Toolbar/Menu Changes (AllowToolbarChanges). To set these properties, click Startup on the Tools menu.

- If your database contains Microsoft Visual Basic code, distribute it as an MDE file. Saving your database as an MDE file compiles all modules, removes all editable source code, and compacts the destination database. Your Visual Basic code will continue to run, but it cannot be viewed or edited, and the size of your database will be reduced due to the removal of the code. Additionally, memory usage is optimized, which will improve performance.

Locating Access Runtime Files

When you use the Packaging Wizard to include the Microsoft Access Runtime in your application, a message prompts you to locate the Access Runtime files if the wizard cannot find the files.

The Access Runtime is not installed to your computer as part of the Microsoft Office Developer setup. Instead, you can use the Packaging Wizard to copy the files from the Microsoft Office CD.

The first time you run the Packaging Wizard and include the Access Runtime in your package, you will be prompted to locate the files. You will be prompted to locate the files for any packages you create in additional languages as well. When the correct files have been copied to your computer, you will not be prompted to locate the files by the Packaging Wizard.

Note that the Access Runtime components are available for all of the different languages that Office is available in. To use the localized version of the Access Runtime, simply point the Packaging Wizard to a folder containing the localized version.

To include the Access Runtime file in your package

1. Use the Packaging Wizard to package an Access application.

2. Add the Access Runtime to your application. For details, see Deploying Microsoft Access Applications using the Access Runtime.

3. Complete the wizard, including selecting a location for the package.

4. When prompted to locate the Access Runtime files, if you have already copied the Access Runtime files for the languages selected on the Access Runtime screen of the Packaging Wizard, select **Browse** and locate the folder that contains the files.

   Note   To identify a network location, you can copy and past the network path into the path field.

5. .To create a new set of Access Runtime components on your computer, select **Create New**.

6. Identify a folder where you would like to save the Access Runtime components.

   Note   To select a network location, you can copy and past the network path into the path field.

7.   Insert Microsoft Office XP CD 1, and select the drive in the tree view.

> **Note**   The Access Runtime files are stored on the Microsoft Office XP CD, not the
> Microsoft Office XP Developer CD. In addition, you must use the Office XP CD that
> corresponds with the language you selected on the Access Runtime screen of the
> Packaging Wizard.

The Packaging Wizard copies the necessary files from the Office XP CD to your computer. The
Access Runtime files are then included in your package.

Programming Concepts

When you program, you store data and manipulate it with a series of instructions. The data and data storage containers are the raw materials of programming. The tools you use to manipulate this raw material are commands, functions, and operators.

In This Section

Writing Solid Code
"Writing solid code" means writing Microsoft® Visual Basic® for Applications (VBA) code or script that performs as expected and is reusable, easy to understand, and easy to maintain.

Working with XML
This section provides information about Office Applications and XML.

Custom Classes and Objects
If you have never used class modules to build custom objects before, this section covers the concepts that you must understand to design, build, and use custom objects with their own methods and properties.

The Windows API and Other Dynamic-Link Libraries
One of the most powerful features of Microsoft® Visual Basic® for Applications (VBA) is its extensibility. You can extend your applications by calling functions in the Microsoft® Windows® application programming interface (API) and other dynamic-link libraries (DLLs).

Writing Solid Code

"Writing solid code" means writing Microsoft® Visual Basic® for Applications (VBA) code or script that performs as expected and is reusable, easy to understand, and easy to maintain. Many developers focus all their time and effort on just getting code to work. If you have ever struggled to understand code, whether written by you or someone else, or rewritten the same procedure to work in different applications, then you understand how writing solid code can make life easier.

One of the most important considerations for an effective Microsoft® Office application is how well it is designed. If your application has a user interface, you should be aware of consistency and ease-of-use issues every time you create a dialog box or add a custom toolbar. You also must be aware of the design and structure of the code you write. The way you design your code, from how you name variables to when you use class modules, can make a big difference in the maintainability and usability of your code.

In This Section

Writing Solid Script
> The benefits associated with writing reusable, understandable, and maintainable code can be realized whether you are writing script or Microsoft® Visual Basic® for Applications (VBA) code.

Using a Naming Convention
> There are many formal naming conventions and each has its adherents and detractors. You can adopt one of the existing conventions or create one of your own.

Structuring and Formatting Your Code
> How you use structured coding conventions directly affects how easy your code is to understand and maintain.

Commenting Code
> All procedures and functions should begin with a brief comment describing the functional characteristics of the procedure (what it does).

Designing Code to Be Used Again
> Reusable code is code that can be used, without modification, to perform a specific service regardless of what application uses the code.

Writing Solid Script

Scripting languages are "loosely typed" and, therefore, all variables used in script have a Variant data type. In addition, script is written directly into the HTML code behind a Web page, and there are no modules used to contain code as there are in VBA and other "strongly typed" languages. Finally, scripting languages do not require you to expressly declare variables before you use them.

Given these unique characteristics, it still makes sense to talk about a naming convention in the context of writing script. The naming conventions and other coding guidelines apply to script in an HTML page as they do to Microsoft® Visual Basic® for Applications (VBA) code in a Microsoft® Office application. The benefits associated with writing reusable, understandable, and maintainable code can be realized whether you are writing script or VBA code. In fact, there is a great deal of work to be done persuading script developers to pay attention to issues of code reuse and maintainability. There are just as many benefits to writing solid script as there are to writing solid code.

Although script is written directly into the HTML code of a Web page, questions of visibility and lifetime are still important. Variables and constants declared within a procedure are local to that procedure and have a lifetime that lasts only as long as the script within the procedure is executing.

Variables and constants declared in script outside a procedure are visible to any script contained in the current HTML page. These variables have the equivalent of the module-level scope described earlier. Variables and constants declared in Visual Basic Scripting Edition (VBScript) by using the Public keyword are visible to all script in the current HTML page and to all script in all other currently loaded pages. For example, if you have an HTML page that contains multiple frames designated by a <FRAMESET> tag pair, a variable or constant declared with the Public keyword will be visible to all pages loaded within all the frames specified by the <FRAMESET> tag.

In addition, although all script variables have a Variant data type, it is important to remember that the Variant data type encompasses many different data types and can coerce a variable to the most appropriate data type in a particular context. Although you cannot declare a variable as a specific data type, you should name your variables as if you could. Naming script variables as if they were strongly typed will not prevent you from assigning an integer value to the `strCompanyName` variable, but it will force you to think about how the variable is used and the data subtype it will contain. You declare VBScript variables by using the Dim statement and Microsoft® JScript® variables by using the var statement.

   Note   Unlike VBScript, JScript is a case-sensitive language; if you name a variable `strCompanyName` but refer to it as `STRCompanyName`, you will encounter errors.

Using the Option Explicit Statement

Neither VBScript nor VBA requires you to declare variables before using them. The default behavior in both languages makes it possible for you to create variables by simply using a variable name in an assignment statement. However, the failure to use the Option Explicit statement to force explicit variable declaration can be a serious mistake. Using undeclared variables can introduce subtle, hard-to-find bugs into your code that are easily avoided by using this simple technique.

To force VBA to insert the Option Explicit statement in every module you create, open the Visual Basic Editor, click Options on the Tools menu, and then click Require Variable Declaration on the Editor tab.

To force variables to be declared in VBScript, type Option Explicit immediately after the first
`<SCRIPT>` tag in your HTML document. For example, `<SCRIPT> Option Explicit`
`</SCRIPT>`.

Using a Naming Convention

There are many formal naming conventions, and each has its adherents and detractors. You can
adopt one of the existing conventions or create one of your own. The important points are that you
adopt some convention that would be self-evident to another Office developer and that you apply it
consistently.

At a minimum, a useful naming convention will identify and distinguish variable type (object
variable, control variable, and data type), variable scope, constants, and procedures, and it should
be simple to understand and use.

Naming Variables and Constants

Naming conventions typically use a lowercase prefix or suffix to specify the variable's type and
scope. The variable itself should have a meaningful name that describes what it is or what it does.
Multiple-word names are concatenated, the first letter of each word is capitalized, and the
underscore character is not used. If you used a variable-name template, it would be in the form
prefixNoun or *prefixNounVerb*.

Constant names should also be descriptive names in the *NOUN* or *NOUN_VERB* format. Constant
names are uppercase and use an underscore character to separate words. Although there is nothing
technically wrong with adding characters to constant names to specify data type and scope, it is not
done often. A constant is really the same thing as a variable in the sense that both are symbolic
representations of data. The difference is that variables can change and constants remain the same.

Both variable and constant names can contain up to 255 characters; however, names that exceed 25
to 30 characters can become unwieldy. Besides, 25 or 30 characters should be plenty of room to
provide descriptive names that clearly convey the purpose of the variable or constant.

Variable Names

Variable names use the mixed-case form (*Noun* or *NounVerb*), specifying what the variable is and
what it does. The mixed-case form is used as the descriptive portion of the variable name where
the first letter of each word is in uppercase and the rest is in lowercase.

Variable names also have a two- or three-character prefix used to specify the variable's data type.
For example, the following statements declare variables with a prefix that specifies the variable's
data type:

```
Dim strRecipientName          As String
Dim intItemsProcessed         As Integer
Dim blnContinueProcessing     As Boolean
```

The two-character prefix is used typically to specify an Office Application object type. For example:

```
Dim xlApp           As Excel.Application
Dim olNameSpace     As Outlook.NameSpace
Dim wdNewDoc        As Word.Document
```

Use the "obj" prefix when declaring a generic, or object variable. Use this prefix even when you are creating a late-bound object variable that represents a Microsoft® Office application. For example:

```
Dim objXLApp        As Object
Dim objWDDocument   As Object
Dim objOLMailItem   As Object
```

Global and module-level variables use an additional single-character prefix to specify their scope. The scope of a variable defines its lifetime and visibility. Global and module-level variables have a permanent lifetime. That is, the memory allocated to the variable remains allocated as long as the application is running. Variables declared within a procedure are visible only within the procedure where they are declared and have a lifetime that lasts only as long as the code within the procedure is executing. The exception to this is when they are declared by using the Static keyword.

Global variables have a lowercase "g" prefix and are declared in the Declarations section of a module by using the Public statement. They are visible to all procedures in all modules in an application. For example, `Public gstrPathToDataSource As String` would be a global variable that contains a string that is the path to the data source used in the application.

Variables always should be defined using the smallest scope possible. Use global variables only when there is no other way to share the data they contain. Global variables can make your code hard to understand and difficult to maintain. If you find you are using more than a few carefully chosen global variables, you might want to redesign your code to eliminate them.

Module-level variables have a lowercase "m" prefix and are declared in the Declarations section of a module by using the Dim or Private statement. They are visible to any procedure within the module in which they are declared. For example, `Dim mrstCustomerRecords As ADODB.Recordset` would be a module-level object variable for customer records. In class modules, module-level variables that are declared with the Private statement have a "p_" prefix. Public module-level variables in class modules appear as properties of the class and should not have any prefix to indicate their data type or scope.

Procedure-level variables are created within a procedure by using the Dim statement. For example, `Dim intCurrentMailItem As Integer` would be a procedure-level variable used as a loop counter. In addition, procedure-level variables can be declared by using the Static keyword. Static variables retain their value even after the procedure in which they are declared has finished running. Static procedure-level variables have a lowercase "s" prefix. For example, `Static scurTotalSales As Currency` would create a procedure-level static variable used to keep an accumulating total in a procedure that calculates current sales.

User-defined type variables are declared in the Declarations section of a module by using an all uppercase type name with "_TYPE" appended to the type name. You could declare a user-defined type in the following manner:

```
Type EMPLOYEEINFO_TYPE
    strFullName As String
    lngEmployeeID As Long
    datStartDate As Date
    strDepartmentCode As String * 4
    curSalary As Currency
End Type
```

You declare a module-level variable of type EMPLOYEEINFO_TYPE by using a "udt" prefix. For example, `Dim mudtEmployeeRecord As EMPLOYEEINFO_TYPE`.

Array variables have a lowercase "a" prefix and, unless the variable is a variant, are followed by a pair of parentheses. An array is a variable that can contain multiple values. Array variables are declared by using the Dim statement; for example, `Dim alngNum()` is an array variable of type Long. Arrays are useful when you must store a number of values of the same type, but you do not want to create individual variables to store them all.

The following are some examples of variable names that use the general naming guidelines described earlier.

Variable	Data type	Scope
strCompanyName	**String**	Procedure
rstCurrentOrders	**Object**	Procedure
intCurrentRecordCount	**Integer**	Procedure
wdWordApplication	**Object**	Procedure
varClipboardData	**Variant**	Procedure
curAmountPastDue	**Currency**	Procedure
blnProcessNextRecord	**Boolean**	Procedure
molOutlookMailItem	**Object**	Module
mcolCurrentUsers	**Object**	Module
gcnnDBConnection	**Object**	Global
gstrLogonID	**String**	Global
gastrContactNames()	**String** (array)	Global
molOutlookMailItem	**Object**	Module
mcolCurrentUsers	**Object**	Module

Variable	Data type	Scope
gcnnDBConnection	**Object**	Global
gstrLogonID	**String**	Global
gastrContactNames()	**String** (array)	Global

Constant Names

Constants use multiple-word descriptive names in all uppercase letters with an underscore character between each word. Constants are declared by using the Const statement along with the name of the constant, its data type, and its value. For example, the following constant could be declared in the Declarations section of a module to provide the path to the data source used by an application:

```
Public Const DATABASE_PATH As String = "C:\Solutions\Source\AppData.mdb"
```

> **Note** By using the Public keyword to declare the constant, that constant can be used by any procedure in any module in the application. If the Public keyword is not used, the constant has a module-level scope, meaning that it is available only to procedures within the module in which it was declared. If the constant is declared within a procedure, it is available only to the code in the procedure and only as long as the code in the procedure is executing.

Here are some examples of constant names that use the general naming guidelines described earlier:

```
ACCESS_CONNECTSTRING
API_MAX_STRINGBUFFER
SQL_STRING
```

> **Note** If you create public enumerated constants in a class module, you can use a different naming convention to distinguish them from other constants.

In addition to the constants you declare yourself, Microsoft® Visual Basic® for Applications (VBA), Visual Basic Scripting Edition (VBScript), and each of the Microsoft® Office applications contain built-in, or intrinsic, constants whose values are predefined. Intrinsic constants always should be used in place of the values they represent. As with user-defined constants, the advantage to using intrinsic constants is that they make your code more understandable. For example, compare the following two code samples, where one sample uses intrinsic constants and the other does not. See if you agree that intrinsic constants can make a big difference in how easy the code is to understand.

```
If MsgBox("Proceed Now?", 48 + 512 + 3 + 16384, "Continue?") = 7 Then
    DoCmd.OpenForm "Customers", 0, , , 1, 3
End If
```

```
If MsgBox("Proceed Now?", vbExclamation + vbDefaultButton3 + _
    vbYesNoCancel + vbMsgBoxHelpButton, "Continue?") = vbNo Then
  DoCmd.OpenForm "Customers", acNormal, , , acFormEdit, acDialog
End If
```

For a complete listing of intrinsic constants available through VBA and each of the Office applications, open the Object Browser, select the appropriate type library from the Projects/Library dialog box, type the appropriate constant prefix in the Search text box, and then click Search on the Object Browser toolbar. The following table is a sampling of the complete listing of intrinsic constants.

Application/type library	Constant prefix
Access	Ac
Excel	Xl
FrontPage	Fp
Office	Mso
Outlook	Ol
PowerPoint	Pp
Word	Wd
VBA	Vb

Naming Objects and Controls

Objects and controls, and variables that represent objects and controls, should be named with a prefix that identifies the item and a mixed-case name that clearly identifies the item's purpose. In this context, the term *objects* refers to object variables that represent items such as documents, workbooks, forms, reports, recordsets, the application itself, and other items exposed through a Microsoft® Office XP application's type library.

When you create a new module or form or add a control to a document, form, or report, the Visual Basic Editor creates a default name for the object, such as Module1, Form3, or TextBox5. You should avoid using these default names in your code. Develop the habit of specifying a meaningful name for an object as soon as you add it to your project. That way, you will not have to revise your code to rename objects later. The name should include a prefix that specifies what the object is and a name that identifies its purpose. For example, you could use modDataAccessCode, frmCustomers, and txtLastName to represent a module, a form, and a text box control. A three-character prefix is preferred, but the important point is that the prefix should be adequate to clearly specify the control type.

Note When you are designing custom object models, you should use object names without prefixes and instead use names that indicate the purpose of the objects in the model. Custom objects are designed to be used by other developers and are exposed through the Object Browser; therefore, prefixes do not make sense in this context.

When you create HTML objects and controls, you must specify a name by using the object's ID parameter. If you use a tool to add controls to an HTML page, the tool often will insert a default name for an object or control, the same way that the Visual Basic Editor does. For example, if you add a Microsoft® Forms 2.0 CommandButton control to an HTML page by using the Microsoft® ActiveX® Control Pad, the control's ID parameter is given the name CommandButton1 by default. These objects and controls should always be renamed according to the guidelines discussed in this section.

HTML element names (tags) should be entered in all capital letters. Although HTML is not case-sensitive, using this convention will help create a visual distinction between HTML elements and other items on the page. You might think of this technique as being equivalent to Microsoft® Visual Basic® for Applications (VBA) keywords being highlighted in the Visual Basic Editor. For example, if you examine the HTML code in the following example, the use of uppercase HTML element names clearly distinguishes them from the other items on the page:

```
<HTML>
<HEAD>

<TITLE>
    Developing Office Deveoper VBA and Workflow Solutions, Formatting HTML
Elements
</TITLE>

<STYLE>
    .CenterThisRed    {position:absolute; left:40%; top:220; font:bold;
color:red}
    .BoldAndBlue      {font:bold; color:blue}
</STYLE>

<SCRIPT LANGUAGE="VBSCRIPT">
<!--
    Option Explicit
    Dim strMessage

    Sub ShowAMessage(strMessage)
        ' Display strMessage in a message box.
```

```
        If Len(strMessage) = 0 Then
            strMessage = "You need to enter some text in the " _
                & "'Enter Text Here' text box before you can " _
                & "see it displayed here!"
        End If
        MsgBox strMessage
    End Sub


    Sub cmdMessage_OnClick()
        ShowAMessage(frmSampleForm.txtMessage.Value)
        frmSampleForm.txtMessage.Value = ""
    End Sub
-->
</SCRIPT>

<BODY>
    <CENTER>
    <H1>Enter HTML Elements Using
    <BR>
    <SPAN CLASS = "BoldAndBlue">
    ALL CAPS
    </SPAN>
    </H1>
    </CENTER>


    <HR>


    <DIV ID="ItemsList" CLASS="CenterThisRed">
        <OL>
            <LI>Item One</LI>
            <LI>Item Two</LI>
            <LI>Item Three</LI>
            <LI>Item Four</LI>
        </OL>
    </DIV>


    <CENTER>
```

```
<FORM NAME="frmSampleForm">
    <DIV ID="divTextBoxLabel"
        STYLE="font:bold;
                color:green">
        Enter Text Here:
    </DIV>

    <INPUT TYPE="Text" NAME="txtMessage" SIZE=50>
    <BR>
    <INPUT TYPE="Button" NAME="cmdMessage" VALUE="Display Text">
</FORM>
</CENTER>
</BODY>
</HTML>
```

Naming Functions and Subroutines

A well-written procedure performs a single specific task and is named to identify the task performed. If you find it difficult to give a specific name to a procedure because it is performing more than one task, consider breaking the procedure down into multiple procedures, so each discrete piece of functionality can be identified clearly.

When naming a procedure, you should use the *NounVerb* or *VerbNoun* style to create a name that clearly identifies what the procedure does. It is not necessary to use a prefix or suffix to specify the data type of the return value. Keep in mind that when you store related procedures in the same module, the Procedures box in the Code window will display those procedures alphabetically. If you stored all your data access code in a module named modDataAccessCode, you could use the *NounVerb* naming style, so related procedures are listed together. For example, the CustomerAdd, CustomerDelete, and CustomerUpdate procedures would all be displayed together in the Procedures dialog box.

When you are creating procedures that use arguments, use argument names that adhere to your variable-naming convention. For example, the following procedure uses arguments consisting of three strings, an integer, and a Boolean value:

```
Function RemoveString(ByVal strSource As String, _
                      strStart As String, _
                      strEnd As String, _
                      Optional intEndCount As Integer = 0, _
                      Optional blnReturnChunk As Boolean = False) As
String
As _
String



    .
    .
    .



End Function
```

When you are calling a built-in or custom method or procedure that accepts optional arguments, always use named arguments instead of positional arguments. Named arguments make your code easier to understand, debug, and maintain. A named argument is an argument name followed by a colon and an equal sign (:=), followed by the argument value. When you use named arguments, you do not have to include placeholders for optional arguments not passed to the procedure. The first line in the following example shows how to call a custom procedure using positional arguments. The second line shows how to call the same procedure using named arguments.

```
strModifiedString = RemoveString(strOriginalString, strStartHere, _
    strEndHere, , True)


strModifiedString = RemoveString(strSource:=strOriginalString, _
    strStart:=strStartHere, strEnd:=strEndHere, blnReturnChunk:=True)
```

The following example shows how to use named arguments to call the Open method of the Word Documents collection. The Open method accepts up to 10 arguments, but only the FileName argument is required.

```
Application.Documents.Open ReadOnly:=True, FileName:="AUTOSHAPE.DOC", _
    Format:=wdOpenFormatAuto
```

If an argument uses a value that represents a built-in enumerated constant, declare the argument's data type by using the enumerated constant name. For example, if you have an argument that is used to specify one of the many Outlook item types, declare the argument As Outlook.OlItemType rather than As Integer. Using this technique means you do not have to validate the argument that is passed to the procedure, because by definition the argument value can contain only an existing Outlook item type. For example:

```
Function CreateNewItemB(intItemType As Outlook.OlItemType, _
                        Optional strName As String = "")
    Dim olApp          As New Outlook.Application
    Dim olNewItem      As Object

    Select Case intItemType
        Case olMailItem
            Set olNewItem = olApp.CreateItem(olMailItem)
        Case olAppointmentItem
            Set olNewItem = olApp.CreateItem(olAppointmentItem)
        Case olContactItem
            Set olNewItem = olApp.CreateItem(olContactItem)
        Case olTaskItem
            Set olNewItem = olApp.CreateItem(olTaskItem)
        Case olNoteItem
            Set olNewItem = olApp.CreateItem(olNoteItem)
        Case Else
    End Select
    .
    .
    .
End Function
```

Structuring and Formatting Your Code

How you use structured coding conventions directly affects how easy your code is to understand and maintain. General principles of applying a structure to your code have effects at the application level, the module level, and the procedure level. The corresponding use of formatting—line breaks, white space, and indentation—helps reveal the logic and structure of each procedure.

Structuring Your Code

At the application level, your code is contained in one or more standard modules or class modules and in modules behind forms, reports, or documents. You apply structure to your code at this level by organizing your code logically within these components in your application. Within any module, the procedures should have some relation to each other. For example, you could keep all data access code in a single module. Form, report, or document modules should contain only code that applies directly to the form, report, or document or to controls it contains.

At the procedure level, applying a structure to the code means breaking up large procedures into smaller ones and using line breaks, white space, and indentation to organize and illustrate the logical structure of the code. Any general-purpose procedures called by code in these objects should be contained in a separate module. In addition, you should add comments at the module level to provide information on the nature and purpose of the procedures contained in the module.

You should use these principles whether you are writing Microsoft® Visual Basic® for Applications (VBA) code or script in an HTML page. You can think of an HTML page as being similar to a VBA application for the purposes of structuring your script. You can think of blocks of script within <SCRIPT> tags as being similar to VBA procedures contained in a module. The script and procedures used between <SCRIPT> tags should be related to other script within the same set of tags. Any general-purpose procedures called from the script in an HTML page should be grouped together within their own pair of <SCRIPT> tags or kept in a scriptlet.

Formatting Code

Some developers believe that although formatting code might make it look pretty, it is not really worth the time. However, properly formatting code has nothing to do with appearance and everything to do with how easy your code is to understand and maintain. The basic techniques used to format code are line breaks, white space, and indentation. In addition to making the code easier to read, these formatting techniques help document the code by showing the logic and flow of a procedure and by grouping logically related sections of code.

Formatting VBScript vs. VBA Code

Even developers of the most feebly written Microsoft® Visual Basic® for Applications (VBA) code usually attempt to name things consistently and add comments and perhaps some white space where appropriate. However, something very different is happening on the Web. It seems there is no attempt to use naming conventions or formatting techniques to make script easier to understand and maintain; in fact, just the opposite appears to be happening. Perhaps it is the forgiving nature of an HTML page as a scripting environment, or perhaps it is because script in an HTML page is viewed easily by others, and the easier it is to understand, the easier it is for someone to borrow.

Line Breaks

In VBA and Visual Basic Scripting Edition (VBScript) code, you break a line by using the line-continuation character—an underscore (_) preceded by a space. You use line breaks to make sure that your code does not extend beyond the right edge of the Code window (usually about 60 characters).

For example, line breaks have been used in the following code, so the entire string can be viewed in the Code window without having to scroll to the right:

```
Dim strMessage As String
strMessage = "Fourscore and seven years ago our fathers " _
    & "brought forth, on this continent, a new nation, " _
    & "conceived in liberty, and dedicated to the " _
    & "proposition that all men are created equal."
MsgBox strMessage
```

Note how an additional tab character is inserted for all lines following the initial line break. This creates the visual cue that the indented text remains a part of the portion of the string that comes before the line break.

If the line following the continued line is indented as much as the continued line would be, add one more tab to the continued line to distinguish it from the next line. For example:

```
If ActiveSheet.ChartObjects(1).Chart.ChartTitle = _
        ActiveSheet.Range("a2").Value Then
    MsgBox "They are equal."
End If
```

Be careful when you are using line-continuation characters in strings. If you must divide the string into two or more strings, place the line-continuation character between the strings, and then concatenate them using the ampersand (&). It is important to preserve all spaces in the string when it is concatenated. For example:

```
Sub LongString()
    ' This will form a correct SQL string.
    strSQL = "SELECT LastName, FirstName FROM Employees WHERE " _
        & "(BirthDate > #1-1-60#);"

    ' This one will be missing the space between WHERE and (BirthDate).
    strSQL = "SELECT LastName, FirstName FROM Employees WHERE" _
        & "(BirthDate > #1-1-60#);"
End Sub
```

Use the ampersand (&) for all concatenation operations; never use the plus sign (+).

In HTML code, you create a line break by entering a carriage return. The browser will ignore these line breaks when it renders the page. For example, text in this HTML page will break only where the <BR> element appears:

```
<BODY>
    <CENTER>
    <H2>Office Programmer's Guide
    <BR>Programming Concepts
    <BR>HTML Sample Page: Line Breaks</H2>
```

```
<HR>
<H3>To see an example, click Source
on the View menu.</H3>
<BR>
<BR>
</CENTER>

Fourscore and seven
years ago our fathers
brought forth, on this
continent, a new nation,
conceived in liberty, and
dedicated to the proposition
that all men are created equal.


</BODY>
```

White Space

Use blank lines to separate logically related blocks of code, introductory (header) comments from the first variable declaration, and the last declared variable from the code itself. Precede all comments with a blank line.

Indentation

Indent code and comments within a procedure by using a two- to four-space tab stop. (The Visual Basic Editor uses a four-space tab stop by default.) As with white space, indents are used to organize code logically and make it visually appealing.

The following list contains some general guidelines regarding where, when, and how to use indentation correctly to make your code more readable and maintainable:

- Indent all code and comments within a procedure at least one tab stop. The only code lines that are not indented are the beginning and ending of the procedure and line labels used in connection with your error handler.

- If you use line breaks to format a procedure's argument list, use tabs to indent the arguments and their data-type declarations, so they are aligned with the first argument in the list.

- Indent declared variables one tab stop. Declare only one variable on a line.

- Indent control structures at least one tab stop. If one control structure is embedded within another, indent the embedded structure one tab stop. Indent code within a control structure one additional tab stop.

- If you use a line-continuation character to break a line of code, indent the new line one extra tab stop. This creates a visual cue that the two (or more) lines belong together. If the line following the continued line is indented as much as the continued line would be, add one more tab to the continued line to distinguish it from the next line.

- Indent comments to the same level as the code to which the comment refers.

Look at how these general techniques are applied in the following procedure:

```
Function GetFileList(strDirPath As String, _
                     Optional strFileSpec As String = "*.*", _
                     Optional strDelim As String = ",") As String


    ' This procedure returns a delimited list of files from the
    ' strDirPath directory that match the strFileSpec argument.
    ' The default delimiter character is a comma. By default, the
    ' procedure returns all files ("*.*") from the designated
    ' directory.

    Dim strFileList     As String ' Used to collect the file list.
    Dim strFileNames    As String ' The full path and criteria to search
for.
    Dim strTemp         As String ' Temporarily holds the matching file
name.

    ' Make sure that strDirPath ends in a "\" character.
    If Right$(strDirPath, 1) <> "\" Then
        strDirPath = strDirPath & "\"
    End If


    ' This will be our file search criteria.
    strFileNames = strDirPath & strFileSpec

    ' Create a list of matching files delimited by the
    ' strDelim character.
    strTemp = Dir$(strFileNames)
    Do While Len(strTemp) <> 0
        strFileList = strFileList & strTemp & strDelim
        strTemp = Dir$()
    Loop
```

```
If Len(strFileList) > 1 Then
    ' If there are matching files, remove the delimiter
    ' character from the end of the list.
    GetFileList = Left(strFileList, Len(strFileList) - 1)
Else
    GetFileList = ""
End If
End Function
```

Commenting Code

If you follow the guidelines discussed in Using a Naming Convention and Structuring and Formatting Your Code, you are using a naming convention that identifies objects, variables, constants, and procedures, and you are using a prefix to indicate each variable's data type and scope. In addition to naming conventions, structured coding conventions, such as code commenting, can greatly improve code readability.

All procedures and functions should begin with a brief comment describing the functional characteristics of the procedure (what it does). This description, preceded by an apostrophe ('), should not describe the implementation details (how it does it), because these often change over time, resulting in unnecessary comment maintenance work, or worse yet, erroneous comments. The code itself and any necessary inline comments will describe the implementation. For example:

```
' This is a comment beginning at the left edge of the
' screen.
Text1.Text = "Hi!"          ' Place friendly greeting in text
                  ' box.
```

Note Comments can follow a statement on the same line or can occupy an entire line. Both are illustrated in the preceding code.

Using Comments Effectively

The purpose of adding comments to code is to provide an understandable description of what your code is doing. Comments should provide information that is not otherwise available from reading the code itself. Good comments are written at a higher level of abstraction than the code itself. Comments that only restate what is already obvious add nothing to the code and should be avoided. In addition, if your comments speak to how the code works, instead of to what it does, you have created an additional code-maintenance problem, because comments that describe how code works must be revised whenever you change the code. Failing to maintain these comments along with the code creates a risk that the comments will no longer describe the code. Some developers often write "how" comments that merely restate what is already obvious from the code itself; for example:

```
' Make sure the length of strSource is not zero and it contains
' a ".txt" extension.
If Len(strSource) > 0 And InStr(strFileName, ".txt") > 0 Then
    ' If strSource does not contain a ":" or a "\" then
    ' return False.
    If InStr(strFileName, ":") = 0 Or InStr(strFileName, "\") = 0 Then
        SaveStringAsTextFile = False
    Else
        ' Get the next available file number.
        intFileNumber = FreeFile
        ' Open the file in Append mode.
        Open strFileName For Append As intFileNumber
        ' Write data to the file on disk.
        Print #intFileNumber, strSource;
        ' Close the file.
        Close intFileNumber
    End If
Else
    ' Return False.
    SaveStringAsTextFile = False
End If
```

These comments add nothing that is not evident from the code itself. The following is the full version of this procedure that lets the code speak for itself and uses comments that describe only what the code is doing:

```
Function SaveStringAsTextFile(strSource As String, _
                        strFileName As String) As Boolean


    ' Save the string in strSource to the file supplied
    ' in strFileName. If the operation succeeds, return True;
    ' otherwise, return False. If the file described by
    ' strFileName already exists, append strSource to any
    ' existing text in the file.

    Dim intFileNumber As Integer


    On Error GoTo SaveString_Err
```

```
' Assume that the operation will succeed.
SaveStringAsTextFile = True


If Len(strSource) > 0 And InStr(strFileName, ".txt") > 0 Then
    If InStr(strFileName, ":") = 0 Or InStr(strFileName, "\") = 0 Then
        ' Invalid file path submitted.
        SaveStringAsTextFile = False
    Else
        ' Save file to disk.
        intFileNumber = FreeFile
        Open strFileName For Append As intFileNumber
        Print #intFileNumber, strSource;
        Close intFileNumber
    End If
Else
    SaveStringAsTextFile = False
End If


SaveString_End:
    Exit Function
SaveString_Err:
    MsgBox Err.Description, vbCritical & vbOKOnly, _
        "Error Number " & Err.Number & " Occurred"
    Resume SaveString_End
End Function
```

At a minimum, you should add comments at the module level to describe the group of related procedures in the module. Add comments at the procedure level to describe the purpose of the procedure itself. For example, the following module-level comments document the public and private procedures (called "methods" in a class module), the properties and their data types, and information about how to use the class as an object:

```
' This class provides services related to creating and sending
' Outlook MailItem objects. It also includes wrappers to handle
' attaching files to a mail message.
'
```

```
'    Public Methods:
'        MailAddRecipient(strName As String, Optional fType As Boolean)
'            strName:    Name of recipient to add to message.
'            fType:      Outlook MailItem Type property setting.
'        SendMail(Optional blnShowMailFirst As Boolean)
'            blnShowMailFirst:   Whether to show the Outlook mail message
'                                before sending it. Set to True
'programmatically
'                                if unable to resolve recipient addresses.
'
'    Private Methods:
'        InitializeOutlook()
'        CreateMail()
'
'    Public Properties:
'        MailSubject:        (Write only, String)
'        MailMessage:        (Write only, String)
'        MailAttachments:    (Write only, String)
'
'    Usage:   From any standard module, declare an object variable of type
'             clsMailMessage. Use that object variable to access the methods
'             and properties of this class.
```

Where appropriate, add comments to describe the functionality of a particular line or block of code. These comments should be used sparingly and should be used to document any unusual aspects of the code. A blank line should precede all comments, and they should be aligned with the code to which they apply. Insert comments before the line or block of code to which they apply, not on the same line as the code itself.

In certain circumstances, you will use comments to document the arguments passed to a procedure, to state whether those arguments should be within a certain range of values, to convey whether global variables are changed within the procedure, and to relate the procedure's return values. It is not unusual to include comments that document a procedure's revision history, the names of other procedures that call the current procedure, the author of a procedure (or a revision), or a sample syntax line showing how the procedure is called.

It is a good practice to write comments at the same time (or earlier than) you write your code. Some developers write the comments for all of their procedures before they write a single line of code. It can be very effective to design procedures using only comments to describe what the code will do. This is a way to sketch out a framework for a procedure, or several related procedures, without getting bogged down in the details of writing the code itself. Later, when you write the code to implement the framework, your original high-level descriptions can be effective comments. Whatever technique you use, always enter or revise your comments as soon as you write the code. Avoid "saving it for later," because there is rarely time to do it later, or, if there is, you will not understand the code as well when you come back to it.

You add comments to an HTML page by wrapping them in comment tags. The HTML element for a comment is the <!— and —> tag pair. At a minimum, add comments to document the HTML where appropriate. Use an introductory (header) comment to document each subroutine and function in the HTML page. How you add comments to script in an HTML page depends on the scripting language you are using. In VBScript, comments are indicated by an apostrophe (') character. In Microsoft® JScript®, you use either //, which indicates that the rest of the line is a comment, or /* *comment text* */, which indicates that all of the *comment text* is a comment, no matter how many lines it spans.

Comments serve an additional purpose when they are used in script in an HTML file. Browsers will ignore any unrecognized HTML tag. However, if the script tags are ignored, the browser will attempt to render the script itself as plain text. The correct way to format script so older browsers will ignore both the script tags and the script itself is to wrap your script (but not the script tags) in the <!— and —> comment tags. If you are using VBScript, you must use the apostrophe character to add comments to script that is nested within the <!— and —> comment tags. The following example uses both forms of comment tags:

```
<SCRIPT LANGUAGE="VBSCRIPT">

<!--

    Option Explicit


    Sub UpdateMessage()
        ' This procedure calls code in a scriptlet to get
        ' values for the current day, month, and year, and then
        ' uses the innerHTML property of a <DIV> tag to dynamically
        ' display those values on the page.

        .

        .

        .

-->
</SCRIPT>
```

Automating Code Commenting

It is a good practice to add thorough comments to any code that you write. Although it might be perfectly clear to you how your code works, it might not be clear to someone else (or even to yourself) when that code must be modified at a later time. Clear comments can save you a lot of time and effort in the future.

The VBA Code Commenter and Error Handler add-in helps you to add consistent comments to your code, including author name, date and time of creation, and other pertinent information. It inserts a header template at the beginning of a procedure; you fill in the blanks. You can choose to add comments to a single procedure, to all of the procedures within a module, or to all procedures in your project at once.

To add comments to your code

1. From the **Add-Ins** menu, select **VBA Code Commenter**.

    Note The VBA Code Commenter menu item is available only when the VBA Code Commenter and Error Handler add-in is loaded.

2. Make a selection from the **Add Comments To** group to determine whether comments will be added to the current procedure, all procedures in the current module, or all procedures in the current project.

3. Verify that the desired template is selected in the **Code Header Template** box.

4. Type the name and initials for the **Author** if desired. With the default template, this information appears as part of the code comments. This information is stored in the registry for future use. If you do not enter information, the name and initials default to the registered user of the product.

5. Click **OK**.

The VBA Code Commenter and Error Handler add-in uses template files (.eht) to control the format of comments. You can edit the standard template (CodeCommenter.eht) or create your own templates using Notepad or another text editor.

Designing Code to Be Used Again

The following topics cover techniques you can use to transform your code into reusable components.

These topics are designed to get you started writing code that can be used in different situations.

In This Section

What Is Reusable Code?
>   Reusable code is code that can be used, without modification, to perform a specific service regardless of what application uses the code.

Writing Reusable Code
>   There are many ways to write code that performs some valuable service.

Source Code Sharing
>   Whether you are working on a team or by yourself, you can integrate source code control, code sharing, and code reuse for your projects, simplifying just about any development project.

Related Sections

Writing Solid Code

"Writing solid code" means writing Microsoft® Visual Basic® for Applications (VBA) code or script that performs as expected and is reusable, easy to understand, and easy to maintain.

Writing Solid Script

The benefits associated with writing reusable, understandable, and maintainable code can be realized whether you are writing script or Microsoft® Visual Basic® for Applications (VBA) code.

Using a Naming Convention

There are many formal naming conventions and each has its adherents and detractors. You can adopt one of the existing conventions or create one of your own.

Structuring and Formatting Your Code

How you use structured coding conventions directly affects how easy your code is to understand and maintain.

Commenting Code

All procedures and functions should begin with a brief comment describing the functional characteristics of the procedure (what it does).

What Is Reusable Code?

Reusable code is code that can be used, without modification, to perform a specific service regardless of what application uses the code.

There are everyday objects that perform a specific service in different circumstances all around you. Think of a calendar. It gives you the ability to look up days and dates. You can use it to determine that this year your birthday falls on a Tuesday, or that Thanksgiving is on the 25th, or that there are two extra days to file tax returns because April 15 is on a Saturday. When you are building software, objects are created in code, and reusable objects that perform specific services in different circumstances are called *components*.

When you use Microsoft® Office to build custom applications, you write code that leverages the power of Office components. Using an Office component means you not only do not have to write the code yourself, but you are using a component that has been tested and found reliable in different conditions. In the past, developers would consider writing a custom program to check spelling. Today, you would call the spelling checker provided with Microsoft® Word. Similarly, nobody would develop custom code to calculate depreciation or determine principal and interest payments on a long-term loan. Instead, you would call the VBA built-in financial functions or use the Microsoft® Excel Application object to handle complex calculations for you.

Just as you can build custom applications based on components supplied as part of Office, you also can build them by using reusable components you have created yourself. You can think of reusable code from the perspective of the code that will call it to perform its service. This reusable code is a black box that accepts a known input value and returns a known output value. What happens inside the box (how the procedure actually works) is irrelevant to the code that calls it.

When you get into the habit of writing reusable procedures, you will find that you often have applications where groups of related procedures work together to perform a single service or a group of related services. For example, you might have a group of procedures that provides data access services or another group that consists of string-handling routines. This is an opportunity to group related procedures in their own module (or in a class module that exposes methods and properties to gain access to the procedures). Then, you can add the module to any application that requires the services it provides.

Writing Reusable Code

There are many ways to write code that performs some valuable service. Options range from recording a macro that can replay a sequence of keystrokes and menu selections to creating a class module that provides a wrapper around complicated Microsoft® Windows® application programming interface (API) functions.

It is not difficult to write reusable code. It is really a matter of how you approach the problem. If you understand how to create and use class modules, then you already know a great deal about how to approach writing reusable code.

The first consideration when you are writing reusable code is writing code that uses a consistent naming convention, that is formatted properly, and that contains useful comments.

Examine your existing code to make sure that your procedures have a single, specific purpose. Can you describe your procedures in a short, plain sentence? For example, "This procedure accepts an SQL string as an argument and returns a Recordset object containing the records described by the string." If you are unable to describe a procedure simply and clearly, it probably does too many things. Break down complicated procedures into smaller ones that do one thing each. Procedures should contain only code that clearly belongs together.

In the first of the following two examples, you have application-specific code that provides an application, but is not reusable. In the second example, you have created a reusable component that can perform its service from within any application.

Avoid making specific reference to named application objects. For example, the following code makes a specific reference to a combo box control and a text box control on a Microsoft® Access form:

```
strEmployeeName = Forms!frmEmployees!cboEmployeeName
strSQL = "SELECT * FROM Employees WHERE LastName = '" & _
    Mid(strEmployeeName, InStr(strEmployeeName, " ") + 1) & "'"
Set rstAddresses = dbs.OpenRecordset(strSQL)
Forms!frmEmployees!txtHireDate = rstAddresses!HireDate
```

It would not be possible to reuse the previous code without revising it substantially. However, the procedure could be rewritten as a function that accepts a table name, a field name, and the record-selection criteria and returns the matching data. The following procedure could be used in any application that must retrieve a value from a field in a table:

```
Function GetDataFromField(strTableName As String, _
                          strFieldName As String, _
                          strCriteria As String) As Variant

    ' Returns a value from the field specified by strFieldName
    ' in the table specified by strTableName according to the
    ' criteria specified by strCriteria.

    Dim rstFieldData    As New ADODB.Recordset
    Dim strSQL          As String

    On Error Resume Next

    strSQL = "SELECT " & strFieldName & " FROM " & _
        strTableName & " WHERE " & strCriteria
    rstFieldData.Open strSQL, DATA_CONNECTSTRING & DATA_PATH
    If Err = 0 Then
        GetDataFromField = rstFieldData(strFieldName)
    Else
        GetDataFromField = ""
    End If
End Function
```

In the previous code sample, notice that two constants were used in place of the database connection string and database path in the Microsoft® ActiveX® Data Object (ADO) Recordset object's Open method. This sample highlights another important consideration when you are writing reusable code: Avoid hard-coding values used in your code. If a string or number is used repeatedly, define a module-level constant and use the constant in your code. If you must use a string or number in more than one module, declare the constant by using the Public keyword. If you have a string or number that is local to a procedure, consider rewriting the procedure to pass the value as an argument or by using a local constant.

Try to minimize the number of arguments in a procedure and pass in only what is actually required by the procedure. In addition, make sure your procedures use all the arguments passed to them.

Group related procedures and the constants they use together in the same module, and where appropriate, consider grouping related procedures together in a class module with a clearly defined interface.

Keep procedures in standard modules and not in modules behind forms or documents. The code in form modules should be only that code that is tied directly to the form itself and the code required for calling general procedures stored in standard modules.

Communicate between procedures by passing data as arguments to the procedures. Persist data by writing it to disk or to the Windows registry. Avoid using a procedure to write to a global variable so another procedure can read data from that global variable. Avoid communicating with another procedure by passing data out of the application, for example, using one procedure to write data to a disk file, .ini file, or the registry so another procedure can read that data.

The same considerations that go into writing reusable code also apply to writing reusable script. The easiest way to reuse script is to group related procedures together in a scriptlet and then link the scriptlet to the HTML page in which you want to use the script.

Source Code Sharing

Whether you are working on a team or by yourself, you can integrate source code control, code sharing, and code reuse for your projects, simplifying just about any development project. Microsoft® Visual SourceSafe™ and the Code Librarian make it easier to share, reuse, and move your code safely among individual programmers, development teams, and project stages.

Visual SourceSafe is a version control system that makes it possible for you and other team members to share files, modify them independently, and later merge the changes. Visual SourceSafe also saves past versions of the files in a database, tracks the date and time of changes, and provides an option to keep a comment log.

The Code Librarian is a database for code snippets, functions, or modules that might be useful to other developers. You can select functions, change the name, change the description, and specify search criteria. In addition, you can create new code snippets and delete existing ones.

Working with XML

Extensible Markup Language (XML) is a meta-markup language that provides a format for describing structured data. This facilitates more precise declarations of content and more meaningful search results across multiple platforms. In addition, XML enables the separation of presentation from data. For example, in HTML, you use tags to tell the browser to display data as bold or italic; in XML, you use tags only to describe data, such as city name, temperature, and barometric pressure. In XML, you use style sheets, such as Extensible Stylesheet Language (XSL) and cascading style sheets (CSS), to present the data in a browser. XML separates the data from the presentation and the process, making it possible for you to display and process the data by applying different style sheets and applications.

XML is a subset of Standard Generalized Markup Language (SGML) that is optimized for delivery over the Web. It is defined by the World Wide Web Consortium (W3C). This standardization makes sure structured data will be uniform and independent of applications or vendors.

XML, which provides a data standard that can encode the content, semantics, and schemata for a wide variety of cases ranging from simple to complex, can be used to mark up the following:

- An ordinary document

- A structured record, such as an appointment record or purchase order

- An object with data and methods, such as the persistent format of an object or Microsoft® ActiveX® control

- A data record, such as the result set of a query

- Meta-content about a Web site, such as Channel Definition Format (CDF)

- Graphical presentation, such as an application's user interface

- Links between information and people on the Web

XML is simple, platform independent, and a widely adopted standard. The power of XML is that it separates the user interface from the structured data. This separation of data from presentation makes it possible for the integration of data from diverse sources. Customer information, purchase orders, research results, bill payments, medical records, catalog data, and other information can be converted to XML.

In This Section

Office Applications and XML

The advent of the Internet has drawn attention to the fact that there is a great amount of information available in a wide variety of shapes and sizes—most of which is interesting, much of which is not available without a great deal of development effort. Sometimes, even the greatest effort has been unsuccessful in sharing the information across applications.

Working with XML in the Design Environment
The XML Designer provides tools for working with XML files.

Office Applications and XML

The advent of the Internet has drawn attention to the fact that there is a great amount of information available in a wide variety of shapes and sizes—most of which is interesting, much of which is not available without a great deal of development effort. Sometimes, even the greatest effort has been unsuccessful in sharing the information across applications.

A primary problem with data interchange is caused by the differences in the structure of the data being shared (word documents not being the same as Microsoft® SQL Server™ data) and/or the schema of that data (last_name and LastName). XML resolves these problems by creating a data interchange format that is agreed upon by an independent standards body.

XML has proven useful as an interchange protocol because it:

- Is readable by a human being
- Supports dynamic content
- Can be navigated and manipulated on the client
- Makes it possible for partial updating of information without round trips to the server (the information is already on client)
- Makes it possible for the exchange of data despite different platforms, applications, data formats, protocols, schemas, business rules, and so on

XML encourages the separation of business rules from data. Therefore, XML is often used as a:

- Transient data aggregator and information normalizer
- Persistent store for metadata
- Means for creating an object paradigm rather than a data paradigm

XML can be used to maintain strong data requirements across sources through the expression of rich relationships, complex linking, metadata, and versioning.

The implications are that, by using XML, Microsoft Access can move information between a variety of sources without losing the metadata required to update the original source, and/or any intermediate sources. Furthermore, XML not only provides the mechanism for moving information among various products on the client, XML also makes it possible for the movement of information between the client and the server—even across servers themselves.

Data alone, however, is not sufficient; presentation of that information also is critical. Typically, presentation on the Internet is accomplished using a browser rendering HTML or DHTML. However, conditioning the data hosted within the XML file is done through XSL.

XSL is a subset of well-formed XML used for defining presentation. An XSL file will contain standard HTML formatting clauses, as well as clauses specific to finding data matches, retrieving data, and so on. XSL files can be used not only to change the presentation of the underlying XML, but also as a filter to limit the XML data displayed.

XML Support in Excel

XML is establishing itself quickly as an important data interchange format. Disparate systems using XML now can communicate, exchange, and share data easily and readily. Information consumers might want to move this data in and out of Microsoft® Excel and the Spreadsheet component. In some cases, Excel might be the final destination for data, for example, a summary report created for analysis. In other cases, users might want to view, update, and review their data in Excel as an intermediate step in the context of a larger business process.

With XML support built into Excel, users can load data into Excel from a broader range of sources, and users can expose data in their spreadsheets, as well as the spreadsheet models themselves, to a wider range of applications that can consume that data.

There are some exciting, new features, with which you can:

- Load any generic XML document

- Utilize Excel XML Spreadsheet Scheme (XML SS) to

    - Hand author XML SS documents (from Microsoft® Visual Basic® for Applications, Microsoft® Active Server Pages, Microsoft® BizTalk™, or other technologies)

    - Extract data from your Excel documents with relative ease

    - Extend Range Value programmability to understand data in the XML SS structure

    - Create web queries to XML data sources, with timed refreshes in your spreadsheet models

XML Data Import in Access

Microsoft® Access now provides you with the ability to import information from an XML document into one of the standard Access data engines: Microsoft® Jet or Microsoft® SQL Server™ 2000 Desktop Engine.

You can import an XML file that contains only data (bulk load), metadata (structure only), both data and metadata (structure and data load) or one that has been transformed using Extensible Stylesheet Language Transformation (XSLT) during the import process.

Access provides choices for using data from many external sources. XML makes it easier to transform the data from almost any external application for use by Access. You can:

- Import XML data to a Jet, SQL Server, or SQL Server Desktop Engine

- Import XML schema data to a Jet, SQL Server, or SQL Server Desktop Engine

- Use an XSLT file to transform the data into an Access data format

As with importing other data into Access, the File | Get External Data | Import option is used to import XML data files into Access. This option brings up the Import dialog box where an XML document can be selected, as well as a schema that describes the structure of the data. Only a single document can be selected for import into Access. To support the import of XML, the data must be in a format that Access recognizes either in a native format or by using a schema.

Note   When importing XML data, you cannot choose a subset of the XML document; the entire file has to be imported.

By choosing Options from the Import XML dialog box, you can select a specific Access format in which to transform the native XML data. In addition, you can specify whether to overwrite any existing tables with the same name and overwrite or append them to existing data.

XML Data Export in Access

Exporting data and database objects to an XML file is a convenient way to move and store your information in a format that can be used across the Web readily. In Microsoft® Access, you can export just the data, just the schema (data structure), or both to XML files. You can:

- Export data to an XML file and, optionally, use an XSLT to transform the data to another format

- Export the data schema using XSD

- Export the data behind forms and reports to an XML file

- Send a table or query, or the data behind a form or report, as an e-mail attachment

In addition, you can transform the data to another presentation format using an Extensible Style Language (XSL) file during the export process. You can export tables, queries, and the data behind forms or reports from an Access database (.mdb) and tables, views, and the data behind forms and reports from an Access project (.adp).

Exporting Tables, Queries, Views, Datasheets, Forms or Reports

When you export a database object as an XML document, Access provides several options:

- You can export just the data from a table, query/view, datasheet, form, or report into an XML file. This data "snapshot" is saved to a file named <filename>.xml.

- You can export just the schema (data structure) from a table, query/view, datasheet, form, or report to an XML schema file. An XML schema file is a formal specification of the rules for an XML document, providing a series of element names, as well as which elements are permitted in the document and in what combinations. If you select to save the schema as XSD, the file is saved as <filename>.xsd.

Note When you export a table to an XML document, you also can export related tables. For example, if you export a table of Customers Orders, you also can choose to export a related Orders Details table and Customers table.

- If selected, you also can save the structure of a table, query/view, datasheet, form, or report into a file that describes the presentation and connection information. For forms and reports, this file is saved in an XML-based language called ReportML, which provides presentation data as well as a data model for creating a data access page. For tables, queries/views, and datasheets, the presentation file is a spreadsheet-like template. This file is saved as <filename>_report.xml.

- In addition, when you choose to save the data as XML, you can specify that the data be transformed to a custom display format by using an existing .xsl file. If no .xsl file is specified, the data is saved in standard XML format. The file is saved as <filename>_report.xml.

  Note If no data is selected for export, then a presentation format is unavailable.

XSL: Technology Backgrounder

XSL is an interpretation mechanism. It interprets, or transforms, XML data structures native to one source into data structures that can be understood by another source. In addition, XSL is used to change the XML presentation of information based upon the requirements of the recipient.

To work, the XSL must make assumptions about the incoming and outgoing XML. That is, the XSL assumes it already "knows" the format of the incoming XML, and, therefore, transforms that format into the known outgoing format.

For example, Microsoft® Access can read only XML data documents that are in the Access XML format, which is element centric. ActiveX data objects only can persist XML data documents in its format, which is attribute centric. Access cannot, therefore, read ADO XML data documents. However, Access does provide an XSL that takes the ADO XML data document, transforms the format, and produces an Access XML data document.

In the case of presentation, Access uses XSL presentation transformations to take the internal report representation, called ReportML, to produce a variety of other outputs, such as an XML-spreadsheet, HTML 4.0, and data access pages.

For export, Access supports the use of XSLs to transform Access XML into input XML documents and into a data shape that is for use by an external processor, or the transformation of Access ReportML into any presentation format. For import, Access supports the use of XSLs to transform the output from an external source into Access XML.

XSL Transformations in Access

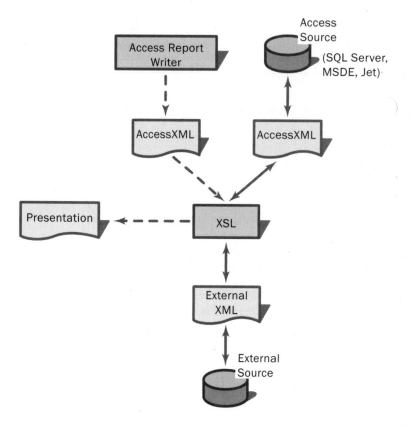

XSL Transformation in Access

The purpose of XML is to act as a data transfer protocol. Unfortunately, the format in which XML can be transported can vary widely. This means to share data between disparate sources, XML still must be interpreted, or transformed from the source to the target format and back again. This is the purpose of XSL/T.

Furthermore, any given XML document, while self-describing, might not contain the presentation information appropriate to the recipient. Transforming the XML document's presentation instructions is the purpose of XSL.

Microsoft® Access will support both the transformation of the XML data document and its presentation or rendering.

Using this feature, you can create an XSL:

- Transformation document that is displayed automatically in the import/export dialogs and is applied by the Access import/export/save as/send to methods

- Presentation document that is displayed automatically in the import/export dialogs and is applied by the Access import/export/save as/send to methods

The XSL architecture is designed to make it possible for third parties to add data and presentation transformations to the export and import dialogs in Access easily. This is done by both adding a meta tag, or header, to the XSL file and by placing the XSL in the directory.

The Access XSL architecture is designed to include any XSL file containing the proper header information when it is located on the appropriate directory. There are three possible locations for the transformation files: program files, application data, and a network server. The following is true regardless of where the file location:

- Access will merge the .XSL files found in these locations whenever possible.

- Administrators can lock down any or all of the locations such that third party transformations cannot be stored or used.

XML Access Reports

ReportML is a language that describes Microsoft® Access objects in XML. The ReportML language is made up of a set of tags that describes a form or report's properties, events, and attributes.

Any XML document produced by Access is, at a minimum, well-formed—which means it conforms to the basic rules of XML. That is:

- Each XML document must have a unique root element (an element encompassing the entire document).

- All start and end tags match. XML tags are case-sensitive.

- For each start tag, there is a corresponding end tag. Empty elements can be denoted by a special shorthand tag. Again, XML tags are case-sensitive.

    Note Access ReportML will not write out any empty tags.

- Elements do not overlap. In other words, start and end tags must be nested properly within other elements.

- Certain reserve characters are part of the XML syntax and will not be interpreted correctly if used in the data portion of an element. You must substitute a special character sequence (called an entity by XML) as follows:

    - < <

    - & &

    - > >

    - " "

    - ' '

If a properly formatted schema is specified while exporting from Access, then the XML documents created are considered valid XML document. This means, in addition to being well-formed, the documents conform to a defined schema.

Working with XML in the Design Environment

The XML Designer provides tools for working with XML files. The designer contains a view for editing XML source code (XML Source view).

The following extensions also are recognized as .xml:

- .tdl—Template Description Language file
- .xslt (no data view)
- .web
- .resx

XML Source View

The XML Source view provides an editor for creating and editing XML, which offers Microsoft® IntelliSense® and statement completion. When you press < key to initiate a new tag, you will be presented with a list of elements that are valid at that location. After you type the element name and press the space bar, you will be presented with a list of attributes that the element supports.

By right-clicking and selecting Synchronize Document Outline from the shortcut menu, you can view the Document Outline window, which makes it possible for you to see the nesting structure of your .xml file and to navigate easily to different elements.

Custom Classes and Objects

Are you ready to take your Microsoft® Visual Basic® for Applications (VBA) programming skills to a new level? If you have never used class modules to build custom objects before, this section covers the concepts that you must understand to design, build, and use custom objects with their own methods and properties. If you have been building your own objects for some time now, this section also covers some exciting new additions to the VBA language in Microsoft® Office XP: the ability to add custom events to your objects, and the ability to extend your objects by implementing interfaces. In addition to describing how to use VBA to build custom objects, this section introduces the basics of using script to create reusable custom objects for Web pages.

In This Section

Why Build Your Own Objects?
> Build entire custom object models that involve complex code behind the scenes, but that present a relatively simple and intuitive object syntax to the programmer.

Basic Class Concepts
> Become familiar with using class modules to build custom objects, and learn the basics of adding a class to your project, creating an instance of a class in memory, and constructing properties and methods.

Creating Property Procedures
> Public module-level variables in a class module function as properties of an object.

Creating Events and Event Procedures
> Take advantage of simple to create events procedures and use ThisDocument, ThisWorkbook, or SheetN objects.

Extending Objects Through Interfaces
> Suppose that in the process of designing your application, you decide that you want to create several objects that are closely related, and, in fact, require at least some of the same properties and methods.

Designing Object Models
> When you design an object model, you are taking abstract processes and imposing concrete relationships upon them.

Creating Custom Objects for Web Pages
> There are two ways to create objects for Web pages that are similar to custom objects created in VBA—by creating scriptlets and by using Microsoft® Internet Explorer version 5 and later behaviors.

Why Build Your Own Objects?

In and of themselves, custom objects do not add new functionality to your code. There is usually another way to arrive at the same result that does not involve creating objects. What they can do is make complex operations appear as simpler, sophisticated applications, more self-documenting and maintainable, and procedures that required hours of coding time more reusable, both for yourself and for other programmers. In fact, creating a custom object is an ideal way to package your code for other Microsoft® Visual Basic® for Applications (VBA) programmers to use, because rather than figuring out how to call your code, they can work with your custom object much as they would with any built-in object.

You can build entire custom object models that involve complex code behind the scenes but present a relatively simple and intuitive object syntax to the programmer. This is, in fact, what all of the Microsoft® Office and VBA object models do for you—they take complex operations and package them into easy-to-use objects, methods, properties, and events. When you set the Visible property of a Microsoft® Excel object to False, for example, you do not have to worry about how VBA, Excel, and Windows cooperate to hide the object. You can focus on the larger-scale goals of building your application.

Naturally, simplicity and reusability come at a price. Creating custom objects and object models requires a different, perhaps even revolutionary, way of thinking than the sort of programming you might be accustomed to doing in VBA. It can take time to get the hang of it. In the long run, though, coding with objects can make you a better programmer by increasing your efficiency, honing your design skills, and making it easier to reuse your code.

When Should You Create Custom Objects?

The following sections outline some situations in which it makes sense to create your own objects.

Reducing Code Complexity

Any time you find yourself writing code for a complex operation that you might have to use more than once, consider building an object. Remember that the object itself does not have to do anything new or profound; simplicity that will save you time in the future is sufficient justification. For example, if you are building an application that involves displaying data from a Microsoft® Access database on a Microsoft® Excel worksheet, you might want to create a combo box that can bind to data in the database. Rather than doing all the binding work every time you must have such a combo box, you can create a new object that has all the functionality of a combo box but also has methods and properties for binding data.

Calling Dynamic-Link Library (DLL) Functions

Calls to the Windows application programming interface (API) and other DLLs lend themselves to being encapsulated in class modules. Creating a class module that handles DLL calls is sometimes called "wrapping" the DLL. Because DLL calls are often complicated, you can write the code to call a DLL function from within a class module, and use it in the future without having to remember the details of calling the DLL function directly. For example, you might create a System object with properties and methods that call various API functions internally to set and return information about the operating system.

Building Custom Data Structures

A custom object can act as a *data structure*, which is a group of related data stored as a unit. For example, you might create a Server object, with properties such as UNCPath and Available, and methods such as SaveFile, and use this object to manage operations between your application and a network server. Of course, you could also store this kind of data in a database; it depends on the requirements of your application. If you are working with small data structures, using a custom object might provide better performance.

Building Component Object Model (COM) Add-ins and Application-Specific Add-ins

If you are building a COM add-in, you will work with the class module provided by the add-in designer. You might want your add-in to provide custom events; at the very least, you might want an event procedure to run in response to the click of a command bar button, which involves some of the concepts discussed later in this section.

Custom objects can be useful in application-specific add-ins as well. They're a good way to add new functionality to a document.

Creating Custom Object Models

You can create a custom object model to represent relationships between different parts of your application. Your custom object model can include objects and collections, just as any built-in object model does. The key to creating a custom object model is that you can use a class module to represent a collection. Because a collection is just an object that groups other objects of a particular type, you can write code within a class module so that the class module acts as a collection.

Basic Class Concepts

In case you are not yet familiar with using class modules to build custom objects, this section covers the basics of adding a class to your project, creating an instance of a class in memory, and constructing properties and methods.

What Is a Class?

A *class* is a definition for an object. It contains information about how an object should behave, including its name, methods, properties, and events. It is not actually an object itself, in that it does not exist in memory. When code runs that refers to a class, a new *instance* of the class, an *object*, is created in memory. Although there is only one class, multiple objects of the same type can be created in memory from that class.

You can think of a class as an object "on paper"—that is, it provides the blueprint for an object, but has no substance in memory itself. Any number of objects can be created from this blueprint. Each object created from a class has the same *members*: its properties, methods, and events. However, each object behaves as an independent entity; for example, one object's properties might be set to different values than those of another object of the same type.

A Microsoft® Visual Basic® for Applications (VBA) project can contain two different varieties of class modules: basic class modules, which do not have any kind of user interface associated with them, and class modules that are associated with a form or another component. Class modules that are associated with a form, for example, are identical to basic class modules, except that they exist in memory only when that form exists in memory. Examples of objects that have associated class modules are UserForms, Microsoft® Access forms and reports, the Microsoft® Word ThisDocument object, and the Microsoft® Excel ThisWorkbook and SheetN objects.

Adding a Class Module

To add a class module to your Microsoft® Visual Basic® for Applications (VBA) project, click Class Module on the Insert menu in the Visual Basic Editor. Then name the class module by setting its Name property in the Properties window. Keep in mind that the class module will be treated as an object, so use a name that suggests the object's functionality. The name that you assign to the class module will also be the name under which it appears in the Classes list in the Object Browser.

If you have been following naming convention for standard modules, you can forgo the three-letter prefix here. It is best to name an object intuitively.

Creating a New Instance of a Class

To work with a custom object from code, you first create a new instance of the class that defines the object. When you create a new instance of a class, the object defined by the class is created in memory.

You can create a new instance of a class from within any type of module. Create an object variable of type *ClassName*, and then use the New keyword to assign a new instance of that class to the object variable.

For example, the following code creates a new instance of a custom class named System and assigns it to an object variable of type System:

```
' Declare an object variable of type System.
Dim sysLocal As System
```

```
' Create a new instance of the System class and assign it to the object
variable.
Set sysLocal = New System
```

In addition, you can declare the object variable and assign a new instance of the class all in one step, as shown in the following code fragment:

```
Dim sysLocal As New System
```

The first method of declaring an object variable is generally preferable because you have control over when the new instance of the class is created in memory and thus more control over when memory resources are consumed. You are less likely to introduce unexpected bugs when your code controls the creation of the instance. In addition, when you are building a custom object model, you often must perform certain operations at the time that an object is created, so it is critical to know where in your code that will happen. If you use the second method, Microsoft® Visual Basic® for Applications (VBA) creates the object in memory the first time that you refer to it, so you cannot check to see whether it is equal to Nothing; performing this check creates the object if it does not already exist.

The Instancing Property

You might notice that a class module has an additional property in the Properties window, the Instancing property. This property specifies whether the class module should be visible from another project when you have set a reference to the project that contains the class module. The property has two settings, Private, which is the default setting, and PublicNonCreatable. If you set the Instancing property to Private, a project that sets a reference to your project will not be able to view that class module in the Object Browser, nor will it be able to work with an instance of the class. If you set it to PublicNonCreatable, a project that sets a reference to your project can see the class module in the Object Browser. The referencing project can work with an instance of the class, but only if the referenced project has first created that instance. The referencing project cannot actually create the instance itself.

For more information about the Instancing property, search the Visual Basic Reference Help index for "Instancing property."

Matters of Scope

When designing a custom object, you should think carefully about the object's scope and lifetime within the project, as well as that of its properties and methods. The following sections outline some things to consider when deciding how to scope object variables and procedures.

Object Variable Scope

When you create a new instance of a class and assign it to an object variable, that instance exists in memory until the object variable goes out of scope, or until you explicitly set it to Nothing in your code. This is an important issue to consider when designing custom objects, because it is easy to leave objects lying around in memory, tying up resources unnecessarily.

The scope of an object variable depends on where you have declared it. If you declare it in the Declarations section of a standard module, it exists from the time code begins running in the project until the project is reset or the file containing the project is closed. If you declare it within a procedure, it exists until the procedure has finished executing. If you declare it in the Declarations section of a class module, it exists for the lifetime of an instance of that class.

When creating a hierarchical object model, you typically want top-level objects or collections to have a global scope, so you should declare the object variables to represent them as public module-level variables in a standard module. That way the object variables will be available throughout the project for the lifetime of the project. Of course, you have to assign to them an instance of a class before you can use them.

If your object model includes an object or collection that belongs to another object or collection, you'll want the lower-level object to exist only after the higher-level object has been created. For example, each ParentWindow object in the ParentWindows collection represents an open application window in the system. Each ParentWindow object has a collection of ChildWindow objects that contains the child windows belonging to the ParentWindow object, if there are any. Because you do not know what window a ChildWindow object will represent until you have created its parent, and because you might have several different collections of ChildWindow objects, you do not want to declare the object variable for the ChildWindows collection globally. Instead, declare a private module-level object variable to represent the ChildWindows collection within the ParentWindow class module. Each instance of the ParentWindow class can then maintain its own ChildWindows collection.

If your project includes objects that do not form an object model, you might simply want to create an instance of the class locally within a procedure, as you require it. In that case, it makes sense to create the System object variable within the procedure that requires it, and destroy it as soon as you are finished using it.

As with any other variable, you should try to scope object variables that point to custom objects as narrowly as possible to optimize performance and to reduce the risk of bugs that might be introduced by having to manage global variables.

Member Scope

The set of public variables, methods, properties, and events described in a class module define the *interface* for an object. The interface consists of the object members that are available to a programmer who's using the object from code.

A class module can also include private members that are not available to a programmer working with the object. You can create private variables, methods, properties, and events that are used by other procedures within the class module but are not part of the object's public interface. Additionally, constants, user-defined types, and Declare statements within a class module must always be private.

By default, Sub, Function, and Property procedures within a class module are public. Variables declared with the Dim statement, on the other hand, are private. It is a good idea to preface variable declarations and procedure definitions with either the Public or Private keyword, so that it is clear to you or any other developer looking at the class which elements are intended to be public or private.

In addition, you can declare a Sub, Function, or Property procedure with the Friend keyword. The Friend keyword makes a procedure private to the project: The procedure is available to any code running within the project, but it is not available to a referencing project. For more information about the Friend keyword, search the Visual Basic Reference Help index for "Friend keyword."

Creating Simple Properties with Variables

A property sets and stores a characteristic of an object. The simplest way to create a property for a custom object is to add a public module-level variable to the class module. This variable behaves as a property of the object—you can set its value, and then retrieve the value later. A module-level variable in a class module exists as long as an instance of the class exists in memory, so you can count on the property being available for the lifetime of the object.

For example, the following line of code is all that you must create a property named FirstName within a hypothetical class named Customer:

```
Public FirstName As String
```

To set this property, create a new instance of the Customer class and provide a value for the property, as shown in the following code fragment:

```
Dim cstCust As New Customer

cstCust.FirstName = "Maria"
```

The property that you create in this manner is always read-write, and there's no way to run other code when you set or return the property's value. Although this is an easy way to create a property when you are first beginning to program with class modules, you'll often find that you want to run code when a property is set or retrieved, or that you must make certain properties read-only.

Creating Methods

A method performs an action on or with an object. Any public Sub or Function procedure that you add to a class module becomes a method of the object. If a method is a Sub procedure, it does not return a value; if it is a Function procedure, it returns a value.

For example, the following procedure is the Multiply method for a hypothetical object named Calculator:

```vb
Public Function Multiply(ParamArray avarOperands() As Variant) As Variant
    ' Multiplies the set of numbers passed in to the procedure.
    Dim lngCount       As Long
    Dim dblResult    As Double
    Dim varElement     As Variant

    ' Initialize result to 1, since multiplying by 0 would
    ' return 0.
    dblResult = 1
    ' Loop through parameter array, from lower bound to upper
    ' bound.
    For lngCount = LBound(avarOperands) To UBound(avarOperands)
        ' Store value of element.
        varElement = avarOperands(lngCount)
        ' Check whether element is numeric.
        If IsNumeric(varElement) Then
            ' Multiply result by element.
            dblResult = dblResult * varElement
        Else
            ' Return Null if any element is not numeric.
            Multiply = Null
            GoTo Multiply_End
        End If
    Next

    Multiply = dblResult

Multiply_End:
    Exit Function
End Function
```

To call this method, create a new object of type Calculator, and pass in the values that you want to multiply, as shown in the following code fragment:

```vb
Dim calCalc As New Calculator

Debug.Print calCalc.Multiply(2.5, 2.5, 2.5)
```

Creating Property Procedures

Public module-level variables in a class module function as properties of an object. However, they're not very sophisticated. If you must run code to set or return a property's value, or you want to make a property read-only, you can create a Property procedure. There are three types of Property procedures: Property Get, Property Let, and Property Set procedures. The Property Get procedure returns the current value of a property, whereas the Property Let procedure sets the value. The Property Set procedure assigns an object to an object property.

To create a read-write property, you must include a pair of Property procedures in the class module. Both procedures must have the same name. If the property stores and returns a scalar value, such as a numeric, text, or date value, you use a Property Let procedure to set the value and a Property Get procedure to retrieve it. If the property stores and returns a reference to an object, you use the Property Set procedure to store the reference and the Property Get procedure to return it.

In addition, you can create read-only, write-only, and write-once properties. The following table outlines which property procedures you must have for each type.

Type of property	Procedures needed
Read-write, scalar	Property Let, Property Get
Read-write, object	Property Set, Property Get
Read-only, scalar	Property Get
Read-only, object	Property Get
Write-only, scalar	Property Let
Write-once, scalar	Property Let, including code to determine whether property has been set previously, Property Get
Write-once, object	Property Set, including code to determine whether object property has been set previously, Property Get

Creating Scalar Properties

The properties that you use to return information about a characteristic of an object are usually scalar properties. For example, a Name property most likely sets or returns a String value, an Age property sets or returns a numeric value, and a Birthdate property sets or returns a Date value. The following sections discuss how to create scalar properties.

Property Let Procedures

A Property Let procedure sets the value for a scalar property. The Property Let procedure takes one argument, which is the value that the property is to store.

Note Because it sets a value, rather than returning one, the Property Let procedure does not have a return value.

The Property Let procedure does not do all of the work for you—if you want to store the value that's passed into the Property Let procedure, you have to actually store the value that you pass into the procedure yourself. You can store it in a private module-level variable. For example, the following Property Let procedure sets the LastName property for a hypothetical Customer object:

```
' Declare private module-level variable to store value.
Private p_strLastName As String


Public Property Let LastName(strLastName As String)
    ' Store value of argument in module-level variable.
    p_strLastName = strLastName
End Property
```

When you work with the Customer object from code in another module, you can set the LastName property as follows:

```
Dim cstCust As Customer


Set cstCust = New Customer
cstCust.LastName = "Andrews"
```

This line of code passes the value "Andrews" to the Property Let LastName procedure. The procedure then assigns this value to the module-level variable p_strLastName.

You do not always have to store a property value in a module-level variable. In some cases, you might use the Property Let procedure to affect some aspect of the application or system. For example, the following Property Let procedure sets the minute portion of the local system time. To do so, it calls the Windows API SetLocalTime function:

```
Public Property Let Minute(intMinute As Integer)
    ' Retrieve current time so that all values will be current.
    ' Then set minute portion of local time.


    GetLocalTime sysSystemTime
    sysSystemTime.wMinute = intMinute
    SetLocalTime sysSystemTime
End Property
```

There's no point in storing the value of the Minute property in a module-level variable; if you retrieve the property value several minutes later, the stored value will be inaccurate. The following section describes how to retrieve the value of the Minute property by calling the Windows API GetLocalTime function.

Property Get Procedures

A Property Get procedure returns the value of a property through the procedure's return value. Note that the Property Get procedure complements the Property Let procedure: The Property Get procedure has a return value, but takes no argument. Note also that the argument passed to the Property Let procedure must have the same data type as the return value of the Property Get procedure.

To return a property value by using a Property Get procedure, you must retrieve the value for the property from within the Property Get procedure. Assuming that the corresponding Property Let procedure has already stored the value assigned to the property in a module-level variable, you would read the value of this variable from within the Property Get procedure, and assign it as the return value for the Property Get procedure. For example, the following Property Get procedure is the companion procedure to the Property Let LastName procedure shown in the previous section. It retrieves the value of the p_strLastName variable and assigns it to the name of the property:

```
Public Property Get LastName As String
    ' Retrieve value stored in module-level variable.
    LastName = p_strLastName
End Property
```

When you work with the Customer object from code in another module, you can retrieve the value of the LastName property as follows:

```
Dim cstCust As Customer


Set cstCust = New Customer
Debug.Print cstCust.LastName
```

> **Note** If the property has not already been set, the p_strLastName variable does not yet have a value; therefore, the Property Get procedure for the LastName property returns an empty string.

In the Property procedures for the LastName property, you can see that both procedures use the p_strLastName variable. The Property Let procedure writes a value to the variable, and the Property Get procedure reads the value from it.

There might be situations in which you must ensure that a Property Get procedure returns the most up-to-date information from the system or application. In this case, you do not want to store the property value in a variable. Instead, you should call a function that always returns current information.

For example, the Property Get Minute procedure is the companion procedure to the Property Let Minute procedure shown in the previous section. If you stored the value set by the Property Let Minute procedure in a variable, and then used the Property Get procedure to retrieve the value several minutes later, it would be out-of-date and incorrect. Instead, you can call the Windows API GetLocalTime function from within the Property Get procedure to retrieve the current local time for the system, and then return the minute portion, as shown:

```
Public Property Get Minute() As Integer
    ' Retrieve current time, then return minute.


    GetLocalTime sysSystemTime
    Minute = sysSystemTime.wMinute
End Property
```

Creating Object Properties

The Property Set procedure behaves the same as the Property Let procedure, except that you use it to assign an object reference to an object property. You can then use a corresponding Property Get procedure to return the object reference.

There are a couple of cases in which it is useful to create an object property. When you want to create a new object that provides all the properties, methods, and events of an existing object, plus additional ones that you have defined, you can create an object property that returns a reference to the existing object. In addition, when you create an object model that has a hierarchy—the object contains other objects or collections—you must create an object property to access a lower-level object in the hierarchy.

Wrapping a Built-in Object

You can use the Property Set procedure to create an object that wraps an existing built-in object; that is, it contains unique properties and methods and provides access to all the built-in properties and methods of the existing object. This way, you can add additional properties, methods, and events to a built-in object.

List boxes and combo boxes on a worksheet differ from those on UserForms; they are Microsoft® ActiveX® controls that belong to the OLEObjects collection of the Worksheet object. The BoundList custom object contains some custom properties and methods, and provides access to all the properties and methods of the OLEObject class that's built into Microsoft® Excel. What makes this possible is an object property that sets and returns a reference to an object of type OLEObject, which refers to the list box or combo box on the worksheet. This property maintains the reference to the OLEObject object for the BoundList class.

The following example shows the Property Set and Property Get procedures for the ActiveXControl object property of the BoundList class. The ActiveXControl object property requires both a Property Set procedure and a Property Get procedure. The Property Set procedure stores a reference to an object of type OLEObject in a private module-level variable, p_oleCtl. The Property Get procedure returns that reference.

```
Private p_oleCtl As OLEObject
```

```
Property Set ActiveXControl(oleCtl As OLEObject)
    If p_oleCtl Is Nothing Then
        Set p_oleCtl = oleCtl
    End If
End Property


Property Get ActiveXControl() As OLEObject
    Set ActiveXControl = p_oleCtl
End Property
```

You can name this property whatever you want; in this case it is named ActiveXControl because it sets and returns a reference to an ActiveX control on a worksheet.

Note that the Property Set procedure makes the ActiveXControl property a write-once property. The Property procedure checks whether the private object variable that stores the reference to the OLEObject object already points to a valid object. If it does, the property has already been set and will not be set again. The write-once property ensures that the reference to the OLEObject object is set only once, when it is first added to the BoundLists collection.

The ActiveXControl property is set in the Add method of the BoundLists class. First, the Add method creates a new instance of the BoundList class. Then, in one line of code, it uses the built-in Add method of the OLEObjects collection to add a new OLEObject object (the new list box or combo box) to the worksheet, and assigns a reference to this OLEObject object to the ActiveXControl property of the BoundList object. Setting the ActiveXControl property passes the reference to the new OLEObject object to the Property Set procedure for the ActiveXControl property. The ActiveXControl property stores the reference to the OLEObject object, to be maintained for the lifetime of that BoundList object.

The Add method of the custom BoundLists collection wraps the built-in Add method of the OLEObjects collection, and the ActiveXControl property wraps the built-in OLEObject object. The code within the custom objects still uses the OLEObject object and OLEObjects collection to control a list box or combo box on a worksheet. A programmer working with the BoundList object and BoundLists collection, however, sees only the properties and methods of those custom objects, rather than the internal code that's managing OLEObject objects.

The Add method for the BoundLists collection is shown here. Also shown is the opgListType custom enumeration, which provides the constants that specify whether to create a list box or a combo box; one of these constants is passed to the procedure for the *lngListType* argument:

```
Enum opgListType
    COMBO_BOX
    LIST_BOX
End Enum
```

```
Public Function Add(strListName As String, _
                    lngListType As opgListType) As BoundList
    ' Add new BoundList object to BoundLists collection and return
reference to object.
    ' This procedure not only creates the BoundList object but also
creates a new
    ' OLEObject on the worksheet and returns a reference to it, which is
then
    ' assigned to the ActiveXControl property of the new BoundList object.
The BoundList
    ' object "wraps" the OLEObject object.
    Dim objBndLst As BoundList


    Set objBndLst = New BoundList


    ' Create either a list box or a combo box.
    Select Case lngListType
        Case opgListType.LIST_BOX
            Set objBndLst.ActiveXControl = _
                ActiveSheet.OLEObjects.Add(ClassType:="Forms.ListBox.1", _
                Link:=False, DisplayAsIcon:=False, Left:=100, _
                Top:=100, Width:=150, Height:=150)
        Case opgListType.COMBO_BOX
            Set objBndLst.ActiveXControl = _
                ActiveSheet.OLEObjects.Add(ClassType:="Forms.ComboBox.1", _
                Link:=False, DisplayAsIcon:=False, Left:=100, _
                Top:=100, Width:=150, Height:=25)
    End Select


    ' Name the new list.
    objBndLst.ListName = strListName


    ' Add BoundList object to BoundLists collection.
    p_colLists.Add objBndLst, objBndLst.ListName


    ' Return added object.
    Set Add = objBndLst
End Function
```

When the ActiveXControl property has been set, you can use it to access the properties and methods of the OLEObject corresponding to the list box or combo box. For example, the following code fragment returns the height of the first bound list in the BoundLists collection to the Immediate window:

```
? BoundLists.Item("Combo1").ActiveXControl.Height
```

> **Note** The Item property of the BoundLists collection is a custom property that's used to return a reference to a BoundList object in the collection. Because the custom BoundLists collection is created from a class module, it does not have a default Item property as built-in collections do. When you build a class to represent a collection, you must implement the Item property yourself, and to return a reference to an object in the collection, you must explicitly refer to the Item property. In addition, you cannot use the For Each...Next statement to loop through a collection that is built from a custom class; instead, you must use a For...Next loop and maintain a counter variable that acts as an index into the collection.

Accessing Objects in a Custom Object Model

If you create an object model that has a hierarchical organization, you must include object properties to access the lower-level members of the object model. For example, in the example below, every ParentWindow object has a ChildWindows collection. To work with the ChildWindows collection, you must return a reference to it that's associated with the ParentWindow object. The sample uses an object property within the ParentWindow object to do this, the ChildWindows property. The ChildWindows property has the same name as the collection it returns, which simplifies its use and makes the custom object model consistent with the built-in object models in Microsoft® Office XP.

Here are the Property Set and Property Get procedures for the ChildWindows property of the ParentWindow object. Note that the Property Set procedure takes an argument of type `ChildWindows`, and the Property Get procedure returns a reference to a ChildWindows collection.

```
Public Property Set ChildWindows(colChildWindows As ChildWindows)
    ' This property sets a reference to the ParentWindow
    ' object's ChildWindows collection.
    ' Write-once property.

    If p_colChildWindows Is Nothing Then
        ' Assign reference to passed-in object to private
        ' module-level variable.
        Set p_colChildWindows = colChildWindows
    End If
End Property
```

```
Public Property Get ChildWindows() As ChildWindows
    ' This property returns a reference to the ParentWindow
    ' object's ChildWindows collection.

    ' Return reference to ChildWindows collection stored in
    ' private module-level variable.
    Set ChildWindows = p_colChildWindows
End Property
```

The Property Set procedure is a write-once property. For each instance of the ParentWindow class, you can set the ChildWindows property only once, although you can return it as many times as you want. Because every ParentWindow object has a ChildWindows collection, whether or not it contains any elements, the ChildWindows property is set in the Class_Initialize event procedure of the ParentWindow class. From the perspective of the programmer using the ParentWindow object, the ChildWindows property is read-only; because the property is set in the Class_Initialize event procedure, the property returns a reference to the ChildWindows collection as soon the object has been created.

Note that every property that is read-only must be set somewhere within your code. The difference between a read-write property and a read-only property is whether the property can be set by the programmer who's using the object, or whether it can only be set internally, by your code.

The line of code that sets the ChildWindows property is shown in the following example, taken from the Class_Initialize event procedure:

```
' Create a new ChildWindows collection and assign it
' to the ParentWindow object's ChildWindows property.
Set Me.ChildWindows = New ChildWindows
```

This statement creates a new instance of the ChildWindows collection. Rather than assigning the reference directly to an object variable, the statement assigns it to the ChildWindows property of the ParentWindow object. The ChildWindows property takes care of handling the reference to the parent window's ChildWindows collection.

After the Object property has been set, it returns a reference to the collection, so that you can use it to traverse the object hierarchy. For example, the following line of code prints the value of the first child window's Caption property to the Immediate window:

```
? ParentWindows.Item(1).ChildWindows.Item(1).Caption
```

Creating Events and Event Procedures

As a Microsoft® Visual Basic® for Applications (VBA) programmer, you understand how to handle form and control events. If you have programmed in Microsoft® Word or Microsoft® Excel, you might also have taken advantage of events on the ThisDocument, ThisWorkbook, or

SheetN objects. These event procedures are simple to create—you just open the class module and construct the event procedure from the Object and Procedure drop-down lists in the Code window.

There are two additional ways to handle events from VBA code in a Microsoft® Office application. You can create event procedures for certain objects that provide built-in events but that do not have associated class modules. In addition, you can create custom events for your own classes.

Creating Event Procedures for Built-in Events by Using the WithEvents Keyword

The objects for which you have commonly written event procedures—UserForms, Microsoft® Access forms and reports, and the ThisDocument, ThisWorkbook, and SheetN objects—have one thing in common: They all have an associated class module. Some other objects in the Microsoft® Office 97, Office 2000 and Office XP object models also provide built-in events, but they do not have associated class modules. For example, if you look at the Object Browser in the Visual Basic Editor in Microsoft® Excel, you'll see that the Excel Application object has several events listed as its members—NewWorkbook, WorkbookOpen, and SheetChange, to name a few. Examples of other Excel objects that provide events include the Chart, OLEObject, and QueryTable objects. The Microsoft® Word Application object and the Microsoft® PowerPoint® Application object also provide events.

You can create event procedures for these events in a generic class module. Though the class module is not associated with the object by default, it can contain event procedures for an object that has events.

If you consider event procedures in a form module, you might realize that those event procedures exist only for a particular instance of the form. For example, UserForm1 and UserForm2 are separate instances of an object of type UserForm. Both have an Initialize event, which occurs only when that form is loaded. The Initialize event procedure for UserForm1 runs only when UserForm1 is loaded, not when UserForm2 is loaded, and vice versa.

The same holds true for events on objects that do not have associated modules—an event occurs for a particular instance of an object. More specifically, it occurs for an instance of an object that you have indicated should respond to events, not for any other instance.

To indicate that an instance of an object should respond to events, you declare a module-level object variable of that type by using the WithEvents keyword in a class module. This keyword notifies Microsoft® Visual Basic® for Applications (VBA) that you want to respond to events for the instance that is assigned to that object variable. You can use the WithEvents keyword only with objects that support events, and only in a class module.

For example, the following line of code in a class module declares a private object variable of type Excel.Application to respond to events:

```
Private WithEvents xlApp As Excel.Application
```

When you have declared an object variable to respond to events, that object variable appears in the Object box in the class module's Code window, and its events appear in the Procedures box in the Code window. To create an event procedure stub, click the object name and event name in these boxes. The Visual Basic Editor inserts an event procedure stub for you that looks similar to the following:

```
Private Sub xlApp_NewWorkbook(ByVal Wb As Excel.Workbook)


End Sub
```

At this point, you have created an object variable that has associated events, and an event procedure. The object variable does not yet point to anything, however. You must assign a reference to it, which you can do in the Initialize event procedure for the class module. The Initialize event occurs as soon as a new instance of the class is created, so if you assign a reference to the object variable here, you can always be sure it will exist when you must have it.

In this case, you want the object variable to point to the current instance of the application:

```
Private Sub Class_Initialize()
    Set xlApp = Application
End Sub
```

Finally, you must create a new instance of the class to trigger the Initialize event and load the event-ready Application object variable into memory. Insert a new standard module, and declare a private module-level object variable that will point to the instance of the class. For example, if the class is named XLEvents, you can declare the following object variable:

```
Private p_evtEvents As XLEvents
```

You must declare this object variable at the module level, so that it will remain in memory until the project is closed or reset, because this object variable points to the class that contains the event-ready object and its event procedures. Otherwise, the object will no longer respond to events when the variable has gone out of scope.

Next, add the procedure that creates the new instance of the class in a standard module:

```
Public Sub InitXLEvents()
    Set p_evtEvents = New XLEvents
End Sub
```

After you run this procedure, any code you have added to the Application object's event procedures will run when the corresponding Application object event occurs.

Note that you have to run the InitXLEvents procedure each time you open Excel to make the Application object event-ready. It is not possible to define events for the Application object once and for all.

Note If you think about the events that are available to you for objects such as the Excel Application object, you might realize that there's no way to use some of them consistently from within their own application. For example, the Excel Application object has an OpenWorkbook event. However, to run a procedure such as InitXLEvents, you are going to have to open a workbook. So there's no way to trap the event for the first workbook that's opened, although after you run InitXLEvents, the event will occur when subsequent workbooks are opened.

Note It makes more sense to use the OpenWorkbook event in the context of a COM component that supports Automation (formerly OLE Automation). For example, you can write an application in Microsoft® Word that includes the class and standard modules described above. You have to make two changes—you must set a reference to the Excel object library, and you must use the New keyword to create a new instance of the Excel Application object, rather than returning the current instance. When you create a new instance of the Application object from Automation by calling the InitXLEvents procedure or one similar to it, Excel loads without opening a workbook. The Application object is now event-ready, and the OpenWorkbook event will occur as soon as you open a workbook through Automation.

Adding Events to Custom Classes

You can include your own events in custom classes, and create event procedures that run when those events occur. Creating a custom event is somewhat more complex than creating an event procedure for a built-in event, because your code has to *raise* the custom event in response to something that happens within the code.

Understanding Custom Events

When you raise an event, you cause its event procedure to run. For the built-in events you are accustomed to working with, this is the job of the application; for example, when you click a button on a form in a Microsoft® Access application, Microsoft® Visual Basic® for Applications (VBA) in Access calls the button's Click event procedure and runs any code that's in it. However, when you create a custom event, the application does not know when your event is supposed to occur; you have to specify that in your code. Then you or other developers who are using your custom object have to create the event procedure and write the code that runs when the event is raised.

The most important thing to understand about custom events is that your code has to cause them to occur. They do not automatically occur in response to something that the user or system does, although you can write code that does cause an event to occur in this manner. The class module that contains a custom event must also include a public method that raises the event. This method raises the event by calling the RaiseEvent statement and passing in any arguments defined for the event. These arguments are in turn passed in to the event procedure that runs in response to the event.

For the event to occur, some code outside the class module must call the method that raises the event. For example, code in a form that runs when a command button is clicked might create a new instance of the custom class, assign it to an object variable that has been declared by using the WithEvents keyword, and then call the method that raises the event. When the event occurs, the event procedure in the form's module runs—if the event procedure exists.

Of course, an event can occur without any code responding to it. Events are occurring all the time, in the operating system and in your applications, and code runs in response to some events but not to others. To run code in response to an event that is occurring in an instance of a class, you must create an event procedure that is associated with that instance.

When Do You Need to Create a Custom Event?

In many cases, it is not necessary to create a custom event—you can call a procedure to do the same thing. On the other hand, creating an event for a custom object can improve the object's flexibility and reusability. If you call a method rather than raising an event, the method will run the same way every time, no matter what code is working with the object. If you raise an event, the programmer who's using the object can decide how to respond to the event and can use the same object in different scenarios. Imagine, for example, if a command button ran the same code every time the user clicked it, instead of providing an event procedure to run whatever code the programmer chooses. Command buttons would not be nearly as useful!

Here are some cases where you'll must create an event rather than use a procedure:

- When you implement an interface in multiple classes, and you want to maintain common code within the class that provides the interface, but you also must provide some customization within each individual class.

- When you want to trap the messages that Microsoft® Windows sends to an application. Windows messages are similar to events—Windows alerts an application when the application gets or loses the focus, for example, and the application can respond accordingly. In some cases you might want your Microsoft® Visual Basic® for Applications (VBA) code to take notice of certain Windows messages and respond to them. To do this you must employ an advanced technique called *subclassing*, which makes it possible for your VBA code to look at a window's messages and take some action before the window's normal code is called. You can correlate particular messages to custom events that you create in your code.

- When two or more objects, components, or applications must know that an event has occurred in an instance of a class that both are aware of. When an event occurs for an instance of a class, every variable that points to that instance in memory is notified of the event, and any event procedure that is tied to that instance runs. For example, if you have two forms that both have a variable pointing to a single instance of a Timer object, and the Timer object has an event that occurs when the timer is stopped, both forms will be notified of the event and will run the corresponding event procedure if it exists.

Creating Custom Events

The sample code in this section is taken from a sample that includes a custom event named ItemAdded on a custom object named DataComboBox. Because creating and responding to a custom event requires code in several places, it might be useful for you to study and run this sample while reading this section.

The DataComboBox object wraps a combo box on a form to provide an additional event, the ItemAdded event, which the MSForms ComboBox control does not have. When the user enters a new item and chooses to add it to the list, the ItemAdded event occurs. The programmer can use the ItemAdded event procedure to run validation code before adding the item to the list. For example, the ItemAdded event procedure in the sample file checks to see whether the item already exists in the list. If it does, the event is cancelled and the item is not added.

To define a custom event in a class module, use the Event keyword. An event might be public or private and must be declared at the module level. It can have any number of arguments, but it cannot return a value. The following statement defines the ItemAdded event in the DataComboBox class:

```
Public Event ItemAdded(strValue As String, _
                    blnCancel As Boolean)
```

After you have defined the event in the DataComboBox class module, you can declare a private module-level variable of type DataComboBox, declared by using the WithEvents keyword, in the module of the frmDataCombo form:

```
Private WithEvents mdcbCombo As DataComboBox
```

This declaration notifies Microsoft® Visual Basic® for Applications (VBA) that the instance of the DataComboBox class that this variable points to will respond to events. When you have added this variable declaration to the form's module, you can create the mdcbCombo_ItemAdded event procedure stub by using the module's Object and Procedure drop-down lists:

```
Private Sub mdcbCombo_ItemAdded(strValue As String, _
                    blnCancel As Boolean)
    ' Code that runs when event occurs.
End Sub
```

When the form loads, the code creates a new instance of the DataComboBox object and sets its custom ComboBox property, which is an object property, to point to the cboData combo box on the form:

```
Private Sub UserForm_Initialize()
    ' Create new instance of DataComboBox object.
    Set mdcbCombo = New DataComboBox

    ' Set ComboBox property of DataComboBox object
    ' to point to combo box on form.
    Set mdcbCombo.ComboBox = Me.cboData
End Sub
```

Note that the ComboBox object property is the key to wrapping the built-in ComboBox object within a custom class. The ComboBox property provides access to all the properties and methods of the built-in ComboBox object.

At this point, the event has been defined in the class module, and the form is set up to respond to the event when it occurs. The next step is to write the procedure that raises the event. This procedure must be in the same module in which the event is defined, namely the DataComboBox class module.

It is reasonable that a combo box would know how to add an item that the user has entered in the text portion of the combo box. There's no built-in way to do this for an MSForms ComboBox control, however, so the DataComboBox class provides one, a method named AddDataItem. When the form calls this method on an instance of the class, the method raises the ItemAdded event, giving the programmer an opportunity to respond through the event procedure and handle the event as required. After the event procedure runs, if the event was not cancelled, the AddDataItem method adds the new item to the list.

Here's the code for the AddDataItem method. Note that the RaiseEvent statement raises the ItemAdded event and passes values for its arguments. When this line executes, the event procedure defined in the form's module runs.

```
Public Function AddDataItem(strValue As String)
    ' Raises ItemAdded event when user chooses to add
    ' item. If item already exists in list, event is
    ' cancelled. Otherwise new item is added to list.
    Dim blnCancel As Boolean

    ' Initialize Boolean variable.
    blnCancel = False

    ' Raise ItemAdded event, passing in new value
    ' and Boolean variable. Boolean variable is passed
    ' by reference, so event procedure might alter its
    ' value.
    RaiseEvent ItemAdded(strValue, blnCancel)

    ' If ItemAdded event is cancelled, then exit.
    ' Otherwise add new item to list.
    If blnCancel = False Then
        Me.ComboBox.AddItem strValue
    End If
End Function
```

Finally, there must be code that calls the AddDataItem method. In the sample file, this method is called from the Click event procedure of the cmdAdd command button:

```
Private Sub cmdAdd_Click()
    Dim strValue As String
```

```
' Store value that's been typed into combo box.
strValue = Me.cboData.Text

' Call AddDataItem method of DataComboBox object.
mdcbCombo.AddDataItem strValue
End Sub
```

In summary, a command button's Click event procedure in the form's module calls the AddDataItem method of the DataComboBox object. The AddDataItem method raises the ItemAdded event, which in turn calls the combo box's ItemAdded event procedure in the form's module.

The ItemAdded event procedure in this example checks to make sure that the item does not already exist in the list and cancels the add operation if it does. You could put whatever code you wanted here, though, and it could be different code for different forms. For example, the ItemAdded event could include code to convert the entry to proper case, or it could trim additional spaces from the text entered, or it could write the entry to a database.

Extending Objects Through Interfaces

Suppose that in the process of designing your application, you decide that you want to create several objects that are closely related, and, in fact, require at least some of the same properties and methods. Also, in the future, you might have to add more objects that are related to these, and you want to make the process as easy as possible for yourself down the road. You can *implement an interface* that defines the properties and methods that these objects have in common.

As noted earlier, an interface is the set of properties, methods, and events that define an object's characteristics and behavior. Every object has an interface, whether it is a built-in or custom object. When you implement an interface in a class module, you take advantage of another object's interface to provide some or all of the properties and methods for that class. In this way you can extend your objects, relate them according to their functionality, and maximize your code's reusability. You can implement interfaces to take advantage of *polymorphism*. Polymorphism refers to the ability to create objects that have specific individual functionality, but that share something in common with a more general object.

> **Note** If you have programmed in object-oriented programming languages, you might be familiar with the concepts of polymorphism and *inheritance*. Inheritance refers to the ability of a class to derive members (and their functionality) from other classes. By implementing an interface, you can achieve polymorphism. However, interfaces do not provide true inheritance, because a class can implement only those members that are defined within an interface that it implements. For example, if Class B implements the interface for Class A, and Class C implements the interface for Class B, Class C must implement all the members of Class B, but it cannot directly implement members of Class A. In true inheritance, objects can derive characteristics from an entire hierarchy of other objects. For example, if Class B inherits from Class A, and Class C inherits from Class B, and so on, Class E can selectively derive all or some characteristics from Classes A, B, C, and D.

As a conceptual example of polymorphism, consider Control objects. There are several different control classes. For example, CommandButton controls are created from the CommandButton class, and TextBox controls are created from the TextBox class. You can create a variable of type CommandButton and assign to it a reference to a CommandButton control. You can do the same with a variable of type TextBox. You cannot, however, assign a reference to a TextBox control to a variable of type CommandButton—you'll get an error if you try it.

On the other hand, both types of controls also have the more general type Control. If you create a variable of type Control, you can assign a reference to either a command button or a text box to the variable. This flexibility is indispensable in cases where you must enumerate through all the controls on a form and set their Visible properties to True, for example. When you know what type of control your code will work with, it is better to create a variable of the more specific type, but when you do not know ahead of time, you can create a variable of type Control.

Interface Basics

Fundamentally, implementing an interface requires two components. One component defines the interface, and the other implements it.

The component that defines the interface can come from a variety of places. It can be a class module in your project or in a referenced project. It can be a referenced component, such as a DLL. It can even be a built-in class. You can implement any interface contained in a type library, as long as that interface supports Automation. The component that implements the interface is a class module in a Microsoft® Visual Basic® for Applications (VBA) project.

This section assumes that you are designing your own interface, and that you are creating it in a class module in the same VBA project that contains the classes in which you are implementing it. The examples shown here are designed in this way: One class module in the project defines the interface, and one or more class modules implement it.

Note that if the component that provides the interface is not part of your project, you must set a reference to its type library before you can implement it within a class in the project.

To notify VBA that you want to implement an interface, you use the Implements keyword, followed by the name of the interface (which is simply the name of the class that defines the interface). To implement the LibraryItem interface in another class named Periodical, you would type the following line in the Declarations section of the Periodical class:

```
Implements LibraryItem
```

After you enter this line, when you click the Object drop-down list in the module's Code window, you'll see that LibraryItem appears in the list of available objects, and all the properties and methods defined for the interface appear in the Procedure drop-down list. For example, if the LibraryItem class includes a property named CheckedOut, the Property Let and Property Get procedures for the CheckedOut property appear in the list. When you select the Property Get procedure from the list, a procedure stub, such as the following one, is added to the class module:

```
Private Property Get LibraryItem_CheckedOut() As Boolean

End Property
```

Note that the name of the interface you have implemented precedes the name of the property itself. In addition, note that the procedure stub created is denoted as private. This means that the LibraryItem_CheckedOut property does not form part of the Periodical object's own interface; it will not appear in the list of available properties for an object of type `Periodical`. Instead, the CheckedOut property will appear in the list of available properties for an object of type `LibraryItem`.

An important thing to understand when you implement an interface is that an interface is similar to a contract. When you implement an interface in a class module, you agree to include all of the interface's public members in the class module. Every procedure that appears in the Procedure list must be included in the class module before your project will compile, and each procedure must contain either code or a comment. For example, the LibraryItem interface has four read-write properties: Name, AllowCheckOut, ItemType, and CheckedOut. Each class that implements the LibraryItem interface must include the Property Let and Property Get procedures for each of these four properties.

Even if you do not require a particular procedure in your class module, you still have to include it to implement the interface. If you omit a procedure that's provided by the interface, the VBA project will not compile.

Only those members of the interface that are public are visible to the class module that's implementing the interface. In other words, only the public members of the interface are part of the contract, and only they can be implemented by other class modules. The class that describes the interface can include private members, but these members will not be part of the interface.

Implementing an Abstract Interface

One way to design an interface is to create a class that describes Sub, Function, and Property procedure definitions, including arguments and return types, without adding any code to the procedures. This is referred to as an *abstract interface*. The advantage to implementing an abstract interface is that the class that implements it can include whatever code you want in the procedures it provides. Two classes that implement the same method can contain entirely different code within that method.

The four different objects that the library offers are all similar, but not identical. Fiction and Nonfiction objects can be checked out, while Periodical and Reference objects cannot. However, the objects are similar enough to share certain common properties. In addition, as the library expands and adds new types of holdings, such as Audio or Film, those new holdings will also have common properties. All of these objects implement the LibraryItem interface, which supplies the common properties that each object must have. Within each object's class module, a property procedure can contain custom code tailored to that object's requirements.

The interface described by the LibraryItem class defines four read-write properties: Name, ItemType, AllowCheckOut, and CheckedOut. The Name property is a simple public module-level variable; the others are paired Property Let and Property Get procedures. Because this is an abstract interface, none of the Property procedures contains any code.

The LibraryItem class also contains a public enumeration that defines numeric constants that represent each of the four existing object types. In the interest of organization, the enumeration appears in the LibraryItem class; however, it could also be defined in a standard module. The enumeration itself does not form part of the interface.

The Fiction, Nonfiction, Periodical, and Reference objects all implement the LibraryItem interface, so each of them has its own property procedures for each property defined by the interface. You can customize these procedures according to the requirements of the object. For example, the AllowCheckOut property indicates whether a particular item can be checked out. For Fiction and Nonfiction objects, this property should return True. For Periodical and Reference objects, it should return False. Compare the LibraryItem_AllowCheckOut property procedures for the Fiction and Periodical classes:

```
' AllowCheckOut property for Fiction object.
Private Property Get LibraryItem_AllowCheckOut() As Boolean
    ' Fiction can be checked out.
    LibraryItem_AllowCheckOut = True
End Property


' AllowCheckOut property for Periodical object.
Private Property Get LibraryItem_AllowCheckOut() As Boolean
    ' Don't allow periodical to be checked out.
    LibraryItem_AllowCheckOut = False
End Property
```

Although it is practical for both Fiction and Periodical objects to have an AllowCheckOut property, it is not practical for both properties to return the same value.

The real power of implementing an abstract class becomes apparent when you begin using the objects to construct an application. The library system must be designed to handle any type of holding, and yet to distinguish between different types at the same time. Because the LibraryItem class is implemented in all four of the specific classes, an item of type LibraryItem can represent any of those objects, just as a Control object can represent any type of control generically.

The concepts of implementing an abstract class are more important than the details of the library application, so the discussion here will focus on explaining the concepts. When the user clicks the Catalog New Items button on the switchboard form (frmLibrary), another form loads (frmCatalog). This form makes it possible for the user to enter a name for a new library holding and select the type of holding from a combo box. When the user clicks the Catalog button, a new object of the appropriate type is created and added to the collection.

Here's the code that creates a new library item in the cmdCatalog_Click event procedure. Note that this code fragment calls the AddLibraryItem procedure, passing in the name of the library item and its type, and returns a reference to an object that is assigned to a variable of type LibraryItem:

```
Dim colItem As LibraryItem
Set colItem = AddLibraryItem(Me.txtItemName, Me.cboItemType.ListIndex)
```

Next, take a look at the AddLibraryItem procedure. This procedure examines the value passed in for the *lngType* argument and creates a new object of type Reference, Fiction, Nonfiction, or Periodical. It then adds this reference to a global Microsoft® Visual Basic® for Applications (VBA) Collection object to store it. Finally, the procedure returns a reference to the new object. Because the procedure's return type is declared as type LibraryItem, it is this type of object that is returned to the calling procedure and assigned to a variable of type LibraryItem:

```
Public Function AddLibraryItem(strName As String, _
                    lngType As opgItemType) As LibraryItem
    ' This function creates a library item of the specified type,
    ' sets its Name property, adds it to the collection,
    ' and returns a reference to the object.
    ' Note that a variable of type LibraryItem is used to store the
    ' reference, even though the code creates a specific object type.
    ' In a more sophisticated application, you would probably include
    ' this method in a collection class as the Add method.

    Dim colNew As LibraryItem

    ' Determine what type of library item this is and
    ' create a new object of the appropriate type.
    Select Case lngType
        Case opgItemType.ITEM_REFERENCE
            Set colNew = New Reference
        Case opgItemType.ITEM_FICTION
            Set colNew = New Fiction
        Case opgItemType.ITEM_NONFICTION
            Set colNew = New NonFiction
        Case opgItemType.ITEM_PERIODICAL
            Set colNew = New Periodical
    End Select

    ' Set object's Name property.
    colNew.Name = strName
```

```
' Add new object to collection, specifying its name as
' the key for the item. The key can be used to retrieve
' the item from the collection.
gcolLibItems.Add colNew, strName


' Return reference to new object.
Set AddLibraryItem = colNew
End Function
```

As you can see from this procedure, implementing the LibraryItem interface in the Reference, Fiction, Nonfiction, and Periodical classes means that a reference to any of those objects can be assigned to a variable of type LibraryItem. You do not have to know ahead of time exactly which object your code will be dealing with. When you set or return a property on the LibraryItem object, the property procedure for the appropriate object runs.

For example, the following event procedure determines whether an item can be checked out, and, if so, checks it out by setting the CheckedOut property to True. All of the available object types have an AllowCheckOut property. For Fiction and Nonfiction objects, this property returns True. For Periodical and Reference objects, it returns False. Without knowing exactly which type of object the colLibItem variable refers to, you can check the property and respond appropriately:

```
Private Sub cmdCheckOut_Click()
    ' Attempt to check out library item.


    Dim colLibItem       As LibraryItem
    Dim strMsg           As String


    ' Locate item in collection and return reference to it.
    ' Assign reference to variable of type LibraryItem.
    ' Note that although the object has a specific type,
    ' you don't need to know what it is to use it.
    ' Value of selected text in combo box is same as
    ' item's key in collection. The key can be used to retrieve
    ' the item from the collection.
    Set colLibItem = gcolLibItems.Item(cboItems.Text)


    ' Check whether this item can be checked out.
    If colLibItem.AllowCheckOut Then
        If colLibItem.CheckedOut Then
            ' If item is already checked out, apologize.
            strMsg = "Sorry, this item is already checked out."
```

```
    Else
        ' Otherwise, check out and give return date.
        colLibItem.CheckedOut = True
        strMsg = "Item is checked out to you; due back " & Date + 14
    End If
Else
    ' If item can't be checked out, apologize.
    strMsg = "Sorry, this item can't be checked out."
End If


' Display message.
    MsgBox strMsg
End Sub
```

In addition, you can add properties or methods that are not part of the interface to any object. For example, you could add a Volume property to the Periodical and Reference classes to set and return the volume number for the object. To set that property, however, you must use an object of type `Periodical` or `Reference`, because the Volume property is not part of the LibraryItem interface. To determine whether the type of object you are working with is a Periodical or Reference object, you can use the If TypeOf construct. For example, the following procedure sets the volume number if the object passed in is a Periodical or Reference object:

```
Public Sub SetVolume(colItem As LibraryItem, _
                strVolNum As String)
    ' Declare object variables of specific types.
    Dim perItem As Periodical
    Dim refItem As Reference


    ' Use Is TypeOf... construct to check whether
    ' library item is a periodical.
    If TypeOf colItem Is Periodical Then
        ' Assign library item reference to object variable
        ' of type Periodical.
        Set perItem = colItem
        ' Set Volume property on Periodical object.
        perItem.Volume = strVolNum
```

```
    Else
        ' Check whether library item is reference material.
        If TypeOf colItem Is Reference Then
            ' Assign library item reference to object variable
            ' of type Reference.
            Set refItem = colItem
            ' Set Volume property on Reference object.
            refItem.Volume = strVolNum
        Else
            ' Library item must be fiction or nonfiction.
            MsgBox "You can't enter a volume label for " _
                & "a fiction or nonfiction item."
        End If
    End If
End Sub
```

Note You could also implement the Volume property shown in the previous example as part of the LibraryItem interface, and simply not add any code to it for the Fiction and Nonfiction classes. This might be a better approach, because then you do not have to use the If TypeOf construct or create an additional object variable.

Implementing a Nonabstract Class

The abstract interfaces discussed in Implementing an Abstract Interface impose a discipline on a set of related objects. Each class contains the same properties and methods, at a minimum, and each class must provide the code that runs for a given property or method, which is desirable if the objects behave differently. In some cases, however, every object in the set might behave in exactly the same manner for a given property. In this case, you can implement an interface that contains the desired code in the Property procedure, and call that Property procedure from the corresponding property for each object.

For example, every class in the Library.xls sample implements the Name property for the object in an identical way. Each time you add a new type of object, you must implement the Name property again. You can save yourself a little effort by moving the code for the Name property into the LibraryItem interface itself. Of course, each class must still implement the Name property. Instead of storing and retrieving the value itself, however, each class can delegate that task to the LibraryItem interface. To call code in the LibraryItem class, each class must contain a private variable of type LibraryItem, which can be initialized in the Class_Initialize event procedure:

```
Private p_colLibItem As LibraryItem
```

```
Private Sub Class_Initialize()
    Set p_colLibItem = New LibraryItem
End Sub
```

To delegate to the LibraryItem interface, the class must set and retrieve the Name property on this object of type `LibraryItem`:

```
Private Property Let LibraryItem_Name(ByVal RHS As String)
    ' Store name.
    p_colLibItem.Name = RHS
End Property
```

```
Private Property Get LibraryItem_Name() As String
    ' Return name.
    LibraryItem_Name = p_colLibItem
End Property
```

The only difference between implementing the Name property by delegating it to the LibraryItem interface and implementing it individually in each class module is that rather than storing a value in a module-level variable that's private to that class, you are storing a value in the Name property of a LibraryItem object, which in turn stores the value in its own private module-level variable.

Finally, note that when a class implements an interface, all the members that it implements are automatically denoted as private. This means that the implemented properties and methods in the Fiction, Nonfiction, Periodical, and Reference classes do not appear as part of the available interfaces for those objects. The implemented properties and methods appear on a variable of type `LibraryItem` only, which is fine if you are using variables of type `LibraryItem` to represent all of the other objects, as is done in the Library.xls sample.

If you want to define a public interface for each object, however, you can create a public property or method that calls the code that's in the private member. For example, if you wanted the Name property to be publicly available on an object, you could write a public Name property procedure that calls the private procedure supplied by the implemented interface, as shown in the following example:

```
Public Property Let Name(strName As String)
    LibraryItem_Name = strName
End Property
```

```
Public Property Get Name As String
    Name = LibraryItem_Name
End Property
```

You have a great deal of flexibility in how you define an interface. It can be fully abstract, nonabstract, or a combination of the two. Often a combination of the two types can be useful. For those members that share the same code, you can group that code in the interface. For those that do not, you can implement the code separately in each class.

Designing Object Models

Designing a custom object model can be a tricky business. If you dive in and start coding right away, you might find yourself realizing in the middle of your development process that your design is less than ideal. It pays to take some time to think through an object model, and even draw diagrams and make notes by hand. You might also want to study other object models to understand how they were constructed. When you design an object model, you are taking abstract processes and imposing concrete relationships upon them. In essence, you are creating artificial conceptual divisions for your code.

In This Section

Planning the Object Model
> Begin by determining how many objects and collections you must have and naming all of them.

Creating Collection Classes
> You can represent a collection with a class module, and use the collection to organize objects of the same type.

Relating Objects with Object Properties
> If an object contains a collection or another object, you must create an object property that returns a reference to the object or collection that it contains.

Sharing Code by Using Interfaces
> If two or more objects share common functionality, consider whether you can implement an interface that the objects can share.

Planning the Object Model

Begin by determining how many objects and collections you must have and naming all of them. You might find it helpful to draw the objects and collections in a hierarchical diagram that shows the relationships between them.

List as many of the properties, methods, and events for each object and collection that you can. Denote which properties can be simple module-level variables, which require Property procedures, and which are object properties. Also indicate whether properties should be read-write, read-only, write-only, or write-once.

Creating Collection Classes

You can represent a collection with a class module, and use the collection to organize objects of the same type. By convention, a collection class is usually given the plural name of the object that it contains; for example, the BoundLists collection contains BoundList objects.

Collection classes usually contain a Count property, for counting the number of objects in the collection, and an Item property, which returns a reference to an object in the collection by its index or key value. Most collection classes also contain an Add method, which adds a new object to the collection and returns a reference to it, and a Remove method, which removes an item from the collection.

You should consider how a top-level collection or object is to be initialized. Somewhere in your project there must be a line of code that creates an instance of the top-level collection or object. From there all other objects can be created from within your object model. If the collection will contain objects that might already exist or are saved with the file, such as bound list boxes or combo boxes, the collection will probably have to be initialized when the application loads. If the collection provides objects on demand, it might not have to be initialized until the objects are required.

You should also consider how objects are to be added to a collection. Does this happen based on user or programmatic input, or based on some change in the state of the system, or both? In addition, do objects have to be added when the application is first loaded?

Relating Objects with Object Properties

If an object contains a collection or another object, you must create an object property that returns a reference to the object or collection that it contains. The object property should have the same name as the object or collection. For example, suppose a ParentWindow object contains a ChildWindows collection. In this case, you would create a ChildWindows property of the ParentWindow object to return a reference to that object's ChildWindows collection.

If an object belongs to another object, you might want to add a Parent property that returns a reference to the parent object. To do so, you must define the Parent property in the class module for the child object, and set the Parent property in the class module for the parent object, after the child object has been created.

> **Note** When you implement a Parent property for an object that belongs to another object or collection, you run the risk of creating circular references. A circular reference exists when a parent object maintains a reference to a child object, and the child object, through its Parent property, maintains a reference to the parent object. The problem with this circular reference is that an object is not destroyed until the last remaining reference to it is destroyed. When you attempt to destroy the parent object by setting the reference to it to Nothing, the parent object will not actually be destroyed because each of its child objects still maintain a reference to the parent object. For example, in the EnumWindows.xls sample file, a ParentWindow object maintains a reference to its collection of ChildWindows objects through the ChildWindows object property. A ChildWindows collection maintains a reference to its ParentWindow object

through its Parent property. Setting a ParentWindow object to Nothing does not destroy the reference to the ParentWindow object that is maintained by the ChildWindows collection's Parent property. To truly destroy a Parent object, you must also destroy the references maintained by the Parent property.

Note   One way to solve the problem of circular references is to include a TearDown method on the parent object. This method should set all of the parent object's object properties to Nothing so that any references maintained indirectly through these object properties are destroyed. After you call the TearDown method on the parent object, you can set the parent object to Nothing. As long as there are no additional references to the parent object in your code, setting the parent object to Nothing will destroy the parent object in memory.

Sharing Code by Using Interfaces

If two or more objects share common functionality, consider whether you can implement an interface that the objects can share. That way you can consolidate your code by moving common code to the interface.

Creating Custom Objects for Web Pages

There are two ways to create objects for Web pages that are similar to custom objects created in Microsoft® Visual Basic® for Applications (VBA): by creating scriptlets, and by using Microsoft® Internet Explorer version 5 and later behaviors.

Dynamic HTML (DHTML) Scriptlets

You can create custom reusable objects for Web pages by using *DHTML scriptlets*. DHTML scriptlets are Web pages in which script procedures have been written according to certain conventions so that these procedures behave similar to methods and properties of the scriptlet. Scriptlets are supported in Internet Explorer version 4.0 and later. You can build scriptlets in either Microsoft® Visual Basic® Scripting Edition (VBScript) or Microsoft® JScript®.

Scriptlets can be script only, or they can have a user interface component in addition to script. You can include a scriptlet in the HTML for other pages to add the functionality that the scriptlet provides to those pages. By building scriptlets, you can componentize the process of developing Web pages in much the same way that you componentize applications with custom objects in Microsoft® Visual Basic® for Applications (VBA).

You refer to a scriptlet in an <OBJECT> tag in the HTML code for the page in which you want to use it. The following HTML code, shows how to refer to the Scriptlet.htm sample file. Note that the DATA attribute contains the name of the scriptlet file, Scriptlet.htm; this is comparable to the name of a class in VBA. The name for the scriptlet, as it is referred to within the script, is scrltDateCode; this name is comparable to the variable that you use to represent an instance of a class in VBA.

```
<OBJECT ID="scrltDateCode"
STYLE=  "position:absolute;
        width:0;
        height:0;"
        type="text/x-scriptlet"
        data="Scriptlet.htm">
</OBJECT>
```

The scriptlet file itself, Scriptlet.htm, contains script procedures that behave similar to methods and properties. The following procedure defines the GetYear property for the scriptlet:

```
Function public_get_GetYear()
' Return the current year.
    public_get_GetYear = Year(Date())
End Function
```

When the scriptlet has been included in a Web page by using the <OBJECT> tag, script in that Web page can call methods and properties of the scriptlet. For example, the following script fragment returns the value of the scriptlet's GetYear property and stores it in a variable.

```
Dim strCurrentYear

strCurrentYear = scrltDateCode.GetYear
```

For more information about creating and using scriptlets, see the Microsoft Scripting Technologies Web site at http://msdn.microsoft.com/scripting/.

DHTML Behaviors

Microsoft® Internet Explorer 5 or later supports DHTML behaviors. DHTML behaviors are lightweight, reusable components that encapsulate specific functionality or behavior on a page. You apply a behavior to a standard HTML element on a page to enhance that element's default functionality. When you have defined a custom DHTML behavior, you or other people on your Web development team can easily apply the behavior to achieve custom interactive effects across multiple pages, without having to write script.

Internet Explorer 5 or later implements several default behaviors. For example, the saveFavorite behavior saves the current state of a page when it is added to the Favorites list. You can use the saveFavorite default behavior to save information that a user has added to a Web page prior to saving it in the user's Favorites list. If your Web page provides stock information, for example, you might use the saveFavorite behavior to make it possible for the user to save selected stock symbols with the user's page.

In addition, you can create custom DHTML behaviors by using scriptlets. For example, you can create a behavior that affects a list item on a Web page, so that when the user rests the mouse pointer on the list item, the item changes color. To apply this behavior to a Web page, you refer to the file containing the behavior within a <STYLE> tag. The following example applies the behavior defined in a file named Hilite.sct to two list items in an HTML file:

```
<BODY><UL>
<LI STYLE="behavior:url(hilite.sct)">Item1
</UL></BODY>


<BODY><UL>
<LI STYLE="behavior:url(hilite.sct)">Item2
</UL></BODY>
```

The scriptlet that defines the behavior must implement certain tags that Internet Explorer recognizes to associate the behavior with an HTML element.

Using the Office Developer Productivity Tools

Build applications with Microsoft® Office XP Developer productivity and team-oriented tools. From code management to rapid application development, you will find enhanced productivity tools and documentation to help make you more productive.

Office Developer provides customization and extensibility tools that can help make you more productive and reduce development time. In addition, Office Developer provides a series of designers that extend the functionality of Microsoft® Visual Basic® for Applications (VBA). For example, the Add-in Designer facilitates building COM Add-ins (fully compiled DLLs) to extend the Office environment. Getting to data is critical. The tools simplify tasks from building reusable complex queries to creating reports that bind to enterprise data.

In This Section

Sharing Code with the Code Librarian
Use the Code Librarian to store and easily access code snippets.

Using Source Code Control
Place your Microsoft® Office applications and source code under source control.

Sharing and Reusing VBA Objects
Import and export Microsoft® Visual Basic® for Applications (VBA) objects between projects.

Rapid Application Development Tools
Develop and deploy applications quickly with Rapid Application Development (RAD) tools.

Sharing Code with the Code Librarian

You can store and manage reusable code in a centralized database. You can add your own code to the existing Code Librarian database, or you can create new code databases. The Code Librarian has a whole new look for Microsoft Office XP Developer, providing more efficient code management and functionality.

The Code Librarian includes a large starter database of prewritten code for standard routines for Microsoft® Office XP, Visual Basic® for Applications (VBA), Office XP Developer projects and the Microsoft Development Environment.

Each code snippet is associated with a category and multiple keywords, making it easy to find the code you are looking for. When you have located a desired piece of code in the Code Librarian, it is easy to add that code to your code module. The Code Librarian supports drag-and-drop as well as cut-and-paste actions.

Opening the Code Librarian

In Office XP Developer, the Code Librarian has been redesigned to improve functionality and accessibility. You can open the Code Librarian from the Windows Start menu or from within the Microsoft Development Environment.

After you first open the Code Librarian, you must attach a Code Librarian database. After attaching a database, the next time you open the Code Librarian, it will open with the previously viewed code library.

To open the Code Librarian from the Start Menu

1. From the **Start** menu, point to **Programs**, then **Microsoft Office XP Developer**, and then **Code Librarian**.

2. From the **Code Librarian** menu, select **Add**, and then **Existing Library**.

3. In the **Open** dialog box, browse to the location of the Code Librarian database.

    To open the Codelib.clb database, browse to the **My Documents** folder.

To open the Code Librarian from the Microsoft Development Environment

1. From the **Start** menu, point to **Programs**, then **Microsoft Office XP Developer**, and then **Microsoft Development Environment**.

2. From the **View** menu, select **Code Librarian**.

3. From the **Code Librarian** menu, select **Add**, and then **Existing Library**.

4. In the **Open** dialog box, browse to the location of the Code Librarian database.

    To open the Codelib.clb database, browse to the **My Documents** folder.

To close a code library

1. Select the code library node in the Code Librarian Explorer.

2. From the **Code Librarian** menu, click **Close.**

Creating a Code Library

In addition to the Codelib.clb database provided with the Code Librarian, you can create your own Code Librarian databases. You might have many projects, each requiring a separate library of its own. For example, you might develop a collection of code samples that you want to distribute with a book. With the Code Librarian, you can organize all of the source code with descriptions, keywords, and searchable text and titles.

To create a new code library

1. Open the **Code Librarian**. For details, see "Opening the Code Librarian."

2. From the **Code Librarian** menu, point to **Add**, and then select **New Library.**

3. In the **Save As** dialog box, enter the name of the new code library and browse to the location where you want to save the file. Click **Save**.

After the new code library has been saved, it appears as a new node in the Code Librarian Explorer. You can then add new categories and code items.

For information about distributing your custom code libraries, see "Distributing Code Samples with the Code Librarian."

Creating Code Librarian Categories

The Code Librarian uses categories and code item types to organize the code items in the Code Librarian Explorer. By creating a hierarchy of categories, you can make it easier to find specific code. The code item type option provides a means to visually organize your code by customizing the icon associated with the code item.

When you add new code to the library, you can associate it with a default category provided with the Code Librarian, or you can create a new category for the item.

To add a new category

1. Open the **Code Librarian**. For details, see "Opening the Code Librarian."

2. In the **Code Librarian Explorer**, select the library node or category you want to create a new category under.

3. From the **Code Librarian** menu, select **Add**, and then select **New Category**. The new category appears in the Code Librarian Explorer.

4. Enter a name for your category by right-clicking on the category in the Code Librarian Explorer, selecting **Rename**, and then typing the new name.

Using Code Snippets from the Code Library

The Code Librarian organizes code snippets and samples using categories, keywords, and item type icons. You can use the Code Librarian Explorer to locate code items, or you can perform searches on the keywords associated with the code items.

When you select a code item in the Code Librarian Explorer, a description of the item is displayed in the field below the explorer.

Searching for Code in the Code Librarian

You can specify search criteria for finding source code in the Code Librarian database. The search engine limits the search based on the selection you make in the Search Options area. The default is to search by title, code, descriptions, and keywords.

To search the Code Librarian for a code item

1. Open the **Code Librarian**. For details, see "Opening the Code Librarian."

2. From the **Code Librarian Menu**, select **Find**.

3. In the **Find in Code Library** dialog box, select the desired search types in the **Options** field.

    If you do not want to search by **Titles**, **Code**, **Descriptions**, or **Keywords**, then clear the check box for the respective option.

4. In the **Find What** field, type what you want to find.

5. In the **Look in** field, select the library you want to look in, and then click **Find**.

After searching, the Search Results window displays the name of the library item, its category, and its type.

To open one of the library items, double-click the item you want to open.

To copy the code item to a new location, you can use the drag-and-drop feature. For example, to copy the item to a different category within the Code Librarian, drag the library item to the new category folder to create a copy in the new location. To add the code item to your application, drag the code item onto your code editor surface.

Inserting Code into your Project from the Code Librarian

When you have found the code snippet you wish to use, you can easily insert it in your code module by dragging it onto your code module or by copying the code to the Clipboard and pasting it into the code module.

To drag code from the Code Librarian into an existing code module

1. In the **Code Librarian Explorer** select the category or code item you want to copy.

2. Double-click the code item to view the code.

3. Using the mouse, drag the selected code from the **Code** window to the desired location in your code module.

When you release the mouse, the selected code is inserted in the location.

To insert code from the Code Librarian into an existing code module

1. In your code module, place the cursor in the location where you want to insert the code.

2. In the **Code Librarian**, select the code snippet you want to copy.

3. From the **Edit** menu, select **Copy** to add the code item to the Clipboard. Place your cursor in the code item where you want to paste the code.

4. From the **Edit** menu, select **Paste**.

The code from the Code Librarian is inserted in your code module.

Customizing Code in the Code Librarian

The Code Librarian uses a database format to store its code so you can easily update the existing information in the Code Librarian, or you can create a new code database.

You can add new code, delete existing code, rename the code, and add or modify keywords, categories, and code item types. With the Code Librarian, you can associate all of the source code with descriptions, keywords, and searchable text and titles.

Modifying Existing Code Databases

If you have write permissions to the Code Librarian database, you can make changes to the code snippets. For example, you can add new code, delete existing code, rename the code, add new keywords, and change the categories or code item types.

Note If you are accessing the Code Librarian database over a network, you might not have write privileges to that database. To make changes to a database, you must have the appropriate permissions.

Note When adding new code, it is recommended that you include keywords and a description that will be helpful to others searching for code.

Defining Categories and Code Items

You can associate the source code in the Code window with categories and code items. By using categories, you can make it easier to find specific code within the Code Librarian. The code item option provides another way to organize your code, and displays a code item's properties.

The Code Librarian provides default values for both category and code item type, but you can create your own categories. A single piece of code can be associated with numerous categories. When you add new code to the library, you can associate it with existing categories, or you can create new categories.

To define categories and code items

1. Open the **Code Librarian**.

2. In the **Code Librarian** menu, select **Add**, and then select either **New Category** or **New Code Item**, depending on what you want to do.

3. When in the **Code Librarian** window, you can rename your category or new code item. To change the category or code item type, display the **Properties** window by selecting the **View** menu, then **Properties Window**. With the code item selected in the Code Librarian, change the **Type** property in the **Properties** window. Select the browse (**...**) button, and then select **Type** to display the dialog box.

4. If you want to create a new item, select the **New** button. If you want to delete an item, select the **Delete** button. If you want to change the icon for your item, select the **Change Icon** button. Follow the instructions for your specific task.

5. Click **OK**.

Associating Keywords with a Code Item

You can use Keywords to search the Code Librarian database for associated source code. A list of keywords is similar to an index. Keywords are a great way to find relevant code items fast.

To associate a keyword with a code item

1. Open the **Code Librarian**. For details, see "Opening the Code Librarian."

2. Select the code item for which you want to edit keywords.

3. Select the browse (**...**) button in the **Keyword** property in the **Property** window to open the **Keyword** Editor. The keywords already associated with the code item are listed in the **Keywords associated with this object** box. The list of available keywords is displayed in **Keywords list**.

4. To associate a keyword from the **Keywords list** with your code item, select the keyword in **Keywords list** and then click the "<" button. The keyword moves to the **Keywords associated with this object** field. To disassociate a keyword from the list, select the keyword and click the ">" button.

To add, edit, or delete keywords

1. To add a keyword that is not on the **Keywords list**, type the name of the new keyword in the **Add a new word** box and click **New**. Your keyword is added to the **Keywords associated with this object** box of the currently selected code item or category, and is also available in the **Keywords list** for association with other code items later.

2. To edit a keyword in the **Keywords list**, select the one keyword you want to edit, and click **Edit**.

3. To delete a keyword in the **Keywords list**, select the one keyword you want to delete, and click **Delete**. Click **OK** to accept the deletion.

Modifying Code Item Keywords

You can use Keywords to search the Code Librarian database for associated source code. A list of keywords is similar to an index. Keywords are a great way to find relevant code items fast.

To associate a keyword with a code item

1. Open the **Code Librarian**. For details, see "Opening the Code Librarian."

2. Select the code item for which you want to edit keywords.

3. Select the browse (**...**) button next to the **Keyword** property in the **Property** window to open the **Keyword** Editor. The keywords already associated with the code item are listed in the **Keywords associated with this object** box. The entire list of keywords is displayed in the **Keywords list** box.

4. If you want to add a keyword from the **Keywords list** to your code item, select the keyword from the **Keywords list** box. Select the "<" button. The keyword is placed in the **Keywords associated with this object** list box and added to your code item. To remove a keyword from the list, select the ">" button.

To add, edit, or delete keywords

1. If you want to add a keyword that is not on the **Keywords list**, type the name of your new keyword in the **Add a new word** text box. To add the keyword you typed, click **New**. Your keyword is added to both your **Keywords associated with this object** list box, and **Keywords list**.

2. If you want to edit a keyword in the **Keywords list**, select the one keyword you want to edit, and click **Edit**. Edit the keyword you selected in the **Keywords list** field. Click **OK** to accept the edit.

3. If you want to delete a keyword in the **Keywords list**, select the one keyword you want to delete, and click **Delete**. Click **OK** to accept the deletion.

Making the Code Librarian Available to Multiple Users

You might want to make the code samples in the Code Librarian available to multiple users.

Place a Code Librarian database on a network share where each user can access it.

To view the code, each user need only open the .clb file in a local copy of the Code Librarian.

Distributing Code Samples with the Code Librarian Viewer

The Code Librarian makes it easy to create libraries of sample code. The Code Librarian Viewer is provided as a redistributable read-only run-time version of the Code Librarian. By distributing the Code Librarian Viewer, your users can browse any code library created using the Code Librarian.

The Code Librarian Viewer makes it possible for users to search for code and copy it to their own projects. Because it is read-only, however, users will not be able to modify, add, or delete items using the Code Librarian Viewer.

> **Note**   You can use Microsoft Access to compress the code library database (.clb file) to reduce the size of the file. For details, see the Microsoft Access online documentation.

To view a library using the Code Librarian Viewer

1. From the **Start** menu, point to **Programs**, then **Microsoft Office XP Developer**, and then **Code Librarian Viewer**.

    > **Note**   The first time the Code Librarian Viewer is launched, there is no database attached. You must first add a database before you can use the Code Librarian Viewer.

2. From the **File** menu, select **Open**.

3. In the **Open** dialog box, browse to the location of the code librarian database you want to open and click **OK**.

The library is opened in the Viewer.

To distribute a library with the Code Librarian Viewer

1. Create a code library using the **Code Librarian** in the **Microsoft Development Environment**. For details, see "Creating a Code Library."

2. Enter the categories, code snippets, and keywords as desired.

3. Close the code library.

4. Launch the **Packaging Wizard**.

5. In the **Identify Application and Package** screen, select the code librarian file (.clb) as the main file for the package.

6. In the **Dependencies** screen, click **Add File**.

7. Browse to the location of the Code Librarian Viewer file (**codelibviewer.exe**) and add the file to your package. This file is installed by default to \Program Files\Microsoft Office Developer\CodeLibrarian.

8. Continue with the wizard.

The Packaging Wizard will create a setup program that will install your code library and the Code Librarian Viewer on your user's computer.

Using Source Code Control

Microsoft® Office XP Developer provides source code control using Microsoft® Visual SourceSafe™, which is available in the Office XP Developer package. As a stand-alone developer, source code control gives you the immediate benefits of versioning. You might have made some recent changes and then decided to revert back to an earlier version. With Visual SourceSafe, you can easily recover the previous code.

Each time you begin a new Office application, you can benefit from source code control by using Visual SourceSafe. If you are part of a team developing a large application, automated source code control provides a significant advantage. When many people work together to create, support, and update source code files for a large application, the coordination of files and updates is a complex process. Visual SourceSafe provides stable, easy-to-use source code management to keep the team's developers in sync with each other's changes.

The following sections acquaint you with how to install and use Visual SourceSafe with your Office application.

In This Section

Setting Up Visual SourceSafe
Getting started with Microsoft® Visual SourceSafe™ begins with setting up and connecting to a Visual SourceSafe project.

Choosing the Right Source Code Control Add-In
There are two Microsoft® Office XP Developer add-ins that provide source code control: Access Source Code Control add-in and VBA Source Code Control add-in.

Using the Visual SourceSafe Add-In with the Visual Basic Environment
The VBA Source Code Control add-in included with Microsoft® Office XP Developer conveniently provides Microsoft® Visual SourceSafe™ functionality within the Office development environment.

Using Visual SourceSafe with Documents and VBA Code

When using the VBA Source Code Control add-in, it is important to understand that Microsoft® Visual SourceSafe™ stores the binary document by using Visual SourceSafe directly and stores the Microsoft® Visual Basic® for Applications (VBA) source code by using the VBA Source Code Control add-in.

Using Source Control with Access

When working with a Microsoft® Access database, you can store the database file (.mdb) and all its contained objects in Microsoft® Visual SourceSafe™ using the Access Source Control add-in.

Setting Up Visual SourceSafe

Getting started with Microsoft® Visual SourceSafe™ begins with setting up and connecting to a Visual SourceSafe project. When you use Visual SourceSafe, your files are stored in a project, providing safe storage, important historical information, and version tracking. With the source control add-ins, you do not have to run Visual SourceSafe separately to realize the advantages of source code control.

The steps to integrating Visual SourceSafe into your Microsoft® Office XP development environment include:

Installing the Visual SourceSafe Application

Generally, your Visual SourceSafe administrator installs Visual SourceSafe on a network server for you and then adds your name to the database user list. Simply run the setup program, and select the option to install Visual SourceSafe.

There are three Visual SourceSafe setup options:

- **Shared Database Server** Installs a database and the necessary software on a network server (used by Administrators). Individual users then install the Visual SourceSafe client from the network server using Netsetup.

- **Custom** Makes it possible for you to choose which components to install.

- **Stand-alone** Installs the components necessary to create and access a private database on your machine. In addition, you can connect to existing databases on a network server.

Assigning User Permissions

Before you can access the database, you must assign the appropriate permissions. In addition, you can assign user permissions to other team members who want to share the files in your database. Use the Visual SourceSafe Administrator to add, change, or delete user permissions and passwords for your database.

Connecting to a Visual SourceSafe Database

You can connect to the database using either the Visual SourceSafe application or the source control add-in.

To connect to a Visual SourceSafe database from the Visual SourceSafe application

1. Start the **Visual SourceSafe** application.

2. From the **File** menu, click **Open SourceSafe Database**, and select one of the databases in the list box.

You can use this command to select an existing database from a Visual SourceSafe project that someone else has already created. This is how you enlist in a multi-developer project that someone has set up already.

To connect to a Visual SourceSafe database from the Source Control add-in

1. For the Visual Basic for Applications (VBA) Source Control add-in, in the **Visual Basic Editor**, select the **VBA Source Control** add-in from the **Add-Ins** menu.

   For the **Access Source Control** add-in, select **SourceSafe** from the **Tools** menu.

2. The first time you access Source Control, a logon box appears. Fill in the appropriate information for your database.

3. The Source Control options change on the menu.

You can now place items in your project under source control.

Choosing the Right Source Code Control Add-In

There are two Microsoft® Office XP Developer add-ins that provide source code control: Access Source Code Control add-in and VBA Source Code Control add-in.

When you are developing your application using Microsoft® Access, you must use the Access Source Code Control add-in. This is because Access is able to store the binary portion as well as the code for its objects as separate items within the Microsoft® Visual SourceSafe™ database.

Developing your application using any other Office application (such as Microsoft® Excel or Microsoft® Word), you must use the VBA Source Code Control add-in. For Office developers, this add-in conveniently provides Visual SourceSafe functionality within the Office development environment.

Using the Visual SourceSafe Add-In with the Visual Basic Environment

The VBA Source Code Control add-in included with Microsoft® Office XP Developer conveniently provides Microsoft® Visual SourceSafe™ functionality within the Office development environment.

Note   To use the VBA Source Code Control add-in, you must first load it into the Office environment.

How Source Code Control Works

While a group of Office developers work together to build a database application, the master copies of all the Microsoft® Visual Basic® for Applications (VBA) objects are kept in a Visual SourceSafe project. Each developer might work on a VBA project on his or her local workstation. Checking out source code objects from the Visual SourceSafe version control system copies them from the Visual SourceSafe project into the developer's project on the local workstation. Checking in source code objects copies them from the developer's local workstation into the Visual SourceSafe database.

Visual SourceSafe provides useful versioning and control functionality. When you install the VBA Source Code Control add-in and place your project under source code control, the following commands are added to the VBA Source Code Control submenu on the **Add-Ins** menu.

- **Get Latest Version**   This command overwrites your local version with the current object in the database. With the Get Latest Version command, some objects might appear in the list box that are not actually part of your database. These are objects that other users have put in Visual SourceSafe that you have not copied yet.

- **Check Out**   This command copies the selected objects to the current project and updates the Project control status window to indicate the files are checked out to a specific team member. Checking out an object gives you the ability to make changes to that object. When you check out an object, no other developer can check out that object until you check it back in.

- **Check In**   This command displays a dialog box that lets you select the objects to check in. You can optionally check the files in but also keep them checked out to continue working on them. You can include a comment describing the latest modifications made to the file. Checking in an object gives other developers the chance to view and use your changes to that object.

- **Undo Check Out**   This command reverts to the last version saved in Visual SourceSafe.

  Note   When you select the Get Latest Version, Check Out, or Undo Check Out commands, the objects on your machine might be different versions than the objects in the Visual SourceSafe project. If so, the objects are synchronized as they are copied from the Visual SourceSafe database to your workstation, overwriting your versions of the objects.

- **Show History**   This command displays a dialog box showing the history of the currently selected object.

- **Show Differences**   This command compares the local copy of an object to the one in the Visual SourceSafe project and shows how they differ using a textual display.

- **SourceSafe Properties**   This command displays Visual SourceSafe object properties (such as comments and check-out status).

- **Add Files to SourceSafe**   This command displays a dialog box with a list of the objects that are currently in your project but are not under source code control. You use this dialog box to add these objects to Visual SourceSafe.

- **Get Object from SourceSafe**   This command copies the object from Visual SourceSafe, drops it into your project on your workstation, and then gives you the option of putting it under source code control within your project. The copied object is essentially a new object that now belongs to your project and is no longer associated with the object's original source. The original object still remains in Visual SourceSafe. This command is one of several ways to reuse existing code. For additional information on code reuse, see "Sharing and Reusing VBA Objects."

- **Run SourceSafe**   This command runs Visual SourceSafe Explorer. If Visual SourceSafe is already running, it is brought to the front of your screen.

- **Refresh File Status**   This command refreshes the data in the source code control window.

These commands typically display a dialog box with a list box of all the objects in the Visual SourceSafe project that the command applies to. For instance, if you choose the Check In command, the list box is filled with all the objects that you currently have checked out. Select the items that apply for the chosen command, and then click OK. Depending on what you had selected before choosing the command, certain items in the list box might already be selected.

Using Visual SourceSafe with Documents and VBA Code

When using the VBA Source Code Control add-in, it's important to understand that Microsoft® Visual SourceSafe™ stores the binary document by using Visual SourceSafe directly and stores the Microsoft® Visual Basic® for Applications (VBA) source code by using the VBA Source Code Control add-in. The VBA Source Code Control add-in cannot store the actual binary document. This affects how you use Visual SourceSafe to protect both documents and VBA code.

The following sections describe the important procedural differences for using Visual SourceSafe to protect both the document file and the associated VBA code files.

Creating the Initial Document

Suppose you are developing a new Microsoft® Excel document named Book1.xls. As a general process, you will use the Visual SourceSafe application to add the document to source control.

To create and add your document to Visual SourceSafe

1. Open **Excel**. From the **File** menu, save the new workbook document that appears as **Book1.xls**.

2. While the document is still open, start the **Visual Basic Editor (ALT+F11)**, and click **Add Project to SourceSafe**. This adds the VSSODE control module to your project.

    Tip   You can specify the name and directory location for your new project folder.

3. Save the Excel document again to capture the new VSSODE module.

4. Close the document, and exit the Excel application.

5. From the **Start** menu, run **Visual SourceSafe**.

6. Create a new project folder for your document.

7. Add the Book1.xls document to your new project folder (using the **Add Files** command).

8. Exit **Visual SourceSafe**.

Visual SourceSafe now protects your document. Because the Book1.xls document is the fundamental basis for your new project, you might set up procedural rules so only you and certain designated developers can modify it.

Modifying the Document

Occasionally, you will want to modify the Book1.xls document to support additional VBA source code enhancements. As a general process, you'll check the document in and out of the Visual SourceSafe application.

To modify a document under source control

1. From the **Start** menu, run **Visual SourceSafe**.

2. Check out the document.

3. Open the document, and start the **Visual Basic Editor (ALT+F11)**.

4. On the **Add-Ins** menu, click **Get Latest Version** to get all the associated VBA files to update recent code changes.

5. Make changes to the document, and save the document.

6. Close the document, and exit the **Excel** application.

7. Check in the document to **Visual SourceSafe**.

8. Exit **Visual SourceSafe**.

Adding VBA Code Modules

You can extend your document's functionality with VBA source code. For storing VBA code, Visual SourceSafe is conveniently available from within the Visual Basic Editor using commands from the VBA Source Code Control add-in. Although the Microsoft® Office document is stored directly in the Visual SourceSafe application, code modules are added to source control using the VBA Source Control add-in.

To create and add VBA code modules to source control

1. From the **Start** menu, run **Visual SourceSafe**.

2. Check out the Office document.

3. Open the document, and start the **Visual Basic Editor (ALT+F11)**.

4. On the **Add-Ins** menu, click **Get Latest Version** to get all the latest code.

5. In the **Project Explorer**, right-click the VBA project folder, click **Insert**, and then click **Module**.

   This creates a new VBA code module associated with the document. As a general practice, you can insert all of the required user forms, modules, and class modules at this time. Additional modules can always be added later using the same procedure.

6. Modify the code module as required.

7. Select the VBA project folder, and, from the **Add-Ins** menu, click **Add Files to SourceSafe**.

8. After selecting a project location directory, click **OK**, and finally select the objects you want to check in to Visual SourceSafe. When you click **OK** again, a temporary dialog box indicates that everything was added successfully. Then, the Source Code Control status window displays the object names, check in/out status, and who currently owns them.

   Tip The floating Source code control status window is also dockable. You can drag it to the left frame to share space with the VBA Project window and the Properties window.

   Note If you are working on several projects, switching context between one project and the other does not update the Source code control status window. You can use the Refresh File Status command to immediately update this window.

9. Save the **Excel** document to capture the new VBA code modules.

10. Close the document, and exit the **Excel** application.

11. Check in the document directly into **Visual SourceSafe**.

12. Exit **Visual SourceSafe**.

Modifying VBA Code Modules

As you develop your VBA enhancements, you'll want to modify the actual VBA source code. Again, your code is stored by the VBA Source Code Control add-in, and the Office document is stored in the Visual SourceSafe application.

To modify your VBA code modules under source control

1. From the **Start** menu, run **Visual SourceSafe**.

2. Check out the document so you have a container for the VBA objects. (If you use the **Get Latest Version** command, be sure to check the option **Make writeable**.)

3. Open the document, and start the **Visual Basic Editor (ALT+F11)**.

4. On the **Add-Ins** menu, click **Get Latest Version** to get all the latest code changes.

5. On the **Add-Ins** menu, check out the VBA source code.

6. Make the changes to the VBA source code.

7. On the **Add-Ins** menu, check in the VBA source code.

8. Close the document, and exit the Excel application.

9. Check in the document directly into Visual SourceSafe.

10. Exit Visual SourceSafe.

Using Source Control with Access

When working with a Microsoft® Access database, you can store the database file (.mdb) and all its contained objects in Microsoft® Visual SourceSafe™ using the Access Source Control add-in.

The Access Source Control add-in is installed as part of the Microsoft® Office XP Developer tools setup and is immediately available from the Tools menu within Access.

Each of your databases is stored in a Visual SourceSafe project. Query, form, report, macro, and module objects are stored as text files in the project associated with the database they are used in. Other objects, known as the Data and Misc. objects, (tables, relationships, toolbars, database properties, import/export specifications, and so on) are stored in a special file with an .acb extension in the Visual SourceSafe project. This .acb file should be treated with care—you should not rename or share this file in Visual SourceSafe, or you risk database corruption.

A shared object can simultaneously exist in many projects. When you modify a shared object in one project, the change is propagated automatically to all the projects that share the object. You can share a form between databases or have multiple teams developing a module simultaneously.

Sharing and Reusing VBA Objects

In developing your Microsoft® Office application, you might have created some useful VBA objects that other developers could use. On the other hand, you might know of some Microsoft® Visual Basic® for Applications (VBA) objects created by other developers that you want to get and modify in your current project. You can easily import and export objects with the VBA Multi-Code Import/Export add-in.

Exporting VBA Objects

Using the VBA Multi-Code Export add-in, you can share Microsoft® Visual Basic® for Applications (VBA) objects by exporting objects from one VBA project to another location to be imported into a different VBA project.

Suppose you have a number of objects within your project that you want to export. In this context, export means to copy the files to a target directory (either on your local workstation or to a network file share). The Multi-Code Export command lists all of the objects within the currently selected VBA project in the Project window.

To export VBA objects

1. From the **Add-Ins** menu, select **Multi-Code Export**.

2. In the **Available Objects** list, select the objects for export and transfer them to the **Selected Objects** lists.

3. Verify that the **Target Folder** is where you want to copy the objects.

4. Click **Export**.

This copies all of the objects to the designated target directory. Document objects are exported as class files (*.cls). Other file types are exported with the original extension.

> **Note** Only the VBA code for the object is exported. The binary portion of the object (such as the content of an Excel worksheet) is not stored. You must use Visual SourceSafe directly to store the binary portion of the object.

Importing VBA Objects

Using the VBA Multi-Code Import add-in, you can share Microsoft® Visual Basic® for Applications (VBA) objects by importing existing objects into the current VBA project.

> **Note**   To use the VBA Multi-Code Import add-in, you must first load it into the Office environment.

To import VBA objects to your project

1.   From the **Add-Ins** menu, select **Multi-Code Import**.

2.   Use the **Browse** button to find the objects you want to import.

     For example, if you just exported some VBA objects, you can browse to the target ..\Export folder to display a list of possible objects for importing.

3.   Select the items you want to import.

4.   Click **Import**, and the objects are added to your current VBA project.

Where necessary to avoid duplicate names, a sequential number is appended to each imported VBA object as it is copied into the Class Modules folder. For example, if the original object name was Sheet2, the imported name in the Class Modules folder is Sheet21.

Imported objects are inserted into your project and—because they are copies—belong to your project. There is no association with the original project where the objects were selected for import.

Rapid Application Development Tools

When it comes to developing applications, no matter how small or how large, one limiting factor almost always comes into play: time. Rapid Application Development (RAD) tools provide the ability to develop and deploy applications quickly by automating much of the development process for you, and eliminating repetitive tasks.

Formatting String Variables

The VBA String Editor add-in assists in the formatting of strings for inclusion in Microsoft® Visual Basic® for Applications (VBA) code. Complex strings, such as SQL statements, can be entered as standard text, and the String Editor then formats the string with the proper quotation marks and other symbols and inserts it into your code.

Using the VBA String Editor reduces the time you spend building strings and hunting syntax errors by making it easier to create strings to embed long scripts or complicated SQL statements into VBA code.

Note The String Editor makes it possible for you to create new strings or to update existing formatted strings easily. To update existing strings, highlight the string you want to update in the code, and select the String Editor Add-in. Then, follow these steps to edit:

To format strings using the VBA String Editor

1. To open the VBA String Editor, launch the **Visual Basic Editor** (ALT + F11) from a Microsoft® Office application.

2. Open a VBA project. Place your cursor in the active code pane where you want to add a formatted string.

    Note The VBA String Editor will not activate unless an active code pane is open.

3. From the **Add-ins** menu, select **VBA String Editor**. If the VBA String Editor is not listed under the **Add-Ins** menu, you must load it into the **Add-Ins** menu through the **Add-In Manager**, located in the **Add-Ins** menu.

4. In the **String Editor** text field, enter the text that you want to format as a string.

5. If there are variables within the entered text, you can designate them in one of two ways.

    a. Select the variable name in the text field, and click the **Toggle to String/NonString** button. This changes the variable name to a bold blue font, distinguishing the variable from the rest of the entered text.

    b. Before you enter the variable name, click the **Toggle to String/NonString** button. All text entered is now in the same bold blue font, indicating that you are in **NonString** mode.

        After you have finished entering the variable name, click the **Toggle to String/NonString** button to toggle back to **String** mode.

6. Select the **Concatenation Symbol** toolbar button to toggle between the "&" and the "+" concatenation symbols for the selected text.

    Note Although either symbol will work as a concatenation operator, the "+" symbol also is used as an addition operator. If a string contains numerical characters, the "+" symbol will cause those numbers to be added together rather than displayed as a string. For best results, always use the "&" symbol when you want to concatenate strings.

7. If you must cut, copy, or paste text, select the appropriate toolbar button.

8. Click **Update** when you are finished. The **VBA String Editor** screen closes, and the formatted string is placed into the code.

Formatting Code Commenter and Error Handler Templates

Using the VBA Code Commenter and Error Handler add-in, you can apply a template to selected procedures in the code. You can choose to apply a given template to only one procedure, to all the procedures in a module, or to all the procedures in a project. By providing this functionality, this add-in saves time by avoiding copying and pasting the same code comments or error handling code over and over. The Code Commenter and Error Handler add-in uses template files (.eht) to control the format of comments. These templates contain replaceable tokens that specify what will be added to your code. As the add-in is inserting text, it searches for these tokens.

Three template files are provided for use with the Code Commenter and Error Handler add-in: CodeCommenter.eht, ErrorHandler.eht, and CC_EH.eht. The CodeCommenter.eht file provides a standard format for comments to be inserted into procedures. The ErrorHandler.eht file provides error-handling code that would otherwise be tedious to insert repeatedly into every procedure. The CC_EH.eht file combines the two previous templates, so you can take advantage of both purposes of this add-in.

In addition, you can create custom template using the Code Commenter and Error Handler Template Editor provided through the add-in or by using Microsoft® Notepad or another text editor. The Template to Apply can then be set to the custom-made template.

To use the Template Editor, click the New button on the Code Commenter and Error Handler add-in. This opens the Template Editor to a new file. Or, if you simply want to modify an existing template, set the Template to Apply to the template file that you want to modify, and click the Edit button. Then, you can change an existing template as you like and save it either under its original name. If you want to retain a copy of the original template file, you can save the modified template under a different name.

The codecommenter.eht and errorhandler.eht templates can be applied to the same procedure. The add-in makes it possible for only one error handling type template and one code commenting type template to be applied to each procedure. If a certain type of template has been applied to a procedure already, applying another template of the same type using the add-in (either the same template or a template of the same type) has no effect.

To format a Code Commenter and Error Handler template

1. To open the Code Commenter and Error Handler, launch the **Visual Basic Editor** (ALT + F11) from a Microsoft® Office application.

2. Open a Microsoft® Visual Basic® for Applications (VBA) project to which you want to add comments or error handling.

3. From the **Add-ins** menu, select **Code Commenter and Error Handler**. If **Code Commenter and Error Handler** is not listed under the **Add-Ins** menu, you must load it into the **Add-Ins** menu through the **Add-In Manager**, located in the **Add-Ins** menu.

4. The **Code Commenter and Error Handler** screen is displayed. In the **Insert** section, select whether comments should be added to the current procedure, all procedures in the current module, or all procedures in the current project.

5. Type the name and initials for the **Author** if desired. With the default template, this information appears as part of the code comments. This information is stored in the registry for future use. If author name and initials are not specified, this information will remain blank when the template is applied.

6. If you want to modify an existing template, enter the template name in the **Template to Apply** box. You can either enter the template file path manually or select the file by clicking the browse (**...**) button and finding the file through the Browse dialog box.

   If you choose to browse for the template that you want to modify, the **Select Code Commenter or Error Handler Templates** dialog box appears after clicking the browse (**...**) button. Select the template that you want to format, and then click **Open**. This closes the browse dialog box and returns you to the main **Code Commenter and Error Handler** add-in screen.

7. Click the **Edit** command button. The **Code Commenter and Error Handler Template Editor** opens with the template that you selected loaded. After modifying the template, you can either save the template under the original name or choose a different name so as not to overwrite the original template. It is suggested that you save the template under a different name, so the original template will remain available should you need it.

8. If you want to design a new template from scratch, select the **New** button. Create your own template in the **Code Commenter and Error Handler Template Editor**. When you are finished creating the template, save the template, and close the Template Editor. You will return to the **Code Commenter and Error Handler** add-in.

9. In the **Code Commenter and Error Handler** add-in, click **Apply**. Your template is then applied to your code.

Microsoft Office Developer Walkthroughs

The topics in this section provide mini-tutorials that walk you through some typical application development scenarios using Microsoft® Office XP Developer. These walkthroughs are intended to provide:

- A guide to accomplish the primary tasks you must have in your own work.

- Step-by-step instructions to be used as a learning exercise.

- A means to get acquainted with Office Developer.

- Pointers to more detailed information in other topics.

In This Section

Walkthrough: Creating a COM Add-in with VBA
Using this walkthrough, you can create a COM add-in using Microsoft® Visual Basic® for Applications (VBA). COM Add-ins can extend your application's functionality without adding complexity for your user.

Walkthroughs: Workflow Applications for Exchange Server
The Workflow Applications for Exchange Server walkthroughs introduce the important areas of the Workflow Designer for Exchange Server. Each walkthrough discusses the development of a specific workflow application type and user interface using a series of steps.

Walkthroughs: Workflow Applications for SQL Server
These walkthroughs provide a hands-on introduction to the numerous features of Microsoft® Office XP Developer, and Workflow Designer for SQL Server in a clear and ordered manner.

Walkthrough: Creating a Digital Dashboard using Web Parts
A Digital Dashboard is a customized application that delivers personal, team, and corporate information directly to a user's desktop.

Creating a COM Add-in with VBA

Using this walkthrough, you can create a COM add-in using Microsoft® Visual Basic® for Applications (VBA). COM add-ins can extend your application's functionality without adding complexity for your user. Underneath the surface, a COM add-in is a dynamic-link library (DLL) that is registered to make it possible for Microsoft® Office XP applications to load and use it. Although an add-in can be written as an executable file (.exe), DLLs generally provide better performance than .exe files.

This walkthrough creates and runs a custom toolbar COM add-in using VBA in Microsoft® Excel. The tasks in this topic assume you are familiar with Office applications and VBA projects, as well as with debugging and running code.

Introduction

You can create COM add-ins in any language that supports COM, such as VBA, Visual Basic, and Microsoft® Visual C++®. Add-ins created with Office Developer are packaged automatically as DLLs and registered for loading in the host application. You can create a single add-in that can work in several applications. For more information, see "Creating COM Add-ins for Multiple Applications."

This walkthrough follows a series of steps to create a COM add-in with VBA. The basic process for creating this COM add-in includes:

1. Configuring the Add-in Designer.

2. Writing code in the Add-in Designer.

3. Integrating a command bar control into the add-in.

4. Debugging and testing the COM add-in.

5. Making a DLL for the COM add-in.

6. Troubleshooting COM add-in development problems.

Configuring the Add-in Designer

Projects created with Add-in Designers provide the work area for developing your add-in. You can use Add-in Designers to create COM add-ins for use in VBA or any Office application. Each Add-in Designer in the project represents a separate add-in that can run in only one Office application.

The resulting DLL can contain multiple add-ins that share forms, modules, and class modules but are targeted for different applications. This walkthrough uses Excel as the host Office application.

If you want your add-in to be available for multiple applications, you must add a separate Add-in Designer for each host application. You can share code through modules; however, in each project, you must reference the object model specific to each host application.

To configure the Add-in Designer

1. Open **Microsoft Excel**.

2. From the **Tools** menu, select **Macros**, and then select **Visual Basic Editor**.

3. From the **File** menu, select **New Project**, and then select **Add-In Project**.

4. Type the name **Greeting Toolbar** in the **Addin Display Name** text box, and type the description **Toolbar add-in that launches a Hello World message in Excel** in the **Addin Description** text box.

5. Select **Microsoft Excel** from the **Application** list.

6. Select **Microsoft Excel 10.0** from the **Application Version** list.

7. Select **Startup** from the **Initial Load Behavior** list.

8. From the **Tools** menu, select **References**, and make sure the following type-libraries are referenced for the project. (This list of references is required for this walkthrough. For your add-ins, be sure to select the type libraries required by each Office application that might use the add-in.)

    *   Visual Basic for Applications

    *   OLE Automation

    *   Microsoft Add-in Designer

    *   Microsoft Office 10.0 Object Library

    *   Microsoft Excel 10.0 Object Library

9. From the **File** menu, select **Save AddInProject1**.

10. In the **Save Project As** dialog box, enter the name **Greetings**, select a folder to save it in, and then click **Save**.

Writing Code in the Add-in Designer

After you have created the project and assigned values to the Add-in Designer, you can add the code that connects the add-in to the host application. This walkthrough shows you the typical procedures and events you must have for the add-in and host application to work together. The IDTExtensibility2 interface supplies the COM objects and events required for the two to connect. Then, your add-in can interface with the host application using the object model exposed by the host application. You can view the object model for your particular application in the Object Browser.

Code that is in the Add-in Designer handles the integration of the add-in with the host application. For example, code that runs when the add-in is loaded or unloaded resides in the Add-in Designer's module. If the add-in contains forms, the Add-in Designer also might contain code to display the forms.

To declare variables and set up procedure stubs

1. In the **Project Explorer** window, select **AddInDesigner1**, and then open the **View** menu, and click **Code**.

2. In the **General Declarations** section, reference the extensibility interface.

   ```
   Implements IDTExtensibility2
   ```

3. Add the module-level variables that provide communication between the add-in and the host. The variable assigned As Application persists as long as the COM add-in is loaded, so all procedures can determine in what application the add-in is running currently. Because the WithEvents keyword is assigned to the cbbButton variable, the menu item's Click event procedure will be triggered when the user clicks the new menu item.

   ```
   'Global object references
   Public appHostApp As Application
   Private WithEvents cbbButton As Office.CommandBarButton
   ```

4. In the **Code Window**, select **IDTExtensibility2** from the **Object** list, and **OnConnection** from the **Event** list. This creates the OnConnection event procedure stub.

   Note You must include the event procedure stub for each event provided by the IDTExtensibility2 interface. If you omit any of the event procedures, your project will not compile.

5. Add an event procedure stub for each of the following events:

   - OnDisconnection
   - OnStartupComplete
   - OnBeginShutdown
   - OnAddinsUpdate

Now, you can add the functionality for your add-in.

Integrating a Command Bar Control into the Add-in

If your COM add-in has a user interface, you can add code that displays a command bar that makes it possible for users to run your add-in. This walkthrough shows how to include code that creates a new command bar control (toolbar button or menu item) in the host application. When your add-in is loaded, the control is loaded as well, and the user can click the button or menu item to open and work with the add-in.

To create the command bar control

1. Find the **OnConnection** event procedure. Between the Private Sub and End Sub lines, add the code to create a new command bar control and assign it to the event-ready **CommandBarButton** object variable. The entire procedure will appear as the following:

```
Private Sub IDTExtensibility2_OnConnection(ByVal _
    Application As Object, ByVal ConnectMode As _
    AddInDesignerObjects.ext_ConnectMode, ByVal AddInInst _
    As Object, custom() As Variant)

    'Store startup reference
    Set appHostApp = Application

    ' Add the commandbar
    Set cbbButton = CreateBar()
End Sub
```

If you are familiar with creating add-ins using Visual Basic, you might notice that you do not set a value for the command bar button **OnAction** property when creating an add-in in VBA. This is because the event is hooked up for you automatically.

2. Find the **OnDisconnection** event procedure. Between the Private Sub and End Sub lines, add code to remove the command bar control when the add-in is unloaded. The entire procedure will appear as the following:

```
Private Sub IDTExtensibility2_OnDisconnection(ByVal _
    RemoveMode As AddInDesignerObjects.ext_DisconnectMode, _
    custom() As Variant)

    RemoveToolbar
    ' remove references to shutdown
    Set appHostApp = Nothing
    Set cbbButton = Nothing
End Sub
```

3. Wherever you generally store functions in your code, add the code for the function you called in the **OnConnection** procedure. This function creates the command bar, sets the properties for the command button, and provides for handling of error messages.

```
Public Function CreateBar() As Office.CommandBarButton
    ' Specify the command bar
    Dim cbcMyBar As Office.CommandBar
    Dim btnMyButton As Office.CommandBarButton
```

```
On Error GoTo CreateBar_Err


Set cbcMyBar = appHostApp.CommandBars.Add(Name:="GreetingBar")


' Specify the commandbar button
Set btnMyButton = cbcMyBar.Controls.Add(Type:=msoControlButton, _
    Parameter:="Greetings")
With btnMyButton
    .Style = msoButtonCaption
    .BeginGroup = True
    .Caption = "&Greetings"
    .TooltipText = "Display Hello World Message"
    .Width = "24"
End With


' Display and return the commandbar
cbcMyBar.Visible = True
Set CreateBar = btnMyButton
Exit Function


CreateBar_Err:
MsgBox Err.Number & vbCrLf & Err.Description
End Function
```

4. Add the code for the function you called in the **OnDisconnection** procedure. This function removes the command bar when the add-in is unloaded.

```
Private Function RemoveToolbar()
    appHostApp.CommandBars("GreetingBar").Delete
End Function
```

5. Add a click event procedure for the **CommandBarButton** object. This procedure will be called when the new command bar button is clicked. The following code displays a message to show that the click event is working:

```
Private Sub cbbButton_Click(ByVal Ctrl As _
    Office.CommandBarButton, CancelDefault As Boolean)
    MsgBox ("Hello World!")
End Sub
```

6. Save your project.

Now, your COM add-in is complete. The remaining steps are to debug and test the code to make sure it works as you expect and then to make the add-in into a DLL file that can be distributed and used on other computers that have Office XP installed.

Debugging and Testing the COM Add-in

When you are developing a COM add-in in VBA, you can debug the add-in by putting the project into run mode. With the project in run mode, you can load and use the COM add-in from within an Office application to test and debug it by using any of the VBA debugging tools.

To debug and test a COM add-in using VBA

1. Place any desired breakpoints, **Stop** statements, or watches in the code.

2. On the **Run** menu, click **Run Project**. In the **Debugging** dialog box, select **Wait for components to be created**, and click **OK**. This compiles your project, alerting you to any compilation errors, and then puts the project into run mode.

3. Verify that **[Published]** appears in the editor's title bar.

   Note   The add-in must be published to make it available to the host application.

4. Start a new instance of Excel. Because you set the load behavior of the add-in to **Startup**, the add-in loads as soon as you start the application, the **OnConnection** event occurs, and the **Greetings** button appears. Now, you can use the breakpoints and **Stop** statements that you added to debug the code.

   If you click the **Greetings** button, the Hello World message will appear in front of the Visual Basic Editor—not in front of Excel—as long as you are running the project in the Editor. After you make the project into a DLL file, the message will appear in front of Excel.

5. When you are finished debugging and testing, open the **Run** menu, and click **Stop Project**. This clears up temporary files and registry entries and puts the project in the correct state to be made into a DLL file.

Making a DLL for the COM Add-in

After you have written and debugged your code, you can make your add-in into a DLL that can be deployed to other computers that have Office XP.

To package the COM add-in as a DLL in VBA

1. From the **File** menu, select **Make Greetings.DLL**.

2. Keep the file name **Greetings** in the **Make Project** dialog box, and choose a location where you want to save your project.

3. Click **OK**.

This step will create the COM add-in, add the appropriate registry entries, and make the COM add-in available for use in your Office host. When you create the add-in DLL, VBA uses the information you have given to the Add-in Designer to register the DLL as a COM add-in. VBA writes the name, description, and initial load behavior setting of the add-in to the registry. The host application of the add-in reads these registry entries and loads the add-in accordingly.

Troubleshooting Common Add-in Development Problems

While working in the development environment and switching between applications, you might encounter some error messages or unexpected behavior. Here are some common problems and their solutions.

Compile errors appear or Statement Completion does not work in the editor

Be sure the appropriate object libraries are referenced for the project.

Nothing happens when I run the project and open a new instance of the host application

- Be sure that the word "Published" appears in the title bar of the add-in you are running. If not, you must run the project.

- Click the window of each open application. Your object might be running, but it might be visible only after you click the first instance of the application that you opened.

- Make sure you have specified and set the module-level variables properly.

- In the host application, make sure your add-in is selected in the COM Add-Ins dialog box. You can customize the host application by adding the COM Add-ins command to a toolbar. This command opens the COM Add-Ins dialog box.

To add the COM Add-ins dialog box to a toolbar

1. Open the **Tools** menu, click **Customize**, and select the **Commands** tab. Under **Categories**, select **Tools**. Scroll down the **Commands** list until you find **COM Add-Ins**. Drag **COM Add-Ins** onto a toolbar to create a new button, and then close the **Customize** dialog box.

2. On the toolbar, click the **COM Add-ins** button you just added.

3. In the **COM Add-Ins** dialog box, verify the check box next to your add-in is selected. To unload the add-in, clear the check box.

> **Note** If your add-in does not appear in the list, make sure that the project is running in the Visual Basic Editor.

The object appears in the host application but does not respond

Multiple instances of your object might be running. Your code for detecting and removing an existing object with that name might not be running. Check and debug your OnDisconnection code.

Creating a Workflow Application Using Exchange Server

In this walkthrough, you will be guided through the process of creating a team application that uses a Microsoft Exchange 2000 public folder, a Microsoft® Outlook® form, and workflow to move a purchase order through a simplified approval process. The workflow created in this example uses values in an Outlook form to determine how the order is sent through the various states in the process. In addition, it uses script to notify users automatically that the order has been submitted and reviewed.

Introduction

Does your department require an application for tracking reports or other items in Exchange? Would you like to automate reminders and notifications based on items in an Exchange folder? You can create such a team application quickly using the Workflow Designer for Exchange 2000 Server.

Using the Workflow Designer for Exchange Server, you can add a workflow process to any items in Exchange folders. A workflow process automates control of items in a folder by moving them through a series of states depending on the transitions and conditions you specify. In addition, you can enhance your workflow application by scripting your own functions that run when the transitions are performed. Your workflow process can track any type of item available in Outlook, such as messages, forms, or tasks, as well as any file, such as documents (.doc), spreadsheets (.xls), or text files (.txt).

The user interface for a workflow process determines how the user submits the item that moves through the process. When designing the user interface for your application, you have a wide variety of options. You can integrate Microsoft® Visual Basic® applications, Web pages, and any other front-end that can access the Exchange folder objects.

By completing this walkthrough, you can create a team application that uses a public folder, an Outlook form, and a workflow to move a purchase order through a simplified approval process.

Because this walkthrough is designed to highlight how to create a simple workflow process, not the user interface for the application, the user interface provided in this example is a simple Outlook form intended only to show how to automate your workflow. The example application created in this walkthrough is not designed to be a real-world application.

Preparing Exchange for a Team Application

To follow along with this walkthrough, you must have access to an Exchange 2000 Server, the Workflow Designer for Exchange Server, and the appropriate permissions on the server. For more information about preparing Exchange for a workflow process, see the documentation in the Exchange SDK download, available from the Microsoft® Developer Network (MSDN®) Exchange Server Developer Center at http://msdn.microsoft.com/exchange/.

Creating a team application requires the following components:

- **Server**: Microsoft Windows 2000 with Exchange 2000 Server as the back-end for the application.

- **Development tool**: Workflow Designer for Exchange Server as the tool for creating the workflow process. This tool can reside on either a client computer with access to the server or the server itself.

Before you can add workflow to your folder, you must have the following:

- **A public folder** in Exchange 2000 Server. For example, you could add a folder called PurchaseOrders to Public Folders.

- **Workflow design permissions** on the Exchange 2000 Server. By creating the folder in Outlook, you automatically have the owner permissions required. For additional information about setting the permissions required for creating workflow processes, see the documentation in the Exchange SDK download, available from the MSDN Exchange Server Developer Center at http://msdn.microsoft.com/exchange/.

- **A set of items your team wants to track**. Using this walkthrough, you can create an Outlook form that shows simple controls that make it possible for users to enter and to track Exchange items. In addition to Outlook, you can use .asp pages, a Visual Basic form, or data access pages as the user interface for your folder and workflow.

- **A plan** for the business process that tracks an item. Using this walkthrough, you can create a simplified workflow process for a purchase order form in Outlook.

To enable Script Execute Permissions

1. Open the **Exchange System Manager** on the Exchange 2000 Server.

2. From the **Servers** menu, select your computer | **Protocols** | **HTTP**, and then **Exchange Virtual Server**.

3. Right-click **Public**, and select **Properties**.

4. In the **Access** tab, select **Scripts** in the **Execute Permissions**.

To add the yourself to the two COM+ Workflow Roles

1. Open the **Component Services** on the Exchange 2000 Server.

2. From the **Component Services** menu, select **Computers | My Computer | COM+ Applications | Workflow Event Sink**, and then **Roles**.

3. Add yourself to the **Can Register Workflow** and **Privileged Workflow Authors** roles.

Creating the User Interface in Outlook

You can use a workflow process created using the Workflow Designer for Exchange Server to track any type of item available in Exchange 2000 Server. This walkthrough demonstrates how to create a workflow team application using a simplified purchase order implemented as an Outlook Post form. The application created in this example is designed only to illustrate how you can integrate a form with a workflow, and it lacks many of the features a real purchase order would require. In this example, the user interface is created first, because the workflow and its script require the values obtained through controls on the user interface form.

The first step is to create a public folder that will be used to post the purchase orders and that will be where you will create the workflow project. For example, you could add a folder called PurchaseOrders to Public Folders.

To add a public folder using Microsoft Outlook

1. Start **Outlook**, and display the folder list if it is not shown already by selecting **Folder List** from the **View** menu.

2. Expand the **Public Folders** node, and then expand **All Public Folders**.

3. Right-click **All Public Folders**, and select **New Folder**.

4. Enter a name for the new folder, such as PurchaseOrders.

5. Navigate to the folder by selecting the folder you just created.

Sometimes it is not convenient to set up Outlook simply to create folders. You also can use Outlook Web Access by using Microsoft® Internet Explorer to navigate to the Exchange Server.

To add a public folder using Internet Explorer

1. Start **Internet Explorer**.

2. In the Address Bar, type http://*server name*/Public to display Outlook Web Access.

3. The public folders will be displayed in the **Folder List** on the left.

4. Right-click the **Public Folders** node, and select the **New Folder** option. The currently logged on user will be set as the folder owner automatically. If you create a sub folder under an existing folder, both the currently logged in user and the owner of the main folder will have owner permissions on the subfolder.

When you have a folder created, it is a good idea to create a Network Place for the folder or at least for the http://*MyServer*/Public location.

To create the user interface for this walkthrough, you create two different views of the Post form in Outlook:

- **Edit Compose Page view**   This view is used by the person submitting the purchase order to input data in the expense fields. It appears when the report is created or composed. You are shown this view automatically when you are designing a form. The text boxes on the form provide values to the script used in the workflow.

- **Edit Read Page view**   This view is used by a manager to approve or reject the purchase order. It contains an approval and rejection combo box in addition to the expense fields.

By completing this walkthrough, you create and publish an Outlook form and set it as the default form for the folder. The fields in this form are used by the workflow process described in Planning the Workflow later in this walkthrough.

To create the Edit Compose Page view of the Outlook form

1. In **Outlook**, open the public folder to which you want to add the workflow.

2. From the **Tools** menu, select **Forms**, and then select **Design a Form**.

3. In the **Design Form** dialog box, select **Post**, and then select **Open**.

4. In the form, resize the message area to create space for the purchase order fields.

5. Right-click the form, and then click **Control Toolbox**.

6. Add the following label controls to the form.

Control	Properties
Office supply	Caption: Office supply
PC software	Caption: PC software
PC hardware	Caption: PC hardware
Misc.	Caption: Misc
Total Expense	Caption: Total Expense

7. Add the following controls to the form to enter and display the expense values. To modify the associated properties, right-click the control and then click **Properties**. On the **Value** tab, click the **New** button to specify a user-defined field that the workflow script can reference.

Control	Properties
Office supply textbox	Name: Office supply Type: Currency
PC software textbox	Name: PC software

Control	Properties
	Type: Currency
PC hardware textbox	Name: PC hardware Type: Currency
Misc. textbox	Name: Misc Type: Currency
Total Expense label (A label box is used because the user cannot change the value.)	Name: TotalExpense Type: Currency Caption: (Null) Select **Set the initial value of this field to**, and enter this formula for the initial value: **[Office supply] + [PC software] + [PC hardware] + [Misc]**. Click **Calculate this formula automatically**.
Submit check box	Name: Submit Type: Yes/No Format: True/False Check **Set the initial value to this field to**, and enter **No** for the initial value.

Edit Compose Page view of the Outlook form

To create the Edit Read Page view of the Outlook form

1. In the **Edit Compose Page** view of the form, select and copy all of the controls you added to the form.

2. Above the tabs for the form, click **Edit Read Page**.

3. Resize the message area to create space for the controls, and then paste them in place.

4. Add a combo box control to the form, right-click the combo box control, and then click **Properties**. Click **New** to specify a user-defined field, and set the properties shown in the following table.

Property	Value
Name	Approved
Type	Text

Property	Value
Format	Text
List type	Dropdown
Possible values	Approve;Reject;Pending
Initial value	Pending

5. Add a label with the caption **Approved?** next to the combo box control.

To make the form available to the workflow, you must publish it. In addition, you can specify it as the default form for the folder. You must have editor, publishing editor, or owner permissions to add forms to a public folder.

> **Note** Do not enable workflow on a folder before publishing the form. If you do, you might get a permissions error even though you are the owner of the folder.

To publish the form and specify it as the default form for the folder

1. On the **Tools** menu, select **Forms**, and then select **Publish Form As**.

2. In the **Publish Form As** dialog box, enter a name for the form, and then select **Publish**.

   > **Note** The name you provide is the name that the user sees when choosing a form to post in the folder. For the purchase order example, you can name it "PurchaseOrders."

3. Close the form, and select **No** when prompted to save your changes (because the form is published already, you are not required to save your changes).

4. In the **Folder list**, right-click the folder to which you want to add workflow, and then click **Properties**.

5. In the **When posting to this folder, use** combo box, select the form you created, and then click **OK**.

Your form will appear when a user decides to post to that folder.

Planning the Workflow

To learn about using the Workflow Designer for Exchange Server, you can use this walkthrough to create a workflow process that includes a series of states through which a purchase order item moves and to define the transitions that move the item.

The Workflow Process

The workflow process in this example is based on the following scenario. An employee creates a purchase order form in a PurchaseOrders folder located in the Public Folder. When the order is created, the item enters the Draft state. To move into the Submit to Manager state, the employee must select a Submit check box and save the order. Otherwise, the employee can modify and save the item as many times as required while the Submit check box is not selected. When the Submit check box is selected, the order is moved automatically to the Submit to Manager state. When the order is moved to the Submit to Manager state, a manager can either approve or reject the order.

If the manager selects "Approve" in the Approved check box, then the purchase order moves into the Approved state. If the manager selects "Reject," then the purchase order returns to the Draft state.

Items in the Approved state or Draft state can be deleted. Items in the Submit to Manager state cannot be deleted, because a Delete transition is not specified for it.

Each workflow state specifies a step in the workflow process. Details about the specifications for the states, transitions, events, and script used to implement the workflow process in this walkthrough are provided in the procedures in the Creating a Workflow Process section later in this walkthrough.

The purchase order workflow example includes the following states:

- Draft

- Submit to Manager

- Approved

Transitions are used to transition an item from one state to another. Each state typically has at least two transitions. One transition moves the item into the state, and one transition moves the item out of the state. Each transition has a condition associated with it that is used in determining which state is transitioned to.

States can have any number of transitions. For example, the Submit to Manager state has four transitions: Manager Approved, Manager Rejected, Manager Pending, and Expiry. Transitions are triggered by a change to the item in the folder. When triggered, the condition is evaluated. If the condition evaluates to True, then the script associated with the transition is executed. In this example, the workflow for the purchase order has the following transitions:

- **Create Draft** The condition for this transition is evaluated after the item in the folder is created. The value of the Submit check box control must be False.

- **Create and Submit** The condition for this transition is evaluated after the item in the folder is created. The value of the Submit check box control must be True.

- **Edit** This transition occurs when the item in the folder is edited in draft state.

- **Manager Submission** The condition for this transition is evaluated after the item in the folder is saved. The value of the Submit check box control must be True.

- **Manager Approved** The condition for this transition is evaluated after the item in the folder is read while in the Submit to Manager state. In this example, the value of the Approved combo box control on the Outlook form must be Approve.

- **Manager Rejected** The condition for this transition is evaluated after the item in the folder is read while in the Submit to Manager state. In this example, the value of the Approved combo box control on the Outlook form must be Reject.

- **Manager Pending** The condition for this transition is evaluated after the item in the folder is read while in the Submit to Manager state. In this example, the value of the Approved combo box control on the Outlook form must be Pending.

- **Expiry** This transition occurs after the report has been in the Submit to Manager state for a user-defined period of time without being opened.

- **Delete1 and Delete2** These transitions make it possible for the report to be deleted while in either the Draft or Approved state. Items in the Submit to Manager state cannot be deleted.

The Workflow Scripts

In your script associated with each transition, you can call user-defined functions. This example uses the following custom functions, along with a set of standard functions that are called from the custom functions. The script used for each function is provided in the Creating the Script Procedures section later in this walkthrough.

Custom Functions

- **SubmitPurchaseOrder** Called from the Manager Submission transition when a purchase order is submitted to a manager. Sends an e-mail message to the approval authority containing a link to the posted item awaiting approval.

- **ApprovePurchaseOrder** Called from the Manager Approved transition and Manager Rejected transition when the manager either approves or rejects a purchase order. Checks the value on the Outlook form for approved/rejected status and sends notification e-mail to the person who submitted the form. If the item is rejected, it also resets the Submit property value and returns it to the Draft state.

- **ExpirePurchaseOrder** Called from the Expiry transition when a purchase order remains submitted to a manager for seven days. Sends a reminder message to the approval authority that the purchase order must be approved.

Standard Functions

- **AddFieldToCurrentMsg** Called from the Create Draft and Create and Submit transitions. Dynamically adds a new property to the item. This is used to add the Approval Authority property, returned from the GetUserManager script, and the SubmittedBy property created in the WorkflowSessionSender script to the item.

- **ClearPermissions** Clears all previously set permissions. This is used to change the permissions for the person who submitted the form to read-only after the item has been submitted for approval.

- **GetPathAndSubject** Returns the path to the public folder and the subject of the current item. This makes it possible for the SubmitPurchaseOrder and ApprovePurchaseOrder functions to add a link to the specific purchase order item in the e-mail message body.

- **GetUserManager** Returns application-defined data. In this example, it returns the e-mail alias of the user's manager.

- **SendMessage** Sends an e-mail message in response to workflow transitions.

- **SetCurrentMessageField** Sets the value of an existing property on an item. This is used to reset the Submit property value when a purchase order is rejected.

- **SetPermissions** Sets permissions making it possible for only the approval authority to make changes to the item and sets read-only permissions to all others.

Creating a Workflow Process

To create a workflow process, you open the Workflow Designer for Exchange Server and specify the states, transitions, and events. Creating a workflow includes the following main tasks:

- Adding a workflow to a public folder.

- Adding states and transitions that the item will move through.

- Adding events that determine how the item is handled and specify conditions for special handling.

- Adding script to automate handling of items, sending notifications, or calling other functions you want to use. Activating the workflow on the folder.

In the sections that follow, the generic procedure describing how to accomplish the designated task is followed by specific instructions for creating the purchase order example.

Creating the Workflow Process

After planning your workflow, you can create the workflow on a public folder. The Workflow Designer for Exchange Server works directly on the folder, so you must create the folder before opening the Workflow Designer for Exchange Server. The Workflow Designer for Exchange Server also automatically generates a new empty workflow process, containing only starting and ending shapes.

To create a project and workflow process

1. From the **Start** menu, select **Programs**, select **Microsoft Office XP Developer,** and then **Microsoft Development Environment**.

2. From the **File** menu, select **New**, and then select **Project**. The **New Project** dialog box is displayed.

3. Select **Office Developer Projects**.

4. Under **Templates:**, select the **Exchange Workflow Project** icon.

5. In the **New Project** dialog box, enter a name for the new project and a folder location in the form of a URL, for example http://myserver/public/myfolder. The folder location will default to the last folder opened.

   Note You cannot browse to an http location unless you have created a network place.

6. Click **OK**. An empty workflow process is created, and the workflow diagram is displayed on the **Design Surface**.

> **Caution** Each Exchange folder location can contain only one Exchange Workflow Project. Each project can contain multiple workflow processes.

Adding States to the Workflow Diagram

You can add states to the workflow diagram representing each stage through which an item might pass during processing. In this example, the states used in the purchase order workflow diagram are: Draft, Submit to Manager, and Approved.

To add a workflow state

1. Select the workflow process from the **Solution Explorer**.

2. From the **View** menu, select **Open**, or double-click the workflow process.

3. Select the **State** tool in the Toolbox, and click the design surface. The **State** shape will be created at the location of the click. **Properties**, such as name and caption, can be set for the state shape in the **Property Page** or **Properties Grid**.

4. To connect this new state with existing states, you must create a new workflow transition.

To create the workflow diagram

Add three states with the following properties.

- State Name: Draft

Property	Value
Name	Draft
Caption	Draft

- State Name: Submit to Manager

Property	Value
Name	SubmitToManager
Caption	Submit to manager
ExpiresIn	7 days

- State Name: Approved

Property	Value
Name	Approved
Caption	Approved

Adding Transitions to States

You can add events to states, such as Enter or Edit, and add transitions, such as Submit or Reject, to establish the relationships between the states in the workflow and to provide a place to add script for automating the workflow. In addition, workflow transitions can be used to evaluate conditions and to trigger scripts that automate your workflow process.

To add a transition to a state in the Workflow Designer for Exchange Server

1. From the **View** menu, select **Open**, or double-click the workflow process.

2. Select the **Transition** tool, click the shape at the start of the transition, and then drag to the shape at the end of the transition. The transition is created between the two shapes. **Properties**, such as name, caption, and type of transition, can be set in the **Property Page** or **Properties Grid**. By default, the transition will be a Change transition type. That means a change to an item will cause the transition.

   If you have multiple states to connect, you can turn on sticky mode. Press **CTRL**, click the transition shape, and then drag to create transitions between the states. Press **ESC** to turn off sticky mode.

   > **Note** Sticky mode can be turned on for any of the workflow tools.

   > **Caution** If you drag one transition directly over anther transition, it might appear that they have merged into one transition, however both transition still exist.

To complete the purchase order example, add the transitions, conditions, and script specified in the following procedure. This script calls user-defined functions specified in the Creating Script Procedures section later in this walkthrough.

If a state has multiple transitions exiting, the next state of the item might vary dependent on the order by which the transitions are evaluated. You can control the order by which transitions are evaluated by setting the evaluation order. To set the evaluation order for transitions exiting a state, select the state on the Design Surface, and then right-click and select Properties. On the Properties dialog box, select the Transitions tab.

To create a functional workflow for the purchase order example

Add the following transitions to the workflow diagram.

- Transition Name: CreateDraft

Property	Value
Caption	Create Draft
Beginning State	Start1
Ending State	Draft
Type	Create

- Transition Name: CreateAndSubmit

Property	Value
Caption	Create and Submit
Beginning State	Start1
Ending State	SubmitToManager
Type	Create

- Transition Name: Edit

Property	Value
Caption	Edit
Beginning State	Draft
Ending State	Draft
Type	Change

- Transition Name: ManagerSubmission

Property	Value
Caption	Manager Submission
Beginning State	Draft
Ending State	SubmitToManager
Type	Change

- Transition Name: Delete1

Property	Value
Caption	Delete1
Beginning State	Draft
Ending State	End1
Type	Delete

- Transition Name: ManagerRejected

Property	Value
Caption	Manager Rejected
Beginning State	SubmitToManager
Ending State	Draft
Type	Change

- Transition Name: ManagerPending

Property	Value
Caption	Manager Pending
Beginning State	SubmitToManager
Ending State	SubmitToManager
Type	Change

- Transition Name: ManagerApproved

Property	Value
Caption	Manager Approved
Beginning State	SubmitToManager
Ending State	Approved
Type	Change

- Transition Name: Expiry

Property	Value
Caption	Expiry
Beginning State	SubmitToManager
Ending State	SubmitToManager
Type	Expiry

- Transition Name: Delete2

Property	Value
Caption	Delete2
Beginning State	Approved
Ending State	End1
Type	Delete

Creating the Script Procedures

Each workflow transition has two associated script functions—a validation script procedure and a transition script procedure. When a workflow transition is triggered, the workflow engine invokes the script engine and executes the validation function. If this validation function returns True, the associated transition and transition script procedure are executed.

To Access the Script Editor and add script

1. From the **View** menu, select **Code**, or double click the transition in the **Design Surface** where you want to add code.

2. Create a procedure, including **Sub** and **End Sub** tags, or a function, including **Function** and **End Function** tags.

    Note Success entries must be enabled to use the Audit trail for debugging. For details, see the "To enable script debugging and success entries procedure" later in this walkthrough.

Many of the procedures and functions in these examples refer to and rely on each other. When using the example script, be sure to verify that all parameters and dependent functions exist in the workflow script.

1. Add the following script event handlers to each transition:

   - Transition Name: CreateDraft

Property	Value
Event	OnCreate
Script	AddFieldToCurrentMsg "SubmittedBy", WorkflowSession.Sender AddFieldToCurrentMsg "ApprovalAuthority", ""

   - Transition Name: CreateAndSubmit

Property	Value
Event	OnCreateValidate
Script	CreateandSubmit_OnCreateValidate = CBOOL(WorkflowSession.Fields("Submit").Value)

Property	Value
Event	OnCreate
Script	AddFieldToCurrentMsg "SubmittedBy", WorkflowSession.Sender AddFieldToCurrentMsg "ApprovalAuthority", "" SubmitPurchaseOrder

   - Transition Name: ManagerSubmission

Property	Value
Event	OnChangeValidate
Script	ManagerSubmission_OnChangeValidate = CBOOL(WorkflowSession.Fields("Submit").Value)

Property	Value
Event	OnChange
Script	SubmitPurchaseOrder

   - Transition Name: ManagerApproved

Property	Value
Event	OnChangeValidate
Script	ManagerApproved_OnChangeValidate = CBOOL(WorkflowSession.FIelds("Approved").Value = "Approve")

Property	Value
Event	OnChange
Script	ApprovePurchaseOrder(TRUE)

- Transition Name: ManagerRejected

Property	Value
Event	OnChangeValidate
Script	ManagerRejected_OnChangeValidate = CBOOL(WorkflowSession.Fields("Approved").Value = "Reject")

Property	Value
Event	OnChange
Script	ApprovePurchaseOrder(FALSE)

- Transition Name: Expiry

Property	Value
Event	OnExpire
Script	ExpirePurchaseOrder

2. Set the evaluation order for transitions as follows:

- State Name: Start1

Order	Transition
1	CreateAndSubmit
2	CreateDraft

- State Name: Draft

Order	Transition
1	ManagerSubmission
2	Delete1
3	Edit

- State Name: SubmitToManager

Order	Transition
1	ManagerApproved
2	ManagerRejected
3	Expiry
4	ManagerPending

AddFieldToCurrentMsg

To use this code, create the AddFieldToCurrentMsg script in the Script Editor. This script is called during the Create Draft and Manager Submission transitions, adding the SubmittedBy and ApprovalAuthority properties to the SubmitPurchaseOrder script.

```
Sub AddFieldToCurrentMsg (strName, Value)
    Dim FieldType
    FieldType = 8 ' BSTR
    WorkflowSession.Fields.Append CStr(strName),FieldType, , , CStr(Value)
    WorkflowSession.Fields.Update
End Sub
```

ApprovePurchaseOrder

To use this code, create the ApprovePurchaseOrder script in the Script Editor.

The ApprovePurchaseOrder is dependent on the GetUserManager (approval authority), GetPathAndSubject, SendMessage, and SetCurrentMessageField scripts. If the parameter is True, then the purchase order is approved, and the e-mail message indicates that it has been approved. If it is False, the e-mail message indicates that the report has been rejected.

```
Sub ApprovePurchaseOrder(bApproved)
    Dim strSMTPAddress
    Dim strBody
    Dim strSubject
    Dim strMessageSubject
    Dim strApproved
    Dim strOutlookURL

strSMTPAddress =
WorkflowSession.Fields("urn:schemas:mailheader:from").Value
strMessageSubject =
WorkflowSession.Fields("urn:schemas:mailheader:subject").Value
```

```
    If bApproved = True Then
        strApproved = "APPROVED"
    Else
        strApproved = "REJECTED"
    End If


    strSubject = strApproved & " -- Purchase Order " & strMessageSubject


    strSubject = "Your purchase order has been " & strApproved & " (" &
strMessageSubject & ")"


    strOutlookURL = GetPathAndSubject
    strBody = "Your purchase order has been " & strApproved & " by " &
WorkflowSession.Fields("ApprovalAuthority").Value & vbCRLF & vbCRLF
    strBody = strBody & "View the purchase order by clicking here.
<outlook://public folders/All public Folders/" & strOutlookURL & ">" &
vbCRLF & vbCRLF
    strBody = strBody & "-----------------------------------" & vbCRLF
    strBody = strBody & "Purchase Starting State: " &
WorkflowSession.StateFrom & vbCRLF
    strBody = strBody & "Purchase Ending State: " &
WorkflowSession.StateTo


    SendMessage strSMTPAddress, strSubject, strBody


    ' Reset submit when rejected
    If bApproved = Falşe Then
        SetCurrentMessageField "Submit", False
    End If


End Sub
```

ClearPermissions

To use this code, create the ClearPermissions script in the Script Editor. This script is called when
the SubmitPurchaseOrder is executed. After the purchase order is submitted, the permissions for
the person who submitted the form change to read-only.

```
Sub ClearPermissions()
    WorkflowSession.ItemAuthors.Clear
End Sub
```

ExpirePurchaseOrder

To use this code, create the ExpirePurchaseOrder script in the Script Editor. This script sends e-mail to the approve authority indicating that a purchase order has been awaiting approval and has now expired.

The ExpirePurchaseOrder is dependent on the GetUserManager (approval authority) and SendMessage scripts.

```
Sub ExpirePurchaseOrder()
    Dim strSubject
    Dim strBody


    strSubject = "Action Required: Purchase Order Approval Request"
    strOutlookURL = GetPathAndSubject
    strBody = "There is a purchase order waiting for your approval."  &
vbCRLF & vbCRLF
    strBody = strBody & "View the purchase order by clicking here.
<outlook://public folders/All public Folders/"  & strOutlookURL & ">" &
vbCRLF & vbCRLF
    strBody = strBody & "----------------------------------------" &
vbCRLF
    strBody = strBody & "Submitted: " & Cstr(Date) & "  " & Cstr(Time) &
vbCRLF
    strBody = strBody & "Purchase ending state: " &
WorkflowSession.StateTo
    strSMTPAddress = WorkflowSession.Fields("ApprovalAuthority").Value
    SendMessage strSMTPAddress, strSubject, strBody
End Sub
```

GetPathAndSubject

To use this code, create the GetPathAndSubject script in the Script Editor. This script makes it possible for the SubmitPurchaseOrder and ApprovePurchaseOrder functions to add a link to the purchase order in the e-mail message body.

```
Function GetPathAndSubject()
    Dim iPos
    Dim iPathLength
    Dim strPath
    Dim strSubject

    strPath = WorkflowSession.Fields("DAV:parentname")
    strSubject = WorkflowSession _
```

```
    .Fields("http://schemas.microsoft.com/mapi/proptag/0x0037001F") _
    .Value


iPathLength = len(strPath)


iPos = Instr(strPath, "backofficestorage") + 18
iPos = Instr(iPos,strPath, "/") + 1
iPos = Instr(iPos,strPath, "/")


iPathLength = iPathLength - iPos
GetPathAndSubject = Right(strPath, iPathLength) & "/~" & strSubject

End Function
```

GetUserManager

To use this code, create the GetUserManager script in the Script Editor. This script is called in the ApprovePurchaseOrder, ExpirePurchaseOrder, and SubmitPurchaseOrder scripts.

```
Function GetUserManager(strUserAddress)
    Dim mgrDN


    With WorkflowSession
        mgrDN = .GetUserProperty(strUserAddress, "manager",0)
        GetUserManager = .GetUserProperty(mgrDN, "mail", 1)
    End With


End Function
```

SendMessage

To use this code, create the SendMessage script in the Script Editor. This script is called in the ApprovePurchaseOrder, ExpirePurchaseOrder, and SubmitPurchaseOrder scripts to send an e-mail message. The parameters used specify to whom the message should be sent, along with the subject and body of the e-mail message.

```
Sub SendMessage (strTo, strSubject, strBody)


    Set oMsg = CreateObject("CDO.Message")
```

```
oMsg.To = strTo
oMsg.From = WorkflowSession.Sender
oMsg.Subject = strSubject
oMsg.TextBody = strBody
oMsg.Send

Set oMsg = Nothing
```

End Sub

SetCurrentMessageField

To use this code, create the SetCurrentMessageField script in the Script Editor. This script is called in the ApprovePurchaseOrder and SubmitPurchaseOrder scripts to reset the Submit property value when moving from Approved to Rejected. The parameters specify the name of the property to set and the value to which to set it.

```
Sub SetCurrentMessageField(strName, Value)
    WorkflowSession.Fields(CStr(strName)).Value = Value
    WorkflowSession.Fields.Update
End Sub
```

SetPermissions

To use this code, create the SetPermissions script in the Script Editor. This script is called in the SubmitPurchaseOrder script; in addition, you must call ClearPermissions prior to setting permissions. The parameter specifies what user (using the user's SMTP e-mail address) should have author access to the item.

```
Sub SetPermissions (strSMTPAddress)
    WorkflowSession.ItemAuthors.Add strSMTPAddress, 0
End Sub
```

SubmitPurchaseOrder

To use this code, create the SubmitPurchaseOrder script in the Script Editor. This script sends the approval authority an e-mail message containing a link to the specific purchase order item awaiting approval. The approval authority is determined after the total expense is evaluated. If the total expense is less than $1000, the approval authority is the manager of the person who submitted the form. If the total is greater than $1000, the approval authority is the manager's manager. In both instances, the GetUserManager script is called and returns an e-mail alias for the appropriate authority.

The SubmitPurchaseOrder is dependent on the AddFieldToCurrentMsg, GetUserManager (approval authority), GetPathAndSubject, SendMessage, ClearPermissions, SetPermissions, and SetCurrentMessageField scripts.

The ClearPermissions and SetPermissions scripts are required for the manager to be able to approve or reject the purchase order.

```
Sub SubmitPurchaseOrder()
    Dim strSMTPAddress
    Dim strSubject
    Dim strBody
    Dim strOutlookURL

    strSubject = "Action Required: Purchase Order Approval Request"
    strOutlookURL = GetPathAndSubject
    strBody = "There is a purchase order waiting for your approval." &
vbCRLF & vbCRLF
    strBody = strBody & "View the purchase order by clicking here.
<outlook://public folders/All public Folders/" & strOutlookURL & ">" &
vbCRLF & vbCRLF
    strBody = strBody & "-------------------------------------" &
vbCRLF
    strBody = strBody & "Submitted: " & CStr(Date) & "   " & CStr(Time) &
vbCRLF
    strBody = strBody & "Purchase ending state: "  &
WorkflowSession.StateTo

    strSMTPAddress = GetUserManager(WorkflowSession.Sender)

    If WorkflowSession.Fields("TotalExpense").Value > 1000 Then
        strSMTPAddress = GetUserManager(strSMTPAddress)
    End If

    SendMessage strSMTPAddress, strSubject, strBody
    SetCurrentMessageField "ApprovalAuthority", strSMTPAddress
    ClearPermissions
    SetPermissions(strSMTPAddress)

End Sub
```

Activating the Workflow Process

After you have completed your workflow, you can implement it on the folder. Before workflow can be enabled, a default workflow process must be set. When workflow is enabled for a folder, items in the folder use the default workflow.

Note Finish your work on the forms before activating the workflow. After the workflow is activated, you might find that you no longer have permissions to save your design changes to the folder.

To set the default workflow process

1. Select the workflow project from the **Solution Explorer**.

2. From the **View** menu, select **Property Pages**. You also can right-click the project in the **Solution Explorer**, and select **Properties** from the context menu.

3. In the **Default Workflow Process:** text box, enter the name of the workflow process you want to set as the default, or select the "**…**" button to browse for other available workflow processes. When browsing for the desired workflow process, only *.wfd files will be filtered. In addition, the name of the default workflow process can be entered into the **Property Grid**, in the **DefaultWorkflow** property field.

    If the selected workflow process is not in the current folder, a URL including the location and name of the process will be entered in the text box. It is important to note that external default workflow process will not be displayed in the **Solution Explorer**; it is displayed only in the **Properties Grid**.

    Note The default workflow process must reside on the same server as the Exchange Server project folder.

To enable a workflow process

1. From the **View** menu, select **Property Pages**. You also can right-click the project in the **Solution Explorer**, and select **Properties** from the context menu.

2. To enable workflow, select the **Workflow enabled on this folder** check box, or in the **Property Grid**, set the **WorkflowEnabled** property to True.

3. Click **OK**.

Using the Workflow Process

When you have completed the creation of the Outlook form and the workflow process, you can test the functionality of your application.

1. In **Outlook**, click the **PurchaseOrder** folder.

2. Click **New** to display the **Purchase Order** form.

3. Enter a name for the purchase order in the **Subject** field.

4. Enter values for the purchase order values. The **Total** field will calculate the total automatically.

5. Select the **Submit** check box to submit your purchase order to a manager for approval.

    An e-mail message is sent to your manager indicating that a purchase order is awaiting approval.

    Note If an error message appears stating that you do not have permission to save the item, make sure that you have manager information specified in the Exchange address book. If your e-mail alias does not have a manager identified, an error will occur when you try to send e-mail to the manager.

6. Edit the newly added purchase order by double-clicking it. The **Purchase Order** form now shows the **Approved?** combo box.

7. In the **Approved?** combo box, click **Approve**, and then on the **File** menu, click **Save**.

An e-mail message is sent to you informing you that your purchase order has been approved.

Developing a Workflow Application Using Workflow Designer for SQL Server

In this walkthrough, you will be guided through the process of creating a workflow application using the Workflow Designer for SQL Server, which is included in Microsoft® Office XP Developer. The easiest way to create a powerful application is by taking advantage of the database interface elements in Microsoft® Access, so the steps in this example include creating an Access data project, building and relating the necessary tables, producing the workflow objects, and building the user interface.

Introduction

An Access data project makes it possible for you to use familiar Access tools to build Microsoft® SQL Server™ databases. When the Workflow Services for SQL Server components are installed, a data project can be enhanced with workflow processes that create and enforce business rules.

A user interface made up of data access pages can be used to create Web views of your database in minutes. The Office Developer Workflow Toolbar control can be added to the page to provide access to the workflow steps.

In this walkthrough, you create a basic application using Access and the Workflow Designer. This application will include a relational database called ProjectTracker, business rules, permissions, and a user interface comprised of data access pages.

Setup Requirements

For this walkthrough, you must have a server and a development/client computer. If you are a system administrator on the server, you are not required to install the Workflow Services components on the server. With system administrator permissions, you can set the workflow application User Directory synchronization options using your development computer.

To develop applications, you must be a member of the Windows group modAppOwners. This group is created during the installation of the Workflow Services. You must be administrator on your development computer, and you minimally must be a server administrator on your local copy of SQL Server or Microsoft® SQL Server™ 2000 Desktop Engine.

For this walkthrough, you must create two additional Microsoft® Windows® user accounts with SQL Server logins. Two users, user1 and user2, can be individuals in your organization who already have Windows accounts and SQL Server logins, or you can use test accounts which your system administrator creates for you.

Building a Workflow Application

There are two ways to build a workflow application—by adding workflow to an existing SQL Server database or by using a database template as a boilerplate for a new application. In this walkthrough, you will add workflow to a database. When you have created your database, you can turn it into an application using the Workflow Designer.

This walkthrough takes you through the following general steps that outline the basic procedure for creating a workflow application:

1. Create a SQL Server database, and open it in **Office XP Developer**.

2. Create a table hierarchy consisting of main, detail, and lookup tables. The table hierarchy makes it possible for you to indicate the tables involved in a workflow process and displays a visual representation of your table relationships.

3. Create a basic workflow process diagram.

4. Test your workflow.

5. Enhance the workflow process by adding additional states and transitions from the Workflow toolbox to the diagram.

6. Add database users, and create roles. Create role permissions, and assign users to roles.

7. Define workflow permissions, and add script to provide added functionality to workflow events.

8. Create a Web-based user interface in Microsoft® Access using data access pages. Use the Office Developer Workflow Toolbar control to add workflow functionality to the pages.

9. Create a template for your application.

After following these steps, your final application includes the following objects:

*   A Web site

*   An Access data project based on a SQL Server database

*   The workflow objects, including a table hierarchy and one or more workflow processes

*   Data access pages, designed in Access and stored in the Web site

Step 1: Create a SQL Server Database

Creating the SQL Server Database Using Access

When you create an Access data project (*.adp), the Access Database window includes objects, such as views, database diagrams, and stored procedures, that you do not see when you create an .mdb. These objects are native to SQL Server.

To create a SQL Server database using Access

1. Start **Microsoft Access**.

2. On the **New File** list, click **Project (New Data)**.

3. Give your project a name, **ProjectTracker**, and click **Create**.

   Note You can save this project in your personal folder or any alternate location. The location is not critical.

Logging into SQL Server

The first step to creating a SQL Server database using Access is to connect to an existing SQL Server and provide a name for the new SQL Server database. To do this you must be a member of the modAppOwners Windows Group on your server. This group has a SQL Server login with database creation privileges.

To log in to SQL Server

1. Open your new **Access** project (**ProjectTracker.adp**). A **SQL Server** wizard opens to help you connect to **SQL Server** and specify a name for the **SQL Server** database.

2. Specify the name of the **SQL Server** you want to use, or select a server from the list.

3. Select **Use Trusted Connection** to use Windows authentication.

4. Provide a database name of **ProjectTrackerSQL**.

5. Click **Next**, and click **Finish** to complete the wizard with the defaults.

   Note A SQL Server progress meter message is displayed. This process might take a few minutes.

When processing is completed, the Access database window is active. Now, you can design your SQL Server schema using Access.

Creating SQL Server Database Tables

In this walkthrough, you are going to create three tables:

- tblProjects
- tblProjectTasks
- tblProjectTaskAssignments

To create the tblProjects table

1. In the **Access Database** window, select **Tables** from the **Objects** list. Double-click **Create table in Design view**.

2. Create the first column **ProjectID** as an **int** datatype (the length defaults to **4**). Clear the **Allow Nulls** column, and set the **Identity** to **Yes**. Click the **Primary Key** button to make this column a primary key.

3. Create a second column **ProjectName** as a datatype of **nvarchar**, with length of **50**.

4. Create a third column **ProjectDescription** as datatype of **nvarchar**, with length of **75**.

5. Create a fourth column **ProjectBeginDate** as a datatype **datetime**, with length of **8**.

6. Create a fifth column **ProjectEndDate** as a datatype **datetime**, with length of **8**.

7. Create a sixth column **Completed** as a datatype **bit**, with length of **1**, and set a **default value** of **(0)**, which is **False**.

8. Create a seventh column **ModifiedBy** as a datatype **nvarchar**, with length of **65**.

9. Click **Save**, and name this table **tblProjects**.

10. Close the table designer.

To create the tblProjectTasks table

1. In the **Access Database** window, select **Tables** from the **Objects** list. Double-click **Create table in Design view**.

2. Create the first column **ProjectTaskID** as an **int** datatype (the length defaults to **4**). Clear the **Allow Nulls** column, and set the **Identity** to **Yes**. Click the **Primary Key** button to make this column a primary key.

3. Create a second column **ProjectID** as an **int** datatype, with length of **4**.

4. Create a third column **TaskName** as datatype of **nvarchar**, with length of **50**.

5. Create a fourth column **TaskDescription** as datatype of **nvarchar**, with length of **75**.

6. Create a fifth column **TaskStartDate** as a datatype **datetime**, with length of **8**.

    Note If you want to set a default for the current date, use the following syntax:
    `(convert(varchar,getdate(),1))`.

7. Create a sixth column **TaskEndDate** as a datatype **datetime**, with length of **8**.

8. Click **Save**, and name this table **tblProjectTasks**.

9. Close the table designer.

To create the tblProjectTaskAssignments table

1. In the **Access Database** window, select **Tables** from the **Objects** list. Double-click **Create table in Design view**.

2. Create the first column **ProjectTaskAssignmentID** as an **int** datatype (the length defaults to **4**). Clear the **Allow Nulls** column, and set the **Identity** to **Yes**. Click the **Primary Key** button to make this column a primary key.

3. Create a second column **ProjectTaskID** as an **int** datatype, with length of **4**.

4. Create a third column **EmployeeID** as datatype of **nvarchar**, with length of **65**. You use this column to link to the application user directory.

5. Create a fourth column **DateAssigned** as a datatype **datetime**, with length of **8**.

> **Note** If you want to set a default for the current date, use the following syntax:
> `(convert(varchar,getdate(),1))`.

6. Create a fifth column **DateCompleted** as a datatype **datetime**, with length of **8**.

7. Click **Save**, and name this table **tblProjectTaskAssignments**.

8. Close the table designer.

Creating Relationships in the Access Database Diagram Designer

When you create a table hierarchy in the Workflow Designer, it examines the table relationships to determine how to create the hierarchy. Therefore, it is important to create your table relationships before registering your application or attempting to set up a table hierarchy. To create relationships in the Access data project, you use a database diagram.

To create table relationships

1. In the **Access Database** window, select **Database Diagrams** in the **Objects** list.

2. Double-click the **Create database diagram in designer** option.

3. Add all three tables from the **Add Tables** list to the diagram window, and click **Close**.

4. To create a relationship between **tblProjects** and **tblProjectTasks**, drag from the primary key, **ProjectID**, in **tblProjects** to the foreign key, **ProjectID**, in **tblProjectTasks**.

5. When you release the mouse button, the **Create Relationship** dialog box appears. Verify that it lists the correct fields, and click **OK**.

Note   Unlike the Relationships feature in an *.mdb, the relationship lines do not necessarily line up primary key to foreign key.

6. To create a relationship between **tblProjectTasks** and **tblProjectTaskAssignments**, drag from the primary key, **ProjectTaskID**, in **tblProjectTasks** to the foreign key, **ProjectTaskID**, in **tblProjectTaskAssignments**.

7. When you release the mouse button, the **Create Relationship** dialog box appears. Verify that it lists the correct fields, and click **OK**.

8. Save the diagram, and name the diagram **Project Tracker**. Click **OK**.

9. Click **Yes** when prompted to save all tables.

10. Close the **Database Diagram**.

Registering Your Database as an Application

After you have created your SQL Server database, you can begin to add workflow using the Workflow Designer.

To enable workflow on a SQL Server database

1. From the **Start** menu, point to Programs, then **Microsoft Office XP Developer**, and then click **Microsoft Development Environment**.

2. On the **File** menu, point to **New**, and click **Project**.

3. The **New Project** dialog box is displayed. Under **Project Types**, select the **Office Developer Projects** folder.

4. Under **Templates**, several icons are displayed.

5. Give your project the name **ProjectTracker**, and double-click the **SQL Server Workflow Project** icon.

6. Select your server and the database **ProjectTrackerSQL** from the lists. The default Web site URL is displayed: http://<Server Name>/ProjectTrackerSQL.

7. Click **OK**, and then click **OK** on the message that informs you that tables will be added to your database.

8. Type in the file name **TrackingTools**, and click **Save**. The database is registered in the Workflow Designer and is ready for you to add a workflow process.

Step 2: Create a Table Hierarchy

Typically, your database includes a combination of main tables, detail tables, and lookup tables. The advantage of this hierarchy is that detail and lookup tables inherit permissions and properties from the parent main table.

To set up your table hierarchy

1. Select the **Project** node (**ProjectTracker**) in the **Solution Explorer**.

2. Open the **Project** menu, and click **Add New Item**. The **Add New Item** dialog box is displayed.

3. Double-click the **Add a Main Table** icon.

4. Select **tblProjects** as your main table. Click **OK**.

5. To view the table hierarchy, expand the **ProjectTracker** node in the **Solution Explorer**, and then expand the **Tables** folder.

Now, the table hierarchy is created, and you can create a workflow process using the main table, tblProjects.

Step 3: Create a Workflow Process

To design a workflow process for a database, you drag a series of states and transitions from the Workflow toolbox to the workflow design surface. Behind the scenes, the Workflow Designer adds a column to your main table called modStateID. This has a foreign key relationship with a table called <*main table*>StateLookup that is created during registration. This lookup table contains the ID number that is assigned to each workflow state as it is added to the diagram.

Before starting to work on your workflow process, determine the type of states you might want to set. For instance, in a payroll application, you might want to create submit, review, and approved workflow states. For this Project Tracker application, we are creating six states: Analyze, Design, Test, Release, Reanalyze, and Redesign.

To add workflow to your application

1. Select the **Project** node (**ProjectTracker**) in the **Solution Explorer**.

2. Open the **Project** menu, and click **Add New Item**. The **Add New Item** dialog box is displayed.

3. Double-click the **Add a Workflow Process** icon.

4. Select **tblProjects** from the list, and click **OK**. **Item Created** and **Item Deleted** shapes are added to the design surface.

5. Drag a state shape from the **Workflow** toolbox to the design surface near the **Item Created** shape. Change the caption to **Analyze**.

6. Drag another state shape from the **Workflow** toolbox next to the first state, and change the caption to **Design**.

7. Add two more states to the diagram, and name them **Test** and **Release**.

8. Locate the **Transition** shape in the **Workflow** toolbox. Press **CTRL**, and click the **Transition** shape; this turns on sticky mode, so you do not have to go back to the toolbox after you add each transition.

9. Click the **Item Created** shape, and drag to **Analyze**. Then, click **Analyze**, and drag to **Design**. Connect **Design** to **Test**, **Test** to **Release**, and **Release** to **Item Deleted** the same way. Click the **Pointer** shape in the **Workflow** toolbox to turn off **Transition**.

10. Select the first transition. In the **Properties** window, change the **Caption** and the **(Name)** properties to **New**.

11. Change the captions and names of the rest of the transitions, so they are identifiable. You might want to use a format such as OriginState_DestinationState, for example, **Analyze_Design**.

12. Change the **(Name)** property of the states to match their captions, so when you add script to the workflow, the names of the states and transitions will be the same in the code as they are in the diagram.

You now have a basic functioning workflow process. When you save the project, all manipulations of tblProjects will be regulated by this workflow process.

> **Note**   In the table hierarchy, if you expand the tblProjectTasks, you see an additional table has been added—tblProjectsStateLookup. In fact, if you switch back to Access and press F5 to refresh the database window, you see many objects have been added to your Access project. (In addition, you can view these objects in the SQL Server Enterprise Manager if you have it installed.)

You could finish the application now by skipping to Step 8 and creating the user interface, because once you have a functioning workflow process you only need to enter a record into the database for the workflow to take effect. However, to learn more about how the workflow process functions and to enhance your workflow, continue on and test what you have so far.

Step 4: Test Your Workflow

After adding a workflow process to a table, you can test the workflow directly in Access or the SQL Server Enterprise Manager. Even without a user interface or any script, the workflow states, transitions, and events are enforced when you enter data into your table.

To test a workflow process

1. Find the modStateID for each state by opening the *<tablename>*StateLookup table in **Access** and noting the ID number beside each state name. You must know the modStateID to be able to move to a particular state in the workflow process when you are working directly in the tables.

2. Open the workflow-enabled table in **Access**, and enter a new record.

    Change from one state to another by changing the ModStateID value. Try to change the status of your record from the first state to the last state. Since you have not added a transition event that makes this transition possible, you are notified that this is not a valid event. In addition, you are not able to delete the record while it is in a state that has no transition to the **Item Deleted** shape.

3. If workflow is not performing as expected, return to your workflow diagram and make sure you have saved your workflow and refreshed the database. In addition, make sure you have added the required transitions to your diagram.

Step 5: Enhance the Workflow Process

When you add a transition, you create a permissible change from one state to another. In the current workflow design, for example, a record cannot go from Analyze to Closed; that transition would be rejected. In addition, when a record is open, it cannot be saved as Analyze again, because there is no Transition Within on the Analyze state; so the record must be saved as Design or closed without saving.

There are script blocks that are called when an item moves from one state to the next: OnExit_previous state, OnChange, and OnEnter_next state. Each script block has two script procedures—a validation script procedure and an event script procedure. The validation procedure must return True for the event script procedure to be triggered. By default, each validation procedure does return True.

In addition, other events can be scripted, such as OnCreate and OnDelete, that are added to a transition from the Item Created shape and to a transition to the Item Deleted shape respectively.

> **Note** You can modify the validation function to interact with your application. For example, perhaps this function only returns a True if a certain user is entering data or if it is a certain day. However, keep in mind that if this function does not return a True, the event script procedure will not fire, and the state transition will not be permitted.

Modifying a Workflow Process

If it turns out that the business process requires more flexibility, you can enhance your workflow process by adding more states and transitions. For this walkthrough, you are adding two states: Reanalyze and Redesign.

To modify a workflow process

1. If required, open the **ProjectTracker** application in the **Workflow Designer**. Open the **Workflow Processes** folder, and double-click **tblProjectsWorkflow**. The **tblProjects** workflow diagram is displayed on the workflow design surface.

2. Add a new state, and change the caption to **Reanalyze**. Put the new state beside the state called **Design**

3. Repeat those steps, and add **Redesign** beside **Test**.

4. Add a transition from **Design** to **Reanalyze**, and then, because transitions only permit movement in one direction, add another from **Reanalyze** back to **Design**.

5. Add a transition from **Test** to **Redesign**, and another from **Redesign** back to **Test**.

Your workflow should look similar to the following illustration:

TblProjects Workflow Diagram

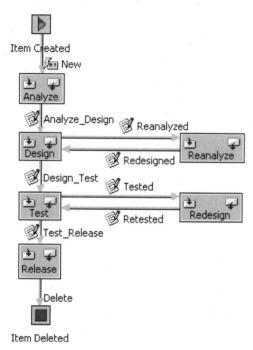

Next, you must set up user information, so you have an accessible list of database users for an employee lookup.

Step 6: Add Database Users and Create Roles

To assign users and groups to database roles, the users and groups must have valid Windows domain accounts and SQL Server logins. This walkthrough is simplified by having two users, user1 and user2, who have the required access. They can be test accounts that your system administrator creates for this walkthrough or any individuals with domain accounts.

> **Note**   Generally, you have Windows group accounts for various categories of users, and you assign these groups to a SQL Server login. Then, this group is added as a database user and assigned to one or more roles. For example, to grant everyone access, you can use the Windows group account Domain Users.

Creating Database Roles

To manage the permissions in your workflow-enabled database, it is recommended you define a set of roles based on job functions and assign each role the permissions that apply to that job.

SQL Server roles exist within a database and cannot span more than one database. Because roles are unique to each database, you can reuse a role name, such as Reviewer, in each database you create. Use the SQL Server Enterprise Manager to create roles and add users to the roles.

To add database users using the Enterprise Manager

1. From the **Start** menu, point to **Programs**, point to **Microsoft SQL Server**, and click **Enterprise Manager**.

2. Expand a server group, and then expand a server.

3. Expand the databases node, and then expand the **ProjectTrackerSQL** database.

4. Right-click **Users**, and then click **New Database User**.

5. Select **Login Name** user1 from the list. By default, the login is added to the **Public database** role.

6. Click **OK**. User1 is listed under database users. Repeat the steps to add user2.

For this walkthrough, there are three database users—dbo, user1, and user2. Now, create two roles and assign these users to specific roles in this database. One is a Developer role, for individuals who review the information but cannot do certain workflow events or make certain transitions. The other is a Manager role, for individuals who create and delete projects and make certain state changes, such as setting a project to the Reanalyze or Redesign state.

To create SQL Server roles using the Enterprise Manager

1. In the **ProjectTrackerSQL** database, right-click **Roles**, and click **New Database Role**.

2. In the **Name** box, type **Manager**.

3. Click the **Add** button to see a list of database users.

4. Select **user1**, and click **OK** to assign it to the **Manager** role.

5. Click **OK**.

6. Click **New Database Role** again, and create a **Developer** role.

7. Assign **user2** to the **Developer** role.

Now, your application has three users—dbo, user1, and user2—and two new roles that you defined, in addition to the default roles created automatically. You can grant and revoke workflow permissions to these roles.

To assign permissions to roles

Now, the roles are created, and you must specify the permissions for these roles. Role permissions are separate from the permissions that you designate for the workflow. Role permissions specify the privileges that members of these roles have on the server. For example, if a role does not have Select permissions, members of the role are not able to see any data, and if the role does not have Insert permissions, members cannot add records.

1. With **Enterprise Manager** open, expand your server and database.

2. Click **Roles**.

3. In the **Details** pane, right-click the **Public** role, and click **Properties**.

4. Click **Permissions**. If required, select **List all objects**. Objects are listed in rows, and permissions are listed in columns.

5. You must grant **Select** permissions on four objects, **tblProjects**, **tblProjectsView**, **tblProjectTaskAssignmentsView**, and **tblProjectTasks**.

6. Click **OK**.

7. Edit **Public** permissions again, and add **Insert**, **Update**, and **Delete** permissions to three tables: **tblProjects**, **tblProjectTasks**, and **tblProjectTaskAssignments**.

8. Click **OK**.

Notice that by granting the required permissions to the Public role, all database users inherit them. In the next step, you modify workflow permissions, so only certain roles can perform certain events. This is one way to manage permissions—being lenient on the role permissions and then tightening security using the workflow permissions.

Synchronizing the User Directory with Your Exchange Server

The workflow application User Directory lists all users of applications on a particular server. This directory information is displayed in a view (called modUserList) in each workflow-enabled database, which limits the list to role members for that particular application.

Before you are able to synchronize with Microsoft® Exchange 2000, an individual with administrative privileges on the server must setup the synchronization options. If you have Windows administrative privileges, then you can do this from your development machine. If you are not a Windows administrator, then the Windows administrator must install the Workflow Designer on the server and launch the Workflow Manager for SQL Server.

To set up workflow application User Directory synchronization

1. From the **Start** button, point to **Programs**, point to **Microsoft Office XP Developer**, and click **Workflow Manager for SQL Server**.

2. Select your SQL Server from the **Server** list, and click **Refresh**.

3. On the **User Information** tab, click **Synchronization**.

4. Select the **Synchronize with Microsoft Exchange Server** option.

5. In the **Exchange Server** field, enter your Exchange Server name.

6. Click **OK**.

7. If a message appears informing you that data could be overwritten, click **Yes**.

8. Click **Synchronize Now**. Your user directory is populated based on information from Exchange. Minimally, you should see three users—you, user1, and user2.

If you want to use the user directory as a source for user information in your application, you can use the modUserList view in your application as a lookup.

Now there is user information available for the application. The next step is to assign permissions to the application roles and to enhance workflow functionality using script.

Step 7: Define Workflow Permissions and Add Workflow Script

Permissions added to workflow transitions make sure only members of designated roles can perform certain events. By default, when a new event is added, all users are permitted to perform the event. In the ProjectTracker, only the Manager role members should be permitted to create and delete projects and to set the states to Reanalyze and Redesign. Therefore, permissions must be revoked for the Public role (because all database users inherit Public permissions), and for the Developer role for these events.

To restrict user permissions for specific workflow events

1. Open the **ProjectTracker** application in the **Workflow Designer**, and expand the **Workflow Processes** folder.

2. Double-click **tblProjectsWorkflow** to open the workflow diagram.

3. Select the first transition, named **New**, in the workflow diagram.

4. Open the **View** menu, and click **Property Pages**.

5. On the **Permissions** tab, clear the check boxes next to **Developer** and **Public**, and click **OK**. Now, only the Manager role will be able to add new records to the database.

6. Repeat these steps for the transitions from **Design** to **Reanalyze**, from **Test** to **Redesign**, and from **Release** to **Item Deleted**.

7. Select **Save** to update your application.

Adding Script to Workflow Transitions

In this walkthrough, you add a sub procedure called SetUser to the Code Editor. When called by an event, this procedure sets the ModifiedBy field in tblProjects to the current user.

To add script to workflow transitions

1. In the **Solution Explorer** of the **Workflow Designer**, open the **Workflow Processes** folder, and double-click **tblProjectsWorkflow**, so the diagram appears on the design surface.

2. Double-click the workflow diagram to open the **Code Editor**.

3. The following procedure enters the current user's SAMAccountName in the ModifiedBy field. You can use this syntax when you want to insert the current user into a field, and you can change the target field by changing the Session.item(*<Field Name>*) to the name of the field you want to update with the current user's name. Type the following code into the **Code Editor**:

```
Sub SetUser()
    'Session object represents the current recordset
    'this snippet sets the ModifiedBy field equal to the current user
    Session.item("ModifiedBy") = Session.User
    Session.item.updateBatch(3)
End Sub
```

4. To set this up so the ModifiedBy field is updated when a new record is created, this procedure must be called from **OnCreate** for the transition called **New**, which goes from the **Item Created** shape to **Analyze**. Double-click the **New** transition to add the event script procedure, which looks like this:

```
Sub New_OnCreate()
End Sub
```

Between the **Sub New_OnCreate()** and the **End Sub**, type **Call SetUser()**. It looks like this:

```
Sub New_OnCreate()
    Call SetUser()
End Sub
```

5. Open the **Tools** menu, and click **Verify Script**.

6. Click **Save**.

This completes the workflow for the ProjectTracker.

Step 8: Create a Web-Based User Interface Using Data Access Pages

You can use any form of user interface that has read/write capabilities on a SQL Server database. However, only data access pages support the full set of Workflow Designer features.

A data access page is a special type of Web page designed for viewing and working with data from the Internet—data that is stored in an Access database or SQL Server database.

Creating Application Data Access Pages

When you create data access pages for an application, you base the page on a view rather than a table, because row-level permissions are enforced through the views. In the following examples, you create pages using the tblProjectsView, the tblProjectTasksView, and the tblProjectTaskAssignmentsView.

To create a new data access page using a wizard in Access

1. Open your data project in **Access**.

2. In the **Objects** list, click **Pages**, and double-click the **Create data access page by using wizard** option.

3. From the **Tables/Queries** list, select **tblProjectsView**.

4. From the **Available Fields** list, add all the columns to the **Selected Fields** list, and click **Next**.

5. Accept the default grouping levels by clicking **Next**.

6. Accept the default sort order by clicking **Next**.

7. Give your Web page the title **Project Information**. Leave the option selected to **Modify the Page's Design**. Click **Finish**.

8. Right-click the design surface of the open page, and click **Section Properties**.

9. Select the **Data** tab.

10. In the **UniqueTable** property, select **tblProjects**. Close the property box.

    Note   This step makes sure that the base table can be updated through the data access pages.

To customize your page

1. Click the data access page where you would like to insert the **Microsoft Office Developer Workflow Toolbar** control. The top portion of the page below the title often works well.

2. From the **Insert** menu, select **ActiveX Control**, and double-click **Microsoft Office Developer Workflow Toolbar**.

3. The toolbar is added to the page. This automatically binds it to the workflow rules by inspecting the **UniqueTable** property on the data source control. Stretch it out horizontally to display all the states and transitions.

4. Click **Save**, and enter the full path to the Web site URL you created when you registered the application: http://<Server Name>/ProjectTrackerSQL.

    Tip   If you accidentally save a data access page to a site other than your Web site, you will not get the option to Save As and change the location. However, you can select the page in the database window and cut it. Then, paste it back into the same database window, and you will get the option to specify the save location.

5. From the **File** menu, select **Web Page Preview** to see the toolbar.

Notice that transitions and events that are not permitted by the workflow process for the current record are not available. When you are in a blank record, the only permissible event is New. Furthermore, New is available only if you are a member of the Manager role.

To enter information in your data page

1. On the toolbar, select **New** to start entering a new project. Notice the value of **modStateID** is set to that of the first state.

2. Enter a **ProjectName** of **Project 1**, a **ProjectDescription** of **First Project**, and a beginning and ending date. Set **Completed** to **False**.

3. Click **Save Record**.

When the record is saved, the **ModifiedBy** field is updated to the current user (courtesy of the SetUser() procedure placed in the workflow script)—in this case, your SAMAccountName.

Now, you can adjust the design of the data page. The design controls are very similar to those in the Access form and report design environments. However, the properties for these pages are quite different. In the Access Help, use the Answer Wizard, and search for "data access page design." You get many helpful topics about designing, creating, and using data access pages.

To create the Project Task Information data access pages

1. In the **Objects** list, click **Pages**, and double-click the **Create data access page by using wizard** option.

2. From the **Tables/Queries** list, select **tblProjectTasksView**.

3. From the **Available Fields** list, add all the columns to the **Selected Fields** list, and click **Next**.

4. Accept the default grouping levels by clicking **Next**.

5. Accept the default sort order by clicking **Next**.

6. Give your Web page the title **Project Tasks**. Leave the option selected to **Modify the Page's Design**. Click **Finish**.

7. Right-click the design surface of the open page, and click **Section Properties**.

8. Select the **Data** tab.

9. In the **UniqueTable** property, select **tblProjectTasks**.

To customize your page

1. Replace the **ProjectID** text box with a lookup by deleting the **ProjectID** field. In the toolbox, click the **DropdownList** control, and add it to the form.

2. When the wizard opens, select the **I want the combo box to look up the values in a table or query** option, and click **Next**.

3. Select the **tblProjects** table, and click **Next**.

4. Add **ProjectID** and **ProjectName** to the **Selected Fields** list. Click **Next**.

5. Make sure the **Hide key column (recommended)** box is selected, so the **ProjectID** column is hidden. Adjust the **ProjectName** column as required to display the expected values, and click **Next**.

6. Click **Finish**.

7. Right-click the **DropdownList** control, and click **Element Properties**.

8. Click the **Data** tab, and set the **ControlSource** to **ProjectID**.

9. Make sure **ListBoundField** is set to **ProjectID**.

10. Make sure **ListDisplayField** is set to **ProjectName**.

11. Close the **Properties** window, and click **Save**. Enter the full path to the Web site URL you created when you registered the application: http://<Server Name>/ProjectTrackerSQL.

To create the Project Task Assignments data access pages

1. In the **Objects** list, click **Pages**, and double-click the **Create data access page by using wizard** option.

2. From the **Tables/Queries** list, select **tblProjectTaskAssignmentsView**.

3. From the **Available Fields** list, add all the columns to the **Selected Fields** list, and click **Next**.

4. Accept the default grouping levels by clicking **Next**.

5. Accept the default sort order by clicking **Next**.

6. Give your Web page the title **Project Task Assignments**. Leave the option selected to **Modify the Page's Design**. Click **Finish**.

7. Right-click the design surface of the open page, and click **Section Properties**.

8. Select the **Data** tab.

9. In the **UniqueTable** property, select **tblProjectTaskAssignments**

To customize your page

1. Delete the **ProjectTaskID** text box, so it can be replaced with a lookup. From the **toolbox**, add the **DropdownList** control to the form.

2. When the wizard opens, select the **I want the combo box to look up the values in a table or query** option. Click **Next**.

3. Select **tblProjectTasks** table, and click **Next**.

4. Add **ProjectTaskID** and **TaskName** to the **Selected Fields** list, and click **Next**.

5. Make sure the **Hide key column (recommended)** box is selected, so the **ProjectTaskID** column is hidden. Adjust the **TaskName** column as required to display the estimated values. Click **Next**.

6. Change the label to **Task**, and click **Finish**.

7. Right-click the **DropdownList** control, and select **Element Properties**.

8. Click the **Data** tab, and set the **ControlSource** to **ProjectTaskID**.

9. Make sure **ListBoundField** is set to **ProjectTaskID**.

10. Make sure **ListDisplayField** is set to **TaskName**.

11. Close the **Properties** window, and click **Save**. Enter the full path to the Web site URL you created when you registered the application: http://<Server Name>/ProjectTrackerSQL.

The final step is to create a lookup to the Workflow Application User Directory information you synchronized earlier. To do this, you must create a drop-down list control that displays information from the modUserList view.

To create a lookup to the User Directory

1. Delete the **EmployeeID** field from the **ProjectTaskAssignments** data page.

2. From the **toolbox**, click the **DropdownList** control, and add it to the form.

3. When the wizard opens, select the **I want the combo box to look up the values in a table or query** option, and click **Next**.

4. Select the **Queries** option, and select **modUserList** view, and click **Next**.

5. Add **SAMAccountName** and **CN** (full name) to the **Selected Fields** list. Click **Next**.

6. Adjust the **CN** column as required to display the values, and click **Next**.

7. Change the label to **Employee**, and click **Finish**.

8. Right-click the **DropdownList** control, and select **Element Properties**.

9. Click the **Data** tab, and set the **ControlSource** to **EmployeeID**.

10. Make sure **ListBoundField** is set to **SAMAccountName**.

11. Make sure **ListDisplayField** is set to **CN**.

12. Close the **Properties** window, and click **Save**. Enter the full path to the Web site URL you created when you registered the application: http://<Server Name>/ProjectTrackerSQL.

Creating Navigation Controls

The final enhancement to the data access page in this walkthrough is the addition of navigation links on the ProjectsInformation page.

These will be hyperlinks added using the Script Editor.

To add navigational links the ProjectInformation page

1. Open the **ProjectInformation** page in **Design** view.

2. Right-click the page, and select **Microsoft Script Editor**.

3. Scroll through the page until you see the tags </OBJECT></P>.

4. Add the following HTML code after the **</P>** tag:

```
<p><a href="Project Tasks.htm">Project Tasks</a>   <a
href="Project Task Assignments.htm">Project
Task Assignments</a></p>
```

Note If you paste the text from a Microsoft® Word document, use the **Paste as HTML** option from the **Edit** menu in the **Script Editor**.

This code creates links to the **Project Tasks** and **Project Task Assignments** pages. Notice that, because all the application pages reside in the Web site, the <a href> tag does not include a server and path.

5. Click **Save**, and close the script editor.

Step 9: Create a Template

A database template is a complete copy of an application. The template contains all of the information required to create an application, including the database schema, workflow, and data access pages.

Templates provide a quick way to create customized applications based on your original schema. You might want to create a template of the ProjectTracker and distribute it to various branch offices, which can then make any minor (or major) modifications required for each office.

To save an application as a template

1. From the **Start** button, point to **Programs**, point to **Microsoft Office XP Developer**, and click **Workflow Manager for SQL Server**.

2. On the **Workflow Applications** tab, click **Create Template**.

3. Click **Next**, select **Workflow Project**, and specify the server that hosts the database for the application you want to include in the template.

4. Click **Connect** and select the application you want to save as a template. Click **Next**.

5. Enter **ProjectTrackingExample** as the name and **Project Tracking Example Template** as the title for the new template. Enter version information and a description if desired. After completing the wizard, you can view this information in the **Workflow Manager** on the **Templates** tab. Click **Next**.

6. There are no additional files to include, so click **Next**.

7. Add all the data to the template by accepting the defaults and clicking **Next**.

8. Click **Next** to accept the default option that excludes current users of the application from the template.

9. Select **Save Template to File** to create a .tpl file that can be distributed to other servers that have **Workflow Services for SQL Server** installed. Click **Next**.

10. Click **Finish**. The wizard backs up the database, truncates all specified tables, removes database users, and stores the backed-up database information in the modTemplates table. It also enumerates all of the files in your Web site and stores them in the table.

    Note This process might take a few minutes.

When this template is created, you can create new applications based on it quickly and easily. All of the work done in this example is rolled up in the template.

You should now have a good understanding of how to use the Workflow Designer to create a workflow process, how to set permissions on the workflow, how to create a basic user interface, and how to save your application as a template for distribution. You can build on these basic ideas as you create your own applications.

Creating a Digital Dashboard using Web Parts

A Digital Dashboard is a customized solution that delivers personal, team, and corporate information directly to a user's desktop. A Digital Dashboard can be as simple as a single Web page that runs inside the Microsoft® Outlook® messaging and collaboration client displaying your daily calendar and favorite links or as complex as a full-featured knowledge-management solution that joins information from enterprise and external sources. This document walks you through building your first dashboard.

Introduction

Using Microsoft® Office XP Developer, you can quickly build and deploy customized Digital Dashboard solutions. A Digital Dashboard is an Active Server Page (ASP) that references one or more Web Parts. Each Web Part is a self-contained module of Extensible Markup Language (XML), HTML, or script (Microsoft® JScript® or Microsoft® Visual Basic® Scripting Edition (VBScript)) and is designed to retrieve and render the information you want to include in the dashboard. When the user loads the dashboard, the dashboard retrieves the Web Parts that it is configured to display.

The basic process for developing a Digital Dashboard using Office Developer is as follows:

1. **Preparing the Exchange Server** To follow along with this walkthrough and create your first Digital Dashboard, you must have access to a Microsoft® Exchange 2000 server.

2. **Creating the Digital Dashboard Project** Add Web Parts. After you create a dashboard, you can tailor its functionality by adding Web Parts. Web Parts determine the content of a Digital Dashboard and can display any type of information or Web format that you would like to implement. A catalog of Web Parts is provided with Office Developer. You can implement these as is or modify them to meet your requirements. In addition, you can create your own Web Parts.

3. **Testing your dashboard** After creating your dashboard and adding Web Parts, you can test your dashboard by viewing it in a browser.

By completing this walkthrough, you can create a Digital Dashboard that uses Web Parts and runs on an Exchange Server.

Because this walkthrough is designed to highlight how to create a simple dashboard project, not a complicated user interface, it is not a real-world Digital Dashboard.

Preparing the Exchange Server

To follow along with this walkthrough, you must have Office XP Developer, access to an Exchange 2000 server, and the appropriate permissions on the server. For more information about preparing Exchange for a Digital Dashboard, see the documentation in the Exchange SDK download, available from the Microsoft® Developer Network (MSDN®) Exchange Server Developer Center at http://msdn.microsoft.com/exchange/.

Creating a Digital Dashboard requires the following components:

- **Server**: Microsoft® Exchange 2000 Server as the back-end for the application.

- **Development tool**: Office Developer as the tool for creating the dashboard. This tool can reside on either a client computer with access to the server or the server itself.

Creating the Digital Dashboard Project

The following process outlines the steps required to create a new dashboard project and the HTML Web Parts it contains.

To create a dashboard

1. From the **Start** menu, select **Programs**, select **Microsoft Office XP Developer**, and then select **Microsoft Development Environment**.

2. From the **File** menu, select **New**, and then select **Project**.

3. The **New Project** dialog box is displayed. Select **Office Developer Projects**. Under **Templates**: three project icons are displayed, **Exchange Workflow Project**, **SQL Server Workflow Project**, and **Dashboard Project**.

4. Select the **Dashboard Project** icon.

5. In the **Location** box, do one of the following:

    - Type the URL to the Exchange 2000 Server public folder location where you want to create your application. Typically, this URL will be in the form http://*ServerName*/Public.

      –or–

    - Click the **Browse** button to specify a folder location by using the **Project Location** dialog box.

6. In the **Folder Name** dialog box, type the name for the folder that will contain your application. This will be part of the URL used to open your application. For example, if you enter MyApplication, the URL to your application will look like http://MyServer/Public/MyApplication.

7. Click **OK**.

Adding Web Parts

A Web Part is a reusable component that can contain any kind of Web-based information.

To add Web Parts to a dashboard project, use the Add New Item command. Using this command, you can add a JScript, VBScript, XML, or HTML Web Part to the dashboard project.

Use the Add Existing Item command to add an existing file to the dashboard. If the item you add is already a Web Part, its property values are preserved and affect the appearance and behavior of the dashboard. If the added file is not a Web Part, it is copied into the dashboard project. When you double-click the imported file, Office Developer starts the registered editor for the file.

To add a new Web Part to a dashboard

1. In the **Solution Explorer**, select the dashboard project.

2. Right-click the dashboard project name, and, from the shortcut menu, select **Add**, and then select **New Item**.

3. Select a part type (for example, HTML), and click **Open**.

To add an existing Web Part to a dashboard

1. In the **Solution Explorer**, select the dashboard project.

2. Right-click the dashboard project name, and, from the shortcut menu, select **Add**, and then select **Existing Item**.

3. Select the **Web Part** that you want to add, and click **OK**.

Previewing and Testing your Dashboard

After creating your dashboard and adding Web Parts, you can preview and test your dashboard by viewing it in a browser.

To preview and test a Digital Dashboard

1. In the **Solution Explorer**, select the dashboard project.

2. Right-click the dashboard project name, and select **View in Browser** from the shortcut menu.

Microsoft Office XP Developer Object Model Guide

This document consists of object model diagrams for each Microsoft® Office XP application, as well as components available for use within an Office application. The object model diagrams show how the objects in an object model fit together.

An application or component programmatically exposes its functionality through objects. You work with an object by using its properties and methods. Objects are named according to the portion of an application they represent, and they are ordered in a hierarchy. The uppermost tier of each application's object hierarchy typically is occupied by a single object: Application. The Application object represents the application itself, and all other objects for that application are below the Application object. The second tier consists of a high-level categorization of objects. The remaining tiers include a variety of additional objects that are used to access the functionality that the second-tier objects contain.

A group of similar objects can be combined in the hierarchy as a collection. You can work with a member of a collection as a single object or as a member of that collection. For example, the Microsoft® Excel object model exposes the Application object as the top-level object in its object model hierarchy. The Application object has a Workbooks collection that contains a Workbook object for each currently open workbook. Similarly, each Workbook object has a Worksheets collection that represents the worksheets in a workbook, and so on.

Using These Object Model Diagrams

You can use these diagrams as a handy shortcut to finding the object you want to work with and understanding how that object fits into the overall object model exposed by an application.

The following table shows how objects and collections are represented in the diagrams:

This type of item	Is designated this way
Object	Object
Collection	Collections

Each diagram contains notes to help you further understand what is depicted. The notes vary from diagram to diagram, but every note includes the name of the type library and its file name, as well as the name of the Help file that contains detailed information about the objects in the object model.

The symbols associated with a diagram indicate special information required to help you understand and work with the objects in the specified object model. Some symbols are used globally throughout the document; the following table explains what these global symbols mean:

Symbol	Meaning
*	Items marked with this symbol are contained in the Office XP library.
**	Items marked with this symbol are contained in the Microsoft® Visual Basic® Extensibility 5.3 library.

Office XP Applications

Microsoft Access Object Model

Application
- Modules
  - Module
- References
  - Reference
- DataAccessPages
  - DataAccessPage
    - WebOptions
- Reports
  - Report
    - Module
    - Controls
      - Control
        - Properties
          - Control
    - Printer
    - Properties
      - Form
- Forms
  - Form
    - Controls
      - Control
        - Properties
          - Control
    - Module
    - Printer
    - Properties
      - Form
- Printers
  - Printer

- DoCmd
- Screen
- VBE ★ ★
- DefaultWebOptions
- Assistant ★
- CommandBars ★
- DBEngine
- FileSearch ★
- COMAddIns ★
- AnswerWizard ★
- LanguageSettings

Repeated Objects
AccessObject
- AccessObjectProperties
  - AccessObjectProperty

- CurrentProject
  - AllForms +
  - AllMacros +
  - AllModules +
  - AccessObjectProperties
    - AccessObjectProperty
  - AllReports +
  - AllDataAccessPages +
- CurrentData
  - AllFunctions
    - AccessObject
  - AllStoredProcedures +
  - AllDatabaseDiagrams +
  - AllTables +
  - AllQueries +
  - AllViews +
- CodeProject
  - AllForms +
  - AllMacros +
  - AllModules +
  - AccessObjectProperties
    - AccessObjectProperty
  - AllReports +
  - AllDataAccessPages +
- CodeData
  - AllFunctions
    - AccessObject
  - AllStoredProcedures +
  - AllDatabaseDiagrams +
  - AllTables +
  - AllQueries +
  - AllViews +

Microsoft Access Object Model (2)

Source (Type Library)

The Microsoft® Access object model is provided by MSACC.OLB, which is included when you install Access.

Reference Information in Help

Help for this object model is available in VBAAC10.CHM.

Notes

A plus sign (+) indicates that additional objects or collections are displayed in the Repeated Objects portion of this object model diagram.

Microsoft Excel Object Model

Application
- AddIns
  - AddIn
- AnswerWizard ★
- Assistant ★
- AutoCorrect
- AutoRecover
- CellFormat
  - Borders
    - Border
  - Font
  - Interior
- COMAddIns ★
- CommandBars
- DefaultWebOptions
- Dialogs
  - Dialog
- ErrorCheckingOptions
- FileSearch ★
- LanguageSettings
- Names
  - Name
- ODBCErrors
  - ODBCError
- OLEDBErrors
  - OLEDBError
- RecentFiles
  - RecentFile
- RTD
- Speech
- SpellingOptions
- UsedObjects
- VBE ★★
- Watches
  - Watch
- Windows
  - Window
    - Panes
      - Pane
- WorksheetFunction

Workbooks
- Workbook
  - Areas
  - Charts
  - Chart
    - Axes
      - Axis
        - AxisTitle
        - DisplayUnitLabel
        - GridLines
        - TickLabels
      - ChartArea
      - ChartGroups
        - ChartGroup
          - DownBars
          - DropLines
          - HiLoLines
          - SeriesCollection
            - Series
              - Border
              - ChartFillFormat
              - DataLabels
                - DataLabel
              - ErrorBars
              - Interior
          - SeriesLines
          - Tab
          - UpBars

CommandBars   (continued) →

(continued) →

- ChartTitle
- Corners
- DataTable
  - Border
  - Font
- Floor
- Legend
  - LegendEntries
    - LegendEntry
      - LegendKey
- PageSetup
  - Graphic
- PivotLayout

- LeaderLines
- Points
  - Point
    - DataLabel
- TrendLines
  - TrendLine

Microsoft Excel Object Model (2)

(continued)

Application
 └ Workbooks
    └ Workbook
       ├ Charts
       │ └ Chart
       │   ├ PlotArea
       │   ├ Scripts   *
       │   ├ SeriesCollections
       │   │ (Repeat from Series)
       │   ├ Shapes   ++
       │   │ (Repeat from Shape)
       │   └ Walls
       ├ CustomViews
       │ └ CustomView
       ├ DocumentProperties *
       ├ HTMLProject   *
       ├ Names
       │ └ Name
       ├ PivotCaches
       │ └ PivotCache
       ├ PublishObjects
       │ └ PublishObject
       ├ RoutingSlip
       └ Styles
          └ Style
             ├ Borders
             │ └ Border
             ├ Font
             └ Interior

       ├ VBProject   ★★
       ├ Windows
       │ └ Window
       │   └ Panes
       │   └ Pane
       ├ WebOptions
       └ Worksheets
          └ Worksheet
             ├ AutoFilter
             │ └ Filters
             │   └ Filter
             ├ Comments
             │ └ Comment
             ├ ChartObjects
             │ └ ChartObject
             │   ├ Chart
             │   │ (Repeat from Chart)
             │   └ PivotLayout
             ├ CustomProperties
             │ └ CustomProperty
             ├ HPageBreaks
             │ └ HPageBreak
             ├ Hyperlinks
             │ └ Hyperlink
             ├ Names
             │ └ Name
             ├ OLEObjects
             │ └ OLEObject
             └ Outline

             ├ PageSetup   ▸▸
             ├ PivotTables
             │ ├ CalculateMembers
             │ │ └ CalculateMember
             │ └ PivotTable
             │   ├ CubeFields
             │   │ └ CubeField
             │   ├ PivotCache
             │   ├ PivotFields
             │   │ └ PivotField
             │   │   └ PivotItems
             │   │   └ PivotItem
             │   └ PivotFormulas
             │   └ PivotFormula
             ├ Protection
             │ ├ AllowEditRanges
             │ │ └ AllowEditRange
             │ ├ Range
             │ └ UserAccessList
             │   └ UserAccess ✎
             └ QueryTables
                └ QueryTable
                   └ Parameters
                      └ Parameter

(continued) ⟶

Microsoft Excel Object Model (3)

(continued)

Application
- Workbooks
  - Workbook
    - Worksheets
      - Worksheet
        - Range
          - Areas
          - Borders
            - Border
          - Characters
            - Font
          - Comment
          - Errors
            - Error
          - Font
          - FormatConditions
            - FormatCondition
          - Hyperlinks
            - Hyperlink
          - Interior
          - Name
          - Phonetics
          - PivotCell
            - PivotField
            - PivotItem
            - PivotItemList
              - PivotItem
            - PivotTable
            - Range   ▸▸
          - Shapes   ++
            - Shape
              (Repeat from Shape)
          - Style
            (Repeat from Style)
          - Validation
        - Scenarios
          - Scenario
        - Shapes   ++
          - Shape
            - Adjustments
            - DiagramNode   ▸▸
            - ConnectorFormat
            - ControlFormat
            - FillFormat   +
            - Hyperlink
            - LineFormat   +
            - LinkFormat
            - OLEFormat
            - PictureFormat
            - Script   ★
            - ShadowFormat   +
            - ShapeRange
              - Diagram
                - DiagramNodes
                  - DiagramNode
                    - DiagramNodeChildren
                      - DiagramNode
              - DiagramNode
            - TextEffectFormat
            - TextFrame
            - ThreeDFormat   +
        - SmartTags
          - SmartTag
            - CustomProperties ▸▸
              - SmartTagActions
                - SmartTagAction
        - Tab
        - VPageBreaks
          - VPageBreak

Microsoft Excel Object Model (4)

Source (Type Library)

The Microsoft® Excel object model is provided by EXCEL.EXE, which is included when you install Excel.

Reference Information in Help

Help for this object model is available in VBAXL10.CHM.

Notes

A single plus sign (+) designates objects with accessors to the ColorFormat object.

A double plus sign (++) indicates that the ShapeRange objects have been omitted from this diagram. For general purposes, you can think of these objects as occupying the same positions as the Shape object.

A double arrow (>>) designates that you can reference the children of this object in another location within this object model.

Microsoft FrontPage Object Model

Application
- ActiveDocument
- ActivePageWindow
- ActiveWeb
- ActiveWebWindow
- AnswerWizard ★
- COMAddIns ★
- CommandBars ★
- DispFPHTMLDocument
- FileSearch ★
- LanguageSettings ★
- System
- Themes
  (Repeat from Theme)
- Webs
  - Web
    - HomeNavigationNode ‡
    - Properties
    - RootFolder ++
      - Files +
        - File +
          - MetaTags
          - Properties
      - Folders ++
        - Folder ++
          - Properties
          - Files +
            (Repeat from File)
          - Folders ++
            (Repeat from Folder)

WebWindows
- WebWindow
  - PageWindows
    - PageWindow
      - Document ⧻
  - Web

BasicList
- ListFields
- WebFolder

ListFieldLookup
- ListField

RootNavigationNode ‡
- NavigationNodes
  - NavigationNode
- Themes
  - Theme
- WebWindows
  (Repeat from WebWindow)

PageWindowEx
- DispFPHTMLDocument
- WebFile

Survey
- ListFields
- WebFolder

WebEX
- Lists
  - List
    - ListFields
      - ListField
    - WebFolder
- NavigationNode
- NavigationNodes
- Properties
- Themes
- WebFile
- WebFiles
- WebFolder
- WebFolders
- WebWindows

DocmentLibrary
ListFieldChoice
ListFieldComputed
ListFieldCounter
ListFieldCurrency
ListFieldDateTime
ListFieldFile
ListFieldInteger
ListFieldMultiLine
ListFieldNumber
ListFieldSingleLine
ListFieldTrueFalse
ListFieldURL

Source (Type Library)

The Microsoft® FrontPage® object model is provided by FPEDITAX.DLL and FRONTPG.EXE, which are included when you install FrontPage.

Microsoft FrontPage Object Model (2)

Reference Information in Help

Help for this object model is available in VBAFPW10.CHM.

Notes

Property names sometimes are shown instead of collection and object names.

A plus sign (+) indicates that the Files and File properties return the WebFiles collection and the WebFile object.

A double plus sign (++) indicates that the Folders property returns the WebFolders collection and that the RootFolder and Folder properties each return a WebFolder object.

A † symbol indicates that the HomeNavigationNode and RootNavigationNode properties return a NavigationNode object.

A †† symbol indicates that the Document property returns the FrontPage document object model.

Microsoft MapPoint Object Model

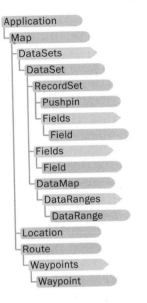

Application
Map
DataSets
DataSet
RecordSet
Pushpin
Fields
Field
Fields
Field
DataMap
DataRanges
DataRange
Location
Route
Waypoints
Waypoint

Source (Type Library)

The Microsoft® MapPoint object model is provided by MPNA80.TLB, which is included when you install Microsoft MapPoint.

Reference Information in Help

Help for this object model is available in MAPPOINT.CHM.

Microsoft Outlook Object Model

Source (Type Library)

The Microsoft® Outlook® object model is provided by MSOUTL.OLB, which is included when you install Outlook.

Reference Information in Help

Help for this object model is available in VBAOL10.CHM.

Microsoft PowerPoint Object Model

Microsoft PowerPoint Object Model (2)

(continued)

Application

└ Presentations

   └ Presentation

     ├ PageSetup
     ├ PrintOptions
     │ └ PrintRanges
     │   └ PrintRange
     ├ PublishObjects
     │ └ PublishObject
     ├ SlideShowSettings
     │ ├ NamedSlideShows
     │ │ └ NamedSlideShow
     │ └ SlideShowWindow +
     │   (Repeat from SlideShowWindow)
     ├ Tags
     ├ VBProject ★★
     └ WebOptions

     ├ Slides ++
     └ Slide
       ├ ColorScheme
       ├ HeadersFooters
       │ └ HeadersFooter
       ├ HyperLinks
       │ └ HyperLink
       ├ Master
       ├ Shapes ++
       │ └ Shape
       ├ SlideShoeTransition   (continued) ⟶
       │ └ SoundEffect
       └ Tags

Microsoft PowerPoint Object Model (3)

(continued)

Application
- Presentations
  - Presentation
    - Slides ++
      - Slide
        - Shapes ++
          - Shape
            - ActionSettings
              - ActionSetting
                - HyperLink
                - SoundEffect
            - Adjustments
            - AnimationSettings +
              - PlaySettings
              - SoundEffect
            - CalloutFormat
            - ConnectorFormat
            - Diagram
              - DiagramNode
              - DiagramNodes
                - DiagramNode
            - DiagramNode
              - Diagram
              - DiagramNode
              - DiagramNodeChildren
                - DiagramNode
              - Shape
            - FillFormat +
            - LineFormat +
            - LinkFormat
            - OLEFormat
              - Object
              - ObjectVerbs
            - PictureFormat
            - Placeholders

Scripts
- Script
ShadowFormat +
ShapeNodes
- ShapeNode
Table
- Columns
  - Column
    - CellRange
      (Repeat from CellRange)
- Rows
  - Row
    - CellRange
      - Borders
        - LineFormat +
      - Cell
        - Borders
          - LineFormat +
        - Shape
          (Repeat from Shape)

Tags
TextEffectFormat
TextFrame
- Ruler
- TextRange
  - ActionSettings
    (Repeat from ActionSettings)
  - Font +
  - ParagraphFormat
ThreeDFormat +

Microsoft PowerPoint Object Model (4)

Source (Type Library)

The Microsoft® PowerPoint® object model is provided by MSPPT.OLB, which is included when you install PowerPoint.

Reference Information in Help

Help for this object model is available in VBAPP10.CHM.

Microsoft Project Object Model

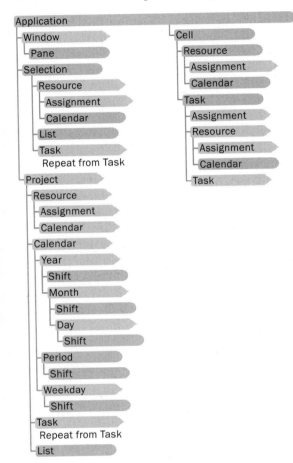

Source (Type Library)

The Microsoft® Project object model is provided by MSPRJ9.OLB, which is included when you install Project.

Microsoft Publisher Object Model

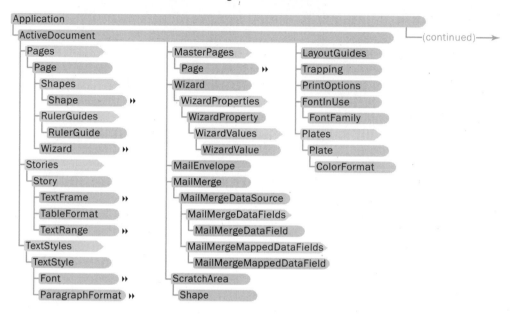

Application
ActiveDocument ────────────────────────────────── (continued)⟶

Pages
  Page
    Shapes
      Shape ▸▸
    RulerGuides
      RulerGuide
    Wizard ▸▸
Stories
  Story
    TextFrame ▸▸
    TableFormat
    TextRange ▸▸
TextStyles
  TextStyle
    Font ▸▸
    ParagraphFormat ▸▸

MasterPages
  Page ▸▸
Wizard
  WizardProperties
    WizardProperty
      WizardValues
        WizardValue
MailEnvelope
MailMerge
  MailMergeDataSource
    MailMergeDataFields
      MailMergeDataField
    MailMergeMappedDataFields
      MailMergeMappedDataField
ScratchArea
  Shape

LayoutGuides
Trapping
PrintOptions
FontInUse
  FontFamily
Plates
  Plate
    ColorFormat

Microsoft Publisher Object Model (2)

Application
- ActiveWindow
  - View
- Assistant
- ComAddIns
- CommandBars
- FileSearch
- Options

- Selection
  - ShapeRange
  - Shape
    - Adjustments
    - BorderArt
    - CalloutFormat
    - ConnectorFormat
    - FillFormat
    - GroupShapes
    - LineFormat
    - ShapeNodes
    - PictureFormat
    - ShadowFormat
    - TextEffectFormat
    - Script
    - Hyperlink
    - LinkFormat
    - OLEFormat
    - TableFormat
    - Tags
    - WebCommandButton
      - WebHiddenFields
    - WebListBox
      - WebListBoxItems
    - WebTextBox
    - WebOptionButton
    - WebCheckBox
    - WrapFormat
    - Wizard ▸▸

──(continued)──▸

- Adjustments
- CalloutFormat
- ConnectorFormat
  - Shape
- FillFormat
  - ColorFormat
- GroupShapes
  - Shape
- LineFormat
  - ColorFormat
- ShapeNodes
  - ShapeNode
- PictureFormat
- ShadowFormat
  - ColorFormat
- TextEffectFormat
- TextFrame
  - TextRange
  - Shape
  - Story
- ThreeDFormat
  - ColorFormat
- Script
- Hyperlink
- LinkFormat
- OLEFormat
  - ObjectVerbs
- TableFormat
- Tags

Microsoft Publisher Object Model (3)

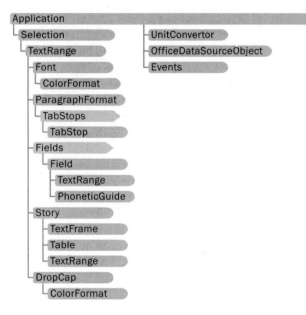

Source (Type Library)

The Microsoft® Publisher object model is provided by MSPUB.TLB, which is included when you install Publisher.

Reference Information in Help

Help for this object model is available in VBAPB10.CHM.

Notes

A double arrow symbol (>>) indicates that additional objects are shown elsewhere in this diagram.

Microsoft Visio Object Model

Source (Type Library)

The Microsoft® Visio object model is provided by MODELENG.DLL, VISLIB32.DLL, and VISGRF32.DLL, which are included when you install Visio.

Reference Information in Help

Help for this object model is available in VISIO.CHM.

Microsoft Word Object Model

Application
- AddIns
  - AddIn
- AnswerWizard   *
- Assistant   *
- AutoCaptions
  - AutoCaption
- AutoCorrect
  - AutoCorrectEntries
    - AutoCorrectEntry
  - FirstLetterExceptions
    - FirstLetterException
  - HangulAndAlphabetExceptions
    - HangulAndAlphabetException
  - OtherCorrectionExceptions
    - OtherCorrectionException
  - TwoInitialCapsExceptions
    - TwoInitialCapsException
- Browser
- CaptionLabels
  - CaptionLabel
- COMAddIns   *
- CommandBars   *
- DefaultWebOptions
- Dialogs
  - Dialog
- Dictionaries
  - Dictionary
- EmailOptions
  - EmailSignature
    - EmailSignatureEntries
      - EmailSignatureEntry
  - Style

——— (continued) ———▶

- FileConverters
  - FileConverter
- FileSearch   *
- FontNames
- HangulHanjaConversionDictionaries
  - Dictionary
- KeyBindings
  - KeyBinding
- KeysBoundTo
  - KeyBinding
- Languages
  - Language
    - Dictionaries   ▸▸
- LanguageSettings
- ListGalleries
  - ListGallery
    - ListTemplates
      - ListTemplate
        - ListLevels
          - ListLevel
            - Font   ▸▸
- MailingLabel
  - CustomLabels
    - CustomLabel
- MailMessage
- Options

Microsoft Word Object Model (2)

(continued)

Application
- Selection
  - Bookmarks
    - Bookmark
  - Borders
    - Border
  - Cells ▸▸
  - Characters
    - Range ▸▸
  - Columns ▸▸
  - Comments
    - Comment
  - Document ▸▸
  - EndnoteOptions
  - Endnotes
    - Endnote
      - Range
    - Range
      - EndnoteOptions
  - Fields
    - Field
  - Find ▸▸
  - Font ▸▸
  - FootnoteOptions
  - Footnotes
    - Footnote
  - FormFields ▸▸
  - Frames
    - Frame
  - HeadersFooters
    - HeaderFooter
  - HTMLDivisions
    - HTMLDivision
      - Borders ▸▸
      - HTMLDivision

- Hyperlinks
  - Hyperlink
- InlineShapes ★
- PageSetup ▸▸
- ParagraphFormat
- Paragraphs ▸▸
  - Range ▸▸
- Revision
- Rows ▸▸
- Sections ▸▸
- Sentences
  - Range ▸▸
- Shading
- ShapeRange
  - CanvasShapes ▸▸
  - DiagramNode
    - Diagram
      - DiagramNodes
        - DiagramNode
    - DiagramNode
    - DiagramNodeChildren
      - DiagramNode
    - Shape ▸▸
  - Shape ▸▸
- Style ▸▸
- Tables ▸▸
- Words
  - Range ▸▸

- HTMLDivisions ▸▸
- Range

- RecentFiles
  - RecentFile
- SpellingSuggestions
  - SpellingSuggestion
- SynonymInfo
- System
- TaskPanes
  - TaskPane
- Tasks
  - Task
- Templates
  - Template
    - AutoTextEntries
      - AutoTextEntry
    - ListTemplates ▸▸
    - VBProject ★★
- VBE ★★
- Windows
  - Selection ▸▸
  - View
    - Reviewers
      - Reviewer
    - Zoom
  - Window
    - Panes
      - Pane
        - Frameset
        - Selection ▸▸
        - View ▸▸
        - Zooms
          - Zoom

(continued) ⟶

Microsoft Word Object Model (3)

(continued)

Application
└ Documents
　└ Document
　　├ Bookmarks »
　　├ Characters »
　　├ CommandBars ★
　　├ Comments »
　　├ DocumentProperties ★
　　├ Email
　　│　└ EmailAuthor
　　├ Endnotes »
　　├ Envelope
　　├ Fields »
　　├ Footnotes »
　　├ FormFields »
　　├ Frames »
　　├ Frameset
　　├ HTMLDivisions
　　├ HTMLProject ★
　　├ Hyperlinks »
　　├ Indexes
　　│　└ Index
　　└ InlineShapes
　　　└ InlineShape
　　　　├ Borders »
　　　　├ Field
　　　　├ FillFormat +
　　　　├ HorizontalLineFormat
　　　　├ Hyperlink
　　　　├ LineFormat +
　　　　└ LinkFormat

├ LetterContent
├ Lists
│　└ List
│　　├ ListParagraphs »
│　　└ Range »
├ ListParagraphs »
├ ListTemplates »
├ MailMerge
│　├ MailMergeDataSource
│　│　└ MappedDataFields
│　│　　└ MappedDataFieldObject
│　└ MailMergeFields
│　　└ MailMergeField
├ PageSetup
│　├ LineNumbering
│　└ TextColumns
│　　└ TextColumn
├ Paragraphs »
├ ProofreadingErrors
└ Range »

(continued) →

├ PictureFormat
├ OLEFormat
├ Range »
├ Script ★
├ Shape »
└ TextEffectFormat

Microsoft Word Object Model (4)

(continued)

Application
- Documents — (continued) →
  - Document
    - Range — (continued) →
      - Bookmarks ▸▸
      - Borders ▸▸
      - Cells ▸▸
      - Characters ▸▸
      - Columns
        - Column
          - Borders ▸▸
          - Cells
            - Cell
              - Borders ▸▸
              - Column ▸▸
              - Range ▸▸
              - Row ▸▸
              - Shading
          - Shading
      - Comments ▸▸
      - Endnotes ▸▸
      - Fields ▸▸
      - Find
        - Font ▸▸
        - Frame
        - ParagraphFormat
        - Replacement
      - FootnoteOptions
      - Footnotes ▸▸
      - Font
        - Borders ▸▸
        - Shading
      - FormFields
        - FormField
          - CheckBox
          - DropDown
          - Range ▸▸
          - TextInput
      - Frames ▸▸
      - HTMLDivisions ▸▸
      - Hyperlinks ▸▸
      - InlineShapes ▸▸
      - ListFormat
        - List
        - ListTemplates ▸▸
      - ListParagraphs ▸▸
      - PageSetup ▸▸
      - ParagraphFormat
      - Paragraphs
        - Paragraph
          - Borders ▸▸
          - DropCap
          - ParagraphFormat
          - Style ▸▸
          - TabStops
            - TabStop
          - ParagraphFormat
          - Range ▸▸
          - Shading ▸▸
          - Style ▸▸
          - TabStops

Microsoft Word Object Model (5)

(continued)

Application
└ Documents
  └ Document
    ├ Range
    │ ├ ProofreadingErrors ➤➤
    │ ├ ReadabilityStatistics ➤➤
    │ ├ Revisions ➤➤
    │ ├ Rows ➤➤
    │ ├ Scripts ★
    │ ├ Sections
    │ │ └ Section
    │ │   └ PageSetup
    │ ├ Sentences ➤➤
    │ ├ Shading
    │ ├ ShapeRange ➤➤
    │ ├ Style ➤➤
    │ ├ Subdocuments ➤➤
    │ ├ SynonymInfo
    │ ├ Tables
    │ │ └ Table
    │ │   ├ Borders ➤➤
    │ │   ├ Cell ➤➤
    │ │   ├ Columns ➤➤
    │ │   ├ Range ➤➤
    │ │   ├ Rows
    │ │   │ └ Row
    │ │   │   ├ Borders ➤➤
    │ │   │   └ Cell ➤➤
    │ │   └ Shading
    │ ├ TextRetrievalMode
    │ └ Words ➤➤
    │
    ├ ReadabilityStatistics   (continued) ──→
    │ └ ReadabilityStatistic
    ├ Revisions
    │ └ Revision
    ├ RoutingSlip
    ├ Scripts ★
    ├ Sentences ➤➤
    ├ Sections ➤➤
    ├ Shapes ++
    │ ├ Range ➤➤
    │ └ Shape
    │   ├ Adjustments
    │   ├ CanvasShapes
    │   │ ├ FreeFormBuilder
    │   │ ├ Shape ➤➤
    │   │ └ ShapeRange ➤➤
    │   ├ CalloutFormat
    │   ├ DiagramNode ➤➤
    │   ├ FillFormat +
    │   ├ Frame
    │   └ FreeformBuilder

    │   ├ GroupShapes
    │   │ └ Shape ➤➤
    │   ├ Hyperlink
    │   ├ InlineShape ➤➤
    │   ├ LineFormat +
    │   ├ LinkFormat
    │   ├ OLEFormat
    │   ├ PictureFormat
    │   ├ Range ➤➤
    │   └ Script ★

    │   ├ ShadowFormat +
    │   ├ Shape ➤➤
    │   ├ ShapeNodes
    │   │ └ ShapeNode
    │   ├ ShapeRange ➤➤
    │   ├ TextEffectFormat
    │   ├ TextFrame
    │   ├ ThreeDFormat +
    │   └ WrapFormat

    Range ➤➤
    Shading ➤➤

Microsoft Word Object Model (6)

(continued)

Application
└ Documents
  └ Document
    ├ SmartTags
    │ └ SmartTag
    │   └ CustomProperties
    │   └ CustomProperty
    │ └ Range
    ├ StoryRanges
    │ └ Range ▸▸
    └ Styles
      └ Style
        ├ Borders ▸▸
        ├ Font ▸▸
        ├ Frame
        ├ ListTemplate ★
        ├ ParagraphFormat
        ├ Shading
        └ TableStyle
          ├ ConditionalStyle
          │ ├ Borders ▸▸
          │ ├ Font ▸▸
          │ ├ ParagraphFormat ▸▸
          │ └ Shading ▸▸
          ├ Borders ▸▸
          └ Shading ▸▸

    ├ StyleSheets
    │ └ StyleSheet
    ├ Subdocuments
    │ └ Subdocument
    ├ Tables ▸▸
    ├ TablesOfAuthorities
    │ └ TableOfAuthorities
    ├ TablesOfAuthoritiesCategories
    │ └ TableOfAuthoritiesCategories
    ├ TablesOfContents
    │ └ TableOfContents
    ├ TablesOfFigures
    │ └ TableOfFigures
    ├ Variables
    │ └ Variable
    ├ VBProject ★★
    ├ Versions
    │ └ Version
    ├ WebOptions
    ├ Windows ▸▸
    └ Words ▸▸

Microsoft Word Object Model (7)

Source (Type Library)

The Microsoft® Word object model is provided by MSWORD.OLB, which is included when you install Word.

Reference Information in Help

Help for this object model is available in VBAWD10.CHM.

Notes

A single plus sign (+) designates objects with accessors to the ColorFormat object.

A double plus sign (++) indicates that the ShapeRange objects have been omitted from this diagram. For general purposes, you can think of these objects as occupying the same positions as the Shape object.

A double arrow symbol (>>) indicates that additional objects are shown elsewhere in this diagram.

Shared Components

Microsoft Office XP Object Model

AnswerWizard
└ AnswerWizardFiles

COMAddIns
└ COMAddIn

DocumentProperties
└ DocumentProperty

HTMLProject
├ HTMLProjectItems
│ └ HTMLProjectItem

LanguageSettings

Scripts
└ Script

WebPageFonts
└ WebPageFont

SignatureSet
└ Signature

NewFile

MSOEnvelope
└ CommandBars
  └ CommandBar
    └ CommandBarControls +
      └ CommandBarControl
        ├ CommandBarButton
        ├ CommandBarComboBox
        └ CommandBarPopup

FileSearch
├ FileTypes
├ FoundFiles
├ PropertyTests
│ └ PropertyTest
├ SearchFolders
│ └ ScopeFolder
└ SearchScopes
  └ SearchScope

Assistant
└ Balloon
  ├ BalloonCheckboxes
  │ └ BalloonCheckbox
  └ BalloonLabels
    └ BalloonLabel

OfficeDataSourceObject
├ ODSOColumns
│ └ ODSOColumn
└ ODSOFilters
  └ ODSOFilter

FileDialog
├ FileDialogFilters
│ └ FileDialogFilter
└ FileDialogSelectedItems

Source (Type Library)

The Microsoft® Office XP object model is provided by MSO.DLL, which is included when you install Office.

Reference Information in Help

Help for this object model is available in VBAOF10.CHM.

Notes

The plus sign (+) indicates that the CommandBarControls collection contains CommandBarControl objects. A CommandBarControl object can be one of 23 types, which are specified by the MsoControlType enumerated constant. Three of those control types (shown in the previous diagram) also are exposed as specific objects.

Microsoft Graph Object Model

Application
- AutoCorrect
- Chart
  - Axes
    - Axis
      - AxisTitle
        - Border
        - Font
      - Border
      - DisplayUnitLabel
      - GridLines
        - Border
      - TickLabels
        - Font
  - ChartArea
    - Border
    - Font
  - ChartGroups
    - ChartGroup
      - DownBars
        - Border
      - DropLines
        - Border
      - HiLoLines
        - Border
      - SeriesLines
        - Border
    - ChartTitle
      - Border
      - Font

CommandBars *
- Corners
- DataTable
  - Border
  - Font
- Floor
  - Border
- Legend
  - Border
  - Font
  - LegendEntries
    - LegendEntry
      - Font
      - LegendKey
        - Border

- PlotArea
  - Border
- Walls
  - Border
- SeriesCollection
  (Repeat from Series)

DataSheet
- Font
- Range

- SeriesCollection
  - Series
    - Border
    - ChartFillFormat
    - DataLabels
      - Border
      - Font
    - DataLabel
      - Border
      - Font

- TickLabels
- ErrorBars
  - Border
- Interior
- LeaderLines
  - Border
- Points
  - Point
    - Border
    - DataLabel

- UpBars
  - Border
- TrendLines
  - TrendLine
    - Border
    - DataLabel

- Interior

Source (Type Library)

The Microsoft® Graph object model is provided by GRAPH.EXE, which is included when you install Microsoft® Office XP.

Reference Information in Help

Help for this object model is available in VBAGR10.CHM.

Microsoft Forms Object Model

Source (Type Library)

The Microsoft Forms object model is provided by FM20.DLL, which is included when you install Microsoft® Office XP.

Reference Information in Help

Help for this object model is available in FM20.CHM.

Visual Basic Editor 6.0 Object Model

```
VBE
├─ AddIns
│   └─ AddIn
├─ CommandBars        *
├─ CodePanes
│   └─ CodePane
├─ Events
│   ├─ CommandBarEvents
│   └─ ReferencesEvents
├─ VBProjects
│   └─ VBProject
│       ├─ References
│       │   └─ Reference
│       └─ VBComponents
│           └─ VBComponent
│               ├─ Properties
│               │   └─ Property
│               └─ CodeModule
└─ Windows
    └─ Window
        └─ LinkedWindows
            └─ Window
```

Source (Type Library)

The Microsoft® Visual Basic® Editor object model is provided by VBE6EXT.OLB, which is included when you install Microsoft® Office XP.

Reference Information in Help

Help for this object model is available in VBOB6.CHM.

Data Access

Microsoft ActiveX Data Objects 2.1 Object Model

```
Connection
 ├─ Errors
 │   └─ Error
 ├─ Command
 │   ├─ Parameters
 │   │   └─ Parameter
 │   └─ Properties
 │       └─ Property
 ├─ RecordSet
 │   ├─ Fields
 │   │   └─ Field
 │   │       └─ Properties
 │   │           └─ Property
 │   └─ Properties
 │       └─ Property
 └─ Properties
     └─ Property
```

Source (Type Library)

The Microsoft® ActiveX® Data Objects 2.1 object model is provided by MSADO15.DLL, which is included when you install Microsoft® Office XP.

Reference Information in Help

Help for this object model is available in ADO210.CHM.

Microsoft ADO Extensions 2.1 for DDL and Security Object Model

Source (Type Library)

The Microsoft ADO Extensions 2.1 for DDL and Security object model is provided by MSADOX.DLL, which is included when you install Microsoft® Office XP.

Reference Information in Help

Help for this object model is available in ADO210.CHM.

Microsoft ActiveX Data Objects (Multi-Dimensional) 1.0 Object Model

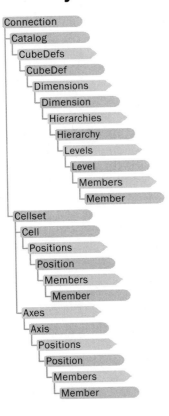

```
Connection
 ├ Catalog
 │   └ CubeDefs
 │       └ CubeDef
 │           └ Dimensions
 │               └ Dimension
 │                   └ Hierarchies
 │                       └ Hierarchy
 │                           └ Levels
 │                               └ Level
 │                                   └ Members
 │                                       └ Member
 └ Cellset
     ├ Cell
     │   └ Positions
     │       └ Position
     │           └ Members
     │               └ Member
     └ Axes
         └ Axis
             └ Positions
                 └ Position
                     └ Members
                         └ Member
```

Source (Type Library)

The Microsoft® ActiveX® Data Objects (Multi-Dimensional) 1.0 object model is provided by MSADOMD.DLL, which is included when you install Microsoft® Office XP.

Reference Information in Help

Help for this object model is available in ADO210.CHM.

Microsoft Data Access Objects (DAO) 3.6 Object Library Object Model

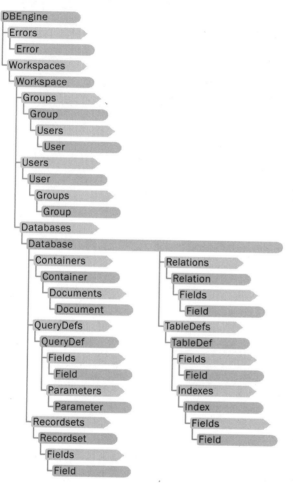

Source (Type Library)

The Data Access Objects 3.6 object model is provided by DAO360.DLL, which is included when you install Microsoft® Office XP.

Reference Information in Help

Help for this object model is available in DAO360.CHM.

Microsoft Jet and Replication Objects 2.1 Library Object Model

JetEngine
Replica
 └ Filters
    └ Filter

Source (Type Library)

The Microsoft® Jet and Replication objects 2.1 object model is provided by MSJRO.DLL, which is included when you install Microsoft® Office XP.

Reference Information in Help

Help for this object model is available in MSJRO.CHM.

Web Technologies

Microsoft Internet Explorer 5 and Document Object Model

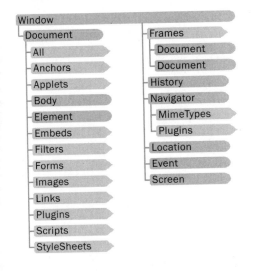

Source (Type Library)

The Microsoft® Internet Explorer 5 object model is provided by MSHTML.TLB, which is included when you install Microsoft® Office XP. The objects in this object model are available whenever Internet Explorer is open, so it is not required that you refer to a specific type library file.

Reference Information in Help

Help for this object model is available in HTMLREF.CHM.

Microsoft Scripting Runtime Object Model

Dictionary

FileSystemObject

Drives
　└ Drive

Folders
　└ Folder

Files
　└ File

TextStream

Source (Type Library)

The Microsoft Scripting Runtime object model is provided by SCRRUN.DLL, which is included when you install Microsoft® Office XP.

Reference Information in Help

Help for this object model is available in VBLR6.CHM.

Microsoft Office XP Chart Component Object Model

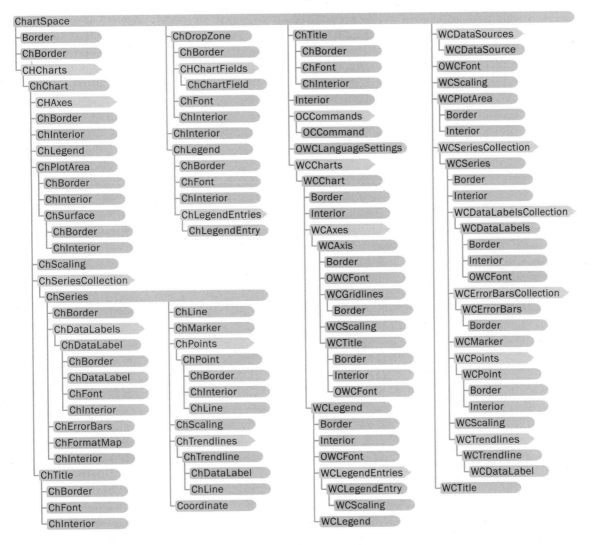

Source (Type Library)

The Microsoft® Office XP Web Components (including the Chart control) object model is provided by MSOWC.DLL, which is included when you install Office.

Reference Information in Help

Help for this object model is available in OWCVBA10.CHM.

Microsoft Office XP Data Source Control Object Model

Source (Type Library)

The Microsoft® Office XP Web Components (including the Data Source control) object model is provided by MSOWC.DLL, which is included when you install Office.

Reference Information in Help

Help for this object model is available in OWCVBA10.CHM.

Microsoft Office XP PivotTable Component Object Model

PivotTable
- PivotView
  - PivotFont
  - PivotTotals
    - PivotTotal
  - PivotFilterAxis
  - PivotFieldSets
    - (Repeat from PivotFieldSet)
    - PivotLabel
      - PivotFont
  - PivotGroupAxis
  - PivotFieldSets
    - (Repeat from PivotFieldSet)
    - PivotLabel
      - PivotFont
  - PivotFieldSets
    - PivotFieldSet
      - PivotFields
        - PivotField
  - PivotDataAxis
    - PivotFieldSets
    - (Repeat from PivotFieldSet)
    - PivotTotals
      - PivotTotal
    - PivotLabel
      - PivotFont

- PivotData
  - PivotCell
    - PivotAggregates
      - PivotAggregate
    - PivotDetailCell
    - PivotDetailRange
      - PivotDetailCell
    - PivotRowMember
  - PivotColumnMembers
    - PivotColumnMember
  - PivotColumnMember
    - PivotAxisMember
    - PivotAxisMembers
      - PivotAxisMember
    - PivotColumnMember
    - PivotColumnMembers
      - PivotColumnMember
    - PivotField
    - PivotHyperlink
    - PivotMember
    - PivotResultGroupAxis
    - PivotResultGroupField
    - PivotResultMemberProperties
      - PivotResultMemberProperty
    - PivotView
  - PivotMember
  - PivotMembers
    - PivotMember
  - PivotRange
    - PivotCell
    - (Repeat from PivotCell)

- PivotResultColumnAxis
- PivotResultDataAxis
- PivotResultFilterAxis
- PivotAxis
- PivotData
- PivotFieldSets
- PivotFilterAxis
- PivotResultLabel
- PivotResultLabel
- PivotResultPageAxis
  - PivotPageMember
    - PivotAxisMember
    - PivotAxisMembers
      - PivotAxisMember
        - PivotAxisMember
        - PivotAxisMembers
        - PivotField
        - PivotHyperlink
        - PivotMember
        - PivotMembers
        - PivotResultGroupAxis
        - PivotResultGroupField
        - PivotResultMemberProperties
        - PivotView

(continued) →

Microsoft Office XP PivotTable Component Object Model (2)

(continued)

PivotTable
- PivotData
  - PivotResultRowAxis
    - PivotAxis
    - PivotAxisMember
      - PivotAxisMember
      - PivotAxisMembers
        - PivotAxisMember
      - PivotField
      - PivotHyperlink
      - PivotMember
      - PivotMembers
      - PivotResultGroupAxis
      - PivotResultGroupField
      - PivotResultMemberProperties
      - PivotView
    - PivotDataObject
    - PivotFields
    - PivotGroupAxis
    - PivotResultGroupFields
      - PivotResultGroupField
    - PivotResultLabel
    - PivotRowMember
  - PivotRowMember
  - PivotRowMembers
    - PivotRowMember
      - PivotAxisMember
      - PivotField
      - PivotHyperlink
      - PivotMember
      - PivotMembers
      - PivotResultGroupAxis
        - PivotAxis
        - PivotAxisMember
        - PivotData
        - PivotFields
          - PivotField
        - PivotResultGroupFields
          - PivotResultGroupField
            - PivotField
            - PivotResultAxis
        - PivotResultLabel
      - PivotResultGroupField
      - PivotResultMemberProperties
      - PivotRowMember
      - PivotRowMembers
      - PivotView
  - PivotView

Source (Type Library)

The Microsoft® Office XP Web Components (including the PivotTable List control) object model is provided by OWC10.DLL, which is included when you install Office.

Reference Information in Help

Help for this object model is available in OWCVBA10.CHM.

Microsoft Office XP Spreadsheet Component Object Model

```
Spreadsheet
├─Pane
├─Range
│  ├─Borders
│  │  └─Border
│  ├─Hyperlink
│  ├─Interior
│  └─OWCFont
├─TitleBar
│  ├─Interior
│  └─OWCFont
└─Worksheet
   ├─AutoFilter
   │  └─Filters
   │     └─Filter
   │        └─Criteria
   ├─Panes
   │  └─Pane
   ├─Protection
   └─Range
```

Source (Type Library)

The Microsoft® Office XP Web Components (including the Spreadsheet control) object model is provided by MSOWC.DLL, which is included when you install Office.

Reference Information in Help

Help for this object model is available in OWCVBA10.CHM.

Microsoft Office XP Server Extensions Object Model

Source (Type Library)

The Microsoft® Office XP Server Extensions object model is provided by OWSCLT.DLL, which is included when you install the Web Discussions feature of Office.

Reference Information in Help

Help for this object model is available in VBAOWS10.CHM.

Additional References

The following books and Web sites provide additional information about developing applications and solutions.

Access Virus Information

Access Virus Information Web site
(http://officeupdate.microsoft.com/Articles/antivirus.htm)

ActiveX Data Objects (ADO)

Microsoft Universal Data Access Web site
(http://www.microsoft.com/data/)

Microsoft ActiveX Data Objects Web site
(http://www.microsoft.com/data/ado/)

Microsoft Office Developer Center
(http://msdn.microsoft.com/office/)

Vaughn, William R. *Hitchhiker's Guide to Visual Basic and SQL Server, Sixth Edition*. Redmond, WA: Microsoft Press, 1998.

Administrator Control over Passwords

Microsoft Office Resource Kit Web site
(http://www.microsoft.com/office/ork/)

Microsoft Office XP Resource Kit. Redmond, WA: Microsoft Press, 1999.

Administrator Control over Internet Explorer

Internet Explorer Administration Kit Web site
(http://ieak.microsoft.com/)

Answer Wizard SDK

Microsoft Office Resource Kit Web site
(http://www.microsoft.com/office/ork/)

Microsoft Office XP Resource Kit. Redmond, WA: Microsoft Press, 1999.

Calling the Windows API from VBA

Appleman, Dan. *Dan Appleman's Visual Basic 5.0 Programmer's Guide to the Win32 API.* Indianapolis, IN: Macmillan Computer Publishing, 1998.

Bockmann, Christopher J., Lars Klander, and Lingyan Tang. *Visual Basic Programmer's Library.* Las Vegas, NV: Jamsa Press, 1998.

Getz, Ken, and Mike Gilbert. *Visual Basic Language Developer's Handbook.* Alameda, CA: Sybex, 1999.

O'Brien, Timothy, Steven Pogge, and Geoffrey White. *Microsoft Access 97 Developer's Handbook.* Redmond, WA: Microsoft Press, 1997.

Creating Add-ins and DLLs in Microsoft® Visual Basic®

Microsoft Developer Network Web site
(http://msdn.microsoft.com/default.asp)

Microsoft Visual Basic 6.0 Programmer's Guide. Redmond, WA: Microsoft Press, 1998.

Cornell, Gary, and Dave Jezak. *Core Visual Basic 6.* Upper Saddle River, NJ: Prentice Hall PTR, 1998.

McKinney, Bruce. *Hardcore Visual Basic, Second Edition.* Redmond, WA: Microsoft Press, 1997.

Creating and Using DHTML Scriptlets

Microsoft Scripting Technologies Web site
(http://msdn.microsoft.com/scripting/default.htm)

Creating Application-Specific Templates and Add-ins

Boctor, David. *Microsoft Office 2000/Visual Basic Fundamentals.* Redmond, WA: Microsoft Press, 1999.

Getz, Ken, Paul Litwin, and Mike Gilbert. *Access 2000 Developer's Handbook, Volume 1: Desktop Edition.* Alameda, CA: Sybex, 1999.

Creating COM Add-ins with Visual C++ and Visual J++

Microsoft Developer Network Web site
(http://msdn.microsoft.com/default.asp)

Creating Object Models in VBA

Getz, Ken, and Mike Gilbert. *Visual Basic Language Developer's Handbook.* Alameda, CA: Sybex, 1999.

Stearns, Dave. "The Basics of Programming Model Design." MSDN Online Web site at http://msdn.microsoft.com/library/techart/msdn_basicpmd.htm.

Creating PivotTable Reports

Microsoft Office Developer Center
(http://msdn.microsoft.com/office/)

Wells, Eric, and Steve Harshberger. *Microsoft Excel 97 Developer's Handbook.* Redmond, WA: Microsoft Press, 1997.

Data Access Objects (DAO)

Microsoft Office Developer Center
(http://msdn.microsoft.com/office/)

Microsoft Jet Database Engine Programmer's Guide, Second Edition. Redmond, WA: Microsoft Press, 1997

Database Design

Hernandez, Michael J. *Database Design for Mere Mortals.* Reading, MA: Addison-Wesley Developers Press, 1997.

Roman, Steven. *Access Database Design and Programming.* Sebastopol, CA: O'Reilly & Associates, 1997.

Debugging VBA Code

Maguire, Steve. *Writing Solid Code.* Redmond, WA: Microsoft Press, 1993.

McConnell, Steve. *Code Complete.* Redmond, WA: Microsoft Press, 1993.

Debugging and Error Handling in Script

Microsoft Scripting Technologies Web site
(http://msdn.microsoft.com/scripting/default.htm)

DHTML

Isaacs, Scott. *Inside Dynamic HTML.* Redmond, WA: Microsoft Press, 1997.

Simpson, Alan. *Official Microsoft Internet Explorer 4 Site Builder Toolkit.* Redmond, WA: Microsoft Press, 1998.

Disabling User Passwords

Microsoft Office XP Resource Kit. Redmond, WA: Microsoft Press, 1999.

General Security Issues

Microsoft Security Advisor Web site
(http://www.microsoft.com/security/)

HTML Help

Steve Wexler. *Official Microsoft HTML Help Authoring Kit.* Redmond, WA: Microsoft Press, 1998.

Internet Information Server Authentication and Encryption Configuration

Microsoft Internet Information Server 4.0 Online documentation
http://www.microsoft.com/ntserver/web/exec/feature/Datasheet.asp)

Macro Viruses

Microsoft Office Anti-Virus Center Web site
(http://officeupdate.microsoft.com/Articles/antivirus.htm)

International Computer Security Association (ICSA) Web site
 http://www.icsa.net)

Microsoft Jet Replication

Microsoft Jet Database Engine Programmer's Guide, Second Edition. Redmond, WA: Microsoft Press, 1997.

Dove, Debra. "Database Replication in Microsoft Jet." (RepJet.doc)

Microsoft Outlook

Byrne, Randy. *Building Applications with Microsoft Outlook 2000.* Redmond, WA: Microsoft Press, 1999.

Microsoft SQL Server

Microsoft SQL Server Web site
(http://www.microsoft.com/sql)

Naming Conventions

Microsoft Knowledge Base article: "*Built-in Constants in Visual Basic for Applications,*" Q112671 (http://support.microsoft.com/support)

OLAP, OLE DB for OLAP, and OLAP Queries

Universal Data Access Web site
http://www.microsoft.com/data

Microsoft SQL Server OLAP Services
(http://www.microsoft.com/sql/techinfo/olap.htm)

OLE DB

Microsoft OLE DB Web site
(http://www.microsoft.com/data/oledb)

Optimizing VBA Code

Balena, Francesco. "88 Optimization Tips." *Visual Basic Programmer's Journal* 7, no. 14
(December 1997): 28–41.

Signcode.exe Utility for Signing COM Add-ins

Microsoft Internet Client SDK Web site
(http://msdn.microsoft.com/workshop/essentials/inetsdk/inetsdk_map.asp)

SQL Server Replication

SQL Server Books Online, *Replication.*

Subclassing Windows Messages

Bockmann, Christopher J., Lars Klander, and Lingyan Tang. *Visual Basic Programmer's Library.*
Las Vegas, NV: Jamsa Press, 1998.

Training Resources for Office XP

http://www.microsoft.com/office/training/training.asp

Universal Data Access Strategy

Microsoft Universal Data Access Web site
(http://www.microsoft.com/data)

Useful Tips and Sample Code

Microsoft Office Developer Center
(http://msdn.microsoft.com/office/)

The Microsoft Knowledge Base
http://support.microsoft.com/support

Useful VBA Sample Code

For samples and how-to articles that may provide interesting code, search the Visual Basic for
Applications section of the Microsoft Knowledge Base for "VBA." The Knowledge Base is
available at http://support.microsoft.com/support.

Using ActiveX Data Objects with MDB Files and the Microsoft Jet Database Engine

Microsoft ActiveX Data Objects Web site at http://www.microsoft.com/data/ado.

Using ActiveX Data Objects with SQL Server

Vaughn, William R. *Hitchhiker's Guide to Visual Basic and SQL Server, Sixth Edition*. Redmond, WA: Microsoft Press, 1998.

SQL Server Books Online, *Building SQL Server Applications*.

Using Scriptlets

Scriptlet Technology Web site
(http://msdn.microsoft.com/developer/sdk/inetsdk/help/scriptlets/scrlt.htm)

Isaacs, Scott. *Inside Dynamic HTML*. Redmond, WA: Microsoft Press, 1997.

Scriptlet Wizard on Microsoft Scripting Technologies Web site
(http://msdn.microsoft.com/scripting)

Using Scriptlets in HTML Files

Microsoft Scripting Technologies Web site
(http://msdn.microsoft.com/scripting/default.htm)

Isaacs, Scott. *Inside Dynamic HTML*. Redmond, WA: Microsoft Press, 1997.

Windows File System Security

Microsoft Windows 95 Resource Kit. Redmond, WA: Microsoft Press, 1995.

Microsoft Windows 98 Resource Kit. Redmond, WA: Microsoft Press, 1998.

Microsoft Windows NT Workstation Resource Kit. Redmond, WA: Microsoft Press, 1996.

Microsoft Windows NT Server Resource Kit. Redmond, WA: Microsoft Press, 1996.

WinHelp 4.0

Microsoft Help Workshop (download from the Microsoft Technical Support Web site at
http://support.microsoft.com/download/support/mslfiles/hcwsetup.exe)

Microsoft Windows 95 Help Authoring Kit. Redmond, WA: Microsoft Press, 1995.

Working with JScript

Microsoft Scripting Technologies Web site
(http://msdn.microsoft.com/scripting/default.htm)

Working with VBA

Getz, Ken, and Mike Gilbert. *Visual Basic Language Developer's Handbook*. Alameda, CA: Sybex, 1999.

Working with VBScript

Microsoft Scripting Technologies Web site
(http://msdn.microsoft.com/scripting/default.htm)

Working with the Visual Basic for Applications Extensibility Library

Getz, Ken, and Mike Gilbert. *Visual Basic Language Developer's Handbook*. Alameda, CA: Sybex, 1999.

Wrapping API Functions

Microsoft Developer Network Web site
(http://msdn.microsoft.com/default.asp)

Appleman, Dan. *Dan Appleman's Visual Basic 5.0 Programmer's Guide to the Win32 API*. Indianapolis, IN: Macmillan Computer Publishing, 1998.

Writing Reusable Code

McConnell, Steve. *Code Complete*. Redmond, WA: Microsoft Press, 1993.

XML

XML Developer Center
(http://msdn.microsoft.com/xml/default.asp)

Index

Master
the building blocks of
32-bit and 64-bit
development

Here's definitive instruction for advancing the next generation of Windows®-based applications—faster, sleeker, and more potent than ever! This fully updated expansion of the best-selling *Advanced Windows* digs even deeper into the advanced features and state-of-the-art techniques you can exploit for more robust Windows development—including authoritative insights on the new Windows 2000 platform.

U.S.A.   **$59.99**
U.K.   £38.99 [V.A.T. included]
Canada $89.99
ISBN 1-57231-996-8

mspress.microsoft.com

Learn to write drivers
the easy way—
with help from a Windows Driver Model authority.

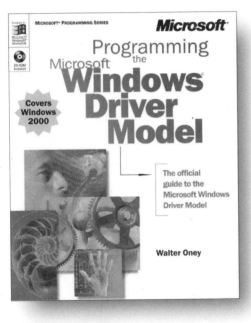

MICROSOFT® PROGRAMMING SERIES

Microsoft®

Programming the Microsoft

Windows® Driver Model

Covers Windows 2000

The official guide to the Microsoft Windows Driver Model

Walter Oney

U.S.A.	**$49.99**
U.K.	£32.99 [V.A.T. included]
Canada	$74.99

ISBN 0-7356-0588-2

The new driver model for Microsoft Windows 98 and Windows 2000 supports Plug and Play, provides power management capabilities, and expands on the driver/ minidriver approach. PROGRAMMING THE MICROSOFT® WINDOWS® DRIVER MODEL is the official guide to the Windows Driver Model. Written by device-driver programming expert Walter Oney in close cooperation with the Microsoft Windows DDK team, it provides extensive practical examples, illustrations, advice, and line-by-line analysis of code samples to clarify real-world programming issues.

Microsoft Press® products are available worldwide wherever quality computer books are sold. For more information, contact your book or computer retailer, software reseller, or local Microsoft Sales Office, or visit our Web site at mspress.microsoft.com. To locate your nearest source for Microsoft Press products, or to order directly, call 1-800-MSPRESS in the U.S. (in Canada, call 1-800-268-2222).

Prices and availability dates are subject to change.

Microsoft®

mspress.microsoft.com

Plan and design
commercial database systems
using
Microsoft technologies.

Step up to professional-quality relational database development with DESIGNING RELATIONAL DATABASE SYSTEMS. This book is an ideal introduction to the core precepts and fundamentals of database design, focusing on critical planning issues that are often overlooked by beginning database designers. It also provides practical discussions and instructive examples of how to develop robust, professional-level database systems using the wide array of Microsoft® database tools and technologies. It even gives you timesaving forms on CD-ROM to use as you design relational database systems.

U.S.A.	**$39.99**
U.K.	£25.99 [V.A.T. included]
Canada	$61.99
ISBN	0-7356-0634-X

Microsoft®
mspress.microsoft.com

Learn to add a *new* *dimension*
to your data with
analysis services!

DEVELOPER LEARNING TOOLS

Microsoft

Windows

CD-ROM Included

Step by Step

Microsoft
SQL Server 2000
Analysis Services

■ Find out how to make the most of online analytical processing (OLAP) technology

■ Learn to create and display data cubes and use multidimensional expressions (MDX)

■ Discover how to build data-analysis solutions that go beyond Microsoft Excel and Access

OLAP Train
Reed Jacobson

This title shows Microsoft® Excel and Access experts, IS managers, and database developers how to build applications that take advantage of the powerful data-analysis services in Microsoft SQL Server™ 2000. You'll discover why these services make it easier to analyze huge amounts of data quickly, and you'll learn how to develop a wide range of advanced dimensional-data applications—from enterprise reporting tools to advanced decision-support systems. The book's easy-to-follow lessons begin with clear objectives and include real-world business examples, with a companion CD full of sample files that support each lesson.

U.S.A.	**$39.99**
U.K.	£25.99 [V.A.T. included]
Canada	$57.99
ISBN: 0-7356-0904-7	

Microsoft®

mspress.microsoft.com

MICROSOFT LICENSE AGREEMENT

Book Companion CD

IMPORTANT—READ CAREFULLY: This Microsoft End-User License Agreement ("EULA") is a legal agreement between you (either an individual or an entity) and Microsoft Corporation for the Microsoft product identified above, which includes computer software and may include associated media, printed materials, and "online" or electronic documentation ("SOFTWARE PRODUCT"). Any component included within the SOFTWARE PRODUCT that is accompanied by a separate End-User License Agreement shall be governed by such agreement and not the terms set forth below. By installing, copying, or otherwise using the SOFTWARE PRODUCT, you agree to be bound by the terms of this EULA. If you do not agree to the terms of this EULA, you are not authorized to install, copy, or otherwise use the SOFTWARE PRODUCT; you may, however, return the SOFTWARE PRODUCT, along with all printed materials and other items that form a part of the Microsoft product that includes the SOFTWARE PRODUCT, to the place you obtained them for a full refund.

SOFTWARE PRODUCT LICENSE

The SOFTWARE PRODUCT is protected by United States copyright laws and international copyright treaties, as well as other intellectual property laws and treaties. The SOFTWARE PRODUCT is licensed, not sold.

1. **GRANT OF LICENSE.** This EULA grants you the following rights:

   a. **Software Product.** You may install and use one copy of the SOFTWARE PRODUCT on a single computer. The primary user of the computer on which the SOFTWARE PRODUCT is installed may make a second copy for his or her exclusive use on a portable computer.

   b. **Storage/Network Use.** You may also store or install a copy of the SOFTWARE PRODUCT on a storage device, such as a network server, used only to install or run the SOFTWARE PRODUCT on your other computers over an internal network; however, you must acquire and dedicate a license for each separate computer on which the SOFTWARE PRODUCT is installed or run from the storage device. A license for the SOFTWARE PRODUCT may not be shared or used concurrently on different computers.

   c. **License Pak.** If you have acquired this EULA in a Microsoft License Pak, you may make the number of additional copies of the computer software portion of the SOFTWARE PRODUCT authorized on the printed copy of this EULA, and you may use each copy in the manner specified above. You are also entitled to make a corresponding number of secondary copies for portable computer use as specified above.

   d. **Sample Code.** Solely with respect to portions, if any, of the SOFTWARE PRODUCT that are identified within the SOFTWARE PRODUCT as sample code (the "SAMPLE CODE"):

      i. **Use and Modification.** Microsoft grants you the right to use and modify the source code version of the SAMPLE CODE, *provided* you comply with subsection (d)(iii) below. You may not distribute the SAMPLE CODE, or any modified version of the SAMPLE CODE, in source code form.

      ii. **Redistributable Files.** Provided you comply with subsection (d)(iii) below, Microsoft grants you a nonexclusive, royalty-free right to reproduce and distribute the object code version of the SAMPLE CODE and of any modified SAMPLE CODE, other than SAMPLE CODE, or any modified version thereof, designated as not redistributable in the Readme file that forms a part of the SOFTWARE PRODUCT (the "Non-Redistributable Sample Code"). All SAMPLE CODE other than the Non-Redistributable Sample Code is collectively referred to as the "REDISTRIBUTABLES."

      iii. **Redistribution Requirements.** If you redistribute the REDISTRIBUTABLES, you agree to: (i) distribute the REDISTRIBUTABLES in object code form only in conjunction with and as a part of your software application product; (ii) not use Microsoft's name, logo, or trademarks to market your software application product; (iii) include a valid copyright notice on your software application product; (iv) indemnify, hold harmless, and defend Microsoft from and against any claims or lawsuits, including attorney's fees, that arise or result from the use or distribution of your software application product; and (v) not permit further distribution of the REDISTRIBUTABLES by your end user. Contact Microsoft for the applicable royalties due and other licensing terms for all other uses and/or distribution of the REDISTRIBUTABLES.

2. **DESCRIPTION OF OTHER RIGHTS AND LIMITATIONS.**

   - **Limitations on Reverse Engineering, Decompilation, and Disassembly.** You may not reverse engineer, decompile, or disassemble the SOFTWARE PRODUCT, except and only to the extent that such activity is expressly permitted by applicable law notwithstanding this limitation.

   - **Separation of Components.** The SOFTWARE PRODUCT is licensed as a single product. Its component parts may not be separated for use on more than one computer.

   - **Rental.** You may not rent, lease, or lend the SOFTWARE PRODUCT.

- **Support Services.** Microsoft may, but is not obligated to, provide you with support services related to the SOFTWARE PRODUCT ("Support Services"). Use of Support Services is governed by the Microsoft policies and programs described in the user manual, in "online" documentation, and/or in other Microsoft-provided materials. Any supplemental software code provided to you as part of the Support Services shall be considered part of the SOFTWARE PRODUCT and subject to the terms and conditions of this EULA. With respect to technical information you provide to Microsoft as part of the Support Services, Microsoft may use such information for its business purposes, including for product support and development. Microsoft will not utilize such technical information in a form that personally identifies you.

- **Software Transfer.** You may permanently transfer all of your rights under this EULA, provided you retain no copies, you transfer all of the SOFTWARE PRODUCT (including all component parts, the media and printed materials, any upgrades, this EULA, and, if applicable, the Certificate of Authenticity), **and** the recipient agrees to the terms of this EULA.

- **Termination.** Without prejudice to any other rights, Microsoft may terminate this EULA if you fail to comply with the terms and conditions of this EULA. In such event, you must destroy all copies of the SOFTWARE PRODUCT and all of its component parts.

3. **COPYRIGHT.** All title and copyrights in and to the SOFTWARE PRODUCT (including but not limited to any images, photographs, animations, video, audio, music, text, SAMPLE CODE, REDISTRIBUTABLES, and "applets" incorporated into the SOFTWARE PRODUCT) and any copies of the SOFTWARE PRODUCT are owned by Microsoft or its suppliers. The SOFTWARE PRODUCT is protected by copyright laws and international treaty provisions. Therefore, you must treat the SOFTWARE PRODUCT like any other copyrighted material **except** that you may install the SOFTWARE PRODUCT on a single computer provided you keep the original solely for backup or archival purposes. You may not copy the printed materials accompanying the SOFTWARE PRODUCT.

4. **U.S. GOVERNMENT RESTRICTED RIGHTS.** The SOFTWARE PRODUCT and documentation are provided with RESTRICTED RIGHTS. Use, duplication, or disclosure by the Government is subject to restrictions as set forth in subparagraph (c)(1)(ii) of the Rights in Technical Data and Computer Software clause at DFARS 252.227-7013 or subparagraphs (c)(1) and (2) of the Commercial Computer Software—Restricted Rights at 48 CFR 52.227-19, as applicable. Manufacturer is Microsoft Corporation/One Microsoft Way/Redmond, WA 98052-6399.

5. **EXPORT RESTRICTIONS.** You agree that you will not export or re-export the SOFTWARE PRODUCT, any part thereof, or any process or service that is the direct product of the SOFTWARE PRODUCT (the foregoing collectively referred to as the "Restricted Components"), to any country, person, entity, or end user subject to U.S. export restrictions. You specifically agree not to export or re-export any of the Restricted Components (i) to any country to which the U.S. has embargoed or restricted the export of goods or services, which currently include, but are not necessarily limited to, Cuba, Iran, Iraq, Libya, North Korea, Sudan, and Syria, or to any national of any such country, wherever located, who intends to transmit or transport the Restricted Components back to such country; (ii) to any end user who you know or have reason to know will utilize the Restricted Components in the design, development, or production of nuclear, chemical, or biological weapons; or (iii) to any end user who has been prohibited from participating in U.S. export transactions by any federal agency of the U.S. government. You warrant and represent that neither the BXA nor any other U.S. federal agency has suspended, revoked, or denied your export privileges.

DISCLAIMER OF WARRANTY

NO WARRANTIES OR CONDITIONS. MICROSOFT EXPRESSLY DISCLAIMS ANY WARRANTY OR CONDITION FOR THE SOFTWARE PRODUCT. THE SOFTWARE PRODUCT AND ANY RELATED DOCUMENTATION ARE PROVIDED "AS IS" WITHOUT WARRANTY OR CONDITION OF ANY KIND, EITHER EXPRESS OR IMPLIED, INCLUDING, WITHOUT LIMITATION, THE IMPLIED WARRANTIES OF MERCHANTABILITY, FITNESS FOR A PARTICULAR PURPOSE, OR NONINFRINGEMENT. THE ENTIRE RISK ARISING OUT OF USE OR PERFORMANCE OF THE SOFTWARE PRODUCT REMAINS WITH YOU.

LIMITATION OF LIABILITY. TO THE MAXIMUM EXTENT PERMITTED BY APPLICABLE LAW, IN NO EVENT SHALL MICROSOFT OR ITS SUPPLIERS BE LIABLE FOR ANY SPECIAL, INCIDENTAL, INDIRECT, OR CONSEQUENTIAL DAMAGES WHATSOEVER (INCLUDING, WITHOUT LIMITATION, DAMAGES FOR LOSS OF BUSINESS PROFITS, BUSINESS INTERRUPTION, LOSS OF BUSINESS INFORMATION, OR ANY OTHER PECUNIARY LOSS) ARISING OUT OF THE USE OF OR INABILITY TO USE THE SOFTWARE PRODUCT OR THE PROVISION OF OR FAILURE TO PROVIDE SUPPORT SERVICES, EVEN IF MICROSOFT HAS BEEN ADVISED OF THE POSSIBILITY OF SUCH DAMAGES. IN ANY CASE, MICROSOFT'S ENTIRE LIABILITY UNDER ANY PROVISION OF THIS EULA SHALL BE LIMITED TO THE GREATER OF THE AMOUNT ACTUALLY PAID BY YOU FOR THE SOFTWARE PRODUCT OR US$5.00; PROVIDED, HOWEVER, IF YOU HAVE ENTERED INTO A MICROSOFT SUPPORT SERVICES AGREEMENT, MICROSOFT'S ENTIRE LIABILITY REGARDING SUPPORT SERVICES SHALL BE GOVERNED BY THE TERMS OF THAT AGREEMENT. BECAUSE SOME STATES AND JURISDICTIONS DO NOT ALLOW THE EXCLUSION OR LIMITATION OF LIABILITY, THE ABOVE LIMITATION MAY NOT APPLY TO YOU.

MISCELLANEOUS

This EULA is governed by the laws of the State of Washington USA, except and only to the extent that applicable law mandates governing law of a different jurisdiction.

Should you have any questions concerning this EULA, or if you desire to contact Microsoft for any reason, please contact the Microsoft subsidiary serving your country, or write: Microsoft Sales Information Center/One Microsoft Way/Redmond, WA 98052-6399.

OWNER REGISTRATION CARD **Register Today!** 0-7356-1242-0

Return the bottom portion of this card to register today.

Microsoft® Office XP Developer's Guide

FIRST NAME   MIDDLE INITIAL   LAST NAME

INSTITUTION OR COMPANY NAME

ADDRESS

CITY   STATE   ZIP

( )

E-MAIL ADDRESS   PHONE NUMBER

U.S. and Canada addresses only. Fill in information above and mail postage-free.
Please mail only the bottom half of this page.

For information about Microsoft Press® products, visit our Web site at

mspress.microsoft.com

Microsoft®

‖‖‖‖